Lecture Notes in Computer Science   14651

The series Lecture Notes in Computer Science (LNCS), including its subseries Lecture Notes in Artificial Intelligence (LNAI) and Lecture Notes in Bioinformatics (LNBI), has established itself as a medium for the publication of new developments in computer science and information technology research, teaching, and education.

LNCS enjoys close cooperation with the computer science R & D community, the series counts many renowned academics among its volume editors and paper authors, and collaborates with prestigious societies. Its mission is to serve this international community by providing an invaluable service, mainly focused on the publication of conference and workshop proceedings and postproceedings. LNCS commenced publication in 1973.

Marc Joye · Gregor Leander
Editors

Advances in Cryptology – EUROCRYPT 2024

43rd Annual International Conference on the Theory
and Applications of Cryptographic Techniques
Zurich, Switzerland, May 26–30, 2024
Proceedings, Part I

 Springer

Editors
Marc Joye 🆔
Zama
Paris, France

Gregor Leander 🆔
Ruhr University Bochum
Bochum, Germany

ISSN 0302-9743   ISSN 1611-3349 (electronic)
Lecture Notes in Computer Science
ISBN 978-3-031-58715-3   ISBN 978-3-031-58716-0 (eBook)
https://doi.org/10.1007/978-3-031-58716-0

This Springer imprint is published by the registered company Springer Nature Switzerland AG
The registered company address is: Gewerbestrasse 11, 6330 Cham, Switzerland

Paper in this product is recyclable.

Preface

EUROCRYPT 2024 is the 43rd Annual International Conference on the Theory and Applications of Cryptographic Techniques. It was held in Zurich, Switzerland, during May 26–30, 2024. EUROCRYPT is an annual conference organized by the International Association for Cryptologic Research (IACR).

EUROCRYPT 2024 received 501 submissions, out of which 469 formally went to the review process. Every submission was assigned in a double blind way to three program committee members and, in some cases, one or two extra reviewers were added. The IACR version of the HotCRP software was used for the whole review process. In total, 1436 reviews were produced and 5200+ comments were made during the whole process. After a first round, 290 papers were pre-selected by the program committee to enter the second round. These remaining papers were offered a rebuttal to answer questions and requests for clarification from the reviewers. After several weeks of subsequent discussions, the committee ultimately selected 105 papers for acceptance.

The program committee was made up of 110 top cryptography researchers, all expert in their respective fields. For some papers, external sub-referees were appointed by the committee members. We warmly thank all the committee members and their sub-referees for the hard work in the peer review and their active participation in the discussions. We greatly benefited from the help of the area chairs: Shweta Agrawal for "Public Key Primitives with Advanced Functionalities", Serge Fehr for "Theoretical Foundations", Pierre-Alain Fouque for "Secure and Efficient Implementation, Cryptographic Engineering, and Real-World Cryptography", María Naya-Plasencia for "Symmetric Cryptology", Claudio Orlandi for "Multi-Party Computation and Zero-Knowledge", and Daniel Wichs for "Classic Public Key Cryptography". They each led the discussions and the paper selection in their respective area. The previous program chairs for IACR flagship conferences were also very helpful; in particular, we are grateful to Carmit Hazay and Martijn Stam for sharing their experience with EUROCRYPT 2023.

The IACR aims to support open and reproducible research within the field of cryptography. For the first time for a flagship conference, authors of accepted papers were invited to submit artifacts associated with their papers, such as software or datasets, for review, in a collaborative process between authors and the artifact review committee. We thank Martin Albrecht for having accepted to chair the artifact committee.

Three papers were awarded this year. The Best Paper Awards went to Pierrick Dartois, Antonin Leroux, Damien Robert and Benjamin Wesolowski for their paper "SQIsignHD: New Dimensions in Cryptography" and to Itai Dinur for his paper "Tight Indistinguishability Bounds for the XOR of Independent Random Permutations by Fourier Analysis". The Early-Career Best Paper Award was given to Maria Corte-Real Santos, Jonathan Komada Eriksen, Michael Meyer, and Krijn Reijnders for their paper "AprèsSQI: Extra Fast Verification for SQIsign Using Extension-Field Signing".

In addition to the contributed papers, EUROCRYPT 2024 featured two invited talks: "Cryptography in the Wild" by Kenny Paterson and "An Attack Became a Tool: Isogeny-based Cryptography 2.0" by Wouter Castryck. The conference also included a panel discussion on the future of publications; the panel was moderated by Anne Canteaut. The traditional rump session featuring short and entertaining presentations was held on Wednesday 29th.

Several people were key to the success of the conference. Our two general chairs, Julia Hesse and Thyla van der Merwe, did a fantastic job with the overall organization of EUROCRYPT 2024. Kevin McCurley ensured everything went smoothly with the review software and in the collection of the final papers. The conference relied on sponsors to help ensure student participation and reduce costs. We gratefully acknowledge the financial support of (in alphabetical order): Apple, AWS, CASA, City of Zürich, Concordium, Cosmian, Ethereum Foundation, Fair Math, Google, Huawei, IBM, Input/Output, NTT Research, SandboxAQ, Swiss National Science Foundation, Starkware, TII, Zama, and ZISC.

May 2024

Marc Joye
Gregor Leander

Organization

General Co-chairs

Thyla van der Merwe   Google, Switzerland
Julia Hesse   IBM Research Zurich, Switzerland

Program Co-chairs

Marc Joye   Zama, France
Gregor Leander   Ruhr-University Bochum, Germany

Area Chairs

Shweta Agrawal   IIT Madras, India
Serge Fehr   CWI Amsterdam and Leiden University,
     The Netherlands
Pierre-Alain Fouque   Université de Rennes, CNRS and Inria, France
María Naya-Plasencia   Inria, France
Claudio Orlandi   Aarhus University, Denmark
Daniel Wichs   Northeastern University and NTT Research, USA

Program Committee

Martin R. Albrecht   King's College London and SandboxAQ, UK
Diego F. Aranha   Aarhus University, Denmark
Nuttapong Attrapadung   AIST, Japan
Christof Beierle   RUB, Germany
Sonia Belaïd   CryptoExperts, France
Tim Beyne   KU Leuven, Belgium
Olivier Blazy   Ecole Polytechnique, France
Jeremiah Blocki   Purdue University, USA
Alexandra Boldyreva   Georgia Tech University, USA
Xavier Bonnetain   Inria, France
Jonathan Bootle   IBM Research Europe – Zurich, Switzerland
Christina Boura   University of Versailles, France

André Schrottenloher	Inria, Université de Rennes, IRISA, France
Peter Schwabe	MPI-SP, Germany, and Radboud University, The Netherlands
Yannick Seurin	Ledger, France
Mark Simkin	Ethereum Foundation, Denmark
Pratik Soni	University of Utah, USA
Akshayaram Srinivasan	University of Toronto, Canada
Damien Stehlé	CryptoLab, France
Siwei Sun	Chinese Academy of Sciences, China
Berk Sunar	Worcester Polytechnic Institute, USA
Yosuke Todo	NTT Social Informatics Laboratories, Japan
Junichi Tomida	NTT Social Informatics Laboratories, Japan
Serge Vaudenay	EPFL, Switzerland
Frederik Vercauteren	KU Leuven, Belgium
Ivan Visconti	University of Salerno, Italy
David Wu	UT Austin, USA
Mark Zhandry	NTT Research, USA

External Reviewers

Marius A. Aardal
Aysajan Abdin
Ittai Abraham
Damiano Abram
Hamza Abusalah
Anasuya Acharya
Léo Ackermann
Amit Agarwal
Ahmet Agirtas
Prabhanjan Ananth
Yoshinoro Aono
Ananya Appan
Nicolas Aragon
Arasu Arun
Gennaro Avitabile
Renas Bacho
Youngjin Bae
David Balbas
Marshall Ball
Fabio Banfi
Zhenzhen Bao
Manuel Barbosa

Augustin Bariant
Cruz Barnum
Khashayar Barooti
James Bartusek
Balthazar Bauer
Amit Behera
Shalev Ben-David
Shany Ben-David
Omri Ben-Eliezer
Loris Bergerat
Ward Beullens
Varsha Bhat
Ritam Bhaumik
Kaartik Bhushan
Alexander Bienstock
Alexander Block
Erica Blum
Jan Bobolz
Nicolas Bon
Charlotte Bonte
Carl Bootland
Joppe Bos

Katharina Boudgoust
Alexandre Bouez
Clemence Bouvier
Cyril Bouvier
Pedro Branco
Nicholas Brandt
Lennart Braun
Alessio Caminata
Matteo Campanelli
Sébastien Canard
Kevin Carrier
Ignacio Cascudo
Gaëtan Cassiers
Guilhem Castagnos
Wouter Castryck
Pierre-Louis Cayrel
André Chailloux
Debasmita Chakraborty
Hubert Chan
Anirudh Chandramouli
Rahul Chatterjee
Rohit Chatterjee
Mingjie Chen
Yanlin Chen
Yilei Chen
Yu Long Chen
Jesús-Javier Chi-Domínguez
Ilaria Chillotti
Hyeongmin Choe
Wonseok Choi
Wutichai Chongchitmate
Arka Ra Choudhuri
Hao Chung
Kai-Min Chung
Michele Ciampi
Sebastian Clermont
Benoît Cogliati
Daniel Collins
Brice Colombier
Sandro Coretti
Alain Couvreur
Daniele Cozzo
Wei Dai
Quang Dao
Debajyoti Das

Sourav Das
Pratish Datta
Emma Dauterman
Gareth T. Davies
Leo de Castro
Thomas De Cnudde
Paola de Perthuis
Giovanni Deligios
Cyprien Delpech de Saint Guilhem
Rafael del Pino
Amit Deo
Julien Devevey
Siemen Dhooghe
Zijing Di
Emanuele Di Giandomenico
Christoph Dobraunig
Rafael Dowsley
Leo Ducas
Jesko Dujmovic
Betül Durak
Avijit Dutta
Christoph Egger
Martin Ekera
Felix Engelmann
Simon Erfurth
Reo Eriguchi
Jonathan Komada Eriksen
Hülya Evkan
Thibauld Feneuil
Giacomo Fenzi
Rex Fernando
Valerie Fetzer
Rune Fiedler
Ben Fisch
Matthias Fitzi
Nils Fleischhacker
Pouyan Forghani
Boris Fouotsa
Cody Freitag
Sapir Freizeit
Daniele Friolo
Paul Frixons
Margot Funk
Phillip Gajland
Daniel Gardham

Rachit Garg
Francois Garillot
Gayathri Garimella
John Gaspoz
Robin Geelen
Paul Gerhart
Diana Ghinea
Satrajit Ghosh
Ashrujit Ghoshol
Emanuele Giunta
Kristian Gjøsteen
Aarushi Goel
Evangelos Gkoumas
Eli Goldin
Rishab Goyal
Adam Groce
Ziyi Guan
Zichen Gui
Antonio Guimaraes
Felix Günther
Kanav Gupta
Nirupam Gupta
Kamil Doruk Gur
Hosein Hadipour
Mohammad Hajiabadi
Ghaith Hammouri
Guillaume Hanrot
Keisuke Hara
Patrick Harasser
Dominik Hartmann
Keitaro Hashimoto
Rachelle Heim
Nadia Heninger
Alexandra Henzinger
Julius Hermelink
Julia Hesse
Hans Heum
Shuichi Hirahara
Taiga Hiroka
Marc Houben
James Hsin-Yu Chiang
Kai Hu
Yungcong Hu
Tao Huang
Zhenyu Huang

Loïs Huguenin-Dumittan
James Hulett
Atsunori Ichikawa
Akiko Inoue
Tetsu Iwata
Joseph Jaeger
Jonas Janneck
Dirmanto Jap
Samuel Jaques
Ruta Jawale
Corentin Jeudy
Ashwin Jha
Dan Jones
Philipp Jovanovic
Bernhard Jungk
Fatih Kaleoglu
Chethan Kamath
Jiayi Kang
Minsik Kang
Julia Kastner
Hannah Keller
Qiao Kexin
Mustafa Khairallah
Dmitry Khovratovich
Ryo Kikuchi
Jiseung Kim
Elena Kirshanova
Fuyuki Kitagawa
Michael Klooß
Christian Knabenhans
Lisa Kohl
Sebastian Kolby
Dimitris Kolonelos
Chelsea Komlo
Anders Konring
Nishat Koti
Mukul Kulkarni
Protik Kumar Paul
Simran Kumari
Norman Lahr
Russell W. F. Lai
Baptiste Lambin
Oleksandra Lapiha
Eysa Lee
Joohee Lee

Jooyoung Lee
Seunghoon Lee
Ryan Lehmkuhl
Tancrède Lepoint
Matthieu Lequesne
Andrea Lesavourey
Baiyu Li
Shun Li
Xingjian Li
Zengpeng Li
Xiao Liang
Chuanwei Lin
Fuchun Lin
Yao-Ting Lin
Fukang Liu
Peiyuan Liu
Qipeng Liu
Patrick Longa
Julian Loss
Paul Lou
George Lu
Steve Lu
Zhenghao Lu
Reinhard Lüftenegger
Vadim Lyubashevsky
Fermi Ma
Varun Madathil
Christian Majenz
Giulio Malavolta
Mary Maller
Nathan Manohar
Mario Marhuenda Beltrán
Ange Martinelli
Elisaweta Masserova
Takahiro Matsuda
Christian Matt
Noam Mazor
Pierrick Méaux
Jeremias Mechler
Jonas Meers
Willi Meier
Kelsey Melissaris
Nikolas Melissaris
Michael Meyer
Pierre Meyer

Charles Meyer-Hilfiger
Peihan Miao
Chohong Min
Brice Minaud
Kazuhiko Minematsu
Tomoyuki Morimae
Hiraku Morita
Mahnush Movahedi
Anne Mueller
Michael Naehrig
Marcel Nageler
Vineet Nair
Yusuke Naito
Varun Narayanan
Hugo Nartz
Shafik Nassar
Patrick Neumann
Lucien K. L. Ng
Ruth Ng
Dinh Duy Nguyen
Jérôme Nguyen
Khoa Nguyen
Ky Nguyen
Ngoc Khanh Nguyen
Phong Nguyen
Phuong Hoa Nguyen
Thi Thu Quyen Nguyen
Viet-Sang Nguyen
Georgio Nicolas
Guilhem Niot
Julian Nowakowski
Koji Nuida
Sabine Oechsner
Kazuma Ohara
Olya Ohrimenko
Jean-Baptiste Orfila
Astrid Ottenhues
Rasmus Pagh
Arghya Pal
Tapas Pal
Mahak Pancholi
Omkant Pandey
Lorenz Panny
Jai Hyun Park
Nikitas Paslis

Alain Passelègue
Rutvik Patel
Shravani Patil
Sikhar Patranabis
Robi Pedersen
Alice Pellet-Mary
Hilder V. L. Pereira
Guilherme Perin
Léo Perrin
Thomas Peters
Richard Petri
Krzysztof Pietrzak
Benny Pinkas
Guru-Vamsi Policharla
Eamonn Postlethwaite
Thomas Prest
Ludo Pulles
Kirthivaasan Puniamurthy
Luowen Qian
Kexin Qiao
Xianrui Qin
Willy Quach
Rahul Rachuri
Rajeev Raghunath
Ahmadreza Rahimi
Markus Raiber
Justin Raizes
Bhavish Raj Gopal
Sailaja Rajanala
Hugues Randriam
Rishabh Ranjan
Shahram Rasoolzadeh
Christian Rechberger
Michael Reichle
Krijn Reijnders
Jean-René Reinhard
Bhaskar Roberts
Andrei Romashchenko
Maxime Roméas
Franck Rondepierre
Schuyler Rosefield
Mike Rosulek
Dragos Rotaru
Yann Rotella
Lior Rotem

Lawrence Roy
Ittai Rubinstein
Luigi Russo
Keegan Ryan
Sayandeep Saha
Yusuke Sakai
Matteo Salvino
Simona Samardjiska
Olga Sanina
Antonio Sanso
Giacomo Santato
Paolo Santini
Maria Corte-Real Santos
Roozbeh Sarenche
Pratik Sarkar
Yu Sasaki
Rahul Satish
Sarah Scheffler
Dominique Schröder
Jacob Schuldt
Mark Schultz-Wu
Gregor Seiler
Sruthi Sekar
Nicolas Sendrier
Akash Shah
Laura Shea
Yixin Shen
Yu Shen
Omri Shmueli
Ferdinand Sibleyras
Janno Siim
Tjerand Silde
Jaspal Singh
Nitin Singh
Rohit Sinha
Luisa Siniscalchi
Naomi Sirkin
Daniel Slamanig
Daniel Smith-Tone
Yifan Song
Yongsoo Song
Eduardo Soria-Vazquez
Nick Spooner
Mahesh Sreekumar Rajasree
Sriram Sridhar

Srivatsan Sridhar
Lukas Stennes
Gilad Stern
Marc Stöttinger
Bing Sun
Ling Sun
Ajith Suresh
Elias Suvanto
Jakub Szefer
Akira Takahashi
Abdullah Talayhan
Abdul Rahman Taleb
Suprita Talnikar
Tianxin Tang
Samuel Tap
Stefano Tessaro
Jean-Pierre Tillich
Ivan Tjuawinata
Patrick Towa
Kazunari Tozawa
Bénédikt Tran
Daniel Tschudi
Yiannis Tselekounis
Ida Tucker
Nirvan Tyagi
LaKyah Tyner
Rei Ueno
Gilles Van Assche
Wessel Van Woerden
Nikhil Vanjani
Marloes Venema
Michiel Verbauwhede
Javier Verbel
Tanner Verber
Damien Vergnaud
Fernando Virdia
Damian Vizár
Benedikt Wagner
Roman Walch
Julian Wälde

Alexandre Wallet
Chenghong Wang
Mingyuan Wang
Qingju Wang
Xunhua Wang
Yuyu Wang
Alice Wanner
Fiona Weber
Christian Weinert
Weiqiangg Wen
Chenkai Weng
Ivy K. Y. Woo
Lichao Wu
Keita Xagawa
Aayush Yadav
Anshu Yadav
Saikumar Yadugiri
Shota Yamada
Takashi Yamakawa
Hailun Yan
Yibin Yang
Kevin Yeo
Eylon Yogev
Yang Yu
Chen Yuan
Mohammad Zaheri
Gabriel Zaid
Riccardo Zanotto
Arantxa Zapico
Maryam Zarezadeh
Greg Zaverucha
Marcin Zawada
Runzhi Zeng
Tina Zhang
Yinuo Zhang
Yupeng Zhang
Yuxi Zheng
Mingxun Zhou
Chenzhi Zhu

Contents – Part I

Public Key Primitives with Advanced Functionalities (I/II)

Awarded Papers

SQIsignHD: New Dimensions in Cryptography

Pierrick Dartois[1,2]([✉]) [iD], Antonin Leroux[3,4] [iD], Damien Robert[1,2] [iD],
and Benjamin Wesolowski[5] [iD]

[1] Univ. Bordeaux, CNRS, INRIA, IMB, UMR 5251, 33400 Talence, France
{pierrick.dartois,damien.robert}@inria.fr
[2] INRIA, IMB, UMR 5251, 33400 Talence, France
[3] DGA-MI, Bruz, France
antonin.leroux@polytechnique.org
[4] IRMAR - UMR 6625, Université de Rennes, Rennes, France
[5] ENS de Lyon, CNRS, UMPA, UMR 5669, Lyon, France
benjamin.wesolowski@ens-lyon.fr

Abstract. We introduce SQIsignHD, a new post-quantum digital signature scheme inspired by SQIsign. SQIsignHD exploits the recent algorithmic breakthrough underlying the attack on SIDH, which allows to efficiently represent isogenies of arbitrary degrees as components of a higher dimensional isogeny. SQIsignHD overcomes the main drawbacks of SQIsign. First, it scales well to high security levels, since the public parameters for SQIsignHD are easy to generate: the characteristic of the underlying field needs only be of the form $2^f 3^{f'} - 1$. Second, the signing procedure is simpler and more efficient. Our signing procedure implemented in C runs in 28 ms, which is a significant improvement compared to SQISign. Third, the scheme is easier to analyse, allowing for a much more compelling security reduction. Finally, the signature sizes are even more compact than (the already record-breaking) SQIsign, with compressed signatures as small as 109 bytes for the post-quantum NIST-1 level of security. These advantages may come at the expense of the verification, which now requires the computation of an isogeny in dimension 4, a task whose optimised cost is still uncertain, as it has been the focus of very little attention. Our experimental sagemath implementation of the verification runs in around 600 ms, indicating the potential cryptographic interest of dimension 4 isogenies after optimisations and low level implementation.

1 Introduction

Isogeny-based cryptography has been a promising area of research in post-quantum cryptography since Couveignes, Rostovtsev and Stolbunov introduced the first key exchange using ordinary isogenies [8,34]. Schemes from this family often distinguish themselves by their compactness, in particular with respect to key sizes. It is notably the case of the digital signature scheme SQIsign [10,13], the most compact post-quantum signature scheme by a decent margin. However,

© International Association for Cryptologic Research 2024
M. Joye and G. Leander (Eds.): EUROCRYPT 2024, LNCS 14651, pp. 3–32, 2024.
https://doi.org/10.1007/978-3-031-58716-0_1

efficiency has been a recurring challenge for isogeny-based schemes, and indeed, SQIsign is much slower than other post-quantum signatures.

In this paper, we introduce SQIsignHD, a new digital signature scheme derived from SQIsign. As in [15], SQIsign uses the Deuring correspondence between supersingular elliptic curves and quaternion orders. This Deuring correspondence is a powerful tool to construct cryptosystems because it is one way: it is easy to turn an order into the corresponding elliptic curve, but the converse direction is the presumably hard *supersingular endomorphism ring problem* [12,41]. In SQIsign, the signer's public key is a supersingular elliptic curve, and a signature effectively proves that the signer knows the associated quaternion order. This requires algorithms to translate between orders (and ideals in these orders) and elliptic curves (and isogenies from these curves). This translation is costly, and crucially requires the ideals (or isogenies) to have smooth norms (or degrees). The original methods have been improved upon [13], but that remains the bottleneck of SQIsign. Another issue with SQIsign is its scalability to higher security levels. Indeed, to set public parameters, one needs to find a prime p such that $p^2 - 1$ has a very large smooth factor. Searching for such primes p becomes harder as the security level grows, and is still an active area of research [1,4,7]. Besides, the security of SQIsign relies on the fact that signatures are computationally indistinguishable from random isogenies of fixed powersmooth degrees. There is no known formal proof of this *ad hoc* heuristic assumption.

The new scheme SQIsignHD follows a similar outline as SQIsign, but resolves its main drawbacks by fundamentally reforging the computational approach. The main ingredient is the ground-breaking technique that has recently led to the downfall of SIDH [5,27,33]. Namely, these attacks use a lemma due to Kani [19] combined with Zahrin's trick, which allows one to "embed" any isogeny into an isogeny of higher dimension. As remarked in [32], this technique allows one to describe an isogeny by listing only the image of a few well-chosen points; from this description, one can efficiently evaluate the isogeny on any other point, regardless of the factorisation pattern of the underlying isogeny. This newly gained freedom on usable isogenies unlocks challenges in efficiency, security, and scalability.

Our Contribution. We introduce the digital signature scheme SQIsignHD. It leverages recent algorithmic breakthroughs [5,27,33] to overcome the main drawbacks of SQIsign. It has the following advantages:

- SQIsignHD scales well to high security levels. Indeed, while SQIsign requires a search for primes p with strong constraints, the primes used in SQIsignHD may be of the form $c2^f 3^{f'} - 1$, where c is some (preferably small) cofactor. Such primes, already used in SIDH [18], are easy to find, and allow for efficient field arithmetic.
- The signing procedure of SQIsignHD is simpler and more efficient than SQIsign. Let us stress that no high dimensional isogeny needs to be computed when signing. Our proof-of-concept implementation, which still lacks many

standard optimisations, is already about ten times faster than the fastest SQIsign implementation. This is discussed in further detail in Sect. 6.2.

- SQIsignHD is easier to analyse, allowing for a much more compelling security reduction to the supersingular endomorphism problem. Unlike in SQIsign, our proof of the zero-knowledge property in SQIsignHD relies on simple and plausible heuristic assumptions. In fact, we propose two variants of SQIsign, one of which is less efficient but benefits from a heuristic-free analysis. In both cases, the zero-knowledge property is based on a simulator which is given access to a non-standard oracle. We carefully discuss the impact of this oracle on the supersingular endomorphism problem.

- SQIsignHD signatures are even more compact than SQIsign, as they are only 6.5λ bits long, for λ bits of security. In particular, they are as small as 109 bytes for the NIST-1 security level. SQIsign already had the most compact signature and public keys combined of all post-quantum signature schemes, and SQIsignHD breaks this record.

These advantages may come at the expense of the verification, which now requires the computation of a chain of 2-isogenies in dimension 4 (or 8 in the less efficient variant). We provide an algorithm for the verification, and an experimental implementation in `sagemath` [28,36]. An optimised low-level implementation is left for future work, hence the true cost of verification is still uncertain. The verification in SQIsign also requires the computation of a (longer!) chain of 2-isogenies, but only in dimension 1.

1.1   A Modular Overview of SQIsignHD

We introduce two distinct versions of SQIsignHD, optimised in different directions. FastSQIsignHD is optimised for speed, while RigorousSQIsignHD is optimised for the security proof. Note that the security proof applies to both: the difference lies in the proof being unconditional for RigorousSQIsignHD when given access to an oracle, but requiring additional heuristics for FastSQIsignHD (see [9, § D.2] and Sect. 5.2). Under the hood, FastSQIsignHD relies on isogenies of dimension 4, while RigorousSQIsignHD relies on isogenies of dimension 8. The reader may sense the parallel with the heuristic (dimension 4) and rigorous (dimension 8) variants of the algorithms of [33].

We present here the main algorithmic building blocks of the identification scheme undelying SQIsignHD to give a modular overview of the protocol (see Fig. 1). Those algorithms are presented in detail in this paper for Fast-SQIsignHD and in [9, § B] for RigorousSQIsignHD. Unsurprisingly, the protocol shares a lot of similarities with SQIsign. The full signature scheme can be derived from there with the Fiat-Shamir transform [14] as in [10, § 3.4] (see [9, § A.1] for details).

Public set-up. We choose a prime p and a supersingular elliptic curve $E_0/\mathbb{F}_{p^2}$ of known endomorphism ring $\mathcal{O}_0 \cong \operatorname{End}(E_0)$ such that E_0 has smooth torsion defined over a small extension of $\mathbb{F}_{p^2}$ (of degree 1 or 2). In practice, one may use the curve $E_0 : y^2 = x^3 + x$ (and $p \equiv 3 \mod 4$).

Key Generation. The prover generates a random secret isogeny $\tau : E_0 \longrightarrow E_A$ of fixed smooth degree D_τ. Then, the prover publishes E_A. Knowing τ, only the prover can compute the endomorphism ring $\text{End}(E_A)$. In the fast method FastKeyGen, the isogeny τ has degree $D_\tau = \Theta(p)$, which is heuristically sufficient to ensure that the distribution of E_A is computationally indistinguishable from uniform. In the alternate method RigorousKeyGen, the degree is chosen a bit larger to make the distribution of E_A statistically close to uniform.

Commitment. The prover generates a random isogeny $\psi : E_0 \longrightarrow E_1$ of smooth degree D_ψ and returns E_1 to the verifier (ψ being secret). The resulting distribution for E_1 is as close as possible to the uniform distribution in the supersingular isogeny graph. As in the key generation, we propose a fast procedure FastCommit(E_0) in Sect. 3.3 resulting in a distribution heuristically indistinguishable from uniform, and a slower variant RigorousCommit(E_0) in [9, § B.2] which guarantees statistical closeness to uniform.

Challenge. The verifier generates a random isogeny $\varphi : E_A \longrightarrow E_2$ of smooth degree D_φ sufficiently large for φ to have high entropy. Then, φ is sent to the prover. The Challenge procedure is described in Sect. 3.2. Unlike SQIsign, we chose to start the challenge from E_A instead of E_1 in order to optimize the response process.

Response. The prover generates an *efficient representation* of an isogeny $\sigma : E_1 \longrightarrow E_2$ of small degree $q \simeq \sqrt{p}$ in the sense of the following definition and returns it to the verifier.

Definition 1. Let $\mathscr{A}$ be an algorithm and $\varphi : E \longrightarrow E'$ be an isogeny defined over a finite field $\mathbb{F}_q$. An *efficient representation* of φ (with respect to $\mathscr{A}$) is some data $D \in \{0, 1\}^*$ of polynomial size in $\log(\deg(\varphi))$ and $\log(q)$ such that, on input D and $P \in E(\mathbb{F}_{q^k})$, $\mathscr{A}$ returns $\varphi(P)$ in polynomial time in $k \log(q)$ and $\log(\deg(\varphi))$.

There always exists an efficient representation of a smooth degree isogeny. For instance, it can be written as a chain of small degree isogenies. Until the recent attacks on SIDH [5,27,33], we did not know how to efficiently represent isogenies with non-smooth degrees without revealing the endomorphism ring of the domain. For that reason, the original version of SQIsign uses smooth degree isogenies for the signature. These smooth degree isogenies are found with a variant of the KLPT algorithm [20] and have very big degree $\simeq p^{15/4}$. This not only hurts efficiency, but also security: the isogeny σ is so carefully crafted that it is hard to simulate, and as a result, the zero-knowledge property of SQIsign is very *ad hoc*.

Now, the methods from [5,27,33] give much more freedom on the isogenies that can be efficiently represented. This allows SQIsignHD to improve both efficiency (using isogenies σ of degree as low as $\simeq \sqrt{p}$), and security (the isogenies σ are now nicely distributed, hence simulatable).

The idea is to "embed" σ into an isogeny of higher dimension — and that only requires knowing the image of a few points through σ. As in the attacks against SIDH, such an isogeny can have dimension 2, 4 or 8. We shall see that dimension 2 has little interest compared to the original SQIsign protocol from an efficiency and security point of view. In SQIsignHD, we propose a response procedure FastRespond to represent σ in dimension 4, and an alternative procedure RigorousRespond based on an isogeny computation in dimension 8. The procedure FastRespond is fast, and its security analysis relies on reasonable heuristics. On the other hand, RigorousRespond is much slower (though still polynomial time), but allows for a rigorous analysis.

In either case, for efficiency reasons, the prover does not actually compute higher dimensional isogenies but only images of some points through σ (we explain how these points are evaluated in the course of the paper). Those points provide an efficient representation of σ (along with $\deg(\sigma)$) and this data is sent to the verifier who can then compute higher dimensional isogenies representing σ.

Verification. The verifier checks that the response returned by the prover (points of E_2) correctly represents an isogeny $\sigma : E_1 \longrightarrow E_2$. We propose two procedures FastVerify and RigorousVerify computing isogenies embedding σ in dimension 4 or 8. So far, isogeny computations in dimension 4 has been the subject of very little literature.

Nonetheless, our proof of concept implementation of dimension 4 isogenies in sagemath [28,36] demonstrates the cryptographic feasibility of this phase. We expect an optimized implementation to be at worse twice as slow as the original SQIsign verification, and hopefully even closer than that. We refer to [9, § F] for an estimate of the number of operations required for the verification.

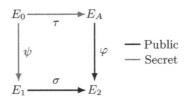

Fig. 1. The SQIsign/SQIsignHD identification protocol.

Content. The rest of this paper is organized as follows. In Sect. 2, we present the core idea of our paper: how to embed signature/response isogenies in higher dimension with Kani's lemma. Section 3 introduces algorithms for key generation, commitment and challenge whereas Sect. 4 presents the response and verification phase for FastSQIsignHD. A security analysis of FastSQIsignHD identification protocol is conducted in Sect. 5. Finally, we discuss the expected performance of the digital signature scheme derived from FastSQIsignHD in Sect. 6. To save space, some preliminaries, proofs and algorithmic details on RigorousSQIsignHD and higher dimensional isogenies are given in [9].

2   Representing the Response Isogeny Efficiently in Higher Dimension

In this section, we explore our main idea to improve SQIsign by embedding the signature isogeny inside an isogeny in higher dimension. We start by recalling how the signature is represented in the original SQIsign protocol in Sect. 2.1 and why this representation is slow to compute. Then, we introduce Kani's lemma and explain how to embed isogenies in higher dimension in Sect. 2.2. Finally, we apply this idea to provide another representation of the signature isogeny in SQIsign in Sect. 2.3.

2.1   State of the Art Isogeny Representation: A Slow Signature Process

With state of the art techniques prior to the attacks against SIDH, we could only efficiently represent isogenies of smooth degrees. That is why in the original versions of SQIsign [10,13], the signature isogeny σ has degree a prime power ℓ^e and is represented as a chain of ℓ-isogenies.

To compute such a signature σ, the prover computes the ideal J associated to the isogeny path given by the secret key, commitment and challenge. They then apply a SigningKLPT algorithm to J, to return a random equivalent ideal $I \sim J$ of norm ℓ^e. Then, the prover converts I into an isogeny. This last computation is very costly because $\mathrm{nrd}(I) = \ell^e$ is close to $p^{15/4}$, while the accessible torsion points have much smaller order. The method introduced in [10] (and later improved in [13]) requires to cut J into several pieces in order to compute σ as a chain of isogenies. This complicated mechanism is by far the bottleneck in the signing algorithm.

In order to avoid this costly ideal to isogeny translation in SQIsignHD, we shall no longer require σ to have smooth degree and embed it in an isogeny of dimension 4 or 8 having smooth degree. This embedding will provide an efficient representation, and is faster to compute than the one in the original SQIsign. We shall also explain why this improves security in Sect. 5.

2.2   Embedding Isogenies in Higher Dimension with Kani's Lemma

In this section, we explain in more detail this idea of embedding isogenies in higher dimension. For that, we need a few definitions first.

Definition 2 (*d-isogeny*). Let $\alpha : (A, \lambda_A) \longrightarrow (B, \lambda_B)$ be an isogeny between principally polarized abelian varieties. We say that α is a *d-isogeny* if $\widehat{\alpha} \circ \lambda_B \circ \alpha = [d]\lambda_A$, where $\widehat{\alpha} : \widehat{B} \longrightarrow \widehat{A}$ is the dual isogeny of α.

Equivalently, α is a d-isogeny if $\tilde{\alpha} \circ \alpha = [d]_A$, where $\tilde{\alpha} := \lambda_A^{-1} \circ \widehat{\alpha} \circ \lambda_B$ is the dual isogeny of α with respect to the principal polarisations λ_A and λ_B.

Definition 3 (Isogeny diamond). *Let $a, b \in \mathbb{N}^*$. An (a,b)-isogeny diamond is a commutative diagram of isogenies between principally polarized abelian varieties*

$$
\begin{array}{ccc}
A' & \xrightarrow{\;\varphi'\;} & B' \\
\psi \uparrow & & \uparrow \psi' \\
A & \xrightarrow{\;\varphi\;} & B
\end{array}
$$

where φ and φ' are a-isogenies and ψ and ψ' are b-isogenies.

Lemma 4 (Kani). *We consider an (a,b)-isogeny diamond as above, with $d := a + b$ prime to the characteristic of the base field of abelian varieties. Then, the isogeny $F : A \times B' \longrightarrow B \times A'$ given in matrix notation by*

$$
F := \begin{pmatrix} \varphi & \widetilde{\psi'} \\ -\psi & \widetilde{\varphi'} \end{pmatrix}
$$

is a d-isogeny with $d = a + b$, for the product polarisations.
If a and b are coprime, the kernel of F is

$$
\ker(F) = \{(\widetilde{\varphi}(x), \psi'(x)) \mid x \in B[d]\}.
$$

This lemma has first been proved in [19, Theorem 2.3]. We also give a proof in [9, §E.1].

Remark 2.1. The existence of $F : A \times B' \to B \times A'$, implies the existence of $\varphi : A \to B$. We can recover φ as $\pi \circ F \circ \iota$ where ι is the embedding morphism $x \in A \longmapsto (x, 0) \in A \times B'$ and π is the projection from $B \times A'$ to B. Hence, F is an efficient representation of φ.

2.3 Application of Kani's Lemma to SQIsign

Let us now see how we propose to use Kani's Lemma (Lemma 4) in SQIsignHD.

Signing in Dimension 4. The idea is to embed the signature $\sigma : E_1 \longrightarrow E_2$ in an isogeny of dimension 4. We consider the 2-dimensional q-isogeny $\Sigma := \mathrm{Diag}(\sigma, \sigma) : E_1^2 \longrightarrow E_2^2$, and for $a_1, a_2 \in \mathbb{Z}$ and $i \in \{1, 2\}$ the $(a_1^2 + a_2^2)$-isogeny

$$
\alpha_i := \begin{pmatrix} a_1 & a_2 \\ -a_2 & a_1 \end{pmatrix} \in \mathrm{End}(E_i^2).
$$

Then, we have an isogeny diamond

$$
\begin{array}{ccc}
E_2^2 & \xrightarrow{\;\alpha_2\;} & E_2^2 \\
\Sigma \uparrow & & \uparrow \Sigma \\
E_1^2 & \xrightarrow{\;\alpha_1\;} & E_1^2
\end{array}
$$

yielding an N-isogeny (with $N := q + a_1^2 + a_2^2$):

$$F := \begin{pmatrix} \alpha_1 & \widetilde{\Sigma} \\ -\Sigma & \widetilde{\alpha_2} \end{pmatrix} \in \text{End}(E_1^2 \times E_2^2).$$

Notation 5. We shall denote $F(\sigma, a_1, a_2)$ when we want to specify the dependence of F on σ, a_1, a_2.

We choose the parameters q, a_1, a_2, so that $N = \ell^e$, with ℓ a small prime and $e \in \mathbb{N}^*$ big enough. Provided that q and ℓ are coprime, we know that

$$\ker(F) = \{(\widetilde{\alpha_1}(P), \Sigma(P)) \mid P \in E_1^2[\ell^e]\}, \tag{1}$$

by Lemma 4. Then, knowing $\ker(F)$ we can compute F as an ℓ-isogeny chain and obtain an efficient representation of σ, as explained in Remark 2.1.

It follows that our idea requires to compute $\ker(F)$, which becomes easy once we know how to evaluate σ on $E_1[\ell^e]$, by formula 1. The idea is to use the alternate isogeny path $\varphi \circ \tau \circ \widehat{\psi} : E_1 \to E_2$. Since the signature requires to compute the three isogenies φ, ψ, τ, it will not cost too much to use them in order to evaluate σ. There are several technicalities to make it work in practice (such as to making sure that this alternate path has degree prime to ℓ) but it is manageable (see [9, §A.5]).

Computing such a representation for the signature is simpler than in the original SQIsign protocol. This shifts the main computation effort to the verification, where the actual isogeny in dimension 4 must be computed.

Parameters. Even though we no longer impose $q = \deg(\sigma)$ to be smooth, we still impose conditions on q to make it work. We shall need $\ell^e - q$ to be a prime congruent to 1 modulo 4 in order to decompose it easily as a sum of two squares $\ell^e - q = a_1^2 + a_2^2$ by Cornacchia's algorithm [6]. This choice of q ensures its coprimality with ℓ, as required to compute $\ker(F)$. The exponent e is fixed to be as small as possible so that there always exists an isogeny $\sigma : E_1 \longrightarrow E_2$ of ℓ^e-*good* degree in the sense of the following definition. In practice, the smallest values for q are close to $\sqrt{p}$ (Sect. 4.2) so ℓ^e will be slightly bigger than $\sqrt{p}$.

Definition 6. We say that an integer q is ℓ^e-*good* when $\ell^e - q$ is a prime number congruent to 1 modulo 4.[1]

Remark 7 (The issue of the signature distribution). Those restrictions on the degree q impact the distribution of signatures. The bound $\ell^e \simeq \sqrt{p}$ is also restrictive (see [9, Theorem 42]). For that reason, we need some plausible heuristic assumptions to prove the zero-knowledge property of our scheme. This can be

---

[1] One could improve slightly the scheme by defining ℓ^e-good integers as integers q such that $\ell^e - q = sq'$, with s a smooth integer whose prime factors are all congruent to 1 modulo 4 and q' is a prime congruent to 1 modulo 4. Indeed, all we really need is that $\ell^e - q$ is easy to factor so Cornacchia's algorithm can be applied efficiently. This alternate definition would improve a bit the search for ℓ^e-good integer, but we went for the simplest definition.

fixed by going to dimension 8 as long as $q < \ell^e$ and $\ell^e = \Omega(p^2)$. This way, we shall obtain a uniform distribution of signatures and a provably zero-knowledge scheme which is the purpose of our scheme in dimension 8 that we present below.

Signing in Dimension 8. By Lagrange's four square theorem [21], if $q < \ell^e$, there always exists $a_1, \cdots, a_4 \in \mathbb{Z}$ such that $q + a_1^2 + \cdots + a_4^2 = \ell^e$. We can find such a decomposition in polynomial time in e with Rabin and Shallit's algorithm [31] improved by Pollack and Treviño [30]. We then consider the endomorphisms

$$
\alpha_i := \begin{pmatrix} a_1 & -a_2 & -a_3 & -a_4 \\ a_2 & a_1 & a_4 & -a_3 \\ a_3 & -a_4 & a_1 & a_2 \\ a_4 & a_3 & -a_2 & a_1 \end{pmatrix} \in \mathrm{End}(E_i^4),
$$

for $i \in \{1, 2\}$, which are $(a_1^2 + \cdots + a_4^2)$-isogenies, and the q-isogeny $\Sigma := \mathrm{Diag}$ $(\sigma, \cdots, \sigma) : E_1^4 \longrightarrow E_2^4$. As previously, by Kani's lemma, we have the ℓ^e-isogeny

$$
F := \begin{pmatrix} \alpha_1 & \widetilde{\Sigma} \\ -\Sigma & \widetilde{\alpha}_2 \end{pmatrix} \in \mathrm{End}(E_1^4 \times E_2^4).
$$

Similarly to dimension 4, we write $F(\sigma, a_1, \cdots, a_4)$ to highlight the dependence of F on $\sigma, a_1, \cdots, a_4$. To ensure the uniformity of the response, in dimension 8 we no longer restrict to the case q prime to ℓ. This means we might have to embed in dimension 8 a factor of σ of degree prime to ℓ instead of σ (see [9, § C] for details). As in dimension 4, can compute $\ker(F)$ by evaluating σ on $E_1[\ell^e]$ and then compute F as an ℓ-isogeny chain. This way, we can represent any signature isogeny σ of degree $q < \ell^e$, with the implications on the security proof that we mentioned before. However, computing isogenies in dimension 8 is much more costly than in dimension 4 (though, still polynomial), so we do not recommend to use this representation and only propose it in the alternate version RigorousSQIsignHD.

More generally, the same techniques allow, given an ideal I representing an isogeny of degree q, to give an efficient representation of the isogeny σ associated to I by the Deuring correspondance, even when q is not smooth (see [9, § A.3–4]). **Why not Signing in Dimension 2?** The cost of computing an isogeny grows exponentially with the dimension [24–26]. For that reason, finding an efficient representation in dimension 2 could be fruitful for SQIsignHD. On the other hand, the higher the dimension, the lesser the constraints on the isogeny σ. We have already seen that going from dimension 4 to 8 relaxes the constraints on $q = \deg(\sigma)$. Unsurprisingly, the constraints on σ are tighter in dimension 2. So far, under those constraints, we have failed to provide an efficient and secure version of SQIsignHD. We leave this question to future works.

3   Key Generation, Commitment and Challenge

To evaluate σ on the ℓ^e-torsion, as required for the response computation, we apply the EvalTorsion procedure ([9, § A.5]) which uses the alternate path $\varphi \circ \tau \circ \widehat{\psi} :$ $E_1 \longrightarrow E_2$ formed by the challenge φ, secret key τ and commitment isogeny ψ

along with their ideals I_φ, I_τ and I_ψ. These ideals are also necessary to compute the ideal I_σ.

For the EvalTorsion procedure to work, the degrees of φ, τ and ψ must be prime to ℓ. The ideals I_ψ and I_τ can be generated directly along with ψ and τ. However, the computation of I_φ uses the procedure IsogenyToIdeal ([9, §A.4]) which requires a precomputation in the key generation phase. Namely, the prover will need to generate an alternate secret path $\tau' : E_0 \longrightarrow E_A$ of degree $D_{\tau'}$ prime to D_φ along with the secret key $\tau : E_0 \longrightarrow E_A$. This will be explained in Sect. 3.3.

3.1 Accessible Torsion and Choice of the Prime Characteristic

The choice of p is usually made to provide enough accessible torsion for our isogeny computations. In FastSQIsignHD, we can choose $p = c\ell^f \ell'^{f'} - 1$ with $\ell \neq \ell'$ two primes, $c \in \mathbb{N}^*$ small and $\ell^f \simeq \ell'^{f'} \simeq \sqrt{p}$, as in SIDH [18]. In practice, $\ell = 2$ and $\ell' = 3$ are the best choice.

We then require $D_\tau = D_\psi = \ell'^{2f'}$, $D_\varphi = \ell^f \ell'^{f'}$ and $D_{\tau'} = \ell^{2f^2}$. This choice ensures that D_τ, D_ψ and D_φ are prime to ℓ and that $D_{\tau'}$ is prime to D_φ, as needed. We also have $D_\tau, D_\psi, D_{\tau'} = \Theta(p)$, which guarantees (at least heuristically) that the public key E_A and the commitment E_1 are computationally indistinguishable from a uniformly random supersingular elliptic curve – which is essential to the security of FastSQIsignHD.

This choice of prime also provides enough accessible torsion to compute the ℓ^e-isogeny F representing the response σ in dimension 4, where $\ell^e > q := D_\sigma$. In fact, we even have much more than the minimum requirement since it will be enough to have $2f \geq e + 4$ (so $\ell^f = \Omega(p^{1/4})$) as will be explained in Sects. 4.3 and 4.4 and Remark 4.2. This freedom is welcome anyway because it allows us to take ℓ^e slightly bigger than $\sqrt{p}$ to make sure that we can always find an ideal I of ℓ^e-good norm $q < \ell^e$ (see Sect. 4.2).

We finally discuss the security requirements regarding the size of p. The best known classical key recovery attacks are the meet-in-the-middle algorithm or the general Delfs and Galbraith attack [11] in the supersingular isogeny graph which both have a complexity in $\tilde{O}(\sqrt{p})$. Using Grover's algorithm [16], we reach a quantum complexity of $\tilde{O}(p^{1/4})$. Hence, to ensure a classical security level of λ bits and a quantum security level of $\lambda/2$ bits, we need to take $p = \Theta(2^{2\lambda})$, as in the original version of SQIsign [10].

We give below some concrete values of primes for NIST levels 1, 3 and 5.

NIST security level	Security parameter λ (bits)	Prime p
NIST-I	128	$13 \cdot 2^{126} \cdot 3^{78} - 1$
NIST-III	192	$5 \cdot 2^{193} \cdot 3^{122} - 1$
NIST-V	256	$11 \cdot 2^{257} \cdot 3^{163} - 1$

---

[2] Actually, we will not have exactly $D_\tau = D_\psi = \ell'^{2f'}$ but D_τ and D_ψ will be divisors of $\ell'^{2f'}$ close to $\ell'^{2f'}$. It will be the same for $D_{\psi'}$ (see Algorithm 1). We assume equality to simplify the exposition.

3.2   Challenge Generation

To ensure a soundness security level of λ bits, the challenge space needs to have size at least $2^\lambda \simeq \sqrt{p}$. We also need the challenge degree D_φ to be prime to ℓ to be able to push the points of order ℓ^f through ψ during the signing procedure. The challenge generation procedure Challenge is the same in the fast and provably secure challenge generation procedure. It simply generates a random element $P \in E_A$ of order D_φ and computes φ of kernel $\langle P \rangle$. Only the degree D_φ changes; in FastSQIsignHD, we take $D_\varphi = \ell'^{f'}$.

3.3   Fast Key Generation and Commitment

We now present FastDoublePath (Algorithm 1) the main algorithmic block for the key generation and commitment of FastSQIsignHD. The goal of this algorithm is to generate two isogeny paths $\phi, \phi' : E_0 \longrightarrow E$ of degree dividing $\ell^{2f} \simeq p$ and $\ell'^{2f'} \simeq p$ respectively, computing the kernel ideals I_ϕ and $I_{\phi'}$ along the way. This algorithm is directly applicable to the key generation procedure FastKeyGen where we need to generate a double path to be able to compute the challenge kernel ideal I_φ (using [9, §A.4] and an ℓ-isogeny path of degree prime to ℓ') in order to apply the EvalTorsion procedure (with the ℓ'-isogeny path of degree prime to ℓ).

For the commitment FastCommit, we only need the ℓ'-isogeny path $\psi = \phi'$ but the algorithm is essentially the same, except that we do not compute ϕ and I_ϕ completely. This is the reason why we changed the side of the challenge: to save time in the commitment phase. Had we started the challenge φ from E_1 as in SQISign, we would have needed to compute a double isogeny path in the commitment phase. Instead, we precompute this double path during the key generation.

Note that generating isogenies of degree $\simeq p$ is essential for security reasons, in order to ensure that the codomain E is heuristically close to a random elliptic curve in the supersingular isogeny graph. To compute such long isogeny paths, however, we are limited by the accessible torsion in E_0 (we have access to the $\ell^f \ell'^{f'}$-torsion only). To circumvent this difficulty, we use pushforward isogenies, as defined in [10, §4.1].

Definition 8. Let $\rho : E \longrightarrow E_1$ and $\theta : E \longrightarrow E_2$ be two isogenies with coprime degree. The *pushforward* of ρ via θ, denoted by $\rho' := [\theta]_* \rho$ is an isogeny $E_2 \longrightarrow E_3$ satisfying $\ker(\rho') = \theta(\ker(\rho))$.

Remark 9. θ and ρ satisfy $[\theta]_* \rho \circ \theta = [\rho]_* \theta \circ \rho$. In particular, $[\theta]_* \rho$ and $[\rho]_* \theta$ have the same codomain. If I and J are the ideals associated to ρ and θ respectively via the Deuring correspondence, we denote by $[J]_* I$ the *pushforward ideal* associated to $[\theta]_* \rho$. By [10, Lemma 3], the ideal $[J]_* I$ can be computed as follows: $[J]_* I = J^{-1} \cdot (I \cap J)$.

The Algorithm. The idea is to construct the isogenies ϕ and ϕ' (of degree dividing ℓ^{2f} and $\ell'^{2f'}$ respectively) by finding an endomorphism γ of degree dividing $\ell^{2f}\ell'^{2f'}$, and factoring it as $\gamma = \hat{\phi}' \circ \phi$. Since $\ell^{2f}\ell'^{2f'} = \Theta(p^2) = \omega(p)$, we can easily find $\gamma \in \mathcal{O}_0$ non divisible by ℓ or ℓ', of norm $\mathrm{nrd}(\gamma) = \ell^{2g}\ell'^{2g'}$ with $g \leq f$ close to f and $g' \leq f'$ close to f', using [22, Algorithm 4].

Since ℓ^{2f} (and $\ell'^{2f'}$) exceeds the available torsion, some "pushforward gymnastics" is required to compute the factorisation. We thus decompose $\varepsilon(\gamma) = \widehat{\rho_2} \circ \rho_1$ where ρ_1 and ρ_2 are isogenies $E_0 \longrightarrow E'$ of degree $\ell^g\ell'^{g'}$ and ε is an isomorphism $\mathcal{O}_0 \xrightarrow{\sim} \mathrm{End}(E_0)$. $\varepsilon(\gamma)$ being cyclic, according to the following lemma, ρ_1 and its associated kernel ideal K_1 are given by:

$$\ker(\rho_1) = \ker(\varepsilon(\gamma)) \cap E_0[\ell^g\ell'^{g'}] \quad \text{and} \quad K_1 = \mathcal{O}_0\gamma + \mathcal{O}_0\ell^g\ell'^{g'}.$$

Similarly, $\ker(\rho_2) = \ker(\widehat{\varepsilon(\gamma)}) \cap E_0[\ell^g\ell'^{g'}]$ and the associated kernel ideal is $K_2 = \mathcal{O}_0\overline{\gamma} + \mathcal{O}_0\ell^g\ell'^{g'}$.

Lemma 10. *Let $\rho : E \longrightarrow E'$ be a cyclic isogeny decomposed into $\rho = \theta \circ \rho_1$. Then we have:*

(i) $\ker(\rho_1) = \ker(\rho) \cap E[d_1]$ *with $d_1 := \deg(\rho_1)$.*
(ii) *If ρ is a cyclic endomorphism $(E = E')$, then the kernel ideal of ρ_1 is $K_1 = \mathcal{O}\rho + \mathcal{O}d_1$, where $\mathcal{O} := \mathrm{End}(E)$.*

Proof. Since $\rho = \theta \circ \rho_1$ and $\deg(\rho_1) = d_1$, we clearly have $\ker(\rho_1) \subseteq \ker(\rho) \cap E[d_1]$. Since ρ is cyclic, there exists a generator $P \in E$ of $\ker(\rho)$ of order $d := \deg(\rho)$ and we have $\ker(\rho) \cap E[d_1] = \langle [d/d_1]P \rangle$, where $[d/d_1]P$ has order d_1, so we conclude that the inclusion is an equality by cardinality, since ρ_1 is separable. (i) follows.

To prove (ii), we remark that $E[\mathcal{O}\rho + \mathcal{O}d_1] = E[\rho] \cap E[d_1] = \ker(\rho_1)$, where the last equality was proved in (i). Then, we conclude that $K_1 = \mathcal{O}\rho + \mathcal{O}d_1$ by injectivity of the Deuring correspondence between left $\mathcal{O}$-ideals and isogenies of domain E [40, Proposition 42.2.16]. This completes the proof. □

Then, we can decompose ρ_1 and ρ_2 into $\rho_1 = \widehat{\theta'}_1 \circ \theta_1$ and $\rho_2 = \widehat{\theta}_2 \circ \theta'_2$ where the θ_i are isogenies of degree ℓ^g and the θ'_i are isogenies of degree $\ell'^{g'}$ for $i \in \{1, 2\}$, as in the following diagram:

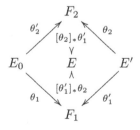

The pushforward isogenies $[\theta'_1]_*\theta_2$ and $[\theta_2]_*\theta'_1$ have the same codomain E and degree ℓ^g and $\ell'^{g'}$ respectively. Hence, $\phi := [\theta'_1]_*\theta_2 \circ \theta_1$ and $\phi' := [\theta_2]_*\theta'_1 \circ \theta'_2$ are isogenies $E_0 \longrightarrow E$ of desired degrees ℓ^{2g} and $\ell^{2g'}$ respectively. By Lemma

---

Algorithm 1: FastDoublePath

Data: A basis of $\mathcal{O}_0$ and an isomorphism $\varepsilon : \mathcal{O}_0 \xrightarrow{\sim} \mathrm{End}(E_0)$.

Result: Two cyclic isogenies $\phi : E_0 \longrightarrow E$ of degree dividing ℓ^{2f} and $\phi' : E_0 \longrightarrow E$ of degree dividing $\ell'^{2f'}$ and their respective kernel ideals J and J'.

1 Use [22, Algorithm 4] to find $\gamma \in \mathcal{O}_0$ non divisible by ℓ and ℓ' of norm $\mathrm{nrd}(\gamma) = \ell^{2g}\ell'^{2g'}$ with $g \leq f$ close to f and $g' \leq f'$ close to f';

2 Evaluate $\varepsilon(\gamma)$ and $\varepsilon(\overline{\gamma})$ on a basis of $E_0[\ell^g\ell'^{g'}]$ and solve discrete logarithm problems to compute $\mathcal{G}_1 := \ker(\varepsilon(\gamma)) \cap E_0[\ell^g\ell'^{g'}]$ and $\mathcal{G}_2 := \ker(\widehat{\varepsilon(\gamma)}) \cap E_0[\ell^g\ell'^{g'}]$;

3 Compute $\rho_i : E_0 \longrightarrow E'$ of kernel $\mathcal{G}_i$ for $i = 1, 2$;

4 Compute $\mathcal{H}_1 := \ker(\varepsilon(\gamma)) \cap E_0[\ell^g]$, $\mathcal{H}_2' := \ker(\widehat{\varepsilon(\gamma)}) \cap E_0[\ell'^{g'}]$, $\mathcal{H}_1' := \ker(\widehat{\rho_1}) \cap E'[\ell'^{g'}]$ and $\mathcal{H}_2 := \ker(\widehat{\rho_2}) \cap E'[\ell^g]$;

5 Compute θ_i of kernel $\mathcal{H}_i$ and θ_i' of kernel $\mathcal{H}_i'$ for $i = 1, 2$;

6 Compute $[\theta_1']_*\theta_2$ and $[\theta_2]_*\theta_1'$ of kernels $\theta_1'(\ker(\theta_2))$ and $\theta_2(\ker(\theta_1'))$ respectively;

7 Let $\phi := [\theta_1']_*\theta_2 \circ \theta_1$ and $\phi' := [\theta_2]_*\theta_1' \circ \theta_2'$;

8 Let $J := \mathcal{O}_0\gamma + \mathcal{O}_0\ell^{2g}$ and $J' := \mathcal{O}_0\overline{\gamma} + \mathcal{O}_0\ell'^{2g'}$;

9 Return ϕ, ϕ', J, J';

10, we can compute $\ker(\theta_1)$, $\ker(\theta_2')$, $\ker(\theta_1')$ and $\ker(\theta_2)$, and obtain the θ_i and θ_i' with Vélu's formulas [38]. We then compute $\ker([\theta_1']_*\theta_2) = \theta_1'(\ker(\theta_2))$ and $\ker([\theta_2]_*\theta_1') = \theta_2(\ker(\theta_1'))$ and use Vélu's formulas again. We then easily get ϕ and ϕ'.

Since $\varepsilon(\gamma) = \widehat{\rho_2} \circ \rho_1$ and $[\theta_1']_*\theta_2 \circ \theta_1' = [\theta_2]_*\theta_1' \circ \theta_2$, we get that $\varepsilon(\gamma) = \hat{\phi}' \circ \phi$. Lemma 10 implies that the ideals $J := \mathcal{O}_0\gamma + \mathcal{O}_0\ell^{2g}$ and $J' := \mathcal{O}_0\overline{\gamma} + \mathcal{O}_0\ell'^{2g'}$ are the respective kernel ideals of ϕ and ϕ'. Algorithm 1 follows.

Remark 3.1. The FastKeyGen procedure calls Algorithm 1 directly. For FastCommit, only ϕ' and J' are necessary, so we use a slightly modified version of Algorithm 1 where $\mathcal{H}_1$ (line 4), θ_1 (line 5), ϕ (line 7), and J (line 8) are not computed.

4   Response and Verification

The goal of this section is to present a precise description of the algorithmic building blocks required by our new signature scheme in dimension 4. We refer to [9, § C] for details on the dimension 8 version.

Throughout this section, we assume that the prover has generated two secret key paths $\tau, \tau' : E_0 \longrightarrow E_A$ of respective degrees $D_\tau = \ell'^{2f'}$ and $D_{\tau'} = \ell^{2f}$ and a secret commitment path $\psi : E_0 \longrightarrow E_1$ of degree $D_\psi = \ell'^{2f'}$. We also assume the prover has access to the challenge $\varphi : E_A \longrightarrow E_2$ of degree $D_\varphi = \ell^f{}'$.

4.1 Overview of the Response Computation

In this section, we present the algorithm FastRespond used to compute the response in the FastSQIsignHD identification protocol (in dimension 4) and its verification counterpart FastVerify.

Those algorithms use the following sub-algorithms that will be introduced in this section (if not already):

- IsogenyToIdeal($\varphi, \tau', I_{\tau'}$) (presented in [9, §A.4]) takes as input a basis of End(E_0) that we can evaluate on points, an isogeny $\varphi : E_A \longrightarrow E_2$ of degree D_φ, an isogeny $\tau' : E_0 \longrightarrow E_A$ of degree prime to D_φ, its ideal $I_{\tau'} \subset \mathcal{O}_0$ and returns the kernel ideal I_φ of φ.
- RandomEquivalentIdeal takes as input an $\mathcal{O}_0$-left ideal J and returns an equivalent ideal I that is uniformly random among ideals of norm $\leq \ell^e$.
- EvalTorsion (presented in [9, §A.5]) evaluates a non-smooth degree isogeny on ℓ^f-torsion points knowing its kernel ideal and an alternate smooth degree path. Namely, it takes as input an ideal I connecting $\mathcal{O} \cong$ End(E) and $\mathcal{O}' \cong$ End(E'), a basis (P_1, P_2) of $E[\ell^f]$, two isogenies $\rho_1 : E_0 \longrightarrow E$ and $\rho_2 : E_0 \longrightarrow E'$ of smooth degrees prime to ℓ, with their respective kernel ideals I_1 and I_2 and returns $(\phi_I(P_1), \phi_I(P_2))$, where $\phi_I : E \longrightarrow E'$ is the isogeny associated to I.
- RepresentIsogeny takes as input an ℓ^e-good integer q, integers a_1, a_2 such that $a_1^2 + a_2^2 + q = \ell^e$, a basis (P_1, P_2) of $E_1[\ell^f]$, $(\sigma(P_1), \sigma(P_2))$, where $\sigma : E_1 \longrightarrow E_2$ is a q-isogeny, and returns a chain of 4-dimensional ℓ-isogenies whose composition is $F(\sigma, a_1, a_2)$ as in Notation 5.
- IsValid, with input $F, E_1, E_2, \ell^e, \ell^f$, checks if F is a valid output of RepresentIsogeny representing an isogeny $\sigma : E_1 \longrightarrow E_2$ in dimension 4.

The prover sends the image of two points P_1, P_2 forming a basis of $E_1[\ell^f]$ by σ and its degree q. The verifier can then use q to compute a_1, a_2 and compute $F(\sigma, a_1, a_2)$ with the RepresentIsogeny procedure. If the computation succeeds and is validated by the IsValid procedure, then the verification is complete. Algorithm 3 follows.

Remark 4.1. (On the ℓ^f-torsion basis). It is sufficient to send the data $(\sigma(P_1), \sigma(P_2), q)$ to the verifier as the basis (P_1, P_2) can be computed canonically knowing E_1 by classical compression techniques developed for SIDH [2,42]. This decreases the communications size at a small computational cost. Later, with the compression/decompression algorithms (see Algorithms 6 and 7), we will see how to further compress this data.

Note that we use a basis of the ℓ^f-torsion with $2f \geq e + 4$ here because we might not have the ℓ^e-torsion accessible. We can still compute F with this partial information as explained in Sect. 4.3.

To respond, the prover starts by computing an ideal $I \sim \overline{I_\psi} \cdot I_\tau \cdot I_\varphi$ connecting $\mathcal{O}_1 \cong$ End(E_1) to $\mathcal{O}_2 \cong$ End(E_2) of ℓ^e-good norm q and prime to ℓ' with uniform distribution using RandomEquivalentIdeal. The coprimality with ℓ' is justified by security reasons (see Sect. 5.1). Then, the prover generates the basis (P_1, P_2) of $E_1[\ell^f]$ canonically and evaluates σ on it with EvalTorsion using I (kernel ideal of σ) and the paths $\psi : E_0 \longrightarrow E_1$ and $\varphi \circ \tau : E_0 \longrightarrow E_2$ of degrees prime to ℓ.

As input of Algorithms 2 and 3, we denote by:

- FastSetup, the public parameters of FastSQIsignHD, $p = c\ell^f \ell'^{f'} - 1$, ℓ, ℓ', f, f', the exponent e and the elliptic curve $E_0/\mathbb{F}_p$;
- SecretKey, the isogenies $\tau, \tau' : E_0 \longrightarrow E_A$ of degrees $D_\tau = \ell'^{2f'}$ and $D_{\tau'} = \ell^{2f}$ respectively along with their kernel ideals I_τ and $I_{\tau'}$;
- CommitData, the isogeny $\psi : E_0 \longrightarrow E_1$ of degree $D_\psi = \ell'^{2f}$ and its kernel ideal I_ψ;
- ChallData, the isogeny $\varphi : E_A \longrightarrow E_2$ of degree $D_\varphi = \ell'^{f'}$.

Algorithm 2: FastRespond

Data: FastSetup, SecretKey, CommitData and ChallData.
Result: $(\sigma(P_1), \sigma(P_2), q)$, where (P_1, P_2) is a canonically determined basis of $E_1[\ell^f]$ and $\sigma : E_1 \longrightarrow E_2$ is an isogeny of ℓ^e-good degree q prime to ℓ'.
1 $I_\varphi \longleftarrow$ IsogenyToIdeal$(\varphi, \tau', I_{\tau'})$;
2 $J \longleftarrow \overline{I_\psi} \cdot I_\tau \cdot I_\varphi$;
3 $I \longleftarrow$ RandomEquivalentIdeal(J) and $q \longleftarrow$ nrd(I);
4 If q is not ℓ^e-good or $q \wedge \ell' \neq 1$, go back to line 3;
5 Compute the canonical basis (P_1, P_2) of $E_1[\ell^f]$;
6 $(\sigma(P_1), \sigma(P_2)) \longleftarrow$ EvalTorsion$(I, P_1, P_2, \psi, \varphi \circ \tau, I_\psi, I_\tau \cdot I_\varphi)$;
7 Return $(\sigma(P_1), \sigma(P_2), q)$;

Algorithm 3: FastVerify

Data: FastSetup, E_1, E_2 and an output R from FastRespond.
Result: Determines if R is a valid response.
1 Try to parse $R := (R_1, R_2, q)$, where $R_1, R_2 \in E_2[\ell^f]$ and $q < \ell^e$ and return False if it fails;
2 If q is not ℓ^e-good or $q \wedge \ell' \neq 1$, return False;
3 Compute the canonical basis (P_1, P_2) of $E_1[\ell^f]$;
4 Find $a_1, a_2 \in \mathbb{Z}$ such that $a_1^2 + a_2^2 = \ell^e - q$ using Cornacchia's algorithm [6];
5 $F \longleftarrow$ RepresentIsogeny$(E_1, E_2, a_1, a_2, P_1, P_2, R_1, R_2)$;
6 if $F \neq$ False then
7 $\quad |$ Return IsValid(F, E_1, E_2, a_1, a_2);
8 else
9 $\quad |$ Return False.
10 end

4.2   Finding a Uniformly Random Tight Response Ideal

In this section, we present the algorithm RandomEquivalentIdeal taking a left
$\mathcal{O}_0$-ideal J as input and returning an ideal I which is uniformly random among
the ideals $I \sim J$ of norm $q < \ell^e$. By [10, Lemma 1], all the equivalent ideals
$I \sim J$ are of the form $\chi_J(\alpha) := J\overline{\alpha}/\mathrm{nrd}(J)$ for some $\alpha \in J$ and α determines
I up to multiplication by an element of $\mathcal{O}_0^\times$. Besides, the norm of $I = \chi_J(\alpha)$ is
$q_J(\alpha) := \mathrm{nrd}(\alpha)/\mathrm{nrd}(J)$, so we need $q_J(\alpha) \leq \ell^e$.

Hence, to sample an ideal $I \sim J$ such that $\mathrm{nrd}(I) \leq \ell^e$ with uniform distribution is equivalent to sample $\alpha \in J \setminus \{0\}$ such that $q_J(\alpha) \leq \ell^e$ with uniform
distribution. If we fix a basis of J, we can see q_J as a primitive positive definite
integral quadratic form with four variables. By the following lemma, which is a
simple generalization of [41, Lemma 3.3], we can sample uniformly $\alpha \in J$ such
that $q_J(\alpha) \leq \ell^e$. RandomEquivalentIdeal calls this procedure to get $\alpha \in J$ uniform and rejects the result if $\alpha = 0$. Then the distribution of α is still uniform
but in $J \setminus \{0\}$. The proofs of the two following lemmas can be found in [9, § E.2].

Lemma 11. *Let f be a primitive positive definite integral quadratic form in k
variables and let $\rho > 0$. Then there exists an algorithm that samples uniformly
random elements from the set*

$$\{x \in \mathbb{Z}^k \mid f(x) \leq \rho\}$$

*in polynomial time in $\log(\rho)$ and the length of f (namely, the maximal number
of bits of the coefficients of f). This algorithm runs in exponential time in k.*

For RandomEquivalentIdeal(J) to terminate, we need to find $\alpha \in J \setminus \{0\}$ such
that $q_J(\alpha) \leq \ell^e$. For such an α to exist, we need $\ell^e = \Omega(\sqrt{p})$ according to the
following lemma (Lemma 12).

Lemma 12. *Let $\mathcal{O}$ be a maximal order and J be a left $\mathcal{O}$-ideal. Then there exists
$\alpha \in J$ such that $q_J(\alpha) \leq 2\sqrt{2p}/\pi$.*

In the procedure FastRespond, we reject the results of RandomEquivalentIdeal
whose norm is not ℓ^e-good or divisible by ℓ'. If it terminates, this rejection
sampling outputs ideals which are uniformly random among the targeted ones,
as desired. However, we can only give a heuristic argument for the termination.
Assuming that $q_J(\alpha)$ behaves like a random integer, we should expect to find a
suitable $\alpha \in J$ with probability $O(1/\log(p))$. Hence, taking ℓ^e a few bits over $\sqrt{p}$
might be sufficient. For that reason, in our choice of parameters, we only have
accessible ℓ^f-torsion with $\ell^f < \sqrt{p} < \ell^e$ (see Sect. 3.1). Proving formally that we
can always find an ℓ^e-good value of $q_J(\alpha)$ would certainly require to increase ℓ^e
by a lot. As [35] indicates, we should expect lower bounds close to $\ell^e = \omega(p^2)$,
causing a huge efficiency loss.

4.3   Dividing the Higher Dimensional Isogeny Computation in Two

As explained in Sect. 4.2, we do not necessarily have enough accessible torsion
to compute the whole kernel of the higher dimensional representation of the

response F. In this section, we explain in plain generality how to circumvent this difficulty. Hence, the following discussion applies to both dimension 4 and 8. Let us keep the notations of Sect. 2.2. Recall that we have the following isogeny

$$F := \begin{pmatrix} \varphi & \widetilde{\psi}' \\ -\psi & \varphi' \end{pmatrix}, \quad \text{with} \quad \ker(F) = \{(\widetilde{\varphi}(x), \psi'(x)) \mid x \in B[d]\}.$$

To compute F, we need to evaluate $\widetilde{\varphi}$ and ψ' on $B[d]$, so we need to have accessible d-torsion. However, we assume that we only have d'-accessible torsion with $d' | d$.

The idea is to decompose $F = F_2 \circ F_1$ where $F_1 : \mathcal{A} := A \times B' \longrightarrow \mathcal{C}$ and $F_2 : \mathcal{C} \longrightarrow \mathcal{B} := B \times A'$ are respectively d_1 and d_2-isogenies such that $d_1, d_2 | d'$ and to use the following proposition (proved in [9, § E.3]) to compute F_1 and $\widetilde{F_2}$ to infer F.

Proposition 13. *Suppose d prime to p so that F is separable. Then:*

(i) *We can always decompose $F = F_2 \circ F_1$, as above.*
(ii) $\ker(F_1) \subseteq \ker(F) \cap \mathcal{A}[d_1]$.
(iii) $\ker(\widetilde{F_2}) \subseteq \ker(\widetilde{F}) \cap \mathcal{B}[d_2] = F(\mathcal{A}[d]) \cap \mathcal{B}[d_2]$.
(iv) *When $\ker(F)$ has rank $g := \dim(\mathcal{A})$, those inclusions are equalities.*

In SQIsignHD, $d_1 = \ell^{e_1}$ and $d_2 = \ell^{e_2}$ with $e = e_1 + e_2$ and we have accessible ℓ^f-torsion such that $f \geq e_1, e_2$. Since $\ker(F)$ has maximal rank $g = 4$ (or 8), we have by point (iv) of the above proposition

$$\ker(F_1) = \ker(F)[\ell^{e_1}] = \{(\widetilde{\alpha_1}(P), \Sigma(P)) \mid P \in E_1^{g/2}[\ell^{e_1}]\}$$

and similarly, $\ker(\widetilde{F_2}) = \ker(\widetilde{F})[\ell^{e_2}] = \{(\alpha_1(P), -\Sigma(P)) \mid P \in E_1^{g/2}[\ell^{e_2}]\}$, with the notations of Sect. 2.3.

In [9, § F], we give an overview of the higher dimensional isogeny computation required in the procedures RepresentIsogeny of our SQIsignHD scheme. We provide a proof of concept sagemath implementation in dimension 4. Optimizing this implementation in a low level programming language is left for future works.

4.4   Computing the Response Isogeny Representation

We finally give algorithms to compute the signature representation in dimension 4 using all the ideas presented in Sect. 4.3 and [9, § F]. We refer to KernelToIsogeny($\mathscr{B}_0$) as the algorithm computing an ℓ-isogeny chain in dimension g given a basis $\mathscr{B}_0$ of its kernel. We refer to [9, § F] for more details on this algorithm.

In dimension 4, RepresentIsogeny (Algorithm 4) computes basis of $\ker(F_1)$ and $\ker(\widetilde{F_2})$ with $F := F_2 \circ F_1$, as in Sect. 4.3. Then, it calls KernelToIsogeny to obtain F_1 and $\widetilde{F_2}$ as isogeny chains. The ideas are the same in dimension 8.

Algorithm 4: RepresentIsogeny

Data: $E_1, E_2, a_1, a_2 \in \mathbb{Z}$, a basis (P_1, P_2) of $E_1[\ell^f]$ and $(\sigma(P_1), \sigma(P_2))$, where
$\quad \sigma : E_1 \longrightarrow E_2$ is a q-isogeny with $a_1^2 + a_2^2 + q = \ell^e$.

Result: An ℓ^{e_1}-isogeny $F_1 : E_1^2 \times E_2^2 \longrightarrow \mathcal{C}$ and a ℓ^{e_2}-isogeny $\widetilde{F_2} : E_1^2 \times E_2^2 \longrightarrow \mathcal{C}$
$\quad$ such that $F(\sigma, a_1, a_2) = F_2 \circ F_1$, with $e_1, e_2 \leq f$ and $e_1 + e_2 = e$.

1   $e_2 \longleftarrow \lceil e/2 \rceil, e_1 \longleftarrow e - e_2$;

2   $Q_i \longleftarrow [\ell^{f-e_1}]P_i, \; R_i \longleftarrow [\ell^{f-e_1}]\sigma(P_i), \; Q_i' \longleftarrow [\ell^{f-e_2}]P_i, \; R_i' \longleftarrow [\ell^{f-e_2}]\sigma(P_i)$
$\quad$ for $i \in \{1, 2\}$;

3   $\mathcal{B}_0 \longleftarrow (([a_1]Q_i, [a_2]Q_i, R_i, 0)_{i \in \{1,2\}}, (-[a_2]Q_i, [a_1]Q_i, 0, R_i)_{i \in \{1,2\}})$;

4   $\mathcal{C}_0 \longleftarrow (([a_1]Q_i', -[a_2]Q_i', -R_i', 0)_{i \in \{1,2\}}, ([a_2]Q_i', [a_1]Q_i', 0, -R_i')_{i \in \{1,2\}})$;

5   **if** $\mathcal{C}_0$ and $\mathcal{B}_0$ are valid kernels of ℓ^{e_1} and ℓ^{e_2}-isogenies **then**

6      $F_1 \longleftarrow$ KernelToIsogeny$(\mathcal{B}_0)$;

7      $\widetilde{F_2} \longleftarrow$ KernelToIsogeny$(\mathcal{C}_0)$;

8   Return F_1 and $\widetilde{F_2}$;

9   **else**

10   Return False;

11   **end**

Proposition 14. *Algorithm 4 is correct. Namely, Algorithm 4 returns $F_1, \tilde{F}_2$ such that $F_2 \circ F_1 = F(\sigma, a_1, a_2)$ on entry $a_1, a_2, P_1, P_2, \sigma(P_2), \; \sigma(P_2)$, where $\sigma : E_1 \longrightarrow E_2$ is a q-isogeny with $a_1^2 + a_2^2 + q = \ell^e$.*

Proof. See [9, § E.4].   □

Remark 4.2. To make sure we have enough accessible torsion, we need $f \geq e_1, e_2$, so that $2f \geq e$. Actually, for KernelToIsogeny to work (with theta coordinates of level 2), we need $4\ell^{e_i}$-torsion points (see [9, § F.3]). Then, when $\ell = 2$, we have $f \geq e_i + 2$, so $2f \geq e + 4$.

4.5 Verification

We describe the verification procedure IsValid taking as input the isogenies F_1 and $\widetilde{F_2}$ outputted by RepresentIsogeny and determining if they represent an isogeny $\sigma : E_1 \longrightarrow E_2$ of degree q. The idea is to check if F_1 and $\widetilde{F_2}$ have the same codomain (computed as principally polarized abelian varieties) and then evaluate $F_2 \circ F_1$ on some points to check that the degree is correct.

The following results (proved in [9, § E.5]) ensure that our verification procedure is correct. In [9, § C], we provide algorithms in dimension 8 achieving similar correctness results.

Proposition 15. *Algorithm 5 is correct. Namely, when given E_1, E_2, a_1, a_2, $F_1, \tilde{F}_2$, if Algorithm 5 returns True, then $F_2 \circ F_1$ is an efficient representation of an isogeny $\sigma : E_1 \longrightarrow E_2$ of degree $q = \ell^e - a_1^2 - a_2^2$.*

Corollary 16. *The verification procedure FastVerify (Algorithm 3) is correct. Namely, on input (R_1, R_2, q), FastVerify returns True if and only if (R_1, R_2, q)*

Algorithm 5: IsValid

Data: Elliptic curves E_1, E_2, integers $a_1, a_2 \in \mathbb{Z}$ and the output $(F_1, \widetilde{F_2})$ of
    RepresentIsogeny$(E_1, E_2, a_1, a_2, *, *, *, *)$.

Result: Determines if $F_2 \circ F_1$ is an efficient repersentation of an isogeny σ :
    $E_1 \longrightarrow E_2$ of degree $q := \ell^e - a_1^2 - a_2^2$.

1 Let $(\mathcal{C}_1, \lambda_1)$ and $(\mathcal{C}_2, \lambda_2)$ be the respective codomains of F_1 and $\widetilde{F_2}$;
2 **if** $(\mathcal{C}_1, \lambda_1) \neq (\mathcal{C}_2, \lambda_2)$ **then**
3 | Return False;
4 **else**
5 | Find a point $Q \in E_1$ of order $\ell^f \ell'^{f'}$;
6 | Compute compute F_2 as the dual of $\widetilde{F_2}$ and $\underline{T} \longleftarrow F_2 \circ F_1(Q, 0, 0, 0)$;
7 | **if** $\underline{T} = ([a_1]Q, -[a_2]Q, *, 0)$ **then**
8 | | Return True;
9 | **else**
10 | | Return False;
11 | **end**
12 **end**

---

defines an efficient representation of an isogeny $\sigma : E_1 \longrightarrow E_2$ of degree q, where
q is ℓ^e-good and prime to ℓ'.

5 Security Analysis

In this section, we prove that the SQIsignHD identification protocol is secure,
namely that it is complete, knowledge sound and honest-verifier zero knowledge.
Recall that by [39, Theorem 7], it is sufficient to ensure that our signature scheme
obtained by Fiat-Shamir transform is universally unforgeable under chosen message attacks in the random oracle model.

Completeness means that a honest execution of the protocol is always
accepted by the verifier. This is true by Proposition 14 and by construction
of IsValid. Knowledge soundness means that an attacker can only "guess" a
response with very low probability. It is proven under the assumption that computing an endomorphism in a supersingular elliptic curve is hard, a well known
difficult problem in isogeny based cryptography.

The honest-verifier zero-knowledge property implies that the response does
not leak any information on the secret key τ. More precisely, we can simulate transcripts of the identification protocol without using the secret key
with the same distribution as real transcripts. To construct such a simulator
of SQIsignHD, we need access to an oracle evaluating isogenies of non-smooth
degrees. In RigorousSQIsignHD, this oracle is very generic and we do not need
any additional hypothesis to prove the zero-knowledge property (hence the name
of this version). On the contrary, in FastSQIsignHD, the oracle definition is *ad
hoc* and we need an additional heuristic assumption to prove the zero-knowledge
property. However, it is very unlikely to build an attack on this assumption as

we argue in Sect. 5.3 and both oracles do not undermine the knowledge soundess. As previously, this section mainly focuses on FastSQIsignHD and refer to [9, § D] for a complete security analysis of RigorousSQIsignHD.

5.1   Knowledge Soundness

The proof that FastSQIsignHD is knowledge sound is a straightforward special soundness argument identical to the original version of SQIsign [10, Theorem 1]. Namely, we prove that given two transcripts with the same commitment but disctinct challenges, we can find an endomorphism in E_A. This *special soundness* property is sufficient to prove that SQIsignHD satisfies *knowledge soundness* [17, Theorem 6.3.2]. However, note that we have to require the prime ideal norm q to be not only ℓ^e-good but also prime to ℓ' in order to complete the proof.

Proposition 17. *Under the assumption that $q = \deg(\sigma)$ is always prime to ℓ', the FastSQIsignHD identification protocol satisfies special soundness. Namely, given two transcripts $(E_1, \varphi, R_1, R_2, q)$ and $(E_1, \varphi', R_1', R_2', q')$ with the same commitment E_1 but different challenges $\varphi \neq \varphi'$, we can extract an efficient representation of a non-scalar endomorphism $\alpha \in \mathrm{End}(E_A)$.*

Proof. Let $(E_1, \varphi, R_1, R_2, q)$ and $(E_1, \varphi', R_1', R_2', q')$ be two FastSQIsignHD transcripts with the same commitment E_1 but different challenges $\varphi \neq \varphi'$. Then, by Corollary 16, (R_1, R_2, q) and (R_1', R_2', q') define efficient representations of isogenies $\sigma : E_1 \longrightarrow E_2$ and $\sigma' : E_1 \longrightarrow E_2'$ of degrees q and q' respectively which are ℓ^e-good and comprime with ℓ'. Knowing $(R_1, R_2) = (\sigma(P_1), \sigma(P_2))$, where (P_1, P_2) is a canonical basis of $E_1[\ell^f]$, we can also find $a_1, a_2 \in \mathbb{Z}$ such that $a_1^2 + a_2^2 + q = \ell^e$ and apply RepresentIsogeny to compute $F := F(\sigma, a_1, a_2)$ by Proposition 14. Then, F provides an efficient representation of $\widehat{\sigma}$.

Hence, we know an efficient representation of $\alpha := \widehat{\varphi'} \circ \sigma' \circ \widehat{\sigma} \circ \varphi \in \mathrm{End}(E_A)$. We now prove that α is not scalar. Indeed, if it was, we would have $\alpha = [\lambda]$ for some $\lambda \in \mathbb{Z}$ and $qq'\ell'^{2f'} = \lambda^2$ where $q := \deg(\sigma)$ and $q' := \deg(\sigma')$ are prime to ℓ'. Hence, $\lambda = \ell'^{f'}\lambda'$ with $\lambda' \in \mathbb{Z}$ prime to ℓ' ($\lambda'^2 = qq'$). It follows that $[q']\widehat{\sigma} \circ \varphi = [\lambda']\widehat{\sigma'} \circ \varphi'$. Since q, q' and λ' are prime to ℓ', we get that $\ker(\varphi) = \ker(\varphi')$ *i.e.* $\varphi = \varphi'$ up to post-composition by an automorphism. Contradiction. This completes the proof. $\square$

For RigorousSQIsignHD, our special soundness argument does not apply because we have no guarantee on q in general. For that reason, we need to come back to the formal definition of knowledge soundess given in [17, Definition 6.3.1]. This analysis is conducted in [9, § D.1].

The previous proof of knowledge would be trivial if it was easy to find an endomorphism. Fortunately, this is a well-known hard problem in isogeny-based cryptography.

Problem 18 (Supersingular Endomorphism Problem). Given a supersingular elliptic curve $E/\mathbb{F}_{p^2}$, find an efficient representation of a non-scalar endomorphism $\alpha \in \mathrm{End}(E)$.

This problem is very similar to [10, Problem 1], except that we do not require the endomorphism to have smooth degree. This does not seem to make the problem easier since the endomorphisms solution to this can be evaluated (which was the reason why smoothness was imposed in the first place). The supersingular endomorphism ring problem (Problem 19) reduces to Problem 18. Problem 19 is notoriously hard and it has been proven it is equivalent to path finding in the supersingular ℓ-isogeny graph [41]. The heuristic reduction from Problem 19 to 18 is given by [12, Algorithm 8]. Basically, if we have an oracle finding endomorphisms of E, we call this oracle until we have found enough endomorphisms to generate $\text{End}(E)$.

Problem 19 (Supersingular Endomorphism Ring Problem). Given a supersingular elliptic curve $E/\mathbb{F}_{p^2}$, find four endomorphisms of E (that we can evaluate) forming a $\mathbb{Z}$-basis of $\text{End}(E)$.

5.2   Heuristic Zero-Knowledge Property

The proof of the zero-knowledge property of SQIsignHD uses an oracle generating isogenies of non-smooth degree. To our knowledge, there is no efficient algorithm implementing such an oracle. Nonetheless, it is believed that access to such an oracle does not affect the hardness of the underlying problem (the endomorphism ring problem, see Sect. 5.3). In RigorousSQIsignHD, the definition of such an oracle is very natural. In FastSQIsignHD, we add (mild) conditions on the degree to account for the computational constraints imposed by the method in dimension 4. These degree constraints are the main reason why the signatures are represented in dimension 8 instead of 4 in RigorousSQIsignHD. Our proof is limited to FastSQIsignHD in this section and we refer to [9, § D.2] for an analysis of RigorousSQIsignHD.

Definition 20. A *random uniform good degree isogeny oracle* (RUGDIO) is an oracle taking as input a supersingular elliptic curve E defined over $\mathbb{F}_{p^2}$ and returning an efficient representation of a random isogeny $\sigma : E \longrightarrow E'$ of ℓ^e-good degree prime to ℓ', such that: **(i)** the distribution of E' is uniform in the supersingular isogeny graph and **(ii)** the conditional distribution of σ given E' is uniform among isogenies $E \longrightarrow E'$ of ℓ^e-good degree prime to ℓ'.

In addition to the constraint on the degree of the RUGDIO output, we add constraints on the distributions of isogenies. Those constraints are necessary to construct a simulator of FastSQIsignHD. We already justified that these constraints can be mathematically satisfied, namely that for all supersingular elliptic curves E and E', there exists $\sigma : E \longrightarrow E'$ of ℓ^e-good norm. As explained in Sect. 4.2, taking ℓ^e slightly bigger than $\sqrt{p}$ by a few bits is heuristically sufficient. Note that to prove the zero-knowledge property, we not only need access to a RUGDIO, but also to make a heuristic assumption on the distribution of the commitment E_1. This assumption is no longer necessary in RigorousSQIsignHD.

Theorem 21. *Assume that the commitment E_1 is computationally indistinguishable from an elliptic curve chosen uniformly at random in the supersingular isogeny graph. Then, the FastSQIsignHD identification protocol is computationally honest-verifier zero knowledge in the RUGDIO model.*

In other words, under this assumption, there exists a random polynomial time simulator S with access to a RUGDIO that simulates transcripts (E_1, φ, R) with a computationally indistinguishable distribution from the transcripts of the FastSQIsignHD identification protocol.

Proof. First, we explain how to construct the simulator S. The simulator starts by generating a challenge $\varphi' : E_A \longrightarrow E_2'$. Then, it applies the RUGDIO on entry E_2' to get an efficient representation of a dual response isogeny $\widehat{\sigma}' : E_2' \longrightarrow E_1'$. We can use this efficient representation to evaluate $\widehat{\sigma}'$ on $E_2'[\ell^f]$ and obtain its degree in polynomial time in $\log(p)^3$. Then, as explained in the proof of Proposition 17, we can compute a dimension 4 isogeny representation of $\widehat{\sigma}'$, which is also to an efficient representation of σ'. Hence, we can compute $R' := (\sigma'(P_1), \sigma'(P_2), q')$ in polynomial time, where (P_1, P_2) is a canonical basis of $E_1'[\ell^f]$ and $q' := \deg(\sigma')$.

We now prove that the transcripts (E_1', φ', R') of S are statistically indistinguishable from the transcripts (E_1, φ, R) of the FastSQIsignHD identification protocol. By construction, φ and φ' have the same distribution. Given E_2', by the definition of the RUGDIO, E_1' is uniformly random in the supersingular isogeny graph. Besides, E_1 is statistically close to uniformly random as well by assumption.

Finally, conditionally to E_1' and E_2', $\widehat{\sigma}'$ (represented by R') is uniformly random among the isogenies $E_2' \longrightarrow E_1'$ of ℓ^e-good degree prime to ℓ' by the definition of the RUGDIO. The dual map $\phi \longmapsto \widehat{\phi}$ being a bijection preserving the degree, conditionally to E_1' and E_2', σ' is also uniformly random among the isogenies $E_2' \longrightarrow E_1'$ of ℓ^e-good degree prime to ℓ'. By construction (see Sect. 4.2), conditionally to E_1 and E_2, σ has the same distribution. This completes the proof. □

It remains to justify that the commitment E_1 is computationally indistinguishable from an elliptic curve chosen uniformly at random in the supersingular isogeny graph. While RigorousCommit satisfies statistical indistinguishability, the variant FastCommit relies on heuristics. Consider the distributions on E_1 induced by the following procedures

1. Return the output E_1 of FastCommit.
2. Generate a uniformly random cyclic endomorphism γ of E_0 of degree $\ell^{2f}\ell'^{2f'}$. Factor it as $\gamma = \widehat{\phi}' \circ \phi$ with $\deg(\phi) = \ell^{2f}$. Return the codomain E_1 of ϕ.
3. Generate a uniformly random cyclic isogeny ϕ from E_0 of degree ℓ^{2f}. Let E_1 be its codomain; let m be the number of cyclic isogenies $\phi' : E_0 \to E_1$ of degree $\ell'^{2f'}$. Return E_1 with probability m/M (for some fixed upper bound M on m, for instance $M = (\ell' + 1)\ell'^{2f'-1}$), otherwise resample.

---

[3] We can compute the norm of σ' on $E_2'[m]$ (which is $\deg(\sigma') \mod m$) for a bunch of small primes m and apply the Chinese remainder theorem.

4. Generate a uniformly random cyclic isogeny ϕ from E_0 of degree ℓ^{2f}; return its codomain E_1.
5. Return a uniformly random elliptic curve E_1.

We argue that each distribution from the list is somewhat close to the next. The difference between 1 and 2 is that in FastCommit, the endomorphism γ is not truly uniform: they follow a distribution biased by the fact that some intermediate result should be easy to factor. Since this property appears somewhat decorrelated from the final distribution of γ it seems plausible to argue that the distribution of γ in 1 is close to the one in 2. The distributions 2 and 3 are actually identical: distribution 3 simulated distribution 2 by rejection sampling. The difference between 3 and 4 is that m is not necessarily a (positive) constant; it is however heuristically expected to be almost a constant: there are about $(\ell'-1)\ell'^{2f'-1}$ possible paths, and about $p/12$ vertices, so we expect about $m \approx 12(\ell'-1)\ell'^{2f'-1}/p$ distinct paths to any fixed vertex. The difference between 4 and 5 is similar, but reasoning about ℓ-paths instead of ℓ'-paths.

Note that the differences at some of these steps are statistically significant. We only argue that they are not computationally detectable, at least when the endomorphism rings are not known.

5.3   On Hardness of the Supersingular Endomorphism Problem with Access to an Auxiliary Oracle

The FastSQIsignHD identification protocol is sound assuming the hardness of the supersingular endomorphism problem 18, and zero-knowledge with respect to a simulator that has access to a RUGDIO (or a RADIO for RigorousSQIsignHD, as defined in [9, § D.2]). For the resulting signature scheme to be secure, one therefore needs to assume that the supersingular endomorphism problem remains hard even when given access to a RUGDIO.

While it currently seems out of reach to prove that the supersingular endomorphism problem is equivalent to the variant with RUGDIO access, let us argue that the RUGDIO indeed does not help. We focus the following discussion on the RUGDIO, but the same arguments apply to the RADIO despite the slightly different distribution.

The RUGDIO allows to generate random isogenies with a chosen domain E. Note that this task is already known to be easy, with isogenies of smooth degree. The RUGDIO only lifts this smoothness restriction and replaces it with other restrictions (ℓ^e-good and prime to ℓ'): it allows to generate random isogenies whose degrees have large prime factors. It does not allow to reach more target curves, nor does it give more control on which specific target to hit: the target curve is uniformly distributed in the supersingular graph, which was already possible with smooth isogenies.

Smoothness of random isogenies has never been an inconvenience in finding endomorphisms. In fact, the current fastest algorithms for this problem only require very smooth degree isogenies, typically a power of 2. The reason is the following: the purpose of constructing a random isogeny from a fixed source is to reach a random target. As very smooth isogenies (even 2-smooth) are sufficient for optimal randomisation, there is no incentive to involve much larger prime factors. More specifically, the best known strategies to solve the supersingular endomorphism problem [11] have classical time complexity $\tilde{O}(\sqrt{p})$ (and quantum time complexity $\tilde{O}(p^{1/4})$ with a Grover argument [16]) and essentially perform a meet-in-the-middle search in the supersingular isogeny graph. Access to a RUG-DIO would allow to use isogenies of a different shape in the search, but would not speed it up, as the probability to find isogenies with matching codomains stays the same. Another illustration that having access to non-smooth degree isogenies does not help is the fact that the discovery of the $\sqrt{}$élu algorithm [3] (which dramatically improved the complexity of computing prime degree isogenies) did not affect the state-of-the-art of the supersingular endomorphism problem.

The above arguments support that random isogenies of non-smooth degrees are not more helpful than random isogenies of smooth degrees. Now, one may be concerned that the encoding of the output of the RUGDIO may leak more information than it should. Non-smooth degree isogenies are represented as a component of a higher dimensional isogeny (Sect. 2.2). This representation is universal, in the sense that any efficient representation of an isogeny can be efficiently rewritten in this form. In particular, this encoding contains no more information than any other efficient representation of the same isogeny.

6   The SQIsignHD Digital Signature Scheme

The SQIsignHD identification protocol that we presented yields a digital signature scheme via the Fiat-Shamir transform. The security of the transform of both versions FastSQIsignHD and RigorousSQIsignHD follows from the analysis conducted in Sect. 5 and [9, § D], so the digital signature is also secure under the same computational assumptions. Namely, we have seen it is universally unforgeable under chosen message attacks in the random oracle and RADIO or RUGDIO model, assuming the hardness of the endomorphism ring problem. In this section, we present the performance of the signature scheme obtained from FastSQIsignHD.

6.1   Compactness

As explained before, the signature is made of the data $(E_1, q, \sigma(P_1), \sigma(P_2))$, with $q < \ell^e$, $\sigma : E_1 \longrightarrow E_2$ a q-isogeny and (P_1, P_2) a basis of $E_1[\ell^f]$ determined canonically.

E_1 can be entirely determined by its j-invariant $j(E_1) \in \mathbb{F}_{p^2}$. Since any element of $\mathbb{F}_{p^2}$ can be represented by 2 integers in $[0 ; p-1]$, storing $j(E_1)$ takes approximately $2 \log_2(p) \simeq 4\lambda$ bits, given that $p = \Theta(2^{2\lambda})$ (where λ is the security level). Similarly, $q < \ell^e \simeq \sqrt{p}$, so q is an integer of $1/2 \log_2(p) \simeq \lambda$ bits.

The points $\sigma(P_1)$ and $\sigma(P_2)$ need not be represented explicitly with coordinates in $\mathbb{F}_{p^2}$. They can be compressed. Indeed, if we generate a canonical basis (Q_1, Q_2) of $E_2[\ell^f]$, then we may write $\sigma(P_1) = a_1 Q_1 + b_1 Q_2$ and

$\sigma(P_2) = a_2Q_1 + b_2Q_2$ with $a_1, b_1, a_2, b_2 \in \mathbb{Z}/\ell^f\mathbb{Z}$. Storing the scalars a_1, b_1, a_2, b_2 requires $4f$ bits (assuming $\ell = 2$, which will be the case in practice).

Actually, we can gain f bits by omitting one of the scalars a_1, b_1, a_2, b_2 if we use the Weil pairing. Indeed, we have

$$e_{\ell^f}(\sigma(P_1), \sigma(P_2)) = e_{\ell^f}(P_1, P_2)^q.$$

$$e_{\ell^f}(\sigma(P_1), \sigma(P_2)) = e_{\ell^f}(a_1Q_1 + b_1Q_2, a_2Q_1 + b_2Q_2) = e_{\ell^f}(Q_1, Q_2)^{a_1b_2 - b_1a_2}.$$

Since (P_1, P_2) and (Q_1, Q_2) are basis of $E_1[\ell^f]$ and $E_2[\ell^f]$ respectively, $e_{\ell^f}(P_1, P_2)$ and $e_{\ell^f}(Q_1, Q_2)$ are both primitive ℓ^f-th root of unity. Hence, we may find $k \in (\mathbb{Z}/\ell^f\mathbb{Z})^\times$ such that $e_{\ell^f}(P_1, P_2) = e_{\ell^f}(Q_1, Q_2)^k$, and we must have

$$a_1b_2 - b_1a_2 \equiv kq \mod \ell^f \tag{2}$$

Since $\ell^f | p - 1$, the ℓ^f-th Weil pairing takes values in $\mathbb{F}_p^*$, so we find k easily by solving a discrete logarithm problem in a subgroup of order ℓ^f of $\mathbb{F}_p^*$ by Pohlig-Hellman [29] techniques (which apply since $p - 1$ is smooth).

Since q is prime to ℓ, $\sigma(P_1)$ have order ℓ^f so either a_1 or b_1 is invertible modulo ℓ^f. If a_1 is invertible, we can recover b_2 from the other scalars using Eq. 2 and we can recover a_2 otherwise. Hence we only need 3 scalars among 4.

We can make the representation of $\sigma(P_1)$ and $\sigma(P_2)$ even more compact. Indeed, by Remark 4.2 the ℓ^e-isogeny F representing σ can be computed as long as $2f \geq e + 4$. But in FastSQIsignHD, $f \simeq e \simeq \lambda$ so we may use points of ℓ^{f_1}-torsion with $f_1 := \lceil e/2 \rceil + 3$ instead of points of ℓ^f-torsion. This reduces the storage cost of $\sigma(P_1)$ and $\sigma(P_2)$ from $3f \simeq 3\lambda$ to $3f_1 \simeq 3/2\lambda$.

On the whole, we can represent the signatures with $s = 13/2\lambda + O(\log(\lambda))$ bits if we use the compression and decompression algorithms given by Algorithms 6 and 7, breaking the previous record of SQIsign. Indeed, in SQIsign, the kernels of the signature isogeny σ (of degree $p^{15/4}$) and of the dual of the challenge (of degree $\sqrt{p}$) need to be transmitted so we get a signature of size $s = 17/2\lambda + O(\log(\lambda))$ at least.

Example: For NIST-I security level ($\lambda = 128$ bits), we can choose the parameters $p = 13 \cdot 2^{126}3^{78} - 1$, $e = 142$ and $f_1 = 73$. The total signature size in SQIsignHD is $2\lceil \log_2(p) \rceil + e + 3f_1 + 1 = 870$ bits or 109 bytes. SQIsign signatures took 177 bytes in the NIST-I implementation [37].

We can use the same techniques in dimension 8 but we output signatures of size $s = 14\lambda + O(\log(\lambda))$ instead of $13/2\lambda + O(\log(\lambda))$ since e is bigger ($\ell^e = \Theta(p^2)$). Details may be found in [9, § C.3].

6.2   Time Efficiency

Low Signing Time (and Key Generation Time). In the latest version of SQIsign [13], the signature time was dominated by the computation of 30 T-isogenies with $T \simeq p^{5/4}$. Each T-isogeny is rather slow as T typically has prime factors as large as a few thousands. FastSQIsignHD signing only requires

---

Algorithm 6: Compression

Data: $E_1, E_2, q, P_1, P_2, \sigma(P_1), \sigma(P_2)$, where $q < \ell^e$, $\sigma : E_1 \longrightarrow E_2$ a q-isogeny
and (P_1, P_2) a basis of $E_1[\ell^{f_1}]$ determined canonically ($f_1 := \lceil e/2 \rceil + 3$).

Result: A word of length $2\lceil \log_2(p) \rceil + e + 3f_1$ bits (assuming $\ell = 2$).

1 Compute $j(E_1) \in \mathbb{F}_{p^2}$;
2 Let ζ be a canonical generator of $\mathbb{F}_{p^2}$. Write $\zeta := n_1 + n_2\zeta$ where $n_1, n_2 \in \mathbb{F}_p$
   are represented by integers in $[\![0 \; ; \; p - 1]\!]$ of length $\lceil \log_2(p) \rceil$ bits each;
3 Compute the canonical basis (Q_1, Q_2) of $E_2[\ell^{f_1}]$;
4 Find $k \in (\mathbb{Z}/\ell^{f_1}\mathbb{Z})^\times$ such that $e_{\ell^{f_1}}(P_1, P_2) = e_{\ell^{f_1}}(Q_1, Q_2)^k$;
5 Find $a_1, b_1, a_2, b_2 \in \mathbb{Z}/\ell^{f_1}\mathbb{Z}$ such that $\sigma(P_1) = a_1Q_1 + b_1Q_2$ and
   $\sigma(P_2) = a_2Q_1 + b_2Q_2$;
6 **if** $\ell \nmid a_1$ **then**
7 | Return $\|n_1\|n_2\|q\|a_1\|b_1\|b_2\|$;
8 **else**
9 | Return $\|n_1\|n_2\|q\|a_1\|b_1\|a_2\|$;
10 **end**

---

a handful of ℓ^f and $\ell'^{f'}$-isogenies, where typically $\ell = 2$ and $\ell' = 3$. Computing these isogenies is orders of magnitude faster than a SQIsign [13] signature.

We have implemented FastSQIsignHD in C, based on the implementation of SQIsign [37]. The signature takes an average time of 28 ms at the 128 bits security level on an Intel(R) Core(TM) i5-1335U 4600MHz CPU (average over 1000 signature computations). Key generation takes 70 ms on average on the same CPU. While signature is already close to ten times faster than the fastest implementations of SQIsign [13,23], we refrain from reporting a detailed clock-cycle comparison, as the bottleneck of our implementation has shifted from isogeny computations to a variety of steps which have not been optimised (as they were negligible in former SQIsign implementations). Most notably, about 29% of the FastSQIsignHD signing time is spent computing two discrete logarithms; a 4.8× speedup is reported in [23] using Tate pairings for comparable discrete logarithm computations. Another 20% is spent solving a quaternion norm equation [22, Algorithm 4], a step that has not been the focus of much attention. In addition, contrary to former implementations of SQIsign, our implementation is purely in C, with no assembly-optimised field arithmetic. Providing a completely optimized implementation is left for future works, yet this first implementation is already compelling.

Verification Time. This efficiency gain in the signature is made at the expense of the verification time where a 4-dimensional ℓ^e-isogeny has to be computed. Of course ℓ-isogenies in dimension 4 are expected to be slower to compute than in dimension 1. Nonetheless, we only have to compute two chains of ℓ-isogenies of length $1/4 \log_\ell(p)$, whereas the verifier had to compute an ℓ-isogeny chain of size $15/4 \log_\ell(p)$ in the last version of SQIsign [13]. Furthermore, our choice of parameters allows for more efficient field arithmetic.

Algorithm 7: Decompression

Data: A word w of $2\lceil\log_2(p)\rceil + e + 3f_1$ bits ($\ell := 2$, $f_1 := \lceil e/2\rceil + 3$), the public key E_A, a message m, and hash functions Φ and H used to generate the challenge in the Fiat-Shamir transform (see [9, § A.1]).

Result: $E_1, E_2, q, P_1, P_2, \sigma(P_1), \sigma(P_2)$, where $q < \ell^e$, $\sigma : E_1 \longrightarrow E_2$ is a q-isogeny and (P_1, P_2) is a basis of $E_1[\ell^{f_1}]$ determined canonically.

1 Parse $\|n_1\|n_2\|q\|a_1\|b_1\|c_2\| \longleftarrow w$;

2 Set $j \longleftarrow n_1 + n_2\zeta$, where ζ is the canonical generator of $\mathbb{F}_{p^2}$;

3 Compute E_1 of j-invariant $j(E_1) = j$;

4 Recover the commitment $\varphi \longleftarrow \Phi(E_1, H(E_1, m))$. Let E_2 be the codomain of φ;

5 Compute the canonical basis (P_1, P_2) of $E_1[\ell^{f_1}]$ and the canonical basis (Q_1, Q_2) of $E_2[\ell^{f_1}]$;

6 Find $k \in (\mathbb{Z}/\ell^{f_1}\mathbb{Z})^\times$ such that $e_{\ell^{f_1}}(P_1, P_2) = e_{\ell^{f_1}}(Q_1, Q_2)^k$;

7 **if** $\ell \nmid a_1$ **then**

8 | $a_2 \longleftarrow c_2$;

9 | Find $b_2 \in \mathbb{Z}/\ell^{f_1}\mathbb{Z}$ such that $a_1b_2 - b_1a_2 \equiv kq \mod \ell^{f_1}$;

10 **else**

11 | $b_2 \longleftarrow c_2$;

12 | Find $a_2 \in \mathbb{Z}/\ell^{f_1}\mathbb{Z}$ such that $a_1b_2 - b_1a_2 \equiv kq \mod \ell^{f_1}$;

13 **end**

14 Return $E_1, E_2, q, P_1, P_2, a_1Q_1 + b_1Q_2, a_2Q_1 + b_2Q_2$;

Our experimental `sagemath` implementation provides an upper bound on the verification time: for 128 bits of security the verification takes around 600 ms on the same CPU as above. We expect this time to be significantly reduced in the future: new optimisations remain to be implemented, and more importantly a low level implementation should lead to a significant gain. Currently, the time spent on verification is as follows: around 60 ms for the challenge computation[4], 510 ms for the two dimension 4 2^{71}-isogenies giving F, and 30 ms for the image of a point through F.

Acknowledgements. We thank Luca De Feo for his advice all along this project and for suggesting the title of this paper. This project was supported by ANR grant CIAO (ANR-19-CE48-0008), PEPR PQ-TLS (the France 2030 program under grant agreement ANR-22-PETQ-0008 PQ-TLS) and the European Research Council under grant No. 101116169 (AGATHA CRYPTY).

---

[4] Which essentially consists in computing a chain of 3-isogenies in dimension 1. The signature also needs to compute similar isogenies, and in this case the low level C implementation only takes 1–2 ms, which shows the potential of improvements of writing a low level implementation of the verification.

References

1. Ahrens, K.: Sieving for large twin smooth integers using single solutions to Prouhet-Tarry-Escott. Cryptology ePrint Archive, Paper 2023/219. (2023). https://eprint.iacr.org/2023/219
2. Azarderakhsh, R., Jao, D., Kalach, K., Koziel, B., Leonardi, C.: Key compression for isogeny-based cryptosystems. In: Proceedings of the 3rd ACM International Workshop on ASIA Public-Key Cryptography, Xi'an, China, pp. 1–10. ACM (2016)
3. Bernstein, D.J., De Feo, L., Leroux, A., Smith, B.: Faster computation of isogenies of large prime degree. In: Open Book Series, Proceedings of the Fourteenth Algorithmic Number Theory Symposium - ANTS XIV 4.1, pp. 39–55 (2020)
4. Bruno, G., et al.: Cryptographic smooth neighbors. Cryptology ePrint Archive, Paper 2022/1439 (2022). https://eprint.iacr.org/2022/1439
5. Castryck, W., Decru, T.: An efficient key recovery attack on SIDH. In: Advances in Cryptology - EUROCRYPT 2023: 42nd Annual International Conference on the Theory and Applications of Cryptographic Techniques, Lyon, France, 23–27 April 2023, Proceedings, Part V, Lyon, Springer, France, pp. 423–447 (2023). ISBN: 978-3-031-30588-7. https://doi.org/10.1007/978-3-031-30589-4_15
6. Cornacchia, G.: Su di un metodo per la risoluzione in numeri interi dell'equazione $\sum_{h=0}^{n} C_h x^{n-h} y^h = P$. Giornale di matematiche di Battaglini **46**, 33–90 (1908)
7. Costello, C., Meyer, M., Naehrig, M.: Sieving for twin smooth integers with solutions to the prouhet-tarry-escott problem. In: Canteaut, A., Standaert, F.-X. (ed.) Advances in Cryptology - EUROCRYPT 2021. Springer, Cham, pp. 272–301 (2021). https://doi.org/10.1007/978-3-030-77870-5_10, ISBN: 978-3-030-77870-5
8. Couveignes, J.-M.: Hard Homogeneous Spaces. Cryptology ePrint Archive, Report 2006/291 (2006). https://eprint.iacr.org/2006/291
9. Dartois, P., Leroux, A., Robert, D., Wesolowski, B.: SQIsignHD: new dimensions in cryptography. Cryptology ePrint Archive, Paper 2023/436 (2023). https://eprint.iacr.org/2023/436
10. De Feo, L., Kohel, D., Leroux, A., Petit, C., Wesolowski, B.: SQISign: compact post-quantum signatures from quaternions and isogenies. In: Moriai, S., Wang, H. (eds.) ASIACRYPT 2020. LNCS, vol. 12491, pp. 64–93. Springer, Cham (2020). https://doi.org/10.1007/978-3-030-64837-4_3
11. Delfs, C., Galbraith, S.D.: Computing isogenies between supersingular elliptic curves over $\mathbb{F}_p$. Des. Codes Cryptography **78**(2), 425–440 (2016). https://doi.org/10.1007/s10623-014-0010-1
12. Eisenträger, K., Hallgren, S., Lauter, K., Morrison, T., Petit, C.: Supersingular isogeny graphs and endomorphism rings: reductions and solutions. In: Nielsen, J.B., Rijmen, V. (eds.) EUROCRYPT 2018. LNCS, vol. 10822, pp. 329–368. Springer, Cham (2018). https://doi.org/10.1007/978-3-319-78372-7_11
13. De Feo, L., Leroux, A., Longa, P., Wesolowski, B.: New algorithms for the deuring correspondence. In: Hazay, C., Stam, M. (eds.) Advances in Cryptology - EUROCRYPT 2023. LNCS, vol. 14008, pp. 659–690. Springer, Cham (2023). https://doi.org/10.1007/978-3-031-30589-4_23
14. Fiat, A., Shamir, A.: How to prove yourself: practical solutions to identification and signature problems. In: Odlyzko, A.M. (ed.) CRYPTO 1986. LNCS, vol. 263, pp. 186–194. Springer, Heidelberg (1987). https://doi.org/10.1007/3-540-47721-7_12
15. Galbraith, Steven D.., Petit, Christophe, Silva, Javier: Identification protocols and signature schemes based on supersingular isogeny problems. J. Cryptology **33**(1), 130–175 (2019). https://doi.org/10.1007/s00145-019-09316-0

16. Grover, L.K.: A fast quantum mechanical algorithm for database search. In: Proceedings of the Twenty-Eighth Annual ACM Symposium on Theory of Computing. STOC 1996. Philadelphia, Pennsylvania, Association for Computing Machinery, USA, pp. 212–219 (1996). ISBN: 0897917855. https://doi.org/10.1145/237814. 237866

17. Hazay, C., Lindell, Y.: Efficient Secure Two-Party Protocols: Techniques and Constructions. 1st. Springer, Berlin (2010). ISBN: 3642143024

18. Jao, D., De Feo, L.: Towards quantum-resistant cryptosystems from supersingular elliptic curve isogenies. In: Yang, B.-Y. (ed.) PQCrypto 2011. LNCS, vol. 7071, pp. 19–34. Springer, Heidelberg (2011). https://doi.org/10.1007/978-3-642-25405-5_2

19. Kani, E.: The number of curves of genus two with elliptic differentials. J. für die reine und angewandte Mathematik **485**, 93–122 (1997). https://doi.org/10.1515/crll.1997.485.93

20. Kohel, D., Lauter, K., Petit, C., Tignol, J.-P.: On the quaternion - isogeny path problem. LMS J. Comput. Math. 17 (2014). https://doi.org/10.1112/S1461157014000151

21. de Lagrange, J. L.: Démonstration d'un théoreme d'arithmétique. In: Nouveau Mémoire de l'Académie Royale des Sciences de Berlin, pp. 123–133 (1770)

22. Leroux, A.: Quaternion algebras and isogeny-based cryptography (2022). http://www.lix.polytechnique.fr/Labo/Antonin.LEROUX/manuscrit_these.pdf

23. Lin, K., Wang, W., Xu, Z., Zhao, C.-A.: A faster software implementation of SQISign. Cryptology ePrint Archive, Paper 2023/753 (2023). https://eprint.iacr.org/2023/753

24. Lubicz, D., Robert, D.: Computing isogenies between abelian varieties. Compos. Math. **148**(5), 1483–1515 (2012). https://doi.org/10.1112/S0010437X12000243

25. Lubicz, D., Robert, D.: Computing separable isogenies in quasi-optimal time. LMS J. Comput. Math. **18**(1), 98–216 (2015). https://doi.org/10.1112/S146115701400045X

26. Lubicz, D., Robert, D.: Fast change of level and applications to isogenies. **9**, 7 (2023). https://doi.org/10.1007/s40993-022-00407-9

27. Maino, L., Martindale, C., Panny, L., Pope, G., Wesolowski, B.: A direct key recovery attack on SIDH. In: Hazay, C., Stam, M. (eds.) Advances in Cryptology - EUROCRYPT 2023. LNCS, vol. 14008, pp. 448–471. Springer, Cham (2023). https://doi.org/10.1007/978-3-031-30589-4_16

28. PARI/GP version 2.13.4. http://pari.math.u-bordeaux.fr/. The PARI Group. Univ. Bordeaux (2022)

29. Pohlig, S.C., Hellman, M.E.: An improved algorithm for computing logarithms over GF(p) and its cryptographic significance. IEEE Trans. Inf. Theor. **24**(1), 106–110 (1978)

30. Pollack, P., Treviño, E.: Finding the four squares in lagrange's theorem. Integers **18A**, A15 (2018)

31. Rabin, J.O., Shallit, M.O.: Randomized algorithms in number theory. Commun. Pure Appl. Math. **39**(S1), S239–S256 (1986). https://doi.org/10.1002/cpa.3160390713

32. Robert, D.: Evaluating isogenies in polylogarithmic time. Cryptology ePrint Archive, Paper 2022/1068 (2022). https://eprint.iacr.org/2022/1068

33. Robert, D.: Breaking SIDH in polynomial time. In: Hazay, C., Stam, M. (eds.) Advances in Cryptology - EUROCRYPT 2023. EUROCRYPT 2023, LNCS, vol. 14008, pp. 472–503. Springer, Cham (2023). https://doi.org/10.1007/978-3-031-30589-4_17

34. Rostovtsev, A., Stolbunov, A.: Public-key cryptosystem based on isogenies. Cryptology ePrint Archive, Report 2006/145 (2006). https://eprint.iacr.org/2006/145
35. Rouse, J., Thompson, K.: Quaternary quadratic forms with prime discriminant (2022). arXiv: 2206.00412 [math.NT]
36. The Sage Developers. SageMath, the Sage Mathematics Software System (Version 10.0) (2023). https://www.sagemath.org
37. The SQIsign team. SQIsign (2023). https://www.sqisign.org
38. Vélu, J.: Isogénies entre courbes elliptiques. In: Comptes-rendus de l'Académie des Sciences, vol. 273, pp. 238–241, July 1971. https://gallica.bnf.fr
39. Venturi, D., Villani, A.: Zero-knowledge proofs and applications, May 2015. http://danieleventuri.altervista.org/files/zeroknowledge.pdf
40. Voight, J.: Quaternion algebras. v.0.9.23, August 2020. https://math.dartmouth.edu/~jvoight/quat.html
41. Wesolowski, B.: The supersingular isogeny path and endomorphism ring problems are equivalent. In: FOCS 2021 - 62nd Annual IEEE Symposium on Foundations of Computer Science. Denver, Colorado, United States, February 2022. https://hal.archives-ouvertes.fr/hal-03340899
42. Zanon, G.H.M., Simplicio, M.A., Pereira, G.C.C.F., Doliskani, J., Barreto, P.S.L.M.: Faster isogeny-based compressed key agreement. In: Lange, T., Steinwandt, R. (eds.) PQCrypto 2018. LNCS, vol. 10786, pp. 248–268. Springer, Cham (2018). https://doi.org/10.1007/978-3-319-79063-3_12

Tight Indistinguishability Bounds for the XOR of Independent Random Permutations by Fourier Analysis

Itai Dinur[✉]

Department of Computer Science, Ben-Gurion University, Beersheba, Israel
dinuri@bgu.ac.il

Abstract. The XOR of two independent permutations (XoP) is a well-known construction for achieving security beyond the birthday bound when implementing a pseudorandom function using a block cipher (i.e., a pseudorandom permutation). The idealized construction (where the permutations are uniformly chosen and independent) and its variants have been extensively analyzed over nearly 25 years.

The best-known asymptotic information-theoretic indistinguishability bound for the XoP construction is $O(q/2^{1.5n})$, derived by Eberhard in 2017.

A generalization of the XoP construction outputs the XOR of $r \geq 2$ independent permutations, and has also received significant attention in both the single-user and multi-user settings. In particular, for $r = 3$, the best-known bound (obtained by Choi et al. [ASIACRYPT'22]) is about $q^2/2^{2.5n}$ in the single-user setting and $\sqrt{u}q_{\max}^2/2^{2.5n}$ in the multi-user setting (where u is the number of users and $q_{\max}$ is the number of queries per user).

In this paper, we prove an indistinguishability bound of $q/2^{(r-0.5)n}$ for the (generalized) XoP construction in the single-user setting, and a bound of $\sqrt{u}q_{\max}/2^{(r-0.5)n}$ in the multi-user setting. In particular, for $r = 2$, we obtain the bounds $q/2^{1.5n}$ and $\sqrt{u}q_{\max}/2^{1.5n}$ in single-user and multi-user settings, respectively. For $r = 3$ the corresponding bounds are $q/2^{2.5n}$ and $\sqrt{u}q_{\max}/2^{2.5n}$. All of these bounds hold assuming $q < 2^n/2$ (or $q_{\max} < 2^n/2$).

Compared to previous works, we improve all the best-known bounds for the (generalized) XoP construction in the multi-user setting, and the best-known bounds for the generalized XoP construction for $r \geq 3$ in the single-user setting (assuming $q \geq 2^{n/2}$). For the basic two-permutation XoP construction in the single-user setting, our concrete bound of $q/2^{1.5n}$ stands in contrast to the asymptotic bound of $O(q/2^{1.5n})$ by Eberhard.

Since all of our bounds are matched (up to constant factors) for $q > 2^{n/2}$ by attacks published by Patarin in 2008 (and their generalizations to the multi-user setting), they are all tight.

We obtain our results by Fourier analysis of Boolean functions. Most of our technical work involves bounding (sums of) Fourier coefficients of the density function associated with sampling without replacement. While the proof of Eberhard relies on similar bounds, our proof is elementary and significantly simpler.

© International Association for Cryptologic Research 2024
M. Joye and G. Leander (Eds.): EUROCRYPT 2024, LNCS 14651, pp. 33–62, 2024.
https://doi.org/10.1007/978-3-031-58716-0_2

1   Introduction

Many cryptosystems such as encryption modes, MAC algorithms and authenticated encryption schemes require pseudorandom functions to achieve security. However, in practice, pseudorandom functions are typically implemented by block ciphers, which are pseudorandom permutations that are only secure up to the birthday bound of $q = 2^{n/2}$ queries (where n is the block length). In order to overcome this limitation, achieving security beyond the birthday bound has become a prominent research area, initiated by the seminal papers by Bellare, Krovetz, and Rogaway [2], and by Hall, Wagner, Kelsey, and Schneier [18].

1.1   The XoP Construction

One of the main constructions analyzed in the literature for achieving security beyond the birthday bound is the XOR of permutations (XoP) construction, which has two main variants. One variant uses two permutations $\pi_1, \pi_2 :$ $\{0,1\}^n \mapsto \{0,1\}^n$ to define $f_{\pi_1, \pi_2} : \{0,1\}^n \mapsto \{0,1\}^n$ by $f(x) = \pi_1(x) \oplus \pi_2(x)$. In practice, π_1 and π_2 are implemented using a block cipher, instantiated with independent keys. In the following, we simply refer to this variant as the XoP construction. Another variant uses a single permutation $\pi : \{0,1\}^n \mapsto \{0,1\}^n$ to define $f_\pi : \{0,1\}^{n-1} \mapsto \{0,1\}^n$ by $f(x) = \pi(0\|x) \oplus \pi(1\|x)$ (where $\|$ denotes concatenation). We refer to this construction as a single-permutation XoP construction. Similarly to the two-permutation variant, π is implemented using a block cipher. However, in information-theoretic security proofs, the block ciphers in both variants are replaced by idealized random permutations.

We note that there are other variants of the XoP construction defined in the literature that we do not deal with in this paper. For example, the recent result [16] by Gunsing et al. analyzes a variant where the underlying permutations are public and the adversary is allowed to query them. Previous works that analyze additional variants include [3,4,7,17].

Previous Results. There have been several works on the security of the (idealized) XoP construction [1,20,24,26], analyzing one or both of its variants. Yet, a simple and verifiable proof that the XoP construction variants achieve security up to $q = O(2^n)$ queries was only published in 2017 in a paper by Dai, Hoang, and Tessaro [10]. Specifically, [10] proved that any adversary that makes q queries to the (two-permutation) XoP construction can distinguish it from a truly random function with advantage of at most (about) $\frac{q^{1.5}}{2^{1.5n}}$.

Independently, in [13, Thm. 1.5] Eberhard proved a substantially better indistinguishability bound of $O(\frac{q}{2^{1.5n}})$, relying and extending results of [14] in additive combinatorics. The bound was given in asymptotic form with an unspecified constant. An additional paper that analyzed the XoP construction is [12].

For the single-permutation XoP variant, the distinguishing advantage was bounded in [10,12] by about $\frac{q}{2^n}$. The works of [8,12], essentially confirm (and improve) the results obtained earlier by Patarin [24,26] (using the so-called mirror theory technique).

The indistinguishability bound $\frac{q}{2^n}$ for the single permutation XoP construction variant is essentially tight. Indeed, it is matched by a simple attack based on the observation that since π is a permutation, for all $x \in \{0,1\}^{n-1}$, $f(x) = \pi(0\|x) \oplus \pi(1\|x) \neq \vec{0}$, while for a random function, $\vec{0}$ is output with probability 2^{-n} for each query.

The attack above does not work for the variant where the permutations are independent, and indeed the bound $O(\frac{q}{2^{1.5n}})$ of [13] for this variant is much better (particularly when q is large). This bound is matched by an attack published by Patarin [25,27], which obtains distinguishing advantage of about $\frac{q}{2^{1.5n}}$, assuming $q = O(2^n)$. Note that if $q = 2^n$, then the distinguishing advantage is close to 1 since the XOR of the outputs of all inputs to $f(x) = \pi_1(x) \oplus \pi_2(x)$ is $\vec{0}$.

Multi-user Setting. The XoP construction also recently received attention in the multi-user setting in [6,7]. A trivial extension of the result in [13] gives a bound of $O(\frac{u \cdot q_{max}}{2^{1.5n}})$ in the multi-user setting, where u is the number of users and q_{max} is the allowed number of queries to each user.

In terms of attacks, one can generically extend the attacks by Patarin [25,27] to the multi-user setting by independently applying the single-user attacker to each user, and then taking the majority of answers (which attempt to deduce whether the oracle is the XoP construction or a random function). Applying a standard Chernoff bound, the attack achieves a distinguishing advantage of about $\frac{\sqrt{u}q_{max}}{2^{1.5n}}$.

Generalized XoP Construction. A natural generalization of the XOR construction defines f by XORing together $r \geq 2$ permutations, where r is a (small) parameter. As in the case of $r = 2$, the generalized construction also has two variants, but we focus on the case where all permutations are independent.

Previous Results. This construction was first analyzed by Lucks [20] and this analysis was improved by Cogliati, Lampe, and Patarin [9], who proved security up to roughly $2^{rn/(r+1)}$ queries (also see [22]). More recently, this analysis has been improved in [10], which obtained an indistinguishability bound to about $(\frac{q}{2^n})^{1.5\lfloor r/2 \rfloor}$ using the generic amplification technique of Maurer, Pietrzak, and Renner [21]. The specific case of $k = 3$ was analyzed in [7] by Choi et al., who proved an indistinguishability bound of about $\frac{\sqrt{u}q_{max}^2}{2^{2.5n}}$ in the multi-user setting.

On the other hand, the best known attacks on the generalized XoP construction, published in [25,27], obtained distinguishing advantage of about $\frac{q}{2^{(r-0.5)n}}$. One can also consider attacks on the generalized XoP construction in the multi-user setting. Similarly to the case of $r = 2$, the best known attack is the generic extension of the single-user attack by Patarin [25,27] to the multi-user setting, which achieves advantage of about $\frac{\sqrt{u} \cdot q_{max}}{2^{(r-0.5)n}}$.

1.2   Our Contribution

Our Results. In this paper, we prove an indistinguishability bound of $\frac{q}{2^{(r-0.5)n}}$ for the (generalized) XoP construction in the single-user setting, and a bound of $\frac{\sqrt{u}q_{\max}}{2^{(r-0.5)n}}$ in the multi-user setting. Specifically, for the basic two-permutation XoP construction, we obtain a bound of $\frac{q}{2^{1.5n}}$ in the single-user setting and $\frac{\sqrt{u}q_{\max}}{2^{1.5n}}$ in the multi-user settings. All of these bounds have no hidden constants. They hold as long as $q < 2^n/2$ (or $q_{\max} < 2^n/2$ in the multi-user setting), assuming $2^n \geq 1000$.

Compared to previous results, we improve all the best-known bounds for the (generalized) XoP construction in the multi-user setting, and the best-known bounds for the generalized XoP construction for $r \geq 3$ in the single-user setting (assuming $q \geq 2^{n/2}$). For the basic XoP construction (with $r = 2$), our concrete bound of $q/2^{1.5n}$ in the single-user setting stands in contrast to the asymptotic bound of $O(q/2^{1.5n})$, derived in [13].

All of our bounds are tight assuming $q \leq 2^{n/2}$, as they match (up to constant factors) the single-user attacks published by Patarin in [25,27], as well as their trivial generalization to the multi-user setting.

Our Techniques. Similarly to [13,14], the main framework that we use to obtain our results is Fourier analysis (of Boolean functions). This is a standard tool for analyzing probability distributions in mathematics, yet it is not commonly used as a main framework in information-theoretic security proofs in symmetric-key cryptography. For example, [5] used Fourier analysis as an auxiliary tool in order to prove an internal lemma, but not as the main framework. The application of Fourier analysis in the more recent work [19] is somewhat more related to ours. We summarize the main ideas of our proof below.

First, the distinguishing advantage of the adversary is bounded by the statistical distance between the distribution generated by the XoP construction and the uniform distribution. Consider a sample in $\mathbb{F}_2^{q \times n}$ composed of q elements in $\{0,1\}^n$, generated by the XoP construction. We can bound the statistical distance of this distribution from the uniform distribution in the "Fourier domain" by bounding the bias (i.e., Fourier coefficient) of each of the $2^{q \cdot n}$ possible masks (i.e., linear equations over $\mathbb{F}_2$) applied to the bits of the sample. To gain intuition, note that for the uniform distribution over $\mathbb{F}_2^{q \times n}$, all non-empty linear equations have 0 bias (i.e., hold with probability 1/2), and thus a distribution that is close to uniform has biases (Fourier coefficients) that are very close to 0.

Our task is thus to bound the Fourier coefficients for the distribution function generated by the XoP construction.[1] Next, we use standard techniques to reduce this task to the task of bounding the Fourier coefficients for the distribution generated by the underlying primitive, namely, a random permutation. Specifically, we consider k elements (for any $1 \leq k \leq q$) drawn uniformly without replace-

---

[1] More accurately, the task is to bound the Fourier coefficients for the normalized distribution function (i.e., density function) generated by the XoP construction.

ment. Our goal is reduced to bounding two quantities of Fourier coefficients on masks that involve all of these k elements (called level-k coefficients).

1. The maximal level-k Fourier coefficient in absolute value.
2. The level-k Fourier weight, which is equal to the sum of squares of all Fourier coefficients of level k.

Intuitively, level-k (Fourier) weight is a measure of dependence between k elements drawn from the distribution. For example, the level-k Fourier weight of a q-wise uniform distribution is 0 for any $1 \leq k \leq q$. We remark that calculating the above two Fourier quantities for various levels has the additional advantage of hinting at the best attack strategy. In particular, we show that for the XoP construction, level-2 Fourier coefficients are dominant. This suggests that the best attack strategy should consider pairwise relations, and indeed, the optimal attacks by Patarin [25, 27] count pairwise collisions.

Most of our technical work involves bounding the two quantities above, which is non-trivial due to intricate dependencies among the bits of the sample. This analysis does not directly deal with the XoP construction, but rather derives fundamental Fourier properties of the sampling without replacement distribution.

Bounding the Quantities. We briefly summarize the main ideas used to bound each of the above quantities. Fix a mask involving bits from exactly k elements. In order to bound the associated bias of the linear equation (in absolute value), we devise an algorithm that allows to partition a subset of the sample space into sample couples with opposite signs (i.e., one satisfies the linear equation and one does not). Thus, the bias (in absolute value) is bounded by the fraction of samples that are not coupled. This fraction is bounded by probabilistic analysis of the algorithm. We note that our analysis does more than merely bound the maximal level-k Fourier coefficients. It actually classifies them into types (or groups) and obtains a refined bound for each type.

Our bound on the maximal level-k Fourier coefficient is tight, yet by itself, it is not sufficient in order to derive tight indistinguishability bounds for the XoP construction. For this purpose, we bound the level-k Fourier weight of the sampling without replacement distribution. While an exact expression for the weight is relatively easy to derive, this expression is a complex sum of terms, and therefore not immediately useful. Hence, we manipulate this expression in two main steps. First, we show how to compute the level-k Fourier weight via a recursive formula, and then we bound this weight by induction. Overall, although the weight is bounded by elementary analysis, it requires insight which is somewhat non-trivial.

Remark 1. Our bounds on the level-k Fourier weight can be formulated in terms of the so-called Efron-Stein orthogonal decomposition [23, Ch. 8] of the density function of sampling without replacement. This decomposition is independent of a specific Fourier basis, and thus these bounds apply more generally to the density function of sampling without replacement from an arbitrary set.

Technical Comparison to Previous Works. Below, we compare our techniques to those of [13,14]. Comparison to additional proof techniques is given in the full version of this paper [11].

Comparison to [13,14]. The papers [13,14] obtained several results in additive combinatorics. One of them is [13, Thm. 1.5], which gives an asymptotic indistinguishability bound of $O(\frac{q}{2^{1.5n}})$ for the two-permutation XoP construction. We compare our techniques to the ones of [13,14], focusing on the aforementioned result.

Both our proof and the one of [13,14] use Fourier analysis and (in our language) bound the (sums of) Fourier coefficients of the density function of sampling without replacement. However, the proof of [13, Thm. 1.5] is significantly more complicated. In particular, it relies on several bounds which are not required to obtain our result. Moreover, it uses complex analysis, whereas our proof is completely elementary.

The two bounds that we use (mentioned above) have comparable bounds in [13,14]. The analog of our first bound (the maximal level-k Fourier coefficient in absolute value) is [13, Lem. 4.1]. After normalization, our bound is identical for even k and slightly better for odd k. It is proved using a completely different technique. The analog of our second bound (the level-k Fourier weight) is [13, Thm 2.3] ([14, Thm. 5.1]). After normalization, our bound is somewhat inferior for small k (e.g., for $k \leq 2^{n/3}$), and becomes better for large k (e.g., denoting $N = 2^n$, it is better by a factor of $2^{\Omega(N)}$ for $k \geq \Omega(N)$). However, such an improvement seems insignificant to the asymptotic results of [13,14]. Our proof of the second bound begins by deriving an exact expression for the weight, as the proof of [14, Thm. 5.1]. On the other hand, our analysis of this expression is elementary, while the one of [14] is based on complex analysis.

In terms of generality of results, [13, Thm. 1.5] was proved for a (generalized variant of the) XoP construction defined over an arbitrary additive abelian group. While our results only apply to the original XoP construction, it is not difficult to extend them to the variant defined over an arbitrary abelian group. In fact, our second bound is already independent of the actual group (see Remark 1), and it only remains to modify the proof of the first bound. However, we leave this to future work.

1.3 Paper Structure

The rest of this paper is organized as follows. We describe preliminaries in Sect. 2. In Sect. 3, we summarize our bounds on the two Fourier properties of sampling without replacement, and use them to prove indistinguishability bounds for the XoP construction. Finally, we prove these bounds in Sect. 4 and Sect. 5. Specifically, in Sect. 4 we bound the maximal (absolute value of the) level-k Fourier coefficient of the sampling without replacement density function, while in Sect. 5, we bound its level-k Fourier weight.

2   Preliminaries

For a natural number m, denote $[m] = \{1, 2, \ldots, m\}$. For natural numbers m_1 and m_2 such that $m_1 \leq m_2$, denote $[m_1, m_2] = \{m_1, m_1 + 1, \ldots, m_2\}$. For a set $\mathcal{A}$, denote its size by $|\mathcal{A}|$. For any integer $k > 0$ and a real number t, define the falling factorial as $(t)_k = t(t-1) \ldots (t - (k-1))$. Further define $(t)_0 = 1$.

Let $\mathbb{F}$ be a field and $v \in \mathbb{F}^{k_1 \times k_2}$ a matrix of elements in $\mathbb{F}$. We index the elements of v in a natural way, namely, for $i \in [k_1]$, $v_i \in \mathbb{F}^{k_2}$ is the i'th row of v and for $j \in [k_2]$, $v_{i,j} \in \mathbb{F}$ is its j'th entry.

For two vectors $v, u \in \mathbb{F}^k$, we denote by $\langle u, v \rangle_{\mathbb{F}} = \sum_{i \in [k]} u_i v_i$ their inner product. Similarly, for matrices $v, u \in \mathbb{F}^{k_1 \times k_2}$, $\langle u, v \rangle_{\mathbb{F}} = \sum_{(i,j) \in [k_1] \times [k_2]} u_{i,j} v_{i,j}$.

In this paper, we typically deal with matrices $x \in \mathbb{F}_2^{k \times n}$, where n is considered a parameter and k may vary. We denote $N = 2^n$. We further denote by $(e_1, e_2, \ldots, e_n)$ the standard basis vectors of $\mathbb{F}_2^n$.

2.1   Probability

Definition 1 (Density function). *A (probability) density function on $\mathbb{F}_2^{q \times n}$ is a nonnegative function $\varphi : \mathbb{F}_2^{q \times n} \mapsto \mathbb{R}^{\geq 0}$ satisfying $\mathrm{E}_{x \in \mathbb{F}_2^{q \times n}}[\varphi(x)] = 1$, where $x \in \mathbb{F}_2^{q \times n}$ is uniformly chosen.*

We write $x \sim \varphi$ to denote that x is a random string drawn from the associated probability distribution, defined by

$$\Pr_{x \sim \varphi}[x = y] = \varphi(y)/2^{n \cdot q} \text{ for every } y \in \mathbb{F}_2^{q \times n}.$$

In particular, the uniform probability density function over $\mathbb{F}_2^{q \times n}$ is the constant function 1, and we denote it by $\mathbf{1}_{q \cdot n}$.

Let $\mathcal{A} \subseteq \mathbb{F}_2^{q \times n}$. We write $x \sim \mathcal{A}$ to denote that x is selected uniformly at random from $\mathcal{A}$.

Definition 2 (Collision probability). *The collision probability of a density function $\varphi : \mathbb{F}_2^{q \times n} \mapsto \mathbb{R}^{\geq 0}$ is*

$$Col[\varphi] = \Pr_{\substack{x, x' \sim \varphi \\ independently}} [x = x'].$$

Definition 3 (Convolution). *Let $f, g : \mathbb{F}_2^{q \times n} \mapsto \mathbb{R}$. Their convolution is the function $f * g : \mathbb{F}_2^{q \times n} \mapsto \mathbb{R}$ defined by*

$$(f * g)(x) = \mathrm{E}_{y \sim \mathbb{F}_2^{q \times n}} [f(y)g(x \oplus y)].$$

For a function $f : \mathbb{F}_2^{q \times n} \mapsto \mathbb{R}$ and a natural number $r \geq 2$, we denote the r-fold convolution of f with itself by $f^{(*r)} = f * f * \ldots * f$ (in particular $f^{(*2)} = f * f$).

Proposition 1 ([23], Proposition 1.26). *If $\varphi, \psi : \mathbb{F}_2^{q \times n} \mapsto \mathbb{R}^{\geq 0}$ are density functions, then so is $\varphi * \psi$. It represents the distribution over $\mathbb{F}_2^{q \times n}$ given by choosing $y \sim \varphi$ and $z \sim \psi$ independently and setting $x = y \oplus z$.*

Definition 4 (Statistical distance). *The statistical distance between two probability density functions $\varphi, \psi : \mathbb{F}_2^{q \times n} \mapsto \mathbb{R}^{\geq 0}$ is*

$$\mathrm{SD}(\varphi, \psi) = 1/2 \cdot \operatorname*{E}_{x \sim \mathbb{F}_2^{q \times n}} |\varphi(x) - \psi(x)|.$$

2.2   Fourier Analysis

We define the Fourier-Walsh expansion of functions on the Boolean cube, adapted to our setting, and state the basic results that we will use. These results are taken from [23].

Definition 5 (Fourier expansion). *Given $\alpha \in \mathbb{F}_2^{q \times n}$, define $\chi_\alpha : \mathbb{F}_2^{q \times n} \mapsto \{-1, 1\}$ by*

$$\chi_\alpha(x) = (-1)^{\langle \alpha, x \rangle_{\mathbb{F}_2}} = \prod_{i \in [q]} (-1)^{\langle \alpha_i, x_i \rangle_{\mathbb{F}_2}} = \prod_{i \in [q], j \in [n]} (-1)^{\alpha_{i,j} \cdot x_{i,j}}.$$

The set $\{\chi_\alpha\}_{\alpha \in \mathbb{F}_2^{q \times n}}$ is an orthonormal basis for the set of functions $\{f \mid f : \mathbb{F}_2^{q \times n} \mapsto \mathbb{R}\}$, with respect to the normalized inner product $\frac{1}{|\mathbb{F}_2^{q \times n}|} \langle f, g \rangle_{\mathbb{R}} = \mathrm{E}_{x \sim \mathbb{F}_2^{q \times n}} [f(x)g(x)]$. Hence each $\{f \mid f : \mathbb{F}_2^{q \times n} \mapsto \mathbb{R}\}$ can be decomposed to

$$f = \sum_{\alpha \in \mathbb{F}_2^{q \times n}} \widehat{f}(\alpha) \chi_\alpha,$$

where $\widehat{f}(\alpha) = \mathrm{E}[\chi_\alpha f]$, and in particular, $\widehat{f}(0) = \mathrm{E}[f]$.

Each element in $\{\chi_\alpha\}_{\alpha \in \mathbb{F}_2^{q \times n}}$ is called a *character*. We refer to α as a *mask*, and to $\widehat{f}(\alpha)$ as the *Fourier coefficient of f on α*. To distinguish the domain of characters from the input domain we write it as $\widehat{\mathbb{F}}_{\mathbb{F}_2^{q \times n}}$, and thus

$$f(x) = \sum_{\alpha \in \widehat{\mathbb{F}}_2^{q \times n}} \widehat{f}(\alpha) \chi_\alpha(x).$$

For a mask $\alpha \in \widehat{\mathbb{F}}_2^{q \times n}$, we write

$$\mathrm{supp}(\alpha) = \{i \mid \alpha_i \neq 0\} \text{ and } \#\alpha = |\mathrm{supp}(\alpha)|.$$

We call $\#\alpha$ the *level* of α, and $\widehat{f}(\alpha)$ is a Fourier coefficient of level $\#\alpha$.

Definition 6 (Fourier weight and maximal magnitude). *For a function $f : \mathbb{F}_2^{q \times n} \mapsto \mathbb{R}$, we define the Fourier weight of f at level k to be*

$$W^{=k}[f] = \sum_{\substack{\alpha \in \widehat{\mathbb{F}}_2^{q \times n} \\ \#\alpha = k}} \widehat{f}(\alpha)^2.$$

The Fourier weight of f up to level k is $W^{\leq k}[f] = \sum_{i=0}^{k} W^{=i}[f]$.
The maximal magnitude of a level-k Fourier coefficient of f is

$$M^{=k}[f] = \max_{\substack{\alpha \in \widehat{\mathbb{F}}_2^{q \times n} \\ \# \alpha = k}} \{|\widehat{f}(\alpha)|\}.$$

Finally, let $M^{\geq 1}[f] = \max_{\substack{\alpha \in \widehat{\mathbb{F}}_2^{q \times n} \\ \alpha \neq 0}} \{|\widehat{f}(\alpha)|\}$ denote the maximal magnitude of a Fourier coefficient on a non-zero mask.

Proposition 2 ([23], Fact 1.21). *If $\varphi : \mathbb{F}_2^{q \times n} \mapsto \mathbb{R}^{\geq 0}$ is a density function and $f : \mathbb{F}_2^{q \times n} \mapsto \mathbb{R}$, then*

$$\mathop{\mathrm{E}}_{x \sim \varphi}[f(x)] = \mathop{\mathrm{E}}_{x \sim \mathbb{F}_2^{q \times n}}[\varphi(x) f(x)].$$

Proposition 3 ([23], Theorem 1.27 – Fourier coefficients of convolution). *Let $f, g : \mathbb{F}_2^{q \times n} \mapsto \mathbb{R}$. Then for all $\alpha \in \widehat{\mathbb{F}}_2^{q \times n}$, $\widehat{f * g}(\alpha) = \widehat{f}(\alpha)\widehat{g}(\alpha)$.*

Proposition 4 ([23], Exercise 1.23 – relation between Fourier weight and collision probability). *For a density function $\varphi : \mathbb{F}_2^{q \times n} \mapsto \mathbb{R}^{\geq 0}$,*

$$W^{\leq q}[\varphi] = Col[\varphi] \cdot 2^{q \cdot n}.$$

Proposition 5 ([23], Proposition 1.13 – variance). *The variance of $f : \mathbb{F}_2^{q \times n} \mapsto \mathbb{R}$ is*

$$\mathrm{Var}[f] = \mathrm{E}[f^2] - \mathrm{E}[f]^2 = \sum_{\substack{\alpha \in \widehat{\mathbb{F}}_2^{q \times n} \\ \alpha \neq 0}} \widehat{f}(\alpha)^2 = \sum_{k=1}^{q} W^{=k}[f].$$

Proposition 6 ([23], Exercise 1.23 – bound on statistical distance from uniform). *Let $\varphi : \mathbb{F}_2^{q \times n} \mapsto \mathbb{R}^{\geq 0}$ be a density function. Then*

$$\mathrm{SD}(\varphi, 1_{q \cdot n}) \leq \frac{1}{2}\sqrt{\mathrm{Var}[\varphi]}.$$

We prove two additional basic results regarding variance.

Proposition 7 (Variance reduction by convolution). *Let $\varphi : \mathbb{F}_2^{q \times n} \mapsto \mathbb{R}^{\geq 0}$ be a density function. Let r_1, r_2 be integers such that $0 < r_2 < r_1$. Then,*

$$\mathrm{Var}[\varphi^{(*r_1)}] \leq (M^{\geq 1}[\varphi])^{2(r_1 - r_2)} \, \mathrm{Var}[\varphi^{(*r_2)}].$$

Proof. By Proposition 5 and Proposition 3,

$$\mathrm{Var}[\varphi^{(*r_1)}] = \sum_{\substack{\alpha \in \widehat{\mathbb{F}}_2^{q \times n} \\ \alpha \neq 0}} \widehat{\varphi^{(*r_1)}}(\alpha)^2 = \sum_{\substack{\alpha \in \widehat{\mathbb{F}}_2^{q \times n} \\ \alpha \neq 0}} \widehat{\varphi}(\alpha)^{2 r_1}$$

$$\leq (M^{\geq 1}[\varphi])^{2(r_1 - r_2)} \sum_{\substack{\alpha \in \widehat{\mathbb{F}}_2^{q \times n} \\ \alpha \neq 0}} \widehat{\varphi}(\alpha)^{2 r_2} = (M^{\geq 1}[\varphi])^{2(r_1 - r_2)} \, \mathrm{Var}[\varphi^{(*r_2)}].$$

∎

Proposition 8 (Variance of independent samples). *Let $\varphi : \mathbb{F}_2^{q \times n} \mapsto \mathbb{R}^{\geq 0}$ be a density function. Let u be a natural number and let $\varphi^{\times u} : \mathbb{F}_2^{(q \cdot u) \times n} \mapsto \mathbb{R}^{\geq 0}$ be the density function obtained by concatenating u independent samples drawn from φ. Then,*

$$\mathrm{Var}[\varphi^{\times u}] \leq 2u \cdot \mathrm{Var}[\varphi], \;\; assuming \; u \cdot \mathrm{Var}[\varphi] \leq 1/2.$$

Proof. By independence of the u samples, we have $\mathrm{Col}[\varphi^{\times u}] = \mathrm{Col}[\varphi]^u$. Applying Proposition 4 and Proposition 5,

$$\mathrm{W}^{\leq q \cdot u}[\varphi^{\times u}] = \mathrm{Col}[\varphi^{\times u}] \cdot 2^{q \cdot n \cdot u} = (\mathrm{Col}[\varphi] \cdot 2^{q \cdot n})^u = (\mathrm{W}^{\leq q}[\varphi])^u = \left(\widehat{\varphi}(0)^2 + \mathrm{Var}[\varphi] \right)^u.$$

Writing $z = \mathrm{Var}[\varphi]$ and noting that $\widehat{\varphi}(0)^2 = 1$ since φ is a density function, we have $\mathrm{W}^{\leq q \cdot u}[\varphi^{\times u}] = (1 + z)^u = 1 + \sum_{i=1}^{u} \binom{u}{i} z^i$. The ratio between two consecutive terms in the sum $\sum_{i=1}^{u} \binom{u}{i} z^i$ is upper bounded by $u \cdot z \leq 1/2$ (by the assumption). Thus, the sum is upper bounded by a geometric series with ratio $1/2$ (i.e., twice the first term). We conclude that

$$\mathrm{W}^{\leq q \cdot u}[\varphi^{\times u}] \leq 1 + 2u \cdot z = \widehat{\varphi^{\times u}}(0)^2 + 2u \cdot z.$$

Hence, by Proposition 5, $\mathrm{Var}[\varphi^{\times u}] = \sum_{k=1}^{q \cdot u} \mathrm{W}^{=k}[\varphi^{\times u}] \leq 2u \cdot z$. $\blacksquare$

2.3 Cryptographic Preliminaries and Sampling Without Replacement

We use the standard notion of PRF security, as defined below. Let $H : \mathcal{K} \times \{0,1\}^{m_1} \mapsto \{0,1\}^{m_2}$ be a family of functions and $\mathrm{Func}(m_1, m_2)$ be the set of all functions $g : \{0,1\}^{m_1} \mapsto \{0,1\}^{m_2}$. Let A be an algorithm with oracle access to a function $f : \{0,1\}^{m_1} \mapsto \{0,1\}^{m_2}$. The PRF advantage of A against H is

$$\mathrm{Adv}_H^{\mathrm{prf}}(A) = \left| \Pr_{K \sim \mathcal{K}}[A^{H_K(\cdot)} \Rightarrow 1] - \Pr_{f \sim \mathrm{Func}(m_1, m_2)}[A^{f(\cdot)} \Rightarrow 1] \right|.$$

We also define the optimal advantage

$$\mathrm{Opt}_H^{\mathrm{prf}}(q) = \max\{\mathrm{Adv}_H^{\mathrm{prf}}(A) \mid A \text{ makes } q \text{ queries}\}.$$

In this paper we also consider the multi-user setting, where we have u users, each with an independent instantiation of the cryptosystem. The adversary can issue (up to) $q_{\max}$ queries to each user with the goal of distinguishing the u instantiations of the cryptosystem from u instantiations of a random function. Extending the single-user definitions, we define the PRF advantage of A against H in the multi-user setting as

$$\mathrm{Adv}_{H,u}^{\mathrm{mu\text{-}prf}}(A) = \Big| \Pr_{K_1,\ldots,K_u \sim \mathcal{K}}[A^{H_{K_1}(\cdot),\ldots,H_{K_u}(\cdot)} \Rightarrow 1]$$

$$- \Pr_{f_1,\ldots,f_u \sim \mathrm{Func}(m_1, m_2)}[A^{f_1(\cdot),\ldots,f_u(\cdot)} \Rightarrow 1] \Big|$$

We further define the optimal advantage

$$\text{Opt}_{H,u}^{\text{mu-prf}}(q_{\max}) = \max\{\text{Adv}_{H,u}^{\text{mu-prf}}(A) \mid A \text{ makes } q_{\max} \text{ queries to each user}\}.$$

The XoP$[r, n]$ Construction and Sampling Without Replacement. Let $\text{Perm}(n)$ be the set of all permutations on $\{0, 1\}^n$ (i.e., the set of all $\pi : \{0, 1\}^n \mapsto \{0, 1\}^n$). For natural numbers r, n such that $r \geq 2$, define the family of functions $\text{XoP}[r, n] : (\text{Perm}(n))^r \times \{0, 1\}^n \mapsto \{0, 1\}^n$ by

$$\text{XoP}[r, n](\pi_1, \ldots, \pi_r, i) = \pi_1(i) \oplus \pi_2(i) \oplus \ldots \oplus \pi_r(i).$$

The main goal of this paper is to bound $\text{Opt}_{\text{XoP}[r,n]}^{\text{prf}}(q)$ as a function of the parameters r, n, q. By symmetry of the randomly chosen permutations $\pi_1, \ldots, \pi_r$, an adversary against $\text{XoP}[r, n]$ obtains the XOR of r independent samples, each containing q elements of $\{0, 1\}^n$, chosen uniformly without replacement (regardless of the actual queries). Below, we formalize this statement.

Definition 7 (Density function of sampling without replacement). *For natural numbers n, q such that $1 \leq q \leq 2^n$, let $\mu_{n,q} : \mathbb{F}_2^{q \times n} \mapsto \mathbb{R}^{\geq 0}$ be the density function associated with the process of uniformly sampling q elements from $\mathbb{F}_2^n$ without replacement. Specifically, for $x \in \mathbb{F}_2^{q \times n}$,*

$$\mu_{n,q}(x) = \begin{cases} \frac{(N-q)!}{N!} \cdot N^q & \text{if } x_i \neq x_j \text{ for all } i, j \in [q] \ (i \neq j), \\ 0 & \text{otherwise.} \end{cases}$$

Furthermore, define $\mu_{n,0}$ to be the constant 1.

Then, by Proposition 1 an adversary against $\text{XoP}[r, n]$ that makes q distinct queries obtains a sample from $\mu_{n,q}^{(*r)}$. By well-known properties of statistical distance,

$$\text{Opt}_{\text{XoP}[r,n]}^{\text{prf}}(q) \leq \text{SD}(\mu_{n,q}^{(*r)}, \mathbf{1}_{q \cdot n}). \tag{1}$$

Therefore, our task reduces to upper bounding $\text{SD}(\mu_{n,q}^{(*r)}, \mathbf{1}_{q \cdot n})$.

We further consider the multi-user setting. Observe that in this setting, an adversary against $\text{XoP}[r, n]$ obtains a sample of $(\mu_{n,q_{\max}}^{(*r)})^{\times u} : \mathbb{F}_2^{(q_{\max} \cdot u) \times n} \mapsto \mathbb{R}^{\geq 0}$, where $(\mu_{n,q_{\max}}^{(*r)})^{\times u}$ is the density function obtained by concatenating u independent samples drawn from $\mu_{n,q_{\max}}^{(*r)}$. Similarly to the single-user setting,

$$\text{Opt}_{\text{XoP}[r,n],u}^{\text{mu-prf}}(q_{\max}) \leq \text{SD}((\mu_{n,q_{\max}}^{(*r)})^{\times u}, \mathbf{1}_{u \cdot q_{\max} \cdot n}). \tag{2}$$

Therefore, in this setting our task reduces to upper bounding $\text{SD}((\mu_{n,q_{\max}}^{(*r)})^{\times u}, \mathbf{1}_{u \cdot q_{\max} \cdot n})$.

3 Indistinguishability Bounds for XoP$[r, n]$ Using Fourier Properties of Sampling Without Replacement

In this section we derive tight indistinguishability bounds for $\text{XoP}[r, n]$ and then extend them to the multi-user setting. For this purpose, we start by stating the fundamental Fourier properties of $\mu_{n,k}$ that we prove in this paper.

3.1 Basic Properties of $\mu_{n,k}$

We will obtain bounds for the maximal magnitude of Fourier coefficients by level, namely $M^{=k}[\mu_{n,q}]$, and Fourier weight by level, namely $W^{=k}[\mu_{n,q}]$. First, note that if $x \sim \mu_{n,q}$, then for every set of k distinct indices $\{i_1, i_2, \ldots, i_k\} \subseteq [q]$, $(x_{i_1}, \ldots, x_{i_k})$ are k elements that are marginally sampled without replacement from $\mathbb{F}_2^{k \times n}$, namely, $(x_{i_1}, \ldots, x_{i_k}) \sim \mu_{n,k}$. Therefore, for $1 \le k \le q$, we have $M^{=k}[\mu_{n,q}] = M^{=k}[\mu_{n,k}]$ and

$$
W^{=k}[\mu_{n,q}] = \sum_{\substack{\alpha \in \widehat{\mathbb{F}}_2^{q \times n} \\ \#\alpha = k}} \widehat{\mu_{n,q}}(\alpha)^2 = \sum_{\{i_1,\ldots,i_k\} \subseteq [q] \text{ distinct}} \sum_{\substack{\beta \in \widehat{\mathbb{F}}_2^{k \times n} \\ \mathrm{supp}(\beta) = \{i_1,\ldots,i_k\}}} \widehat{\mu_{n,k}}(\beta)^2
$$

$$
= \sum_{\{i_1,\ldots,i_k\} \subseteq [q] \text{ distinct}} W^{=k}[\mu_{n,k}] = \binom{q}{k} W^{=k}[\mu_{n,k}].
$$

Consequently, our main results bound $M^{=k}[\mu_{n,k}]$ and $W^{=k}[\mu_{n,k}]$. Lemma 1 below is proved in Sect. 4, while Lemma 2 is proved in Sect. 5.

Lemma 1 (Bounds on magnitude of level-k Fourier coefficients). *We have $M^{=2}[\mu_{n,2}] \le \frac{1}{N-1}$. Generally,*

$$
M^{=k}[\mu_{n,k}]^2 \le \begin{cases} \frac{1}{\binom{N}{k}} & \text{if } k < N/2 \text{ is even,} \\ \frac{1}{\binom{N}{k}} \cdot \frac{k+1}{N-k} < \frac{1}{\binom{N}{k}} & \text{if } k < N/2 \text{ is odd.} \end{cases}
$$

Note that the bound $M^{=2}[\mu_{n,2}] \le \frac{1}{N-1}$ is slightly better (by a factor of about $\sqrt{2}$) than the generic bound for $k = 2$. The quantity $M^{=2}[\mu_{n,2}]$ plays a significant role in our analysis, as it is the maximal magnitude of a Fourier coefficient with a non-zero mask ($M^{=1}[\mu_{n,1}] = 0$ can be deduced from Lemma 2 below).

Lemma 2 (Bounds on weight of level-k Fourier coefficients). *We have*

$$
W^{=1}[\mu_{n,1}] = 0, \quad W^{=2}[\mu_{n,2}] = \frac{1}{N-1}, \quad \text{and} \quad W^{=3}[\mu_{n,3}] = \frac{4}{(N-1)(N-2)}.
$$

Generally,

$$
W^{=k}[\mu_{n,k}] \le \begin{cases} \frac{(N(k-1))^{k/2}}{(N)_k} \le \Psi_N(k) & \text{if } k \ge 2 \text{ is even,} \\ \frac{(N(k-1))^{(k+1)/2}}{(N)_{k+1}} \le \Psi_N(k+1) & \text{if } k \ge 3 \text{ is odd,} \end{cases}
$$

where

$$
\Psi_N(k) = \left(\frac{k}{N-k}\right)^{k/2} \exp\left(-\frac{k(k-2)}{8N(N-k) + 2 \cdot k^2}\right)^{k/2}.
$$

Remark 2. The fact that $W^{=1}[\mu_{n,1}] = 0$ is obvious since $\mu_{n,1}$ is the uniform distribution over $\{0,1\}^n$, and thus all non-empty linear equations on these bits are unbiased.

Remark 3. For $k < N/2$, $\frac{k}{N-k} < 1$. Therefore, the lemma shows that the Fourier weight of $\mu_{n,k}$ at level k is exponentially small in k up to $k < N/2$. In particular, in the extreme case of $k \approx N/2$, we have

$$\exp\left(-\frac{k(k-2)}{8N(N-k)+2\cdot k^2}\right)^{k/2} \approx \exp\left(-\frac{N^2/4}{4N^2+N^2/2}\right)^{N/4} = e^{-N/72} \approx e^{-k/36}.$$

Nevertheless, we will only use a simpler bound of the form $\mathrm{W}^{=k}[\mu_{n,k}] \leq \left(\frac{k}{N-k}\right)^{k/2}$ in our application. Furthermore, since $\mathrm{W}^{=k}[\mu_{n,q}] = \binom{q}{k}\mathrm{W}^{=k}[\mu_{n,k}]$, the number of queries q obviously also plays a significant role in the analysis.

3.2 Application to Indistinguishability Bounds for XoP[r, n]

We now use the results about $\mu_{n,k}$ in our main application to derive indistinguishability bounds for $\mathrm{XoP}[r,n]$, starting with $r = 2$.

Theorem 1. *For $N \geq 1000$ and $q < N/2$,*

$$Opt^{prf}_{XoP[2,n]}(q) \leq \frac{q}{2 \cdot (N-1)^{3/2}} < \frac{q}{N^{3/2}}.$$

Proof. Using (1), and applying Proposition 6,

$$\mathrm{Opt}^{prf}_{\mathrm{XoP}[2,n]}(q) \leq \mathrm{SD}(\mu_{n,q} * \mu_{n,q}, \mathbf{1}_{q \cdot n}) \leq \frac{1}{2}\sqrt{\mathrm{Var}[\mu_{n,q} * \mu_{n,q}]}.$$

Thus, it remains to prove that

$$\mathrm{Var}[\mu_{n,q} * \mu_{n,q}] \leq \frac{q^2}{(N-1)^3}. \tag{3}$$

Applying Proposition 5, and then Proposition 3, we have

$$\mathrm{Var}[\mu_{n,q}^{(*2)}] = \sum_{\substack{\alpha \in \widehat{\mathbb{F}}_2^{q \times n} \\ \alpha \neq 0}} \widehat{\mu_{n,q} * \mu_{n,q}}(\alpha)^2 = \sum_{\substack{\alpha \in \widehat{\mathbb{F}}_2^{q \times n} \\ \alpha \neq 0}} \widehat{\mu_{n,q}}(\alpha)^4 = \sum_{k=1}^{q} \sum_{\substack{\alpha \in \widehat{\mathbb{F}}_2^{q \times n} \\ \#\alpha = k}} \widehat{\mu_{n,q}}(\alpha)^4$$

$$\leq \sum_{k=1}^{q} \mathrm{M}^{=k}[\mu_{n,q}]^2 \sum_{\substack{\alpha \in \widehat{\mathbb{F}}_2^{q \times n} \\ \#\alpha = k}} \widehat{\mu_{n,q}}(\alpha)^2 = \sum_{k=1}^{q} \mathrm{M}^{=k}[\mu_{n,q}]^2 \cdot \mathrm{W}^{=k}[\mu_{n,q}]$$

$$= \sum_{k=1}^{q} \mathrm{M}^{=k}[\mu_{n,k}]^2 \cdot \binom{q}{k} \mathrm{W}^{=k}[\mu_{n,k}],$$

where the final equality exploits the symmetry of $\mu_{n,q}$. Next, applying Lemma 1, and using the fact that $W^{=1}[\mu_{n,1}] = 0$ (by Lemma 2),

$$\text{Var}[\mu_{n,q}^{(*2)}] \leq \frac{1}{(N-1)^2} \cdot \binom{q}{2} \cdot W^{=2}[\mu_{n,2}] + \sum_{k=3}^{q} \frac{\binom{q}{k}}{\binom{N}{k}} W^{=k}[\mu_{n,k}]$$

$$\leq \frac{q^2}{(N-1)^2} \cdot (1/2) \cdot W^{=2}[\mu_{n,2}] + \sum_{k=3}^{q} \frac{(q)(q-1)\ldots(q-(k-1))}{(N)(N-1)\ldots(N-(k-1))} W^{=k}[\mu_{n,k}]$$

$$\leq \frac{q^2}{(N-1)^2} \cdot (1/2) \cdot W^{=2}[\mu_{n,2}] + \sum_{k=3}^{q} (q/N)^k \cdot W^{=k}[\mu_{n,k}]$$

$$\leq \frac{q^2}{(N-1)^2} \left((1/2) \cdot W^{=2}[\mu_{n,2}] + \sum_{k=3}^{q} (q/N)^{k-2} \cdot W^{=k}[\mu_{n,k}] \right)$$

We now apply Lemma 2. We will also separate the term $W^{=3}[\mu_{n,3}] = \frac{4}{(N-1)(N-2)}$ from the sum of terms for $k \geq 4$. For these we use a simple bound

$$W^{=k}[\mu_{n,k}] \leq \left(\frac{k+1}{N-k-1} \right)^{k/2} \leq \left(\frac{2(k+1)}{N} \right)^{k/2},$$

which holds both for even and odd k, and uses the fact that $k \leq q < N/2$. We will further split the remaining sum at $k = 4n$ and use once again the fact that $q/N < 1/2$. Thus, $\text{Var}[\mu_{n,q}^{(*2)}]$ is upper bounded by

$$\frac{q^2}{(N-1)^2} \cdot \left((1/2) \cdot W^{=2}[\mu_{n,2}] + (q/N) \cdot W^{=3}[\mu_{n,3}] + \sum_{k=4}^{4n} (q/N)^{k-2} \cdot W^{=k}[\mu_{n,k}] \right)$$

$$+ \sum_{k=4n+1}^{q} (q/N)^k \cdot W^{=k}[\mu_{n,k}]$$

$$\leq \frac{q^2}{(N-1)^2} \cdot \left(\frac{1}{2(N-1)} + \frac{2}{(N-1)(N-2)} + 4 \sum_{k=4}^{4n} 2^{-k} \cdot \left(\frac{2(k+1)}{N} \right)^{k/2} \right) + \sum_{k=4n+1}^{q} 2^{-k}$$

$$\leq \frac{q^2}{(N-1)^2} \cdot \left(\frac{1}{2(N-1)} + \frac{2}{(N-1)(N-2)} + 4 \sum_{k=4}^{4n} \left(\frac{k+1}{2N} \right)^{k/2} \right) + N^{-4}.$$

We now upper bound $\sum_{k=4}^{4n} \left(\frac{k+1}{2N} \right)^{k/2}$. The (inverse) squared ratio between two consecutive terms is

$$\frac{((k+1)/2N)^k}{((k+2)/2N)^{k+1}} = \left(\frac{k+1}{k+2} \right)^k \cdot \frac{2N}{k+2} = \left(1 - \frac{1}{k+2} \right)^k \cdot \frac{2N}{k+2}$$

$$\geq e^{-2k/(k+2)} \frac{2N}{k+2} \geq e^{-2} \frac{2N}{k+2} \geq \frac{2N}{(4n+2)e^2}.$$

where we have used the inequality $1 - (x/2) > e^{-x}$, which holds for $0 < x \leq 1$, as well as the fact that $k \leq 4n$ in the analyzed sum. Since $\frac{2N}{(4n+2)e^2} \geq 4$ holds for $N \geq 1000$, the sum is upper bounded by the sum of a geometric series with ratio at most $1/2$. Hence, $\sum_{k=4}^{4n} \left(\frac{k+1}{2N}\right)^{k/2} \leq 2 \left(\frac{5}{2N}\right)^2 = \frac{25}{2N^2}$. Also, noting that $N^{-4} \leq (q^2/(N-1)^2) \cdot 1/N^2$, we plug these into the above bound and obtain

$$\mathrm{Var}[\mu_{n,q}^{(*2)}] \leq \frac{q^2}{(N-1)^2} \cdot \left(\frac{1}{2(N-1)} + \frac{2}{(N-1)(N-2)} + \frac{50}{N^2} + \frac{1}{N^2}\right).$$

As each one of the last three summands is bounded by $\frac{1}{8(N-1)}$ assuming $N \geq 1000$, we conclude that $\mathrm{Var}[\mu_{n,q}^{(*2)}] \leq \frac{q^2}{(N-1)^3}$ as in (3).

■

Next, we generalize Theorem 1 to derive indistinguishability bounds for $\mathrm{XoP}[r, n]$ for arbitrary $r \geq 2$.

Theorem 2. *For $N \geq 1000$, $q < N/2$ and $r \geq 2$,*

$$Opt_{XoP[r,n]}^{prf}(q) \leq \frac{q}{2 \cdot (N-1)^{r-(1/2)}} < \frac{q}{N^{r-(1/2)}},$$

where the last inequality assumes $r \leq N/2$.

Proof. By (1) and Proposition 6, $Opt_{XoP[r,n]}^{prf}(q) \leq \mathrm{SD}(\mu_{n,q}^{(*r)}, 1_{q \cdot n}) \leq \frac{1}{2}\sqrt{\mathrm{Var}[\mu_{n,q}^{(*r)}]}$, and thus it remains to prove that

$$\mathrm{Var}[\mu_{n,q}^{(*r)}] \leq \frac{q^2}{(N-1)^{2r-1}}. \tag{4}$$

Applying Proposition 6 and then Proposition 7 (with $r_2 = 2$),

$$\mathrm{Var}[\mu_{n,q}^{(*r)}] \leq (\mathrm{M}^{\geq 1}[\mu_{n,q}])^{2r-4} \cdot \mathrm{Var}[\mu_{n,q}^{(*2)}] = (\max_{0<k\leq q}\{\mathrm{M}^{=k}[\mu_{n,k}]\})^{2r-4} \cdot \mathrm{Var}[\mu_{n,q}^{(*2)}],$$

where the final equality is by symmetry of $\mu_{n,q}$. Next, note from Lemma 1 that (the bound on) $\mathrm{M}^{=k}[\mu_{n,k}]$ is maximized for $k = 2$ assuming $q < N/2$, and $\mathrm{M}^{=2}[\mu_{n,2}] \leq \frac{1}{N-1}$. Moreover $\mathrm{Var}[\mu_{n,q}^{(*2)}] \leq \frac{q^2}{(N-1)^3}$ by (3). Hence,

$$\mathrm{Var}[\mu_{n,q}^{(*r)}] \leq \frac{1}{(N-1)^{2r-4}} \frac{q^2}{(N-1)^3} = \frac{q^2}{(N-1)^{2r-1}}.$$

■

The Multi-user Setting. We extend Theorem 2 to derive indistinguishability bounds for $\mathrm{XoP}[r, n]$ in the multi-user setting.

Theorem 3. *For $N \geq 1000$, $q < N/2$ and $r \geq 2$,*

$$Opt_{XoP[r,n],u}^{mu\text{-}prf}(q_{max}) \leq \frac{\sqrt{u/2} \cdot q_{max}}{(N-1)^{r-(1/2)}} \leq \frac{\sqrt{u} \cdot q_{max}}{N^{r-(1/2)}},$$

assuming $\frac{\sqrt{u/2} \cdot q_{max}}{(N-1)^{r-(1/2)}} \leq 1/2$ (and $r \leq N/3$ for the last inequality).

Proof. By (2) and Proposition 6,

$$\mathrm{Opt}^{\mathrm{mu\text{-}prf}}_{\mathrm{XoP}[r,n],u}(q_{max}) \leq \mathrm{SD}((\mu^{(*r)}_{n,q_{\max}})^{\times u}, \mathbf{1}_{u \cdot q_{\max} \cdot n}) \leq \frac{1}{2}\sqrt{\mathrm{Var}[(\mu^{(*r)}_{n,q_{\max}})^{\times u}]},$$

and thus is remains to prove that $\mathrm{Var}[(\mu^{(*r)}_{n,q_{\max}})^{\times u}] \leq \frac{2u \cdot q^2_{\max}}{(N-1)^{2r-1}}$.

Applying Proposition 8 (assuming $u \cdot \mathrm{Var}[\mu^{(*r)}_{n,q_{\max}}] \leq 1/2$), we have

$$\mathrm{Var}[(\mu^{(*r)}_{n,q_{\max}})^{\times u}] \leq 2u \cdot \mathrm{Var}[\mu^{(*r)}_{n,q_{\max}}] \leq \frac{2u \cdot q^2_{\max}}{(N-1)^{2r-1}},$$

where the final inequality is by (4). Finally, note that by (4), $u \cdot \mathrm{Var}[\mu^{(*r)}_{n,q_{\max}}] \leq \frac{u \cdot q^2_{\max}}{(N-1)^{2r-1}}$, so the condition for applying Proposition 8 is assured if $\frac{u \cdot q^2_{\max}}{(N-1)^{2r-1}} \leq 1/2$, namely $\frac{\sqrt{u/2} \cdot q_{\max}}{(N-1)^{r-(1/2)}} \leq 1/2$.

∎

4   Bounding $\mathrm{M}^{=k}[\mu_{n,k}]$ (Proof of Lemma 1)

The goal of this section is to prove Lemma 1. We first bound the Fourier coefficients on a specific subset of masks (called masks of type $K = (k)$). We will later generalize these results to all mask.

4.1   Bounding $|\widehat{\mu_{n,k}}(\alpha)|$ for α of Type $K = (k)$

Definition 8 (Mask of type $K = (k)$). *Let $\alpha \in \widehat{\mathbb{F}}^{k \times n}_2$ be a non-zero mask such that $\#\alpha = k$ (i.e., $\alpha_i \neq 0$ for all $i \in [k]$). We define the type of α to be $K = (k)$, if for every $i \in [k]$, $\alpha_{i,1} = 1$.*

In other words, α is of type $K = (k)$ if the first bit of all of its k elements is 1. The bounds on the Fourier coefficients are formulated using the following function.

Definition 9. *For natural numbers a, b such that b is even and $a \geq b$ let*

$$\Gamma(a,b) = \prod_{i=1,3,\dots,b-1} \frac{b-i}{a-i}.$$

The main result of this section is as follows.

Proposition 9. *Let $\alpha \in \widehat{\mathbb{F}}^{k \times n}_2$ be of type $K = (k)$. Then,*

$$|\widehat{\mu_{n,k}}(\alpha)| \leq \Gamma(N,k) = \prod_{i=1,3,\dots,k-1} \frac{k-i}{N-i}$$

if k is even and 0 otherwise.

In particular,

$$|\widehat{\mu_{n,1}}(\alpha)| = 0, |\widehat{\mu_{n,2}}(\alpha)| \leq \frac{1}{N-1}, |\widehat{\mu_{n,3}}(\alpha)| = 0, |\widehat{\mu_{n,4}}(\alpha)| \leq \frac{3}{(N-1)(N-3)},$$

etc. We need the following definitions.

Definition 10 (Pairing of two elements). *Two elements $a, b \in \mathbb{F}_2^n$ are paired on bit $j \in [n]$ if $a \oplus b = e_j$ (where $e_j \in \mathbb{F}_2^n$ is the j'th vector of the standard basis).*

Definition 11 (Pairing of a sequence of elements). *Let $x = (x_1, \ldots, x_k) \in \mathbb{F}_2^{k \times n}$. Then, x is self-paired on bit $j \in [n]$ if $(x_1, \ldots, x_k)$ are distinct (i.e., $x_{i_1} \neq x_{i_2}$ for $i_1 \neq i_2$), and for every $i_1 \in [k]$, there exists $i_2 \in [k]$ such that (x_{i_1}, x_{i_2}) are paired on bit j.*

Note that since $(x_1, \ldots, x_k)$ are distinct, each element x_i cannot be paired to more than one other element on bit j, and thus if x is self-paired (on any $j \in [n]$), then k is even.

In order to prove Proposition 9, we define the following algorithm.

---
1. Sample $x \sim \mu_{n,k}$.
2. If x is self-paired on bit 1, return 1. Else, return 0.

Define the random variable $T(x)$ for the output of the algorithm.

We will prove the following two claims, whose combination immediately implies Proposition 9.

Proposition 10 (Magnitude of Fourier coefficient bounded by success probability). $|\widehat{\mu_{n,k}}(\alpha)| \leq \Pr_{x \sim \mu_{n,k}}[T(x) = 1]$.

Proposition 11 (Bound on success probability).

$$\Pr_{x \sim \mu_{n,k}}[T(x) = 1] = \begin{cases} \Gamma(N, k) & \text{if } k \text{ is even,} \\ 0 & \text{if } k \text{ is odd.} \end{cases}$$

Proof (of Proposition 10). By Proposition 2,

$$|\widehat{\mu_{n,k}}(\alpha)| = |\mathop{\mathrm{E}}_{x \sim \mathbb{F}_2^n}[\mu_{n,k}(x)\chi_\alpha(x)]| = |\mathop{\mathrm{E}}_{x \sim \mu_{n,k}}[\chi_\alpha(x)]|$$

$$= |\Pr_{x \sim \mu_{n,k}}[T(x) = 1] \mathop{\mathrm{E}}_{x \sim \mu_{n,k}}[\chi_\alpha(x) \mid T(x) = 1]$$

$$+ \Pr_{x \sim \mu_{n,k}}[T(x) = 0] \mathop{\mathrm{E}}_{x \sim \mu_{n,k}}[\chi_\alpha(x) \mid T(x) = 0]|$$

$$\leq |\Pr_{x \sim \mu_{n,k}}[T(x) = 1] \mathop{\mathrm{E}}_{x \sim \mu_{n,k}}[\chi_\alpha(x) \mid T(x) = 1]|$$

$$+ |\Pr_{x \sim \mu_{n,k}}[T(x) = 0] \mathop{\mathrm{E}}_{x \sim \mu_{n,k}}[\chi_\alpha(x) \mid T(x) = 0]| \qquad (5)$$

$$\leq |\Pr_{x \sim \mu_{n,k}}[T(x) = 1] \mathop{\mathrm{E}}_{x \sim \mu_{n,k}}[|\chi_\alpha(x)| \mid T(x) = 1]|$$

$$+ |\Pr_{x \sim \mu_{n,k}}[T(x) = 0] \mathop{\mathrm{E}}_{x \sim \mu_{n,k}}[\chi_\alpha(x) \mid T(x) = 0]|$$

$$= \Pr_{x \sim \mu_{n,k}}[T(x) = 1] + |\Pr_{x \sim \mu_{n,k}}[T(x) = 0] \mathop{\mathrm{E}}_{x \sim \mu_{n,k}}[\chi_\alpha(x) \mid T(x) = 0]|.$$

Next, we prove that $\mathbb{E}_{x \sim \mu_{n,k}}[\chi_\alpha(x) \mid T(x) = 0] = 0$, which concludes the proof. This is proved by partitioning the sample space of the algorithm conditioned on $T(x) = 0$ into couples of the form (x, x') such that $\chi_\alpha(x) = -\chi_\alpha(x')$. Since all samples in the space (conditioned on $T(x) = 0$) have identical probability, the total contribution of each couple to the expectation is $\chi_\alpha(x) + \chi_\alpha(x') = 0$, which proves that $\mathbb{E}_{x \sim \mu_{n,k}}[\chi_\alpha(x) \mid T(x) = 0] = 0$.

We now define how to couple the samples. Assume that $T(x) = 0$. Then, there exists an element of x that is not paired. Define $in(x) \in [k]$ to be the index of the first unpaired element in $[k]$. Then, $x' = (x_1, \ldots, x_{in(x)-1}, x_{in(x)} \oplus e_1, x_{in(x)+1}, \ldots, x_k)$ is a valid sample from the space (conditioned on $T(x) = 0$). We couple together (x, x'). Note that we need to prove that this is a valid coupling, i.e., if x is coupled to x', then x' is coupled to x. This indeed holds since $in(x') = in(x)$, as x and x' only differ on the element with index $in(x)$.

Finally, we prove that $\chi_\alpha(x) = -\chi_\alpha(x')$ or $\chi_\alpha(x)\chi_\alpha(x') = -1$. As $\alpha \in \widehat{\mathbb{F}}_2^{k \times n}$ is of type $K = (k)$, then $\alpha_{i,1} = 1$ for any $i \in [k]$. Therefore,

$$\chi_\alpha(x)\chi_\alpha(x') = (-1)^{\langle \alpha, x \rangle_{\mathbb{F}_2}}(-1)^{\langle \alpha, x' \rangle_{\mathbb{F}_2}} = (-1)^{\langle \alpha, x \oplus x' \rangle_{\mathbb{F}_2}}$$
$$= (-1)^{\langle \alpha_{in(x)}, e_1 \rangle_{\mathbb{F}_2}} = (-1)^{1 \cdot 1} = -1.$$

∎

Proof (of Proposition 11). First, if k is odd, then x cannot be self-paired. Hence, $\Pr_{x \sim \mu_{n,k}}[T(x) = 0] = 1$ and $\Pr_{x \sim \mu_{n,k}}[T(x) = 1] = 0$.

Next, assume that k is even and consider x_1. There is a single element it can be paired to on bit 1, which is $x_1 \oplus e_1$. The probability that $x_1 \oplus e_1$ appears among $x_2, \ldots, x_k$ is $\frac{k-1}{N-1}$. Next, assuming x_1 is paired, continue by induction after removing the pair from the set of available elements. We obtain

$$\Pr_{x \sim \mu_{n,k}}[T(x) = 1] = \frac{k-1}{N-1}\frac{k-3}{N-3} \cdots \frac{1}{N-k+1} = \Gamma(N, k),$$

as claimed. ∎

4.2 Classification of Masks

Towards proving bounds on the magnitude of Fourier coefficients on general masks, we define two basic operations on masks and prove that they preserve Fourier coefficients. These operations will allow us to focus on a subset of masks whose associated Fourier coefficient is easier to bound. Bounds on the magnitude of Fourier coefficients on the remaining masks will follow by preservation of Fourier coefficients.

Proposition 12 (Permuting elements preserves Fourier coefficients). *Let $\alpha \in \widehat{\mathbb{F}}_2^{k \times n}$. Let $\pi : [k] \mapsto [k]$ be a permutation and define the mask $\alpha^\pi \in \widehat{\mathbb{F}}_2^{k \times n}$ by $\alpha_i^\pi = \alpha_{\pi(i)}$ for $i \in [k]$. Then, $\widehat{\mu_{n,k}}(\alpha^\pi) = \widehat{\mu_{n,k}}(\alpha)$.*

Proof. Similarly to the definition of α^π, for $x \in \mathbb{F}_2^{k \times n}$, define $x^\pi \in \mathbb{F}_2^{k \times n}$ by $x_i^\pi = x_{\pi(i)}$ for $i \in [k]$. Observe that since π merely permutes the elements of x, it preserves equality and inequality among elements, and thus $\mu_{n,k}(x) = \mu_{n,k}(x^\pi)$. Furthermore $\chi_\alpha(x) = \chi_{\alpha^\pi}(x^\pi)$ as inner product in invariant under permutation of elements of α and x. Combining these observations,

$$\widehat{\mu_{n,k}}(\alpha) = \mathop{\mathrm{E}}_{x \sim \mathbb{F}_2^{k \times n}} [\mu_{n,k}(x) \chi_\alpha(x)] = \mathop{\mathrm{E}}_{x \sim \mathbb{F}_2^{k \times n}} [\mu_{n,k}(x^\pi) \chi_{\alpha^\pi}(x^\pi)]$$

$$= \mathop{\mathrm{E}}_{y \sim \mathbb{F}_2^{k \times n}} [\mu_{n,k}(y) \chi_{\alpha^\pi}(y)] = \widehat{\mu_{n,k}}(\alpha^\pi).$$

∎

Proposition 13 (Invertible element-wise linear operations preserve Fourier coefficients). *Let* $\alpha \in \widehat{\mathbb{F}}_2^{k \times n}$. *Let* $L : \mathbb{F}_2^{n \times n} \mapsto \mathbb{F}_2^{n \times n}$ *be an invertible matrix and define the mask* $\alpha^L \in \widehat{\mathbb{F}}_2^{k \times n}$ *by* $\alpha_i^L = \alpha_i \cdot L$ *for* $i \in [k]$ *(where we view* α_i *as a row vector in* $\mathbb{F}_2^n$, *multiplied with* L). *Then,* $\widehat{\mu_{n,k}}(\alpha^L) = \widehat{\mu_{n,k}}(\alpha)$.

Proof. For $x \in \mathbb{F}_2^{k \times n}$, define $x^L \in \mathbb{F}_2^{k \times n}$ similarly to the definition of α^L. By the properties of the inner product, for any $a, b \in \mathbb{F}_2^n$,

$$\langle a, b \rangle_{\mathbb{F}_2} = \langle a \cdot L \cdot L^{-1}, b \rangle_{\mathbb{F}_2} = \langle a \cdot L, b \cdot L^{-T} \rangle_{\mathbb{F}_2},$$

where L^T is the transpose of L and L^{-T} is the inverse of L^T. Hence, $\chi_\alpha(x) = \chi_{\alpha^L}(x^{L^{-T}})$. Furthermore, since L^{-T} is an invertible transformation on the elements of x, it preserves equality and inequality among elements, and thus $\mu_{n,k}(x) = \mu_{n,k}(x^{L^{-T}})$. Therefore,

$$\widehat{\mu_{n,k}}(\alpha) = \mathop{\mathrm{E}}_{x \sim \mathbb{F}_2^{k \times n}} [\mu_{n,k}(x) \chi_\alpha(x)] = \mathop{\mathrm{E}}_{x \sim \mathbb{F}_2^{k \times n}} [\mu_{n,k}(x^{L^{-T}}) \chi_{\alpha^L}(x^{L^{-T}})]$$

$$= \mathop{\mathrm{E}}_{y \sim \mathbb{F}_2^{k \times n}} [\mu_{n,k}(y) \chi_{\alpha^L}(y)] = \widehat{\mu_{n,k}}(\alpha^L).$$

∎

These two propositions motivate the following definition.

Definition 12 (Equivalence of masks). *Masks* $\alpha, \beta \in \widehat{\mathbb{F}}_2^{k \times n}$ *are called equivalent (with respect to* $\mu_{n,k}$) *if* β *can be obtained from* α *by permuting its elements and performing invertible element-wise linear operations.*

By invertibility of the basic operations, equivalence of masks is a well-defined equivalence relation. By the above propositions, if α and β are equivalent, then $\widehat{\mu_{n,k}}(\alpha) = \widehat{\mu_{n,k}}(\beta)$ (and obviously $\#\alpha = \#\beta$).

We now define a classification of masks that will later be used to bound their associated Fourier coefficients.

Definition 13 (Rank of mask). *Let* $\alpha \in \widehat{\mathbb{F}}_2^{k \times n}$ *be a non-zero mask. We define the rank of* α *as its rank when viewed as a* $k \times n$ *matrix over* $\mathbb{F}_2$.

The following definition generalizes Definition 8.

Definition 14 (Type of mask). *Let $\alpha \in \widehat{\mathbb{F}}_2^{k \times n}$ be a mask such that $\#\alpha = k > 0$. Let $K = (k_1, k_2, \ldots, k_t)$ be a t-tuple of natural positive indices such that $k_j < k_{j+1}$ for all $j \in [t-1]$ and $k_t = k$. Define $k_0 = 0$. We define the type of α to be K, if for every $j \in [t]$, the following two conditions hold:*

1. *For every $i \in [k_{j-1} + 1, k_j]$, $\alpha_{i,j} = 1$.*
2. *For every $i \in [k_j + 1, k]$, $\alpha_{i,j} = 0$.*

If α is not of type K for any tuple K, then we define its type to be NULL.

In other words, α is of type $K = (k_1, k_2, \ldots, k_t)$ if the first bit of its first k_1 elements is 1, and the first bits of elements $x_{k_1+1}, \ldots, x_k$ is 0. Next, bit 2 of elements $x_{k_1+1}, \ldots, x_{k_2}$ is 1, while bit 2 of elements $x_{k_2+1}, \ldots, x_k$ is 0, and so forth.

Example 1. Let $n = 4$ and $k = 3$ and assume the leftmost bit is the first bit. Then, the mask $(1011, 1101, 1001)$ is of type (3), $(1011, 0110, 0101)$ is of type $(1, 3)$, $(1011, 0110, 0011)$ is of type $(1, 2, 3)$, while $(1011, 0101, 1001), (1011, 0010, 0101)$ and $(1011, 0110, 0001)$ are all of type NULL.

While many non-zero masks have type NULL, they can be easily transformed to a non-NULL type by basic operations. More specifically, the following holds.

Proposition 14 (Every non-zero mask is equivalent to a mask of non-NULL type). *Let $\alpha \in \widehat{\mathbb{F}}_2^{k \times n}$ have $\#\alpha = k > 0$ and rank r. Then, α is equivalent to some $\beta \in \widehat{\mathbb{F}}_2^{k \times n}$ of type $K = (k_1, \ldots, k_t)$, such that $k_t = k$ and $t = r$.*

Proposition 14 thus allows us to focus on bounding the Fourier coefficients on masks of non-NULL type.

Proof. We transform α to β by basic operations as follows. First, since the rank of α is r, it contains r linearly independent elements. Define and apply to α an invertible linear transformation that maps the first r linearly independent elements (in lexicographical order) to the first r vectors of the standard basis of $\mathbb{F}_2^n$, $e_1, \ldots, e_r$. Denote the outcome by α'.

Next, permute the elements of α' by moving all elements α'_i such that $\alpha'_{i,1} = 1$ to be first, and elements with $\alpha'_{i,1} = 0$ to be last. Let k_1 be the index such that $\alpha'_{i,1} = 1$ if $i \leq k_1$ and $\alpha'_{i,1} = 0$ if $i > k_1$. Note that $k_1 \geq 1$ since the first bit of e_1 is 1 and $k_1 \leq k - r + 1$, as the first bit of all the elements $e_2, \ldots, e_r$ is 0. If $r = 1$, then since $\#\alpha = k$ we must have $k_1 = k$ (otherwise, α has two linearly independent elements). Thus, define $\beta = \alpha'$, which is of type (k), and we are done after 1 step. If $r > 1$, define k_2 after permuting the elements $\alpha'_{k_1+1}, \ldots, \alpha'_k$ according to their second bit and continue inductively. After the process terminates, define $\beta = \alpha'$.

Denote by t the total number of steps in the process. The process cannot end with $t < r$ as the first bit set to j in e_j has index j, and thus e_j will be among the elements $\alpha'_{k_{j-1}+1}, \ldots, \alpha'_{k_j}$. On the other hand, the process cannot end with $t > r$ steps, since vectors $\alpha'_{k_1}, \ldots, \alpha'_{k_t}$ are linearly independent. Therefore, $t = r$. Furthermore, $k_t = k$ since $\#\alpha = k$. We conclude that α is equivalent to $\beta = \alpha'$ of type $K = (k_1, \ldots, k_t)$ such that $k_t = k$ and $t = r$.   ∎

4.3   Bounding $|\widehat{\mu_{n,k}}(\alpha)|$ for General α

In this section we prove bounds on the magnitude of Fourier coefficients on general masks. The main result of this section is the following.

Proposition 15 (Bounds on Fourier magnitude for general masks). *We have*

$$M^{=k}[\mu_{n,k}] \leq \begin{cases} \Gamma(N,k) & \text{if } k < N/2 \text{ is even,} \\ \Gamma(N,k-1) \cdot \frac{k}{N-k} & \text{if } k < N/2 \text{ is odd.} \end{cases}$$

Equivalently, let $\alpha \in \widehat{\mathbb{F}}_2^{k \times n}$ have $\#\alpha = k$. Then,

$$|\widehat{\mu_{n,k}}(\alpha)| \leq \begin{cases} \Gamma(N,k) & \text{if } k < N/2 \text{ is even,} \\ \Gamma(N,k-1) \cdot \frac{k}{N-k} & \text{if } k < N/2 \text{ is odd.} \end{cases}$$

Lemma 1 (stated in Sect. 3) is proved in Appendix A based on this proposition by a straightforward bound on $\Gamma(N,k)$.

Proposition 15 is a consequence of the following proposition.

Proposition 16 (Bounds on Fourier magnitude for masks of non-NULL type). *Let $\alpha \in \widehat{\mathbb{F}}_2^{k \times n}$ be of type $K = (k_1, \ldots, k_t)$ where $k_t = k$. Then,*

$$|\widehat{\mu_{n,k}}(\alpha)| \leq \begin{cases} \Gamma(N,k) & \text{if } k < N/2 \text{ is even,} \\ \Gamma(N,k-1) \cdot \frac{k}{N-k} & \text{if } k < N/2 \text{ is odd.} \end{cases}$$

Proof (of Proposition 15). Let $\alpha \in \widehat{\mathbb{F}}_2^{k \times n}$ have $\#\alpha = k$. Then, by Proposition 14, it is equivalent to some $\beta \in \widehat{\mathbb{F}}_2^{k \times n}$ of type $K = (k_1, \ldots, k_t)$ where $k_t = k$ (with the same rank as α). This proposition follows by applying Proposition 16 to β.

                ∎

It remains to prove Proposition 16. We need the following additional definition.

Definition 15 (Pairing of a subsequence of elements). *Let $x = (x_1, \ldots, x_k) \in \mathbb{F}_2^{k \times n}$. Let $k' \in [k]$. Define $(x_{k'}, \ldots, x_k)$ as paired within $x = (x_1, \ldots, x_k)$ on bit $j \in [n]$ if $(x_1, \ldots, x_k)$ are distinct (i.e., $x_{i_1} \neq x_{i_2}$ for $i_1 \neq i_2$), and for every $i_1 \in [k', k]$, there exists $i_2 \in [k]$ such that (x_{i_1}, x_{i_2}) are paired on bit j.*

We define the following algorithm that generalizes the algorithm of Sect. 4.1 to handle a mask with arbitrary non-NULL type. It takes as input the tuple $K = (k_1, \ldots, k_t)$ (recall the $k_0 = 0$ by definition).

---

1. Sample $x \sim \mu_{n,k}$.
2. For all $j \in [t]$:
   (a) If $(x_{k_{j-1}+1}, \ldots, x_{k_j})$ are paired within $(x_1, \ldots, x_{k_j})$ on bit j, continue by incrementing j.
   (b) Otherwise, return 0.
3. Return 1.

For $j \in [t]$, define the random variable $T_j(x)$ to be equal to 1 if the algorithm has not returned 0 in iterations $1, \ldots, j$, and let $T_j(x) = 0$ otherwise. Furthermore, define $T(x) = T_t(x)$ to be the output of the algorithm.

We need the following definition.

Definition 16. *For integers $a, b \geq 0, c \geq 1$ such that $a \geq b+c$ ($a > b+c$ if c is odd), define*

$$\Lambda(a, b, c) = \begin{cases} \prod_{i=1,3\ldots,c-1} \frac{b+c-i}{a-b-i} = \frac{b+c-1}{a-b-1} \frac{b+c-3}{a-b-3} \cdots \frac{b+1}{a-b-c+1} & \text{if } c \text{ is even}, \\ \prod_{i=1,3\ldots,c} \frac{b+c-i}{a-b-i} = \frac{b+c-1}{a-b-1} \frac{b+c-3}{a-b-3} \cdots \frac{b}{a-b-c} & \text{if } c \text{ is odd}. \end{cases}$$

Note that for even k, $\Gamma(N, k) = \Lambda(N, 0, k)$.

Proposition 16 immediately follows from the three propositions below (that refer to the type of α, namely $K = (k_1, \ldots, k_t)$).

Proposition 17 (Magnitude of Fourier coefficient bounded by success probability). $|\widehat{\mu_{n,k}}(\alpha)| \leq \Pr_{x \sim \mu_{n,k}}[T(x) = 1]$.

Proposition 18 (Bound on success probability). *If k_1 is even, then*

$$\Pr_{x \sim \mu_{n,k}}[T(x) = 1] \leq \Gamma(N, k_1) \cdot \prod_{j=2}^{t} \Lambda(N, k_{j-1}, k_j - k_{j-1}),$$

while if k_1 is odd then, $\Pr_{x \sim \mu_{n,k}}[T(x) = 1] = 0$.

Proposition 19. *For even k_1, we have*

$$\Gamma(N, k_1) \cdot \prod_{j=2}^{t} \Lambda(N, k_{j-1}, k_j - k_{j-1}) \leq \begin{cases} \Gamma(N, k) & \text{if } k = k_t < N/2 \text{ is even}, \\ \Gamma(N, k-1) \cdot \frac{k}{N-k} & \text{if } k = k_t < N/2 \text{ is odd}. \end{cases}$$

In the rest of this section we will prove Proposition 17 and Proposition 18. Proposition 19 is proved in the full version of this paper [11] by elementary analysis.

Proof (of Proposition 17). The proof is a generalization of the proof of Proposition 10, and we focus on the differences. As in (5),

$$|\widehat{\mu_{n,k}}(\alpha)| \leq \Pr_{x \sim \mu_{n,k}}[T(x) = 1] + |\Pr_{x \sim \mu_{n,k}}[T(x) = 0] \underset{x \sim \mu_{n,k}}{\mathrm{E}}[\chi_\alpha(x) \mid T(x) = 0]|,$$

and it remains to prove that $\mathbb{E}_{x \sim \mu_{n,k}}[\chi_\alpha(x) \mid T(x) = 0] = 0$. Once again this is proved by partitioning the sample space conditioned on $T(x) = 0$ into couples (x, x') that satisfy $\chi_\alpha(x) = -\chi_\alpha(x')$. However, this time the coupling depends on the iteration $j \in [t]$ which the algorithm executed and returned 0, namely, $T_\ell(x) = 1$ for $\ell \in [j-1]$ and $T_j(x) = 0$. Fix this iteration $j \in [t]$, let $in(x) \in [k_{j-1}+1, k_j]$ be the index of the first unpaired element among $(x_{k_{j-1}+1}, \ldots, x_{k_j})$.

We now consider two cases depending on whether $x_{in(x)} \oplus e_j$ appears among $x_{k_j+1}, \ldots, x_k$ (note that it does not appear among $(x_1, \ldots, x_{k_j})$ since $x_{in(x)}$ is not paired to any of these elements).

If $x_{in(x)} \oplus e_j$ does not appear among $(x_{k_j+1}, \ldots, x_k)$, then it does not appear among $(x_1, \ldots, x_k)$, and thus we couple x and $x' = (x_1, \ldots, x_{in(x)-1}, x_{in(x)} \oplus e_j, x_{in(x)+1}, \ldots, x_k)$, as in the proof of Proposition 10. Specifically, in this case we have $in(x) = in(x')$. Moreover, since α is of type K, then $\alpha_{i,j} = 1$ for all $i \in [k_{j-1} + 1, k_j]$, and in particular, $\alpha_{in(x),j} = 1$. Since $x_{in(x),j} \neq x'_{in(x),j}$ and they are they equal otherwise, $\chi_\alpha(x) = -\chi_\alpha(x')$. The proof of this case is thus essentially the same as the one of Proposition 10.

We remain with the case that there exists $i \in [k_j + 1, k]$ such that $x_i = x_{in(x)} \oplus e_j$. In this case, we couple (x, x'), where x' is defined by exchanging the positions of elements $x_{in(x)}$ and x_i in x, namely, $x'_{in(x)} = x_i$, $x'_i = x_{in(x)}$ and $x'_\ell = x_\ell$ for all $\ell \notin \{in(x), i\}$.

This is indeed a valid coupling since the execution of the algorithm on x' returns 0 for the same iteration j and $in(x) = in(x')$. Moreover, since α is of type K, then $\alpha_{in(x),j} = 1$, but $\alpha_{i,j} = 0$ (as $i \in [k_j + 1, k]$). Thus,

$$\chi_\alpha(x)\chi_\alpha(x') = (-1)^{\langle \alpha, x \oplus x' \rangle_{\mathbb{F}_2}} = (-1)^{\langle \alpha_{in(x)}, e_j \rangle_{\mathbb{F}_2}} (-1)^{\langle \alpha_i, e_j \rangle_{\mathbb{F}_2}} = -1 \cdot 1 = -1,$$

i.e., $\chi_\alpha(x) = -\chi_\alpha(x')$. This concludes the proof. ∎

Proof (of Proposition 18). First, if k_1 is odd then already $T_1(x) = 0$ and $\Pr_{x \sim \mu_{n,k}}[T(x) = 1] = 0$.

Next, assume that k_1 is even. We prove by induction on $j \in [t]$ that

$$\Pr_{x \sim \mu_{n,k}}[T_j(x) = 1] \leq \Gamma(N, k_1) \cdot \prod_{\ell=2}^{j} \Lambda(N, k_{\ell-1}, k_\ell - k_{\ell-1}).$$

The result then follows since $T(x) = T_t(x)$.

For the base case of $j = 1$, we have $\Pr_{x \sim \mu_{n,k}}[T_1(x) = 1] \leq \Gamma(N, k_1)$ as in the proof of Proposition 11. For the induction step, we have

$$\Pr_{x \sim \mu_{n,k}}[T_j(x) = 1] = \Pr_{x \sim \mu_{n,k}}[T_{j-1}(x) = 1] \cdot \Pr_{x \sim \mu_{n,k}}[T_j(x) = 1 \mid T_{j-1}(x) = 1].$$

Thus, we need to prove that

$$\Pr_{x \sim \mu_{n,k}}[T_j(x) = 1 \mid T_{j-1}(x) = 1] \leq \Lambda(N, k_{j-1}, k_j - k_{j-1}).$$

Fix any values for $x_1, \ldots, x_{k_{j-1}}$ which have positive probability. We prove the above inequality by taking the probability only over the selection of $x_{k_{j-1}+1}, \ldots, x_{k_j}$ (which we may assume are only selected in iteration j of the algorithm).

We show that $\Lambda(N, k_{j-1}, k_j - k_{j-1})$ is an upper bound on the probability to pair $(x_{k_{j-1}+1}, \ldots, x_{k_j})$ within $(x_1, \ldots, x_{k_j})$ on bit j. For this purpose, we assume that all $x_1, \ldots, x_{k_{j-1}}$ are available for pairing on bit j, namely, they are not paired among themselves on bit j (this assumption can only increase the success probability of the algorithm, i.e., its pairing probability).

We upper bound $\Pr_{x \sim \mu_{n,k}}[T_j(x) = 1 \mid T_{j-1}(x) = 1]$ as follows: the probability that the first element in $(x_{k_{j-1}+1}, \ldots, x_{k_j})$ is paired with one of the $k_j - 1$ other elements in $x_1, \ldots, x_{k_j}$ is (at most) $\frac{k_j - 1}{N - k_{j-1} - 1}$. Assuming this occurs, we remove both of these elements and then the probability that the next element in $(x_{k_{j-1}+1}, \ldots, x_{k_j})$ is paired is either $\frac{k_j - 3}{N - k_{j-1} - 3}$ (if the first element was paired among $(x_{k_{j-1}+1}, \ldots, x_{k_j})$ or $\frac{k_j - 3}{N - k_{j-1} - 2}$ (if the first element was paired among $(x_1, \ldots, x_{k_{j-1}})$). In any case, this probability is at most $\frac{k_j - 3}{N - k_{j-1} - 3}$. Continue this way until all elements in $(x_{k_{j-1}+1}, \ldots, x_{k_j})$ are paired. Clearly, if $k_j - k_{j-1}$ is even, then at least $(k_j - k_{j-1})/2$ pairings are required (which occurs if $(x_{k_{j-1}+1}, \ldots, x_{k_j})$ are only paired among themselves).

Taking the product of the corresponding $(k_j - k_{j-1})/2$ terms,

$$\Pr_{x \sim \mu_{n,k}}[T_j(x) = 1 \mid T_{j-1}(x) = 1]$$

$$\leq \frac{k_j - 1}{N - k_{j-1} - 1} \frac{k_j - 3}{N - k_{j-1} - 3} \cdots \frac{k_{j-1} + 1}{N - k_j + 1} = \Lambda(N, k_{j-1}, k_j - k_{j-1}),$$

as claimed. If $k_j - k_{j-1}$ is odd, then at least $(k_j - k_{j-1} + 1)/2$ pairing are required. Similarly,

$$\Pr_{x \sim \mu_{n,k}}[T_j(x) = 1 \mid T_{j-1}(x) = 1]$$

$$\leq \frac{k_j - 1}{N - k_{j-1} - 1} \frac{k_j - 3}{N - k_{j-1} - 3} \cdots \frac{k_{j-1}}{N - k_j} = \Lambda(N, k_{j-1}, k_j - k_{j-1}).$$

∎

5   Bounding $\mathrm{W}^{=k}[\mu_{n,k}]$ (Proof of Lemma 2)

The goal of this section is to prove Lemma 2. We start by deriving an exact (but unwieldy) expression for $\mathrm{W}^{=k}[\mu_{n,k}]$.

Proposition 20.

$$\text{For } 0 \leq k \leq 2^n, \quad \mathrm{W}^{=k}[\mu_{n,k}] = \sum_{i=0}^{k} (-1)^{k-i} \binom{k}{i} \frac{N^i}{(N)_i}.$$

Proof. For any integer $0 \leq i \leq k$, $\mathrm{Col}[\mu_{n,i}] = \mathrm{Pr}_{x,x' \sim \mu_{n,i}}[x = x'] = \frac{(N-i)!}{N!} = \frac{1}{(N)_i}$. Hence, by Proposition 4,

$$W^{\leq i}[\mu_{n,i}] = \mathrm{Col}[\mu_{n,i}] \cdot N^i = \frac{N^i}{(N)_i}. \tag{6}$$

For a subset $\mathcal{S} \subseteq [k]$ of size $|\mathcal{S}|$, define the functions $h(\mathcal{S}) = W^{=|\mathcal{S}|}[\mu_{n,|\mathcal{S}|}]$ and $g(\mathcal{S}) = W^{\leq |\mathcal{S}|}[\mu_{n,|\mathcal{S}|}]$. Then, $g(\mathcal{S}) = \sum_{\mathcal{R} \subseteq \mathcal{S}} h(\mathcal{R})$, and by the inclusion-exclusion principle [15, Pg. 1049], $h(\mathcal{S}) = \sum_{\mathcal{R} \subseteq \mathcal{S}} (-1)^{|\mathcal{S}|-|\mathcal{R}|} g(\mathcal{R}) = \sum_{\mathcal{R} \subseteq \mathcal{S}} (-1)^{|\mathcal{S}|-|\mathcal{R}|} W^{\leq |\mathcal{R}|}[\mu_{n,|\mathcal{R}|}]$. Therefore,

$$W^{=k}[\mu_{n,k}] = h([k]) = \sum_{\mathcal{S} \subseteq [k]} (-1)^{k-|\mathcal{S}|} W^{\leq |\mathcal{S}|}[\mu_{n,|\mathcal{S}|}] = \sum_{i=0}^{k} (-1)^{k-i} \binom{k}{i} W^{\leq i}[\mu_{n,i}]$$

$$= \sum_{i=0}^{k} (-1)^{k-i} \binom{k}{i} \frac{N^i}{(N)_i},$$

where the third equality is by the symmetry of $\mu_{n,k}$, and the final equality is by (6). ∎

The following definition will be useful in deriving a useful bound on $W^{=k}[\mu_{n,k}]$ for all k.

Definition 17. *For a positive integer N and non-negative integers k, a such that $N \geq k + a$, let*

$$F_N(k,a) = \sum_{i=0}^{k} (-1)^{k-i} \binom{k}{i} \frac{N^i}{(N-a)_i}.$$

Note that by Proposition 20, $W^{=k}[\mu_{n,k}] = F_N(k,0)$. We now derive a recursive formula which will allow to analyze $W^{=k}[\mu_{n,k}]$.

Proposition 21 (Recursive formula for level-k weight). *For $k \geq 2$, $F_N(k,a)$ satisfies the recurrence relation*

$$F_N(k,a) = \frac{a}{N-a} \cdot F_N(k-1, a+1) + \frac{(k-1)N}{(N-a)(N-a-1)} \cdot F_N(k-2, a+2),$$

with the starting conditions $F_N(0,a) = 1$ and $F_N(1,a) = \frac{N}{N-a} - 1 = \frac{a}{N-a}$.

Proof. The starting conditions are easily checked by plugging in the parameters into the explicit formula for $F_N(k,a)$. We now prove the recurrence relation holds assuming $k \geq 2$.

To simplify notation, denote $G_i = \frac{N^i}{(N-a)_i}$ and write $F_N(k,a) = \sum_{i=0}^{k} (-1)^{k-i} \binom{k}{i} G_i$. For $1 \leq i \leq k-1$, substitute $\binom{k}{i} = \binom{k-1}{i} + \binom{k-1}{i-1}$ and

$\binom{k}{0} = \binom{k-1}{0}$, $\binom{k}{k} = \binom{k-1}{k-1}$ into the expression, which divides each term into a pair of terms. We obtain

$$F_N(k,a) = \sum_{i=0}^{k}(-1)^{k-i}\binom{k}{i}G_i$$

$$= \left((-1)^k\binom{k-1}{0}\cdot G_0 + (-1)^{k-1}\binom{k-1}{0}G_1\right)$$

$$+ \left((-1)^{k-1}\binom{k-1}{1}G_1 + (-1)^{k-2}\binom{k-1}{1}G_2\right)$$

$$+\ldots+ \left((-1)^{k-(k-1)}\binom{k-1}{k-1}G_{k-1} + (-1)^{k-k}\binom{k-1}{k-1}G_k\right)$$

$$= \sum_{i=1}^{k}(-1)^{k-i}\binom{k-1}{i-1}(G_i - G_{i-1}).$$

We have $G_i = G_{i-1}\cdot\frac{N}{N-a-(i-1)}$, so $G_i - G_{i-1} = G_{i-1}\cdot\left(\frac{N}{N-a-(i-1)}-1\right) = G_{i-1}\cdot\frac{a+(i-1)}{N-a-(i-1)}$. Therefore, the above expression is equal to

$$\sum_{i=1}^{k}(-1)^{k-i}\binom{k-1}{i-1}G_{i-1}\cdot\frac{a+(i-1)}{N-a-(i-1)}$$

$$= \sum_{i=1}^{k}(-1)^{k-i}\binom{k-1}{i-1}\frac{(a+(i-1))N^{i-1}}{(N-a)(N-a-1)\ldots(N-a-(i-1))}$$

$$= \frac{1}{N-a}\cdot\sum_{i=1}^{k}(-1)^{k-i}\binom{k-1}{i-1}\frac{(a+(i-1))N^{i-1}}{(N-a-1)_{i-1}}$$

$$= \frac{1}{N-a}\cdot\sum_{i=0}^{k-1}(-1)^{k-1-i}\binom{k-1}{i}\frac{(a+i)N^i}{(N-a-1)_i}$$

$$= \frac{a}{N-a}\cdot\sum_{i=0}^{k-1}(-1)^{k-1-i}\binom{k-1}{i}\frac{N^i}{(N-a-1)_i}$$

$$+ \frac{1}{N-a}\cdot\sum_{i=1}^{k-1}(-1)^{k-1-i}\binom{k-1}{i}\frac{i\cdot N^i}{(N-a-1)_i}$$

$$= \frac{a}{N-a}\cdot F_N(k-1,a+1)$$

$$+ \frac{N}{(N-a-1)(N-a)}\cdot\sum_{i=1}^{k-1}(-1)^{k-1-i}\binom{k-1}{i}\frac{i\cdot N^{i-1}}{(N-a-1)_{i-1}}.$$

To complete the proof, it remains to show that

$$\sum_{i=1}^{k-1}(-1)^{k-1-i}\binom{k-1}{i}\frac{i\cdot N^{i-1}}{(N-a-1)_{i-1}} = (k-1)\cdot F_N(k-2,a+2).$$

Observe that $i \cdot \binom{k-1}{i} = (k-1) \cdot \binom{k-2}{i-1}$. Therefore,

$$\sum_{i=1}^{k-1}(-1)^{k-1-i}\binom{k-1}{i}\frac{i \cdot N^{i-1}}{(N-a-1)_{i-1}}$$

$$= (k-1) \cdot \sum_{i=1}^{k-1}(-1)^{k-1-i}\binom{k-2}{i-1}\frac{N^{i-1}}{(N-a-1)_{i-1}}$$

$$= (k-1) \cdot \sum_{i=0}^{k-2}(-1)^{k-i}\binom{k-2}{i}\frac{N^{i}}{(N-a-2)_{i}}$$

$$= (k-1) \cdot F_N(k-2, a+2).$$

This completes the proof. ∎

Next, we use the recurrence relation to bound $F_N(k, a)$.

Proposition 22.

$$F_N(k,a) \leq \begin{cases} \frac{(N(a+k-1))^{k/2}}{(N-a)_k} & \text{if } k \text{ is even,} \\ \frac{(N(a+k-1))^{(k-1)/2} \cdot (a+k-1)}{(N-a)_k} & \text{if } k \text{ is odd.} \end{cases}$$

Proof. We prove the result using Proposition 21 by induction on k. It is easy to verify that it holds for $k = 0$ and $k = 1$ by the starting conditions. We prove the induction step.

If k is odd, then by the assumption

$$F_N(k,a) = \frac{a}{N-a} \cdot F_N(k-1, a+1) + \frac{(k-1)N}{(N-a)(N-a-1)} \cdot F_N(k-2, a+2)$$

$$\leq \frac{a}{N-a} \cdot \frac{(N(a+k-1))^{(k-1)/2}}{(N-a-1)_{k-1}}$$

$$+ \frac{(k-1)N}{(N-a)(N-a-1)} \cdot \frac{(N(a+k-1))^{(k-3)/2}(a+k-1)}{(N-a-2)_{k-2}}$$

$$= a \cdot \frac{(N(a+k-1))^{(k-1)/2}}{(N-a)_k} + (k-1) \cdot \frac{(N(a+k-1))^{(k-1)/2}}{(N-a)_k}$$

$$= \frac{(N(a+k-1))^{(k-1)/2} \cdot (a+k-1)}{(N-a)_k},$$

as desired. If k is even, then

$$F_N(k,a) \leq \frac{a}{N-a} \cdot \frac{(N(a+k-1))^{(k-2)/2} \cdot (a+k-1)}{(N-a-1)_{k-1}}$$

$$+ \frac{(k-1)N}{(N-a)(N-a-1)} \cdot \frac{(N(a+k-1))^{(k-2)/2}}{(N-a-2)_{k-2}}$$

$$= a \cdot \frac{(N(a+k-1))^{(k-2)/2} \cdot (a+k-1)}{(N-a)_k} + (k-1)N \cdot \frac{(N(a+k-1))^{(k-2)/2}}{(N-a)_k}$$

$$= \frac{(N(a+k-1))^{(k-2)/2}}{(N-a)_k} \cdot (a(a+k-1) + (k-1)N).$$

It remains to prove that $a(a+k-1)+(k-1)N \leq N(a+k-1)$ or $a+k-1 \leq N$, which indeed holds (as the quantity $a+k$ is preserved throughout the recursive calls).

∎

Finally, Lemma 2 is proved in the full version of this paper [11] by straightforward manipulation of the bound on $F_N(k,a)$ of Proposition 22, and based on the fact that by Proposition 20, $W^{=k}[\mu_{n,k}] = F_N(k,0)$.

Acknowledgements. The author was supported by the Israel Science Foundation through grant no. 1903/20. The author would like to thank Samuel Neves for pointing him to the prior works [13,14].

A   Missing Proofs from Section 4

Proof (of Lemma 1). We use Proposition 15 to bound $M^{=k}[\mu_{n,k}]$. First we have $M^{=2}[\mu_{n,2}] \leq \Gamma(N,2) = \frac{1}{N-1}$.

Next, for even k, by Proposition 15,

$$M^{=k}[\mu_{n,k}]^2 \leq \Gamma(N,k)^2 = \left(\frac{k-1}{N-1}\right)^2 \left(\frac{k-3}{N-3}\right)^2 \cdots \left(\frac{1}{N-(k-1)}\right)^2$$

$$\leq \frac{k}{N} \frac{k-1}{N-1} \frac{k-2}{N-2} \frac{k-3}{N-3} \cdots \frac{2}{N-(k-2)} \frac{1}{N-(k-1)} = \frac{1}{\binom{N}{k}}.$$

Similarly, for odd k,

$$M^{=k}[\mu_{n,k}]^2 \leq \Gamma(N,k-1)^2 \cdot \left(\frac{k}{N-k}\right)^2 \leq \frac{1}{\binom{N}{k-1}} \cdot \left(\frac{k}{N-k}\right)^2$$

$$= \frac{1}{\binom{N}{k}} \cdot \frac{N-(k-1)}{k} \left(\frac{k}{N-k}\right)^2 = \frac{1}{\binom{N}{k}} \cdot \frac{N-(k-1)}{N-k} \frac{k}{N-k}$$

$$< \frac{1}{\binom{N}{k}} \cdot \frac{N-(k-1)}{N-k} \frac{k+1}{N-(k-1)} = \frac{1}{\binom{N}{k}} \cdot \frac{k+1}{N-k}.$$

∎

References

1. Bellare, M., Impagliazzo, R.: A tool for obtaining tighter security analyses of pseudorandom function based constructions, with applications to PRP to PRF conversion. IACR Cryptol. ePrint Arch, p. 24 (1999). http://eprint.iacr.org/1999/024
2. Bellare, M., Krovetz, T., Rogaway, P.: Luby-Rackoff backwards: increasing security by making block ciphers non-invertible. In: Nyberg, K. (ed.) EUROCRYPT 1998. LNCS, vol. 1403, pp. 266–280. Springer, Heidelberg (1998). https://doi.org/10.1007/BFb0054132
3. Bhattacharya, S., Nandi, M.: Revisiting variable output length XOR pseudorandom function. IACR Trans. Symmetric Cryptol. **2018**(1), 314–335 (2018). https://doi.org/10.13154/tosc.v2018.i1.314-335
4. Bhattacharya, S., Nandi, M.: Luby-Rackoff backwards with more users and more security. In: Tibouchi, M., Wang, H. (eds.) ASIACRYPT 2021, Part III. LNCS, vol. 13092, pp. 345–375. Springer, Cham (2021). https://doi.org/10.1007/978-3-030-92078-4_12
5. Chen, S., Lampe, R., Lee, J., Seurin, Y., Steinberger, J.P.: Minimizing the two-round even-Mansour cipher. J. Cryptol. **31**(4), 1064–1119 (2018). https://doi.org/10.1007/s00145-018-9295-y
6. Chen, Y.L., Choi, W., Lee, C.: Improved multi-user security using the squared-ratio method. In: Handschuh, H., Lysyanskaya, A. (eds.) CRYPTO 2023. LNCS, vol. 14082, pp. 694–724. Springer, Cham (2023). https://doi.org/10.1007/978-3-031-38545-2_23
7. Choi, W., Kim, H., Lee, J., Lee, Y.: Multi-user security of the sum of truncated random permutations. In: Agrawal, S., Lin, D. (eds.) ASIACRYPT 2022. LNCS, vol. 13792, pp. 682–710. Springer, Cham (2022). https://doi.org/10.1007/978-3-031-22966-4_23
8. Cogliati, B., Dutta, A., Nandi, M., Patarin, J., Saha, A.: Proof of mirror theory for a wide range of ξ_{max}. In: Hazay, C., Stam, M. (eds.) EUROCRYPT 2023. Lecture Notes in Computer Science, vol. 14007, pp. 470–501. Springer, Cham (2023). https://doi.org/10.1007/978-3-031-30634-1_16
9. Cogliati, B., Lampe, R., Patarin, J.: The indistinguishability of the XOR of k permutations. In: Cid, C., Rechberger, C. (eds.) FSE 2014. LNCS, vol. 8540, pp. 285–302. Springer, Heidelberg (2015). https://doi.org/10.1007/978-3-662-46706-0_15
10. Dai, W., Hoang, V.T., Tessaro, S.: Information-theoretic indistinguishability via the chi-squared method. In: Katz, J., Shacham, H. (eds.) CRYPTO 2017, Part III. LNCS, vol. 10403, pp. 497–523. Springer, Cham (2017). https://doi.org/10.1007/978-3-319-63697-9_17
11. Dinur, I.: Tight indistinguishability bounds for the XOR of independent random permutations by Fourier analysis. IACR Cryptol. ePrint Arch. (2024). http://eprint.iacr.org/2024/338
12. Dutta, A., Nandi, M., Saha, A.: Proof of mirror theory for $\xi_{max} = 2$. IEEE Trans. Inf. Theory **68**(9), 6218–6232 (2022). https://doi.org/10.1109/TIT.2022.3171178
13. Eberhard, S.: More on additive triples of bijections (2017). https://arxiv.org/abs/1704.02407
14. Eberhard, S., Manners, F., Mrazović, R.: Additive triples of bijections, or the toroidal semiqueens problem. J. Eur. Math. Soc. **21**(2), 441–463 (2018). https://doi.org/10.4171/JEMS/841

15. Gessel, I.M., Stanley, R.P.: Algebraic enumeration. In: Handbook of Combinatorics, vol. 2, pp. 1021–1061. MIT Press, Cambridge (1996)
16. Gunsing, A., Bhaumik, R., Jha, A., Mennink, B., Shen, Y.: Revisiting the indifferentiability of the sum of permutations. In: Handschuh, H., Lysyanskaya, A. (eds.) CRYPTO 2023. NCS, vol. 14083, pp. 628–660. Springer, Cham (2023). https://doi.org/10.1007/978-3-031-38548-3_21
17. Gunsing, A., Mennink, B.: The summation-truncation hybrid: reusing discarded bits for free. In: Micciancio, D., Ristenpart, T. (eds.) CRYPTO 2020. LNCS, vol. 12170, pp. 187–217. Springer, Cham (2020). https://doi.org/10.1007/978-3-030-56784-2_7
18. Hall, C., Wagner, D., Kelsey, J., Schneier, B.: Building PRFs from PRPs. In: Krawczyk, H. (ed.) CRYPTO 1998. LNCS, vol. 1462, pp. 370–389. Springer, Heidelberg (1998). https://doi.org/10.1007/BFb0055742
19. Liu, T., Tessaro, S., Vaikuntanathan, V.: The t-wise independence of substitution-permutation networks. In: Malkin, T., Peikert, C. (eds.) CRYPTO 2021. LNCS, vol. 12828, pp. 454–483. Springer, Cham (2021). https://doi.org/10.1007/978-3-030-84259-8_16
20. Lucks, S.: The sum of PRPs is a secure PRF. In: Preneel, B. (ed.) EUROCRYPT 2000. LNCS, vol. 1807, pp. 470–484. Springer, Heidelberg (2000). https://doi.org/10.1007/3-540-45539-6_34
21. Maurer, U., Pietrzak, K., Renner, R.: Indistinguishability amplification. In: Menezes, A. (ed.) CRYPTO 2007. LNCS, vol. 4622, pp. 130–149. Springer, Heidelberg (2007). https://doi.org/10.1007/978-3-540-74143-5_8
22. Mennink, B., Preneel, B.: On the XOR of multiple random permutations. In: Malkin, T., Kolesnikov, V., Lewko, A.B., Polychronakis, M. (eds.) ACNS 2015. LNCS, vol. 9092, pp. 619–634. Springer, Cham (2015). https://doi.org/10.1007/978-3-319-28166-7_30
23. O'Donnell, R.: Analysis of Boolean Functions. Cambridge University Press, New York (2014)
24. Patarin, J.: A proof of security in $O(2^n)$ for the Xor of Two Random Permutations. In: Safavi-Naini, R. (ed.) ICITS 2008. LNCS, vol. 5155, pp. 232–248. Springer, Heidelberg (2008). https://doi.org/10.1007/978-3-540-85093-9_22
25. Patarin, J.: Generic attacks for the XOR of K random permutations. IACR Cryptol. ePrint Arch. p. 9 (2008). http://eprint.iacr.org/2008/009
26. Patarin, J.: Introduction to mirror theory: analysis of systems of linear equalities and linear non equalities for cryptography. IACR Cryptol. ePrint Arch., p. 287 (2010). http://eprint.iacr.org/2010/287
27. Patarin, J.: Generic attacks for the Xor of k random permutations. In: Jacobson, M., Locasto, M., Mohassel, P., Safavi-Naini, R. (eds.) ACNS 2013. LNCS, vol. 7954, pp. 154–169. Springer, Heidelberg (2013). https://doi.org/10.1007/978-3-642-38980-1_10

AprèsSQI: Extra Fast Verification for SQIsign Using Extension-Field Signing

Maria Corte-Real Santos[1]([✉]), Jonathan Komada Eriksen[2], Michael Meyer[3], and Krijn Reijnders[4]

[1] University College London, London, UK
maria.santos.20@ucl.ac.uk
[2] Norwegian University of Science and Technology, Trondheim, Norway
jonathan.k.eriksen@ntnu.no
[3] University of Regensburg, Regensburg, Germany
michael@random-oracles.org
[4] Radboud University, Nijmegen, The Netherlands
krijn@cs.ru.nl

Abstract. We optimise the verification of the SQIsign signature scheme. By using field extensions in the signing procedure, we are able to significantly increase the amount of available rational 2-power torsion in verification, which achieves a significant speed-up. This, moreover, allows several other speed-ups on the level of curve arithmetic. We show that the synergy between these high-level and low-level improvements gives significant improvements, making verification 2.07 times faster, or up to 3.41 times when using size-speed trade-offs, compared to the state of the art, without majorly degrading the performance of signing.

Keywords: post-quantum cryptography · isogenies · SQIsign · verification

1 Introduction

Research has shown that large-scale quantum computers will break current public-key cryptography, such as RSA or ECC, whose security relies on the hardness of integer factorization or the discrete logarithm, respectively [29]. Post-quantum cryptography seeks to thwart the threat of quantum computers by developing cryptographic primitives based on alternative mathematical problems that cannot be solved efficiently by quantum computers. In recent years, lattice-based cryptography has developed successful post-quantum schemes for essential primitives such as key encapsulation mechanisms (KEMs) and digital signatures that will be standardized by NIST. Lattice-based signatures are able

Author list in alphabetical order; see https://www.ams.org/profession/leaders/CultureStatement04.pdf. This work has been supported by UK EPSRC grant EP/S022503/1 and by the German Federal Ministry of Education and Research (BMBF) under the project 6G-RIC (ID 16KISK033).
The full version of this paper is available at https://ia.cr/2023/1559.

M. Joye and G. Leander (Eds.): EUROCRYPT 2024, LNCS 14651, pp. 63–93, 2024.
https://doi.org/10.1007/978-3-031-58716-0_3

to provide fast signing and verification, but have to resort to larger key and signature sizes than were previously acceptable in pre-quantum signatures. For applications where the amount of data transmitted is crucial, these lattice-based schemes may not be a practical option. NIST is therefore looking for other digital signature schemes with properties such as smaller combined public key and signature sizes to ensure a smooth transition to a post-quantum world [32].

A potential solution to this problem is provided by the sole isogeny-based candidate in NIST's new call for signatures – SQIsign [18] – as it is currently the candidate that comes closest to the data sizes transmitted (i.e. the combined size of the signature and the public key) in pre-quantum elliptic curve signatures [23,24]. SQIsign is most interesting in scenarios that require small signature sizes and fast verification, particularly in those applications where the performance of signing is not the main concern. A few common examples include long-term signatures, specifically public-key certificates, code updates for small devices, authenticated communication with embedded devices or other microcontrollers that solely run verification, and smart cards. For such use cases it is imperative to bring down the cost of verification as much as possible.

Performance Bottlenecks in SQIsign. The bottleneck of verification in SQIsign is the computation of an isogeny of fixed degree 2^e with $e \approx (15/4) \log(p)$, where p denotes the prime one is working over, e.g. $\log(p) \approx 256$ for NIST Level I security. However, the rational 2-power torsion, from here on denoted as the $2^\bullet$-torsion, is limited, since we work with supersingular elliptic curves over $\mathbb{F}_{p^2}$ of order $(p+1)^2$ and $(p-1)^2$. This sets a theoretical limit of $2^{\log p}$ for the $2^\bullet$-torsion. Therefore, the verifier needs to perform several *blocks* of degree $2^\bullet$ to complete the full 2^e-isogeny, where each of these blocks involves costly steps such as computing a $2^\bullet$-torsion basis or isogeny kernel generator. Hence, in general, a smaller number of blocks improves the performance of verification.

On the other hand, the bottleneck in signing is the computation of several T-isogenies for odd smooth $T \approx p^{5/4}$. Current implementations of SQIsign therefore require $T \mid (p-1)(p+1)$, such that $\mathbb{F}_{p^2}$-rational points are available for efficient T-isogeny computations. The performance of this step is dominated by the smoothness of T, i.e., its largest prime factor.

While this additional divisibility requirement theoretically limits the maximal $2^\bullet$-torsion to roughly $p^{3/4}$, current techniques for finding SQIsign-friendly primes suggest that achieving this with acceptable smoothness of T is infeasible [7, 8,11,15,18]. In particular, the NIST submission of SQIsign uses a prime with rational 2^{75}-torsion and 1973 as largest factor of T. Since $e \approx (15/4) \cdot 256 = 960$, this means that the verifier has to perform $\lceil e/75 \rceil = 13$ costly isogeny blocks. Increasing the $2^\bullet$-torsion further is difficult as it decreases the probability of finding a smooth and large enough T for current implementations of SQIsign.

Our Contributions. In this work, we deploy a range of techniques to increase the $2^\bullet$-torsion and push the SQIsign verification cost far below the state of the art. Alongside these technical contributions, we aim to give an accessible description of SQIsign, focusing primarily on verification, which solely uses elliptic curves and isogenies and does not require knowledge of quaternion algebras.

Even though we target faster verification, our main contribution is signing with field extensions. From this, we get a much weaker requirement on the prime p, which in turn enables us to increase the size of the $2^\bullet$-torsion.

Focusing on NIST Level I security, we study the range of possible $2^\bullet$-torsion to its theoretical maximum, and measure how its size correlates to verification time through an implementation that uses an equivalent to the number of field multiplications as cost metric. Compared to the state of the art, increasing the $2^\bullet$-torsion alone makes verification almost 1.7 times faster. Further, we implement the new signing procedure as proof-of-concept in SageMath and show that signing times when signing with field extensions are in the same order of magnitude as when signing only using operations in $\mathbb{F}_{p^2}$.

For verification, in addition to implementing some known general techniques for improvements compared to the reference implementation provided in the NIST submission of SQIsign, we show that increasing the $2^\bullet$-torsion also opens up a range of optimisations that were previously not possible. For instance, large $2^\bullet$-torsion allows for an improved challenge-isogeny computation and improved basis and kernel generation. Furthermore, we show that size-speed trade-offs as first proposed by De Feo, Kohel, Leroux, Petit, and Wesolowski [18] become especially worthwhile for large $2^\bullet$-torsion. When pushing the $2^\bullet$-torsion to its theoretical maximum, this even allows for uncompressed signatures, leading to significant speed-ups at the cost of roughly doubling the signature sizes.

For two specific primes with varying values of $2^\bullet$-torsion, we combine all these speed-ups, and measure the performance of verification. Compared to the implementation of the SQIsign NIST submission [8], we reach a speed-up up to a factor 2.70 at NIST Level I when keeping the signature size of 177 bytes. When using our size-speed trade-offs, we reach a speed-up by a factor 3.11 for signatures of 187 bytes, or a factor 4.46 for uncompressed signatures of 322 bytes. Compared to the state of the art [26], these speed-ups are factors 2.07, 2.38 and 3.41 respectively.

Related Work. De Feo, Kohel, Leroux, Petit, and Wesolowski [18] published the first SQIsign implementation, superseded by the work of De Feo, Leroux, Longa, and Wesolowski [19]. Subsequently, Lin, Wang, Xu, and Zhao [26] introduced several improvements for this implementation. The NIST submission of SQIsign [8] features a new implementation that does not rely on any external libraries. Since this is the latest and best documented implementation, we will use it as a baseline for performance comparison, and refer to it as SQIsign (NIST). Since the implementation from [26] is not publicly available, we included their main improvement for verification in SQIsign (NIST), and refer to this as SQIsign (LWXZ).

Dartois, Leroux, Robert, and Wesolowski [16] recently introduced SQIsignHD, which massively improves the signing time in SQIsign, in addition to a number of other benefits, but at the cost of a still unknown slowdown in verification.

This could make SQIsignHD an interesting candidate for applications that prioritise the combined cost of signing and verification over the sole cost of verification.

Recent work by Eriksen, Panny, Sotáková, and Veroni [21] explored the feasibility of computing the Deuring correspondence (see Sect. 2.2) for *general* primes p via using higher extension fields. We apply the same techniques and tailor them to *specialised* primes for use in the signing procedure of SQIsign.

Overview. The rest of the paper is organised as follows. Section 2 recalls the necessary background, including a high-level overview of SQIsign. Section 3 describes how using field extensions in signing affects the cost and relaxes requirements on the prime. Section 4 analyses how the size of the $2^\bullet$-torsion correlates to verification time. Section 5 presents optimisations enabled by the increased $2^\bullet$-torsion, while Sect. 6 gives further optimisations enabled by increased signature sizes. Finally, Sect. 7 gives some example parameters, and measures their performance compared to the state of the art.

Availability of Software. We make our Python and SageMath software publically available under the MIT licence at

$$\text{https://github.com/TheSICQ/ApresSQI.}$$

2   Preliminaries

Throughout this paper, p denotes a prime number and $\mathbb{F}_{p^k}$ the finite field with p^k elements, where $k \in \mathbb{Z}_{>0}$.

2.1   Elliptic Curves and Their Endomorphism Rings

We first give the necessary geometric background to understand the SQIsign signature scheme. For a more general exposition we refer to Silverman [31].

Isogenies. An isogeny $\varphi : E_1 \to E_2$ between two elliptic curves E_1, E_2 is a non-constant morphism that sends the identity of E_1 to the identity of E_2. The degree $d = \deg(\varphi)$ of an isogeny is its degree as a rational map. If the degree d of an isogeny φ has the prime factorisation $d = \prod_{i=1}^n \ell_i^{e_i}$, we can decompose φ into the composition of e_i isogenies of degree ℓ_i for $i = 1$ to n. For every isogeny $\varphi : E_1 \to E_2$, there is a (unique) *dual* isogeny $\widehat{\varphi} : E_2 \to E_1$ that satisfies $\widehat{\varphi} \circ \varphi = [\deg(\varphi)]$, the multiplication-by-$\deg(\varphi)$ map on E_1. Similarly, $\varphi \circ \widehat{\varphi}$ is the multiplication-by-$\deg(\varphi)$ map on E_2.

A *separable* isogeny is described, up to isomorphism, by its kernel, a group of order d. Given a kernel G of prime order d, we can compute the corresponding isogeny $\phi : E \to E/G$ using Vélu's formulas [34] in $\widetilde{O}(d)$. Leroux, and Smith [5] showed that this can be asymptotically reduced to $\widetilde{O}(\sqrt{d})$ using $\sqrt{\text{élu}}$ formulas. In Sect. 2.5, we return to the topic of computing isogenies and give a more detailed discussion.

Endomorphism Rings. An isogeny from a curve E to itself is called an *endomorphism*. For example, for any integer n, the multiplication-by-n map is an endomorphism. Another, not necessarily distinct, example for elliptic curves defined over $\mathbb{F}_q$ is the *Frobenius endomorphism* $\pi : (x, y) \mapsto (x^q, y^q)$.

The set of endomorphisms $\mathrm{End}(E)$ of an elliptic curve E forms a ring under (pointwise) addition and composition of isogenies. The endomorphism ring of $E/\overline{\mathbb{F}}_p$ is either isomorphic to an imaginary quadratic order, or to a maximal order in a quaternion algebra ramified at p and ∞ (which will be defined in Sect. 2.2). In the latter case, we say that E is *supersingular*, and from this point forward, E will denote a supersingular curve.

Supersingular Elliptic Curves and Their Isomorphism Classes. We will mostly consider supersingular elliptic curves *up to isomorphism*, and thus work with isomorphism classes of these curves. Throughout, we will exploit the fact that every isomorphism class of supersingular curves has a model over $\mathbb{F}_{p^2}$, such that the p^2-power Frobenius π is equal to the multiplication-by-$(-p)$ map. Such curves E are $\mathbb{F}_{p^2}$-isogenous to curves defined over $\mathbb{F}_p$, and satisfy

$$E(\mathbb{F}_{p^{2k}}) = E\left[p^k - (-1)^k\right] \cong \mathbb{Z}/\left(p^k - (-1)^k\right)\mathbb{Z} \oplus \mathbb{Z}/\left(p^k - (-1)^k\right)\mathbb{Z}, \qquad (1)$$

while their quadratic twist over $\mathbb{F}_{p^{2k}}$, which we will denote E_k^t, satisfies

$$E_k^t(\mathbb{F}_{p^{2k}}) = E\left[p^k + (-1)^k\right] \cong \mathbb{Z}/\left(p^k + (-1)^k\right)\mathbb{Z} \oplus \mathbb{Z}/\left(p^k + (-1)^k\right)\mathbb{Z}. \qquad (2)$$

For such curves, for any positive integer $N \mid p^k \pm 1$, the full N-torsion group $E[N]$ is defined over $\mathbb{F}_{p^{2k}}$, either on the curve itself, or on its twist.

The Isogeny Problem. The fundamental hard problem underlying the security of all isogeny-based primitives is the following: given two elliptic curves E_1, E_2 defined over $\mathbb{F}_{p^2}$ find an isogeny $\phi : E_1 \to E_2$. The best classical attack against this problem is due to Delfs and Galbraith [20] which runs in time $\widetilde{O}(\sqrt{p})$, and quantum attack due to Biasse, Jao, and Sankar [6] that runs in $\widetilde{O}(\sqrt[4]{p})$. A related problem, which will be useful in the context of SQIsign, is the *endomorphism ring problem*, which asks, given a supersingular elliptic curve $E/\mathbb{F}_{p^2}$, to find the endomorphism ring $\mathrm{End}(E)$. Wesolowski [36] showed that this is equivalent to the isogeny problem under reductions of polynomial expected time, assuming the generalised Riemann hypothesis, and further, Page and Wesolowski [28] recently showed that the endomorphism ring problem is equivalent to the problem of computing one endomorphism.

2.2 Quaternion Algebras and the Deuring Correspondence

We give the necessary arithmetic background to understand the signing procedure of SQIsign at a high level.[1] The heart of the signing procedure in SQIsign

---

[1] This section is only necessary for Sect. 2.3 and Sect. 3, as all other sections are concerned only with SQIsign verification, which will only use well-known isogeny terminology. In contrast, signing heavily relies on the arithmetic of quaternion algebras.

lies in the Deuring correspondence, which connects the geometric world of supersingular curves from Sect. 2.1 to the arithmetic world of quaternion algebras. For more details on quaternion algebras, we refer to Voight [35].

Quaternion Algebras, Orders and Ideals. Quaternion algebras are four-dimensional $\mathbb{Q}$-algebras, generated by four elements $1, i, j, k$ following certain multiplication rules. For SQIsign, we work in the quaternion algebra *ramified* at p and ∞. When $p \equiv 3 \pmod 4$, one representation of such a quaternion algebra is given by $\mathcal{B}_{p,\infty} = \mathbb{Q} + i\mathbb{Q} + j\mathbb{Q} + k\mathbb{Q}$ with multiplication rules $i^2 = -1$, $j^2 = -p$, $ij = -ji = k$. For an element $\alpha = x + yi + zj + wk \in \mathcal{B}_{p,\infty}$ with $x, y, z, w \in \mathbb{Q}$, we define its *conjugate* to be $\bar{\alpha} = x - yi - zj - wk$, and its *reduced norm* to be $n(\alpha) = \alpha\bar{\alpha}$.

We are mainly interested in *lattices* in $\mathcal{B}_{p,\infty}$, defined as full-rank $\mathbb{Z}$-modules contained in $\mathcal{B}_{p,\infty}$, i.e., abelian groups of the form $\alpha_1\mathbb{Z} + \alpha_2\mathbb{Z} + \alpha_3\mathbb{Z} + \alpha_4\mathbb{Z}$, where $\alpha_1, \alpha_2, \alpha_3, \alpha_4 \in \mathcal{B}_{p,\infty}$ are linearly independent. If a lattice $\mathcal{O} \subset \mathcal{B}_{p,\infty}$ is also a subring of $\mathcal{B}_{p,\infty}$, i.e., it contains 1 and is closed under multiplication, then $\mathcal{O}$ is called an *order*. Orders that are not strictly contained in any other order are called *maximal* orders. From this point on, we only consider maximal orders.

A lattice I that is closed under multiplication by an order $\mathcal{O}$ on the left is called a *left* (resp. *right*) $\mathcal{O}$-ideal. We refer to $\mathcal{O}$ as the left (resp. right) order of I. When $\mathcal{O}$ is the left order of I and $\mathcal{O}'$ the right order of I, we define I to be a *connecting* $(\mathcal{O}, \mathcal{O}')$-*ideal*.[2] A left $\mathcal{O}$-ideal I that is also contained in $\mathcal{O}$ is called an *integral* ideal. From this point on, we only deal with integral left ideals and simply refer to them as ideals.

The *norm* of an ideal I is the greatest common divisor of the reduced norms of the elements of I, whereas the *conjugate* $\bar{I}$ of an ideal I is the ideal consisting of the conjugates of the elements of I. Two ideals I and J are said to be equivalent if $I = J\alpha$ for some $\alpha \in \mathcal{B}_{p,\infty}^\times$ and is denoted $I \sim J$. Equivalent ideals have equal left orders and isomorphic right orders.

The Deuring Correspondence. Given an elliptic curve E with $\mathrm{End}(E) \cong \mathcal{O}$, there is a one-to-one correspondence between separable isogenies from E and left $\mathcal{O}$-ideals I of norm coprime to p.

Given an isogeny φ, we denote the corresponding ideal I_φ, and conversely, given an ideal I, we denote the corresponding isogeny φ_I. The Deuring correspondence acts like a dictionary: a given isogeny $\varphi : E \to E'$ corresponds to an ideal I_φ with left order $\mathcal{O} \cong \mathrm{End}(E)$ and right order $\mathcal{O}' \cong \mathrm{End}(E')$. Furthermore, the degree of φ is equal to the norm of I_φ and the dual isogeny $\hat{\varphi}$ corresponds to the conjugate $\overline{I_\varphi} = I_{\hat{\varphi}}$. Equivalent ideals I, J have isomorphic right orders and the corresponding isogenies φ_I, φ_J have isomorphic codomains.

The (Generalised) KLPT Algorithm. The KLPT algorithm, introduced by Kohel, Lauter, Petit, and Tignol [25], is a purely quaternionic algorithm,

---

[2] Note that $\mathcal{O}$ and $\mathcal{O}'$ need not be distinct.

but has seen a variety of applications in isogeny-based cryptography due to the Deuring correspondence. Given an ideal I, KLPT finds an equivalent ideal J of prescribed norm. The drawback is that the norm of the output J will be comparatively large.

For example, the KLPT algorithm is used to compute isogenies between two curves of known endomorphism ring. Given two maximal orders $\mathcal{O}, \mathcal{O}'$, translating the standard choice[3] of connecting ideal I to its corresponding isogeny is hard. However, by processing I through KLPT first, we can find an equivalent ideal J of smooth norm, allowing us to compute φ_J. This is essential for computing the response in SQIsign.

The original KLPT algorithm only works for $\mathcal{O}_0$-ideals, where $\mathcal{O}_0$ is a maximal order of a special form.[4] This was generalised by De Feo, Kohel, Leroux, Petit, and Wesolowski [18] to work for arbitrary orders $\mathcal{O}$, albeit at the cost of an even larger norm bound for the output. Note that SQIsign utilizes both versions.

2.3   SQIsign

Next, we give a high-level description of signing and verification in SQIsign. SQIsign is a signature scheme based on an underlying Sigma protocol that proves knowledge of a *secret* (non-scalar) endomorphism $\alpha \in \mathrm{End}(E_A)$ for some *public* curve E_A. At its core, the prover shows this knowledge by being able to compute an isogeny φ from E_A to some random curve E_2.

A high-level description of the SQIsign Sigma protocol is given below.

Setup: Fix a prime number p and supersingular elliptic curve $E_0/\mathbb{F}_{p^2}$ with known endomorphism ring.

Key generation: Compute a secret key $\varphi_A : E_0 \to E_A$, giving the prover knowledge of $\mathrm{End}(E_A)$, with corresponding public verification key E_A.

Commit: The prover generates a random commitment isogeny $\varphi_{\mathrm{com}} : E_0 \to E_1$, and sends E_1 to the verifier.

Challenge: The verifier computes a random challenge isogeny $\varphi_{\mathrm{chall}} : E_1 \to E_2$, and sends φ_{chall} to the prover.

Response: The prover uses the knowledge of φ_{com} and φ_{chall} to compute $\mathrm{End}(E_2)$, allowing the prover to compute the response isogeny $\varphi_{\mathrm{resp}} : E_A \to E_2$, by translating an ideal computed using the generalised KLPT algorithm, as described at the end of Sect. 2.2.

The verifier needs to check that φ_{resp} is an isogeny from E_A to E_2.[5] Assuming the hardness of the endomorphism ring problem, the protocol is sound: if the prover is able to respond to two different challenges φ_{chall}, $\varphi'_{\mathrm{chall}}$ with φ_{resp} and φ'_{resp}, the prover knows an endomorphism of the public key E_A, namely

---

[3] $I = N\mathcal{O}\mathcal{O}'$, where N is the smallest integer making I integral.

[4] Specifically, it only works for special, p-extremal orders. An example of such an order when $p \equiv 3 \pmod 4$ is $\mathrm{End}(E_0)$ where $j(E_0) = 1728$.

[5] Additionally, $\widehat{\varphi_{\mathrm{chall}}} \circ \varphi_{\mathrm{resp}}$ needs to be cyclic. Observe that otherwise, the soundness proof might return a scalar endomorphism.

$\widehat{\varphi'_{\text{resp}}} \circ \varphi'_{\text{chall}} \circ \widehat{\varphi_{\text{chall}}} \circ \varphi_{\text{resp}}$. Proving zero-knowledge is harder and relies on the output distribution of the generalised KLPT algorithm. Note that KLPT is needed for computing the response:[6] while setting $\varphi_{\text{resp}} = \varphi_{\text{chall}} \circ \varphi_{\text{com}} \circ \widehat{\varphi_A}$ gives an isogeny from E_A to E_2, this leaks the secret φ_A.[7] For a further discussion on zero-knowledge, we refer to the original SQIsign articles [18,19].

Remark 1. The best-known attacks against SQIsign are the generic attacks against the endomorphism ring problem. As discussed in Sect. 2.1, their run time depends only on the size of p and, with high probability, do not recover the original secret isogeny, but rather a different isogeny between the same curves. Therefore, their complexity should be unaffected by the changes we introduce to the SQIsign protocol in Sect. 3, as for these attacks it does not matter whether the original secret isogeny had kernel points defined over a larger extension field. In short, the changes in this work do not affect the security of SQIsign.

Verification. Using the Fiat–Shamir heuristic, the SQIsign Sigma protocol is transformed into a signature scheme. This means that a signature on the message msg is of the form $\sigma = (\varphi_{\text{resp}}, \text{msg}, E_1)$. For efficiency, φ_{resp} is compressed, and E_1 is replaced by a description of φ_{chall}. Thus, given the signature σ and public key E_A, the verifier recomputes the response isogeny $\varphi_{\text{resp}} : E_A \to E_2$ and the (dual of the) challenge isogeny $\widehat{\varphi_{\text{chall}}} : E_2 \to E_1$, and then verifies that the hash $H(\text{msg}, E_1)$ indeed generates φ_{chall}.

The isogeny φ_{resp} is of degree 2^e with $e = \lceil \frac{15}{4} \log(p) \rceil + 25$ [8, Sect. 7.2.3], where 2^e corresponds to the output size of the generalised KLPT algorithm. The bottleneck in verification is the (re)computation of φ_{resp} in $\lceil e/f \rceil$ steps of size 2^f. Accelerating this will be the focus of this paper.

2.4   SQIsign-Friendly Primes

Next, we give more details on the parameter requirements in SQIsign. We refer to the original SQIsign works [8,18,19] for a detailed description of their origins.

SQIsign Prime Requirements. The main bottleneck of SQIsign is the computation of isogenies. Recall from Eqs. (1) and (2) that, when working with supersingular elliptic curves $E/\mathbb{F}_{p^2}$, we have $E(\mathbb{F}_{p^2}) = E[p \pm 1]$. Thus, to use x-only arithmetic over $\mathbb{F}_{p^2}$, SQIsign restricts to computing isogenies of *smooth* degree $N \mid (p^2 - 1)$. Finding SQIsign-friendly primes reduces to finding primes p, with $p^2 - 1$ divisible by a large, smooth number. More explicitly, for a security level λ, the following parameters are needed:

---

[6] Alternatively, one can replace the connecting ideal with the shortest equivalent ideal, and translate it by embedding it in an isogeny between higher-dimensional abelian varieties, as shown in SQIsignHD [16].

[7] Further, this is not a valid response, since the composition with $\widehat{\varphi_{\text{chall}}}$ is not cyclic.

- A prime p of bitsize $\log_2(p) \approx 2\lambda$ with $p \equiv 3 \mod 4$.
- The torsion group $E[2^f]$ as large as possible, that is $2^f \mid p + 1$.
- A smooth odd factor $T \mid (p^2 - 1)$ of size roughly $p^{5/4}$.
- The degree of φ_{com}, $D_{\text{com}} \mid T$, of size roughly $2^{2\lambda} \approx p$.
- The degree of φ_{chall}, $D_{\text{chall}} \mid 2^f T$, of size roughly $2^\lambda \approx p^{1/2}$.
- Coprimality between D_{com} and D_{chall}.

To achieve NIST Level I, III, and V security, we set the security parameter as $\lambda = 128, 192, 256$, respectively. Concretely, this means that, for each of these security parameters, we have $\log p \approx 256, 384, 512$, and $\log T \approx 320, 480, 640$, with f as large as possible given the above restrictions. The smoothness of T directly impacts the signing time, and the problem of finding primes p with a large enough T that is reasonably smooth is difficult. We refer to recent work on this problem for techniques to find suitable primes [7,8,11,15,18,19].

The crucial observation for this work is that T occupies space in $p^2 - 1$ that limits the size of f, hence current SQIsign primes balance the smoothness of T with the size of f.

Remark 2. SQIsign (NIST) further requires $3^g \mid p + 1$ such that $D_{\text{chall}} = 2^f \cdot 3^g \geq p^{1/2}$ and $D_{\text{chall}} \mid p + 1$. While this is not a strict requirement in the theoretical sense, it facilitates efficiency of computing φ_{chall}. From this point on, we ensure that this requirement is always fulfilled.

Remark 3. Since the curves E and their twists E^t satisfy

$$E(\mathbb{F}_{p^2}) \cong \mathbb{Z}/(p \pm 1)\mathbb{Z} \oplus \mathbb{Z}/(p \pm 1)\mathbb{Z},$$

and we work with both simultaneously, choosing T and f is often incorrectly described as choosing divisors of $p^2 - 1$. There is a subtle issue here: even if 2^f divides $p^2 - 1$, $E[2^f]$ may not exist as a subgroup of $\langle E(\mathbb{F}_{p^2}), \rho^{-1}(E^t(\mathbb{F}_{p^2})) \rangle \subseteq E(\mathbb{F}_{p^4})$, where $\rho : E \to E^t$ is the twisting isomorphism. While this does not usually matter in the case of SQIsign (we pick 2^f as a divisor of $p + 1$, and T is odd), this becomes a problem when working over multiple extension fields. In Sect. 3.2, we make this precise and reconcile it using Theorem 1.

2.5 Computing Rational Isogenies from Irrational Generators

Finally, to facilitate signing with field extensions, we recall the techniques for computing $\mathbb{F}_{p^2}$-rational isogenies, i.e., isogenies defined over $\mathbb{F}_{p^2}$, generated by *irrational* kernel points, that is, not defined over $\mathbb{F}_{p^2}$. In the context of this paper, we again stress that such isogenies will only be computed by the signer; the verifier will only work with points in $\mathbb{F}_{p^2}$.

The main computational task of most isogeny-based cryptosystems (including SQIsign) lies in evaluating isogenies given the generators of their kernels. Explicitly, given an elliptic curve $E/\mathbb{F}_q$, a point $K \in E(\mathbb{F}_{q^k})$ such that $\langle K \rangle$ is *defined over* $\mathbb{F}_q$,[8] and a list of points $(P_1, P_2, \ldots, P_n)$ in E, we wish to compute

---

[8] That is, the group $\langle K \rangle$ is closed under the action of $\text{Gal}(\bar{\mathbb{F}}_q/\mathbb{F}_q)$.

the list of points $(\varphi(P_1), \varphi(P_2), \ldots, \varphi(P_n))$, where φ is the separable isogeny with $\ker \varphi = \langle K \rangle$. Since we work with curves E whose p^2-Frobenius π is equal to the multiplication-by-$(-p)$ map (see Sect. 2.1), *every* subgroup of E is closed under the action of $\mathrm{Gal}(\overline{\mathbb{F}}_{p^2}/\mathbb{F}_{p^2})$, hence every isogeny from E can be made $\mathbb{F}_{p^2}$-rational, by composing with the appropriate isomorphism.

Computing Isogenies of Smooth Degree. Recall from Sect. 2.1 that the isogeny factors as a composition of small prime degree isogenies, which we compute using Vélu-style algorithms. For simplicity, for the rest of the section, we therefore assume that $\langle K \rangle$ is a subgroup of order $\ell > 2$, where ℓ is a small prime.

At the heart of these Vélu-style isogeny formulas is evaluating the kernel polynomial. Pick any subset $S \subseteq \langle K \rangle$ such that $\langle K \rangle = S \sqcup -S \sqcup \{\infty\}$. Then the kernel polynomial can be written as

$$f_S(X) = \prod_{P \in S} (X - x(P)). \tag{3}$$

Here, the generator K can be either a rational point, i.e., lying in $E(\mathbb{F}_q)$, or an irrational point, i.e., lying in $E(\mathbb{F}_{q^k})$ for $k > 1$, but whose group $\langle K \rangle$ is defined over $\mathbb{F}_q$. Next, we discuss how to solve the problem efficiently in the latter case.

Irrational Generators. For $K \notin E(\mathbb{F}_q)$ of order ℓ, we can speed up the computation of the kernel polynomial using the action of Frobenius. This was used in two recent works [4,21], though the general idea was used even earlier [33].

As $\langle K \rangle$ is defined over $\mathbb{F}_q$, we know that the q-power Frobenius π acts as an endomorphism on $\langle K \rangle \subseteq E(\mathbb{F}_{p^k})$ and thus maps K to a multiple $[\gamma]K$ for some $\gamma \in \mathbb{Z}$. This fully determines the action on $\langle K \rangle$, i.e., $\pi|_{\langle K \rangle}$ acts as $P \mapsto [\gamma]P$ for all $P \in \langle K \rangle$. For the set S as chosen above, this action descends to an action on its x-coordinates $X_S = \{x(P) \in \mathbb{F}_{q^k} \mid P \in S\}$ and thus partitions X_S into orbits $\{x(P), x([\gamma]P), x([\gamma^2]P), \ldots\}$ of size equal to the order of γ in $(\mathbb{Z}/\ell\mathbb{Z})^\times/\{1, -1\}$.

If we pick one representative $P \in S$ per orbit, and call this set of points S_0, we can compute the kernel polynomial (3) as a product of the minimal polynomials $\mu_{x(P)}$ of the $x(P) \in \mathbb{F}_{q^k}$ for these $P \in S_0$, with each $\mu_{x(P)}$ defined over $\mathbb{F}_q$, as

$$f_S(X) = \prod_{P \in S_0} \mu_{x(P)}(X), \tag{4}$$

where μ_β denotes the minimal polynomial of β over $\mathbb{F}_q$.

To compute $f_S(\alpha)$ for $\alpha \in \mathbb{F}_q$, we only require the smaller polynomial $f_{S_0}(X)$ and compute $\mathrm{Norm}_{\mathbb{F}_{q^k}/\mathbb{F}_q}(f_{S_0}(\alpha))$, as

$$\mathrm{Norm}_{\mathbb{F}_{q^k}/\mathbb{F}_q}(f_{S_0}(\alpha)) = \prod_{\pi \in G} \pi(f_{S_0}(\alpha)) = \prod_{P \in S_0} \prod_{\pi \in G} (\alpha - \pi(x(P))) = \prod_{P \in S_0} \mu_{x(P)}(\alpha),$$

where $G = \mathrm{Gal}(\mathbb{F}_{q^k}/\mathbb{F}_q)$, as per Banegas, Gilchrist, Le Dévéhat, and Smith [4]. This allows us to compute the image under f_S of x-values of points in $E(\mathbb{F}_q)$, but only works for values in $\mathbb{F}_q$. To evaluate $f_S(\alpha)$ for general $\alpha \in \overline{\mathbb{F}}_p$, i.e., to compute the image of a point in $E(\overline{\mathbb{F}}_p)$, we instead use the larger polynomial $f_S(X)$, which we compute, as in Eq. (4), as a product of the minimal polynomials $\mu_{x(P)}$, where we use Shoup's algorithm [30] to compute each $\mu_{x(P)}$ given $x(P)$. Computing $f_S(X)$ requires a total of $O(\ell k) + \widetilde{O}(\ell)$ operations, with k such that each $x(P) \in \mathbb{F}_{q^k}$. Evaluation f_S at α takes $\widetilde{O}(\ell k')$ operations, with k' the smallest value such that $\alpha \in \mathbb{F}_{q^{k'}}$ [21, Sect. 4.3].

Remark 4. The biggest drawback to using this technique is that $\sqrt{\text{élu}}$ is no longer effective, as we would need to work in the smallest field where both the isogeny generator and the x-value of the point we are evaluating are defined in.

3 Signing with Extension Fields

By allowing torsion T from extension fields, we enable more flexibility in choosing SQIsign primes p, thus enabling a larger $2^\bullet$-torsion. Such torsion T requires us to compute rational isogenies with kernel points in extension fields $\mathbb{F}_{p^{2k}}$. This section describes how to adapt SQIsign's signing procedure to enable such isogenies, and the increased cost this incurs. In particular, we describe two approaches for T: allowing torsion T from a particular extension field $\mathbb{F}_{p^{2k}}$, or from all extension fields $\mathbb{F}_{p^{2n}}$ for $1 \leq n \leq k$. The first approach means that we can look for T dividing an integer of bit size $\Theta(k \log p)$, and the second approach allows for $\Theta(k^2 \log p)$. In Sect. 4, we explore how increased $2^\bullet$-torsion affects verification.

Throughout this section, we will reuse the notation from Sect. 2.4 to describe the various parameters related to SQIsign.

3.1 Changes in the Signing Procedure

Recall from Sect. 2.3 that the signing operation in SQIsign requires us to work with both elliptic curves and quaternion algebras, and to translate back and forth between these worlds. Note that the subroutines that work solely with objects in the quaternion algebra $\mathcal{B}_{p,\infty}$, including all operations in KLPT and its derivatives, are indifferent to what extension fields the relevant torsion groups lie in. Hence, a large part of signing is unaffected by torsion from extension fields.

In fact, the only subroutines that are affected by moving to extension fields are those relying on Algorithm 1, IdealToIsogeny$_D$, which translates $\mathcal{O}_0$-ideals I of norm dividing D to their corresponding isogenies φ_I. IdealToIsogeny$_D$ is not used during verification, and is used only in the following parts of signing:

Commitment: The signer translates a random ideal of norm D_{com} to its corresponding isogeny, using one execution of IdealToIsogeny$_{D_{\text{com}}}$.

Response: The signer translates an ideal of norm 2^e to its corresponding isogeny, requiring $2 \cdot \lceil e/f \rceil$ executions of IdealToIsogeny$_T$ (see [19]).

Remark 5. We will choose parameters such that $2^f \mid p + 1$ and $D_{\text{chall}} \mid p + 1$, so that $E[2^f]$ and $E[D_{\text{chall}}]$ are defined over $\mathbb{F}_{p^2}$. As a result, the verifier only works in $\mathbb{F}_{p^2}$ and the added complexity of extension fields applies only to the signer.

Algorithm 1. IdealToIsogeny$_D(I)$

Input: I a left $\mathcal{O}_0$-ideal of norm dividing D
Output: φ_I
1: Compute α such that $I = \mathcal{O}_0\langle\alpha, \mathrm{nrd}(I)\rangle$
2: Let $\mathbf{A} = [1, i, \frac{i+j}{2}, \frac{1+k}{2}]$ denote a basis of $\mathcal{O}_0$
3: Compute $\mathbf{v}_{\bar{\alpha}} := [x_1, x_2, x_3, x_4]^T \in \mathbb{Z}^4$ such that $\mathbf{A}\mathbf{v}_{\bar{\alpha}} = \bar{\alpha}$
4: **for** $\ell^e \,\|\, D$ **do**
5:     $\bar{\alpha}|_{\langle P_{\ell^e}, Q_{\ell^e}\rangle} := x_1\mathbf{I} + x_2(i|_{\langle P_{\ell^e}, Q_{\ell^e}\rangle}) + x_3(\frac{i+j}{2}|_{\langle P_{\ell^e}, Q_{\ell^e}\rangle}) + x_4(\frac{1+k}{2}|_{\langle P_{\ell^e}, Q_{\ell^e}\rangle})$
6:     Let a, b, c, d be integers such that $\bar{\alpha}|_{\langle P_{\ell^e}, Q_{\ell^e}\rangle} = \begin{pmatrix} a & b \\ c & d \end{pmatrix}$
7:     $K_{\ell^e} := [a]P_{\ell^e} + [c]Q_{\ell^e}$
8:     **if** $\mathrm{ord}(K_{\ell^e}) < \ell^e$ **then**
9:        $K_{\ell^e} = [b]P_{\ell^e} + [d]Q_{\ell^e}$
10: Set φ_I to be the isogeny generated by the points K_{ℓ^e}.
11: **return** φ_I

Adapting Ideal-to-Isogeny Translations to Field Extensions. To facilitate signing with field extensions, we slightly adapt IdealToIsogeny$_D$ so that it works with prime powers separately. Note that the additional cost of this is negligible compared to the cost of computing the isogeny from the generators because finding the action of the relevant endomorphisms consists of simple linear algebra. See Algorithm 1 for details.

In Line 5 of Algorithm 1, the notation $\beta|_{\langle P_{\ell^e}, Q_{\ell^e}\rangle}$ refers to the action of an endomorphism β on a fixed basis P_{ℓ^e}, Q_{ℓ^e} of $E[\ell^e]$. This action is described by a matrix in $M_2(\mathbb{Z}/\ell^e\mathbb{Z})$. These matrices can be precomputed, hence the only operations in which the field of definition of $E[\ell^e]$ matters are the point additions in Lines 7 and 9, and isogenies generated by each K_{ℓ^e} in Line 10.

3.2 Increased Torsion Availability from Extension Fields

Next, we detail the two approaches to allow torsion groups from extension fields, which permits more flexibility in choosing the final prime p.

Working with a Single Field Extension of $\mathbb{F}_{p^2}$. Although the choice of solely working in $\mathbb{F}_{p^2}$ occurs naturally,[9] there is no reason a priori that this choice is optimal. Instead, we can choose to work in the field $\mathbb{F}_{p^{2k}}$. We emphasise that this does *not* affect signature sizes; the only drawback is that we now perform more expensive $\mathbb{F}_{p^{2k}}$-operations during signing in IdealToIsogeny. The upside, however, is a relaxed prime requirement: we are no longer bound to $E[T] \subseteq \langle E(\mathbb{F}_{p^2}), \rho^{-1}(E^t(\mathbb{F}_{p^2}))\rangle$ and can instead use $E[T] \subseteq \langle E(\mathbb{F}_{p^{2k}}), \rho^{-1}(E^t(\mathbb{F}_{p^{2k}}))\rangle$.

By Eqs. (1) and (2), we have $E(\mathbb{F}_{p^{2k}}) \cong E[p^k \pm 1]$ and $E^t(\mathbb{F}_{p^{2k}}) \cong E[p^k \mp 1]$, thus we simply get

$$E[T] \subseteq E\left[\frac{p^{2k} - 1}{2}\right],$$

---

[9] It is the smallest field over which every isomorphism class of supersingular elliptic curves has a model.

since $\langle E[A], E[B] \rangle = E[\mathrm{lcm}(A, B)]$. Hence, by using torsion from $E(\mathbb{F}_{p^{2k}})$, we increase $T \mid (p^2 - 1)/2$ to $T \mid (p^{2k} - 1)/2$. This implies there are $2(k - 1) \log p$ more bits available to find T with adequate smoothness.

Working with Multiple Field Extensions of $\mathbb{F}_{p^2}$. Instead of fixing a single higher extension field $\mathbb{F}_{p^{2k}}$, we can also choose to work with multiple field extensions, in particular all fields $\mathbb{F}_{p^{2n}}$, where $1 \leq n \leq k$. The torsion group we can access by this relaxed requirement is described by the following definition.

Definition 1. *Let E be a supersingular elliptic curve over $\mathbb{F}_{p^2}$ and let E_n^t denote an arbitrary quadratic twist of E over $\mathbb{F}_{p^{2n}}$ with respect to the twisting isomorphism $\rho_n : E \to E_n^t$. We define the k-available torsion of E to be the group generated by $E(\mathbb{F}_{p^{2n}})$ and $\rho_n^{-1}(E_n^t(\mathbb{F}_{p^{2n}}))$ for $1 \leq n \leq k$.*

Any point P in the k-available torsion can thus be written as a sum $P = \sum_{i=1}^{k}(P_i + \rho_n^{-1}(P_i^t))$ of points $P_i \in E(\mathbb{F}_{p^{2n}})$ and $P_i^t \in E_n^t(\mathbb{F}_{p^{2n}})$. Since the twisting isomorphism keeps the x-coordinate fixed, the computation of this isomorphism can be ignored when using x-only arithmetic, and we simply obtain a sum of points whose x-coordinates lie in $\mathbb{F}_{p^{2n}}$ for $1 \leq n \leq k$. This justifies the name k-available torsion, as we do not have to go beyond $\mathbb{F}_{p^{2k}}$ to do arithmetic with P by working with the summands separately.

The structure of the k-available torsion is completely captured by the following result, which we prove in the full version of our paper [10, Sect. 3.2].

Theorem 1. *Let $p > 2$ be a prime, and let $E/\mathbb{F}_{p^2}$ be a supersingular curve with $\mathrm{tr}(\pi) = \pm 2p$, where π is the Frobenius endomorphism. Then the k-available torsion is precisely the group $E[N]$ with*

$$N = \prod_{n=1}^{k} \Phi_n(p^2)/2,$$

where Φ_n denotes the n-th cyclotomic polynomial.

We find that using all extension fields $\mathbb{F}_{p^{2n}}$, for $1 \leq n \leq k$, increases $T \mid p^2 - 1$ to $T \mid N$, with N as given by Theorem 1. Given that

$$\log(N) = \sum_{n=1}^{k} \log(\Phi_n(p^2)/2) \approx 2 \sum_{n=1}^{k} \phi(n) \log(p),$$

and the fact that $\sum_{n=1}^{k} \phi(n)$ is in the order of $\Theta(k^2)$, where ϕ denotes Euler's totient function, we find that $T \mid N$ gives roughly $k^2 \log(p)$ more bits to find T

with adequate smoothness, compared to the $\log(p)$ bits in the classical case of working over $\mathbb{F}_{p^2}$, and $k\log(p)$ bits in the case of working over $\mathbb{F}_{p^{2k}}$. Due to this, we only consider working in multiple field extensions from this point on.

3.3   Cost of Signing Using Extension Fields

In SQIsign, operations over $\mathbb{F}_{p^2}$ make up the majority of the cost during signing [19, Sect. 5.1]. Hence, we can roughly estimate the cost of signing by ignoring purely quaternionic operations, in which case the bottleneck of the signing procedure becomes running IdealToIsogeny$_T$ as many times as required by the IdealToIsogenyEichler algorithm [19, Algorithm 5] in the response phase. In other words, we estimate the total signing cost from the following parameters:

- f, such that $2^f \mid p+1$.
- T, the chosen torsion to work with.
- For each $\ell_i^{e_i} \mid T$, the smallest k_i such that $E[\ell_i^{e_i}]$ is defined over $\mathbb{F}_{p^{2k_i}}$.

Since Algorithm 1 works with prime powers separately, we can estimate the cost of a single execution by considering the cost per prime power.

Cost per Prime Power. For each $\ell_i^{e_i} \mid T$, let k_i denote the smallest integer so that $E[\ell_i^{e_i}] \subseteq E(\mathbb{F}_{p^{2k_i}})$, and let $M(k_i)$ denote the cost of operations in $\mathbb{F}_{p^{2k_i}}$ in terms of $\mathbb{F}_{p^2}$-operations. Computing the generator $K_{\ell_i^{e_i}}$ consists of a few point additions in $E[\ell_i^{e_i}]$, hence is $O(M(k) \cdot e \log \ell)$, while the cost of computing the isogeny generated by $K_{\ell_i^{e_i}}$ comes from computing e isogenies of degree ℓ at a cost of $O(\ell k) + \tilde{O}(\ell)$, using the techniques from Sect. 2.5.

   To compute the whole isogeny, we need to push the remaining generators $K_{\ell_j^{e_j}}$, through this isogeny. To minimize the total cost, we pick the greedy strategy of always computing the smaller ℓ first. This bounds the cost of evaluating K_{ℓ^e} in *other* isogenies by $O(M(k) \cdot \ell)$.

Total Cost of Signing. Based on the analysis above, we let

$$\text{COST}_p(\ell_i^{e_i}) = c_1 M(k_i)e\log\ell + c_2 e_i \ell_i k_i + c_3 e_i \ell_i \log(\ell_i) + c_4 M(k_i)\ell$$

where k_i, and $M(k)$ are as before, and c_i are constants corresponding to the differences in the asymptotic complexities. Since we can estimate the total cost of executing IdealToIsogeny$_T$ by summing the cost of each maximal prime power divisor of T, and observing that signing consists of executing IdealToIsogeny$_{D_\text{com}}$ one time, and IdealToIsogeny$_T$ a total of $2 \cdot \lceil e/f \rceil$ times, we get a rough cost estimate of signing as

$$\text{SIGNINGCOST}_p(T) = (2 \cdot \lceil e/f \rceil + 1) \cdot \sum_{\ell_i^{e_i} \mid T} \text{COST}_p(\ell_i^{e_i}).$$

In Sect. 7, we use this function to pick p and T minimising this cost. While this cost metric is very rough, we show that our implementation roughly matches the times predicted by this function. Further, we show that this cost metric suggests that going to extension fields gives signing times within the same order of magnitude as staying over $\mathbb{F}_{p^2}$, even when considering the additional benefit of using $\sqrt{\text{élu}}$ to compute isogenies in the latter case.

4   Effect of Increased $2^\bullet$-Torsion on Verification

In Sect. 3, we showed that signing with extension fields gives us more flexibility in choosing the prime p, and, in particular, allows us to find primes with rational 2^f-torsion for larger f. In this section, we analyse how such an increase in $2^\bullet$-torsion affects the cost of SQIsign verification, e.g., computing φ_{resp} and $\widehat{\varphi_{\text{chall}}}$, in terms of $\mathbb{F}_p$-multiplications,[10] taking the SQIsign (NIST) implementation (with no further optimisations) as the baseline for comparison.

4.1   Detailed Description of Verification

Before giving an in-depth analysis of verification performance, we give a detailed description of how verification is executed. Recall that a SQIsign signature σ for a message msg created by a signer with secret signing key $\varphi_A : E_0 \to E_A$ proves knowledge of an endomorphism on E_A by describing an isogeny $\varphi_{\text{resp}} : E_A \to E_2$ of degree 2^e. A given message msg is hashed on E_1 to a point K_{chall} of order D_{chall}, hence represents an isogeny $\varphi_{\text{chall}} : E_1 \to E_2$. A signature is valid if the composition of φ_{resp} with $\widehat{\varphi_{\text{chall}}}$ is cyclic of degree $2^e \cdot D_{\text{chall}}$.

Thus, to verify a signature σ, the verifier must **(a)** recompute φ_{resp}, **(b)** compute the dual of φ_{chall}, to confirm that both are well-formed, and finally **(c)** recompute the hash of the message msg to confirm the validity of the signature.

In SQIsign, the size of the sample space for φ_{chall} impacts soundness, a key security property for signature schemes. In SQIsign (NIST), to obtain negligible soundness error (in the security parameter λ) the message is hashed to an isogeny of degree $D_{\text{chall}} = 2^f \cdot 3^g$ so that the size of cyclic isogenies of degree D_{chall} is larger than 2^λ. In contrast, when $f \geq \lambda$, we can simply set $D_{\text{chall}} = 2^\lambda$.

The signature σ consists of a compressed description of the isogenies φ_{resp} and $\widehat{\varphi_{\text{chall}}}$. For $f < \lambda$ and $D_{\text{chall}} = 2^f \cdot 3^g$ it is of the form

$$\sigma = (b, s^{(1)}, \ldots, s^{(n)}, r, b_2, s_2, b_3, s_3)$$

with $s^{(j)}, s_2 \in \mathbb{Z}/2^f\mathbb{Z}$, $s_3 \in \mathbb{Z}/3^g\mathbb{Z}$, $r \in \mathbb{Z}/2^f 3^g\mathbb{Z}$, and $b, b_2, b_3 \in \{0,1\}$. If $f \geq \lambda$, we set $D_{\text{chall}} = 2^f$ and have $s_2 \in \mathbb{Z}/2^\lambda\mathbb{Z}$ and $r \in \mathbb{Z}/2^f\mathbb{Z}$, while b_3, s_3 are omitted. Algorithmically, the verification process mostly requires three subroutines.

FindBasis. Given a curve E, find a deterministic basis (P, Q) of $E[2^f]$.

---

[10] As standard, we denote multiplications by **M**, squarings by **S**, and additions by **a**.

FindKernel. Given a curve E with basis (P, Q) for $E[2^f]$ and $s \in \mathbb{Z}/2^f\mathbb{Z}$, compute the kernel generator $K = P + [s]Q$.

ComputeIsogeny. Given a curve E and a kernel generator K, compute the isogeny $\varphi : E \to E/\langle K \rangle$ and $\varphi(Q)$ for some $Q \in E$.

Below we detail each of the three verification steps **(a)–(c)**.

Step (a). Computing φ_{resp} is split up into $n - 1$ *blocks* $\varphi^{(j)} : E^{(j)} \to E^{(j+1)}$ of size 2^f, and a last block of size 2^{f_0}, where $f_0 = e - (n - 1) \cdot f$. For every $\varphi^{(j)}$, the kernel $\langle K^{(j)} \rangle$ is given by the generator $K^{(j)} = P^{(j)} + [s^{(j)}]Q^{(j)}$ for a deterministic basis $(P^{(j)}, Q^{(j)})$ of $E^{(j)}[2^f]$.

In the first block, after sampling $(P^{(1)}, Q^{(1)})$ via FindBasis, the bit b indicates whether $P^{(1)}$ and $Q^{(1)}$ have to be swapped before running FindKernel. For the following blocks, the verifier pushes $Q^{(j)}$ through the isogeny $\varphi^{(j)}$ to get a point $Q^{(j+1)} \leftarrow \varphi^{(j)}(Q^{(j)})$ on $E^{(j+1)}$ of order 2^f above $(0,0)$.[11] Hence, for $j > 1$ FindBasis only needs to find a suitable point $P^{(j)}$ to complete the basis $(P^{(j)}, Q^{(j)})$. Furthermore, $K^{(j)}$ is never above $(0,0)$ for $j > 1$, which ensures cyclicity when composing $\varphi^{(j)}$ with $\varphi^{(i-1)}$. In all cases we use $s^{(j)}$ from σ to compute the kernel generator $K^{(j)}$ via FindKernel and $\varphi^{(j)}$ via ComputeIsogeny.

The last block of degree 2^{f_0} uses $Q^{(n)} \leftarrow [2^{f-f_0}]\varphi^{(n-1)}(Q^{(n-1)})$ and samples another point $P^{(n)}$ as basis of $E^{(n)}[2^{f_0}]$. In the following, we will often assume $f_0 = f$ for the sake of simplicity.[12]

Step (b). Computing $\widehat{\varphi_{\mathrm{chall}}}$ requires a single isogeny of smooth degree $D_{\mathrm{chall}} \approx 2^\lambda$. For the primes given in SQIsign (NIST), we have $E_2[D_{\mathrm{chall}}] \subseteq E_2(\mathbb{F}_{p^2})$. Thus, we compute φ_{chall} by deterministically computing a basis (P, Q) for $E_2[D_{\mathrm{chall}}]$ and finding the kernel $\langle K \rangle$ for $\widehat{\varphi_{\mathrm{chall}}} : E_2 \to E_1$. For $f < \lambda$, we have $D_{\mathrm{chall}} = 2^f \cdot 3^g$, and split this process into two parts.

Given the basis (P, Q) for $E_2[D_{\mathrm{chall}}]$, we compute $(P_2, Q_2) = ([3^g]P, [3^g]Q)$ as basis of $E_2[2^f]$, and use $K_2 = P_2 + [s_2]Q_2$, where b_2 indicates whether P_2 and Q_2 have to be swapped prior to computing K_2. We compute $\varphi_2 : E_2 \to E_2'$ with kernel $\langle K_2 \rangle$, and $P_3 = [2^f]\varphi_2(P)$ and $Q_3 = [2^f]\varphi_3(Q)$ form a basis of $E_2'[3^g]$. Then b_3 indicates a potential swap of P_3 and Q_3, while $K_3 = P_3 + [s_3]Q_3$ is the kernel generator of the isogeny $\varphi_3 : E_2' \to E_1$. Thus, we have $\widehat{\varphi_{\mathrm{chall}}} = \varphi_3 \circ \varphi_2$. If $f \geq \lambda$, we require only the first step.

We furthermore verify that the composition of φ_{resp} and $\widehat{\varphi_{\mathrm{chall}}}$ is cyclic, by checking that the first 2-isogeny step of φ_2 does not revert the last 2-isogeny step of $\varphi^{(n)}$. This guarantees that $\widehat{\varphi_{\mathrm{chall}}} \circ \varphi_{\mathrm{resp}}$ is non-backtracking, hence cyclic.

Step (c). On E_1, the verifier uses the point $Q' \leftarrow \widehat{\varphi_{\mathrm{chall}}}(Q')$, where Q' is some (deterministically generated) point, linearly independent from the generator of $\widehat{\varphi_{\mathrm{chall}}}$, and r (given in σ) to compute $[r]Q'$, and checks if $[r]Q'$ matches the hashed point $K_{\mathrm{chall}} = H(\mathtt{msg}, E_1)$ with hash function H.

---

[11] A point P is said to be *above* a point R if $[k]P = R$ for some $k \in \mathbb{N}$.

[12] In contrast to earlier versions, SQIsign (NIST) fixes $f_0 = f$. However, our analysis benefits from allowing $f_0 < f$.

4.2   Impact of Large f on Verification

The techniques of Sect. 3 extend the possible range of f to any size below $\log(p)$. This gives two benefits to the cost of verification, especially when $f \geq \lambda$.

Number of Blocks in φ_{resp}. The larger f is, the fewer blocks of size 2^f are performed in **Step (a)**. Per block, the dominating part of the cost are FindBasis and FindKernel as we first need to complete the torsion basis $(P^{(j)}, Q^{(j)})$ for $E^{(j)}[2^f]$ (given $Q^{(j)}$ if $j > 1$), followed by computing $K^{(j)} = P^{(j)} + [s^{(j)}]Q^{(j)}$. By minimizing the number of blocks n, we minimize the amount of times we perform FindBasis and FindKernel, and the cost of each individual FindKernel only mildly increases, as $s^{(j)}$ increases in size. The overall cost of ComputeIsogeny, that is, performing the n isogenies of degree 2^f given their kernels $K^{(j)}$, only moderately increases with growing f.

We further note that larger f requires fewer T-isogeny computations for the signer, hence signing performance also benefits from smaller n.

Challenge Isogeny. When $f \geq \lambda$, we can simply set $D_{\text{chall}} = 2^\lambda$, which has two main benefits. Firstly, the cost of FindBasis for this step is reduced as finding a basis for $E[2^\lambda]$ is much easier than a basis search for $E[2^f \cdot 3^g]$. Secondly, the cost for ComputeIsogeny for φ_{chall} decreases as we only have to compute a chain of 2-isogenies instead of additional 3-isogenies.

4.3   Implementation and Benchmark of Cost in $\mathbb{F}_p$-Multiplications

To measure the influence of the size of f on the performance, we implemented SQIsign verification for the NIST Level I security parameter set in Python, closely following SQIsign (NIST). As is standard in isogeny-based schemes, we use x-only arithmetic and represent points and curve coefficients projectively. The benchmark counts $\mathbb{F}_p$-operations and uses a cost metric that allows us to estimate the runtime of real-world implementations for 256-bit primes $p^{(f)}$, where $p^{(f)}$ denotes a prime such that 2^f divides $p^{(f)} + 1$. We benchmark primes $p^{(f)}$ for all values $50 \leq f \leq 250$. These results serve as a baseline to which we compare the optimisations that we introduce in Sects. 5 and 6.

We briefly outline how SQIsign (NIST) implements the three main subroutines FindBasis, FindKernel, and ComputeIsogeny.

FindBasis. We search for points of order 2^f by sampling x-coordinates in a specified order,[13] and check if the corresponding point P lies on E (and not on its twist E^t). We then compute $P \leftarrow [\frac{p+1}{2^f}]P$ and verify that $[2^{f-1}]P \neq \infty$. Given two points $P, Q \in E$ of order 2^f, we verify linear independence by checking that $[2^{f-1}]P \neq [2^{f-1}]Q$, and discard and re-sample the second point otherwise.

FindKernel. Given a basis (P, Q), FindKernel computes $K = P + [s]Q$ via the 3ptLadder algorithm as used in SIKE [22]. In addition to the x-coordinates x_P

---

[13] SQIsign (NIST) fixes the sequence $x_k = 1 + k \cdot i$ with $i \in \mathbb{F}_{p^2}$ such that $i^2 = -1$ and picks the smallest k for which we find a suitable point.

and x_Q of P and Q, it requires the x-coordinate x_{P-Q} of $P - Q$. Hence, after running FindBasis, we further compute x_{P-Q} as described in SQIsign (NIST) [8].

ComputeIsogeny. Given a kernel generator K of order 2^f, ComputeIsogeny follows the approach of SIKE [22], and computes the 2^f-isogeny $\varphi^{(j)}$ as a chain of 4-isogenies for efficiency reasons. If f is odd, we further compute a single 2-isogeny. Following SQIsign (NIST), ComputeIsogeny proceeds as follows:

1. Compute $R = [2^{f-2}]K$ and the corresponding 4-isogeny φ with kernel $\langle R \rangle$. Note that the point $(0,0)$ might be contained in $\langle R \rangle$ for the first block in φ_{resp}, which requires a special 4-isogeny formula. Thus, we check if this is the case and call the suitable 4-isogeny function. We set $K \leftarrow \varphi(K)$.
2. If f is odd, we compute $R = [2^{f-3}]K$, the 2-isogeny φ with kernel $\langle R \rangle$, and $K \leftarrow \varphi(K)$.
3. Compute the remaining isogeny of degree $2^{f'}$ with even f' as a chain of 4-isogenies, where $(0,0)$ is guaranteed not to lie in any of the kernels.

In the last step, SQIsign (NIST) uses *optimal strategies* as in SIKE [22] to compute a chain of 4-isogenies. Naive multiplicative strategies would compute $R = [2^{f'-2j}]K$, the 4-isogeny φ with kernel $\langle R \rangle$, and $K \leftarrow \varphi(K)$ for $j = 1, \ldots, f'/2$. However, this strategy is dominated by costly doublings. Instead, we can save intermediate multiples of K during the computation of $R = [2^{f'-2j}]K$, and push them through isogenies to save multiplicative effort in following iterations. Optimal strategies that determine which multiples are pushed through isogenies and minimise the cost can be found efficiently [17,22].

We note that for $f < \lambda$ the computation of $\widehat{\varphi_{\text{chall}}}$ requires small adaptations to these algorithms to allow for finding a basis of $E[D_{\text{chall}}]$ and computing 3-isogenies. Most notably, SQIsign (NIST) does *not* use optimised formulas or optimal strategies for 3-isogenies from SIKE [22], but uses a multiplicative strategy and general odd-degree isogeny formulas [13,27]. We slightly deviate from SQIsign (NIST) by implementing optimised 3-isogeny formulas, but note that the performance difference is minor and in favor of SQIsign (NIST).

Cost Metric. In implementations, $\mathbb{F}_{p^2}$-operations usually call underlying $\mathbb{F}_p$-operations. We follow this approach and use the total number of $\mathbb{F}_p$-operations in our benchmarks. As cost metric, we express these operations in terms of $\mathbb{F}_p$-multiplications, with $\mathbf{S} = 0.8 \cdot \mathbf{M}$, ignoring $\mathbb{F}_p$-additions and subtractions due to their small impact on performance. $\mathbb{F}_p$-inversions, $\mathbb{F}_p$-square roots, and Legendre symbols over $\mathbb{F}_p$ require exponentiations by an exponent in the range of p, hence we count their cost as $\log p$ $\mathbb{F}_p$-multiplications. In contrast to measuring clock cycles of an optimised implementation, our cost metric eliminates the dependence on the level of optimisation of finite field arithmetic and the specific device running SQIsign, hence, can be considered more general.

Benchmark Results. Figure 1 shows the verification cost for the NIST Level I-sized primes $p^{(f)}$ for $50 \leq f \leq 250$, fixing $e = 975$, using our cost metric. For more efficient benchmarking, we sample random public key curves and signatures σ of the correct form instead of signatures generated by the SQIsign signing procedure.

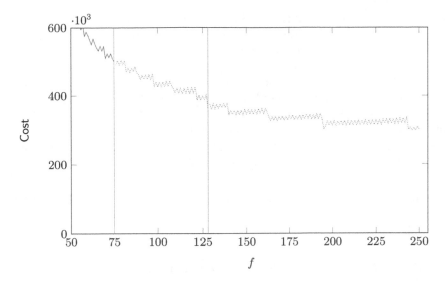

Fig. 1. Cost in $\mathbb{F}_p$-multiplications for verification at NIST Level I security, for varying f and $p^{(f)}$, averaged over 1024 runs per prime. The green vertical lines mark $f = 75$ as used in SQIsign (NIST) for signing without extension fields, and $f = \lambda = 128$, beyond which we can set $D_{\text{chall}} = 2^\lambda$. The dotted graph beyond $f = 75$ is only accessible when signing with extension fields. (Color figure online)

The graph shows the improvement for $f \geq 128$. Furthermore, we can detect when the number of blocks n decreases solely from the graph (e.g. $f = 122, 140, 163, 195, 244$). The cost of sampling a 2^f-torsion basis is highly variable between different runs for the same prime, which is visible from the oscillations of the graph. The performance for odd f is worse in general due to the inefficient integration of the 2-isogeny, which explains the zigzag-shaped graph.

From the above observations, we conclude that $f \geq \lambda$ is significantly faster for verification, with local optima found at $f = 195$ and $f = 244$, due to those being (almost) exact divisors of the signing length $e = 975$.

Remark 6. The average cost of FindBasis differs significantly between primes p even if they share the same 2^f-torsion. This happens because SQIsign (NIST) finds basis points from a pre-determined sequence $[x_1, x_2, x_3, \ldots]$ with $x_j \in \mathbb{F}_{p^2}$. As we will see in Sect. 5, these x_j values can not be considered random: some values x_j are certain to be above a point of order 2^f, while others are certain not to be, for any supersingular curve over p.

5 Optimisations for Verification

In this section, we show how the improvements from Sect. 3 that increase f beyond λ together with the analysis in Sect. 4 allow several other optimisations that improve the verification time of SQIsign in practice. Whereas the techniques in Sect. 3 allow us to decrease the *number* of blocks, in this section, we focus on the operations occurring *within* blocks. We optimise the cost of FindBasis, FindKernel and ComputeIsogeny.

We first analyse the properties of points that have full 2^f-torsion, and use these properties to improve FindBasis and FindKernel for general f. We then describe several techniques specifically for $f \geq \lambda$. Altogether, these optimisations significantly change the implementation of verification in comparison to SQIsign (NIST). We remark that the implementation of the signing procedure must be altered accordingly, as exhibited by our implementation.

Notation. As we mostly focus on the subroutines *within* a specific block $E^{(j)} \to E^{(j+1)}$, we will omit the superscripts in $E^{(j)}, K^{(j)}, P^{(j)}, \ldots$ and write $E, K, P, \ldots$ to simplify notation.

5.1   Basis Generation for Full 2-Power Torsion

We first give a general result on points having full 2^f-torsion that we will use throughout this section. This theorem generalises previous results [14,26] and will set the scene for easier and more efficient basis generation for $E[2^f]$. Its proof can be found in the full version of our paper [10, Sect. 5.1].

Theorem 2. *Let $E : y^2 = (x - \lambda_1)(x - \lambda_2)(x - \lambda_3)$ be an elliptic curve over $\mathbb{F}_{p^2}$ with $E[2^f] \subseteq E(\mathbb{F}_{p^2})$ the full 2-power torsion. Let $L_i = (\lambda_i, 0)$ denote the points of order 2 and $[2]E$ denote the image of E under $[2] : P \mapsto P + P$ so that $E \setminus [2]E$ are the points with full 2^f-torsion. Then*

$$Q \in [2]E \text{ if and only if } x_Q - \lambda_i \text{ is square for } i = 1, 2, 3.$$

More specifically, for $Q \in E \setminus [2]E$, Q is above L_i if and only if $x_Q - \lambda_i$ is square and $x_Q - \lambda_j$ is non-square for $j \neq i$.

Note that for Montgomery curves $y^2 = x^3 + Ax^2 + x = x(x - \alpha)(x - 1/\alpha)$, the theorem above tells us that non-squareness of x_Q for $Q \in E(\mathbb{F}_{p^2})$ is enough to imply Q has full 2^f-torsion and is not above $(0, 0)$ [26, Thorem 3].

Finding Points with 2^f-Torsion Above (0, 0). We describe two methods to efficiently sample Q above $(0, 0)$, based on Theorem 2.

1. **Direct x sampling.** By deterministically sampling $x_Q \in \mathbb{F}_p$, we ensure that x_Q is square in $\mathbb{F}_{p^2}$. Hence, if Q lies on E and $x_Q - \alpha \in \mathbb{F}_{p^2}$ is non-square, where α is a root of $x^2 + Ax + 1$, then Theorem 2 ensures that $Q \in E \setminus [2]E$ and above $(0, 0)$.

2. **Smart x sampling.** We can improve this using the fact that α is always square [2,12]. Hence, if we find $z \in \mathbb{F}_{p^2}$ such that z is square and $z - 1$ is non-square, we can choose $x_Q = z\alpha$ square and in turn $x_Q - \alpha = (z - 1)\alpha$ non-square. Again, by Theorem 2 if Q is on E, this ensures Q is above $(0, 0)$ and contains full 2^f-torsion. Hence, we prepare a list $[z_1, z_2, \ldots]$ of such values z for a given prime, and try $x_j = z_j\alpha$ until x_j is on E.

Both methods require computing α, dominated by one $\mathbb{F}_{p^2}$-square root. Direct sampling computes a Legendre symbol of $x^3 + Ax^2 + x$ per x to check if the corresponding point lies on E. If so, we check if $x - \alpha$ is non-square via the Legendre symbol. On average, this requires four samplings of x and six Legendre symbols to find a suitable x_Q with $Q \in E(\mathbb{F}_{p^2})$, and, given that we can choose x_Q to be small, we can use fast scalar multiplication on x_Q.

In addition to computing α, smart sampling requires the Legendre symbol computation of $x^3 + Ax^2 + x$ per x. On average, we require two samplings of an x to find a suitable x_Q, hence saving four Legendre symbols in comparison to direct sampling. However, we can no longer choose x_Q small, which means that improved scalar multiplication for small x_Q is not available.

Finding Points with 2^f-Torsion *Not* Above (0, 0). As shown in [26], we find a point P with full 2^f-torsion *not* above $(0,0)$ by selecting a point on the curve with non-square x-coordinate. Non-squareness depends only on p, not on E, so a list of small non-square values can be precomputed. In this way, finding such a point P simply becomes finding the first value x_P in this list such that the point $(x_P, -)$ lies on $E(\mathbb{F}_{p^2})$, that is, $x_P^3 + Ax_P^2 + x_P$ is square. On average, this requires two samplings of x, hence two Legendre symbol computations.

5.2   General Improvements to Verification

In this section, we describe improvements to SQIsign verification and present new optimisations, decreasing the cost of the three main subroutines of verification.

Known Techniques from Literature. There are several state-of-the-art techniques in the literature on efficient implementations of elliptic curve or isogeny-based schemes that allow for general improvements to verification, but are not included in SQIsign (NIST). We implemented such methods, e.g., to improve scalar multiplication $P \mapsto [n]P$ and square roots. The details are described in the full version of our paper [10, Appendix A]. In particular, we use that $P \mapsto [n]P$ is faster when x_P is small.

Improving the Subroutine FindBasis. In SQIsign (NIST), to find a complete basis for $E[2^f]$ we are given a point $Q \in E[2^f]$ lying above $(0,0)$ and need to find another point $P \in E(\mathbb{F}_{p^2})$ of order 2^f not lying above $(0,0)$. We sample P directly using x_P non-square, as described above and demonstrated by [26], and in particular can choose x_P small. We then compute $P \leftarrow [\frac{p+1}{2^f}]P$ via fast scalar multiplication to complete the torsion basis (P, Q).

Improved Strategies for ComputeIsogeny. Recall that ComputeIsogeny follows three steps in SQIsign (NIST): it first computes a 4-isogeny that may contain $(0,0)$ in the kernel, and a 2-isogeny if f is odd, before entering an optimal strategy for computing the remaining chain of 4-isogenies. However, the first two steps include many costly doublings. We improve this by adding these first two steps in the optimal strategy. If f is even, this is straightforward, with a simple check for $(0,0)$ in the kernel in the first step. For odd f, we add the additional 2-isogeny in this first step.[14] For simplicity of the implementation, we determine optimal strategies as in SIKE [22], thus we assume that only 4-isogenies are used.

Note that techniques for strategies with variable isogeny degrees are available from the literature on CSIDH implementations [9]. However, the performance difference is very small, hence our simplified approach appears to be preferable.

In addition to optimising 4-isogeny chains, we implemented optimised 3-isogeny chains from SIKE [22] for the computation of $\widehat{\varphi_{\text{chall}}}$ when $f < 128$.

5.3   To Push, or Not to Push[15]

In SQIsign (NIST), the point Q is pushed through φ so that we easily get the basis point above $(0,0)$ on the image curve, and we can then use Theorem 2 to sample the second basis point P. Instead of pushing Q, one can also use Theorem 2 to efficiently sample this basis point Q above $(0,0)$. Although pushing Q seems very efficient, for larger f we are pushing Q through increasingly larger isogeny chains, whereas sampling becomes increasingly more efficient as multiplication cost by $\frac{p+1}{2^f}$ decreases. Furthermore, sampling *both* P and Q allows us to use those points as an *implicit basis* for $E[2^f]$, even if their orders are multiples of 2^f, as described in more detail below. We observe experimentally that this makes sampling Q, instead of pushing Q, more efficient for $f > 128$.

Using Implicit Bases. Using Theorem 2, it is possible to find points P and Q efficiently so that both have full 2^f-torsion. The pair (P, Q) is not an *explicit basis* for $E[2^f]$, as the orders of these points are likely to be multiples of 2^f. However, instead of multiplying both points by the cofactor to find an explicit basis, we can use these points implicitly, as if they were a basis for $E[2^f]$. This allows us to compute $K = P + [s]Q$ first, and only then multiply K by the cofactor. This saves a full scalar multiplication by the cofactor $\frac{p+1}{2^f}$. We refer to such a pair (P, Q) as an *implicit basis* of $E[2^f]$. Algorithmically, implicit bases combine FindBasis and FindKernel into a single routine FindBasisAndKernel.

5.4   Improved Challenge for $f \geq \lambda$

Recall from Sect. 4.2 that when $f \geq \lambda$, we can simply set $D_{\text{chall}} = 2^\lambda$. This decreases the cost of FindBasis for the challenge computation considerably, as we can now use Theorem 2 to find a basis for $E[2^\lambda]$.

Improving FindBasis for the Challenge Isogeny When $f \geq \lambda$. We use Theorem 2 twice, first to find P not above $(0,0)$ having full 2^f-torsion and then to find Q above $(0,0)$ having full 2^f-torsion. We choose x_P and x_Q small such that faster scalar multiplication is available. We find the basis for $E[2^\lambda]$ by

---

[14] In particular, we compute $R' = [2^{f-3}]K$ and $R = [2]R'$, a 4-isogeny with kernel $\langle R \rangle$, push R' through, and compute a 2-isogeny with kernel $\langle R' \rangle$.

[15] –that is, the Q.

$P \leftarrow [\frac{p+1}{2^f}]P$ followed by $f - \lambda$ doublings, and $Q \leftarrow [\frac{p+1}{2^f}]Q$ followed by $f - \lambda$ doublings.[16] Alternatively, if Q is pushed through isogenies, we can reuse $Q \leftarrow \varphi^{(n)}(Q^{(n)}) \in E[2^f]$ from the computation of the last step of φ_{resp}, so that we get a basis point for $E[2^\lambda]$ by $f - \lambda$ doublings of Q. Reusing this point Q also guarantees cyclicity of $\widehat{\varphi_{\text{chall}}} \circ \varphi_{\text{resp}}$.

Remark 7. For SQIsign without extension fields, obtaining $f \geq \lambda$ seems infeasible, hence the degree D of φ_{chall} is $2^f \cdot 3^g$. Nevertheless, some optimizations are possible in the computation of φ_{chall} in this case. FindBasis for $E[2^f \cdot 3^g]$ benefits from similar techniques as previously used in SIDH/SIKE, as we can apply known methods to improve generating a torsion basis for $E[3^g]$ coming from 3-descent [14, Sect. 3.3]. Such methods are an analogue to generating a basis for $E[2^f]$ as described in Theorem 2 and [26, Thorem 3].

6   Size-Speed Trade-Offs in SQIsign Signatures

The increase in f also enables several size-speed trade-offs by adding further information in the signature or by using uncompressed signatures. Some trade-offs were already present in earlier versions of SQIsign [18], however, by using large f and the improvements from Sect. 5, they become especially worthwhile.

We take a slightly different stance from previous work on SQIsign as for many use cases the main road block to using SQIsign is the efficiency of verification in cycles. In contrast, in several applications the precise size of a signature is less important as long as it is below a certain threshold.[17] For example, many applications can handle the combined public key and signature size of RSA-2048 of 528 bytes, while SQIsign (NIST) features a combined size of only 241 bytes. In this section, we take the 528 bytes of RSA-2048 as a baseline, and explore size-speed trade-offs for SQIsign verification with data sizes up to this range.

We note that the larger signatures in this section encode the same information as standard SQIsign signatures, hence have no impact on the security.

6.1   Adding Seeds for the Torsion Basis in the Signature

We revisit an idea that was previously present in SQIsign verification [18] (but no longer in [8] or [19]), and highlight its particular merits whenever $f \geq \lambda$, as enabled by signing with extension fields. So far, we have assumed that completing or sampling a basis for $E[2^f]$ is done by deterministically sampling points. Recall from Sect. 5.1 that sampling x_P resp. x_Q (when not pushing Q) on average requires the computation of several Legendre symbols resp. square roots. We instead suggest using a seed to find x_P (when pushing Q) or x_P and x_Q (otherwise), which we include in the signature, so that the verifier saves all of the above cost for finding x_P, resp. x_Q. Finding these seeds adds negligible overhead

---

[16] Algorithmically, this is faster than a single scalar multiplication by $2^{f-\lambda} \cdot \frac{p+1}{2^f}$.

[17] See https://blog.cloudflare.com/sizing-up-post-quantum-signatures/.

for the signer, while verification performance improves. Signer and verifier are assumed to agree upon all precomputed values.

Seeding a Point *Not* Above (0, 0). For x_P *not* above $(0,0)$, we fix a large enough $k > 0$ and precompute the 2^k smallest values $u_j \in \mathbb{F}_p$ such that $u_j + i \in \mathbb{F}_{p^2}$ is non-square (where i is the same as in Sect. 5). During signing, we pick the smallest u_j such that $x_P = u_j + i$ is the x-coordinate of a point $P \in E(\mathbb{F}_{p^2})$, and add the index j to the signature as a seed for x_P. Theorem 2 ensures that any $P \in E(\mathbb{F}_{p^2})$ for non-square x_P is a point with full 2^f-torsion not above $(0,0)$. This furthermore has the advantage of fast scalar multiplication for x_P as the x-coordinate is very small.

Seeding a Point *Above* (0, 0). As noted above, when f is large, it is faster to deterministically compute a point of order 2^f above $(0,0)$ than to push Q through φ. We propose a similar seed here for fixed large enough $k > 0$, using Theorem 2 and the "direct sampling" approach from Sect. 5.1. During signing, we pick the smallest $j \leq 2^k$ such that $x_Q = j$ is the x-coordinate of a point $Q \in E(\mathbb{F}_{p^2})$ and $x_Q - \alpha$ is non-square. We add $x_Q = j$ to the signature as seed.

Note that when using both seeding techniques, we do not explicitly compute $[\frac{p+1}{2^f}]P$ or $[\frac{p+1}{2^f}]Q$, but rather use the seeded points P and Q as an implicit basis, as described in Sect. 5.3.

Size of Seeds. Per seeded point, we add k bits to the signature size. Thus, we must balance k such that signatures are not becoming too large, while failure probabilities for not finding a suitable seed are small enough. In particular, seeding x_P resp. x_Q via direct sampling has a failure probability of $\frac{1}{2}$ resp. $\frac{3}{4}$ per precomputed value. For the sake of simplicity, we set $k = 8$ for both seeds, such that every seed can be encoded as a separate byte.[18] This means that the failure rate for seeding Q is $(\frac{3}{4})^{256} \approx 2^{-106.25}$ for our choice, while for P it is 2^{-256}. Theoretically it is still possible that seeding failures occur. In such a case, we simply recompute KLPT. We furthermore include similar seeds for the torsion basis on E_A and E_2, giving a size increase of $(n + 1) \cdot 2$ bytes.

The synergy with large f now becomes apparent. The larger f gets, the fewer blocks n are required, hence adding fewer seeds overall. For $f = 75$, the seeds require an additional 28 bytes when seeding both P and Q. For $f = 122, 140, 163, 195, 244$ this drops to 18, 16, 14, 12, and 10 additional bytes, respectively, to the overall signature size of 177 bytes for NIST Level I security.

Remark 8. Instead of using direct sampling for Q with failure probability $\frac{3}{4}$, we can reduce it to $\frac{1}{2}$ via "smart sampling" (see Sect. 5.1). However, this requires the verifier to compute α via a square root to set $x_Q = z\alpha$ with seeded z. We thus prefer direct sampling for seeded Q, which incurs no such extra cost.

---

[18] Note that for equal failing rates the number of possible seeds for P can be chosen smaller than for Q, hence slightly decreasing the additional data sizes.

6.2   Uncompressed Signatures

In cases where f is very large, and hence the number of blocks is small, in certain cases it is worthwhile to replace the value s in the signature by the full x-coordinate of $K = P + [s]Q$. In essence, this is the uncompressed version of the SQIsign signature σ, and we thus refer to this variant as *uncompressed* SQIsign.

Speed of Uncompressed Signatures. Adding the precise kernel point K removes the need for both FindBasis and FindKernel, leaving ComputeIsogeny as the sole remaining cost. This speed-up is significant, and leaves little room for improvement beyond optimizing the cost of computing isogenies. The cost of verification in this case is relatively constant, as computing an 2^e-isogeny given the kernels is only slightly affected by the size of f, as is visible in the black dashed line in Fig. 2. This makes uncompressed SQIsign an attractive alternative in cases where the signature size, up to a certain bound, is less relevant.

Size of Uncompressed Signatures. Per step, this increases the size from $\log(s) \approx f$ to $2 \cdot \log(p)$ bits, which is still relatively size efficient when f is close to $\log(p)$. For recomputing φ_{chall}, we take a slightly different approach than before. We add the Montgomery coefficient of E_1 to the signature, and seeds for a basis of $E[2^f]$. From this, the verifier can compute the kernel generator of φ_{chall}, and verify that the j-invariant of its codomain matches E_2. Hence this adds $2 \cdot \log(p)$ bits for E_1 and two bytes for seeds to the signature, for a total of $(n+1) \cdot (\log p/4) + 2$ bytes.

For $f = 244$, this approach less than doubles the signature size from 177 bytes to 322 bytes for NIST Level I security, for $f = 145$, the signature becomes approximately 514 bytes, while for the current NIST Level I prime with $f = 75$, the size would become 898 bytes. When adding the public key size of 64 bytes, especially the first two cases still appear to be reasonable alternatives to RSA-2048's combined data size of 528 bytes.

Remark 9. Uncompressed signatures significantly simplify verification, as many functionalities required for compressed signatures are not necessary. Hence, this allows for a much more compact code base, which might be important for use cases featuring embedded devices with strict memory requirements.

7   Primes and Performance

In this section we show the performance of verification for varying f, using the optimisations from the previous sections. Further, we find specific primes with suitable f for $n = 4$ and $n = 7$, and report their signing performance using our SageMath implementation, comparing it with the current SQIsign (NIST) prime.

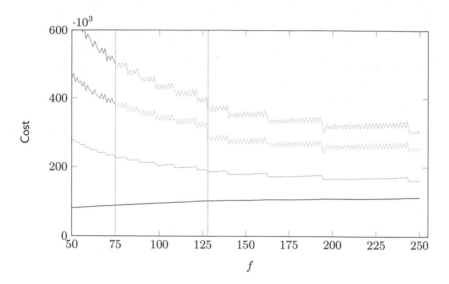

Fig. 2. Extended version of Fig. 1 showing the cost in $\mathbb{F}_p$-multiplications for verification at NIST Level I security, for varying f and $p^{(f)}$, averaged over 1024 runs per prime. In addition to SQIsign (NIST) in blue, it shows the performance of SQIsign (LWXZ) in red, our fastest compressed AprèsSQI variant in brown, and uncompressed AprèsSQI in black. (Color figure online)

7.1 Performance of Optimised Verification

To compare the verification performance of our optimised variants with compressed signatures to SQIsign (NIST) and SQIsign (LWXZ), we run benchmarks in the same setting as in Sect. 4.3. In particular, Fig. 2 shows the cost of verification for the NIST Level I primes $p^{(f)}$ for $50 \leq f \leq 250$. As before, we sample random public key curves and signatures σ of the correct form instead of using signatures generated by the SQIsign signing procedure.

For the sake of simplicity, Fig. 2 displays only the fastest compressed AprèsSQI variant, namely the version that does not push Q through isogenies and uses seeds to sample P and Q. This variant significantly outperforms both SQIsign (NIST) and SQIsign (LWXZ) already at $f = 75$, at the cost of slightly larger signatures. A detailed description and comparison of all four compressed variants is in the full version of our paper [10, Appendix C], which shows that our unseeded variants achieve similar large speed-ups with no increase in signature size. Lastly, the uncompressed variant achieves the fastest speed, although at a significant increase in signature size.

7.2 Finding Specific Primes

We now give two example primes, one prime optimal for 4-block verification, as well as the best we found for 7-block verification. The "quality" of a prime p is measured using the cost metric SIGNINGCOST_p defined in Sect. 3.3.

Optimal 4-Block Primes. For 4-block primes, taking $e = 975$ as a baseline, we need f bigger than 244. In other words, we are searching for primes of the form $p = 2^{244}N - 1$ where $N \in [2^4, 2^{12}]$ (accepting primes between 250 and 256 bits). This search space is quickly exhausted. For each prime of this form, we find the optimal torsion T to use, minimising $\text{SIGNINGCOST}_p(T)$. The prime with the lowest total cost in this metric, which we denote p_4, is

$$p_4 = 2^{246} \cdot 3 \cdot 67 - 1$$

Balanced Primes. Additionally, we look for primes that get above the significant $f > 128$ line, while minimizing $\text{SIGNINGCOST}_p(T)$. To do this, we adopt the "sieve-and-boost" technique used to find the current SQIsign primes [8, Sect. 5.2.1]. However, instead of looking for divisors of $p^2 - 1$, we follow Theorem 1 and look for divisors of $\prod_{n=1}^{k} \Phi_n(p^2)/2$ to find a list of good candidate primes. This list is then sorted with respect to their signing cost according to SIGNINGCOST_p. The prime with the lowest signing cost we could find, which we call p_7, is

$$p_7 = 2^{145} \cdot 3^9 \cdot 59^3 \cdot 311^3 \cdot 317^3 \cdot 503^3 - 1.$$

Remark 10. This method of searching for primes is optimised for looking for divisors of $p^2 - 1$, hence it might be suboptimal in the case of allowing torsion in higher extension fields. We leave it as future work to find methods which further take advantage of added flexibility in the prime search.

7.3   Performance for Specific Primes

We now compare the performance of the specific primes p_4, p_7, as well as the current NIST Level I prime p_{1973} used in SQIsign (NIST).

Signing Performance. We give a summary of the estimated signing costs in Table 1. For p_{1973}, we include the metric "Adjusted Cost", which we compute as SIGNINGCOST with the isogeny computations scaling as $\sqrt{\ell} \log \ell$ to (rather optimistically) account for the benefit of $\sqrt{\text{élu}}$. Further, we ran our proof-of-concept SageMath implementation on the three primes, using SageMath 9.8, on a laptop with an Intel-Core i5-1038NG7 processor, averaged over five runs. An optimised C implementation will be orders of magnitude faster; we use these timings simply for comparison.

We note that the SIGNINGCOST-metric correctly predicts the ordering of the primes, though the performance difference is smaller than predicted. A possible explanation for this is that the SIGNINGCOST-metric ignores all overhead, such as quaternion operations, which roughly adds similar amounts of cost per prime.

Our implementation uses $\sqrt{\text{élu}}$ whenever the kernel generator is defined over $\mathbb{F}_{p^2}$ and ℓ is bigger than a certain crossover point. This mainly benefits p_{1973}, as this prime only uses kernel generators defined over $\mathbb{F}_{p^2}$. The crossover point is experimentally found to be around $\ell > 300$ in our implementation, which

Table 1. Comparison between estimated cost of signing for three different primes.

p	largest $\ell \mid T$	largest $\mathbb{F}_{p^{2k}}$	$\text{SigningCost}_p(T)$	Adj. Cost	Timing
p_{1973}	1973	$k = 1$	8371.7	1956.5	11 m, 32 s
p_7	997	$k = 23$	4137.9	-	9 m, 20 s
p_4	2293	$k = 53$	9632.7	-	15 m, 52 s

Table 2. Comparison between verification cost for different variants and different primes, with cost given in terms of 10^3 $\mathbb{F}_p$-multiplications, using $\mathbf{S} = 0.8 \cdot \mathbf{M}$.

p	f	Implementation	Variant	Verif. cost	Sig. size
p_{1973}	75	SQIsign (NIST) [8]	-	500.4	177 B
		SQIsign (LWXZ) [26]	-	383.1	177 B
		AprèsSQI	unseeded	276.1	177 B
		AprèsSQI	seeded	226.8	195 B
p_7	145	AprésSQI	unseeded	211.0	177 B
		AprèsSQI	seeded	178.6	193 B
		AprèsSQI	uncompressed	103.7	514 B
p_4	246	AprésSQI	unseeded	185.2	177 B
		AprèsSQI	seeded	160.8	187 B
		AprèsSQI	uncompressed	112.2	322 B

is not optimal, compared to an optimised C implementation.[19] Nevertheless, we believe that these timings, together with the cost metrics, provide sufficient evidence that extension field signing in an optimised implementation stays in the same order of magnitude for signing time as staying over $\mathbb{F}_{p^2}$.

Verification Performance. In Table 2, we summarise the performance of verification for p_{1973}, p_7, and p_4, both in terms of speed, and signature sizes.

Two highlights of this work lie in using p_7, both with and without seeds, having (almost) the same signature sizes as the current SQIsign signatures, but achieving a speed-up of factor 2.37 resp. 2.80 in comparison to SQIsign (NIST) and 1.82 resp. 2.15 in comparison to SQIsign (LWXZ), using p_{1973}. Another interesting alternative is using uncompressed p_4, at the cost of roughly double signature sizes, giving a speed-up of factor 4.46 in comparison to SQIsign (NIST) and 3.41 in comparison to SQIsign (LWXZ).

Remark 11. We analyse and optimise the cost of verification with respect to $\mathbb{F}_p$-operations. However, primes of the form $p = 2^f \cdot c - 1$ are considered to be particularly suitable for fast optimised finite field arithmetic, especially when

---

[19] For instance, work by Adj, Chi-Domínguez, and Rodríguez-Henríquez [1] gives the crossover point at $\ell > 89$, although for isogenies defined over $\mathbb{F}_p$.

f is large [3]. Hence, we expect primes like p_4 to improve significantly more in comparison to p_{1973} in low-level field arithmetic, leading to a larger speed-up than predicted in Table 2. Furthermore, other low-level improvements, such as fast non-constant time GCD for inversions or Legendre symbols, will improve the performance of primes in terms of cycles, which is unaccounted for by our cost metric.

Acknowledgement. We thank Craig Costello for helpful suggestions and comments on an earlier version of this work. We thank the anonymous Eurocrypt 2024 reviewers for their constructive feedback.

References

1. Adj, G., Chi-Domínguez, J.-J., Rodríguez-Henríquez, F.: Karatsuba-based square-root Vélu's formulas applied to two isogeny-based protocols. J. Cryptogr. Eng. **13**(1), 89–106 (2023). https://doi.org/10.1007/s13389-022-00293-y
2. Auer, R., Top, J.: Legendre elliptic curves over finite fields. J. Number Theor. **95**(2), 303–312 (2002). ISSN 0022-314X. https://doi.org/10.1006/jnth.2001.2760. https://www.sciencedirect.com/science/article/pii/S0022314X0192760X
3. Bajard, J.-C., Duquesne, S.: Montgomery-friendly primes and applications to cryptography. J. Cryptogr. Eng. **11**(4), 399–415 (2021). https://doi.org/10.1007/s13389-021-00260-z
4. Banegas, G., Gilchrist, V., Le Dévéhat, A., Smith, B.: Fast and Frobenius: rational isogeny evaluation over finite fields. In: Aly, A., Tibouchi, M. (eds.) Progress in Cryptology, LATINCRYPT 2023. LATINCRYPT 2023. LNCS, vol. 14168, pp. 129–148. Springer, Cham (2023). https://doi.org/10.1007/978-3-031-44469-2_7
5. Bernstein, D.J., De Feo, L., Leroux, A., Smith, B.: Faster computation of isogenies of large prime degree. In: Open Book Series, vol. 4, no. 1, pp. 39–55 (2020)
6. Biasse, J.-F., Jao, D., Sankar, A.: A quantum algorithm for computing isogenies between supersingular elliptic curves. In: Meier, W., Mukhopadhyay, D. (eds.) INDOCRYPT 2014. LNCS, vol. 8885, pp. 428–442. Springer, Cham (2014). https://doi.org/10.1007/978-3-319-13039-2_25
7. Bruno, G., et al.: Cryptographic Smooth Neighbors. IACR Cryptol. ePrint Arch., p. 1439 (2022). https://eprint.iacr.org/2022/1439
8. Chavez-Saab, J., et al.: SQIsign: algorithm specifications and supporting documentation (2023). National Institute of Standards and Technology. https://csrc.nist.gov/csrc/media/Projects/pqc-dig-sig/documents/round-1/spec-files/sqisign-spec-web.pdf
9. Chi-Domínguez, J.-J., Rodríguez-Henríquez, F.: Optimal strategies for CSIDH. Adv. Math. Commun. **16**(2), 383–411 (2022)
10. Santos, M.C.-R., Eriksen, J.K., Meyer, M., Reijnders, K.: AprésSQI: extra fast verification for SQIsign using extension-field signing. Cryptology ePrint Archive, Paper 2023/1559 (2023). https://eprint.iacr.org/2023/1559
11. Costello, C.: B-SIDH: supersingular isogeny Diffie-Hellman using twisted torsion. In: Moriai, S., Wang, H. (eds.) ASIACRYPT 2020, Part II. LNCS, vol. 12492, pp. 440–463. Springer, Cham (2020). https://doi.org/10.1007/978-3-030-64834-3_15
12. Costello, C.: Computing supersingular isogenies on Kummer surfaces. In: Peyrin, T., Galbraith, S. (eds.) ASIACRYPT 2018, Part III. LNCS, vol. 11274, pp. 428–456. Springer, Cham (2018). https://doi.org/10.1007/978-3-030-03332-3_16

13. Costello, C., Hisil, H.: A simple and compact algorithm for SIDH with arbitrary degree isogenies. In: Takagi, T., Peyrin, T. (eds.) ASIACRYPT 2017, Part II. LNCS, vol. 10625, pp. 303–329. Springer, Cham (2017). https://doi.org/10.1007/978-3-319-70697-9_11

14. Costello, C., Jao, D., Longa, P., Naehrig, M., Renes, J., Urbanik, D.: Efficient compression of SIDH public keys. In: Coron, J.-S., Nielsen, J.B. (eds.) EUROCRYPT 2017, Part I. LNCS, vol. 10210, pp. 679–706. Springer, Cham (2017). https://doi.org/10.1007/978-3-319-56620-7_24

15. Costello, C., Meyer, M., Naehrig, M.: Sieving for twin smooth integers with solutions to the Prouhet-Tarry-Escott problem. In: Canteaut, A., Standaert, F.-X. (eds.) EUROCRYPT 2021, Part I. LNCS, vol. 12696, pp. 272–301. Springer, Cham (2021). https://doi.org/10.1007/978-3-030-77870-5_10

16. Dartois, P., Leroux, A., Robert, D., Wesolowski, B.: SQISignHD: new dimensions in cryptography. IACR Cryptol. ePrint Arch., p. 436 (2023). https://eprint.iacr.org/2023/436

17. De Feo, L., Jao, D., Plût, J.: Towards quantum-resistant cryptosystems from supersingular elliptic curve isogenies. J. Math. Cryptol. $8(3)$, 209–247 (2014). https://doi.org/10.1515/jmc-2012-0015

18. De Feo, L., Kohel, D., Leroux, A., Petit, C., Wesolowski, B.: SQISign: compact post-quantum signatures from quaternions and isogenies. In: Moriai, S., Wang, H. (eds.) ASIACRYPT 2020, Part I. LNCS, vol. 12491, pp. 64–93. Springer, Cham (2020). https://doi.org/10.1007/978-3-030-64837-4_3

19. De Feo, L., Leroux, A., Longa, P., Wesolowski, B.: New algorithms for the deuring correspondence. In: Hazay, C., Stam, M. (eds.) Advances in Cryptology, EUROCRYPT 2023. LNCS, vol. 14008, pp. 659–690. Springer, Cham (2023). https://doi.org/10.1007/978-3-031-30589-4_23

20. Delfs, C., Galbraith, S.D.: Computing isogenies between supersingular elliptic curves over $\mathbb{F}_p$. Des. Codes Crypt. $\mathbf{78}$, 425–440 (2016)

21. Eriksen, J.K., Panny, L., Sotáková, J., Veroni, M.: Deuring for the people: supersingular elliptic curves with prescribed endomorphism ring in general characteristic. IACR Cryptol. ePrint Arch., p. 106 (2023). https://eprint.iacr.org/2023/106

22. Jao, D., R., et al.: SIKE. Technical report, National Institute of Standards and Technology (2022). https://csrc.nist.gov/Projects/post-quantum-cryptography/round-4-submissions

23. Johnson, D., Menezes, A., Vanstone, S.A.: The elliptic curve digital signature algorithm (ECDSA). Int. J. Inf. Sec. $\mathbf{1}(1)$, 36–63 (2001). https://doi.org/10.1007/s102070100002

24. Josefsson, S., Liusvaara, I.: Edwards-curve digital signature algorithm (EdDSA). RFC: 8032, pp. 1–60 (2017). https://doi.org/10.17487/RFC8032

25. Kohel, D., Lauter, K., Petit, C., Tignol, J.-P.: On the quaternion-isogeny path problem. LMS J. Comput. Math. $\mathbf{17}$(A), 418–432 (2014)

26. Lin, K., Wang, W., Xu, Z., Zhao, C.-A.: A faster software implementation of SQISign. Cryptology ePrint Archive, Paper 2023/753 (2023). https://eprint.iacr.org/2023/753

27. Meyer, M., Reith, S.: A faster way to the CSIDH. In: Chakraborty, D., Iwata, T. (eds.) INDOCRYPT 2018. LNCS, vol. 11356, pp. 137–152. Springer, Cham (2018). https://doi.org/10.1007/978-3-030-05378-9_8

28. Page, A., Wesolowski, B.: The supersingular endomorphism ring and one endomorphism problems are equivalent. CoRR abs/2309.10432. arXiv arXiv:2309.10432 (2023). https://doi.org/10.48550/arXiv.2309.10432

29. Shor, P.W.: Polynomial-time algorithms for prime factorization and discrete logarithms on a quantum computer. SIAM Rev. **41**(2), 303–332 (1999)
30. Shoup, V.: Efficient computation of minimal polynomials in algebraic extensions of finite fields. In: Proceedings of the 1999 International Symposium on Symbolic and Algebraic Computation, pp. 53–58 (1999)
31. Silverman, J.H.: The Arithmetic of Elliptic Curves, vol. 106. Springer, New York (2009). https://doi.org/10.1007/978-1-4757-1920-8
32. National Institute of Standards and Technology (NIST): Call for Additional Digital Signature Schemes for the Post-Quantum Cryptography Standardization Process (2022). https://csrc.nist.gov/csrc/media/Projects/pqc-dig-sig/documents/call-for-proposals-dig-sig-sept-2022.pdf
33. Tsukazaki, K.: Explicit isogenies of elliptic curves. Ph.D. thesis, University of Warwick (2013)
34. Vélu, J.: Isogénies entre courbes elliptiques. Comptes-Rendus de l'Académie des Sciences **273**, 238–241 (1971)
35. Voight, J.: Quaternion Algebras. GTM, vol. 288. Springer, Cham (2021). https://doi.org/10.1007/978-3-030-56694-4
36. Wesolowski, B.: The supersingular isogeny path and endomorphism ring problems are equivalent. In: 2021 IEEE 62nd Annual Symposium on Foundations of Computer Science (FOCS), pp. 1100–1111. IEEE (2022)

Symmetric Cryptology

The Exact Multi-user Security
of (Tweakable) Key Alternating Ciphers
with a Single Permutation

Yusuke Naito[1]($\boxtimes$), Yu Sasaki[2], and Takeshi Sugawara[3]

[1] Mitsubishi Electric Corporation, Kanagawa, Japan
`Naito.Yusuke@ce.MitsubishiElectric.co.jp`
[2] NTT Social Informatics Laboratories, Tokyo, Japan
`yusk.sasaki@ntt.com`
[3] The University of Electro-Communications, Tokyo, Japan
`sugawara@uec.ac.jp`

Abstract. We prove the tight multi-user (mu) security of the (tweakable) key alternating cipher (KAC) for any round r with a single permutation and r-wise independent subkeys, providing a more realistic provable-security foundation for block ciphers. After Chen and Steinberger proved the single-user (su) tight security bound of r-round KAC in 2014, its extension under more realistic conditions has become a new research challenge. The state-of-the-art includes (i) single permutation by Yu et al., (ii) the mu security by Hoang and Tessaro, and (iii) correlated subkeys by Tessaro and Zhang. However, the previous works considered these conditions independently, and the tight security bound of r-round KACs with all of these conditions is an open research problem. We address it by giving the new mu-bound with an n-bit message space, approximately $q \cdot \left(\frac{p+rq}{2^n}\right)^r$, wherein p and q are the number of primitive and construction queries, respectively. The bound ensures the security up to the $O(2^{\frac{rn}{r+1}})$ query complexity and is tight, matching the conventional attack bound. Moreover, our result easily extends to the r-round tweakable KAC when its subkeys generated by a tweak function is r-wise independent. The proof is based on the re-sampling method originally proposed for the mu-security analysis of the triple encryption. Its extension to any rounds is the core technique enabling the new bound.

Keywords: (Tweakable) Key Alternating Cipher · Single Permutation · Any Round · Multi-user Security · Tight Bound · Re-sampling Method

1 Introduction

An r-round key alternating cipher (KAC) constructs a block cipher using r permutations $\pi_1, \ldots, \pi_r$ and $r+1$ subkeys $K_0, \ldots, K_r$ as

$$K_r \oplus \pi_r(K_{r-1} \oplus \pi_{r-1}(\cdots \pi_2(K_1 \oplus \pi_1(K_0 \oplus M))\cdots))). \qquad (1)$$

© International Association for Cryptologic Research 2024
M. Joye and G. Leander (Eds.): EUROCRYPT 2024, LNCS 14651, pp. 97–127, 2024.
https://doi.org/10.1007/978-3-031-58716-0_4

Table 1. Tight bounds of KAC with different conditions.

Reference	Round w/ Tight Bound	Identical Permutation	Independent Subkeys[†]	Multi-user Security	Tweakable KAC
Even-Mansour [12]	1	N/A	All	—	—
Bogdanov et al. [3]	2	—	All	—	—
Steinberger [24]	3	—	All	—	—
Lampe et al. [16]	Asymptotic	—	All	—	—
Chen-Steinberger [5]	Any	—	All	—	—
Chen et al. [4]	2	✓	1	—	—
Wu et al. [27]	3	✓	All	—	—
Yu et al. [28]	Any	✓	All	—	—
Dunkelman et al. [10]	1	N/A	1	—	—
Tessaro-Zhang [25]	Any	—	$r-1$	—	—
Mouha-Luykx [19]	1	N/A	1	✓	—
Hoang-Tessaro [14]	Any	—	All	✓	—
Cogliati et al. [7]	2	—	2	—	✓
Cogliati et al. [7]	Asymptotic	—	r	—	✓
Cogliati-Seurin [8]	4	—	2	—	✓
Dutta [11]	4	—[‡]	2	—	✓
This Work	Any	✓	r	✓	✓

[†]The number of required independent subkeys.

[‡]Single permutation for 2 rounds and two independent permutations for 4 rounds.

The 1-round KAC is also known as the Even-Mansour (EM) cipher, and the r-round KAC is also referred to as the r-round iterated EM. KAC describes the computational structure of block ciphers commonly used in the real world, such as AES and other substitution-permutation networks (SPN) ciphers, and the provable security of KAC is their theoretical foundation. Consequently, obtaining tight security bounds for KAC has been an important challenge in symmetric-key cryptography research. As summarized in Table 1, the tight security bounds of KAC have been studied for different directions, i.e., the number of rounds, correlated subkeys, a reduced number of identical permutations, multi-user (mu) security, and tweakable KAC (TKAC).

To prove security, each component of the scheme is often assumed to behave randomly. Several studies assumed that each subkey and each permutation were independent and proved the security for as many rounds as possible. Although the original EM cipher has been known since 1991, Dunkelman et al. [10] finally obtained its tight bound for $r = 1$ in 2012, which is $O(2^{n/2})$ queries, including both queries to the construction and the internal permutation, with the message space $\{0,1\}^n$. In the same year, Bogdanov et al. [3] tackled $r \geq 2$ and proved the lower bound for $r \geq 2$ to be $O(2^{2n/3})$. This is tight for $r = 2$, and they further conjectured the one with general r to be $O(2^{\frac{rn}{r+1}})$. Steinberger extended the result to show the lower bound of $O(2^{3n/4})$ for $r \geq 3$, which is tight for $r = 3$ [24]. Lampe et al. [16] tackled the problem with any r, proving the security up to

$O(2^{\frac{rn}{r+2}})$ queries. Chen and Steinberger [5] finally resolved the conjecture and proved the $O(2^{\frac{rn}{r+1}})$-security bound for any r.

Unlike the the above works using independent random permutations for each round [3,5,16,24], practical block ciphers use the same round function iteratively. Consequently, proving security of KAC with a single permutation, i.e., $\pi_1 = \pi_2 = \cdots = \pi_r$, has become a new research challenge [4,27,28]. Chen et al. initiated this direction by proving the security bounds for $r = 2$ in 2014 [4], and Wu et al. proved for $r = 3$ in 2020 [27]. Finally, in 2023, Yu et al. proved the tight bound for any r [28].

Assuming that $r+1$ subkeys $K_0, \ldots, K_r$ are independent is another gap from practical block ciphers that use correlated subkeys generated from a single secret key and a key-schedule algorithm. Addressing the issue, the other researchers tackled the security of KAC with correlated subkeys [4,10,25]. Dunkelman et al. [10] addressed the problem for single-key EM cipher, i.e., $r = 1$ with $K_0 = K_1$. Chen et al. [4] tackled $r = 2$ with an identical permutation and proved the security with 1-wise independent subkeys, i.e., $K_0 = K_2$ and $K_1 = f(K_0)$ with a linear map f. Finally, Tessaro and Zhang [25] extended to any r with $(r-1)$-wise independent subkeys, i.e., $r - 1$ independent and two dependent subkeys.

Yet another extension is KAC's tight security bounds under the mu setting. Unlike the conventional single-user (su) setting, the mu security considers multiple users with independent secret keys. An adversary wins by breaking any of the keys, which better represents the real-world attacks targeting a particular service rather than a particular user. Researchers have studied the mu security of the standard algorithms, including AES-GCM [1,15,18], ChaCha20-Poly1305 [9], and TDES [20]. Popular internet protocols determine the AES-GCM's rekeying frequency based on the mu-security bound [22,23,26].

The mu-security bound is generally lower than the su-security bound. In particular, in block ciphers, the key collision attack presented by Biham [2] allows one user's k-bit key to be recovered with a query of $2^k/u$ when there are u users. In the mu-setting, an adversary can distribute q queries to multiple users as desired. The number of queries each user receives is not fixed in advance. In the most extreme case, a user will be queried q times. Thus, by the naive hybrid argument, the mu-security bound has an additional multiplicative factor u compared to the su-security bound, where u is an upper bound on the number of users, which again is upper bounded by q. Unfortunately, this multiplicative factor q can be significant.

On the other hand, Mouha and Luykx [19] proved the mu-security bound of the Even-Mansour construction, i.e., $r = 1$ of KAC, in a dedicated manner without using a hybrid argument, showing no security degradation in the mu setting. Hoang and Tessaro [14] further extended the result to r-round KAC with independent subkeys and permutations and showed that the mu-security bound is not degraded from the su-security bound even for any r.

The other researchers studied the security of TKAC, also known as the tweakable EM, KAC extended with additional tweak input. Cogliati et al. initiated this direction by proving the tight 2-round bound while giving the asymptotic bound for more general cases [7]. Then, Cogliati and Seurin extended the tight security bound from 2 to 4 [8]. Finally, Dutta showed that the 4-round TKAC achieves the same security using two independent permutations only [11].

1.1   Research Question

The previous works pushed forward KAC's tight security bounds toward different directions, as shown in Table 1. Yu et al. proved the su security of r-round KAC with single permutation and independent subkeys [28]. Tessaro and Zhang gave the su security of the r-round KAC with independent permutations and $(r-1)$-wise independent subkeys [25]. Hoang and Tessaro obtained the mu security of r-round KAC with independent permutations and subkeys [14]. In other words, the tight security bound of KAC with all of these conditions, i.e., getting mu-security of the r-round KAC with identical permutation and correlated subkeys, is still an open research problem. Obtaining tight security bounds of TKAC is another open research problem, but the provable tight bound is limited to four [11] and an r-round bound is unknown even without the above conditions.

1.2   Contributions

We address the above open research problems by proving the mu-security of the r-round (tweakable) KAC with identical permutation and correlated subkeys. Below we summarize the main contributions.

Tight Security Bound. The security bound of the r-round KAC with a single permutation with the message space $\{0,1\}^n$ and ϵ r-wise independent subkeys, where ϵ is the probability that one subkey results in some value, is

$$\left(\frac{4^r r^4}{12} + r + 1 \right) \cdot q \left((p + rq) \cdot \max \left\{ \epsilon, \frac{2}{2^n} \right\} \right)^r + 2r^2 \cdot \frac{q}{2^n} , \qquad (2)$$

wherein p and q are the number of the primitive and construction queries, respectively. When using the optimal probability $\epsilon = \frac{1}{2^n}$, the first term becomes $O\left(q \left(\frac{p+rq}{2^n} \right)^r \right)$. Then, the adversary's advantage becomes constant when the number of queries, including both p and q, and reaches $O(2^{\frac{rn}{r+1}})$, which matches Bogdanov et al.'s conjectured lower bound $O(2^{\frac{rn}{r+1}})$.

Compared to the tight bound given by Hoang and Tessaro [14] for independent subkeys and independent permutations, which is $2q \left(\frac{4(p+rq)}{2^n} \right)^r$, our bound is the same up to the constant, indicating that using an identical permutation for all rounds would not degrade security if all the subkeys are independent.

We next extend our KAC result to TKAC that consists of a tweak function h_K and KAC. Given a tweak tw and a plaintext M, the tweak function h_K first generates the subkeys $K_0, \ldots, K_r$ using tw, and then KAC uses these subkeys to encrypt M. With the assumption that each tuple of subkeys defined by h_K are

ϵ r-wise independent, the mu-security of TKAC can be reduced to that of KAC, and we obtain the same bound given in Eq. (2).

Our result improves the state-of-the-art tight security bounds of KAC in multiple ways, as summarized in Table 1. First, we extend the security of the r-round KAC with identical permutation [28] for the mu-setting with r-wise independent subkeys. Second, compared with the state-of-the-art result on the r-round KAC with correlated subkeys [25], our result supports identical permutation in the mu-setting at the cost of using one additional independent subkey, i.e., r-wise instead of $(r-1)$-wise independence. Third, our result extends the mu security of the r-round KAC [14] with identical permutation and correlated subkeys. Finally, we extend the provable tight security bound of TKAC from four [11] to any under the aforementioned relaxed conditions.

Our Technique. Our proof is based on the re-sampling method for the triple encryption by Naito et al. [20]. However, the re-sampling method in [20] is only for the 3-round scheme, whereas our target scheme KAC is an arbitrary-round one. Hence, we update their re-sampling method to support arbitrary round.

Original Re-sampling Method for a Small r. The re-sampling method [20] was originally proposed as a novel way of defining ideal-world dummy internal values in the proof based on the coefficient-H technique [21]. The dummy internal values, as well as dummy keys, are finally revealed to an adversary at the end of the query stage, which makes good-transcript analysis easier. Without this treatment, the previous proofs [4,14] suffered from complicated counting of the number of solutions of the internal values with a huge number of cases.[1] The re-sampling method successfully obtained a tight mu-bound with triple encryption [20].

A naive method to define dummy internal values is to perform only the forward sampling that defines the values from the first round to the last round for each construction query-response pair. This method fails if a defined internal value collides with some primitive query-response or an internal value of some previous construction query. The collision probability is $O\left(q\left(\frac{p+q}{2^{k+n}}\right)\right)$ for the triple encryption with a k-bit key and an n-bit-block block cipher, which was insufficient for getting a tight bound. The original re-sampling method solves the problem by introducing the inverse sampling in addition to the forward sampling. Thus, in the re-sampling method, if the forward sampling fails, i.e., a collision with some construction query-response pair occurs at the i-th round, then the internal values are re-defined from the last round to the i-th round. As the number of chances to define compatible internal values increases, the failure probability of defining the internal values can be improved to $O\left(q\left(\frac{p+q}{2^{k+n}}\right)^2\right)$.

Re-sampling Method for any r (Section 4.5). The re-sampling method offers the bound $O\left(q\left(\frac{p+q}{2^n}\right)^2\right)$ for KAC as $k=0$, but the bound is not tight for $r \geq 3$. To

---

[1] Yu et al. recently simplified the proof technique, and derived the tight su-bound for KAC. The proof is limited to the su-setting, and proving the mu-security is still open.

obtain the tight bound for KAC, we update the method by taking into account all chains involved in the inverse sampling. Intuitively, the original re-sampling method defines a bad event of the inverse sampling as the collision with some primitive query-response or some previous internal value. However, not all such collisions yield incompatible internal values. Namely, the naive extension of the original re-sampling method to 3-rounds or more will result in a loose evaluation of bad events. That is because a longer-round analysis involves a collision with a long chain, a sequence of primitive query-responses or previous internal values with the user's key, which could be ignored in the analysis for 2 rounds or less. Hence, we update the inverse sampling by revisiting the bad event such that a collision of such a chain is taken into account. As such a chain includes the user's key, which is secret and random, we can improve the failure probability of the inverse sampling. Consequently, the updated re-sampling method can define compatible internal values up to the tight bound, offering the tight bound of KAC for any round.

1.3   Organization

This paper is organized as follows. We begin by giving basic notations in Sect. 2. We define KAC with a Single Permutation and their security in Sect. 3. Section 4 summarizes the main results, followed by the formal proofs in Sect. 5. The results are extended to TKAC in Sect. 6. Section 7 is conclusion.

2   Basic Notation

Let ε be an empty string and $\emptyset$ an empty set. For an integer $i \geq 0$, let $\{0,1\}^i$ be the set of all i-bit strings and $\{0,1\}^0 := \{\varepsilon\}$. For integers $0 \leq i \leq j$, let $[i,j] := \{i, i+1, \ldots, j\}$ and $[j] := [1,j]$. If $j < i$ then $[i,j] := \emptyset$. For a value or a set X, $Y \leftarrow X$ means that X is assigned to Y. For a non-empty set $\mathcal{T}$, $T \xleftarrow{\$} \mathcal{T}$ means that an element is chosen uniformly at random from $\mathcal{T}$ and assigned to T. For two sets $\mathcal{T}_1$ and $\mathcal{T}_2$, $\mathcal{T}_1 \xleftarrow{\cup} \mathcal{T}_2$ means that $\mathcal{T}_1 \leftarrow \mathcal{T} \cup \mathcal{T}_2$. For integers s and t, "$i \in \overrightarrow{[s,t]}$ (resp. $i \in \overleftarrow{[s,t]}$)" means that in a for statement, i is chosen from $[s,t]$ in ascending (resp. descending) order from s (resp. from t). If $s > t$, then there is no choice for i. Note that if $s = 1$, then s is omitted such as $\overrightarrow{[t]}$.

3   KACs: Specification and Security Definition

We show the specification of KAC with a single permutation. We then define an mu-PRP security notion with KAC.

3.1   KACs with a Single Permutation

Let n be the bit-length of plaintext and ciphertext blocks of KAC. Let r be the number of rounds of KAC. Let $K = (K_0, K_1, \ldots, K_r)$ be n-bit subkeys of KAC and π the underlying n-bit permutation of KAC. The inverse of π is denoted by π^{-1}. Let $\pi^{\pm} := (\pi, \pi^{-1})$. Let $\mathcal{K}$ be the key space of KAC. Then, the encryption of KAC with K and $\pi^{\pm}$ is defined as follows. For a plaintext block $M \in \{0,1\}^n$, the ciphertext block is defined as

$$\mathsf{KAC}_r[K,\pi](M) = K_r \oplus \pi(K_{r-1} \oplus \pi(\cdots \pi(K_1 \oplus \pi(K_0 \oplus M) \cdots))) \ .$$

The decryption of $\mathsf{KAC}_r[K,\pi]$ is denoted by $\mathsf{KAC}_r^{-1}[K,\pi^{-1}]$. For a ciphertext block $C \in \{0,1\}^n$, the plaintext block is defined as

$$\mathsf{KAC}_r^{-1}[K,\pi^{-1}](C) = K_0 \oplus \pi^{-1}(K_1 \oplus \pi^{-1}(\cdots \pi^{-1}(K_{r-1} \oplus \pi^{-1}(K_r \oplus C) \cdots))) \ .$$

Let $\mathsf{KAC}_r^{\pm}[K,\pi^{\pm}] := (\mathsf{KAC}_r[K,\pi], \mathsf{KAC}_r^{-1}[K,\pi^{-1}])$.

3.2   Definition of Mu-SPRP Security of KACs

We consider multi-user (mu) strong-pseudo-random-permutation (SPRP) security of KAC in the random permutation (RP) model. Let u be the number of users. Let Perm be the set of all n-bit permutations. In the security game, an adversary **A** tries to distinguish between the real and ideal worlds, and has oracle access to the following oracles.

- Real-world oracles:
  - u instantiations of KAC: $\mathsf{KAC}_r^{\pm}[K^{(1)},\pi^{\pm}], \ldots, \mathsf{KAC}_r^{\pm}[K^{(u)},\pi^{\pm}]$, and
  - a RP: $\pi^{\pm}$,

  where $\pi \xleftarrow{\$} \mathsf{Perm}$, and for each $\nu \in [u]$, $K^{(\nu)} \xleftarrow{\$} \mathcal{K}$.
- Ideal-world oracles:
  - u RPs: $\Pi_1^{\pm}, \ldots, \Pi_u^{\pm}$, and
  - a RP: $\pi^{\pm}$,

  where $\pi \xleftarrow{\$} \mathsf{Perm}$, and for each $\nu \in [u]$, $\Pi_\nu \xleftarrow{\$} \mathsf{Perm}$ and $\Pi_\nu^{\pm} := (\Pi_\nu, \Pi_\nu^{-1})$.

At the end of the game, **A** returns a decision bit. Let $\mathbf{A}^{\mathcal{O}} \in \{0,1\}$ denotes an output of **A** with oracle access to the set of oracles $\mathcal{O}$. Then, the advantage function of **A** is defined as

$$\mathbf{Adv}_{\mathsf{KAC}}^{\mathsf{mu\text{-}sprp}}(\mathbf{A}) :=$$
$$\Pr[\mathbf{A}^{\mathsf{KAC}_r^{\pm}[K^{(1)},\pi^{\pm}],\ldots,\mathsf{KAC}_r^{\pm}[K^{(u)},\pi^{\pm}],\pi^{\pm}} = 1] - \Pr[\mathbf{A}^{\Pi_1^{\pm},\ldots,\Pi_u^{\pm},\pi^{\pm}} = 1] \ ,$$

where the real (resp. ideal)-world probability is taken over $K^{(1)}, \ldots, K^{(u)}$ (resp. $\Pi_1, \ldots, \Pi_u$), π, and **A**. We refer the particular queries to as follows:

- Primitive queries: queries to $\pi^{\pm}$;
- Forward (resp. Inverse) queries: queries to π (resp. π^{-1});
- Construction queries (to the ν-th user): queries to $\mathsf{KAC}_r^{\pm}[K^{(\nu)},\pi^{\pm}]$ or $\Pi_\nu^{\pm}$;
- Encryption (resp. decryption) queries (to the ν-th user): construction queries to $\mathsf{KAC}_r[K^{(\nu)},\pi]$ or Π_ν (resp. $\mathsf{KAC}_r^{-1}[K^{(\nu)},\pi^{-1}]$ or Π_ν^{-1}).

4   Mu-Security of KACs with a Single Permutation

We first define r-wise independence which is a requirement for the subkeys of KAC. We then show an upper-bound for the mu-SPRP security of KAC followed by the tools to prove the mu-SPRP security. Our proof is based on the re-sampling method [20] originally introduced for triple encryption. We briefly recall the original method, and show our extension to arbitrary round schemes.

4.1 r-Wise Independent Subkeys

We prove the mu-SPRP security of KAC with r-wise independent subkeys. The definition of r-wise independent keys is given below.

Definition 1. *Subkeys* $K_0^{(\nu)}, K_1^{(\nu)}, \ldots,$ *and* $K_r^{(\nu)}$ *are* ϵ *r-wise independent if for any subset* $S \subseteq [0, r]$ *and* $|S|$ *values* $V_j \in \{0,1\}^n$ *for* $j \in S$ *that are defined independently of the subkeys, we have* $\Pr[\forall j \in S : K_j^{(\nu)} = V_j] \leq \epsilon^{\min\{|S|, r\}}$.

We show examples of r-wise independent subkeys.

Example 1 (r-wise independent subkeys). Let $i \in [0, r-1]$. For each $j \in [0, r-1]$, R_j is chosen uniformly at random from $\{0,1\}^n$. Then, the following subkeys are r-wise independent, since the ranks are both r regarding the subkeys.

- $K_j = R_j$ for each $j \in [0, r]\backslash\{i\}$, and $K_i = \bigoplus_{j \in [0,r]\backslash\{i\}} K_j$.
- $K_0 = R_1$, $K_i = R_{i-1} \oplus R_i$ for each $i \in [r-1]$, and $K_r = R_r$.

4.2   Mu-SPRP Security Bounds of KACs

The following theorem shows the upper-bound of the mu-SPRP security of KAC. The proof is given in Sect. 5.

Theorem 1. *Assume that for each user the subkeys are* ϵ *r-wise independent. Let* $\delta = \max\{\epsilon, \frac{2}{2^n}\}$. *Let* **A** *be an adversary that makes at most* p *primitive queries and* q *construction queries. Let* $\sigma := p + rq$. *Then, we have*

$$\mathbf{Adv}_{KAC}^{\mathsf{mu\text{-}sprp}}(\mathbf{A}) \leq \left(\frac{4^r r^4}{12} + r + 1\right) \cdot q(\sigma\delta)^r + 2r^2 \cdot \frac{q}{2^n} \ .$$

When ϵ is optimal, i.e., $\epsilon = \frac{1}{2^n}$, the above bound becomes

$$8^r \cdot \left(\frac{r^4}{12} + r + 1\right) \cdot q\left(\frac{\sigma}{2^n}\right)^r + 2r^2 \cdot \frac{q}{2^n} \ .$$

The second term becomes a constant only when making full code-book queries. Ignoring the term, i.e., $q \ll O(\frac{2^n}{r^2})$, the bound becomes $O\left(q\left(\frac{\sigma}{2^n}\right)^r\right)$ and is tight.

Algorithm 1. Random Permutations with Lazy Sampling

Random Permutation $\pi^{\pm}$

Forward query X to π

1: $Y \leftarrow \mathcal{L}_0^2[X]$; **if** $\mathcal{L}_0^2[X] = \varepsilon$ **then** $Y \xleftarrow{\$} \{0,1\}^n \backslash \mathcal{L}_0^2$; $\mathcal{L}_0 \xleftarrow{\cup} \{(X,Y)\}$ **end if**
2: **return** Y

Inverse query Y to π^{-1}

1: $X \leftarrow \mathcal{L}_0^1[Y]$; **if** $\mathcal{L}_0^1[Y] = \varepsilon$ **then** $X \xleftarrow{\$} \{0,1\}^n \backslash \mathcal{L}_0^1$; $\mathcal{L}_0 \xleftarrow{\cup} \{(X,Y)\}$ **end if**
2: **return** X

Random Permutations $\Pi_\nu^{\pm}$ for $\nu \in [u]$

Encryption query M to Π_ν

1: $C \leftarrow \mathcal{L}_\nu^2[M]$; **if** $\mathcal{L}_\nu^2[M] = \varepsilon$ **then** $C \xleftarrow{\$} \{0,1\}^n \backslash \mathcal{L}_\nu^2$; $\mathcal{L}_\nu \xleftarrow{\cup} \{(M,C)\}$ **end if**
2: **return** C

Decryption query C to Π_ν^{-1}

1: $M \leftarrow \mathcal{L}_\nu^1[C]$; **if** $\mathcal{L}_\nu^1[C] = \varepsilon$ **then** $M \xleftarrow{\$} \{0,1\}^n \backslash \mathcal{L}_\nu^1$; $\mathcal{L}_\nu \xleftarrow{\cup} \{(M,C)\}$ **end if**
2: **return** M

4.3 Tools for the Mu-SPRP Security Proof

Coefficient-H Technique. In this paper, we refer to the set of responses that an adversary obtains in a security game as a "transcript." Let T_R be a transcript obtained by sampling in the real world, i.e., sampling of $K^{(1)}, \ldots, K^{(u)}$ and π. Let T_I be a transcript obtained by sampling in the ideal world, i.e., sampling of $\Pi_1, \ldots, \Pi_u$ and π. We call a transcript τ *valid* if $\Pr[\mathsf{T}_I = \tau] > 0$. Let $\mathcal{T}$ be the set of all valid transcripts such that $\forall \tau \in \mathcal{T} : \Pr[\mathsf{T}_R = \tau] \leq \Pr[\mathsf{T}_I = \tau]$. Then, we have $\mathbf{Adv}_{\mathsf{KAC}}^{\mathsf{mu\text{-}sprp}}(\mathbf{A}) \leq \mathsf{SD}(\mathsf{T}_R, \mathsf{T}_I) := \sum_{\tau \in \mathcal{T}} (\Pr[\mathsf{T}_I = \tau] - \Pr[\mathsf{T}_R = \tau])$.

We derive the mu-SPRP bound using the coefficient-H technique [21].

Lemma 1. *Let $\mathcal{T}_{\mathsf{good}}$ and $\mathcal{T}_{\mathsf{bad}}$ be good and bad transcripts into which $\mathcal{T}$ is partitioned. If $\forall \tau \in \mathcal{T}_{\mathsf{good}} : \frac{\Pr[\mathsf{T}_R = \tau]}{\Pr[\mathsf{T}_I = \tau]} \geq 1 - \varepsilon$ s.t. $0 \leq \varepsilon \leq 1$, then $\mathsf{SD}(\mathsf{T}_R, \mathsf{T}_I) \leq \Pr[\mathsf{T}_I \in \mathcal{T}_{\mathsf{bad}}] + \varepsilon$.*

We thus show the following three points: (1) define good and bad transcripts; (2) upper-bound $\Pr[\mathsf{T}_I \in \mathcal{T}_{\mathsf{bad}}]$; (3) lower-bound $\frac{\Pr[\mathsf{T}_R = \tau]}{\Pr[\mathsf{T}_I = \tau]}$. Then, putting these bounds into the above lemma, we obtain an upper-bound of $\mathbf{Adv}_{\mathsf{KAC}}^{\mathsf{mu\text{-}sprp}}(\mathbf{A})$.

Lazy Sampled Random Permutations. Our proof makes use of lazy sampled RPs for $\pi^{\pm}$ and $\Pi_\nu^{\pm}$ ($\nu \in [u]$). The lazy sampled RPs use the following tables.

- $\mathcal{L}_0$ (resp. $\mathcal{L}_\nu$): a table that is initially empty and keeps query-response pairs of $\pi^{\pm}$ (resp. $\Pi_\nu^{\pm}$).
- $\mathcal{L}_0^1$ (resp. $\mathcal{L}_0^2$): a table that keeps the first (resp. second) elements of pairs defined in $\mathcal{L}_0$.
- $\mathcal{L}_\nu^1$ (resp. $\mathcal{L}_\nu^2$): a table that keeps the first (resp. second) elements of pairs defined in $\mathcal{L}_\nu$.

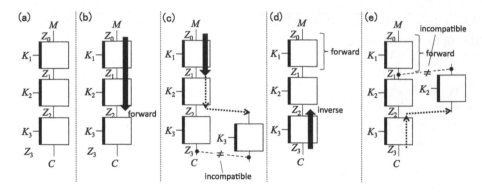

Fig. 1. (a) Structure of the triple encryption; (b) Forward sampling. The forward sampling is success and defines all internal values; (c) Bad event for the forward sampling. The forward sampling is success in the first round but fails in the second one; (d) Inverse sampling after the forward sampling fails in (c). The inverse sampling is success in the last round; (e) Bad event for the inverse sampling after the forward sampling fails in (c). The inverse sampling fails in the last round; Black (resp. dot) arrows show successful (resp. failure) samplings.

- $\mathcal{L}_0^2[X] := Y$ and $\mathcal{L}_0^1[Y] := X$ if $(X, Y) \in \mathcal{L}_0$, and $\mathcal{L}_0^2[X] = \varepsilon$ (resp. $\mathcal{L}_0^1[Y] = \varepsilon$) if $X \notin \mathcal{L}_0^1$ (resp. $Y \notin \mathcal{L}_0^2$).
- $\mathcal{L}_\nu^2[M] := C$ and $\mathcal{L}_\nu^1[C] := M$ if $(M, C) \in \mathcal{L}_\nu$, and $\mathcal{L}_\nu^2[M] = \varepsilon$ (resp. $\mathcal{L}_\nu^1[C] = \varepsilon$) if $M \notin \mathcal{L}_\nu^1$ (resp. $C \notin \mathcal{L}_\nu^2$).

The procedures of the lazy sampled RPs are given in Algorithm 1.

4.4 Re-Sampling Method for Triple Encryption [20]

Our proof makes use of the re-sampling method for the triple encryption by Naito et al. [20]. It was originally proposed only for a 3-round scheme, and we update it to arbitrary rounds for KAC.

We first recall the previous method. Let E be a k-bit key and n-bit block ideal cipher. The structure of the triple encryption is given in Fig. 1(a). The security proof is given in the ideal cipher model, and uses the coefficient-H technique.

The re-sampling method is a novel way of defining dummy internal values in the ideal world, and the dummy internal values and dummy keys are revealed to an adversary after finishing all queries. This method makes good-transcript analysis easier than the existing proofs for the triple encryption. The previous proofs, such as [5,14], do not reveal internal values to the adversary, which makes the analysis of good transcripts complicated since one needs to count the number of solutions of the internal values with a huge number of cases.

A naive method for defining dummy internal values is to define all internal values only by the forward sampling, as shown in Fig. 1(b). This method can avoid such a heavy counting step but cannot offer a tight bound. The bad event for this method is that some internal value is connected with some primitive query-response tuple with the user's key, which yields duplication of the internal value at the next round (See Fig. 1(c)).[2] If the forward sampling fails, then we cannot obtain compatible internal values anymore. Let p (resp. q) be the number of primitive (resp. construction) queries. Then, the probability that the naive method fails is roughly $O(\frac{p}{2^{k+n}})$, since the key (resp. the internal value) is chosen uniformly at random from 2^k (resp. about 2^n) elements. As the number of dummy internal values is at most $3q$, the probability that the naive method fails is at most $O(\frac{qp}{2^{k+n}})$. When making a full codebook construction queries, i.e., $q = O(2^n)$, the naive method yields the $O(2^k)$ security regarding primitive queries, which is not tight for the triple encryption.

The re-sampling method improves the bound by introducing the inverse sampling. This method first tries the forward sampling as described above using E for each construction query-response pair (M, C). If the forward sampling fails, then the remaining internal values, including the (incompatible) internal value, are (re)defined by E^{-1} (the inverse of E) from the last round. This step is called the inverse sampling. Figure 1(d) exemplifies the procedure of the inverse sampling after the failure of the forward sampling in Fig. 1(c). In this example, the internal value Z_2 is (re)defined by the inverse sampling. By the re-sampling method, internal values that are compatible with construction query-response pairs and primitive ones can be defined up to the tight bound.

The inverse sampling fails if some internal value is connected with some primitive query-response tuple with the user's key, which is the bad event of the re-sampling method. Figure 1(e) exemplifies the bad event: if the value Z_2 connects with some primitive query-response tuple with the user's key K_2, then the internal value Z_1 is duplicately defined, and the re-sampling method fails. The probability that the bad event occurs is upper-bounded by the probability that forward and inverse samplings fail within the same construction query-response pair. For each construction query, the probability that an internal value by the forward (resp. inverse) sampling is connected with some primitive query-response tuple with the user's key is roughly $\frac{p}{2^{n+k}}$ (resp. $\frac{p}{2^{n+k}}$). Hence, the probability that the bad event occurs is at most roughly $q(\frac{p}{2^{n+k}})^2$. The bound is tight as long as $q \leq 2^n$ (the bound becomes $\frac{p^2}{2^{2k+n}}$).

For good transcripts τ, we need to evaluate $\frac{\Pr[\mathsf{T}_R=\tau]}{\Pr[\mathsf{T}_I=\tau]}$, the ratio of the real-world and ideal-world probabilities. As transcripts include all internal values, we can avoid the heavy counting step. On the other hand, the re-sampling method increases the number of chances to satisfy the target good transcript, i.e., $\Pr[\mathsf{T}_I = \tau]$ is increased. In the real world, all input-output tuples are defined by an ideal cipher E. In the ideal world, responses to construction queries are defined by a random permutation, and those to primitive queries are defined by an ideal cipher E, which is independent of the random permutation. Hence, the output space of the ideal world is larger than that of the real world. Naito et al. [20] proved that regarding the triple encryption, the influence of the increase can be

---

[2] This is because in the ideal world, a random permutation and the underlying ideal cipher are independently defined.

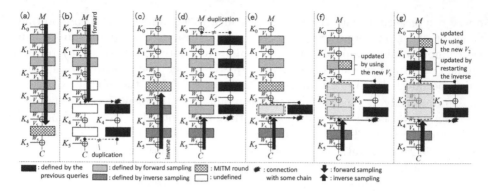

Fig. 2. Updated re-sampling method for $r = 5$. (a) Forward sampling. (b) Bad event of the forward sampling. (c) Inverse sampling. (d) Bad event of the inverse sampling. (e) Inverse sampling with a 1-chain. (f) Inverse sampling with a 2-chain. The pair (V_2, W_2) in the forward sampling has not been defined by the previous queries and is updated by the 2-chain. (g) Inverse sampling with a 2-chain. The pair (V_2, W_2) in the forward sampling were defined by some previous query and is updated by restarting the inverse sampling. For Figs. (f)(g), the left (resp. right) side of the box at the second round shows the value defined by the forward (resp. inverse) sampling.

canceled out by using the budget of the output space of the ideal world, and the ratio can be greater than or equal to 1.

4.5   Updating the Re-Sampling Method for Arbitrary Round KACs

We explain our updated re-sampling method that supports arbitrary round KACs and offers the tight bound of KACs $O\left(q\left(\frac{p+rq}{2^n}\right)^r\right)$. The procedure of defining dummy internal values in the ideal world is similar to the one for the triple encryption. For each construction query-response pair, firstly, the internal values are defined by the forward sampling, and if the forward sampling fails, then the remaining internal values are defined by the inverse sampling.

The failure probability is essential in updating the re-sampling method to longer rounds. The original method in [20] provides the bound $O\left(q\left(\frac{p}{2^{n+k}}\right)^2\right)$ for the triple encryption. This evaluation offers the bound $O\left(q\left(\frac{p}{2^n}\right)^2\right)$ for KACs as $k = 0$, which is not tight for $r \geq 3$. To obtain the tight bound for KACs, the updated method takes into account all chains involved in the inverse sampling. Here, a chain is a sequence of input-output pairs $(V_1, W_1), \ldots, (V_\ell, W_\ell)$ defined by previous queries. The key of the ℓ-chain is defined as $((W_1 \oplus V_2) \| (W_2 \oplus V_3) \| \cdots \| (W_{\ell-1} \oplus V_\ell))$.

In our updated method, even if some internal values are duplicately defined, i.e., in the inverse sampling some internal value connects with some long chain, the duplication is avoided by replacing the internal values defined by the forward sampling with those defined by the inverse sampling. We explain the method by using Fig. 2 that considers the 5-round KAC.

Firstly, as the original method, the forward sampling is performed. Figure 2(a) shows a successful case of the forward sampling, where the forward sampling starts from the first round[3] and ends with the fourth round. The input-output pair of the fifth round, which is called MITM round, is defined by $(W_5 \oplus K_4, C \oplus K_5)$. However, the forward sampling fails if an output of some round connects with a chain that offers an incompatible internal value. Then, the inverse sampling is performed. Figure 2(b) shows the failure event, where after the third round, the result V_4 $(= K_3 \oplus W_3)$ connects with a 2-chain with the key K_4, and by the output of the 2-chain and $K_5 \oplus C$, the internal value W_5 is duplicately defined. In this case, the forward sampling defines the internal values up to the second round, and the inverse sampling defines the remaining internal values. Figure 2(c) shows a successful case of the inverse sampling. The inverse sampling is performed until the fourth round. The third round is the MITM round, i.e., the input-output pair is defined by using the results of the forward and inverse samplings, i.e., $(V_3, W_3) = (K_2 \oplus W_2, K_3 \oplus V_4)$.

As the original re-sampling method, the inverse sampling fails if some internal value connects with a chain that offers duplication of some internal value. Figure 2(d) shows the failure case: the internal value W_4 defined by the inverse sampling connects with a 4-chain with keys K_1, K_2, K_3. Regarding the connection with some chain, the original re-sampling method can define compatible internal values even when in the inverse sample some internal value connects with some chain. The chain must not reach the last round in the forward sampling. Figure 2(e) exemplifies the cases: even if W_4 connects with a 1-chain, we can define compatible internal values as the chain does not reach the second round. However, the original method gives up on cases for connections with longer chains (the lengths are two or longer for the example in Fig. 2(e)).

We update the inverse sampling to salvage the cases by introducing a new procedure that updates internal values defined by the forward sampling with new values defined by the inverse sampling. Figures 2(f)(g) show examples of the updated method. In Fig. 2(f), the 2-chain reaches the second round that has been defined by the forward sampling, and the updated method replaces the previous internal value W_2 with the new one in the 2-chain. Then, the MITM round is also updated from the third round to the second one, and the new method succeeds in defining compatible internal values. Figure 2(g) is similar to Fig. 2(f), but the types of the second round are different. In Fig. 2(g), the input-output pair at the second round was defined by some previous query, and the 2-chain in the inverse sampling reaches the second round, i.e., the values V_3 from the forward sampling and from the inverse one were both fixed by some previous queries. Unlike Fig. 2(f), the value V_3 cannot be directly updated. The updated method salvages the case by going back to the round at which the input-output pair is defined by the forward sampling and is not fixed by previous queries (the

---

[3] Note that if first some internal values have been defined by previous queries, the forward sampling starts from the round at which the internal value is not defined.

first round in Fig. 2(g)). By performing the inverse sampling up to the round, the duplications can be eluded.

Regarding the bad event, as explained before, the updated inverse sampling fails if some internal value connects with a chain that reaches the first round in Fig. 2. The bad event requires avoidance of the updating procedure or connections with long chains. Our proof shows that the probability of the bad event is bounded by the tight one $O\left(q\left(\frac{(p+rq)}{2^n}\right)^r\right)$, assuming the optimal probability $\epsilon = O\left(\frac{1}{2^n}\right)$.

4.6   Evaluation for Good Transcript

Our updated re-sampling method can define dummy internal values up to the tight bound. Thus, we can avoid the heavy counting step, which is required for the ideal-world analysis for a good transcript without dummy internal values. On the other hand, as mentioned in Sect. 4.4, the inverse sampling could increase the ideal-world probability of a good transcript. We thus need to carefully evaluate the ideal-world probability so that the inverse sampling does not cause a dominant term. As the original inverse sampling, the influence of the increase can be canceled out by using the budget of the output space of the ideal world, and the ratio $\frac{\Pr[T_R=\tau]}{\Pr[T_I=\tau]}$ can be greater than or equal to 1.

5   Proof of Theorem 1

Without loss of generality, we assume that an adversary is deterministic, makes no repeated construction query to the same user, and makes no repeated primitive query.

5.1   Notations and Definitions

We use the following notations and definitions.

- q_ν: the number of construction queries to the ν-th user.
- $K^{(\nu)} = K_0^{(\nu)} \| K_1^{(\nu)} \| \cdots \| K_r^{(\nu)}$: the key of the ν-th user.
- $K_{i,j}^{(\nu)} := K_i^{(\nu)} \| \cdots \| K_j^{(\nu)}$ where $i,j \in [0,r]$. If $i = j$ then $K_{i,j}^{(\nu)} := K_i^{(\nu)}$, and if $i > j$ then $K_{i,j}^{(\nu)} := \varepsilon$.
- $(X^{(\alpha)}, Y^{(\alpha)})$: the α-th primitive query-response pair, where $Y^{(\alpha)} = \pi(X^{(\alpha)})$, and $X^{(\alpha)} = \pi^{-1}(Y^{(\alpha)})$.
- $(M^{(\nu,\alpha)}, C^{(\nu,\alpha)})$: the α-th construction query-response pair to the ν-th user.
- $W_0^{(\nu,\alpha)} := M^{(\nu,\alpha)}$ and $V_{r+1}^{(\nu,\alpha)} := C^{(\nu,\alpha)}$.
- $V_i^{(\nu,\alpha)} := K_{i-1}^{(\nu)} \oplus W_{i-1}^{(\nu,\alpha)}$ and $W_i^{(\nu,\alpha)} := \pi(V_i^{(\nu,\alpha)})$: the input and output of π at the i-th round of $\mathsf{KAC}_r[K^{(\nu)}, \pi](M^{(\nu,\alpha)})$.[4]

---

[4]   For   a   pair $(M^{(\nu,\alpha)}, C^{(\nu,\alpha)})$ of   plaintext   and   ciphertext   defined   by $\mathsf{KAC}_r^{-1}[K^{(\nu)}, \pi^{-1}](C^{(\nu,\alpha)})$, the input-output pairs of π^{-1} can be written by the definition with $\mathsf{KAC}_r[K^{(\nu)}, \pi](M^{(\nu,\alpha)})$ since $\mathsf{KAC}_r^{-1}[K^{(\nu)}, \pi^{-1}](C^{(\nu,\alpha)})$ is the inverse of $\mathsf{KAC}_r[K^{(\nu)}, \pi](M^{(\nu,\alpha)})$.

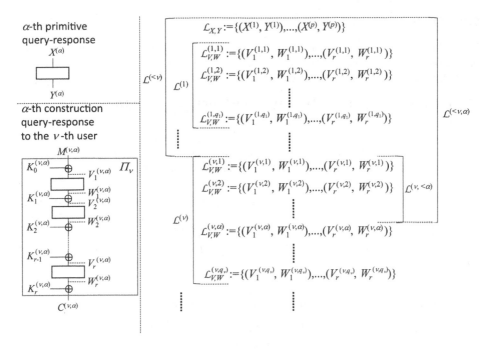

Fig. 3. Diagrams of primitive query-response pairs, internal values for construction queries, and the sets $\mathcal{L}_{X,Y}$, $\mathcal{L}_{V,W}^{(\nu,\alpha)}$, $\mathcal{L}_{V,W}^{(\nu,<\alpha)}$, $\mathcal{L}^{(<\nu)}$, and $\mathcal{L}^{(<\nu,\alpha)}$.

- $\mathcal{L}_K := \{K^{(\nu)} \mid \nu \in [u]\}$: the set of user's keys.
- $\mathcal{L}_{X,Y} := \{(X^{(\alpha)}, Y^{(\alpha)}) \mid \alpha \in [p]\}$: the set of primitive query-response pairs.
- $\mathcal{L}_{V,W} := \{(V_i^{(\nu,\alpha)}, W_i^{(\nu,\alpha)}) \mid \nu \in [u], \alpha \in [q_\nu], i \in [r]\}$: the set of all input-output pairs defined by construction queries.
- $\mathcal{L}^{(<\nu,\alpha)}$: the set of primitive query-responses, input-output pairs from the first to $(\nu - 1)$-th users, and input-output pairs up to the $(\alpha - 1)$-th construction query to the ν-th user.
- $\mathcal{L}^{(<\nu)} := \mathcal{L}^{(<\nu,1)}$: the set of primitive query-responses and input-output pairs defined by construction queries from the first to $(\nu - 1)$-th users.
- $\mathcal{L}_{V,W}^{(\nu,\alpha)} := \{(V_i^{(\nu,\alpha)}, W_i^{(\nu,\alpha)}) \mid \alpha \in [q_\nu], i \in [r], (V_i^{(\nu,\alpha)}, W_i^{(\nu,\alpha)}) \notin \mathcal{L}^{(<\nu,\alpha)}\}$.[5]
- $\mathcal{L}_{V,W}^{(\nu,<\alpha)} := \bigcup_{\beta \in [\alpha-1]} \mathcal{L}_{V,W}^{(\nu,\beta)}$: the set of fresh input-output pairs defined from the first to $(\alpha - 1)$-th construction queries to the ν-th user.
- Query stage: the stage that an adversary makes queries.
- Decision stage: the stage after the query stage.

Diagrams of primitive query-response pairs, internal values for construction queries, the sets $\mathcal{L}_{X,Y}$, $\mathcal{L}_{V,W}^{(\nu,\alpha)}$, $\mathcal{L}_{V,W}^{(\nu,<\alpha)}$, $\mathcal{L}^{(<\nu)}$, and $\mathcal{L}^{(<\nu,\alpha)}$ are given in Fig. 3.

---

[5] In the ideal world, the pairs are freshly defined at the α-th construction query by our algorithm defined in Sect. 5.3.

5.2   Definition of Chain

We define bad events by using chains which are sequences of input-output pairs of π. For each α-th construction query to the ν-th user, the chain is defined from $\mathcal{L}^{(<\nu,\alpha)}$. The definition is given below.

Definition 2 (Chains for the α-th construction query to the ν-th user).
A sequence of ℓ pairs in $\mathcal{L}^{(<\nu,\alpha)}$, $((X_1, Y_1), \ldots, (X_\ell, Y_\ell))$, is called an ℓ-chain from $\mathcal{L}^{(<\nu,\alpha)}$. $(Y_1 \oplus X_2)\|(Y_2 \oplus X_3)\| \cdots \|(Y_{\ell-1} \oplus X_\ell)$ is called a key of the chain. If $\ell = 1$, then the key is ε. X_1 is called a head of the chain, and Y_ℓ is called a tail of the chain. Let ℓ-$\mathbf{Chain}[\mathcal{L}^{(<\nu,\alpha)}, K^*]$ be the set of all ℓ-chains from $\mathcal{L}^{(<\nu,\alpha)}$ whose keys are equal to $K^* \in \{0,1\}^{(\ell-1)n}$. Let ℓ-$\mathrm{Chain}^H[\mathcal{L}^{(<\nu,\alpha)}, K^*]$ be an ℓ-chain from $\mathcal{L}^{(<\nu,\alpha)}$ whose key and head are respectively equal to K^* and H. If there does not exist such chain or $\ell \leq 0$, then ℓ-$\mathrm{Chain}^H[\mathcal{L}^{(<\nu,\alpha)}, K^*] := \varepsilon$. Let ℓ-$\mathrm{Chain}_T[\mathcal{L}^{(<\nu,\alpha)}, K^*]$ be an ℓ-chain from $\mathcal{L}^{(<\nu,\alpha)}$ whose key and tail are respectively equal to K^* and T. If there does not exist such chain or $\ell \leq 0$, then ℓ-$\mathrm{Chain}_T[\mathcal{L}^{(<\nu,\alpha)}, K^*] := \varepsilon$.

5.3   Dummy Internal Values in the Ideal World

In our poof, by using Algorithm 2, dummy keys and dummy internal input-output pairs of the ideal world are defined in the decision stage. $K^{(\nu)}$ is a dummy key of the ν-th user and $(V_i^{(\nu,\alpha)}, W_i^{(\nu,\alpha)})$ is an internal input-output pair at the i-th round of the α-th construction query to the ν-th user. Note that for the sake of simplicity, the superscript symbol ν on the values defined in the algorithm is omitted, i.e., $M^{(\alpha)}$, $C^{(\alpha)}$, K_i, $V_i^{(\alpha)}$, and $W_i^{(\alpha)}$ in the algorithm respectively represent $M^{(\nu,\alpha)}$, $C^{(\nu,\alpha)}$, $K_i^{(\nu)}$, $V_i^{(\nu,\alpha)}$, and $W_i^{(\nu,\alpha)}$. Figure 4 illustrates the algorithm.

In this algorithm, dummy internal input-output pairs $(V_i^{(\alpha)}, W_i^{(\alpha)})$ are defined in the order of user numbers from 1 to u. r_1 (resp. r_2) is the round number such that input-output pairs up to the r_1-th (resp. from the r_2-th) round have been defined before the α-th loop. The remaining input-output pairs are defined by the updated re-sampling method. The forward sampling is from the steps 11 to 17 (Fig. 4(a)), and the inverse one is from the steps 18 to 31 (Fig. 4(b)(c)(d)).

In the forward sampling, input-output pairs are defined up to the $(r_2 - 1)$-th round and are kept as temporary pairs (V_i', W_i'). If the forward sampling fails, i.e., the condition on Step 14 is satisfied (V_{i+1}' connects with some chain with the user's subkey that influences the r_2-th round; see Fig. 4(a)[6]), then the round number where the sampling fails is recorded on r_m. Then, the inverse sampling is performed. Note that if the forward sampling succeeds, then the inverse one is not performed.

---

[6] In the forward (resp. inverse) sampling, the internal value after the 4th (before the 5th) round connects with the 2-chain (resp. 4-chain) with the user's subkeys that influences the 7th (resp. 1st) round. Since the pair at the 7th (resp. 1st) round is fixed by some previous query, the duplication of the internal value cannot be fixed. .

Algorithm 2. Procedure to define internal values in the ideal world

---

1: $\mathsf{flag}_{\mathsf{sample}} \leftarrow \mathsf{false}$

2: **for** $\nu \in \overrightarrow{[u]}$ **do**   ▷ The symbol "ν" is omitted from the following values.

3:     $K \xleftarrow{\$} \mathcal{K}$ ▷ $K = K_0\|K_1\|\cdots\|K_r$

4:     **for** $\alpha \in \overrightarrow{[q_\nu]}$ **do**   ▷ Define internal pairs of the α-th construction query.

5:         $r_1 \leftarrow \max\left(\left\{i \in [r] \mid i\text{-Chain}^{M^{(\alpha)}\oplus K_0}[\mathcal{L}^{(<\nu,\alpha)}, K_{1,i-1}] \neq \varepsilon\right\} \cup \{0\}\right)$

6:         $r_2 \leftarrow \min\Big(\left\{i \in [r] \mid (r - i + 1)\text{-Chain}_{K_r\oplus C^{(\alpha)}}[\mathcal{L}^{(<\nu,\alpha)}, K_{i,r-1}] \neq \varepsilon\right\}$
$$\cup\{r+1\}\Big)$$

7:         $W_0^{(\alpha)} \leftarrow M^{(\alpha)}; V_{r+1}^{(\alpha)} \leftarrow C^{(\alpha)}$

8:         **for** $i \in \overrightarrow{[r_1]}$ **do** $V_i^{(\alpha)} \leftarrow K_{i-1} \oplus W_{i-1}^{(\alpha)}; W_i^{(\alpha)} \leftarrow \pi(V_i^{(\alpha)})$ **end for**

9:         **for** $i \in \overleftarrow{[r_2,r]}$ **do** $W_i^{(\alpha)} \leftarrow K_i \oplus V_{i+1}^{(\alpha)}; V_i^{(\alpha)} \leftarrow \pi^{-1}(W_i^{(\alpha)})$ **end for**

10:         $V_{r_1+1}' \leftarrow K_{r_1} \oplus W_{r_1}^{(\alpha)}; W_{r_2-1}^* \leftarrow K_{r_2-1} \oplus V_{r_2}^{(\alpha)}; r_m \leftarrow r_2 - 1$

11:         **for** $i \in \overrightarrow{[r_1+1,r_2-2]}$ **do**   ▷ Forward sampling

12:             $W_i' \leftarrow \mathcal{L}_0^2[V_i']$; **if** $\mathcal{L}_0^2[V_i'] = \varepsilon$ **then** $W_i' \xleftarrow{\$} \{0,1\}^n \backslash \mathcal{L}_0^2$ **end if**

13:             $V_{i+1}' \leftarrow K_i \oplus W_i'$

14:             **if** $(r_2 - i - 1)\text{-Chain}^{V_{i+1}'}[\mathcal{L}^{(<\nu,\alpha)}, K_{i+1,r_2-2}] \neq \varepsilon$ **then**

15:                 $r_m \leftarrow i$; **goto** Step 18

16:             **end if**

17:         **end for**

18:         **for** $i \in \overleftarrow{[r_m+1,r_2-1]}$ **do**   ▷ Inverse sampling

19:             $V_i^* \leftarrow \mathcal{L}_0^1[W_i^*]$; **if** $\mathcal{L}_0^1[W_i^*] = \varepsilon$ **then** $V_i^* \xleftarrow{\$} \{0,1\}^n \backslash \mathcal{L}_0^1$ **end if**

20:             $W_{i-1}^* \leftarrow K_{i-1} \oplus V_i^*$

21:             $\rho \leftarrow \min\Big(\{r+1\} \cup \Big\{\rho^* \in [r_1+1, r_m] \mid$
$$(i - \rho^*)\text{-Chain}_{W_{i-1}^*}[\mathcal{L}^{(<\nu,\alpha)}, K_{\rho^*,i-2}] \neq \varepsilon\Big\}\Big)$$

22:             **if** $\rho = r_1 + 1$ **then** $\mathsf{fail}_{\mathsf{sample}} \leftarrow \mathsf{true}$ **end if**

23:             **if** $\rho \neq r_1 + 1 \wedge \rho \neq r + 1$ **then**

24:                 **for** $j \in \overleftarrow{[\rho, i-1]}$ **do** $V_j^* \leftarrow \pi^{-1}(W_j^*); W_{j-1}^* \leftarrow K_{j-1} \oplus V_j^*$ **end for**

25:                 **if** $(V_{\rho-1}', W_{\rho-1}') \in \mathcal{L}^{(<\nu,\alpha)}$ **then**   ▷ Duplication for $W_{\rho-1}$

26:                     $r_m \leftarrow \min\Big\{j \in [r_1+1, \rho-1] \mid$
$$(\rho - j)\text{-Chain}_{W_{\rho-1}'}[\mathcal{L}^{(<\nu,\alpha)}, K_{j,\rho-2}] \neq \varepsilon\Big\} - 1$$

27:                     **goto** Step 18

28:                 **end if**

29:                 $r_m \leftarrow \rho - 1$; **goto** Step 32

30:             **end if**

31:         **end for**

32:         **for** $i \in \overrightarrow{[r_1+1,r_m-1]}$ **do** $V_i^{(\alpha)} \leftarrow V_i'; W_i^{(\alpha)} \leftarrow W_i'$ **end for**

33:         **for** $i \in \overleftarrow{[r_m+1,r_2-1]}$ **do** $V_i^{(\alpha)} \leftarrow V_i^*; W_i^{(\alpha)} \leftarrow W_i^*$ **end for**

34:         $V_{r_m}^{(\alpha)} \leftarrow K_{r_m-1} \oplus W_{r_m-1}^{(\alpha)}; W_{r_m}^{(\alpha)} \leftarrow K_{r_m} \oplus V_{r_m+1}^{(\alpha)}$

35:         **for** $i \in \overrightarrow{[r]}$ **do** $\mathcal{L}_0 \leftarrow \mathcal{L}_0 \cup \{(V_i^{(\alpha)}, W_i^{(\alpha)})\}$ **end for**

36:     **end for**

37: **end for**

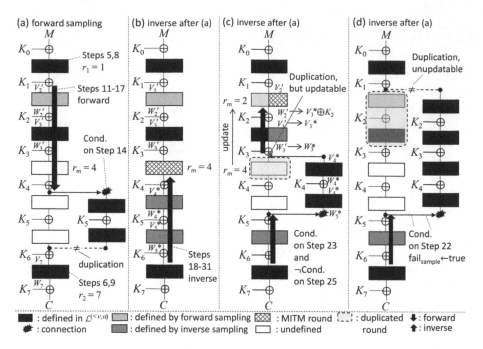

Fig. 4. Algorithm 2 with $r = 7$, $r_1 = 1$, and $r_2 = 7$. (a) Forward sampling with the bad event where V_5 connects with a 2-chain with the key K_5 that influences the r_2-th round. (b) Inverse sampling. (c) Inverse sampling with a 2-chain and with updating W_3. For the second and third rounds, the left (resp. right) side of the box shows the value defined by the forward (resp. inverse) sampling. (d) Bad event for the updated re-sampling method where W_5 connects with a 4-chain with the key $K_2\|K_3\|K_4$ that influences the r_1-th round.

In the inverse sampling, input-output pairs are defined from the $(r_2 - 1)$-th round down to the $(r_m + 1)$-th one, and are kept as temporary pairs (V_i^*, W_i^*). The step 21 searches a chain with the tail W_{i-1}^* that reaches the r_m-th round. If there is no such chain, then the round number is defined as $\rho := r + 1$. Throughout the inverse sampling, if there is no such chain, then input-output pairs from the $(r_2 - 1)$-th round down to the $(r_m + 1)$-th one are defined, and a pair at the r_m-th round, called "meet-in-the-middle (or MITM)" one, is defined by using the results of the forward and inverse samplings (See Fig. 4(b)). If the condition on Step 22 is satisfied, i.e., W_{i-1}^* connects with some chain with the user's subkeys that influences the r_1-th round (See Fig. 4(d) and the footnote 6), then the internal value W_{r_1} is duplicately defined, and the inverse sampling fails. On the other hand, if the condition is not satisfied, then we can continue the inverse sampling. After the condition on Step 23 is satisfied, i.e., W_{i-1}^* connects with some chain that reaches some round defined in the forward sampling but does not influence the r_1-th round, the input-output pairs in the chain are kept as temporary pairs (V_i^*, W_i^*), and r_m is updated to $\rho - 1$ in Step 29. If the condition on Step 25 is satisfied, i.e., the internal value V_ρ is duplicately defined, then to avoid the duplication, the algorithm updates r_m to the round number whose pair is not in $\mathcal{L}^{(<\nu,\alpha)}$, and continues the inverse sampling until all pairs are defined or the sampling fails (See Fig. 4(c)).

Finally, the internal input-output pairs are defined by using the temporary values (V_i', W_i') for $i \in [r_1 + 1, r_m - 1]$ and (V_i^*, W_i^*) for $i \in [r_m + 1, r_2 - 1]$, and the input-output pair $(V_{r_m}^{(\alpha)}, W_{r_m}^{(\alpha)})$ at the r_m-th round is defined by using the results of the forward and inverse sampling. Then, these pairs are added to the RP's table $\mathcal{L}_0$.[7]

5.4 Adversary's View

In the decision stage, all user's keys and all internal input-output pairs are revealed to an adversary **A**. Hence, before outputting a decision bit, **A** obtains a transcript τ which consists of

- (dummy) user's keys $\mathcal{L}_K$,
- primitive query-response tuples $\mathcal{L}_{X,Y}$, and
- (dummy) internal input-output pairs $\mathcal{L}_{V,W}$.

Note that construction query-response pairs can be obtained by combining $\mathcal{L}_{V,W}$ with $\mathcal{L}_K$, and thus are omitted.

5.5 Bad Events and Definitions of Good and Bad Transcripts

We define bad events below.

- Chain_0: $\exists \nu \in [u], \alpha \in [q_\nu]$ s.t. $r\text{-}\mathsf{Chain}^{K_0^{(\nu)} \oplus M^{(\nu,\alpha)}}[\mathcal{L}^{(<\nu,\alpha)}, K_{1,r-1}^{(\nu)}] \neq \varepsilon$.
- Chain_i $(i \in [r-1])$: $\exists \nu \in [u], \alpha \in [q_\nu]$ s.t.
  - $(r-i)\text{-}\mathsf{Chain}^{K_0^{(\nu)} \oplus M^{(\nu,\alpha)}}[\mathcal{L}^{(<\nu,\alpha)}, K_{1,r-i-1}^{(\nu)}] \neq \varepsilon$ and
  - $i\text{-}\mathsf{Chain}_{K_r^{(\nu)} \oplus C^{(\nu,\alpha)}}[\mathcal{L}^{(<\nu,\alpha)}, K_{r-i+1,r-1}^{(\nu)}] \neq \varepsilon$
- Chain_r: $\exists \nu \in [u], \alpha \in [q_\nu]$ s.t. $r\text{-}\mathsf{Chain}_{K_r^{(\nu)} \oplus C^{(\nu,\alpha)}}[\mathcal{L}^{(<\nu,\alpha)}, K_{1,r-1}^{(\nu)}] \neq \varepsilon$.
- $\mathsf{Coll}_{V,W}$: $\exists \nu \in [u], \alpha \in [q_\nu], i, j \in [r]$ s.t. $i \neq j$, $(V_i^{(\nu,\alpha)}, W_i^{(\nu,\alpha)}) \in \mathcal{L}_{V,W}^{(\nu,\alpha)}$, $(V_j^{(\nu,\alpha)}, W_j^{(\nu,\alpha)}) \in \mathcal{L}_{V,W}^{(\nu,\alpha)}$, and $\left(V_i^{(\nu,\alpha)} = V_j^{(\nu,\alpha)} \vee W_i^{(\nu,\alpha)} = W_j^{(\nu,\alpha)} \right)$.
- Fail_π: $\exists \nu_1, \nu_2 \in [u], \alpha_1 \in [q_{\nu_1}], \alpha_2 \in [q_{\nu_2}], i_1, i_2 \in [r]$ s.t. $\left(V_{i_1}^{(\nu_1,\alpha_1)} = V_{i_2}^{(\nu_2,\alpha_2)} \wedge W_{i_1}^{(\nu_1,\alpha_1)} \neq W_{i_2}^{(\nu_2,\alpha_2)} \right)$ or $\left(V_{i_1}^{(\nu_1,\alpha_1)} \neq V_{i_2}^{(\nu_2,\alpha_2)} \wedge W_{i_1}^{(\nu_1,\alpha_1)} = W_{i_2}^{(\nu_2,\alpha_2)} \right)$

---

[7] Note that in a loop of Algorithm 2, each fresh value is sampled from a set including values defined in the same loop. Hence, the sampling method probabilistically yields a collision within the same loop. The collision event is handled in the bad transcript analysis. On the other hand, the sampling method contributes to obtaining a nice ratio for a good transcript.

Let bad = $\mathsf{Chain}_0 \vee \mathsf{Chain}_1 \vee \cdots \vee \mathsf{Chain}_r \vee \mathsf{Coll}_{V,W} \vee \mathsf{Fail}_\pi$. Note that the condition for the event $\mathsf{fail}_{\mathsf{sample}}$ is satisfied in only the ideal world. Then, $\mathcal{T}_{\mathsf{bad}}$ is a set of transcripts that satisfy bad, and $\mathcal{T}_{\mathsf{good}} := \mathcal{T} \backslash \mathcal{T}_{\mathsf{bad}}$.

The bad events Chain_i for $i \in [0, r]$ consider the case that for some $\nu \in [u]$ and $\alpha \in [q_\nu]$, all the internal values of the α-th construction query to the ν-th user have been defined before the construction query. Under the events, there is no randomness for the α-th construction query and thus the difference between the real and ideal worlds arises. The event $\mathsf{Coll}_{V,W}$ considers a collision in internal inputs or outputs defined in the same construction query. The bad event Fail_π is an event that breaks the property of a permutation. Note that the event never occurs in the real world.

5.6   Deriving the Upper-Bound in Theorem 1

In Sect. 5.7, we evaluate the probability for the bad transcripts in the ideal world $\Pr[\mathsf{T}_I \in \mathcal{T}_{\mathsf{bad}}]$, and show the upper-bound in Eq. (3). In Sect. 5.8, we evaluate the ratio of the real-world and ideal-word probabilities for the good transcripts, and prove that for any good transcript τ, $\frac{\Pr[\mathsf{T}_R = \tau]}{\Pr[\mathsf{T}_I = \tau]} \geq 1$. Using these bounds, we obtain the upper-bound in Theorem 1.

5.7   Upper-Bounding $\Pr[\mathsf{T}_I \in \mathcal{T}_{\mathsf{bad}}]$

For $\mathsf{E} \in \mathbf{E} := \{\mathsf{Chain}_0, \ldots, \mathsf{Chain}_r, \mathsf{Coll}_{V,W}, \mathsf{Fail}_\pi\}$, let $\Pr[\mathsf{E}]$ be the probability that E occurs before the other bad events $\mathbf{E} \backslash \{\mathsf{E}\}$. We then have

$$\Pr[\mathsf{T}_I \in \mathcal{T}_{\mathsf{bad}}] = \Pr[\mathsf{bad}] \leq \left(\sum_{i \in (r)} \Pr[\mathsf{Chain}_i] \right) + \Pr[\mathsf{Coll}_{V,W}] + \Pr[\mathsf{Fail}_\pi] \ ,$$

and evaluate these probabilities below.[8] The upper-bounds are given in Eqs. (8), (9), (10), (11) and (13). Using the bounds, we have

$$\Pr[\mathsf{T}_I \in \mathcal{T}_{\mathsf{bad}}] \leq \left(\frac{4^r r^4}{12} + r + 1 \right) \cdot q(\sigma\delta)^r + 2r^2 \cdot \frac{q}{2^n} \ . \tag{3}$$

Upper-Bounding Collision Probabilities for $\mathcal{L}^{(<\nu,\alpha)}$. Before evaluating the probabilities of the bad events, we show upper-bounds of collision probabilities involving $\mathcal{L}^{(<\nu,\alpha)}$, subkeys, $M^{(\nu,\alpha)}$, and $C^{(\nu,\alpha)}$. These upper-bounds are used to evaluate the probability of constructing a chain with user's subkeys considered in the bad events.

---

[8] The bound comes from the fact that if bad occurs, then one of $\mathbf{E}$ occurs before the other bad events occur.

Lemma 2. *Let* $\delta = \max\left\{\epsilon, \frac{2}{2^n}\right\}$. *Consider* $\nu \in [u]$, $\alpha \in [q_\nu]$, $2j+2$ *pairs* (S,T), (S',T'), (S_1,T_1), $\ldots$, $(S_{2j},T_{2j}) \in \mathcal{L}^{(<\nu,\alpha)}$, *and* $a_1, \ldots, a_j \in [r-1]$ *such that* $0 \le j \le r-1$ *and* $a_1, \ldots, a_j$ *are all distinct. Then, we have*

$$\Pr\left[\left(\forall i \in [j] : T_{2i-1} \oplus S_{2i} = K_{a_i}^{(\nu)}\right)\right] \le \delta^j, \tag{4}$$

$$\Pr\left[\left(\forall i \in [j] : T_{2i-1} \oplus S_{2i} = K_{a_i}^{(\nu)}\right) \wedge \left(M^{(\nu,\alpha)} \oplus S = K_0^{(\nu)}\right)\right] \le \delta^{j+1}, \tag{5}$$

$$\Pr\left[\left(\forall i \in [j] : T_{2i-1} \oplus S_{2i} = K_{a_i}^{(\nu)}\right) \wedge \left(C^{(\nu,\alpha)} \oplus T' = K_r^{(\nu)}\right)\right] \le \delta^{j+1}, \tag{6}$$

$$\Pr\left[\left(\forall i \in [j] : T_{2i-1} \oplus S_{2i} = K_{a_i}^{(\nu)}\right) \wedge \left(M^{(\nu,\alpha)} \oplus S = K_0^{(\nu)}\right)\right.$$
$$\left. \wedge \left(C^{(\nu,\alpha)} \oplus T' = K_r^{(\nu)}\right)\right] \le \delta^{\min\{j+2,r\}}. \tag{7}$$

In the above equations, we take into account the cases that several pairs are the same, as we consider KAC with a single permutation. Since the equations include r-wise independent subkeys, we can ensure that the exponents of the bounds are equal to the number of equations that are less than or equal to r. Note that $\mathcal{L}^{(<\nu,\alpha)} = \mathcal{L}^{(<\nu)} \cup \mathcal{L}_{V,W}^{(\nu,<\alpha)}$ is satisfied, and $\mathcal{L}_{V,W}^{(\nu,<\alpha)}$ is defined after the key $K^{(\nu)}$ is defined. Hence, for each equation, if there is a pair in $\mathcal{L}_{V,W}^{(\nu,<\alpha)}$, then instead of the subkey, the randomness of the pair is used, which is chosen uniformly at random from at least $2^n - \sigma \ge 2^{n-1}$ elements in $\{0,1\}^n$. The detailed proof is given in Subsect. 5.9.

Upper-Bounding $\Pr[\mathsf{Chain}_0]$. The number of r-chains from $\mathcal{L}^{(<\nu,\alpha)}$ is at most σ^r. For each r-chain, the probability that the key and the head are respectively equal to $K_{1,r-1}^{(\nu)}$ and $K_0^{(\nu)} \oplus M^{(\nu,\alpha)}$ is at most δ^r by Eq. (5) in Lemma 2. Hence, for each ν, α, we have $p_{0,\nu,\alpha} := \Pr\left[r\text{-Chain}^{K_0^{(\nu)} \oplus M^{(\nu,\alpha)}}[\mathcal{L}^{(<\nu,\alpha)}, K_{1,r-1}^{(\nu)}] \ne \varepsilon\right] \le (\sigma\delta)^r$. Using the bound, we have

$$\Pr[\mathsf{Chain}_0] \le \sum_{\nu \in [u]} \sum_{\alpha \in [q_\nu]} p_{0,\nu,\alpha} \le \sum_{\nu \in [u]} \sum_{\alpha \in [q_\nu]} (\sigma\delta)^r = q(\sigma\delta)^r. \tag{8}$$

Upper-Bounding $\Pr[\mathsf{Chain}_r]$. The evaluation of $\Pr[\mathsf{Chain}_r]$ is the same as that of $\Pr[\mathsf{Chain}_0]$. In this evaluation, a tail collision (a collision with $K_r^{(\nu)} \oplus C^{(\nu,\alpha)}$) is considered instead of the head collision in Chain_0 (the collision with $K_0^{(\nu)} \oplus M^{(\nu,\alpha)}$). Using Eq. (6) in Lemma 2, we have

$$\Pr[\mathsf{Chain}_r] \le q(\sigma\delta)^r. \tag{9}$$

Upper-Bounding $\Pr[\mathsf{Chain}_i]$ ($i \in [r-1]$). We fix $i \in [r-1]$ and evaluate $\Pr[\mathsf{Chain}_i]$.

We fix $\nu \in [u]$ and $\alpha \in [q_\nu]$. The number of $(r-i)$-chains from $\mathcal{L}^{(<\nu,\alpha)}$ is at most σ^{r-i}, and the number of i-chains from $\mathcal{L}^{(<\nu,\alpha)}$ is at most σ^i. For each pair of $(r-i)$-chain and i-chain, the probability that the key and the head of the $(r-i)$-chain are respectively equal to $K_{1,i-1}^{(\nu)}$ and $K_0^{(\nu)} \oplus M^{(\nu,\alpha)}$; and the key and the tail of i-chain are respectively equal to $K_{i+1,r-1}^{(\nu)}$ and $K_r^{(\nu)} \oplus C^{(\nu,\alpha)}$ is at most $(\sigma\delta)^r$, by using Eq. (7) in Lemma 2. Hence, we have

$$p_{i,\nu,\alpha} := \Pr\Big[(r-i)\text{-Chain}^{K_0^{(\nu)} \oplus M^{(\nu,\alpha)}}[\mathcal{L}^{(<\nu,\alpha)}, K_{1,r-i-1}^{(\nu)}] \neq \varepsilon$$
$$\wedge\ i\text{-Chain}_{K_r^{(\nu)} \oplus C^{(\nu,\alpha)}}[\mathcal{L}^{(<\nu,\alpha)}, K_{r-i+1,r-1}^{(\nu)}] \neq \varepsilon\Big] \leq (\sigma\delta)^r.$$

Using the bound, we have

$$\Pr[\mathsf{Chain}_i] \leq \sum_{\nu \in [u]} \sum_{\alpha \in [q_\nu]} p_{i,\nu,\alpha} \leq q\,(\sigma\delta)^r \tag{10}$$

Upper-Bounding $\Pr[\mathsf{Coll}_{V,W}]$. Fix $\nu \in [u], \alpha \in [q_\nu], i, j \in [r]$ s.t. $(V_i^{(\nu,\alpha)}, W_i^{(\nu,\alpha)}) \in \mathcal{L}_{V,W}^{(\nu,\alpha)}$ and $(V_j^{(\nu,\alpha)}, W_j^{(\nu,\alpha)}) \in \mathcal{L}_{V,W}^{(\nu,\alpha)}$.

We first evaluate $\Pr[V_i^{(\nu,\alpha)} = V_j^{(\nu,\alpha)}]$. Without loss of generality, we assume that $V_j^{(\nu,\alpha)}$ is defined after $V_i^{(\nu,\alpha)}$ is defined. Then, $j \neq 1$ is satisfied, since $V_j^{(\nu,\alpha)} = M^{(\nu,\alpha)} \oplus K_j^{(\nu)}$. Since $V_j^{(\nu,\alpha)} = W_{j-1}^{(\nu,\alpha)} \oplus K_{j-1}^{(\nu)}$ and $V_j^{(\nu,\alpha)}$ or $W_{j-1}^{(\nu,\alpha)}$ is chosen uniformly at random from at least $2^n - \sigma \geq 2^{n-1}$ elements in $\{0,1\}^n$, we have $\Pr[V_i^{(\nu,\alpha)} = V_j^{(\nu,\alpha)}] \leq \frac{2}{2^n}$.

We next evaluate $\Pr[W_i^{(\nu,\alpha)} = W_j^{(\nu,\alpha)}]$. Without loss of generality, we assume that $W_j^{(\nu,\alpha)}$ is defined after $W_i^{(\nu,\alpha)}$ is defined. Then, $j \neq r$ is satisfied, since $W_j^{(\nu,\alpha)} = C^{(\nu,\alpha)} \oplus K_j^{(\nu)}$. $W_j^{(\nu,\alpha)} = V_{j+1}^{(\nu,\alpha)} \oplus K_j^{(\nu)}$ is satisfied and $W_j^{(\nu,\alpha)}$ or $V_{j+1}^{(\nu,\alpha)}$ is chosen uniformly at random from at least 2^{n-1} elements in $\{0,1\}^n$. Using the randomness of $W_j^{(\nu,\alpha)}$, we have $\Pr[W_i^{(\nu,\alpha)} = W_j^{(\nu,\alpha)}] \leq \frac{2}{2^n}$.

Using these bounds, we have

$$\Pr[\mathsf{Coll}_{V,W}] \leq \sum_{\nu \in [u]} \sum_{\alpha \in [q_\nu]} 2 \cdot \binom{r}{2} \cdot \frac{2}{2^n} \leq 2r^2 \cdot \frac{q}{2^n}\ . \tag{11}$$

Upper-Bounding $\Pr[\mathsf{Fail}_\pi]$. In this proof, we use the following lemma. The proof is given in Subsect. 5.10.

Lemma 3. *Assume that* $\mathsf{Chain}_0, \ldots, \mathsf{Chain}_r$, *and* $\mathsf{Coll}_{V,W}$ *do not occur.* Fail_π *occurs if and only if* $\mathsf{fail}_{\mathsf{sample}}$ *becomes* true.

Hence, we evaluate $\Pr[\mathsf{fail}_{\mathsf{sample}}]$, the probability that $\mathsf{fail}_{\mathsf{sample}}$ becomes true under the assumption that $\mathsf{Chain}_0, \ldots, \mathsf{Chain}_r$, and $\mathsf{Coll}_{V,W}$ do not occur.

For $\nu \in [u]$ and $\alpha \in [q_\nu]$, let $\mathsf{fail}_{\mathsf{sample}}(\nu, \alpha)$ be an event that $\mathsf{fail}_{\mathsf{sample}}$ occurs for the α-th loop of the ν-th user in Algorithm 2. The upper-bound of $\Pr[\mathsf{fail}_{\mathsf{sample}}(\nu, \alpha)]$ is given in Eq. (13), which gives

$$\Pr[\mathsf{Fail}_\pi] \leq \Pr[\mathsf{fail}_{\mathsf{sample}}] \leq \sum_{\nu \in [u]} \sum_{\alpha \in [q_\nu]} \Pr[\mathsf{fail}_{\mathsf{sample}}(\nu, \alpha)]$$

$$\leq \sum_{\nu \in [u]} \sum_{\alpha \in [q_\nu]} \frac{4^r r^4}{12} \cdot (\sigma\delta)^r = \frac{4^r r^4}{12} \cdot q\,(\sigma\delta)^r. \tag{12}$$

Fix $\nu \in [u]$ and $\alpha \in [q_\nu]$, and evaluate the probability $\Pr[\mathsf{fail}_{\mathsf{sample}}(\nu, \alpha)]$. In this evaluation, we first fix round numbers r_1, r_2, and r_f, and sets of round numbers $\mathcal{R}_f$ and $\mathcal{R}_i$ such that $\mathcal{R}_f \cup \mathcal{R}_i = [r_1 + 1, r_f]$. r_1 and r_2 are the (target) round numbers defined on the α-th loop of the ν-th user in Algorithm 2. r_f is the (target) round number at which forward sampling fails, i.e., the condition on Step 14 is satisfied of Algorithm 2. $\mathcal{R}_f$ and $\mathcal{R}_i$ are respectively (target) non-fresh round numbers defined by the forward and inverse samplings, i.e., for each $i \in \mathcal{R}_f$ (resp. $i \in \mathcal{R}_i$), the sampling satisfies $(V_i', W_i') \in \mathcal{L}^{(<\nu, \alpha)}$ (resp. $(V_i^*, W_i^*) \in \mathcal{L}^{(<\nu, \alpha)}$). We then consider the following conditions C1-C4. If $\mathsf{fail}_{\mathsf{sample}}(\nu, \alpha)$ occurs, then for some r_1, r_2, r_f, $\mathcal{R}_f$, and $\mathcal{R}_i$ such that $\mathcal{R}_f \cup \mathcal{R}_i = [r_1 + 1, r_f]$, these conditions are satisfied. The condition C1 (resp. C2) implies that internal input-output pairs up to the r_1-th round (resp. from the r_2-th round) have been defined before the α-th loop. The condition C3 implies that the forward sampling fails at the r_f-th round. The conditions C4 and C5 imply that the inverse sampling fails. If $\mathsf{fail}_{\mathsf{sample}}(\nu, \alpha)$ occurs, then there is no MITM round, and thus we have $\mathcal{R}_f \cup \mathcal{R}_i = [r_1 + 1, r_f]$. See Fig. 5 for these conditions. Note that in the following evaluation, the superscript symbol ν is omitted except for the set $\mathcal{L}^{(<\nu, \alpha)}$.

- C1: $r_1\text{-Chain}^{M^{(\alpha)} \oplus K_0}[\mathcal{L}^{(<\nu, \alpha)}, K_{1, r_1 - 1}] \neq \varepsilon$
- C2: $(r - r_2 + 1)\text{-Chain}_{C^{(\alpha)} \oplus K_r}[\mathcal{L}^{(<\nu, \alpha)}, K_{r_2, r-1}] \neq \varepsilon$
- C3: $(r_2 - r_f - 1)\text{-Chain}^{K_{r_f} \oplus W_{r_f}'}[\mathcal{L}^{(<\nu, \alpha)}, K_{r_f + 1, r_2 - 2}] \neq \varepsilon$
- C4: $\forall i \in \mathcal{R}_f : (V_i', W_i') \in \mathcal{L}^{(<\nu, \alpha)}$
- C5: $\forall i \in \mathcal{R}_i : (V_i^*, W_i^*) \in \mathcal{L}^{(<\nu, \alpha)}$.

Regarding the condition C1, each r_1-chain has r_1 equations (2 equations in Fig. 5). Using Eq. (5) in Lemma 2, we have $\Pr[\text{C1}] \leq (\sigma \delta)^{r_1}$.

Regarding the condition C2, each $(r - r_2 + 1)$-chain has $r - r_2 + 1$ equations (1 equation in Fig. 5). Using Eq. (6) in Lemma 2, we have $\Pr[\text{C2}] \leq (\sigma \delta)^{r - r_2 + 1}$.

Regarding the condition C3, each $(r_2 - r_f - 1)$-chain has $(r_2 - r_f - 2)$ equations (1 equation in Fig. 5). As W_{r_f}' is chosen uniformly at random from at least $2^n - \sigma \geq 2^{n-1}$ elements in $\{0, 1\}^n$, for each $(r_2 - r_f - 1)$-chain, the probability that W_{r_f}' is equal to the head of the $(r_2 - r_f - 1)$-chain is at most $\frac{2}{2^n}$. Using Eq. (4) in Lemma 2, we have $\Pr[\text{C3}] \leq \sigma^{r_2 - r_f - 1} \cdot \delta^{r_2 - r_f - 2} \cdot \frac{2}{2^n} \leq (\sigma \delta)^{r_2 - r_f - 1}$.

We consider the condition C4. We split $\mathcal{R}_f$ into sequences of consecutive round numbers. Let n_f be the number of the sequences in $\mathcal{R}_f$. For $i \in [n_f]$, let $\mathcal{R}_f[i]$ be the i-th sequence, $n_{f,i} = |\mathcal{R}_f[i]|$, $r_{\max, i} = \max(\mathcal{R}_f[i])$, and $r_{\min, i} = \min(\mathcal{R}_f[i])$, i.e., $\mathcal{R}_f = \bigcup_{i \in [n_f]} \mathcal{R}_f[i]$, $n_f = \sum_{i \in [n_f]} n_{f,i}$, and $\forall i < j \in [n_f] : r_{\max, i} < r_{\min, j} + 1$. For example, in Fig. 5, $n_f = 2$, $\mathcal{R}_f[1] = \{4, 5\}$, and $\mathcal{R}_f[2] = \{7, 8\}$. The first condition on C4 implies that $\forall i \in [n_f] : n_{f,i}\text{-Chain}^{K_{r_{\min, i} - 1} \oplus W_{r_{\min, i} - 1}'}[\mathcal{L}^{(<\nu, \alpha)}, K_{r_{\min, i}, r_{\max, i} - 1}] \neq \varepsilon$. Similar to the evaluation of the condition C3, we have

$$\Pr[\text{C4}] \leq \Pr\left[\forall i \in [n_f] : n_{f,i}\text{-Chain}^{K_{r_{\min, i} - 1} \oplus W_{r_{\min, i}}' \; 1}[\mathcal{L}^{(<\nu, \alpha)}, K_{r_{\min, i}, r_{\max, i} - 1}] \neq \varepsilon\right]$$

$$\leq \prod_{i \in [n_f]} (\sigma \delta)^{n_{f,i}} = (\sigma \delta)^{|\mathcal{R}_f|} .$$

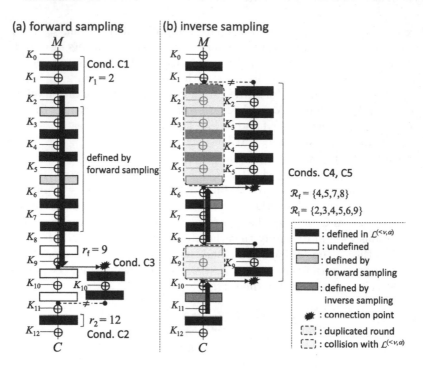

Fig. 5. Failure case of the re-sampling method. $r = 12$, $r_1 = 2$, $r_2 = 12$, $r_f = 9$, $\mathcal{R}_f := \{4, 5, 7, 8\}$, and $\mathcal{R}_i = \{2, 3, 4, 5, 6, 9\}$.

Regarding the condition C5, the evaluation is the same as that of the condition C4, and we have $\Pr[C4] \leq (\sigma\delta)^{|\mathcal{R}_i|}$.

By the above bounds, for each r_1, r_2, r_f, $\mathcal{R}_f$, and $\mathcal{R}_i$, we have

$$\Pr\left[\wedge_{i\in[5]}Ci\right] \leq (\sigma\delta)^{r_1+(r-r_2+1)+(r_2-r_f-1)+|\mathcal{R}_f|+|\mathcal{R}_i|} \leq (\sigma\delta)^r \ ,$$

where the last inequality is due to the relation $\mathcal{R}_f \cup \mathcal{R}_i = [r_1 + 1, r_f]$.

Since $0 \leq r_1 < r_f < r_i < r_2 \leq r$ and the numbers of choices of $\mathcal{R}_f$ and of $\mathcal{R}_i$ are respectively at most 2^r (for each round the pair is either fresh or non-fresh), we have

$$\Pr[\mathsf{fail}_{\mathsf{sample}}(\nu, \alpha)] \leq 2^r \cdot 2^r \cdot \sum_{0 \leq r_1 < r_f < r_i < r_2 \leq r} \Pr\left[\wedge_{i\in[5]}Ci\right]$$

$$\leq 4^r \cdot \binom{r+1}{4}(\sigma\delta)^r \leq \frac{4^r r^4}{12} \cdot (\sigma\delta)^r . \tag{13}$$

5.8 Lower-Bounding $\frac{\Pr[T_R=\tau]}{\Pr[T_I=\tau]}$

The following analysis shows that $\frac{\Pr[T_R=\tau]}{\Pr[T_I=\tau]} \geq 1$.

Fix a good transcript τ which consists of user's keys $\mathcal{L}_K$, primitive query-response pairs $\mathcal{L}_{X,Y}$, and internal input-output pairs $\mathcal{L}_{V,W}$. For a set $\mathcal{L}'$, let $T_R \vdash \mathcal{L}'$ (resp. $T_I \vdash \mathcal{L}'$) be an event that T_R (resp. T_I) satisfies elements in $\mathcal{L}'$.

Evaluating $\Pr[\mathsf{T}_R \vdash \mathcal{L}_{X,Y}]$ and $\Pr[\mathsf{T}_I \vdash \mathcal{L}_{X,Y}]$. Firstly, we define responses to primitive queries. As there is no difference between the real-world sampling and the ideal-world one, we have $\Pr[\mathsf{T}_R \vdash \mathcal{L}_{X,Y}] = \Pr[\mathsf{T}_I \vdash \mathcal{L}_{X,Y}]$. Hereafter, we assume that $\mathsf{T}_R \vdash \mathcal{L}_{X,Y}$ and $\mathsf{T}_I \vdash \mathcal{L}_{X,Y}$ are satisfied.

Evaluating $\Pr[\mathsf{T}_R \vdash \mathcal{L}_K]$ and $\Pr[\mathsf{T}_I \vdash \mathcal{L}_K]$. Next, we define user's keys. In both worlds, for each $\nu \in [u]$, the key $K^{(\nu)}$ is chosen uniformly at random from $\mathcal{K}$, we have $\Pr[\mathsf{T}_R \vdash \mathcal{L}_K] = \Pr[\mathsf{T}_I \vdash \mathcal{L}_K]$. Hereafter, we assume that $\mathsf{T}_R \vdash \mathcal{L}_K$ and $\mathsf{T}_I \vdash \mathcal{L}_K$ are satisfied.

Evaluating $\Pr[\mathsf{T}_R \vdash \mathcal{L}_{V,W}]$ and $\Pr[\mathsf{T}_I \vdash \mathcal{L}_{V,W}]$. Finally, we define internal input-output pairs $(V_i^{(\nu,\alpha)}, W_i^{(\nu,\alpha)})$ for $\nu \in [u]$ and $\alpha \in [q_\nu]$.

For $\nu \in [u]$ and $\alpha \in [q_\nu]$, we show $\frac{\Pr[\mathsf{T}_R \vdash \mathcal{L}_{V,W}^{(\nu,\alpha)}]}{\Pr[\mathsf{T}_I \vdash \mathcal{L}_{V,W}^{(\nu,\alpha)}]} \geq 1$ under the condition $\forall U \in \{R, I\} : \mathsf{T}_U \vdash \mathcal{L}^{(<\nu,\alpha)}$, ensuring $\frac{\Pr[\mathsf{T}_R \vdash \mathcal{L}_{V,W}]}{\Pr[\mathsf{T}_I \vdash \mathcal{L}_{V,W}]} \geq 1$.

For $\nu \in [u]$ and $\alpha \in [q_\nu]$, let $\omega_{\nu,\alpha} := |\mathcal{L}_{V,W}^{(\nu,\alpha)}|$ and $\omega_{<\nu,\alpha} := |\mathcal{L}^{(<\nu,\alpha)}|$. Thus, before the α-th construction query to the ν-th user, $\omega_{<\nu,\alpha}$ input-output pairs have been defined, and at the α-th construction query, $\omega_{\nu,\alpha}$ input-output ones are freshly defined. Since $\forall i \in [0, r] : \neg\mathsf{Chain}_i$, $\omega_{\nu,\alpha} \geq 1$ must be satisfied. Let $\gamma_1, \ldots, \gamma_{\omega_{\nu,\alpha}}$ be the round numbers at which the input-output pairs are not defined before the α-th construction query such that $\gamma_1 < \cdots < \gamma_{\omega_{\nu,\alpha}}$, i.e.,
$$\left(\forall i \in \{\gamma_1, \ldots, \gamma_{\omega_{\nu,\alpha}}\} : (V_i^{(\nu,\alpha)}, W_i^{(\nu,\alpha)}) \notin \mathcal{L}^{(<\nu,\alpha)}\right) \wedge \left(\forall i \in [r]\backslash\{\gamma_1, \ldots, \gamma_{\omega_{\nu,\alpha}}\} : (V_i^{(\nu,\alpha)}, W_i^{(\nu,\alpha)}) \in \mathcal{L}^{(<\nu,\alpha)}\right) \wedge \left(\gamma_1 < \cdots < \gamma_{\omega_{\nu,\alpha}}\right).$$

- *Real-World Probability.* In the real world, we define the internal input-output pairs $(V_i^{(\nu,\alpha)}, W_i^{(\nu,\alpha)})$ $(i \in [r])$ by forward queries to π. Then, we have $\Pr[\mathsf{T}_R \vdash \mathcal{L}_{V,W}^{(\nu,\alpha)}] = \prod_{i \in [\omega_{\nu,\alpha}]} \frac{1}{2^n - (\omega_{<\nu,\alpha} + (i-1))}$.

- *Ideal-World Probability.* In the ideal world, we first define $C^{(\nu,\alpha)}$ by the encryption query $\Pi_\nu(M^{(\nu,\alpha)})$, and define $V_{r+1}^{(\nu,\alpha)} := C^{(\nu,\alpha)} \oplus K_r^{(\nu)}$. Then, we have $\Pr[\mathsf{T}_I \vdash \{V_{r+1}^{(\nu,\alpha)*}\}] = \frac{1}{2^n - (\alpha-1)}$, where $V_{r+1}^{(\nu,\alpha)*}$ is the value in $\mathcal{L}_{V,W}^{(\nu,\alpha)}$ corresponding with $V_{r+1}^{(\nu,\alpha)}$.

We next evaluate the probability that T_I satisfies the remaining $(\omega_{\nu,\alpha} - 1)$ internal values in $\mathcal{L}_{V,W}^{(\nu,\alpha)}$. For $\eta \in [\omega_{\nu,\alpha}]$, let $\mathsf{Fail}_{\mathsf{fwd}}[\eta]$ be an event that the forward sampling fails at the γ_η-th round, i.e., $(V_{\gamma_\eta}^{(\nu,\alpha)}, W_{\gamma_\eta}^{(\nu,\alpha)})$ is defined in Step 12 of Algorithm 2 and satisfies the condition on Step 14. For the sake of convenience, let $\mathsf{Fail}_{\mathsf{fwd}}[\omega_{\nu,\alpha}]$ be an event that the forward sampling does not fail. Let $\mathcal{R}_{\eta,f}$ (resp. $\mathcal{R}_{\eta,i}$) be the set of target round numbers at which the input-output pairs are defined by the forward (resp. inverse) sampling under the condition that $\mathsf{Fail}_{\mathsf{fwd}}[\eta]$ occurs. Hence, for each $i \in \mathcal{R}_{\eta,f}$ (resp. $i \in \mathcal{R}_{\eta,i}$), $W_i^{(\nu,\alpha)}$ (resp. $V_i^{(\nu,\alpha)}$) is defined by the forward (resp. inverse) sampling. Let $\mathcal{R}_\eta := \{\mathcal{R}_{\eta,f}, \mathcal{R}_{\eta,i}\}$. We abuse the notation $\vdash$ for these sets, i.e., $\mathsf{T}_I \vdash \mathcal{R}_\eta$ denotes an event that input-output pairs from T_I at the rounds in $\mathcal{R}_{f,\eta}$ and in $\mathcal{R}_{f,\eta}$ are respectively defined by the forward sampling and the inverse one. Assuming that $\mathsf{Fail}_{\mathsf{fwd}}[\eta]$ occurs, each fresh internal value is chosen uniformly at random from $(2^n - \omega_{<\nu,\alpha})$ elements in $\{0,1\}^n$ by Algorithm 2, and thus the probability that T_I satisfies the remaining $(\omega_{\nu,\alpha} - 1)$ internal values in $\mathcal{L}_{V,W}^{(\nu,\alpha)}$ is $\left(\frac{1}{2^n - \omega_{<\nu,\alpha}}\right)^{\omega_{\nu,\alpha}-1}$. Then, we have

$$\Pr\left[\mathsf{T}_I \vdash \mathcal{L}_{V,W}^{(\nu,\alpha)}\right] = \sum_{\eta \in [\omega_{\nu,\alpha}]} \sum_{\mathcal{R}_{f,\eta}, \mathcal{R}_{i,\eta}} \left(\Pr\left[\mathsf{T}_I \vdash \mathcal{L}_{V,W}^{(\nu,\alpha)} \mid \mathsf{T}_I \vdash \mathcal{R}_\eta \wedge \mathsf{Fail}_{\mathsf{fwd}}[\eta]\right]\right.$$

$$\left. \times \Pr\left[\mathsf{T}_I \vdash \mathcal{R}_\eta\right] \cdot \Pr[\mathsf{Fail}_{\mathsf{fwd}}[\eta]]\right)$$

$$\leq \frac{1}{2^n - (\alpha - 1)} \cdot \left(\frac{1}{2^n - \omega_{<\nu,\alpha}}\right)^{\omega_{\nu,\alpha}-1} \cdot \Pr[\mathsf{Fail}_{\mathsf{fwd}}[\omega_{\nu,\alpha}]]$$

$$+ \frac{1}{2^n - (\alpha - 1)} \cdot \left(\frac{1}{2^n - \omega_{<\nu,\alpha}}\right)^{\omega_{\nu,\alpha}-1} \cdot \underbrace{\left(\sum_{\eta \in [\omega_{\nu,\alpha}-1]} \Pr[\mathsf{Fail}_{\mathsf{fwd}}[\eta]]\right)}_{=:p_{\nu,\alpha}}.$$

We next evaluate the probability $p_{\nu,\alpha} := \sum_{\eta \in [\omega_{\nu,\alpha}-1]} \Pr[\mathsf{Fail}_{\mathsf{fwd}}[\eta]]$, where

$$\Pr[\mathsf{Fail}_{\mathsf{fwd}}[\eta]] \leq \Pr\left[(r_2 - \gamma_\eta - 1)\text{-Chain}^{K_{\gamma_\eta}^{(\nu)} \oplus W_{\gamma_\eta}'}[\mathcal{L}_{V,W}^{(<\nu,\alpha)}, K_{\gamma_\eta+1, r_2-2}^{(\nu)}] \neq \varepsilon\right].$$

Let

$$c_\eta := \left|(r_2 - \gamma_\eta - 1)\text{-Chain}[\mathcal{L}_{V,W}^{(<\nu,\alpha)}, K_{\gamma_\eta+1, r_2-2}^{(\nu)}]\right| \text{ and } c_0 := (\alpha - 1).$$

Note that c_0 is the number of (trivial) chains with (a part of) the user's key $K^{(\nu)}$ that are defined from the first to $(\alpha - 1)$-th loops for the ν-th user. Since $(r_2 - \gamma_\eta - 1)\text{-Chain}[\mathcal{L}_{V,W}^{(<\nu,\alpha)}, K_{\gamma_\eta+1, r_2-2}^{(\nu)}]$ include all chains in $(r_2 - \gamma_{\eta-1} - 1)\text{-Chain}[\mathcal{L}_{V,W}^{(<\nu,\alpha)}, K_{\gamma_{\eta-1}+1, r_2-2}^{(\nu)}]$ where the first $(\gamma_{\eta-1} - \gamma_\eta)$ rounds are removed, we have $\Pr[\mathsf{Fail}_{\mathsf{fwd}}[\eta]] \leq \frac{c_\eta - c_{\eta-1}}{2^n - \omega_{<\nu,\alpha}}$, and

$$p_{\nu,\alpha} \leq \sum_{\eta \in [\omega_{\nu,\alpha}-1]} \frac{c_\eta - c_{\eta-1}}{2^n - \omega_{<\nu,\alpha}} = \frac{c_{\omega_{\nu,\alpha}-1} - (\alpha - 1)}{2^n - \omega_{<\nu,\alpha}} \leq \frac{\omega_{<\nu,\alpha} - (\alpha - 1)}{2^n - \omega_{<\nu,\alpha}}.$$

Using the bound, we have

$$\Pr[\mathsf{T}_I \vdash \mathcal{L}_{V,W}^{(\nu,\alpha)}] \leq \frac{1}{2^n - (\alpha - 1)} \cdot \left(\frac{1}{2^n - \omega_{<\nu,\alpha}}\right)^{\omega_{\nu,\alpha}-1} \cdot \left(1 + \frac{\omega_{<\nu,\alpha} - (\alpha - 1)}{2^n - \omega_{<\nu,\alpha}}\right).$$

- *Conclusion of the Evaluation.* Using the above probabilities, we have

$$\frac{\Pr[\mathsf{T}_R \vdash \mathcal{L}_{V,W}]}{\Pr[\mathsf{T}_I \vdash \mathcal{L}_{V,W}]} \geq \prod_{\nu \in [u], \alpha \in [q_\nu]} \frac{\prod_{i \in [\omega_{\nu,\alpha}]} \frac{1}{2^n - (\omega_{<\nu,\alpha} + (i-1))}}{\frac{1}{2^n - (\alpha-1)} \cdot \left(\frac{1}{2^n - \omega_{<\nu,\alpha}}\right)^{\omega_{\nu,\alpha}-1} \cdot \left(1 + \frac{\omega_{<\nu,\alpha} - (\alpha-1)}{2^n - \omega_{<\nu,\alpha}}\right)}$$

$$\geq \prod_{\nu \in [u], \alpha \in [q_\nu]} \left(\frac{2^n - \omega_{<\nu,\alpha}}{2^n - (\alpha - 1)} \cdot \left(1 + \frac{\omega_{<\nu,\alpha} - (\alpha - 1)}{2^n - \omega_{<\nu,\alpha}}\right)\right)^{-1} = 1.$$

5.9   Proof of Lemma 2

We fix $\nu \in [u]$, $\alpha \in [q_\nu]$, and $a_1, \ldots, a_j \in [r-1]$ such that $a_1, \ldots, a_j$ are all distinct. We consider $2j+2$ pairs (S,T), (S',T'), (S_1,T_1), ..., $(S_{2j}, T_{2j}) \in \mathcal{L}^{(<\nu,\alpha)}$.

We first evaluate the probability in Eq. (7): $\Pr\Big[\Big(\forall i \in [j] : T_{2i-1} \oplus S_{2i} = K_{a_i}^{(\nu)} \Big)$ $\wedge \Big(M^{(\nu,\alpha)} \oplus S = K_0^{(\nu)} \Big) \wedge \Big(C^{(\nu,\alpha)} \oplus T' = K_r^{(\nu)} \Big) \Big]$, where the subkeys are r-wise independent. Hence, there are $\min\{j+2, r\}$ independent random variables in these equations. For an equation $T_{2i-1} \oplus S_{2i} = K_{a_i}^{(\nu)}$, by Algorithm 2, if $(S_{2i-1}, T_{2i-1}) \in \mathcal{L}_{V,W}^{(\nu,<\alpha)}$ (resp. $(S_{2i}, T_{2i}) \in \mathcal{L}_{V,W}^{(\nu,<\alpha)}$), then T_{2i-1} (resp. S_{2i}) is defined after the subkey $K_{a_i}^{(\nu)}$ is defined. Hence, the randomness is used to evaluate the probability, instead of the subkey. For each $Z \in \{0,1\}^n$ and $(S^*, T^*) \in \mathcal{L}_{V,W}^{(\nu,<\alpha)}$, since S^* (resp. T^*) is defined by using $\pi^{\pm}$ or by XORing a sub-key with the previous output (resp. following input) of π, the probability that $S^* = Z$ is at most $\max\left\{\epsilon, \frac{1}{2^n - \sigma}\right\} \leq \max\left\{\epsilon, \frac{2}{2^n}\right\} =: \delta$, and the one that $T^* = Z$ is at most δ, assuming $\sigma \leq 2^{n-1}$. The evaluation holds for the equations $T_{2i-1} \oplus S_{2i} = K_{a_i}^{(\nu)}$, $M^{(\nu,\alpha)} \oplus S = K_0^{(\nu)}$ and $C^{(\nu,\alpha)} \oplus T' = K_r^{(\nu)}$. Using the randomnesses of the subkeys and of $\mathcal{L}_{V,W}^{(\nu,<\alpha)}$, we have

$$\Pr\Big[\Big(\forall i \in [j] : T_{2i-1} \oplus S_{2i} = K_{a_i}^{(\nu)} \Big) \wedge \Big(M^{(\nu,\alpha)} \oplus S = K_0^{(\nu)} \Big)$$
$$\wedge \Big(C^{(\nu,\alpha)} \oplus T' = K_r^{(\nu)} \Big) \Big] \leq \delta^{\min\{j+2,r\}} .$$

Regarding Eqs. (4), (5) and (6), as the above evaluation, using the randomnesses of the subkeys and of $\mathcal{L}_{V,W}^{(\nu,<\alpha)}$, we obtain the bounds.

5.10   Proof of Lemma 3

Fix $\nu \in [u]$ and $\alpha \in [q_\nu]$. Assume that $\mathsf{Chain}_0, \ldots, \mathsf{Chain}_r$, and $\mathsf{Coll}_{V,W}$ do not occur. Also assume that Fail_π does not occur before the α-th loop of the ν-th user. In Algorithm 2, the internal input-output pairs of the α-th loop except for the pair of the MITM round, $(V_i^{(\alpha)}, W_i^{(\alpha)})$ ($i \in [r] \setminus \{r_m\}$), are defined at Steps 8, 9, 12 or 19. The sampling method and the assumption ensure that Fail_π does not occur due to these pairs. Hence, Fail_π occurs if and only if $(V_{r_m}^{(\alpha)}, W_{r_m}^{(\alpha)})$ breaks the property of the permutation, i.e., $\mathsf{fail}_{\mathsf{sample}}$ becomes true (See Fig. 4(d), wherein $r_m = 4$ and the value V_4 is duplicately defined).

6   The Exact Mu-Security of Tweakable KACs

We drive the mu-security bound of the single-permutation-based tweakable KAC TKAC, a.k.a tweakable Even-Mansour, from the mu-security of KAC in Theorem 1. Let $\mathcal{TW}$ be a set of tweaks. Let $h_K : [0, r] \times \mathcal{TW} \to \{0,1\}^n$ be a tweak function with a hash key K that takes a round number $i \in [0, r]$ and a tweak $tw \in \mathcal{TW}$, and returns the i-th round subkey K_i. Then, TKAC is defined as

$$\mathsf{TKAC}[h_K, \pi](tw, M) = \mathsf{KAC}_r[h_K(0, tw)\|h_K(1, tw)\| \cdots \|h_K(r, tw), \pi](M) \ .$$

Assume that the tweak function h is an ϵ r-wise independent function, that is, for each key K and tweak $tw \in \mathcal{TW}$, the subkeys $h_K(0, tw), h_K(1, tw), \dots, h_K(r, tw)$ are ϵ r-wise independent and for each pair of distinct tweaks the subkeys are independent. Then, one can apply the bound of Theorem 1 to the mu-security of TKAC with respect to multi-user strong tweakable PRP (mu-STPRP). Hence, we have the following tight bound.

Theorem 2. *Assume that h is an ϵ r-wise independent function. Let $\delta = \max\left\{\epsilon, \frac{2}{2^n}\right\}$. Let $\mathbf{A}$ be an adversary that makes at most p primitive queries and q construction queries. Let $\sigma := p + rq$. Then, we have*

$$\mathbf{Adv}_{\mathsf{TKAC}}^{\mathsf{mu\text{-}stprp}}(\mathbf{A}) \leq \left(\frac{4^r r^4}{12} + r + 1\right) \cdot q(\sigma\delta)^r + 2r^2 \cdot \frac{q}{2^n} \ .$$

Remark 1. When the permutation π is secret, TKAC is r-CLRW2 that is the r-round cascading LRW2 (with a single-key block cipher). Hence, putting $p = 0$ into the bound of Theorem 2, we have the $\frac{r}{r+1}n$-bit mu-bound of r-CLRW2 that is better than the existing bounds [7,17].

7 Conclusion

We proved the tight security bound of the r-round KAC with a single permutation and correlated subkeys under the mu setting. The new bound $q \cdot \left(\frac{p+rq}{2^n}\right)^r$ matches with the conventional attack bound [3] and is tight both in the su and mu settings. Based on the previous works separately proved the r-round KAC's tight security bounds either with (i) a single permutation, (ii) correlated subkeys, or (iii) the mu setting, this work pushes one step further by proving the security with all three conditions combined. Moreover, our result easily supports the tweakable KAC, extending its provable tight security bound from 4 to any even with the aforementioned relaxed conditions. The key technique is the updated re-sampling method; the original method was limited to 3 rounds, i.e., triple encryption, and we extend it to any round. This result gives a more realistic provable-security foundation for practical block ciphers, including AES.

There are several future research directions. The updated re-sampling method can be applied to other block-cipher constructions, such as the Feistel networks [13] and substitution-permutation networks [6]. Also, further reducing the number of independent subkeys, e.g., $(r-1)$-wise independence [25] is another important open problem.

Acknowledgement. We thank anonymous reviewers for useful comments.

References

1. Bellare, M., Tackmann, B.: The multi-user security of authenticated encryption: AES-GCM in TLS 1.3. In: Robshaw, M., Katz, J. (eds.) CRYPTO 2016. LNCS, vol. 9814, pp. 247–276. Springer, Heidelberg (2016). https://doi.org/10.1007/978-3-662-53018-4_10
2. Biham, E.: How to decrypt or even substitute DES-encrypted messages in 2^{28} steps. Inf. Process. Lett. **84**(3), 117–124 (2002)
3. Bogdanov, A., Knudsen, L.R., Leander, G., Standaert, F.-X., Steinberger, J., Tischhauser, E.: Key-alternating ciphers in a provable setting: encryption using a small number of public permutations. In: Pointcheval, D., Johansson, T. (eds.) EUROCRYPT 2012. LNCS, vol. 7237, pp. 45–62. Springer, Heidelberg (2012). https://doi.org/10.1007/978-3-642-29011-4_5
4. Chen, S., Lampe, R., Lee, J., Seurin, Y., Steinberger, J.: Minimizing the two-round even-mansour cipher. In: Garay, J.A., Gennaro, R. (eds.) CRYPTO 2014, pp. 39–56. Springer Berlin Heidelberg, Berlin, Heidelberg (2014). https://doi.org/10.1007/978-3-662-44371-2_3
5. Chen, S., Steinberger, J.: Tight security bounds for key-alternating ciphers. In: Nguyen, P.Q., Oswald, E. (eds.) EUROCRYPT 2014, pp. 327–350. Springer Berlin Heidelberg, Berlin, Heidelberg (2014). https://doi.org/10.1007/978-3-642-55220-5_19
6. Cogliati, B., et al.: Provable security of (tweakable) block ciphers based on substitution-permutation networks. In: Shacham, H., Boldyreva, A. (eds.) CRYPTO 2018: 38th Annual International Cryptology Conference, Santa Barbara, CA, USA, August 19–23, 2018, Proceedings, Part I, pp. 722–753. Springer International Publishing, Cham (2018). https://doi.org/10.1007/978-3-319-96884-1_24
7. Cogliati, B., Lampe, R., Seurin, Y.: Tweaking even-mansour ciphers. In: Gennaro, R., Robshaw, M. (eds.) CRYPTO 2015: 35th Annual Cryptology Conference, Santa Barbara, CA, USA, August 16-20, 2015, Proceedings, Part I, pp. 189–208. Springer Berlin Heidelberg, Berlin, Heidelberg (2015). https://doi.org/10.1007/978-3-662-47989-6_9
8. Cogliati, B., Seurin, Y.: Beyond-birthday-bound security for tweakable even-mansour ciphers with linear tweak and key mixing. In: Iwata, T., Cheon, J.H. (eds.) ASIACRYPT 2015: 21st International Conference on the Theory and Application of Cryptology and Information Security, Auckland, New Zealand, November 29 – December 3, 2015, Proceedings, Part II, pp. 134–158. Springer Berlin Heidelberg, Berlin, Heidelberg (2015). https://doi.org/10.1007/978-3-662-48800-3_6
9. Degabriele, J.P., Govinden, J., Günther, F., Paterson, K.G.: The Security of ChaCha20-Poly1305 in the Multi-User Setting. In: CCS '21, pp. 1981–2003. ACM (2021)
10. Dunkelman, O., Keller, N., Shamir, A.: Minimalism in cryptography: the even-mansour scheme revisited. In: Pointcheval, D., Johansson, T. (eds.) EUROCRYPT 2012, pp. 336–354. Springer Berlin Heidelberg, Berlin, Heidelberg (2012). https://doi.org/10.1007/978-3-642-29011-4_21
11. Dutta, A.: Minimizing the two-round tweakable even-mansour cipher. In: Moriai, S., Wang, H. (eds.) ASIACRYPT 2020: 26th International Conference on the Theory and Application of Cryptology and Information Security, Daejeon, South Korea, December 7–11, 2020, Proceedings, Part I, pp. 601–629. Springer International Publishing, Cham (2020). https://doi.org/10.1007/978-3-030-64837-4_20

12. Even, S., Mansour, Y.: A construction of a cipher from a single pseudorandom permutation. J. Cryptol. **10**(3), 151–162 (1997)
13. Guo, C., Wang, L.: Revisiting key-alternating Feistel ciphers for shorter keys and multi-user security. In: Peyrin, T., Galbraith, S. (eds.) ASIACRYPT 2018: 24th International Conference on the Theory and Application of Cryptology and Information Security, Brisbane, QLD, Australia, December 2–6, 2018, Proceedings, Part I, pp. 213–243. Springer International Publishing, Cham (2018). https://doi.org/10.1007/978-3-030-03326-2_8
14. Hoang, V.T., Tessaro, S.: Key-alternating ciphers and key-length extension: exact bounds and multi-user security. In: Robshaw, M., Katz, J. (eds.) CRYPTO 2016: 36th Annual International Cryptology Conference, Santa Barbara, CA, USA, August 14-18, 2016, Proceedings, Part I, pp. 3–32. Springer Berlin Heidelberg, Berlin, Heidelberg (2016). https://doi.org/10.1007/978-3-662-53018-4_1
15. Hoang, V.T., Tessaro, S., Thiruvengadam, A.: The multi-user security of GCM, revisited: tight bounds for nonce randomization. In: CCS 2018, pp. 1429–1440. ACM (2018)
16. Lampe, R., Patarin, J., Seurin, Y.: An asymptotically tight security analysis of the iterated even-mansour cipher. In: Wang, X., Sako, K. (eds.) ASIACRYPT 2012, pp. 278–295. Springer Berlin Heidelberg, Berlin, Heidelberg (2012). https://doi.org/10.1007/978-3-642-34961-4_18
17. Lampe, R., Seurin, Y.: Tweakable blockciphers with asymptotically optimal security. In: Moriai, S. (ed.) FSE 2013. LNCS, vol. 8424, pp. 133–151. Springer, Heidelberg (2014). https://doi.org/10.1007/978-3-662-43933-3_8
18. Luykx, A., Mennink, B., Paterson, K.G.: Analyzing multi-key security degradation. In: Takagi, T., Peyrin, T. (eds.) ASIACRYPT 2017. LNCS, vol. 10625, pp. 575–605. Springer, Cham (2017). https://doi.org/10.1007/978-3-319-70697-9_20
19. Mouha, N., Luykx, A.: Multi-key security: the even-mansour construction revisited. In: Gennaro, R., Robshaw, M. (eds.) CRYPTO 2015: 35th Annual Cryptology Conference, Santa Barbara, CA, USA, August 16-20, 2015, Proceedings, Part I, pp. 209–223. Springer Berlin Heidelberg, Berlin, Heidelberg (2015). https://doi.org/10.1007/978-3-662-47989-6_10
20. Naito, Y., Sasaki, Y., Sugawara, T., Yasuda, K.: The multi-user security of triple encryption, revisited: exact security, strengthening, and application to TDES. In: CCS 2022, ACM (2022)
21. Patarin, J.: The "Coefficients H" Technique. In: Avanzi, R.M., Keliher, L., Sica, F. (eds.) SAC 2008. LNCS, vol. 5381, pp. 328–345. Springer, Heidelberg (2009). https://doi.org/10.1007/978-3-642-04159-4_21
22. Rescorla, E.: RFC 8446: The transport layer security (TLS) protocol version 1.3. https://doi.org/10.17487/RFC8446 (2018)
23. Rescorla, E., Tschofenig, H., Modadugu, N.: The datagram transport layer security (DTLS) protocol version 1.3 - draft-ietf-tls-dtls13-43. https://tools.ietf.org/html/draft-ietf-tls-dtls13-43 (2021)
24. Steinberger, J.P.: Improved Security Bounds for Key-Alternating Ciphers via Hellinger Distance. IACR Cryptol. ePrint Arch., p. 481 (2012). http://eprint.iacr.org/2012/481
25. Tessaro, S., Zhang, X.: Tight Security for Key-Alternating Ciphers with Correlated Sub-keys. In: Tibouchi, M., Wang, H. (eds.) ASIACRYPT 2021: 27th International Conference on the Theory and Application of Cryptology and Information Security, Singapore, December 6–10, 2021, Proceedings, Part III, pp. 435–464. Springer International Publishing, Cham (2021). https://doi.org/10.1007/978-3-030-92078-4_15

26. Thomson, M., Turner, S.: Using TLS to secure QUIC. RFC **9001**, 1–52 (2021). https://doi.org/10.17487/RFC9001
27. Wu, Y., Yu, L., Cao, Z., Dong, X.: Tight security analysis of 3-round key-alternating cipher with a single permutation. In: Moriai, S., Wang, H. (eds.) ASIACRYPT 2020: 26th International Conference on the Theory and Application of Cryptology and Information Security, Daejeon, South Korea, December 7–11, 2020, Proceedings, Part I, pp. 662–693. Springer International Publishing, Cham (2020). https://doi.org/10.1007/978-3-030-64837-4_22
28. Yu, L., Wu, Y., Yu, Yu., Cao, Z., Dong, X.: Security proofs for key-alternating ciphers with non-independent round permutations. In: Rothblum, G., Wee, H. (eds.) Theory of Cryptography: 21st International Conference, TCC 2023, Taipei, Taiwan, November 29 – December 2, 2023, Proceedings, Part I, pp. 238–267. Springer Nature Switzerland, Cham (2023). https://doi.org/10.1007/978-3-031-48615-9_9

Partial Sums Meet FFT: Improved Attack on 6-Round AES

Orr Dunkelman[1], Shibam Ghosh[1(✉)], Nathan Keller[2], Gaëtan Leurent[3(✉)], Avichai Marmor[2], and Victor Mollimard[1]

[1] Computer Science Department, University of Haifa, Haifa, Israel
orrd@cs.haifa.ac.il, sghosh03@campus.haifa.ac.il
[2] Department of Mathematics, Bar Ilan University, Ramat Gan, Israel
Nathan.Keller@biu.ac.il, avichai@elmar.co.il
[3] Inria, Paris, France
gaetan.leurent@inria.fr

Abstract. The *partial sums* cryptanalytic technique was introduced in 2000 by Ferguson et al., who used it to break 6-round AES with time complexity of 2^{52} S-box computations – a record that has not been beaten ever since. In 2014, Todo and Aoki showed that for 6-round AES, partial sums can be replaced by a technique based on the Fast Fourier Transform (FFT), leading to an attack with a comparable complexity.

In this paper we show that the partial sums technique can be combined with an FFT-based technique, to get the best of the two worlds. Using our combined technique, we obtain an attack on 6-round AES with complexity of about $2^{46.4}$ additions. We fully implemented the attack experimentally, along with the partial sums attack and the Todo-Aoki attack, and confirmed that our attack improves the best known attack on 6-round AES by a factor of more than 32.

We expect that our technique can be used to significantly enhance numerous attacks that exploit the partial sums technique. To demonstrate this, we use our technique to improve the best known attack on 7-round Kuznyechik by a factor of more than 80.

1 Introduction

The *partial sums* cryptanalytic technique was introduced by Ferguson et al. [21] as a tool for enhancing the Square attack [16] on AES [1]. Informally, the Square attack requires computing the XOR of 2^{32} 8-bit values extracted from partially decrypted ciphertexts under each of 2^{40} candidate subkeys, which amounts to 2^{72} operations. The partial sums technique divides the attack into several steps where at each step, the adversary guesses several key bits and computes a 'partial sum', which allows reducing the number of partially decrypted values whose

---

Supplementary Information The online version contains supplementary material available at https://doi.org/10.1007/978-3-031-58716-0_5.

XOR should be computed. As a result, the overall complexity of the attack is significantly reduced to 2^{52} operations.

In the 23 years since the introduction of the partial sums technique, it was shown to enhance not only the Square attack but also several other attacks (e.g., integral, linear, zero-correlation linear, and multi-set algebraic attacks, see [4,6, 8,12,17]) in various scenarios, and was applied to attack numerous ciphers (AES, Kuznyechik, MISTY1, CLEFIA, Skinny, Zorro, Midori, and LBlock, to mention a few). Yet, its best known application remained the original one – the attack on 6-round AES which remained the best attack on 6-round AES, despite many attempts to supersede it (see Table 2).

In 2014, Todo and Aoki [30] showed that an FFT-based technique can replace partial sums in enhancing the Square attack. The idea is to represent the XOR of the 2^{32} partially decrypted ciphertexts which the adversary has to compute as a *convolution* of two tailor-made functions and then to use the Fast Fourier Transform (FFT) in order to compute this value for all guessed subkeys at once, at the cost of about $4 \cdot 2^{32} \cdot \log(2^{32})$ addition operations. While at a first glance, this technique seems clearly advantageous over partial sums, subtle practical difficulties counter its advantages, making the two techniques comparable. First, the technique can be applied only after guessing 8 bits of the key. Secondly, as the output of the FFT is an element in $\mathbb{Z}$ and not an element in the finite field $GF(2^8)$, one has to repeat the procedure for each of the 8 bits in which the XOR should be computed. Thirdly, while partial sums can exploit partial knowledge of the subkeys the adversary needs to guess, it seems that the FFT-based technique does not gain anything from partial knowledge. According to the authors of [30], the complexity of their attack on 6-round AES is $6 \cdot 2^{50}$ addition operations, which is roughly equal to the complexity of the partial sums attack.

In the last decade, the Todo-Aoki technique was used as a comparable alternative of partial sums, with several authors mentioning advantages of each attack technique in different scenarios (see [4,6,15,32]). Yet, it seemed that one has to choose between the benefits of the two techniques in each application.

In this paper we show that one can combine partial sums with an FFT-based technique, getting the best of the two worlds in many cases. The basic idea behind our technique is to use the general structure of partial sums, but to replace particular key-guessing steps used in partial sums (or combinations of several such steps) by FFT-based steps, which include embedding finite field elements into $\mathbb{Z}$. We show that this allows computing the XOR in all 8 output bits at once, exploiting partial key knowledge, and even *packing* several computations together in the same 64-bit word addition and multiplication operations. As a result, we obtain the speedup of FFT over key guessing, without the disadvantages it carries in the Todo-Aoki technique. In addition, the new technique allows for much more flexibility, as we may choose which steps we group together and in which steps we use FFT instead of key guessing. The choice depends on multiple step-dependent parameters, such as the number of subkey bits guessed in the step, the ability to pre-compute some of the operations required for the FFT, and partial knowledge of subkey bits. Thus, the flexibility may be very helpful.

Table 1. Cost comparison of three best attacks on 6-Round AES in Amazon's AWS

Attack (Source)	AWS Instance	Running Time (in minutes)	Total Cost (in US$)
Square & Partial sums [21]	m6i.32xlarge	4859	497
Square & FFT [30]	r6i.32xlarge	3120	418
Square & Partial sums & FFT (Sect. 3.5)	m6i.32xlarge	48	5

We use our technique to mount an improved attack on 6-round AES. We obtain an attack which requires 2^{33} chosen plaintexts (compared to $2^{34.5}$ in the partial sums attack of [21]), time complexity of about $2^{46.4}$ additions (compared to 2^{52} S-box computations in partial sums), and memory complexity of 2^{27} 128-bit blocks (roughly the same as in partial sums). As it is hard to compare additions with S-box applications, we experimentally compared the attacks by fully implementing our attack, the partial sums attack, and the Todo-Aoki attack, using Amazon AWS servers. We optimized the instance which best fits the attacks (optimizing for performance/cost tradeoff). Our experiments show that our attack takes 48 minutes (and costs 5 US$), the partial sums attack takes 4859 minutes (and costs 497 US$), and the Todo-Aoki attack takes 3120 minutes (and costs 418 US$). Thus, our attack provides a speedup by a factor of more than 65 over both the partial sums attack and Todo-Aoki's attack, and allows breaking 6-round AES in about 48 minutes at the cost of only 5 US$. This breaks a 23-year old record in practical attacks on 6-round AES. Table 1 summarizes the costs of running the attacks. The source code is publicly available at the following link

https://github.com/ShibamCrS/Partial_Sums_Meet_FFT.

Our attack improves the partial sums attack of [21] on 7-round AES by the same factor. In addition, it might be applicable to other primitives that use 6-round AES as a component like the tweakable block cipher TNT-AES [5].

Due to the flexibility of our technique, it can be used to improve various attacks that use the partial sums technique. We demonstrate this applicability by presenting improved attack on Kuznyechik [18] the Russian Federation encryption standard. The best-known attack on Kuznyechik is a multiset-algebraic attack on 7 rounds (out of 9) with the complexity of $2^{154.5}$ encryptions, presented by Biryukov et al. [12]. We show that this attack can be improved by a factor of more than 80 to about 2^{148} encryptions, thus providing the best-known attack on Kuznyechik. A comparison of our results on 6-round AES and reduced Kuznyechik with previously known results is presented in Table 2.

The full version of this paper [19] presents our techniques with two other targets MISTY1 and CLEFIA. We improve the Bar-On and Keller [8] attack by a factor 6 (to 2^{67}) and obtain the best known attacks against full MISTY1. We also improved multiple attacks against CLEFIA [13,23,28] for 11, 12, and 14 rounds. Most strikingly, we improve the 12-round attack of Sasaki and Wang [28] by a factor of about 2^{30}.

Table 2. Comparison of our results with previous key recovery attacks on 6-Round AES and reduced Kuznyechik. The results are listed in chronological order.

Cipher	Rounds	Data	Time	Technique and Source
AES	6	2^{32} CP	2^{71} Enc.	Square [16]
		$6 \cdot 2^{32}$ CP	2^{52} S-box Eval.	Square & Partial sums [21]
		2^{71} ACPC	2^{71} Enc.	Boomerang [11]
		2^{33} CP	2^{52} S-box Eval.	Square & Partial sums [31]
		$6 \cdot 2^{32}$ CP	2^{52} Add.	Square & FFT [30]
		2^{26} CP	2^{80} Enc.	Mixture Differential [7]
		2^{55} ACPC	2^{80} Enc.	Retracing Boomerang [20]
		$2^{79.7}$ ACPC	2^{78} Enc.	Boomeyong [27]
		2^{59} ACPC	2^{61} Enc.	Truncated Boomerang [9]
		2^{33} CP	$2^{46.4}$ Add.	Square & Partial sums & FFT (Sect. 3)
Kuznyechik	7	2^{128} KP	$2^{154.5}$ Enc.	Integral & Partial sums [12]
		2^{128} KP	2^{148} Enc.	Integral & Partial sums & FFT (Sect. 4)
	6	2^{120} CP	$2^{146.5}$ Enc.	Integral & Partial sums [12]
		2^{120} CP	$2^{140.9}$ Enc.	Integral & Partial sums & FFT (Sect. 4)

The paper is organized as follows. In Sect. 2, we describe the structure of the AES, the Square attack, and the two previously known methods for enhancing it – partial sums and the Todo-Aoki FFT-based method. Section 3 presents our new technique, along with its application to 6-round AES. Section 4 presents application of the new technique to the cipher Kuznyechik.

2 Background

2.1 Description of AES

AES [1] is a 128-bit block cipher, designed by Rijmen and Daemen in 1997 (originally, under the name Rijndael). In 2001, it was selected by the US National Institute of Standards (NIST) as the Advanced Encryption Standard, and since then, it has gradually become the most widely used block cipher worldwide.

AES is a Substitution-Permutation Network operating on a 128-bit state organized as a 4×4 array of 8-bit words. The encryption process is composed of 10, 12, or 14 rounds (depending on the key length: 10 rounds for 128-bit keys, 12 rounds for 192-bit keys, and 14 rounds for 256-bit keys). Each round of AES is composed of four operations, presented in Fig. 1.

SUBBYTES. Apply a known 8-bit S-box independently to the bytes of the state;
SHIFTROWS. Shift each row of the state to the left by the position of the row;
MIXCOLUMNS. Multiply each column by the same known invertible 4-by-4 matrix over the finite field $GF(2^8)$;
ADDROUNDKEY. Add a 128-bit round key computed from the secret key to the state, using a bitwise XOR operation.

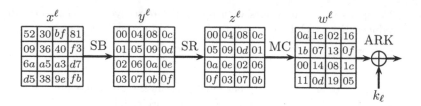

Fig. 1. An AES Round

An additional ADDROUNDKEY operation is applied before the first round, and the last MIXCOLUMNS operation is omitted. As properties of the key schedule of AES are not used in this paper, we refer the reader to [1] for its description.

The rounds are numbered from 0 to $Nr - 1$, where Nr is the number of rounds. The subkey used in the ADDROUNDKEY operation of round ℓ is denoted by k^ℓ, and the j'th byte in its i'th row is denoted by k^ℓ_{4j+i}. The whitening key added before the initial round is denoted by k^{-1}. The j'th byte in the i'th row of the state before the SUBBYTES, SHIFTROWS, MIXCOLUMNS, ADDROUNDKEY operations of round ℓ is denoted by $x^\ell_{4j+i}, y^\ell_{4j+i}, z^\ell_{4j+i},$ and w^ℓ_{4j+i}, respectively. A set of bytes $\{v_i, v_j, v_k\}$ is denoted by $v_{i,j,k}$.

2.2   The Square Attack on AES

AES was designed as a modification of the block cipher Square [16], which came together with a dedicated attack, called 'the Square attack'. This attack, in its basic application to AES, uses the following observation.

Lemma 1. *Consider the encryption by 3-round AES of a set of 256 plaintexts, $P_0, P_1, \ldots, P_{255}$, which are equal in all bytes except for a single byte, such that the single byte assumes each possible value exactly once. Then the corresponding ciphertexts $C_0, C_1, \ldots, C_{255}$ satisfy $\bigoplus_{i=0}^{255} C_i = 0$.*

As was shown in [16], this property can be used to attack 6-round Square, and also 6-round AES, with a complexity of about 2^{80} S-box computations. The adversary asks for the encryption of 2^{32} plaintexts which are equal in all bytes except for the main diagonal (i.e., bytes 0,5,10,15) and assume all 2^{32} possible values in the main diagonal. Then, he guesses bytes $0, 5, 10, 15$ of k^{-1}, and for each guess, he partially encrypts the plaintexts through round 0 and finds a set of 2^8 inputs to round 1 which satisfy the assumption of Lemma 1. Then, he partially guesses the subkeys k^4, k^5, partially decrypts the 2^8 corresponding ciphertexts through rounds 4,5 and checks whether the XOR of the 2^8 corresponding values at the state x_0^4 (i.e., at byte 0 before the SUBBYTES operation of round 4) is zero, as is stated by Lemma 1. If not, the subkey guess is discarded.

While it seems that in order to compute byte x_0^4 from the ciphertext, the adversary must know 64 subkey bits (specifically, key bytes $k^5_{0,7,10,13}$ and $k^4_{0,1,2,3}$), in fact knowing 40 subkey bits is sufficient. Indeed, since MIXCOLUMNS is a linear operation, it can be interchanged with the ADDROUNDKEY operation after it, at the cost of replacing k^4 with the equivalent subkey $\bar{k}^4 = \text{MIXCOLUMNS}^{-1}(k^4)$.

The knowledge of the key bytes $k_{0,7,10,13}^5$ and $\bar{k}_0^4$ is sufficient for computing the state byte x_0^4 from the ciphertext of 6-round AES.[1] Each check whether 2^8 values XOR to zero provides an 8-bit filtering, and hence, checking several sets is sufficient for discarding all wrong subkey guesses. The attack recovers 9 subkey bytes $(k_{0,5,10,15}^{-1}, \bar{k}_0^4, k_{0,7,10,13}^5)$ with complexity of about $2^{32} \cdot 2^{40} \cdot 2^8 = 2^{80}$ S-box computations.

In [21], Ferguson et al. observed that the Square attack can be improved by replacing Lemma 1 with the following lemma on 4-round AES.

Lemma 2. *Consider the encryption by 4-round AES of a set of 2^{32} plaintexts, $P_0, P_1, \ldots, P_{2^{32}-1}$, which are equal in all bytes except for the main diagonal (i.e., bytes 0,5,10,15), such that the diagonal assumes each possible value exactly once. Then the corresponding ciphertexts $C_0, C_1, \ldots, C_{2^{32}-1}$ satisfy $\bigoplus_{i=0}^{2^{32}-1} C_i = 0$.*

Lemma 2 can be used to attack 6-round AES using the same strategy described above. The adversary asks for the encryption of a few sets of 2^{32} plaintexts which satisfy the assumption of Lemma 2. Then, for each set, he guesses subkey bytes $\bar{k}_0^4, k_{0,7,10,13}^5$ and checks whether the XOR of the 2^{32} intermediate values at the state byte x_0^4 is zero, as is stated by Lemma 2. The attack recovers 5 subkey bytes $(\bar{k}_0^4, k_{0,7,10,13}^5)$ and its complexity is about $2^{32} \cdot 2^{40} = 2^{72}$ S-box computations.

2.3 The Partial Sums Attack

In the same paper [21], Ferguson et al. showed that the complexity of the Square attack described above can be significantly reduced, by dividing the key guessing and partial decryption into several steps and gradually reducing the number of values whose XOR should be computed. By the structure of AES, the state byte x_0^4 is computed from the ciphertext C using the following formula:

$$x_0^4 = S^{-1}\big(\bar{k}_0^4 \oplus 0\mathsf{e}_\mathsf{x} \cdot S^{-1}(C_0 \oplus k_0^5) \oplus 09_\mathsf{x} \cdot S^{-1}(C_7 \oplus k_7^5) \oplus \tag{1}$$
$$\oplus\ 0\mathsf{d}_\mathsf{x} \cdot S^{-1}(C_{10} \oplus k_{10}^5) \oplus 0\mathsf{b}_\mathsf{x} \cdot S^{-1}(C_{13} \oplus k_{13}^5)\big),$$

where the coefficients $0\mathsf{e}_\mathsf{x}, 09_\mathsf{x}, 0\mathsf{d}_\mathsf{x}, 0\mathsf{b}_\mathsf{x}$ come from the inverse MixColumns operation and the multiplication is performed in the finite field $GF(2^8)$.

Note that the right hand side of (1) depends only on bytes 0,7,10,13 of the ciphertext. This means that if two ciphertexts are equal in these four bytes, then their contributions to the XOR of x_0^4 values cancel each other. Thus, we may replace the list of ciphertexts with a list A of 2^{32} binary indices which indicates whether each of the 2^{32} possible values of bytes 0,7,10,13 of the ciphertext appears an even or an odd number of times in the list of ciphertexts. The goal of the subsequent steps is to reduce the number of needed binary indices, in parallel to guessing subkey bytes.

---

[1] Here and in the sequel, we assume that in 6-round AES, the MixColumns operation of round 5 is omitted. If this operation is not omitted, the attack works almost without change; we only have to replace the key k^5 with the equivalent key $\bar{k}^5 = $ MixColumns$^{-1}(k^5)$.

At the first step, the adversary guesses bytes 0,7 of k^5, and reduces the size of the list to 2^{24}. Denote $a_1 = 0e_x \cdot S^{-1}(C_0 \oplus k_0^5) \oplus 09_x \cdot S^{-1}(C_7 \oplus k_7^5)$. Observe that if two ciphertexts are equal in the bytes a_1, C_{10}, C_{13}, then their contributions to the XOR of x_0^4 values cancel each other. As the guess of bytes $k_{0,7}^5$ allows computing a_1 for each ciphertext, the adversary can construct a list A_1 of 2^{24} binary values which indicates whether each possible value of (a_1, C_{10}, C_{13}) appears an even or an odd number of times in the list of intermediate values. The complexity of this step is about $2^{16} \cdot 2^{32} = 2^{48}$ S-box evaluations.

At the second step, the adversary guesses the byte k_{10}^5 and reduces the list to a list A_2 of size 2^{16} that corresponds to the possible values of (a_2, C_{13}), where $a_2 = a_1 \oplus 0d_x \cdot S^{-1}(C_{10} \oplus k_{10}^5)$. At the third step, the adversary guesses the byte k_{13}^5 and reduces the list to a list A_3 of size 2^8 that corresponds to the possible values of a_3, where $a_3 = a_2 \oplus 0b_x \cdot S^{-1}(C_{13} \oplus k_{13}^5)$. Finally, at the fourth step, the adversary guesses the byte $\bar{k}_0^4$, computes $\oplus_{\{x \in \{0,1\}^8 : A_3[x]=1\}} S^{-1}(\bar{k}_0^4 \oplus x)$, which is equal to the right hand side of (1), and checks whether it is equal to zero. The complexity of each step is about 2^{48} S-box computations, and thus, the overall complexity for a single set of 2^{32} plaintexts is 2^{50} S-box computations.

As the attack recovers 5 subkey bytes, six sets of 2^{32} plaintexts are required to recover their value uniquely with a high probability. Note that after the check of the first set, only about $2^{40} \cdot 2^{-8} = 2^{32}$ suggestions for the 40 subkey bits remain undiscarded. This means that for each possible value of $k_{0,7,10,13}^5$, at most a few values of $\bar{k}_0^4$ that correspond to them are expected to remain. Hence, when examining the second set of 2^{32} plaintexts, the complexity of the fourth step becomes negligible as it is performed only for a few values of $\bar{k}_0^4$. Similarly, when examining the third set, the two last steps become negligible, etc. In total, the complexity of checking all six plaintext sets of size 2^{32} is equivalent to the cost of $4 + 3 + 2 + 1 = 10$ steps, or $2^{51.3}$ S-box computations.[2]

The attack is given as Algorithm 1. To simplify the notation, we rewrite equation (1) in a more generic way, using S_0 for $0e_x \cdot S^{-1}(\cdot)$, S_1 for $09_x \cdot S^{-1}(\cdot)$, S_2 for $0d_x \cdot S^{-1}(\cdot)$, S_3 for $0b_x \cdot S^{-1}(\cdot)$, and renaming the keys and the ciphertext bytes to k_0, k_1, k_2, k_3, k_4 and c_0, c_1, c_2, c_3, respectively:

$$a_4 = S^{-1}\left(k_4 \oplus S_0(c_0 \oplus k_0) \oplus S_1(c_1 \oplus k_1) \oplus S_2(c_2 \oplus k_2) \oplus S_3(c_3 \oplus k_3)\right). \quad (2)$$

Reducing the Data Complexity. In [31], Tunstall observed that the data complexity of the attack can be reduced to 2^{33} chosen plaintexts by examining two sets of 2^{32} plaintexts instead of six sets. The idea is to check an analogue of Eq. (1) for three additional bytes – x_5^4, x_{10}^4, and x_{15}^4 – using the same set of 2^{32} plaintexts. Note that in order to compute each of these three bytes from the ciphertext, the adversary needs the subkey bytes $k_{0,7,10,13}^5$ (which are the same as in Eq. (1)), along with a different byte of $\bar{k}^4$. When two sets are checked at

---

[2] We note that in [21], the authors performed a similar analysis and concluded that the complexity is 2^{52} S-box computations. This value was used in all subsequent papers. For the sake of consistency, we use the same value in Table 2, but note that the actual complexity is lower, as is shown here, and use the lower estimate when comparing the partial sums attack with our new attack.

Algorithm 1. Partial-sum algorithm for key recovery [21].

1: Input: Array A of bits such that the jth value of A denotes the parity of the number of occurrences of j in the list of ciphertexts
2: **for all** k_0, k_1 **do**
3:     Declare an empty bit-array A_1 of size 2^{24}
4:     **for all** c_0, c_1, c_2, c_3 **do**
5:         **if** $A[c_0, c_1, c_2, c_3] = 1$ **then**
6:             $a_1 \leftarrow S_0(c_0 \oplus k_0) \oplus S_1(c_1 \oplus k_1)$
7:             $A_1[a_1, c_2, c_3] \leftarrow A_1[a_1, c_2, c_3] \oplus 1$
8:     **for all** k_2 **do**
9:         Declare an empty bit-array A_2 of size 2^{16}
10:         **for all** a_1, c_2, c_3 **do**
11:             **if** $A_1[a_1, c_2, c_3] = 1$ **then**
12:                 $a_2 \leftarrow a_1 \oplus S_2(c_2 \oplus k_2)$
13:                 $A_2[a_2, c_3] \leftarrow A_2[a_2, c_3] \oplus 1$
14:         **for all** k_3 **do**
15:             Declare an empty bit-array A_3 of size 2^8
16:             **for all** a_2, c_3 **do**
17:                 **if** $A_2[a_2, c_3] = 1$ **then**
18:                     $a_3 \leftarrow a_2 \oplus S_3(c_3 \oplus k_3)$
19:                     $A_3[a_3] \leftarrow A_3[a_3] \oplus 1$
20:             **for all** k_4 **do**
21:                 $a_4 \leftarrow 0$
22:                 **for all** a_3 **do**
23:                     **if** $A_3[a_3] = 1$ **then**
24:                         $a_4 \leftarrow a_4 \oplus S^{-1}(k_4 \oplus a_3)$
25:                 **if** $a_4 \neq 0$ **then**
26:                     k_0, k_1, k_2, k_3, k_4 is not a valid key candidate

---

the same byte, they provide a 16-bit filtering, which in particular yields an 8-bit filtering on the value $k^5_{0,7,10,13}$ which is common to all examined bytes. Hence, information from different bytes can be combined to recover $k^5_{0,7,10,13}$ with a high probability.

The data complexity can be further reduced to 2^{32} by examining a single set and checking the XOR in all 16 bytes of x^4. The algorithm is more complex and uses a meet-in-the-middle procedure based on the properties of the AES key schedule. We omit the description here, as it will not be needed in the sequel.

In [31], it is claimed that when the same set of plaintexts is used to check the parity in several bytes, the complexity of checking the first byte is dominant, as some of the computations performed for computing the XOR in different bytes are identical. However, this claim seems incorrect, as in the variant of Eq. (1) for other bytes, the order of the coefficients $0e_x, 09_x, 0d_x, 0b_x$ which stems from the inverse MIXCOLUMNS operation is changed, and hence, the operations performed for different bytes are not identical and only knowledge of subkeys can be 'reused'. Therefore, the complexity of the attack that uses two sets is about $(4 + 3 + 2 + 2 + 1 + 1) \cdot 2^{48} = 2^{51.7}$ S-box computations, and the attack that uses one set takes about $16 \cdot 2^{50} = 2^{54}$ S-box computations.

The idea of using two sets of size 2^{32} instead of six was independently suggested in [2] by Alda et al., who also experimentally verified it.

2.4 The FFT-Based Attack of Todo and Aoki

The general idea of using the Fast Fourier Transform (FFT) for speeding up cryptanalytic attacks on block ciphers goes back to Collard et al. [14] who used the FFT to speed up linear cryptanalysis. This idea was extended to several other techniques, including multi-dimensional linear attacks [25,26], zero-correlation attacks [13], differential-linear attacks [10], etc.

In [30], Todo and Aoki proposed to replace the partial sums technique by an FFT-based technique. The basic idea behind the Todo-Aoki technique is that the sum of the values in the right hand side of Eq. (1) which we want to compute can be written in the form of a *convolution* of tailor-made functions, as seen in Algorithm 2.

Consider a set S of 2^{32} ciphertexts for which we want to compute the XOR of the intermediate values at the state byte x_0^4. Like in the partial sums attack, denote by A a bit array of size 2^{32}, such that $A(c_0, c_1, c_2, c_3) = 1$ if and only if $C_{0,7,10,13} = (c_0, c_1, c_2, c_3)$ holds for an odd number of ciphertexts in S. Let $f : \{0,1\}^{32} \to \{0,1\}$ be the indicator function of the array, that is, $f(c_0, c_1, c_2, c_3) = \mathbb{1}(A(c_0, c_1, c_2, c_3) = 1)$. Assume that the subkey k_4 was guessed, and let $g_i : \{0,1\}^{32} \to \{0,1\}$, for $0 \le i \le 7$, be defined by

$$g_i(t_0, t_1, t_2, t_3) = \left[S^{-1} \left(k_4 \oplus S_0(t_0) \oplus S_1(t_1) \oplus S_2(t_2) \oplus S_3(t_3) \right) \right]_i, \qquad (3)$$

where $[S^{-1}(t)]_i$ denotes the i'th bit of $S^{-1}(t)$. Then, denoting by $[x(C, k_0, k_1, k_2, k_3)]_i$ the i'th bit of the value x_0^4 corresponding to the ciphertext C for a given guess of k_0, k_1, k_2, k_3 (see Eq. (2)), we have

$$\bigoplus_{C \in S} [x(C, k_0, k_1, k_2, k_3)]_i = \bigoplus_{\{(c_0,c_1,c_2,c_3):A[c_0,c_1,c_2,c_3]=1\}} g_i(c_0 \oplus k_0, c_1 \oplus k_1, c_2 \oplus k_2, c_3 \oplus k_3)$$

$$= \bigoplus_{c_0,c_1,c_2,c_3} f(c_0, c_1, c_2, c_3) \cdot g_i(c_0 \oplus k_0, c_1 \oplus k_1, c_2 \oplus k_2, c_3 \oplus k_3)$$

$$= (f * g_i)(k_0, k_1, k_2, k_3).$$

Therefore, we can compute the sum for all 2^{32} possible guesses of (k_0, k_1, k_2, k_3) at once by guessing the byte k_4 and computing the convolution of two functions on 32 bits, that takes time of about $4 \cdot 2^{32} \log_2(2^{32})$ additions, as was shown by Collard et al. [14]. As the summation is performed for each bit separately, the complexity of examining a single set S of 2^{32} ciphertexts is $8 \cdot 2^8 \cdot 4 \cdot 2^{32} \log_2(2^{32}) = 2^{50}$ additions, which is roughly equal to the number of operations required for examining a single set of ciphertexts in the partial sums attack.

A disadvantage of the Todo-Aoki technique, compared to the partial sums attack, is that it cannot use partial knowledge of the subkey to obtain a speedup. Indeed, as the computation is performed for all values of (k_0, k_1, k_2, k_3) at the same time, partial knowledge (e.g., knowledge of k_3) cannot be exploited. As

Algorithm 2. FFT-based algorithm for key recovery [30]. The blue colored step has naive complexity $2^{32} \times 2^{32}$, but can be replaced by several Hadamard transformations of size 2^{32} with complexity 2^{37} each.

1: Input: Array A of bits such that the jth value of A denotes the parity of the number of occurrences of j in the list of ciphertexts
2: **for all** k_4 **do**
3:     **for all** k_0, k_1, k_2, k_3 **do**
4:         $A_1[k_0, k_1, k_2, k_3] \leftarrow \bigoplus_{c_0, c_1, c_2, c_3} A[c_0, c_1, c_2, c_3] \cdot S^{-1} \begin{pmatrix} k_4 \oplus S_0(c_0 \oplus k_0) \oplus S_1(c_1 \oplus k_1) \\ \oplus S_2(c_2 \oplus k_2) \oplus S_3(c_3 \oplus k_3) \end{pmatrix}$
5:     **for all** k_0, k_1, k_2, k_3 **do**
6:         **if** $A_1[k_0, k_1, k_2, k_3] \neq 0$ **then**
7:             k_0, k_1, k_2, k_3, k_4 is not a valid key candidate

---

a result, when six sets of 2^{32} ciphertexts are examined, the complexity of the Todo-Aoki attack becomes $6 \cdot 2^{50} = 2^{52.6}$ additions, while the overall complexity of partial sums is only $2^{51.3}$ S-box computations, as was shown above.

The question, whether there is a way to use partial knowledge of the key in an FFT-based attack, was explicitly mentioned as an open question in [30].

Using Precomputation of the FFT to Speed Up the Attack. In the eprint version of the same paper [29], Todo showed that the complexity of the attack can be reduced by precomputing some of the Fast Fourier Transforms that should be computed in the course of the attack.

Recall that the computation of the convolution of $f, g : \{0, 1\}^n \to \{0, 1\}$ using the FFT consists of three stages:

1. Computing the Fourier transforms $\hat{f}, \hat{g} : \{0, 1\}^n \to \mathbb{Z}$.
2. Computing the pointwise product $h : \{0, 1\}^n \to \mathbb{Z}$ defined by $h(x) = \hat{f}(x) \cdot \hat{g}(x)$.
3. Computing the inverse Fourier transform (which is the same as computing the Fourier transform and dividing by 2^n) to obtain $f * g = \hat{h} \cdot 2^{-n}$.

Here, we use the convention that the Fourier transform $\hat{f}$ is obtained from f by writing f as a 2^n-dimensional vector and multiplying it by the Hadamard matrix H_n, defined recursively as $H_n = \begin{pmatrix} H_{n-1} & H_{n-1} \\ H_{n-1} & -H_{n-1} \end{pmatrix}$, where $H_1 = \begin{pmatrix} 1 & 1 \\ 1 & -1 \end{pmatrix}$.

The cost of each computation of the FFT is $n2^n$ addition operations. In order to avoid overflow the additions should have at least $2n$ bits of precision, but since we only want one bit of the result the computation can be done with $n + 1$ bits of precision. For the 6-round AES attack we have $n = 32$ and the FFT will typically be implemented with 64-bit additions. The cost of the pointwise product is about 2^n multiplication operations, which is not much more than the cost of 2^n addition operations for small n (in particular for a software implementation with $n \leq 32$, as in the attack on 6-round AES).[3] Hence, the overall cost of the convolution computation in our case is about $3 \cdot 32 \cdot 2^{32}$ additions.

---

[3] We note that in [30], the authors conservatively estimate that pointwise multiplication of two vectors of size 2^n whose entries are n-bit integers takes $n2^n$ addition

Todo observed that the Fourier transforms $\hat{f}$ and $\hat{g}$ can be precomputed. As the function f does not depend on the guess of k_4, one can compute it once, store the result (which requires at most 2^{32} 64-bit words), and re-use it for each value of k_4. As the cost of this FFT computation is $32 \cdot 2^{32}$ additions, the amortization over guesses of k_4 makes it negligible. The function g cannot be precomputed since it depends on k_4. On the other hand, as it does not depend on the ciphertexts, it can be reused for other sets of ciphertexts. Therefore, the complexity of computing the XOR for a single set of 2^{32} ciphertexts is reduced to about $8 \cdot 2^8 \cdot 2 \cdot 32 \cdot 2^{32} = 2^{49}$ addition operations, and the complexity of computing the XOR for six sets is reduced to about $2^{49} + 5 \cdot 2^{48} = 2^{50.8}$ addition operations. If only two sets are examined and the XOR is computed in four bytes (as was described above), then the complexity becomes $2^{49} + 7 \cdot 2^{48} = 2^{51.2}$ addition operations. This complexity seems a bit lower than the complexity of partial sums, but it is still quite close and the different types of operations make comparison between the techniques tricky.

3   The New Technique: Partial Sums Meet FFT

In this section, we describe our new technique which allows combining the advantages of the partial sums technique with those of the Todo-Aoki FFT-based technique. We begin with a basic variant of the technique in Sect. 3.1, then we show how the complexity can be reduced significantly by packing several FFT computations together in Sect. 3.2, afterward, we present several additional enhancements and other variants of the basic technique in Sect. 3.3, and we conclude this section with a comparison of our technique with partial sums and the Todo-Aoki technique in Sect. 3.4. For the sake of concreteness, we present the attack in the case of 6-round AES and reuse the notations of Sect. 2. It will be apparent from the description how our technique can be applied in general.

3.1   The Basic Technique

Our basic observation is that we can follow the general structure of the partial sums attack, and replace each step by computing a convolution of properly chosen functions. This is shown in Algorithm 3 which is a rearrangement of the operations of Algorithm 1, making convolution appear. As we use somewhat different convolutions for different steps of the attack, we present them separately.

First Step. As described in Sect. 2.3, before the first step of the partial sums attack, the list of ciphertexts is replaced with a list A of 2^{32} binary indices which indicate whether each of the 2^{32} possible values of the bytes c_0, c_1, c_2, c_3 appears an even or an odd number of times in the list of ciphertexts. At the first step, the adversary guesses the bytes k_0, k_1, and replaces the list by a list A_1 of size 2^{24} which corresponds to the bytes a_1, c_2, c_3, where $a_1 = S_0(c_0 \oplus k_0) \oplus S_1(c_1 \oplus k_1)$.

---

operations. For the sake of consistency with [30] and fairness, we use the conservative estimate in the table of results and the less conservative estimate when we compare the Todo-Aoki technique to our technique.

We observe that the list A_1 can be computed for all values k_0, k_1 simultaneously by computing a convolution. Let $\chi : \{0,1\}^{32} \to \{0,1\}$ be the indicator function of the list A. That is, $\chi(c_0, c_1, c_2, c_3) = 1$ if and only if the value $(C_0, C_7, C_{10}, C_{13}) = (c_0, c_1, c_2, c_3)$ appears an odd number of times in the list of ciphertexts. For any $c_2, c_3 \in \{0,1\}^8$, define $\chi^1_{c_2,c_3}(c_0, c_1) = \chi(c_0, c_1, c_2, c_3)$.

For any $a_1 \in \{0,1\}^8$, let $I^1_{a_1}(x, y) = \mathbb{1}(S_0(x) \oplus S_1(y) = a_1)$. Both $\chi^1_{c_2,c_3}$ and $I^1_{a_1}$ are indicator functions on $\{0,1\}^{16}$. For any $a_1, c_2, c_3 \in \{0,1\}^8$, we have

$$(\chi^1_{c_2,c_3} * I^1_{a_1})(k_0, k_1) = \sum_{c_0,c_1 \in \{0,1\}^8} \chi^1_{c_2,c_3}(c_0, c_1) \cdot I^1_{a_1}(c_0 \oplus k_0, c_1 \oplus k_1)$$

$$= \sum_{c_0,c_1 \in \{0,1\}^8} \chi(c_0, c_1, c_2, c_3) \cdot \mathbb{1}(S_0(c_0 \oplus k_0) \oplus S_1(c_1 \oplus k_1) = a_1).$$

Therefore, the entry which corresponds to (a_1, c_2, c_3) in the list $A_1[k_0, k_1]$ created for the subkey guess (k_0, k_1) is

$$A_1[k_0, k_1][a_1, c_2, c_3] = ((\chi^1_{c_2,c_3} * I^1_{a_1})(k_0, k_1)) \mod 2. \tag{4}$$

(Formally, we define A_1, which is a list of size 2^{24} that depends on two key bytes, as an array of size $2^{16} \times 2^{24}$ which includes the guessed bytes.) As was shown in Sect. 2.4, the computation of this convolution requires $3 \cdot 16 \cdot 2^{16}$ addition operations for each value of a_1, c_2, c_3, or a total of $48 \cdot 2^{40}$ additions. This compares favorably with the first step of the partial sums attack which requires 2^{48} S-box computations. As we shall see below, the actual advantage of our technique is significantly larger. However, this requires to store the full A_1 for all values of (k_0, k_1), of size 2^{40} bits.

Second Step. At the second step of the partial sums attack, the adversary guesses the byte k_2 and reduces the list A_1 to a list A_2 of size 2^{16} that corresponds to the possible values of (a_2, c_3), where $a_2 = a_1 \oplus S_2(c_2 \oplus k_2)$.

We compute the entries of the list A_2 using a convolution, as follows. For any $k_0, k_1, c_3 \in \{0,1\}^8$, define

$$\chi^2_{k_0,k_1,c_3}(a_1, c_2) = \mathbb{1}(A_1[k_0, k_1][a_1, c_2, c_3]) \qquad I^2(x, y) = \mathbb{1}(x = S_2(y)).$$

Both $\chi^2_{k_0,k_1,c_3}$ and I^2 are indicator functions on $\{0,1\}^{16}$. For any $k_0, k_1, c_3 \in \{0,1\}^8$, we have

$$(\chi^2_{k_0,k_1,c_3} * I^2)(a_2, k_2) = \sum_{a_1,c_2 \in \{0,1\}^8} \chi^2_{k_0,k_1,c_3}(a_1, c_2) \cdot I^2(a_1 \oplus a_2, c_2 \oplus k_2)$$

$$= \sum_{a_1,c_2 \in \{0,1\}^8} \mathbb{1}(A_1[k_0, k_1][a_1, c_2, c_3]) \cdot \mathbb{1}(a_1 \oplus a_2 = S_2(c_2 \oplus k_2))$$

$$= \sum_{a_1,c_2 \in \{0,1\}^8} \mathbb{1}(A_1[k_0, k_1][a_1, c_2, c_3]) \cdot \mathbb{1}(a_2 = a_1 \oplus S_2(c_2 \oplus k_2)).$$

Therefore, the entry which corresponds to (a_2, c_3) in the list A_2 created for the subkey guess (k_0, k_1, k_2) is

$$A_2[k_2][a_2, c_3] = \big((\chi_{k_0,k_1,c_3}^2 * I^2)(a_2, k_2)\big) \bmod 2. \tag{5}$$

(Note that formally, we define A_2, which is a list of size 2^{16} that depends on three key bytes, as an array of size $2^8 \times 2^{16}$, which depends on k_0, k_1). As above, the complexity of this step is $48 \cdot 2^{40}$ additions.

Third Step. This step is similar to the second step. Thus, we present it briefly. At the third step of the partial sums attack, the adversary guesses the byte k_3 and reduces the list A_2 to a list A_3 of size 2^8 that corresponds to the possible values of a_3, where $a_3 = a_2 \oplus S_3(c_3 \oplus k_3)$. We obtain the list A_3 by defining

$$\chi_{k_0,k_1,k_2}^3(a_2, c_3) = \mathbb{1}(A_2[k_2][a_2, c_3]) \qquad \text{and} \qquad I^3(x, y) = \mathbb{1}(x = S_3(y)),$$

and setting

$$A_3[k_3][a_3] = \big((\chi_{k_0,k_1,k_2}^3 * I^3)(a_3, k_3)\big) \bmod 2. \tag{6}$$

(Note that formally, we define A_3 as an array of size $2^8 \times 2^8$, which depends on k_0, k_1, k_2). As above, the complexity of this step is $48 \cdot 2^{40}$ additions.

Fourth Step. At the fourth step of the partial sums attack, the adversary guesses the byte k_4, and computes $\bigoplus_{\{x \in \{0,1\}^8 : A_3[x]=1\}} S^{-1}(k_4 \oplus x)$, which is equal to the right hand side of (2), and checks whether it is equal to zero.

We cannot compute this XOR directly using a convolution, since in order to apply the FFT we need functions whose output is an integer and not an element of $GF(2^8)$. A basic solution, that was adopted by Todo and Aoki [30], is to compute the XOR in each bit separately. To this end, we define the functions $\chi_{k_0,k_1,k_2,k_3}^4, I^{4,j} : \{0,1\}^8 \to \{0,1\}$ for $j = 0, 1, \ldots, 7$ by

$$\chi_{k_0,k_1,k_2,k_3}^4(a_3) = 1(A_3[k_3][a_3]) \qquad \text{and} \qquad I^{4,j}(x) = [S^{-1}(x)]_j,$$

where $[S^{-1}(x)]_j$ denotes the j'th bit of $S^{-1}(x)$. We have

$$(\chi_{k_0,k_1,k_2,k_3}^4 * I^{4,j})(k_4) = \sum_{a_3 \in \{0,1\}^8} \chi_{k_0,k_1,k_2,k_3}^4(a_3) \cdot I^{4,j}(a_3 \oplus k_4)$$

$$= \sum_{a_3 \in \{0,1\}^8} \mathbb{1}(A_3[k_3][a_3]) \cdot [S^{-1}(a_3 \oplus k_4)]_j.$$

Therefore, the j'th bit of the XOR we would like to compute for the key guess $(k_0, k_1, k_2, k_3, k_4)$ is equal to

$$\big((\chi_{k_0,k_1,k_2,k_3}^4 * I^{4,j})(k_4)\big) \bmod 2. \tag{7}$$

Algorithm 3. The following is the Algorithm for key recovery. The function $\mathbb{1}$ is the indicator function. All the blue colored steps are of complexity $2^{16} \times 2^{16}$ and can be replaced by a 3 Hadamard transformations of size 2^{16} with total complexity 3×2^{20}. The red colored step has complexity $2^8 \times 2^8$, which can be replaced by 3 Hadamard transformations of size 2^8 with total complexity 3×2^{11}.

1: Input: Array A of bits such that the jth value of A denotes the parity of ciphertext j

2: Declare an empty 2D bit-array A_1 of size $2^{16} \times 2^{24}$; $\triangleright$ 2^{40} memory

3: **for all** a_1, c_2, c_3 **do**

4:      **for all** k_0, k_1 **do**

5:          $A_1[k_0, k_1][a_1, c_2, c_3] \leftarrow \bigoplus\limits_{c_0, c_1} A[c_0, c_1, c_2, c_3] \cdot \mathbb{1}(S_0(c_0 \oplus k_0) \oplus S_1(c_1 \oplus k_1) = a_1)$

6: **for all** k_0, k_1 **do**

7:      Declare an empty 2D bit-array A_2 of size $2^8 \times 2^{16}$;

8:      **for all** c_3 **do**

9:          **for all** k_2, a_2 **do**

10:              $A_2[k_2][a_2, c_3] \leftarrow \bigoplus\limits_{a_1, c_2} A_1[k_0, k_1][a_1, c_2, c_3] \cdot \mathbb{1}(a_1 \oplus S_2(c_2 \oplus k_2) = a_2)$

11:      **for all** k_2 **do**

12:          Declare an empty 2D bit-array A_3 of size $2^8 \times 2^8$;

13:          **for all** k_3, a_3 **do**

14:              $A_3[k_3][a_3] \leftarrow \bigoplus\limits_{a_2, c_3} A_2[k_2][a_2, c_3] \cdot \mathbb{1}(a_2 \oplus S_3(c_3 \oplus k_3) = a_3)$

15:          **for all** k_3 **do**

16:              Declare an empty 1D byte-array A_4 of size 2^8;

17:              **for all** k_4 **do**

18:                  $A_4[k_4] \leftarrow \bigoplus\limits_{a_3} A_3[k_3][a_3] \cdot S^{-1}(a_3 \oplus k_4)$

19:              **for all** k_4 **do**

20:                  **if** $A_4[k_4] \neq 0$ **then**

21:                      k_0, k_1, k_2, k_3, k_4 is not a valid key candidate

Hence, we can check the XOR by initializing a list of 2^{40} binary indicators which corresponds to the possible values of $(k_0, k_1, k_2, k_3, k_4)$, computing the convolutions $\chi^4_{k_0, k_1, k_2, k_3} * I^{4,j}$ for $j = 0, 1, \ldots, 7$, and discarding all keys $(k_0, k_1, k_2, k_3, k_4)$ for which at least one of the results of (7) is not equal to zero modulo 2.

The complexity of this step is $2^{32} \cdot 8 \cdot (3 \cdot 8 \cdot 2^8) = 192 \cdot 2^{40}$ additions, which is slightly better than the complexity of the fourth step of the partial sums technique. As we shall show below, the complexity can be reduced significantly, by using a new method to pack several FFTs together, and exploiting enhancements from previous attacks based on the re-use of computations.

3.2 Packing Several FFTs Together by Embedding into $\mathbb{Z}$

We now show that the complexity of the basic attack can be significantly reduced by packing several convolution computations into a single convolution.

We assume that the attack is implemented using 64-bit operations, which is typical for a software implementation. For reference, the 6-round AES attack of Todo and Aoki requires 64-bit additions to avoid overflow.

Improving the Fourth Step of the Attack. Consider the fourth step of our basic attack described above. The step consists of computing the convolution of the function $\chi^4_{k_0,k_1,k_2,k_3}$ with the eight functions $I^{4,j}$ ($j = 0, 1, \ldots, 7$). These eight convolutions can be replaced by a single computation of convolution.

Let s be a 'separation parameter' that will be determined below, and define a function $I^4 : \{0,1\}^8 \to \mathbb{Z}$ by $I^4(x) = \sum_{j=0}^{7} 2^{js}[S^{-1}(x)]_j$.

We claim that for an appropriate choice of s, the convolution $\chi^4_{k_0,k_1,k_2,k_3} * I^4$ allows recovering the value of the XOR in all 8 bits we are interested in, with a high probability. Indeed, we have

$$(\chi^4_{k_0,k_1,k_2,k_3} * I^4)(k_4) = \sum_{a_3 \in \{0,1\}^8} \chi^4_{k_0,k_1,k_2,k_3}(a_3) \cdot I^4(a_3 \oplus k_4)$$

$$= \sum_{a_3 \in \{0,1\}^8} \mathbb{1}(A_3[k_3][a_3]) \cdot \sum_{j=0}^{7} 2^{sj}[S^{-1}(a_3 \oplus k_4)]_j$$

$$= \sum_{j=0}^{7} 2^{sj} \sum_{a_3 \in \{0,1\}^8} \mathbb{1}(A_3[k_3][a_3]) \cdot [S^{-1}(a_3 \oplus k_4)]_j$$

$$= \sum_{j=0}^{7} 2^{sj} (\chi^4_{k_0,k_1,k_2,k_3} * I^{4,j})(k_4),$$

where the penultimate equality uses the change of the order of summation.

Recall that for each value of k_4, we want to compute the eight parity bits $(\chi^4_{k_0,k_1,k_2,k_3} * I^{4,j}(k_4))$ mod 2. Let us reformulate our goal, for the sake of convenience. Denoting $b_j = \chi^4_{k_0,k_1,k_2,k_3} * I^{4,j}(k_4)$, we have $\chi^4_{k_0,k_1,k_2,k_3} * I^4(k_4) = \sum_{j=0}^{7} 2^{sj} b_j$. Thus, for non-negative integers $b_0, b_1, \ldots, b_7$, we are given $\sum_{j=0}^{7} 2^{sj} b_j$ and we want to compute from it the eight parity bits (b_j) mod 2.

Observe that if for all $0 \le j \le 7$, we have $b_j < 2^s$, then the multiplications by 2^{sj} separate the values b_j, and thus, we can simply read the values (b_j) mod 2 from $2^{sj} b_j$, as in this case,

$$\forall j : \left[\sum_{j=0}^{7} 2^{sj} b_j\right]_{sj} = [2^{sj} b_j]_{sj} = (b_j) \bmod 2.$$

How Large Should s be so that $b_j < 2^s$ Holds with a High Probability for All j's? Note that each b_j is the sum of 128 elements, which correspond to the 128 values of c_3 such that $[S^{-1}(c_3 \oplus k_4)]_j = 1$. Each such element is $\chi^4_{k_0,k_1,k_2,k_3}(c_3)$, which can be viewed as a randomly distributed indicator. Hence, b_j is distributed like $Bin(128, 1/2)$. The expectation of such a variable is 64, and its standard deviation is $4\sqrt{2}$. This means that the values b_j are strongly concentrated around 64, and the probability $\Pr[b_j \geq 2^7]$ is extremely small. Therefore, by taking $s = 7$, we can derive the eight parity bits $(b_j) \bmod 2$ from the sum $\sum_{j=0}^{7} 2^{sj} b_j$, easily and with a very low error probability.

How Small Should s be in Order to Perform the Entire Computation with 64-bit Words? For the sake of efficiency, we compute the convolution using 64-bit word operations and disregard overflow beyond the 64'th bit. If s is too large, this may cause an error in the computation of the sum $\sum_{j=0}^{7} 2^{sj} b_j$, and consequently, in the computation of the parity bits $(b_j) \bmod 2$.

To overcome this, note that in the computation of a convolution of f, g : $\{0,1\}^n \to \mathbb{Z}$, all operations are additions and multiplications, except for division by 2^n at the last step. Hence, when we neglect overflow beyond the 64'th bit, this causes an additive error of $m \cdot 2^{64}$ for some $m \in \mathbb{Z}$ until the last step, and an additive error of $m \cdot 2^{64-n}$ at the final result. Assuming that $b_j < 2^s$ for all j, this error does not affect the parity bits as long as $7s < 64 - n$ (as the error affects only the top n bits of $\sum_{j=0}^{7} 2^{sj} b_j$).

In our case, $n = 8$ and hence, for all $s \leq 7$, the possible error does not affect the parity bits we compute.

Reducing s Even Further. Note that we can allow random errors in the convolution computations that do not correspond to the right subkey guess, as such random errors do not increase the probability of a wrong key guess to pass the filtering. Hence, we only have to make sure that for the right key, we obtain the correct value of the parity bits with a high probability.

As was explained above, the values b_j are concentrated around 64. Formally, by evaluating the cumulative distribution function of the binomial law, we have $\Pr[48 < b_j < 80] > 0.99$, and thus, $0 < b_j - 48 < 2^5$ with a very high probability. To make use of this concentration, we subtract from the value $\sum_{j=0}^{7} 2^{sj} b_j$ the integer $u = 48 \sum_{j=0}^{7} 2^{sj}$, to obtain

$$\sum_{j=0}^{7} 2^{sj} b_j - \sum_{j=0}^{7} 48 \cdot 2^{sj} = \sum_{j=0}^{7} (b_j - 48) 2^{sj}.$$

Since $0 < b_j - 48 < 2^5$, we can compute the parity bits $(b_j) \bmod 2$ also for $s = 6$ and for $s = 5$, with a very low error probability.

Summary of improving the fourth step. To summarize, the eight convolutions can be computed using a single convolution of functions over $\{0,1\}^8$. This reduces the complexity of this step to $2^{32} \cdot 3 \cdot 8 \cdot 2^8 = 24 \cdot 2^{40}$ operations.

Improving the Other Steps of the Attack. Once we acquired the ability to compute several convolutions in parallel, we can use it at the other steps of the attack as well. The idea is to pack the convolutions that correspond to several subkey guesses into a single convolution. We exemplify this approach by showing how the first step of the attack can be improved; the improvement of the second and the third steps are similar.

Recall that at the first step of our attack, for any values $c_2, c_3 \in \{0, 1\}^8$, we compute the parity of the convolution $(\chi^1_{c_2,c_3} * I^1_{a_1})(k_0, k_1)$, for all $k_0, k_1 \in \{0, 1\}^8$. We may pack up to seven such computations in parallel. For example, in order to pack four computations, we write $c_2 = (c_2^h, c_2^l)$, where c_2^h denotes the two most significant bits of c_2 and is identified with an integer between 0 and 3, via the binary expansion. We define

$$\chi^1_{c_2^h,c_2^l,c_3}(c_0, c_1) = \chi(c_0, c_1, c_2, c_3), \text{ and } \bar{\chi}^1_{c_2^l,c_3} = \sum_{j=0}^{3} 2^{sj} \chi^1_{j,c_2^l,c_3}.$$

Then, for any $c_2^l \in \{0, 1\}^6$, and $k_0, k_1, c_3 \in \{0, 1\}^8$, we compute the convolution $(\bar{\chi}^1_{c_2^l,c_3} * I^1_{a_1})(k_0, k_1)$, and using the technique described above we derive from it the four parity bits $((\chi^1_{c_2,c_3} * I^1_{a_1})(k_0, k_1))$ mod 2 with $c_2 \in \{(0, c_2^l), \ldots, (3, c_2^l)\}$.

To see what is the maximal value of s we may take, note that each convolution value $b' = (\chi^1_{c_2,c_3} * I^1_{a_1})(k_0, k_1)$ is the sum of 256 elements, which correspond to the 256 values of (c_0, c_1) such that $S_0(c_0 \oplus k_0) \oplus S_1(c_1 \oplus k_1) = a_1$. Each such element can be viewed as a randomly distributed indicator. Hence, b' is distributed like $Bin(256, 1/2)$. When analyzing step 4, we could tolerate a low probability of errors for the right key, but in the first step, there are 2^{24} values of A_1 that are involved in the computation for the right key, and we want all of them to be correct. Therefore, we use $s \geq 7$, since $\Pr[64 < b' < 192] > 1 - 2^{-50}$. Hence, by subtracting $64 \cdot \sum_{j=0}^{3} 2^{js}$ from the convolution value $(\bar{\chi}^1_{c_2^l,c_3} * I^1_{a_1})(k_0, k_1)$, we can correctly compute the parity bits $((\chi^1_{c_2,c_3} * I^1_{a_1})(k_0, k_1))$ mod 2 with a very high probability for $s \geq 7$, and the 2^{24} relevant values are simultaneously correct with probability at least $1 - 2^{-26}$.

Unfortunately, with $s = 7$ we can only pack 7 parallel convolutions within 64-bit words. Indeed, at this step, the convolution is computed for functions over $\{0, 1\}^{16}$ (instead of 8-bit functions in the fourth step), and thus, we need $7s < 64 - 16 = 48$ in order to pack 8 FFTs and avoid errors due to overflow. (We exemplified the idea of packing 4 parallel convolutions for the sake of convenience).

This reduces the complexity of the first step of the attack from $2^{24} \cdot 3 \cdot 16 \cdot 2^{16} = 48 \cdot 2^{40}$ to $48/7 \cdot 2^{40}$ addition operations. The complexity of the second step can be reduced similarly from $48 \cdot 2^{40}$ to $48/7 \cdot 2^{40}$. For the third step, we can actually use $s = 6$ and pack 8 parallel convolutions within a 64-bit word, because we only need 2^8 correct computations, and we have $\Pr[96 < b' < 160]^{256} > 0.98$; the complexity is reduced from $48 \cdot 2^{40}$ to $6 \cdot 2^{40}$.

Improving the Fourth Step Even Further. Finally, we can reduce the complexity of the fourth step even further by packing 12 FFTs in a 64-bit word with $s = 5$. This requires changing as described above the way we do the packing:

instead of packing 8 different $I^{4,j}$ with a fixed χ^4, we consider each function $I^{4,j}$ separately and pack a fixed $I^{4,j}$ with 12 χ^4 functions corresponding to different key guesses. This reduces the complexity of the fourth step from $24 \cdot 2^{40}$ to $16 \cdot 2^{40}$.

3.3 Enhancements and Other Variants of the Basic Technique

In this section, we present two enhancements that reduce the complexity of the attack, along with another variant of the technique that provides us with flexibility that will be useful in the application of our technique to other ciphers.

Precomputing Some of the FFT Computations. At each step of the attack, we perform three FFT computations. As was described in Sect. 2.4 regarding the FFT-based attack of Todo and Aoki, some of these computations do not depend on the guessed key material, and hence, they can be precomputed at the beginning of the attack, thus reducing the overall time complexity.

Specifically, the functions I^2, I^3, I^4, and $I^1_{a_1}$ (for all $a_1 \in \{0,1\}^8$) do not depend on any guessed subkey bits, and thus, their FFTs can be precomputed with overall complexity of about $2^8 \cdot 16 \cdot 2^{16} = 2^{28}$ addition operations, which is negligible compared to other steps of the attack. The results can be stored in lists that require about 2^{24} 64-bit words of memory.

The function $\chi^1_{c_2,c_3}$ does not depend on the value of a_1, and thus, its FFT can be computed once (for each value of (c_2, c_3)) and reused for all values of a_1. This reduces the time complexity of this FFT computation (in total, for all values of c_2, c_3) to $2^{16} \cdot 16 \cdot 2^{16} = 2^{36}$ additions, which is negligible compared to other steps of the attack. As we need to store in memory at each time only the result of the FFT that corresponds to a single value of c_2, c_3, the memory requirement of this step is 2^{16} 64-bit words of memory.

These precomputations reduce the time complexity of the first step (in which two FFTs can be precomputed) from $48/7 \cdot 2^{40}$ to $16/7 \cdot 2^{40}$ additions, the time complexity of the second, third, and fourth steps (in which one FFT can be precomputed) to $32/7 \cdot 2^{40}, 4 \cdot 2^{40}$, and $32/3 \cdot 2^{40}$ additions, respectively.

If the fourth step is implemented by packing 12 χ^4 functions together, as was described above, we can reduce its complexity further by precomputing the FFT of the function $\bar{\chi}^4$ which represents the 'packed' function and reusing it for computing convolutions with the eight functions $I^{4,j}$ ($j = 0, 1, \ldots, 7$). This reduces the time complexity of the fourth step to $(16 + (16/8))/3 \cdot 2^{40} = 6 \cdot 2^{40}$ additions.

Therefore, the time complexity of examining a set of 2^{32} plaintexts is reduced to $2^{40} \cdot (16/7 + 32/7 + 4 + 6) \approx 16.9 \cdot 2^{40} \approx 2^{44.1}$ additions.

Lower Cost for Examining Additional Sets of Plaintexts. As was described in Sect. 2.3 regarding the partial sums attack, when we check the XOR of additional sets of 2^{32} values at a byte which we already checked for one set, the complexity of the check is reduced. Indeed, after the first set was checked, we expect that for each value of $(k^5_0, k^5_7, k^5_{10}, k^5_{13})$, only a few values of

$\bar{k}_0^4$ are not discarded. Hence, instead of performing the fourth step of the attack by computing a convolution, we can simply compute the sum directly for each of the remaining candidate subkeys. The average complexity of such a step is $2^{32} \cdot 1 \cdot 2^7 = 2^{39}$ S-box evaluations and the same number of XORs, which is equivalent to about $1 \cdot 2^{40}$ addition operations. Note that since the fourth step is the most time consuming step of our attack, this gain is more significant than the gain which the partial sums attack achieves in the same case.

After two sets were checked, we expect that for each value of (k_0^5, k_7^5, k_{10}^5), only a few values of $(k_{13}^5, \bar{k}_0^4)$ are not discarded. Hence, instead of performing the third and the fourth steps of the attack by computing convolutions, we can simply perform each of them for each of the remaining candidate subkeys. This reduces the complexity of the third step to 2^{40} additions and the complexity of the fourth step to 2^{32} additions.

Attack that Examines Six Sets of 2^{32} Plaintexts. By continuing the reasoning in the same manner, we see that the complexity of considering six sets of 2^{32} ciphertexts and computing the XOR of the values x_0^4 that correspond to them, is about

$$2^{40} \cdot \left(\left(\frac{16+32}{7} + 4 + 6 \right) + \left(\frac{16+32}{7} + 4 + 1 \right) + \left(\frac{16+32}{7} + 1 \right) + \left(\frac{16}{7} + 1 \right) + 1 \right)$$
$$\approx 40.8 \cdot 2^{40} \approx 2^{45.4} \text{ additions.}$$

Attack that Examines Two Sets of 2^{32} Plaintexts. If we consider two sets of 2^{32} ciphertexts and examine 4 different bytes (as was suggested by Tunstall [31] for the partial sums attack), then we may begin with checking the XOR of both sets at the byte x_0^4, which requires $2^{40}(16.9 + 11.9)$ additions as was described above. Then, we must move to another byte, and it seems that we have to pay a 'full price' again. However, note that after the first two filterings, for each value of (k_0^5, k_7^5, k_{10}^5) we are left with one value of k_{13}^5 on average. As these four subkey bytes are reused in the examination of the XOR in the byte x_5^4 (along with a different byte from $\bar{k}^4$), we can replace the third step by computing the sum directly for each remaining value of k_{13}^5 and replace the fourth step by computing the sum directly for each remaining value of $(k_{13}^5, \bar{k}_1^4)$. This reduces the complexity of each of these two steps to 2^{40} additions. When we examine the second set of 2^{32} ciphertexts at the byte x_5^4, the complexity of the fourth step can be further reduced to 2^{32} additions, since for any value of (k_0^5, k_7^5, k_{10}^5) we are left with one value of $(k_{13}^5, \bar{k}_1^4)$ on average.

Continuing in the same manner, we see that the complexity of considering two sets of 2^{32} ciphertexts and computing the XOR of the values $x_{0,5,10,15}^4$ that correspond to them, is about

$$2^{40} \cdot \left(\left(\frac{16+32}{7} + 4 + 6 \right) + \left(\frac{16+32}{7} + 4 + 1 \right) + \left(\frac{16+32}{7} + 1 + 1 \right) + \right.$$
$$\left. \left(\frac{16+32}{7} + 1 \right) + \left(\frac{16}{7} + 1 \right) + \left(\frac{16}{7} + 1 \right) + 1 \right) \approx 62.8 \cdot 2^{40} \approx 2^{46} \text{ additions.}$$

Attack that Examines One Set of 2^{32} Plaintexts. As was explained in Sect. 2.3, in this case we examine each byte with only a single set of ciphertexts, and thus, we do not obtain information that can be reused in other computations. Therefore, the complexity of our attack in this case is $16 \cdot 16.9 \cdot 2^{40} = 2^{48.1}$ addition operations, which is 16 times the complexity of checking a single set of ciphertexts (like in the partial sums and the Todo-Aoki attacks with only a single set of 2^{32} ciphertexts examined).

Alternative Way of Performing the First Step. Recall that at the first step we are given a list A of 2^{32} binary indices which correspond to (c_0, c_1, c_2, c_3) and our goal is to compute the 2^{24} entries of the list A_1 which corresponds to triples of the form (a_1, c_2, c_3) where $a_1 = S_0(c_0 \oplus k_0) \oplus S_1(c_1 \oplus k_1)$, for all values of (k_0, k_1). We may divide this step into two sub-steps as follows:

- *Step 1.1:* At this sub-step, we guess the subkey k_0 and update the list A into a list A_0 of 2^{32} binary indices that correspond to (a_0, c_1, c_2, c_3), where $a_0 = S_0(c_0 \oplus k_0)$. The complexity of this step is about $2^{32} \cdot 2^8 = 2^{40}$ S-box computations.
- *Step 1.2:* At this sub-step, performed for each guess of k_0, our goal is to replace the list A_0 with a list of size 2^{24} that corresponds to the values (a_1, c_2, c_3) where $a_1 = a_0 \oplus S_1(c_1 \oplus k_1)$, for each value of k_1. This task is exactly the same as the task handled at the second and third steps of our attack described above, and hence, it can be performed in exactly the same way. Specifically, the convolution we have to compute is

$$A_1[k_0, k_1][a_1, c_2, c_3] = \left((\bar{\chi}^1_{k_0, c_2, c_3} * \bar{I}^1)(a_1, k_1) \right) \bmod 2, \qquad (8)$$

where

$$\bar{\chi}^1_{k_0, c_2, c_3}(a_0, c_1) = \mathbb{1}(A_0(a_0, c_1, c_2, c_3) = 1), \text{ and } \bar{I}^1(x, y) = \mathbb{1}(x = S_1(y)).$$

Like in the second step of our attack described above, we can precompute one FFT and perform the computation of 7 FFTs in parallel. Hence, the complexity of this sub-step is $32/7 \cdot 2^{40}$ additions.

The alternative version of the attack is presented in Algorithm 4.

Formally, the complexity of the alternative way is higher than the complexity of the original way of performing this step described above—$39/7 \cdot 2^{40}$ additions instead of $16/7 \cdot 2^{40}$ additions. As a result, the complexity of the attack with two sets of 2^{32} plaintexts becomes about $82.5 \cdot 2^{40} \approx 2^{46.4}$ additions (which is the complexity we mention in the introduction). However, this alternative has several advantages:

1. *Lower memory complexity.* In the attack described above, the most memory-consuming part is the first step which requires a list of 2^{40} bit entries. Thus, its memory complexity is about 2^{33} 128-bit blocks.
   The alternative way reduces the memory complexity of the first step to 2^{32}

Algorithm 4. Low-memory version of the attack.

1: Input: Array A of bits such that the jth value of A denotes the parity of ciphertext j

2: **for all** k_0 **do**

3:     Declare an empty 1D bit-array A_0 of size 2^{32};   ▷ 2^{32} memory

4:     **for all** c_0, c_1, c_2, c_3 **do**

5:         $a_0 \leftarrow S_0(c_0 \oplus k_0)$

6:         $A_0[a_0, c_1, c_2, c_3] \leftarrow A[c_0, c_1, c_2, c_3]$

7:     Declare an empty 2D bit-array A_1 of size $2^8 \times 2^{24}$;   ▷ 2^{32} memory

8:     **for all** c_2, c_3 **do**

9:         **for all** k_1, a_1 **do**

10:            $A_1[k_1][a_1, c_2, c_3] \leftarrow \bigoplus_{a_0, c_1} A_0[a_0, c_1, c_2, c_3] \cdot \mathbb{1}(a_0 \oplus S_1(c_1 \oplus k_1) = a_1)$

11:    **for all** k_1 **do**

12:        Declare an empty 2D bit-array A_2 of size $2^8 \times 2^{16}$;

13:        **for all** c_3 **do**

14:            **for all** k_2, a_2 **do**

15:                $A_2[k_2][a_2, c_3] \leftarrow \bigoplus_{a_1, c_2} A_1[k_1][a_1, c_2, c_3] \cdot \mathbb{1}(a_1 \oplus S_2(c_2 \oplus k_2) = a_2)$

16:        **for all** k_2 **do**

17:            Declare an empty 2D bit-array A_3 of size $2^8 \times 2^8$;

18:            **for all** k_3, a_3 **do**

19:                $A_3[k_3][a_3] \leftarrow \bigoplus_{a_2, c_3} A_2[k_2][a_2, c_3] \cdot \mathbb{1}(a_2 \oplus S_3(c_3 \oplus k_3) = a_3)$

20:            **for all** k_3 **do**

21:                Declare an empty 1D byte-array A_4 of size 2^8;

22:                for all k_4 do

23:                    $A_4[k_4] \leftarrow \bigoplus_{a_3} A_3[k_3][a_3] \cdot S^{-1}(a_3 \oplus k_4)$

24:                **for all** k_4 **do**

25:                    **if** $A_4[k_4] \neq 0$ **then**

26:                        k_0, k_1, k_2, k_3, k_4 is not a valid key candidate

---

bits. We observe that all other steps of the attack can be performed with at most 2^{34} bits of memory. Indeed, all ciphertexts can be transformed immediately into entries of the table A whose size is 2^{32} bits. The table A_0 (which should be stored for one value of k_0 at a time) requires 2^{32} bits. The subsequent tables used in the attack are smaller, and the arrays used in the FFTs are also smaller (as all FFTs are performed on 16-bit or 8-bit functions). By checking two sets of 2^{32} plaintexts in parallel, we reduce the number of remaining keys after examining the byte x_0^4 to 2^{24}, and then the storage of these keys requires less than 2^{30} bits of memory. Therefore, the total memory complexity of the attack is reduced to about $2 \cdot 2^{32} + 2^{32} < 2^{34}$ bits, i.e., 2^{27} 128-bit blocks.

2. *Lower average-case time complexity.* While it is common to measure the complexity of attacks using the worst-case scenario (e.g., the complexity of

exhaustive search over an n-bit key is computed as 2^n, although on average, the attack finds the key after 2^{n-1} trials), the average-case complexity has clear practical significance. In the partial sums attack and in the Todo-Aoki attack, the average-case time complexity is half of the worst-case complexity, since the attack is applied for 2^8 'external' guesses of a subkey, and the right key is expected to be found after trying half of these subkeys. In the original version of our attack, since the last step is performed for all keys in parallel, our average-case complexity is no better than the worst-case complexity, and so, we lose a factor of 2. In the alternative way described here, the attack is performed for each guess of the subkey k_0^5, and hence, we regain the factor 2 loss in the average-case complexity.

3. *Practical effect on the time complexity.* The lower memory complexity of the alternative variant of the attack is expected to have an effect on the time complexity as well. Indeed, our experiments show that the memory accesses to the 2^{40}-bit sized array slow down our attack considerably. As the alternative variant requires only 2^{34} bits of memory, it may be even faster in practice than the original variant.

The alternative way of performing the first step is also used in our improved attack on the full MISTY1 [24] presented in the full version of this paper [19].

3.4   Our Technique vs. Partial Sums and the Todo-Aoki Technique

In this section, we present a comparison between our new technique and the partial sums technique and the Todo-Aoki FFT-based technique. First, we discuss the case of 6-round AES, and then we discuss applications to general ciphers.

The Case of 6-Round AES. Here, we considered three attacks:

1. *Attack with 6 structures of 2^{32} chosen plaintexs.* The partial sums attack requires $2^{51.3}$ S-box computations, the Todo-Aoki attack requires $2^{50.8}$ additions, and our attack requires $2^{45.4}$ additions. Hence, our attack is at least 32 times faster than both previous attacks. In the experiments presented in Sect. 3.5, the advantage of our attack was even bigger.
2. *Attack with 2 structures of 2^{32} chosen plaintexs.* The partial sums attack requires $2^{51.7}$ S-box computations, the Todo-Aoki attack requires $2^{51.2}$ additions, and our attack requires 2^{46} additions. Hence, our attack is at least 32 times faster than both previous attacks.
3. *Attack with 1 structure of 2^{32} chosen plaintexs.* The partial sums attack requires 2^{54} S-box computations, the Todo-Aoki attack requires 2^{53} additions, and our attack requires $2^{48.1}$ additions. Hence, our attack is almost 32 times faster than both previous attacks.

General Comparison. The speedup of our technique over the partial sums technique stems from two advantages: First, we replace key guessing steps with computation of convolutions. Second, we may pack the computation of several convolutions in a single convolution computation. The effect of the first advantage depends on the number of subkey bits guessed at the most time consuming steps of the attack: For a 4-bit subkey guess our gain is negligible, for an 8-bit key guess we get a speedup by a factor of more than 10 (without using packing), and for a 32-bit key guess our speedup factor may be larger than 2^{25} as demonstrated in our attack on CLEFIA [22] presented in the full version of this paper [19]. The effect of the second advantage is also dependent on the number of guessed subkey bits (since it determines the size of the functions whose convolution we have to compute, which in turn affects the number of convolutions we may pack together). Usually, between 4 and 8 convolutions can be packed together, which leads to a speedup by a factor of at least 4. Interestingly, when the number of guessed subkey bits is small (e.g., 4 bits), more convolutions can be packed together, and hence, a stronger effect of the second advantage compensates for a weaker effect of the first advantage.

The speedup of our technique over the Todo-Aoki technique stems from two advantages: First, our attack provides us with more flexibility, meaning that instead of replacing the whole attack by a single FFT-based step, we can consider each step (or a few steps) of the partial sums procedure separately and decide whether it will be better to perform it with key guessing or with an FFT-based technique. Second, we may pack the computation of several convolutions in a single convolution computation. The first advantage allows us to make use of partial knowledge of the subkey. A particular setting in which this advantage plays a role is analysis of additional plaintext sets after one set was used to obtain some key filtering. While our technique and the partial sums technique can make use of this partial knowledge, the Todo-Aoki technique must repeat the entire procedure. In the case of 6-round AES, this makes our attack 6 times faster than the Todo-Aoki attack without using packing. A more complete comparison between our method and the Todo-Aoki technique is available in the full version of this paper [19].

The second advantage provides a speedup by a factor of at least 4, as was described above. Yet another advantage that is worth mentioning is that while the Todo-Aoki technique applies the FFT to functions in high dimensions (e.g., dimension 72 in the Todo-Aoki attack on 12-round CLEFIA-128 presented in [30]), our technique applies the FFT to functions of a significantly lower dimension (e.g., dimension 16 in our improved attack on 12-round CLEFIA-128 presented in Appendix B of the full version of this paper [19]). Computation of the FFT in high dimensions is quite cumbersome from the practical point of view, and hence, avoiding this is a practical advantage of our technique. Moreover, higher dimension FFTs require additions with more precision; without using packing the Todo-Aoki attack on 6-round AES requires 64-bit additions while our attack can use 32-bit additions.

Two advantages of the partial sums technique and the Todo-Aoki technique over our technique are a somewhat lower memory complexity (about 2^{27} 128-bit blocks for partial sums and about 2^{31} 128-bit blocks for Todo-Aoki) and the fact that on average, the attack finds the right key after trying half of the possible keys while our attack must try all keys. However, both advantages can be countered by implementing the first step of our attack in the alternative way presented in Sect. 3.3, which makes the memory complexity equal to that of the partial sums attack and regains the 'lower average-case complexity', as was explained in Sect. 3.3.

3.5 Experimental Verification of Our Attack on 6-Round AES

We have experimentally verified our attack on Amazon's AWS infrastructure. For comparison, we also implemented the partial sums attack of [21] and the Todo-Aoki attack [30]. All implementations in C are publicly available at the following link:

https://github.com/ShibamCrS/Partial_Sums_Meet_FFT.

We note that the FFT implementations were based on the "Fast Fast Hadamard Transform" library [3].

The AWS Instances Used in the Experiment. For each attack we had to pick the most optimal AWS instance, depending on the computational and memory requirements.

The partial sums attack is quite easy to parallelize, and its memory requirement is low. (Specifically, the memory requirement is 2^{34} bits, or 16 GB, as was shown above. Furthermore, only an 2^{32}-bit list that stores the parities of (c_0, c_1, c_2, c_3) combinations should be stored in a memory readable by all threads). As a result, we took the Intel-based instance (that has the AES-NI instruction set) with the maximal number of cores per US$. At the time the experiment was performed (January, 2023) this was the m6i.32xlarge instance.[4]

For our attack (in its original variant) and for the Todo-Aoki attack, we needed instances that support a larger amount of memory. The optimal choice for our attack was the same instance as the one for the partial sums attack—the m6i.32xlarge instance. For the Todo-Aoki attack, we needed 64 GB of RAM for each thread of the attack. Hence, the optimal instance we found was the r6i.32xlarge instance.[5] We note that in the Todo-Aoki attack, we do not exploit all the vCPUs, but we do exploit the whole memory space (of 1 TB of RAM).

Experimental Results. The partial sums attack took 4859 minutes to complete, and its cost was 497 US$ (we used the US-east-2 region (Ohio) which offered the cheapest cost-per-hour for a Linux machine of 6.144 US$, before VAT). The Todo-Aoki approach took 3120 minutes to complete, and its cost was 418 US$ (at 8.064 US$ per hour). We note that due to the costs of these

---

[4] The m6i.32xlarge instance has 128 Intel-based vCPUs and 512GB of RAM.
[5] The r6i.32xlarge instance has 128 Intel-based vCPUs and 1024 GB of RAM.

attacks, they were run only once, but none of those attacks (nor our attack) is expected to show high variance in the running time.

To evaluate the running time of our attack, we ran Algorithm 3 and Algorithm 4 ten times each. In both algorithms, we used only 4 FFTs packed in parallel at each of Steps 1,2,3 and 8 FFTs packed in parallel at Step 4, for ease of implementation. The average running time of Algorithm 3 is 90 minutes, and its average cost is 9.21 US$. The average running time of Algorithm 4 is 48 minutes and its cost is 5 US$. Hence, in the experiment our attack was 83-times cheaper and 65 times faster than both partial sums and Todo-Aoki's attacks.

4   Improved Attack on Kuznyechik

The flexibility of our techniques improves attacks against various other ciphers that use the partial sums technique. In this section, we demonstrate this by presenting an attack on 7-round Kuznyechik, which improves over the multiset-algebraic attack on the cipher presented in [12] by a factor of more than 80. In the supplementary material of the full paper [19], we present improved attacks on the full MISTY1, and variants of CLEFIA-128 with 11 and 12 rounds. Our attacks on Kuznyechik and MISTY1 are the best known attacks on these ciphers.

4.1   The Structure of Kuznyechik

The block cipher Kuznyechik [18] is the current encryption standard of the Russian Federation. It is an SPN operating on a 128-bit state organized as a 4×4 array of 8-bit words. The key length is 256 bits, and the encryption process is composed of 9 rounds. Each round of Kuznyechik is composed of three operations:

Substitution. Apply an 8-bit S-box independently to every byte of the state;
Linear Transformation. Multiply the state by an invertible 16-by-16 matrix M over $GF(2^8)$;
Key Addition. XOR a 128-bit round key computed from the secret key to the state.

An additional key addition operation is applied before the first round. As properties of the key schedule of Kuznyechik are not used in this paper, we omit its description and refer the reader to [18].

4.2   The Multiset-Algebraic Attack of Biryukov et al.

In [12], Biryukov et al. presented an algebraic attack on up to 7 rounds of Kuznyechik. The attack is based on the following observation:

Lemma 3. *Consider the encryption by 4-round Kuznyechik of a set of 2^{127} distinct plaintexts, $P^0, P^1, \ldots, P^{2^{127}-1}$, which form a subspace of degree 127 of $\{0,1\}^{128}$. Then the corresponding ciphertexts satisfy $\bigoplus_{i=0}^{2^{127}-1} C^i = 0$.*

The attack uses Lemma 3 in the same way as the Square attack on AES uses Lemma 1. The adversary asks for the encryption of the entire codebook of 2^{128} plaintexts. Then he guesses a single byte of the whitening subkey and for each guess, he finds a set of 2^7 values in that byte such that the corresponding values after the substitution operation form a 7-dimensional subspace of $\{0,1\}^8$. By taking these values along with all 2^{120} possible values in the other 15 bytes, the adversary obtains a set of 2^{127} plaintexts, whose corresponding intermediate values after one round satisfy the assumption of Lemma 3.

By the lemma, the XOR of the corresponding values at the end of the 5'th round is zero. In order to check this, the adversary guesses some subkey bytes in the last two rounds and partially decrypts the ciphertexts to compute the XOR in a single byte at the end of the 5'th round. The situation is similar to the AES, with the 'only' difference that since the linear transformation is a 16-by-16 matrix (and not a 4-by-4), one has to guess all 16 bytes of the last round subkey. The adversary guesses the last round subkey and one byte of the equivalent subkey of the penultimate round, partially decrypts the ciphertexts, and checks whether the values XOR to zero. Biryukov et al. suggested to significantly speed up this procedure using partial sums. Borrowing the notation from Sect. 2.3, the value of the byte in which the XOR should be computed can be written as:

$$x_0^5 = S^{-1}(\bar{k}_0^5 \oplus e_0 \cdot S^{-1}(C_0 \oplus k_0^6) \oplus e_1 \cdot S^{-1}(C_1 \oplus k_1^6) \oplus \dots$$
$$\oplus e_{14} \cdot S^{-1}(C_{14} \oplus k_{14}^6) \oplus e_{15} \cdot S^{-1}(C_{15} \oplus k_{15}^6)), \tag{9}$$

where the constants $e_0, e_1, \dots, e_{15}$ are obtained from the matrix M^{-1} and the multiplication is defined over $GF(2^8)$. In the attack of Biryukov et al., the sum in the right hand side of (9) is computed using 16 steps of partial sums, where we begin with a list of 2^{128} binary indices which indicate the parity of occurrence of each ciphertext value, and at each step, another subkey byte k_i^6 is guessed and the size of the list is reduced by a factor of 2^8. Like in the partial sums attack on the AES, the two outstanding steps are the first step in which two subkeys are guessed and the list is squeezed to a list of size 2^{120}, and the last step in which the XOR of 2^8 values is computed under the guess of 17 subkey bytes.

The complexity of each step is 2^{144} S-box computations, and hence, the complexity of the entire procedure is 2^{148} S-box computations. Since the procedure provides only an 8-bit filtering, the adversary has to repeat it for each of the 16 bytes (and for each guess of the subkey byte at the first round). Therefore, the total time complexity of the attack is $2^8 \cdot 16 \cdot 2^{148} = 2^{160}$ S-box computations, which are equivalent (according to [12]) to $2^{154.5}$ encryptions.

The authors of [12] present also an attack on 6-round Kuznyechik. In this attack, they use the fact that for 3-round Kuznyechik, taking a vector space of degree 120 of plaintexts (instead of degree 127 above) is sufficient for guaranteeing that the ciphertexts XOR to zero. Hence, in order to attack 6-round Kuznyechik, an adversary can ask for the encryption of 2^{120} plaintexts which are equal in a single byte and assume all possible values in the other bytes. The corresponding intermediate values after one round form a vector space of degree 120, and hence, the corresponding intermediate values after 4 rounds XOR to zero. This allows applying the same attack like above, where the overall complexity is reduced by a factor of 2^8 since there is no need to guess a subkey byte at the first round. Hence, the overall data complexity is 2^{120} chosen plaintexts and the time complexity is $2^{146.5}$ encryptions.

The attacks of [12] are the best known attacks on reduced-round Kuznyechik.

4.3 Improvement Using Our Technique

Just like for AES, we can replace each step of the partial sums procedure performed in [12] by computing a convolution. We can compute several convolutions in parallel by embedding into $\mathbb{Z}$ as well as precompute two FFTs required for the first step and one FFT required for each subsequent step. However, we can only compute 6 FFTs in parallel rather than 7, as we need 2^{120} values to be correct in the first step. This requires $s \geq 8$ and cannot accommodate 7 parallel FFTs; instead we use 6 parallel FFTs with $s = 9$ which guarantees no overflow. The complexity of the first step is reduced to $2^{120} \cdot 16 \cdot 2^{16}/6 = 8/3 \cdot 2^{136}$ additions and the complexity of the subsequent steps is reduced to $2^{120} \cdot 2 \cdot 16 \cdot 2^{16}/6 = 16/3 \cdot 2^{136}$ additions. At the last step (which computes the XOR of the values) we have to compute FFTs for the 8 bits of the SBox individually, but we use FFTs on 8-bit functions (instead of 16-bit ones), we can pack 8 computations in parallel, and we can precompute an additional FFT and reuse it for the computations of the eight bits. Hence, its amortized complexity is $2^{128} \cdot (1 + (1/8)) \cdot 8 \cdot 2^8 = 9 \cdot 2^{136}$ additions. We conclude that the analysis of a single set of 2^{127} ciphertexts, with a given guess of the whitening key, takes $(8/3 + 14 \cdot 16/3 + 9)2^{136} = 259/3 \cdot 2^{136} = 2^{142.4}$ additions.

Instead of examining the other 15 bytes using the same set of 2^{127} ciphertexts, we may construct additional sets of 2^{127} ciphertexts by taking other 127-dimensional subspaces at the end of the first round (which is possible since we ask for the encryption of the entire codebook and guess a subkey byte at the first round) and examining their XOR at the same byte at the end of the 5'th round. Like in the case of AES, when we examine the XOR at the same byte for a second set of ciphertexts, the complexity of the last step becomes negligible (as it is performed only for a few possible values of the subkey). When a third set of ciphertexts is examined, the two last steps become negligible, etc. By using seven sets of 2^{127} ciphertexts and examining each of them in three bytes, the complexity of the attack becomes

$$2^8 \cdot 2^{136} \cdot 1/3 \cdot ((259 + 232 + 216 + 200 + 184 + 168 + 152) +$$
$$+ (136 + 136 + 120 + 104 + 88 + 72 + 56) + (40 + 40 + 24 + 8))$$
$$= 2^{144} \cdot 745 = 2^{153.5}$$

additions, which are equivalent to about 2^{148} encryptions – a speedup by a factor of more than 80 compared to the attack of [12].

The attack on 6-round Kuznyechik can be improved similarly. The only difference is that we cannot use additional sets of plaintexts without increasing the data complexity. Hence, for the same data complexity, the time complexity is reduced to $2^{146.4}$ additions, which are equivalent to $2^{140.9}$ encryptions – a speedup by a factor of more than 40.

5   Summary

In this paper we showed that the partial sums technique of Ferguson et al. [21] and the FFT-based technique of Todo and Aoki [30] can be combined into a new technique that allows enjoying *the best of the two worlds*. The combination improves over the best previously known attacks on 6-round AES by a factor of more than 32, as we verified experimentally.

Furthermore, the new technique allows improving other attacks—most notably, we improve the best known attack against Kuznyechik [18] by a factor of more than 80. Our method also yields the best known attack against the full MISTY1 [24] where we improve previous best result by a factor of 6, and improve the partial sums attacks against reduced-round CLEFIA [22] by varying factors (including a huge factor of 2^{30}, on 12-round CLEFIA-128) as shown in the full version of this paper [19]. We expect that our new technique will be used to improve other cryptanalytic attacks, and will (again) highlight the strength and potential of FFT-based techniques in improving cryptanalytic attacks.

Acknowledgements. The research was conducted in the framework of the workshop 'New directions in the cryptanalysis of AES', supported by the European Research Council under the ERC starting grant agreement n. 757731 (LightCrypt). The authors thank all the participants of the workshop for valuable discussions and suggestions.

The first, second and sixth authors were supported in part by the Center for Cyber, Law, and Policy in conjunction with the Israel National Cyber Directorate in the Prime Minister's Office and by the Israeli Science Foundation through grants No. 880/18 and 3380/19. The third and the fifth authors were supported by the European Research Council under the ERC starting grant agreement n. 757731 (LightCrypt) and by the BIU Center for Research in Applied Cryptography and Cyber Security in conjunction with the Israel National Cyber Bureau in the Prime Minister's Office. The fourth author is partially supported by ANR grants ANR-20-CE48-001 and ANR-22-PECY-0010.

References

1. Advanced Encryption Standard (AES). National Institute of Standards and Technology, NIST FIPS PUB 197, U.S. Department of Commerce, November 2001
2. Aldà, F., Aragona, R., Nicolodi, L., Sala, M.: Implementation and improvement of the partial sum attack on 6-round AES. In: Baldi, M., Tomasin, S. (eds.) Physical and Data-Link Security Techniques for Future Communication Systems. LNEE, vol. 358, pp. 181–195. Springer, Cham (2016). https://doi.org/10.1007/978-3-319-23609-4_12
3. Andoni, A., Indyk, P., Laarhoven, T., Razenshteyn, I., Schmidt, L.: Fast Fast Hadamard Transform. https://github.com/FALCONN-LIB/FFHT

4. Ankele, R., Dobraunig, C., Guo, J., Lambooij, E., Leander, G., Todo, Y.: Zero-correlation attacks on tweakable block ciphers with linear TWEAKEY expansion. Cryptology ePrint Archive, Report 2019/185 (2019). https://eprint.iacr.org/2019/185

5. Bao, Z., Guo, C., Guo, J., Song, L.: TNT: how to tweak a block cipher. In: Canteaut, A., Ishai, Y. (eds.) EUROCRYPT 2020, Part II. LNCS, vol. 12106, pp. 641–673. Springer, Cham (2020). https://doi.org/10.1007/978-3-030-45724-2_22

6. Bar-On, A., Dinur, I., Dunkelman, O., Lallemand, V., Keller, N., Tsaban, B.: Cryptanalysis of SP networks with partial non-linear layers. In: Oswald, E., Fischlin, M. (eds.) EUROCRYPT 2015. LNCS, vol. 9056, pp. 315–342. Springer, Heidelberg (2015). https://doi.org/10.1007/978-3-662-46800-5_13

7. Bar-On, A., Dunkelman, O., Keller, N., Ronen, E., Shamir, A.: Improved key recovery attacks on reduced-round AES with practical data and memory complexities. J. Cryptol. **33**(3), 1003–1043 (2020)

8. Bar-On, A., Keller, N.: A 2^{70} attack on the full MISTY1. In: Robshaw, M., Katz, J. (eds.) CRYPTO 2016, Part I. LNCS, vol. 9814, pp. 435–456. Springer, Heidelberg (2016). https://doi.org/10.1007/978-3-662-53018-4_16

9. Bariant, A., Leurent, G.: Truncated boomerang attacks and application to AES-based ciphers. In: Hazay, C., Stam, M. (eds.) EUROCRYPT 2023. LNCS, vol. 14007, pp. 3–35. Springer, Cham (2023). https://doi.org/10.1007/978-3-031-30634-1_1

10. Beierle, C., Leander, G., Todo, Y.: Improved differential-linear attacks with applications to ARX ciphers. In: Micciancio, D., Ristenpart, T. (eds.) CRYPTO 2020, Part III. LNCS, vol. 12172, pp. 329–358. Springer, Cham (2020). https://doi.org/10.1007/978-3-030-56877-1_12

11. Biryukov, A.: The boomerang attack on 5 and 6-round reduced AES. In: Dobbertin, H., Rijmen, V., Sowa, A. (eds.) AES 2004. LNCS, vol. 3373, pp. 11–15. Springer, Heidelberg (2005). https://doi.org/10.1007/11506447_2

12. Biryukov, A., Khovratovich, D., Perrin, L.: Multiset-algebraic cryptanalysis of reduced Kuznyechik, Khazad, and secret SPNs. IACR Trans. Symm. Cryptol. **2016**(2), 226–247 (2016). https://tosc.iacr.org/index.php/ToSC/article/view/572

13. Bogdanov, A., Geng, H., Wang, M., Wen, L., Collard, B.: Zero-correlation linear cryptanalysis with FFT and improved attacks on ISO standards Camellia and CLEFIA. In: Lange, T., Lauter, K., Lisoněk, P. (eds.) SAC 2013. LNCS, vol. 8282, pp. 306–323. Springer, Heidelberg (2014). https://doi.org/10.1007/978-3-662-43414-7_16

14. Collard, B., Standaert, F.-X., Quisquater, J.-J.: Improving the time complexity of Matsui's linear cryptanalysis. In: Nam, K.-H., Rhee, G. (eds.) ICISC 2007. LNCS, vol. 4817, pp. 77–88. Springer, Heidelberg (2007). https://doi.org/10.1007/978-3-540-76788-6_7

15. Cui, J., Hu, K., Wang, Q., Wang, M.: Integral attacks on Pyjamask-96 and round-reduced Pyjamask-128. In: Galbraith, S.D. (ed.) CT-RSA 2022. LNCS, vol. 13161, pp. 223–246. Springer, Cham (2022). https://doi.org/10.1007/978-3-030-95312-6_10

16. Daemen, J., Knudsen, L., Rijmen, V.: The block cipher Square. In: Biham, E. (ed.) FSE 1997. LNCS, vol. 1267, pp. 149–165. Springer, Heidelberg (1997). https://doi.org/10.1007/BFb0052343

17. Demirbaş, F., Kara, O.: Integral characteristics by keyspace partitioning. Des. Codes Crypt. **90**(2), 443–472 (2022)

18. Dolmatov, V., e.: Gost r 34.12-2015: Block cipher "Kuznyechik" (2016). https://www.rfc-editor.org/rfc/rfc7801.html

19. Dunkelman, O., Ghosh, S., Keller, N., Leurent, G., Marmor, A., Mollimard, V.: Partial sums meet FFT: Improved attack on 6-round AES. Cryptology ePrint Archive, Paper 2023/1659 (2023). https://eprint.iacr.org/2023/1659

20. Dunkelman, O., Keller, N., Ronen, E., Shamir, A.: The retracing boomerang attack. In: Canteaut, A., Ishai, Y. (eds.) EUROCRYPT 2020, Part I. LNCS, vol. 12105, pp. 280–309. Springer, Cham (2020). https://doi.org/10.1007/978-3-030-45721-1_11

21. Ferguson, N., Kelsey, J., Lucks, S., Schneier, B., Stay, M., Wagner, D.: Improved cryptanalysis of Rijndael. In: Goos, G., Hartmanis, J., van Leeuwen, J., Schneier, B. (eds.) FSE 2000. LNCS, vol. 1978, pp. 213–230. Springer, Heidelberg (2001). https://doi.org/10.1007/3-540-44706-7_15

22. Katagi, M.: The 128-bit blockcipher CLEFIA (2011). https://www.rfc-editor.org/rfc/rfc6114

23. Li, Y., Wu, W., Zhang, L.: Improved integral attacks on reduced-round CLEFIA block cipher. In: Jung, S., Yung, M. (eds.) WISA 2011. LNCS, vol. 7115, pp. 28–39. Springer, Heidelberg (2012). https://doi.org/10.1007/978-3-642-27890-7_3

24. Matsui, M.: New block encryption algorithm MISTY. In: Biham, E. (ed.) FSE 1997. LNCS, vol. 1267, pp. 54–68. Springer, Heidelberg (1997). https://doi.org/10.1007/BFb0052334

25. Nguyen, P.H., Wei, L., Wang, H., Ling, S.: On multidimensional linear cryptanalysis. In: Steinfeld, R., Hawkes, P. (eds.) ACISP 2010. LNCS, vol. 6168, pp. 37–52. Springer, Heidelberg (2010). https://doi.org/10.1007/978-3-642-14081-5_3

26. Nguyen, P.H., Wu, H., Wang, H.: Improving the algorithm 2 in multidimensional linear cryptanalysis. In: Parampalli, U., Hawkes, P. (eds.) ACISP 2011. LNCS, vol. 6812, pp. 61–74. Springer, Heidelberg (2011). https://doi.org/10.1007/978-3-642-22497-3_5

27. Rahman, M., Saha, D., Paul, G.: Boomeyong: embedding yoyo within boomerang and its applications to key recovery attacks on AES and Pholkos. IACR Trans. Symmetric Cryptol. **2021**(3), 137–169 (2021)

28. Sasaki, Y., Wang, L.: Meet-in-the-middle technique for integral attacks against feistel ciphers. In: Knudsen, L.R., Wu, H. (eds.) SAC 2012. LNCS, vol. 7707, pp. 234–251. Springer, Heidelberg (2013). https://doi.org/10.1007/978-3-642-35999-6_16

29. Todo, Y.: FFT-based key recovery for the integral attack. Cryptology ePrint Archive, Report 2014/187 (2014). https://eprint.iacr.org/2014/187

30. Todo, Y., Aoki, K.: FFT key recovery for integral attack. In: Gritzalis, D., Kiayias, A., Askoxylakis, I. (eds.) CANS 2014. LNCS, vol. 8813, pp. 64–81. Springer, Cham (2014). https://doi.org/10.1007/978-3-319-12280-9_5

31. Tunstall, M.: Improved "partial sums"-based square attack on AES. In: Proceedings of the International Conference on Security and Cryptography - SECRYPT, (ICETE 2012), pp. 25–34. INSTICC, SciTePress (2012)

32. Yi, W., Chen, S., Wei, K.: Zero-correlation linear cryptanalysis of reduced round ARIA with partial-sum and FFT. arXiv preprint arXiv:1406.3240 (2014)

New Records in Collision Attacks on SHA-2

Yingxin Li[1], Fukang Liu[2], and Gaoli Wang[1(✉)]

[1] Shanghai Key Laboratory of Trustworthy Computing, Software Engineering
Institute, East China Normal University, Shanghai, China
glwang@sei.ecnu.edu.cn
[2] Tokyo Institute of Technology, Tokyo, Japan
liu.f.ad@m.titech.ac.jp

Abstract. The SHA-2 family including SHA-224, SHA-256, SHA-384,
SHA-512, SHA-512/224 and SHA512/256 is a U.S. federal standard published by NIST. Especially, there is no doubt that SHA-256 is one of the
most important hash functions used in real-world applications. Due to
its complex design compared with SHA-1, there is almost no progress
in collision attacks on SHA-2 after ASIACRYPT 2015. In this work, we
retake this challenge and aim to significantly improve collision attacks
on the SHA-2 family. First, we observe from many existing attacks on
SHA-2 that the current advanced tool to search for SHA-2 characteristics
has reached the bottleneck. Specifically, longer differential characteristics
could not be found, and this causes that the collision attack could not
reach more steps. To address this issue, we adopt Liu et al.'s MILP-based
method and implement it with SAT/SMT for SHA-2, where we also add
more techniques to detect contradictions in SHA-2 characteristics. This
answers an open problem left in Liu et al.'s paper to apply the technique
to SHA-2. With this SAT/SMT-based tool, we search for SHA-2 characteristics by controlling its sparsity in a dedicated way. As a result, we
successfully find the first practical semi-free-start (SFS) colliding message
pair for 39-step SHA-256, improving the best 38-step SFS collision attack
published at EUROCRYPT 2013. In addition, we also report the first
practical free-start (FS) collision attack on 40-step SHA-224, while the
previously best theoretic 40-step attack has time complexity 2^{110}. Moreover, for the first time, we can mount practical and theoretic collision
attacks on 28-step and 31-step SHA-512, respectively, which improve the
best collision attack only reaching 27 steps of SHA-512 at ASIACRYPT
2015. In a word, with new techniques to find SHA-2 characteristics, we
have made some notable progress in the analysis of SHA-2 after the major
achievements made at EUROCRYPT 2013 and ASIACRYPT 2015.

Keywords: practical collision attack · SHA-2 · SAT/SMT

1 Introduction

Before the devastating attacks in 2005 [38–41] on the MD-SHA hash family,
there was a trend to design fast hash functions with a similar structure to MD4,

ⓒ International Association for Cryptologic Research 2024
M. Joye and G. Leander (Eds.): EUROCRYPT 2024, LNCS 14651, pp. 158–186, 2024.
https://doi.org/10.1007/978-3-031-58716-0_6

including MD5, SHA-0, SHA-1, SHA-2, RIPEMD-128 and RIPEMD-160, just to name a few. After 2005, we have witnessed efficient collision attacks on full MD4 [38], MD5 [40], SHA-0 [2,41], and SHA-1 [15,16,36,39] as well as the SFS collision attack on full RIPEMD-128 [14]. In spite of these successful attacks on the MD-SHA hash family, SHA-2 survived this game, mainly due to its more conservative and complex design. Since SHA-2 has been used worldwide, studying its collision and preimage resistances is always of practical interest, though it is also challenging.

Preimage Attacks on SHA-2. In the past few years, there have been many results for the preimage attacks on SHA-256 and SHA-512. The first preimage attack on SHA-256 and SHA-512 [11] based on the meet-in-the-middle (MITM) technique reached 24 steps with a complexity of about 2^{240} and 2^{480}, respectively. These preimage attacks were significantly improved at ASIACRYPT 2009 [1], which were improved to 43-step SHA-256 and 46-step SHA-512, respectively. Then, at ASIACRYPT 2010, Guo et al. [9] presented advanced MITM preimage attacks on 42-step SHA-256 and SHA-512, respectively. At FSE 2012, the biclique technique was applied to find preimages of SHA-2 [12], where preimage attacks on 45-step SHA-256 and 50-step SHA-512 with time complexity of $2^{255.5}$ and $2^{511.5}$ were achieved, respectively. It should be noted that the authors in [12] also presented pseudo-preimage attacks on 52-step SHA-256 and 57-step SHA-512 with a complexity of 2^{255} and 2^{511}, respectively. However, all these preimage attacks are far from practical.

Distinguishing Attacks on the Compression Function of SHA-2. Compared with preimage and collision attacks, distinguishing attacks are less meaningful for a hash function, though they can help better understand its security. At the rump session of EUROCRYPT 2008 [43], the non-randomness of 39-step SHA-256 was presented, and a practical example for 33 steps was given by Yu and Wang. In [10], free-start (FS) near-collisions for up to 31 steps of SHA-256 were presented. Then, Lamberger and Mendel gave a second-order differential attack on 46 steps of SHA-256 with a practical complexity in [13]. Later, this attack was extended to 47 steps of SHA-256 with a practical complexity at ASIACRYPT 2011 [3]. At INSCRYPT 2014 [42], Yu and Bai further utilized the attack strategy in [3] to mount a practical distinguishing attack on 48 steps of SHA-512.

Collision Attacks on SHA-2. The first practical collision attack on SHA-256 [30] was presented at FSE 2006, only reaching 18 steps. At FSE 2008, Nikolic and Biryukov [33] improved this practical attack to 21 steps, and they also gave a SFS collision attack on 23 steps of SHA-256. This attack was later further extended to 24 steps of SHA-256 and SHA-512 in [10,34]. Then, at ASIACRYPT 2011, the first major improvement was achieved, where the advanced guess-and-determine (GnD) technique to search for SHA-2 characteristics was invented [26], and the SFS collision for 32-step SHA-256 and the collision for 27-step SHA-256 were presented, respectively. After this work at ASIACRYPT 2011, this advanced automatic tool has been gradually improved in 3 papers published at EURO-CRYPT 2013 [28], FSE 2014 [8] and ASIACRYPT 2015 [6]. In addition, much more complex message differences are used to mount (FS/SFS) collision attacks on SHA-2 in these 3 papers. A summary of these collision attacks is shown in Table 1.

Automatic Tools to Search for SHA-2 Characteristics. Although major achievements have been made in collision attacks on SHA-2 in [6,8,26,28], the corresponding advanced automatic tool to find SHA-2 characteristics is not open-source. Due to the complex design of SHA-2, this significantly increased the difficulty to follow these works without this tool, let alone to improve this tool. Although Stevens open sourced his dedicated tools [35–37] to find MD5 and SHA-1 characteristics, they could not be applied to SHA-2 as SHA-2 is too complex, and contradictions easily occur in its differential characteristics [26]. Recently, to make finding collision-generating signed differential characteristics easier, Liu et al. invented a novel MILP-based method [24] and it works quite well for RIPEMD-160. As can be observed in [24], two main techniques are how to describe signed difference transitions through each component of the step function and how to automatically detect contradictions in an efficient way. At the end of [24], the authors left an interesting problem whether it is possible to apply this technique to SHA-2 because it is required for the model to detect more contradictions in SHA-2 characteristics.

Our Contributions. We briefly summarize our contributions as follows:

1. We demonstrate for the first time that the technique developed in [24] can be applied to SHA-2, and this obviously gives a positive answer to the question left in [24]. Specifically, we develop a SAT/SMT-based tool to efficiently search for valid SHA-2 differential characteristics based on the technique to search for signed differential characteristics in [24] and the technique to automatically verify the correctness of a differential characteristic in [21].
2. We shed new insight into the (free-start/semi-free-start) collision attacks on SHA-2. For the first time, we are able to propose:
   - the first practical SFS colliding message pair for 39-step SHA-256, breaking the record of 38 steps kept by Mendel et al. at EUROCRYPT 2013 [28] after 10 years;
   - the first practical free-start colliding message pair for 40-step SHA-224, improving the previously best theoretic 40-step attack with time complexity 2^{110} published at FSE 2012 [17];
   - the first practical colliding message pair for 28-step SHA-512, updating the previously best record given at ASIACRYPT 2015 [6] by 1 step.
   - the first collision attack on 31-step SHA-512 with time complexity $2^{115.6}$, improving the previously best one published at ASIACRYPT 2015 [6] by 4 steps.

In addition to these notable progress, we also improved the best collision attack on 31-step SHA-256 published at EUROCRYPT 2013 [28], reducing the time complexity from $2^{65.5}$ to $2^{49.8}$. Our results are summarized in Table 1. Especially, we note that there is gap between the previous (SFS) collision attacks on SHA-256 and SHA-512. Specially, due to the similarity between SHA-256 and SHA-512, a (SFS) collision attack on r steps of SHA-256 should have been applicable to r steps of SHA-512, and vice versa. However, this is not the case in previous attacks, as shown in Table 1. We believe this is caused by the infeasibility to find the corresponding valid SHA-2 characteristics with the current GnD technique. Based on our new technique, we have made the (SFS) collision attacks on SHA-256 and SHA-512 reach the same number of steps.

Moreover, based on our results for SHA-2, it indicates that the SAT/SMT-based method performs much better than the dedicated but non-open-source ones developed in [6,8,26,28]. This also contradicts the claims made in [8] that the performance of SAT-based method for SHA-2 is bad. Note that our SAT/SMT-based method is completely different from the one used in [8], which simply uses a model to describe two parallel instances of the value transitions as in [32].

Table 1. Summary of collision attacks on SHA-2, where FS collision* denotes the free-start collision without considering padding, and SFS collision denotes the semi-free-start collision.

State size	Hash size	Attack type	Steps	Time	Memory	References	Year
256	All	collision	28	*practical*	\	[28]	2013
			31	$2^{65.5}$	2^{34}	[28]	2013
			31	$2^{49.8}$	2^{48}	**Section 4.2**	**2023**
		SFS collision	38	*practical*	\	[28]	2013
			39	***practical***	\	**Section 4.1**	**2023**
	256	FS collision	52	$2^{127.5}$	\	[17]	2012
	224	FS collision*	39	*practical*	\	[6]	2015
		FS collision	40	2^{110}	\	[17]	2012
		FS collision*	**40**	***practical***	\	**Section 4.5**	**2023**
512	All	collision	27	*practical*	\	[6]	2015
			28	***practical***	\	**Section 4.4**	**2023**
			31	$2^{115.6}$	$2^{77.3}$	**Section 4.3**	**2023**
		SFS collision	38	*practical*	\	[8]	2014
			39	*practical*	\	[6]	2015
	384	FS collision	40	2^{183}	\	[17]	2012
		FS collision*	41	*practical*	\	[6]	2015
	256	FS collision*	43	*practical*	\	[6]	2015
	224	FS collision*	44	*practical*	\	[6]	2015

The source code to search for the differential characteristics and verify the (SFS/FS) collisions for SHA-256 and SHA-512 is available at https://github.com/Peace9911/sha_2_attack.git.

Outline. This paper is organized as follows. The notations and some preliminary works of this paper are introduced in Sect. 2. A high-level overview of how to implement the MILP-based method with an SAT/SMT-based method and how to overcome more contradictions in the differential characteristics of SHA-2 in is given Sect. 3. Then, we show how to find the differential characteristics to mount the (SFS/FS) collisions for SHA-2 in Sect. 4. Finally, we conclude this paper in Sect. 5.

2   Preliminaries

2.1   Notations

For a better understanding of this paper, we introduce the following notations.

1. $\boxplus$ and $\boxminus$ represent modulo addition and modulo subtraction on $32/64$ bits, respectively.
2. $\gg$, $\ggg$, $\oplus$, $\neg$, $\vee$ and $\wedge$ represent *shift right, rotate right, exclusive or, not, or,* and *and*, respectively.
3. $x[i]$ denotes the i-th bit of x and $x[0]$ is the least significant bit.
4. δx denotes the modular difference, i.e., $\delta x = x' \boxminus x$.
5. Δx denotes the signed difference between x' and x. We use the same notation as in [22,24], i.e.,

$$\Delta x[i] = \begin{cases} \mathtt{n} & (x[i] = 0, x'[i] = 1) \\ \mathtt{u} & (x[i] = 1, x'[i] = 0) \\ \mathtt{=} & (x[i] = x'[i]) \\ \mathtt{0} & (x[i] = x'[i] = 0) \\ \mathtt{1} & (x[i] = x'[i] = 1) \end{cases} \tag{1}$$

6. $M = (m_0, m_1, \ldots, m_{15})$ and $M' = (m'_0, m'_1, \ldots, m'_{15})$ represent two message blocks.

Definition 1 *[24]. The signed difference Δx is said to be an expansion of the modular difference δx only when Δx corresponds to the modular difference δx.*

Definition 2 *[24]. The hamming weight of the signed difference Δx is denoted by $H(\Delta x)$ and $H(\Delta x)$ is the number of indices i such that $\Delta x[i] \in \{n, u\}$.*

For example, let

$$\Delta x_0 = [\mathtt{====\ nu==\ ====\ ====\ ====\ ====\ ====\ ====}],$$
$$\Delta x_1 = [\mathtt{====\ =n==\ ====\ ====\ ====\ ====\ ====\ ====}].$$

Then, both Δx_0 and Δx_1 are the expansions of $\delta x = 2^{26}$. Moreover, we have $H(\Delta x_0) = 2$ and $H(\Delta x_1) = 1$. As each signed difference corresponds to a unique modular difference, for convenience, when computing $\delta x \boxplus \delta y$ for a given $(\Delta x, \Delta y)$, we also simply denote $\delta x \boxplus \delta y$ by $\Delta x \boxplus \Delta y$. For the above example, we have $\Delta x_0 \boxplus \Delta x_1 = 2^{27}$.

2.2   Description of SHA-2

The SHA-2 family is a series of hash functions standardized by NIST as part of the Secure Hash Standard (SHS) [7]. This family mainly consists of two versions, namely SHA-256 and SHA-512. Furthermore, NIST defines a general truncation procedure for SHA-256 and SHA-512, which includes SHA-224, SHA-512/224, SHA-512/256 and SHA-384. SHA-2 adopts the well-known Merkle-Damgård construction [5,31], and its compression functions employ the Davies-Meyer construction. As the two main versions of SHA-2, SHA-256 and SHA-512 have 32-bit and 64-bit state words, respectively. SHA-256 and SHA-512 utilize 512-bit message words and 1024-bit message words as input, with their chaining variables and final outputs being 256 bits and 512 bits, respectively.

The compression functions of SHA-256 and SHA-512 are computed through iterative updates to internal states. The number of steps, which is denoted by r, is 64 for SHA-256 and 80 for SHA-512. In the following, we provide a brief overview of their compression functions. They consist of two main parts: the message expansion and the state update transformation. A complete description of SHA-2 is given in [7].

Message Expansion. The 512-bit message block for SHA-256 and the 1024-bit message block for SHA-512 are divided into 16 message words of sizes 32 bits and 64 bits, respectively, which are denoted by $(m_1, \ldots, m_{15})$. Then, the 16 message words are expanded to r expanded message words W_i, i.e., $W_0, W_1, \ldots, W_{r-1}$:

$$W_i = \begin{cases} m_i & 0 \le i \le 15, \\ \sigma_1(W_{i-2}) \boxplus W_{i-7} \boxplus \sigma_0(W_{i-15}) \boxplus W_{i-16} & 16 \le i \le r-1. \end{cases}$$

The functions $\sigma_0(x)$ and $\sigma_1(x)$ in SHA-256 are given by

$$\sigma_0(x) = (x \ggg 7) \oplus (x \ggg 18) \oplus (x \gg 3),$$
$$\sigma_1(x) = (x \ggg 17) \oplus (x \ggg 19) \oplus (x \gg 10).$$

The functions $\sigma_0(x)$ and $\sigma_1(x)$ in SHA-512 are given by

$$\sigma_0(x) = (x \ggg 1) \oplus (x \ggg 8) \oplus (x \gg 7),$$
$$\sigma_1(x) = (x \ggg 19) \oplus (x \ggg 61) \oplus (x \gg 6).$$

State Update Transformation. We utilize the alternate description for the state update of SHA-256 and SHA-512, as illustrated in Fig. 1.

The state update transformation starts from a 256-bit (resp. 512-bit) chaining value $iv = (A_{-1}, \ldots, A_{-4}, E_{-1}, \ldots, E_{-4})$ for SHA-256 (resp. SHA-512), and updates it by applying the step function r times. In each step $i = 0, \ldots, r-1$, one expanded message word W_i is used to compute the two state words E_i and A_i as follows, where K_i is a predefined constant and can be referred to [7].

$$E_i = A_{i-4} \boxplus E_{i-4} \boxplus \Sigma_1(E_{i-1}) \boxplus \mathrm{IF}(E_{i-1}, E_{i-2}, E_{i-3}) \boxplus K_i \boxplus W_i,$$
$$A_i = E_i \boxminus A_{i-4} \boxplus \Sigma_0(A_{i-1}) \boxplus \mathrm{MAJ}(A_{i-1}, A_{i-2}, A_{i-3}).$$

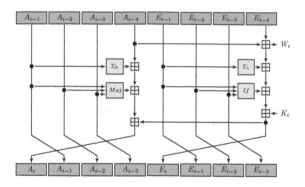

Fig. 1. The state update transformation of SHA-2.

Both SHA-256 and SHA-512 utilize the same Boolean functions IF and MAJ, as defined below:

$$\text{IF}(x, y, z) = (x \wedge y) \oplus (x \wedge z) \oplus z,$$
$$\text{MAJ}(x, y, z) = (x \wedge y) \oplus (x \wedge z) \oplus (y \wedge z).$$

However, the linear functions Σ_0 and Σ_1 are different for SHA-256 and SHA-512. For SHA-256, they are defined below:

$$\Sigma_0(x) = (x \ggg 2) \oplus (x \ggg 13) \oplus (x \ggg 22),$$
$$\Sigma_1(x) = (x \ggg 6) \oplus (x \ggg 11) \oplus (x \ggg 25).$$

For SHA-512, they are defined below:

$$\Sigma_0(x) = (x \ggg 28) \oplus (x \ggg 34) \oplus (x \ggg 39),$$
$$\Sigma_1(x) = (x \ggg 14) \oplus (x \ggg 18) \oplus (x \ggg 41).$$

After the last step of the state update transformation, the previous chaining value is added to the output of the state update. The result of this feed-forward sum is the chaining value h:

$$h = (A_{63} \boxplus A_{-1}, \ldots, A_{60} \boxplus A_{-4}, E_{63} \boxplus E_{-1}, \ldots, E_{60} \boxplus E_{-4}).$$

On Finding (FS/SFS) Collisions. Denote the compression function of SHA-2 by $h_i = H(h_{i-1}, M_i)$. To find a collision with j message blocks, we need to find $(M_1, \ldots, M_j)$ and $(M'_1, \ldots, M'_j) \neq (M_1, \ldots, M_j)$ such that $h_j = h'_j$ where $h'_i = H(h'_{i-1}, M'_i)$ and $h_0 = h'_0$ is a *predefined constant*. In most cases, only $M_j \neq M'_j$ is required and we have $M_k = M'_k$ for $1 \leq k < j$. To find SFS collisions, we need to find $H(h, M) = H(h, M')$ where $M \neq M'$ and h can be an *arbitrary value*. To find FS collisions, we need to find $H(h, M) = H(h', M')$ where $M \neq M'$ and (h, h') can be *arbitrary values*.

2.3   Previous Methods to Search for Differential Characteristics

Almost all effective collision attacks on the MD-SHA hash family rely on Wang et al.'s techniques [38–40]. One of the most important steps is to find a collision-generating differential characteristic. For this purpose, there are three methods in the literature, as summarized below.

- **Hand-crafted method:** This remarkable work was first done by Wang et al. in their ground-breaking works on MD4 [38], MD5 [40], SHA-0 [41], and SHA-1 [39]. However, for complex designs like SHA-256 and RIPEMD-160, finding such differential characteristics for a large number of steps by hand is almost impossible, or at least considerably time-consuming.
- **Ad-hoc heuristic search tools:** De Cannière and Rechberger developed the first heuristic search tool for this problem based on the guess-and-determine (GnD) technique, and successfully applied it to SHA-1 [4]. Subsequently, this heuristic search tool were further developed and it has been applied to many hash functions like RIPEMD-128, RIPEMD-160, SHA-256, and SHA-512 [6,8,14,19,20,23,25–29]. However, the implementation of this GnD-based tool is not open-source. Although Stevens made his tools for MD5 and SHA-1 [35–37] open-source, it requires a significant amount of work to tweak them for SHA-2 because contradictions much more easily occur in the differential characteristics of SHA-2, and no existing tools for SHA-2 are based on this method.
- **Off-the-shelf solvers:** The method was first explored in [32] with SAT solvers after Wang et al.'s attacks and it was later also applied to SHA-1 in [36]. The main idea is to construct a model to describe two parallel instances of the value transitions. A new MILP-based method proposed by Liu et al. [24] is to model the pure signed difference transitions through each component of the round function, aided with some contradiction-detecting techniques. Especially, this technique [24] works quite well for RIPEMD-160.

3   SAT/SMT-Based Tools for the MD-SHA Hash Family

The first SAT-based method to find collision-generating differential characteristics was proposed in 2006 [32], but the model is to simply describe two parallel instances of the value transitions. To efficiently capture the information of the signed difference propagation, the MILP-based method was proposed in [24]. Although the authors of [24] only target RIPEMD-160, since the MD-SHA hash functions share similar structures, the authors also mention that there are indeed much more applications beyond RIPEMD-160. Especially, whether it is applicable to SHA-2 is left as an interesting problem.

We answer this question in this paper. First, we show how to implement the MILP-based method [24] with an SAT/SMT-based method, and how to detect more contradictions in SHA-2 characteristics. Then, we demonstrate how to utilize our tools to find suitable differential characteristics to significantly improve the (SFS) collision attacks on SHA-2.

For the MILP-based method in [24], the constraints are already in Conjunctive Normal Form (CNF) due to the usage of the software Friday, which can output the minimized CNF for a given truth table with the Quine-McCluskey (QM) algorithm. However, they choose to further convert CNF into linear inequalities in order to use the solver Gurobi [24]. In this sense, we can not claim any novelty for how to re-implement the propagation of signed difference transitions with SAT/SMT. To make this paper self-contained, we briefly describe the idea to model the signed difference propagation with SAT/SMT. Note that when applying it to searching for valid SHA-2 characteristics, nontrivial additional techniques are required, as can be seen later in our detailed description of the search strategy.

For the MD-SHA hash family, it can be observed that in their round functions, there are three basic operations:

- modular addition;
- logic shift;
- Boolean functions.

Hence, we only describe how to describe the signed difference transitions through the modular addition and Boolean functions. For the logic shift, it does affect the model for RIPEMD-160 as shown in [24]. However, in the case of SHA-2, there is no such problem and it only affects the order of the variables. Hence, we simply omit it in this section.

Since we will target both SHA-256 and SHA-512, and their state sizes are 32 and 64 bits, respectively, to make the description of the model general, we treat the state size as n bits, i.e., the modular addition is within modulo 2^n.

3.1 SAT/SMT Models for the Signed Difference Transitions

Similar to [24], we use 2 binary variables (v, d) to describe the signed difference. Specifically, $(0,0)$, $(0,1)$ and $(1,1)$ correspond to [=], [n] and [u], respectively, while we always exclude $(1,0)$ as it carries the same information as $(0,0)$. For the n-bit signed difference Δx, throughout this paper, the signed difference at the i-th ($0 \leq i \leq n-1$) bit is always represented by $(x_v[i], x_d[i])$. For example, if $n = 5$ and $\Delta x = $ [=u==n], we have

$$(x_v[0], x_d[0]) = (0,0), (x_v[1], x_d[1]) = (1,1), (x_v[2], x_d[2]) = (0,0),$$
$$(x_v[3], x_d[3]) = (0,0), (x_v[4], x_d[4]) = (0,1).$$

Modelling the Modular Addition. As explained in [24], given the signed difference Δx and Δy, it is sufficient to pick only 1 signed difference Δz to describe the modular difference $\delta z = \delta x \boxplus \delta y$.

To achieved this, the intermediate variable Δc with $\Delta c[0] = $ [=] is introduced and the propagation rules for

$$(\Delta x[i], \Delta y[i], \Delta c[i]) \xrightarrow{Add} (\Delta z[i], \Delta c[i+1])$$

Table 2. The propagation rules for $(\Delta x[i], \Delta y[i], \Delta c[i]) \xrightarrow{Add} (\Delta z[i], \Delta c[i+1])$ in [24]

[=== → ==],	[==n → n=],	[==u → u=],	[=n= → n=],
[=u= → u=],	[=nn → =n],	[=un → ==],	[=nu → ==],
[=uu → =u],	[n== → n=],	[u== → u=],	[n=n → =n],
[u=n → ==],	[n=u → ==],	[u=u → =u],	[nn= → =n],
[nun → n=],	[unn → n=],	[nnu → n=],	[uun → u=],
[unu → u=],	[nuu → u=],	[uuu → uu].	

are shown in Table 2, where $0 \le i \le n-1$.

With the above method to describe the signed difference, there are 27 possible values for

$$(x_v[i], x_d[i], y_v[i], y_d[i], c_v[i], c_d[i], z_v[i], z_d[i], c_v[i+1], c_d[i+1])$$

based on Table 2. With the software LogicFriday, we can obtain the corresponding CNF to describe that this tuple can only take these 27 possible values. For convenience, we denote the CNF by $\mathcal{C}_{Add}(i)$. In this way, the complete model for the modular addition can be described with $\mathcal{C}_{Add}(i)$ for $0 \le i \le n-1$ and $(c_v[0], c_d[0]) = (0, 0)$.

For convenience, we denote the model for the modular addition $\delta z = \delta x \boxplus \delta y$ by $\mathcal{C}_{Add}(\Delta x, \Delta y, \Delta z, \Delta c)$.

Modelling the Expansions of the Modular Difference [24]. In the above model, the signed difference transition through the modular addition is deterministic. To obtain all possible signed differences corresponding to the same modular difference, the authors of [24] introduce a model to describe the expansions of the modular difference. Given one Δz, the aim is to find all possible $\Delta \xi$ such that $\delta \xi = \delta z$, i.e., $\Delta \xi$ and Δz correspond to the same modular difference. To achieve this, as in [24], an intermediate variable Δc is introduced and there are two methods to model it, as shown in Table 3.

Table 3. Two methods to describe the propagation rules for the expansion of modular difference [24]

Method 1 $(\Delta z[i], \Delta c[i]) \xrightarrow{Exp} (\Delta \xi[i], \Delta c[i+1])$	[nn → =n], [uu → =u], [nu → ==], [un → ==], [n= → n=], [n= → un], [u= → u=], [u= → nu], [=n → n=], [=n → un], [=u → u=], [=u → nu], [== → ==].
Method 2 $(\Delta \xi[i], \Delta z[i], \Delta c[i]) \xrightarrow{Exp} (\Delta c[i+1])$	[=un → n], [=nn → =], [=uu → =], [=nu → u], [u=n → =], [n=n → n], [u=u → u], [n=u → =], [nu= → n], [nn= → =], [uu= → =], [un= → u], [=== → =].

Similarly, based on the above way to describe the signed difference and using the software LogicFriday, the corresponding CNF to describe the constraints on

$$(z_v[i], z_d[i], c_v[i], c_d[i], \xi_v[i], \xi_d[i], c_v[i+1], c_d[i+1])$$

for Method 1 can be obtained, which is denoted by $\mathcal{C}_{Exp}(i)$. The complete model for the expansion of the modular difference is thus $\mathcal{C}_{Exp}(i)$ for $0 \leq i \leq n-1$ and $(c_v[0], c_d[0]) = (0,0)$ for Method 1.

In the same way, we can also obtain the corresponding CNF denoted by $\mathcal{C}'_{Exp}(i)$ to describe the constraints on

$$(\xi_v[i], \xi_d[i], z_v[i], z_d[i], c_v[i], c_d[i], c_v[i+1], c_d[i+1])$$

for Method 2. The complete model for the expansion of the modular difference is thus $\mathcal{C}'_{Exp}(i)$ for $0 \leq i \leq n-1$ and $(c_v[0], c_d[0]) = (0,0)$ for Method 2.

For convenience, we denote the model for the expansions of the modular addition in Method 1 and Method 2 by $\mathcal{C}_{Exp}(\Delta z, \Delta \xi, \Delta c)$ and $\mathcal{C}'_{Exp}(\Delta z, \Delta \xi, \Delta c)$.

Modelling the Vectorial Boolean Functions $w = f(x, y, z)$ [24]. In SHA-2, there are some vectorial Boolean functions, i.e., f can be XOR, IF or MAJ where $XOR(x, y, z) = x \oplus y \oplus z$. Note that σ_0, σ_1, Σ_0 and Σ_1 in SHA-2 are basically the same as XOR. Generally speaking, we can have

$$w[i] = f_i(x[i], y[i], z[i])$$

where f_i is a Boolean function $\mathbb{F}_2^3 \mapsto \mathbb{F}_2$ and $0 \leq i \leq n-1$. As described in [24], there are two models for $(f_i)_{0 \leq i \leq n-1}$: (i) the fast filtering model; (ii) the full model.

For the fast filtering model, we first need to build a table to include all valid propagation rules for $(\Delta x[i], \Delta y[i], \Delta z[i], \Delta w[i])$ and then obtain the corresponding valid values for

$$(x_v[i], x_d[i], y_v[i], y_d[i], z_v[i], z_d[i], w_v[i], w_d[i]).$$

Finally, LogicFriday is used to obtain the corresponding CNF for the constraints on this tuple.

For the full model, we need to involve both the signed difference and bit values. Specifically, the first step is to list all possible propagation rules for

$$(\Delta x[i], \Delta y[i], \Delta z[i], \Delta w[i], x[i], y[i], z[i]),$$

where $(x[i], y[i], z[i])$ can make the signed difference transition

$$(\Delta x[i], \Delta y[i], \Delta z[i]) \xrightarrow{f_i} \Delta w[i]$$

hold with probability 1. Then, we can obtain all the possible valid values for

$$(x_v[i], x_d[i], y_v[i], y_d[i], z_v[i], z_d[i], w_v[i], w_d[i], x[i], y[i], z[i]).$$

Finally, with LogicFriday, we obtain the corresponding CNF to describe the constraints on this tuple.

For convenience, we denote the fast filtering model and full model for $w = f(x, y, z)$ by $\mathcal{C}^f_{fast}(\Delta x, \Delta y, \Delta z, \Delta w)$ and $\mathcal{C}^f_{full}(\Delta x, \Delta y, \Delta z, \Delta w, x, y, z)$, respectively.

3.2 SAT/SMT Models for the Value Transitions

In SHA-2, contradictions easily occur in the collision-generating differential char-acteristics. To avoid this, we use the technique proposed by Liu et al. at CRYPTO 2020 [21]: using one model for the differential characteristic and another model for the value transitions. In the above model for the differential characteristic, we have included the relations between the value and the differential characteristic if using the full model for the Boolean functions. Specially, if the full model is applied to step i, the conditions on the internal states at step $i-1$, $i-2$ and $i-3$ to ensure the difference transitions have been added. Then, we can further build a model to optionally describe how to compute the internal state $i-1$ or $i-2$ or $i-3$ in order to test whether these conditions can hold, which is the model for the value transitions. It is easy to build the model for the value transitions as we only need to model the modular addition and Boolean functions.

To compute $z = x \boxplus y$, we can simply introduce a variable c with $c[0] = 0$ to denote the carry. Then, we list all possible values for the tuple $(x[i], y[i], c[i], z[i])$ and get the corresponding CNF for the model addition. For convenience, we denote the model for the modular addition of the value by $\mathcal{C}_{Val}^{Add}(x, y, z, c)$.

To compute $w = f(x, y, z)$, we can simply list all possible valid values for the tuple $(x[i], y[i], z[i], w[i])$ and get the corresponding CNF. For convenience, the model for the vectorial Boolean function f is denoted by $\mathcal{C}_{Val}^{f}(x, y, z, c)$.

With the two basic models $\mathcal{C}_{Val}^{Add}$ and $\mathcal{C}_{val}^{f}$, we can simply build the model for the value transitions through the step function of SHA-2 by decomposing the step function with intermediate variables. For convenience, the models to compute E_i, A_i and W_i are denoted by $\mathcal{C}_{Val}^{E}(i)$, $\mathcal{C}_{Val}^{A}(i)$ and $\mathcal{C}_{Val}^{W}(i)$, respectively.

Remark 1. With the model for value transitions, we can also use it to search for conforming input pairs for some dense parts of the differential characteristic. Specially, after a differential characteristic is obtained, we first derive all the differential conditions. Then, to find the conforming input pairs for the dense part of the characteristic, we simply use the value transitions for this part and add the corresponding differential conditions on the internal states to the model. This will be frequently used in our attacks in order to search for conforming message pairs automatically. Indeed, it is not surprising that this method has been used in [21,32].

3.3 Models for SHA-2

With the above basic models, it is easy to combine them to fully describe how the signed difference propagates through the step function of SHA-2, and how to detect contradictions by involving the value transitions. We refer the interested readers to the full version of this paper for more details [18].

4 New (SFS/FS) Collision Attacks on SHA-2

In the (FS/SFS) collision attacks on SHA-2 [6,8,26,28] with the GnD tools, a crucial step is to first search for a relatively complex local collision in the message expansion, where nonzero message differences exist in the middle steps, and the differences will be cancelled in as many consecutive steps as possible in the forward and backward directions.

Basically, after determining the local collision in the message expansion, the number of attacked steps is also known. However, finding a valid attack further requires attackers to finish the following two tasks:

Task 1: searching for a corresponding differential characteristic in (A_i, E_i);
Task 2: finding the conforming message pair to ensure the validity of the differential characteristic since contradictions easily occur.

In some cases, even though we know there may exist a good local collision in the message expansion, it may be still infeasible to find a valid attack due to the difficulty of Task 1 or Task 2. For example, the SFS collision attack can reach 39 steps of SHA-512, but could not reach 39 steps of SHA-256. Moreover, the best collision attack on SHA-256 could reach 31 steps, while it is only 27 steps for SHA-512.

4.1 The First Practical SFS Collision for 39-Step SHA-256

We note that there is a practical SFS collision attack on 39-step SHA-512 published at ASIACRYPT 2015 [6]. However, the authors did not report any attacks on 39-step SHA-256, even though SHA-256 and SHA-512 share almost the same message expansion and state update function, i.e., only with different state sizes and different rotation numbers in Σ and σ. Specifically, the strategy to construct the local collision for 39-step SHA-512 should have been applicable to 39-step SHA-256, and this cannot be the bottleneck. We thus believe that the difficulty exists in either Task 1 or Task 2.

Hence, we aim to retake this challenge with the new SAT/SMT-based technique. First, we observe that in the differential characteristic for 39-step SHA-512 in [6], the local collision spans over 19 steps (steps 8–26), and the nonzero message differences exist in 9 words ($W_8, \ldots, W_{12}, W_{16}, W_{17}, W_{24}, W_{26}$). In addition, in ($W_{26}, W_{17}, A_{18}$), there is only a one-bit difference, respectively.

In our new attack on 39-step SHA-256, we use the same strategy to construct the local collision, as shown in Fig. 2(a). Different from the ad-hoc GnD techniques [6,8,28], it is efficient to use our SAT/SMT-based technique to find a sparse differential characteristic by minimizing the Hamming weight of the signed differences. This is crucial to improve the uncontrolled differential probability and to make the message modification more practical. Our general procedure to search for the differential characteristic for 39-step SHA-256 is summarized below:

Step 1: **Minimize the Hamming weight of** ΔW_i. Specifically, find the minimal value of $t_w = \sum_{i=0}^{38} \mathbf{H}(\Delta W_i)$ such that the nonzero differences only exist in the 9 expanded message words ($W_8, \ldots, W_{12}, W_{16}, W_{17}$, W_{24}, W_{26}). Note that the concrete message differences are not specified at this step and the only goal is to find the minimal value t_w.

Step 2: **Minimize the Hamming weight of** ΔA_i. Specifically, under the conditions

$$\forall i \in [19, 38] : \delta A_i = 0,$$
$$\forall i \in [23, 38] : \delta E_i = 0,$$
$$\forall i \in [0, 38] \text{ and } i \notin \{8, \ldots, 12, 16, 17, 24, 26\} : \delta W_i = 0,$$
$$\sum_{i=0}^{38} \mathbf{H}(\Delta W_i) = t_w,$$

find the minimal value of $t_A = \sum_{i=0}^{38} \mathbf{H}(\Delta A_i)$ such that there exists a solution of a 39-step collision-generating differential characteristic, i.e., there is a solution to $(\Delta W_i, \Delta A_i, \Delta E_i)$ for $0 \le i \le 38$ to allow a 39-step attack. Still, we only aim at the minimal value t_A, and do not fix $(\Delta W_i, \Delta A_i, \Delta E_i)$ according to the solution at this step.

Step 3: **Minimize the Hamming weight of** ΔE_i. In addition to the conditions at Step 2, we further add the condition

$$\sum_{i=0}^{38} \mathbf{H}(\Delta A_i) = t_A.$$

Under these conditions, find and output the solution of $(\Delta W_i, \Delta A_i, \Delta E_i)$ for $0 \le i \le 38$ that minimizes $\sum_{i=0}^{38} \mathbf{H}(\Delta E_i)$.

Following the above procedure, we successfully found a corresponding 39-step differential characteristic, as shown in Table 4. By our procedure, this differential characteristic can be kept as sparse as possible and hence it is expected to be valid.

Remark 2. Our strategy to search for a concrete 39-step differential characteristic is different from the GnD technique in [6] because we first minimize the Hamming weight of $(\Delta W_i, \Delta A_i)$ and then search the solution under such constraints. However, there is no such a minimization procedure when searching for the differential characteristic in 39-step SHA-512 in [6]. Without this strategy, the differential characteristic may be dense and there is a high chance that it is invalid, which may somehow explain why the technique in [6] failed for 39-step SHA-256.

Message Modification. As the differential characteristic is still relatively dense, we could not ensure that there must exist a conforming message pair. To verify this, we first extract all the constraints on $(A_i, E_i)_{-4 \le i \le 22}$ and $(W_i)_{0 \le i \le 38}$ for this differential characteristic. Then add these constraints to the SAT/SMT model for the value transitions of SHA-256, and solve the model to find a solution of these variables. We succeed in finding a practical SFS colliding message pair for 39-step SHA-256 in 120 s with 26 threads, as shown in Table 5.

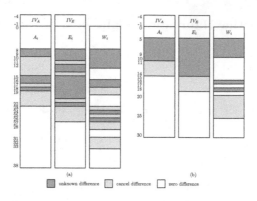

Fig. 2. (a) represent the shape of the 39-step differential SHA-256 and (b) represent the shape of the differential characteristic for 31-step SHA-256

4.2 Improved Collision Attacks on 31-Step SHA-256

The best existing collision attack on SHA-256 reaches 31 steps, which was published at EUROCRYPT 2013 [28]. The main idea is to use a two-block method to convert a SFS collision into a collision by utilizing the available degrees of freedom in the first few message words. To achieve this purpose, the first step is to find a suitable differential characteristic for 31-step SHA-256. In [28], this 31-step differential characteristic relies on a properly constructed local collision in the message expansion, which spans over 14 steps (steps 5−18). Specifically, the nonzero message differences only exist in 7 expanded message words

$$(W_5, W_6, W_7, W_8, W_9, W_{16}, W_{18}).$$

Moreover, there are no conditions on the first 5 expanded message words $(W_i)_{0 \le i \le 4}$ and hence they can be freely chosen to efficiently convert a SFS collision into a collision. The shape of the 31-step differential characteristic is shown in Fig. 2(b).

The method in [28] to convert SFS collisions into collisions is described below:

Step 1: Find 2^ℓ solutions of $(A_i)_{-3 \le i \le 12}$, $(E_i)_{1 \le i \le 12}$ and $(W_i)_{5 \le i \le 12}$ that satisfy the differential conditions on steps 5−12. Store them in a table denoted by TAB$_1$.

Step 2: Compute $2^{96-\ell}$ arbitrary first message blocks and get $2^{96-\ell}$ chaining inputs $(A_{-4}, \ldots, A_{-1})$ and $(E_{-4}, \ldots, E_{-1})$. Check TAB$_1$ and find a match in (A_{-3}, A_{-2}, A_{-1}). Then, $(W_i)_{0 \le i \le 4}$ and E_0 are all determined for this match.

Step 3: At this step, $(W_i)_{0 \le i \le 12}$ have been fixed. Use the degrees of freedom in (W_{13}, W_{14}, W_{15}) to fulfill the remaining uncontrolled conditions on $(E_{13}, E_{14}, E_{15}, W_{16}, W_{18})$. If it fails, go to Step 2.

Supposing Step 3 succeeds with probability $2^{-\gamma}$, the time complexity for this two-block method to find a collision is $2^{96-\ell+\gamma} + 2^\ell \cdot T_{\texttt{tool}}$, where $T_{\texttt{tool}}$ denotes

Table 4. The differential characteristic for 39 steps of SHA-256

i	ΔA_i	ΔE_i	ΔW_i
-4	================================	================================	
-3	================================	================================	
-2	================================	================================	
-1	================================	================================	
0	================================	================================	================================
1	================================	================================	================================
2	================================	================================	================================
3	================================	================================	================================
4	================================	================================	================================
5	================================	================================	================================
6	================================	===0============================	================================
7	================================	===1========11=====11======0===	================================
8	===u===========================	unnn1=1110=0=0101==00011==11110=	===u============================
9	============n=u===u====n===	010n0n0111010nu01001un011n10n=10	======n===u==========u=========
10	--=============.===============	0101u1n=1n0n010=u0=11nuu=1u00=n1	===n===========================
11	================================	=100010000=0101=0===0010=10=1=0=	======nn=======n==n===nn==uu=n
12	================================	=unn010000=1000011=00011==0=101=	==========u======nn===========
13	================================	10110nuuuuuuuuu0u101un000010n111	================================
14	================================	=111=0000000000=0=1=001111111=1=	================================
15	======================n===	1100110110100000001nuuuuuuuu001	================================
16	======u=u======u==============	010100unu00001001u1000110unn=n1	=====n===u==========u=========
17	================================	1100111u00nn=100110=u1u00unn000n	==n=============================
18	==n============================	uuu1uuuu01000=110n000111101=0101	================================
19	================================	000u0n1000101=0un01=1100=u11n000	================================
20	================================	011100un0u001unnnn1100000001111	================================
21	================================	=110=111=0===000=1======1==1===	================================
22	================================	=nuu==0110===00101=0110=====110=	================================
23	================================	=000===========================	================================
24	================================	=111===========================	======n=n=======n==============
25	================================	================================	================================
26	================================	================================	===u===========================
27	================================	================================	================================
28	================================	================================	================================
29	================================	================================	================================
30	================================	================================	================================
31	================================	================================	================================
32	================================	================================	================================
33	================================	================================	================================
34	================================	================================	================================
35	================================	================================	================================
36	================================	================================	================================
37	================================	================================	================================
38	================================	================================	================================

Table 5. The SFS colliding message pair for 39 steps of SHA-256

cv	02b19d5a	88e1df04	5ea3c7b7	f2f7d1a4	86cb1b1f	c8ee51a5	1b4d0541	651b92e7
M	c61d6de7	755336e8	5e61d618	18036de6	a79f2f1d	f2b44c7b	4c0ef36b	a85d45cf
	f72b8c2f	0def947c	a0eab159	8021370c	4b0d8011	7aad07f6	33cd6902	3bad5d64
M'	c61d6de7	755336e8	5e61d618	18036de6	a79f2f1d	f2b44c7b	4c0ef36b	a85d45cf
	e72b8c2f	0fcf907c	b0eab159	81a1bfc1	4b098611	7aad07f6	33cd6902	3bad5d64
hash	431cadcd	ce6893bb	d6c9689a	334854e8	3baae1ab	038a195a	ccf54a19	1c40606d

the time to find a solution of $(A_i)_{-3 \leq i \leq 12}$, $(E_i)_{1 \leq i \leq 12}$ and $(W_i)_{5 \leq i \leq 12}$ at Step 1. The memory complexity is 2^ℓ. In [28], $\ell \approx 34$, $\gamma \approx 3.5$ and $T_{\texttt{tool}}$ is negligible. Hence the time complexity is estimated as $2^{65.5}$ and the memory complexity is 2^{34}.

According to the above analysis, it is clear that ℓ and γ should be improved to get better attacks. Moreover, the best time-memory trade-off cannot be achieved with their 31-step differential characteristic [28]. Note that the maximal value of ℓ is dominated by the number of differential conditions on steps 5−12 and hence we can expect a relatively larger ℓ with a sparser differential characteristic. Therefore, we are interested whether it is possible to find a new sparser differential characteristic with our tool that can help achieve the optimal time-memory trade-off, i.e., with time and memory complexity close to $2^{96/2} = 2^{48}$. The overall searching procedure is stated as follows:

1. **Minimize the Hamming weight of ΔW_i.** Specifically, find the minimal value of $t_w = \sum_{i=0}^{30} \mathbf{H}(\Delta W_i)$ while keeping the minimal $\mathbf{H}(\Delta W_{16})$ and the minimal $\mathbf{H}(\Delta W_{18})$ such that the nonzero differences only exist in the 7 expanded message words $(W_5, W_6, W_7, W_8, W_9, W_{16}, W_{18})$. Note that the concrete message differences are not specified at this step.
2. **Minimize the Hamming weight of ΔA_i.** Specifically, under the conditions

$$\forall i \in [11, 30] : \quad \delta A_i = 0,$$
$$\forall i \in [15, 30] : \quad \delta E_i = 0,$$
$$\forall i \in [0, 30] \text{ and } i \notin \{5, \ldots, 9, 16, 18\} : \delta W_i = 0,$$
$$\sum_{i=0}^{30} \mathbf{H}(\Delta W_i) = t_w,$$

find the minimal value of $t_A = \sum_{i=0}^{30} \mathbf{H}(\Delta A_i)$ such that there is a solution to $(\Delta W_i, \Delta A_i, \Delta E_i)$ for $0 \leq i \leq 30$ to allow a 31-step attack. Still, we only aim at the minimal value t_A, and do not fix $(\Delta W_i, \Delta A_i, \Delta E_i)$ according to the solution at this step.
3. **Minimize the Hamming weight of ΔE_i.** In addition to the conditions at Step 2, we further add the condition

$$\sum_{i=0}^{30} \mathbf{H}(\Delta A_i) = t_A.$$

Under these conditions, find and output the solution minimizing $\sum_{i=0}^{30} \mathbf{H}(\Delta E_i)$ to allow a 31-step attack.

As already mentioned in our SAT/SMT models, to further detect the contradictions caused by the complex relationship between (A_i, E_i, W_i), we sometimes add the value transitions at certain steps to ensure its validity. In our model for the 31-step differential characteristic, this strategy is applied to

$(A_i, E_i, W_i)_{7 \leq i \leq 10}$. Without this strategy, we found that the obtained differential characteristic was indeed invalid[1]. Our new 31-step differential characteristic is shown in Table 6.

Estimating ℓ and γ. We use a dedicated method to find valid solutions of $(A_i)_{-3 \leq i \leq 12}$, $(E_i)_{1 \leq i \leq 12}$ and $(W_i)_{5 \leq i \leq 12}$ such that ℓ can be better estimated. First, use the model for the value transitions to find a solution of $(A_i)_{1 \leq i \leq 12}$, $(E_i)_{5 \leq i \leq 12}$ and $(W_i)_{9 \leq i \leq 12}$ that satisfy the differential conditions on steps $5-12$. For simplicity, this solution is called a starting point for 31-step SHA-256. Due to

$$A_i = E_i \boxminus A_{i-4} \boxplus \Sigma_0(A_{i-1}) \boxplus \text{MAJ}(A_{i-1}, A_{i-2}, A_{i-3}), \tag{2}$$

$(A_{-3}, A_{-2}, A_{-1}, A_0)$ will then depend on (E_1, E_2, E_3, E_4) for this starting point. Moreover, according to

$$E_i = A_{i-4} \boxplus E_{i-4} \boxplus \Sigma_1(E_{i-1}) \boxplus \text{IF}(E_{i-1}, E_{i-2}, E_{i-3}) \boxplus K_i \boxplus W_i, \tag{3}$$

(E_1, E_2, E_3, E_4) will depend on (W_5, W_6, W_7, W_8) for this starting point. By analyzing the conditions on (W_5, W_6, W_7, W_8) to ensure the local collision in the message expansion, we find that there are in total 2^{14}, 2^{23}, 2^{27} and 2^{25} possible values of W_5, W_6, W_7 and W_8, respectively. Since there are no conditions on (E_1, E_2) or $(A_{-3}, A_{-2}, A_{-1}, A_0)$ for this differential characteristic to hold, we only need to check how many (W_7, W_8) are left to ensure the conditions on (E_3, E_4) for this starting point. Experiments suggest that there are 2^{11} valid (W_7, W_8) left. Hence, based on this starting point, we can expect to generate $2^{14+23+11} = 2^{48}$ valid solutions of $(A_i)_{-3 \leq i \leq 12}$, $(E_i)_{1 \leq i \leq 12}$ and $(W_i)_{5 \leq i \leq 12}$. For γ, since we do not have enough degrees of freedom in (W_{13}, W_{14}, W_{15}), we found that $\gamma \approx 1.3$ by 100 tests. If we can generate 2^{ℓ_1} starting points, then we have $2^\ell = 2^{\ell_1 + 48}$. Hence, the time complexity of the new collision attack on 31-step SHA-256 is estimated as

$$2^{96-48-\ell_1+1.3} + 2^{48+\ell_1} + 2^{\ell_1} \cdot T_{\text{model}},$$

where $T_{\text{model}} \approx 2^{31.7}$ denotes the time to generate a starting point and is always negligible. With $\ell_1 = 0$, i.e., only using one starting point, the time complexity is about $2^{49.8}$ and the memory complexity is 2^{48}. With this improved attack, we are much closer to a practical collision attack on 31-step SHA-256 and the bottleneck is the memory consumption. A possible practical implementation is to use less memory at the cost of increased time complexity.

4.3   The First Collision Attack on 31-Step SHA-512

While the best existing collision attack on SHA-256 reaches 31 steps, the best collision attack on SHA-512 could only reach up to 27 steps, which was reported

---

[1] When searching for the differential characteristic for 39-step SHA-256, this strategy was not applied because we found that the obtained differential characteristic was valid.

Table 6. The differential characteristic for 31 steps of SHA-256

i	ΔA_i	ΔE_i	ΔW_i
-4	================================	================================	
-3	================================	================================	
-2	================================	================================	
-1	================================	================================	
0	================================	================================	================================
1	================================	================================	================================
2	================================	================================	================================
3	================================	==================10====	================================
4	================================	==========0===0========01===0	================================
5	================n=unnnnnnn=n=	000111010001111110nu=11111unnnu1	==============nuuu======0=uu=
6	========n===================u	101011=11==0n0==u11110=1110011n	========u====u===u=====n===u
7	===u===n==n======n=======n=u	un0u1100n=01u11111001u1=n110u10n	u=u=====n====n=nu=n====nun=
8	=============================n=	1u01un0u0=1=1=11n=0=u0=001001u0=	=u=nn=======u===u===u==1====
9	================================	01100001110=0=010===00=11101u0=1	============u=========1=u=
10	==============u==========u=	=1n1uuuuu0100=1un0=10unnnnnnn010	================================
11	================================	=01u1010uu1==11100===1000001n=0=	================================
12	================================	==110001=11====1n====0011110n=0=	================================
13	================================	===0====01=====1===============	================================
14	================================	===============u=========0u==	================================
15	================================	===============0=========1==	================================
16	================================	===============1=========1==	==========unnnunnnnnnnnnnn==
17	================================	================================	================================
18	================================	================================	===========1=n=0========n==
19	================================	================================	================================
20	================================	================================	================================
21	================================	================================	================================
22	================================	================================	================================
23	================================	================================	================================
24	================================	================================	================================
25	================================	================================	================================
26	================================	================================	================================
27	================================	================================	================================
28	================================	================================	================================
29	================================	================================	================================
30	================================	================================	================================

at ASIACRYPT 2015 [6]. The authors also stated in [6] that they could not find better collision attacks on SHA-512 because they could not find a suitable differential characteristic with their tools. In this part, we show how to overcome this obstacle.

Our practical SFS collision attack on 39-step SHA-256 benefits much from the practical SFS collision attack on 39-step SHA-512 due to their similarity. Hence, we feel interested to know whether it is possible to find a suitable differential characteristic for 31-step SHA-512 based on the collision attack on 31-step SHA-256 [28] with our new tool.

Specifically, similar to the 31-step attack on SHA-256, the nonzero message differences are injected in

$$(W_5, W_6, W_7, W_8, W_9, W_{16}, W_{18}),$$

and the local collision in the message expansion spans over 14 steps (steps 5−28), as shown in Fig. 2(b). Similar to the collision attack on 31-step SHA-256, we first find SFS collisions and then convert them into collisions with the two-block method. The general procedure to convert SFS collisions into collisions is essentially the same and we refer the readers to the above improved attack on 31-step SHA-256.

The most challenging step to achieve the collision attack on 31-step SHA-512 is how to find a valid differential characteristic. In what follows, we describe how to use our tool to solve this problem.

Step 1: Find a solution of $(\Delta W_i)_{0 \leq i \leq 30}$ with the minimal $\sum_{i=0}^{30} \mathbf{H}(\Delta W_i)$, while keeping the minimal $\mathbf{H}(\Delta W_{16})$ and the minimal $\mathbf{H}(\Delta W_{18})$, which allows a local collision in the message expansion.

Step 2: With the fixed solution of $(\Delta W_i)_{0 \leq i \leq 30}$ obtained at Step 1, find a valid solution of $(\Delta A_i, \Delta E_i)_{0 \leq i \leq 30}$, which follows the shape of the 31-step differential characteristic shown in Fig. 2(b). Here, set a threshold to $\sum_{i=0}^{30} \mathbf{H}(\Delta A_i)$. Specifically, choose an integer tr and add the constraint

$$\sum_{i=0}^{30} \mathbf{H}(\Delta A_i) \leq tr$$

to the model. If the solver cannot output a solution in a reasonable time, e.g., 72 h, increase tr until a valid solution of $(\Delta A_i, \Delta E_i)_{0 \leq i \leq 30}$ is found. Keep the solution of $(\Delta A_i)_{0 \leq i \leq 30}$.

Step 3: With the fixed solution of $(\Delta A_i, \Delta W_i)_{0 \leq i \leq 30}$, find a valid solution of $(\Delta E_i)_{0 \leq i \leq 30}$ with the minimal $\sum_{i=0}^{30} \mathbf{H}(\Delta E_i)$, which allows a 31-step collision attack.

It is found that the obtained 31-step differential characteristic is invalid. Therefore, we propose to use the following method to correct this obtained solution.

Step 1: Set $(\Delta E_i)_{5 \leq i \leq 7}$ as unknown variables. For the remaining $(\Delta E_i)_{0 \leq i \leq 30}$ where $i \notin \{5, 6, 7\}$, keep them the same as those in the obtained solution. For $(\Delta A_i)_{0 \leq i \leq 30}$ and $(\Delta W_i)_{0 \leq i \leq 30}$, they are also kept the same as those in the obtained solution.

Step 2: Add the constraints describing the value transitions for $(A_i, E_i, W_i)_{7 \leq i \leq 12}$ to the model.

In summary, we utilize the degrees of freedom in $(\Delta A_i, \Delta E_i)_{5 \leq i \leq 7}$ and the model for value transitions to correct an invalid 31-step differential characteristic. In our search, the corresponding 31-step differential characteristic is shown in Table 7.

Complexity Evaluation. As already mentioned, the only challenge to achieve the collision attack on 31-step SHA-512 is to find a suitable differential characteristic. Once it is found, the two-block method for 31-step SHA-256 can be directly applied. For consistency, we use the same notation, i.e., use (ℓ, γ, ℓ_1) to describe the time complexity and memory complexity as in the above collision attack on 31-step SHA-256. For our 31-step differential characteristic, there are in total 2^{36}, 2^{26}, 2^{25} and 2^{43} possible values for W_5, W_6, W_7 and W_8, respectively. For each starting point, i.e., the solution of $(A_i)_{1 \leq i \leq 12}$, $(E_i)_{5 \leq i \leq 12}$ and

$(W_i)_{9 \leq i \leq 12}$, we have experimentally found that there are on average $2^{15.3}$ possible (W_7, W_8) that can make the conditions on (E_3, E_4) hold. Therefore, for each starting point, we can generate $2^{36+26+15.3} = 2^{77.3}$ candidate solutions of $(A_i)_{-3 \leq i \leq 12}$, $(E_i)_{1 \leq i \leq 12}$ and $(W_i)_{5 \leq i \leq 12}$. For 2^{ℓ_1} starting points, we thus can expect to generate $2^\ell = 2^{\ell_1+77.3}$ such many solutions. For γ, similarly, we found $\gamma \approx 0.9$ according to 100 experiments. Since the time complexity to generate a starting point is negligible, the whole time complexity is estimated as

$$2^{64 \times 3 - (\ell_1 + 77.3) + 0.9} + 2^{\ell_1 + 77.3}$$

and the memory complexity is $2^{\ell_1+77.3}$. With $\ell_1 = 0$, i.e., only one starting point, the time and memory complexity are $2^{115.6}$ and $2^{77.3}$, respectively.

4.4   The Practical Collision Attack on 28-Step SHA-512

Similar to the 28-step attack on SHA-256 [28], the nonzero message differences are injected in

$$(W_8, W_9, W_{13}, W_{16}, W_{18}),$$

and the local collision in the message expansion spans over 11 steps (steps 8−18), resulting in a collision on 28-step SHA-512.

The most challenging step to achieve the collision attack on 28-step SHA-512 is how to find a valid differential characteristic. In what follows, we describe how to use our tool to solve this problem.

Step 1: Find a solution of $(\Delta W_i)_{0 \leq i \leq 27}$ with the minimal $\sum_{i=0}^{27} \mathbf{H}(\Delta W_i)$ while keeping the minimal $\mathbf{H}(\Delta W_{16})$ and the minimal $\mathbf{H}(\Delta W_{18})$, which allows a local collision in the message expansion.

Step 2: **Find the suitable ΔE_i.** With the fixed solution of $(\Delta W_i)_{0 \leq i \leq 27}$ obtained at Step 1, find a valid solution of $(\Delta A_i, \Delta E_i)_{0 \leq i \leq 27}$.

To improve the efficiency of the message modification, we have tried three strategies for Step 2, as detailed below:

Strategy 1: First, with the fixed solution of $(\Delta W_i)_{0 \leq i \leq 27}$, find a valid solution of $(\Delta A_i, \Delta E_i)_{0 \leq i \leq 27}$, and we minimize $\sum_{i=0}^{27} \mathbf{H}(\Delta A_i)$.
Then, with the fixed solution of $(\Delta W_i, \Delta A_i)_{0 \leq i \leq 27}$, find a valid solution of $(\Delta E_i)_{0 \leq i \leq 27}$ with the minimal $\sum_{i=0}^{27} \mathbf{H}(\Delta E_i)$.

Strategy 2: With the fixed solution of $(\Delta W_i)_{0 \leq i \leq 27}$, find a valid solution of $(\Delta A_i, \Delta E_i)_{0 \leq i \leq 27}$, and we minimize $\sum_{i=0}^{27} \mathbf{H}(\Delta E_i)$.

Strategy 3: With the fixed solution of $(\Delta W_i)_{0 \leq i \leq 27}$, find a valid solution of $(\Delta A_i, \Delta E_i)_{0 \leq i \leq 27}$, and we minimize $\sum_{i=11}^{27} \mathbf{H}(\Delta E_i)$.

After testing, it is found that Strategy 3 is more suitable for message modifications. However, such a 28-step differential characteristic is invalid. Similar to the method to correct the SHA-512 31-step differential characteristic, we also use the same technique to correct this invalid 28-step differential characteristic.

Table 7. The differential characteristic for 31-step SHA-512

Step 1: Set $(\Delta E_i)_{8 \leq i \leq 10}$ as unknown variables. For the remaining $(\Delta E_i)_{0 \leq i \leq 27}$ where $i \notin \{8, 9, 10\}$, keep them the same as those in the obtained solution. For $(\Delta A_i)_{0 \leq i \leq 27}$ and $(\Delta W_i)_{0 \leq i \leq 27}$, they are also kept the same as those in the obtained solution.

Step 2: Add the constraints describing the value transitions for $(A_i, E_i, W_i)_{10 \leq i \leq 12}$ to the model.

With this method, we eventually found a valid 28-step differential characteristic, as shown in Table 8.

Message Modification. We use a different message modification technique than in [28]. In our message modification technique, we first determine all expanded message words and state variables in steps 8–12. Since the first 8 message words can be (almost) freely chosen, it is easy to connect the $(A_i, E_i)_{-4 \leq i \leq -1}$ and $(A_i, E_i)_{8 \leq i \leq 12}$ by using $(W_i)_{0 \leq i \leq 7}$. Currently, $(A_i, E_i)_{-4 \leq i \leq 12}$ and $(W_i)_{0 \leq i \leq 12}$ has been determined. Then, the degree of freedom in message words $W_{13} - W_{15}$ can be used to fulfill the conditions on $E_{13} - E_{15}$ and (W_{16}, W_{18}). With this method, the cost to find the colliding message pair is almost negligible. The colliding message pair is shown in Table 9.

4.5   The First Practical FS Collision for 40-Step SHA-224

In SHA-224, the last one output word $(E_{60} + E_{-4})$ was truncated. Therefore, similar to [6], we inject differences in E_{-4} to mount a FS collision attack. The best practical FS collision attack on SHA-224 was presented in [6] and it reaches 39 steps. With our tool, we could find a practical FS collision for 40-step SHA-224 for the first time. Specifically, we inject message differences at 10 expanded words

$$(W_0, W_9, W_{10}, W_{11}, W_{12}, W_{13}, W_{17}, W_{18}, W_{25}, W_{27}),$$

and then search for the corresponding 40-step differential characteristic. The searching strategy is almost the same as in our attack on 39-step SHA-256.

The 40-step differential characteristic and the conforming message pair are shown in Tables 10 and 11, respectively.

5   Summary and Future Work

Although there was major progress on collision attacks on SHA-2 between 2011 and 2015, which essentially benefited from the development of the GnD technique to search for SHA-2 characteristics, no other progress has been made for nearly 8 years. One reason we believe is that the GnD technique has reached the bottleneck. In addition, the code for this GnD technique is not open source, which may further increase the difficulty to follow these works. Given the importance of SHA-2, there is no doubt that advancing the understanding of its collision resistance is always of practical interest.

Table 8. The differential characteristic for 28-step SHA-512

i	ΔA_i	ΔE_i	ΔW_i
-4			
-3			
-2			
-1			
0			
1			
2			
3			
4			
5			
6		=1=100=10=10111101=10001001=11=1200101=0=0=0=011==110==1001100====1=0	
7		=001=11000100110010000101=0=111101001==101011101011000110000=0u=0=0=01	
8		1un=01un=1mmmmmm=0mmmmm0nnn1111un110=mmmmmmmm=0mm10mm1u1u=0=01mm	
9			1000000000nnunnnn=010001111
10		=01000=101111u1=0111=0=101n101010100001111=01=11110101010010=mmm	
11		=0100mmmm00n1n0n11010101u0000n=000=1011n10u010000010=0um0111101	
12		=100==0111n10=1=1===11=u1=10=====1=1=10=0=11=1	
13		=1==1111110n1=101======1=10==0==0=1=1=1=1=1==1===0=11==	
14		=0==0=1===0==0=	
15		=1===0	
16		==1=	
17			
18		==1=	
19			==11=
20			
21			
22			
23			
24			
25			
26			
27			

Table 9. The colliding message pair for 28 steps of SHA-512

M	1f736d69a0368ef6	7277e5081ad1c198	e953a3cdc4cbe577	bd05f6a203b2f75f
	dd18b3e39f563fca	cad0a5bb69049fcd	4d0dd2a06e2efdc0	86db19c26fc2e1cf
	0184949e92cdd314	82fb3c1420112000	e4930d9b8295ab26	5500d3a2f30a3402
	26f0aa8790cb1813	a9c09c5c5015bc0d	53892c5a64e94edb	8e60d500013a1932
M′	1f736d69a0368ef6	7277e5081ad1c198	e953a3cdc4cbe577	bd05f6a203b2f75f
	dd18b3e39f563fca	cad0a5bb69049fcd	4d0dd2a06e2efdc0	86db19c26fc2e1cf
	037a8f464c0bb995	83033bd41e111fff	e4930d9b8295ab26	5500d3a2f30a3402
	26f0aa8790cb1813	a9809e5c4015bc45	53892c5a64e94edb	8e60d500013a1932
hash	dceb3d88adf54bd2	966c4cb1ab0cf400	01e701fdf10ab603	796d6e5028a5e89a
	f29a7517b216c09f	46dbae73b1db8cce	8ea44d45041010ea	26a7a6b902f2632f

Table 10. The differential characteristic for 40 steps of SHA-224

i	ΔA_i	ΔE_i	ΔW_i
-4	================================	===u============================	
-3	================================	================================	
-2	================================	================================	
-1	================================	================================	
0	================================	================================	===n============================
1	================================	================================	================================
2	================================	================================	================================
3	================================	================================	================================
4	================================	================================	================================
5	================================	================================	================================
6	================================	================================	================================
7	================================	0111============================	================================
8	================================	1000=========10======1===1==1===	================================
9	========u=======================	unnn1=0=00=0=00=01=1=100=0110=1=	==u=============================
10	=========n=u===u==u=====n===	100n0n110111=nu00011un101n11n=00	======n==u===========u=========
11	================================	0101u0n=1n0n010=u0=10nun=1u01=n1	===n============================
12	================================	=10001000010001=0===0110=10=1=0=	======nn=======n===n==nn==uu=u
13	================================	=unn0000001100011=00011==0=101=	================u======nn=======
14	================================	11100nuuuuuuuuu1u=01un000001n001	================================
15	================================	=111=0000000000=0=1=001111111==1=	================================
16	============================n===	1100110110100000101nuuuuuuuu001	================================
17	=====u=u====u===u===========	010100unu00000100101u1000110unn=n1	===n==u============u===========
18	================================	1100111u00nn=100110=u1u00unn000n	==n============================
19	==n=============================	uuu1uuuu01000=110n000111101=0101	================================
20	================================	000u0n1000101=0un01=1100=u11n000	================================
21	================================	011100un1u001unnnn1000000101111	================================
22	================================	=110=111=0==11101======1==1===	================================
23	================================	=nuu==0110===00101=0110====110=	================================
24	================================	=000============================	================================
25	================================	=111============================	=======n=n=======n=============
26	================================	================================	================================
27	================================	================================	==u============================
28	================================	================================	================================
29	================================	================================	================================
30	================================	================================	================================
31	================================	================================	================================
32	================================	================================	================================
33	================================	================================	================================
34	================================	================================	================================
35	================================	================================	================================
36	================================	================================	================================
37	================================	================================	================================
38	================================	================================	================================
39	================================	================================	================================

Table 11. The FS colliding message pair for 40 steps of SHA-224

CV	791c9c6b	baa7f900	f7c53298	9073cbbd	c90690c5	5591553c	43a5d984	af92402d
CV'	791c9c6b	baa7f900	f7c53298	9073cbbd	c90690c5	5591553c	43a5d984	bf92402d
M	f41d61b4	ce033ba2	dd1bc208	a268189b	ee6bda2c	5ddbe94d	9675bbd3	32c1ba8a
	7eba797d	88b06a8f	3bc3015c	d36f38cc	cfcb88e0	3c70f7f3	faa0c1fe	35c62535
M'	e41d61b4	ce033ba2	dd1bc208	a268189b	ee6bda2c	5ddbe94d	9675bbd3	32c1ba8a
	7eba797d	98b06a8f	39e3055c	c36f38cc	ce4b002d	3c74f1f3	faa0c1fe	35c62535
hash	9af50cac	c165a72f	b6f1c9f3	ef54bad9	af0cfb1f	57d357c9	c6462616	

By this work, we report for the first time that it is possible to overcome the obstacle to find SHA-2 characteristics with a SAT/SMT-based method, which is supported by several new improved attacks on the SHA-2 family. As can be observed, these new attacks highly depend on our SAT/SMT-based tool and how to use it in a dedicated way. Especially, we could find useful SHA-2 characteristics that could not be found with the GnD technique.

Through this work, we also expect that there could be more efforts to further improve this SAT/SMT-based method in the future, and that more and more researchers can easily perform analysis of SHA-2 with our tool.

Acknowledgement. We would like to thank the anonymous reviewers for their insightful comments. Yingxin Li and Gaoli Wang are supported by the National Key Research and Development Program of China (No. 2022YFB2701900), the National Natural Science Foundation of China (No. 62072181). Fukang Liu is supported by JSPS KAKENHI Grant Numbers JP22K21282, JP24K20733.

References

1. Aoki, K., Guo, J., Matusiewicz, K., Sasaki, Yu., Wang, L.: Preimages for step-reduced SHA-2. In: Matsui, M. (ed.) ASIACRYPT 2009. LNCS, vol. 5912, pp. 578–597. Springer, Heidelberg (2009). https://doi.org/10.1007/978-3-642-10366-7_34
2. Biham, E., Chen, R., Joux, A., Carribault, P., Lemuet, C., Jalby, W.: Collisions of SHA-0 and reduced SHA-1. In: Cramer, R. (ed.) EUROCRYPT 2005. LNCS, vol. 3494, pp. 36–57. Springer, Heidelberg (2005). https://doi.org/10.1007/11426639_3
3. Biryukov, A., Lamberger, M., Mendel, F., Nikolić, I.: Second-order differential collisions for reduced SHA-256. In: Lee, D.H., Wang, X. (eds.) ASIACRYPT 2011. LNCS, vol. 7073, pp. 270–287. Springer, Heidelberg (2011). https://doi.org/10.1007/978-3-642-25385-0_15
4. De Cannière, C., Rechberger, C.: Finding SHA-1 characteristics: general results and applications. In: Lai, X., Chen, K. (eds.) ASIACRYPT 2006. LNCS, vol. 4284, pp. 1–20. Springer, Heidelberg (2006). https://doi.org/10.1007/11935230_1
5. Damgård, I.B.: A design principle for hash functions. In: Brassard, G. (ed.) CRYPTO 1989. LNCS, vol. 435, pp. 416–427. Springer, New York (1990). https://doi.org/10.1007/0-387-34805-0_39

6. Dobraunig, C., Eichlseder, M., Mendel, F.: Analysis of SHA-512/224 and SHA-512/256. In: Iwata, T., Cheon, J.H. (eds.) ASIACRYPT 2015. LNCS, vol. 9453, pp. 612–630. Springer, Heidelberg (2015). https://doi.org/10.1007/978-3-662-48800-3_25

7. Draft, F.: Public comments on the draft federal information processing standard (FIPS) draft FIPS 180-2, secure hash standard (SHS)

8. Eichlseder, M., Mendel, F., Schläffer, M.: Branching heuristics in differential collision search with applications to SHA-512. In: Cid, C., Rechberger, C. (eds.) FSE 2014. LNCS, vol. 8540, pp. 473–488. Springer, Heidelberg (2015). https://doi.org/10.1007/978-3-662-46706-0_24

9. Guo, J., Ling, S., Rechberger, C., Wang, H.: Advanced meet-in-the-middle preimage attacks: first results on full tiger, and improved results on MD4 and SHA-2. In: Abe, M. (ed.) ASIACRYPT 2010. LNCS, vol. 6477, pp. 56–75. Springer, Heidelberg (2010). https://doi.org/10.1007/978-3-642-17373-8_4

10. Indesteege, S., Mendel, F., Preneel, B., Rechberger, C.: Collisions and other non-random properties for step-reduced SHA-256. In: Avanzi, R.M., Keliher, L., Sica, F. (eds.) SAC 2008. LNCS, vol. 5381, pp. 276–293. Springer, Heidelberg (2009). https://doi.org/10.1007/978-3-642-04159-4_18

11. Isobe, T., Shibutani, K.: Preimage attacks on reduced tiger and SHA-2. In: Dunkelman, O. (ed.) FSE 2009. LNCS, vol. 5665, pp. 139–155. Springer, Heidelberg (2009). https://doi.org/10.1007/978-3-642-03317-9_9

12. Khovratovich, D., Rechberger, C., Savelieva, A.: Bicliques for preimages: attacks on Skein-512 and the SHA-2 family. In: Canteaut, A. (ed.) FSE 2012. LNCS, vol. 7549, pp. 244–263. Springer, Heidelberg (2012). https://doi.org/10.1007/978-3-642-34047-5_15

13. Lamberger, M., Mendel, F.: Higher-order differential attack on reduced SHA-256. IACR Cryptol. ePrint Arch, p. 37 (2011). http://eprint.iacr.org/2011/037

14. Landelle, F., Peyrin, T.: Cryptanalysis of full RIPEMD-128. In: Johansson, T., Nguyen, P.Q. (eds.) EUROCRYPT 2013. LNCS, vol. 7881, pp. 228–244. Springer, Heidelberg (2013). https://doi.org/10.1007/978-3-642-38348-9_14

15. Leurent, G., Peyrin, T.: From collisions to chosen-prefix collisions application to full SHA-1. In: Ishai, Y., Rijmen, V. (eds.) EUROCRYPT 2019. LNCS, vol. 11478, pp. 527–555. Springer, Cham (2019). https://doi.org/10.1007/978-3-030-17659-4_18

16. Leurent, G., Peyrin, T.: SHA-1 is a shambles: first chosen-prefix collision on SHA-1 and application to the PGP web of trust. In: USENIX, pp. 1839–1856. USENIX Association (2020). https://www.usenix.org/conference/usenixsecurity20/presentation/leurent

17. Li, J., Isobe, T., Shibutani, K.: Converting meet-in-the-middle preimage attack into pseudo collision attack: application to SHA-2. In: Canteaut, A. (ed.) FSE 2012. LNCS, vol. 7549, pp. 264–286. Springer, Heidelberg (2012). https://doi.org/10.1007/978-3-642-34047-5_16

18. Li, Y., Liu, F., Wang, G.: New records in collision attacks on SHA-2. IACR Cryptol. ePrint Arch, p. 37 (2024). https://eprint.iacr.org/2024/349

19. Liu, F., Dobraunig, C., Mendel, F., Isobe, T., Wang, G., Cao, Z.: Efficient collision attack frameworks for RIPEMD-160. In: Boldyreva, A., Micciancio, D. (eds.) CRYPTO 2019. LNCS, vol. 11693, pp. 117–149. Springer, Cham (2019). https://doi.org/10.1007/978-3-030-26951-7_5

20. Liu, F., Dobraunig, C., Mendel, F., Isobe, T., Wang, G., Cao, Z.: New semi-free-start collision attack framework for reduced RIPEMD-160. IACR Trans. Symmetric Cryptol. **2019**(3), 169–192 (2019). https://doi.org/10.13154/tosc.v2019.i3.169-192

21. Liu, F., Isobe, T., Meier, W.: Automatic verification of differential characteristics: application to reduced gimli. In: Micciancio, D., Ristenpart, T. (eds.) CRYPTO 2020. LNCS, vol. 12172, pp. 219–248. Springer, Cham (2020). https://doi.org/10.1007/978-3-030-56877-1_8
22. Liu, F., Meier, W., Sarkar, S., Wang, G., Ito, R., Isobe, T.: New cryptanalysis of ZUC-256 initialization using modular differences. IACR Trans. Symmetric Cryptol. **2022**(3), 152–190 (2022). https://doi.org/10.46586/tosc.v2022.i3.152-190
23. Liu, F., Mendel, F., Wang, G.: Collisions and semi-free-start collisions for round-reduced RIPEMD-160. In: Takagi, T., Peyrin, T. (eds.) ASIACRYPT 2017. LNCS, vol. 10624, pp. 158–186. Springer, Cham (2017). https://doi.org/10.1007/978-3-319-70694-8_6
24. Liu, F., et al.: Analysis of RIPEMD-160: new collision attacks and finding characteristics with MILP. In: Hazay, C., Stam, M. (eds.) EUROCRYPT(4). Lecture Notes in Computer Science, vol. 14007, pp. 189–219. Springer, Cham (2023). https://doi.org/10.1007/978-3-031-30634-1_7
25. Mendel, F., Nad, T., Scherz, S., Schläffer, M.: Differential attacks on reduced RIPEMD-160. In: Gollmann, D., Freiling, F.C. (eds.) ISC 2012. LNCS, vol. 7483, pp. 23–38. Springer, Heidelberg (2012). https://doi.org/10.1007/978-3-642-33383-5_2
26. Mendel, F., Nad, T., Schläffer, M.: Finding SHA-2 characteristics: searching through a minefield of contradictions. In: Lee, D.H., Wang, X. (eds.) ASIACRYPT 2011. LNCS, vol. 7073, pp. 288–307. Springer, Heidelberg (2011). https://doi.org/10.1007/978-3-642-25385-0_16
27. Mendel, F., Nad, T., Schläffer, M.: Collision attacks on the reduced dual-stream hash function RIPEMD-128. In: Canteaut, A. (ed.) FSE 2012. LNCS, vol. 7549, pp. 226–243. Springer, Heidelberg (2012). https://doi.org/10.1007/978-3-642-34047-5_14
28. Mendel, F., Nad, T., Schläffer, M.: Improving local collisions: new attacks on reduced SHA-256. In: Johansson, T., Nguyen, P.Q. (eds.) EUROCRYPT 2013. LNCS, vol. 7881, pp. 262–278. Springer, Heidelberg (2013). https://doi.org/10.1007/978-3-642-38348-9_16
29. Mendel, F., Peyrin, T., Schläffer, M., Wang, L., Wu, S.: Improved cryptanalysis of reduced RIPEMD-160. In: Sako, K., Sarkar, P. (eds.) ASIACRYPT 2013. LNCS, vol. 8270, pp. 484–503. Springer, Heidelberg (2013). https://doi.org/10.1007/978-3-642-42045-0_25
30. Mendel, F., Pramstaller, N., Rechberger, C., Rijmen, V.: Analysis of step-reduced SHA-256. In: Robshaw, M. (ed.) FSE 2006. LNCS, vol. 4047, pp. 126–143. Springer, Heidelberg (2006). https://doi.org/10.1007/11799313_9
31. Merkle, R.C.: One way hash functions and DES. In: Brassard, G. (ed.) CRYPTO 1989. LNCS, vol. 435, pp. 428–446. Springer, New York (1990). https://doi.org/10.1007/0-387-34805-0_40
32. Mironov, I., Zhang, L.: Applications of SAT solvers to cryptanalysis of hash functions. In: Biere, A., Gomes, C.P. (eds.) SAT 2006. LNCS, vol. 4121, pp. 102–115. Springer, Heidelberg (2006). https://doi.org/10.1007/11814948_13
33. Nikolić, I., Biryukov, A.: Collisions for step-reduced SHA-256. In: Nyberg, K. (ed.) FSE 2008. LNCS, vol. 5086, pp. 1–15. Springer, Heidelberg (2008). https://doi.org/10.1007/978-3-540-71039-4_1
34. Sanadhya, S.K., Sarkar, P.: New collision attacks against up to 24-step SHA-2. In: Chowdhury, D.R., Rijmen, V., Das, A. (eds.) INDOCRYPT 2008. LNCS, vol. 5365, pp. 91–103. Springer, Heidelberg (2008). https://doi.org/10.1007/978-3-540-89754-5_8

35. Stevens, M.: New collision attacks on SHA-1 based on optimal joint local-collision analysis. In: Johansson, T., Nguyen, P.Q. (eds.) EUROCRYPT 2013. LNCS, vol. 7881, pp. 245–261. Springer, Heidelberg (2013). https://doi.org/10.1007/978-3-642-38348-9_15

36. Stevens, M., Bursztein, E., Karpman, P., Albertini, A., Markov, Y.: The First collision for full SHA-1. In: Katz, J., Shacham, H. (eds.) CRYPTO 2017. LNCS, vol. 10401, pp. 570–596. Springer, Cham (2017). https://doi.org/10.1007/978-3-319-63688-7_19

37. Stevens, M., Lenstra, A., de Weger, B.: Chosen-prefix collisions for MD5 and colliding X.509 certificates for different identities. In: Naor, M. (ed.) EUROCRYPT 2007. LNCS, vol. 4515, pp. 1–22. Springer, Heidelberg (2007). https://doi.org/10.1007/978-3-540-72540-4_1

38. Wang, X., Lai, X., Feng, D., Chen, H., Yu, X.: Cryptanalysis of the hash functions MD4 and RIPEMD. In: Cramer, R. (ed.) EUROCRYPT 2005. LNCS, vol. 3494, pp. 1–18. Springer, Heidelberg (2005). https://doi.org/10.1007/11426639_1

39. Wang, X., Yin, Y.L., Yu, H.: Finding collisions in the full SHA-1. In: Shoup, V. (ed.) CRYPTO 2005. LNCS, vol. 3621, pp. 17–36. Springer, Heidelberg (2005). https://doi.org/10.1007/11535218_2

40. Wang, X., Yu, H.: How to break MD5 and other hash functions. In: Cramer, R. (ed.) EUROCRYPT 2005. LNCS, vol. 3494, pp. 19–35. Springer, Heidelberg (2005). https://doi.org/10.1007/11426639_2

41. Wang, X., Yu, H., Yin, Y.L.: Efficient collision search attacks on SHA-0. In: Shoup, V. (ed.) CRYPTO 2005. LNCS, vol. 3621, pp. 1–16. Springer, Heidelberg (2005). https://doi.org/10.1007/11535218_1

42. Yu, H., Bai, D.: Boomerang attack on step-reduced SHA-512. In: Lin, D., Yung, M., Zhou, J. (eds.) Inscrypt 2014. LNCS, vol. 8957, pp. 329–342. Springer, Cham (2015). https://doi.org/10.1007/978-3-319-16745-9_18

43. Yu, H., Wang, X.: Non-randomness of 39-step SHA-256. In: Presented at rump session of EUROCRYPT (2008)

Improving Linear Key Recovery Attacks Using Walsh Spectrum Puncturing

Antonio Flórez-Gutiérrez$^{(\boxtimes)}$ (ID) and Yosuke Todo (ID)

NTT Social Informatics Laboratories, Tokyo, Japan
{antonio.florez,yosuke.todo}@ntt.com

Abstract. In some linear key recovery attacks, the function which determines the value of the linear approximation from the plaintext, ciphertext and key is replaced by a similar map in order to improve the time or memory complexity at the cost of a data complexity increase. We propose a general framework for key recovery map substitution, and introduce *Walsh spectrum puncturing*, which consists of removing carefully-chosen coefficients from the Walsh spectrum of this map. The capabilities of this technique are illustrated by describing improved attacks on reduced-round Serpent (including the first 12-round attack on the 192-bit key variant), GIFT-128 and NOEKEON, as well as the full DES.

Keywords: Linear cryptanalysis · Serpent · GIFT · NOEKEON · DES

1 Introduction

Linear cryptanalysis [35] is one of the most popular techniques in the analysis of symmetric cryptographic primitives such as block ciphers. It exploits the statistical bias or correlation of one or more *linear approximations*, which are linear combinations of bits of the input and output of the cipher. These linear approximations can be extended over additional rounds by guessing all possible values of a segment of the key and computing the experimental value of the correlation for each one, as we expect the correct guess to exhibit a larger bias.

Algorithm 2. The linear key recovery attack was introduced by Matsui as Algorithm 2 [35]. There have been multiple improvements, such as the introduction of a distillation phase [36] and the fast Walsh transform or FFT technique [23]. Recently, the Walsh transform pruning approach was introduced [27]. The map describing the value of the linear approximation as a function of the plaintext, ciphertext and key is the *key recovery map*. In [27], the complexity of the attack is highly-dependent on the structure of the non-zero values of this map.

Modifying the Key Recovery Map. There are several examples of substitution of the key recovery map for an approximation which lowers the attack complexity, which can be another Boolean function which is highly correlated to the original [2,5,11], or a function which rejects some plaintext-ciphertext pairs [11,27,37]. This substitution is compensated by increasing the data complexity.

© International Association for Cryptologic Research 2024
M. Joye and G. Leander (Eds.): EUROCRYPT 2024, LNCS 14651, pp. 187–216, 2024.
https://doi.org/10.1007/978-3-031-58716-0_7

Our Contribution. We propose a statistical model for key recovery map approximation which generalises the aforementioned situations and which can be used to compute the required data complexity increase. We introduce a third type of key recovery map approximation, which we call *Walsh spectrum puncturing*. It consists of removing nonzero coefficients of the Walsh spectrum to reduce the cost of the pruned Walsh transform-based attack of [27] and other key recovery algorithms. We find that removing a fraction of ε of the squared 2-norm of the Walsh spectrum (that is, deleting Walsh coefficients so that the sum of their squares is a proportion ε of the total sum), the data complexity must be increased by a factor of $\frac{1}{1-\varepsilon}$. We also describe some puncturing strategies which can be used in common block cipher cryptanalysis scenarios.

As applications, we present improved attacks against Serpent [7,8], GIFT-128 [4], NOEKEON [26], and DES [1], as summarized in Table 1. Of particular significance is, to the best of our knowledge, the first key recovery attack on 12-round Serpent-192. We also improve the best linear attack against GIFT-128, although the best attacks on GIFT-128 are differential rather than linear [45]. Nevertheless, unlike differential cryptanalysis, linear cryptanalysis is still applicable when GIFT-128 is used in COFB mode. The attack on this setting is improved from 16 to 17 rounds. We reduce the memory complexity of the best attack on DES [27] from 3.3TB to 186.1 GB. We also provide the best attack against 12-round NOEKEON in terms of data and time complexities.

Paper layout. Sect. 2 includes preliminary notions on pseudoboolean functions and their spectra, as well as linear cryptanalysis. Section 3 introduces the statistical model for key recovery map approximation, applies it to spectrum puncturing, and shows some validation experiments. Section 4 discusses some puncturing strategies for common cipher constructions. Sections 5, 6, 7 and 8 briefly describe applications to Serpent, GIFT-128, the DES, and NOEKEON, respectively. These are covered in more detail in the paper's extended version [29].

2   Preliminaries

This section covers notions used in the paper, including some definitions and notations about Boolean functions and their Walsh spectra as covered in books like [19,41], and some essential concepts on linear cryptanalysis.

2.1   Binary Vector Spaces

We denote the field with two elements as $\mathbb{F}_2 = \{0,1\}$. For clarity, we use the typeface x, y, u, v to denote vectors of binary vector spaces $\mathbb{F}_2^l$, and the typeface $\mathbf{x}, \mathbf{y}, \mathbf{u}, \mathbf{v}$ to denote (column) vectors of real vector spaces $\mathbb{R}^l$. We use x_i and $\mathbf{x}[i]$ to denote the ith coordinates of a binary vector x and a real vector $\mathbf{x}$, respectively. The rightmost, least significant bit of x is x_0. The top coordinate of $\mathbf{x}$ is $\mathbf{x}[0]$. The sum in $\mathbb{F}_2^l$ is denoted by $+$ and by $\oplus$ when confusion is possible

Table 1. Comparison of attacks on the application target ciphers

Target	Attack	Rds.	Data	Time	Memory	P_S	Source
Serpent (192-bit)	Linear	11	$2^{121.23}$ KP	$2^{121.23}$	2^{108}	79%	[23,38]
	Diff-lin	11	$2^{125.7}$ CC	$2^{125.7}$	$2^{99.00}$	85%	[34]
	Linear[†]	**12**	$2^{127.5}$ KP	$2^{189.74}$	$2^{133.00}$	80%	Sect. 5
	Linear	**12**	$2^{127.5}$ KP	$2^{189.74}$	$2^{182.00}$	80%	Sect. 5
Serpent (256-bit)	Multdim-lin	12	$2^{125.8}$ KP	$2^{253.8}$	$2^{125.8}$	79%	[17,38,39]
	Multdim-lin	12	$2^{125.8}$ KP	2^{242}	2^{236}	79%	[17,38,39]
	Diff-lin	12	2^{127} CC	2^{251}	2^{127}	77%	[17,34]
	Diff-lin[†]	12	$2^{127.92}$ CP	$2^{233.55}$	$2^{127.92}$	10%	[17]
	Diff-lin[†]	12	$2^{125.74}$ CP	$2^{236.91}$	$2^{125.74}$	10%	[17]
	Diff-lin[†]	12	$2^{118.40}$ CP	$2^{242.93}$	$2^{118.40}$	10%	[17]
	Linear	12	$2^{125.16}$ KP	$\mathbf{2^{214.36}}$	$2^{125.16}$	81%	Sect. 5
	Linear	12	$2^{126.30}$ KP	$\mathbf{2^{210.36}}$	$2^{125.16}$	80%	Sect. 5
GIFT-128 (General)	Differential	27	$2^{123.53}$ CP	$2^{124.83}$	$2^{80.00}$	–	[45]
	Linear	25	$2^{124.75}$ KP	$2^{126.77}$	$2^{96.00}$	50%	[44]
	Linear	25	$2^{125.75}$ KP	$2^{127.77}$	$2^{96.00}$	75%	[44]
	Linear	25	$\mathbf{2^{123.02}}$ KP	$\mathbf{2^{124.61}}$	$2^{112.00}$	**80%**	Sect. 6
GIFT-128 (COFB)	Linear*	16	$2^{62.10}$ KP	$2^{122.80}$	$2^{62.10}$	80%	[44]
	Linear	**17**	$2^{62.10}$ KP	$2^{125.09}$	$2^{62.10}$	80%	Sect. 6
DES[‡]	Differential	Full	$2^{47.00}$ CP	$2^{37.00}$	$\mathcal{O}(1)$	58%	[12]
	Linear	Full	$2^{43.00}$ KP	$2^{39.00}$	$2^{26.00}$	50%	[36]
	Multiple-lin	Full	$2^{42.78}$ KP	$2^{38.86}$	$2^{30.00}$	85%	[16]
	Conditional-lin	Full	$2^{42.00}$ KP	$2^{42.00}$	$2^{28.00}$	90%	[11]
	Linear	Full	$2^{41.62}$ KP	$2^{41.76}$	$\mathbf{2^{34.54}}$	70%	Sect. 7
	Linear	Full	$2^{41.50}$ KP	$2^{42.13}$	$2^{38.75}$	70%	[27]
NOEKEON	Linear	12	$2^{122.35}$ KP	$2^{123.82}$	$2^{121.00}$	80%	[18]
	Linear	12	$\mathbf{2^{119.55}}$ KP	$\mathbf{2^{120.63}}$	$\mathbf{2^{115.00}}$	80%	Sect. 8

[†] The attack assumes that a-bit advantage of the subkey implies a-bit advantage of the master key without any extra cost. [‡] For the DES application, the data collection cost is excluded from the time complexity for historical reasons. For other applications, the time includes the data collection. * We have corrected the memory complexity for the sake of comparison. The authors of [44] insisted that the memory complexity is 2^{47}. However, the attack accesses each plaintext-ciphertext pair multiple times. Therefore, storing the data is necessary. We contacted the authors and confirmed that they did not consider the cost of storing the data.

and in cipher specifications. The inner product of binary vectors is

$$\langle x, y \rangle = \sum_{i=0}^{l-1} x_i \cdot y_i.$$

The inner product is linear: $\langle x + y, z \rangle = \langle x, z \rangle \langle y, z \rangle$ and $\langle x, y + z \rangle = \langle x, y \rangle \langle x, z \rangle$. If $\langle x, y \rangle = 0$, we say that x and y are orthogonal and write $x \perp y$.

2.2 Pseudoboolean Functions and Their Walsh Spectra

A *pseudoboolean function* is a map $f : \mathbb{F}_2^l \longrightarrow \mathbb{R}$. If $f(x) \in \{1, -1\}$ for all $x \in \mathbb{F}_2^l$, it is a Boolean function. This is because we can identify $0 \in \mathbb{F}_2$ with $(-1)^0 \in \mathbb{R}$ and $1 \in \mathbb{F}_2$ with $(-1)^1 \in \mathbb{R}$ so that addition in $\mathbb{F}_2$ is the same as multiplication in $\mathbb{R}$. Pseudoboolean functions form a real vector space of dimension 2^l, which is denoted $\mathbb{RF}_2^l$ and can be identified with $\mathbb{R}^{2^l}$. Given a pair of pseudoboolean functions $f, g : \mathbb{F}_2^l \longrightarrow \mathbb{R}$, their inner product and 2-norm are:

$$\langle f, g \rangle = \frac{1}{2^l} \sum_{x \in \mathbb{F}_2^l} f(x)g(x), \qquad \|f\|_2 = \sqrt{\langle f, f \rangle}.$$

If f, g are traditional Boolean functions, their inner product is often denoted $\text{cor}(f, g)$ and called *correlation*. The 2-norm of Boolean functions is always 1. If $\langle f, g \rangle = 0$, we say that f and g are orthogonal and write $f \perp g$.

The *Hadamard basis* of $\mathbb{RF}_2^l$ consists of the *parity functions* $\mathbf{h}_u : \mathbb{F}_2^l \longrightarrow \mathbb{R}$, where $\mathbf{h}_u(x) = (-1)^{\langle u, x \rangle}$. It satisfies $\mathbf{h}_u \perp \mathbf{h}_v$ if $u \neq v$, and $\langle \mathbf{h}_u, \mathbf{h}_v \rangle = 1$ if $u = v$. Given $f : \mathbb{F}_2^l \longrightarrow \mathbb{R}$, its *Walsh spectrum* is the map $\widehat{f} : \mathbb{F}_2^l \longrightarrow \mathbb{R}$ given by

$$\widehat{f}(u) = \frac{1}{2^l} \sum_{x \in \mathbb{F}_2^l} (-1)^{\langle u, x \rangle} f(x).$$

The Walsh spectrum $\widehat{f}$ is the representation of f in the Hadamard basis:

$$f = \sum_{u \in \mathbb{F}_2^l} \widehat{f}(u) \mathbf{h}_u.$$

A pseudoboolean function is *balanced* if $\widehat{f}(0) = \sum_{x \in \mathbb{F}_2^l} f(x) = 0$.

The Walsh spectrum of a function defined in $\mathbb{F}_2^l$ can be obtained with the fast Walsh transform algorithm [24] in $l2^l$ additions and subtractions.

The Walsh spectrum follows several properties:

Involutivity: $\qquad \widehat{\widehat{f}} = 2^{-l} f,$

Linearity: $\qquad \widehat{af + bg} = a\widehat{f} + b\widehat{g},$

Parseval Identity: $\qquad \|f\|_2 = \sqrt{2^l} \|\widehat{f}\|_2,$

Plancherel identity: $\qquad \langle f, g \rangle = 2^l \langle \widehat{f}, \widehat{g} \rangle.$

Given $f, g : \mathbb{F}_2^l \longrightarrow \mathbb{R}$, their *convolution* is a map $(f * g) : \mathbb{F}_2^l \longrightarrow \mathbb{R}$ given by

$$(f * g)(k) = \frac{1}{2^l} \sum_{x \in \mathbb{F}_2^l} f(k)g(x + k).$$

The *convolution theorem* states that

$$\widehat{f * g} = \widehat{f} \odot \widehat{g},$$

where $\odot$ denotes the component-wise product of real vectors. Given g, we can compute $f * g$ by applying the fast Walsh transform on g, multiplying by $\widehat{f}$ component-wise, and applying the fast Walsh transform again.

Given $f : \mathbb{F}_2^l \longrightarrow \mathbb{R}$, if we assume that $x \in \mathbb{F}_2^l$ is uniformly distributed, then $f(x)$ is a real random variable whose mean and variance are:

$$\mathrm{E}[f(x)] = \frac{1}{2^l} \sum_{x \in \mathbb{F}_2^l} f(x) = \widehat{f}(0),$$

$$\mathrm{Var}(f(x)) = \mathrm{E}[f(x)^2] - \mathrm{E}[f(x)]^2 = \frac{1}{2^l} \sum_{x \in \mathbb{F}_2^l} f(x)^2 - \widehat{f}(0)^2$$

$$= \sum_{u \in \mathbb{F}_2^l \setminus \{0\}} \widehat{f}(u)^2 = \|f\|_2^2 - \widehat{f}(0)^2,$$

$$\mathrm{Cov}(f(x), g(x)) = \mathrm{E}[f(x)g(x)] - \mathrm{E}[f(x)]\mathrm{E}[g(x)] = \frac{1}{2^l} \sum_{x \in \mathbb{F}_2^l} f(x)g(x) - \widehat{f}(0)\widehat{g}(0)$$

$$= \langle f, g \rangle - \widehat{f}(0)\widehat{g}(0) = 2^l \langle \widehat{f}, \widehat{g} \rangle - \widehat{f}(0)\widehat{g}(0)$$

If f is balanced, then $\mathrm{E}[f(x)] = \widehat{f}(0) = 0$. For traditional balanced functions, since $\|f\|_2 = 1$, we conclude that $\mathrm{Var}(f(x)) = 1$ and $\mathrm{Cov}(f(x), g(x)) = \mathrm{cor}(f, g)$.

2.3   Vectorial Boolean Functions

Given a vectorial Boolean function $f : \mathbb{F}_2^l \longrightarrow \mathbb{F}_2^m$, its correlation matrix or Walsh spectrum is a $2^l \times 2^m$ matrix containing the spectra of all of its components $f_v : \mathbb{F}_2^l \longrightarrow \mathbb{F}_2$, $f_v(x) = \langle v, f(x) \rangle$:

$$\widehat{f}(u, v) = \widehat{f}_v(u) = \frac{1}{2^l} \sum_{x \in \mathbb{F}_2^l} (-1)^{\langle u, x \rangle \oplus \langle v, f(x) \rangle}.$$

The spectrum of a composition $f = f_r \circ \cdots \circ f_1$ is matrix product of the spectra:

$$\widehat{f} = \widehat{f}_r \times \cdots \times \widehat{f}_1, \qquad \widehat{f}(u, v) = \sum_{u_1} \cdots \sum_{u_{r-1}} \widehat{f}_1(u, u_1) \cdots \widehat{f}_r(u_{r-1}, v).$$

The correlation matrix of a map f consisting of the parallel application of several functions $f_1, \ldots, f_r$ is the Kronecker product of the correlation matrices:

$$\widehat{f} = \widehat{f}_1 \otimes \cdots \otimes \widehat{f}_r, \qquad \widehat{f}(u_1 | \ldots | u_r, v_1 | \ldots | v_r) = \widehat{f}_1(u_1, v_1) \cdots \widehat{f}_r(u_r, v_r).$$

2.4   Linear Appproximations

Let $E_K : \mathbb{F}_2^n \longrightarrow \mathbb{F}_2^n$ be a block cipher with key K. A *linear approximation* ν is a pair of masks $\alpha, \beta \in \mathbb{F}_2^n$. The evaluation of the linear approximation is the XOR of the inner product of the input and output masks by the plaintext and ciphertext, respectively: $\nu(p, c) = \langle \alpha, p \rangle \oplus \langle \beta, c \rangle$. Its *correlation* is:

$$\mathrm{cor}_K(\alpha, \beta) = \frac{1}{2^n} \sum_{p \in \mathbb{F}_2^n} (-1)^{\langle \alpha, p \rangle \oplus \langle \beta, E_K(p) \rangle} = \widehat{E_K}(\alpha, \beta).$$

The correlation is key-dependent, and thus follows some statistical distribution over the keyspace. The average is usually zero due to positive and negative correlations canceling each other, so we use the *expected linear potential* [40]:

$$\mathrm{ELP}(\alpha, \beta) = \mathrm{E}\left[\mathrm{cor}_K(\alpha, \beta)^2\right] = \mathrm{Var}\left(\mathrm{cor}_K(\alpha, \beta)\right) + \mathrm{E}\left[\mathrm{cor}_K(\alpha, \beta)\right]^2.$$

Computing the ELP of a given approximation is generally a difficult problem. For *key-alternating block ciphers*, which feature multiple rounds which consist of a round subkey addition and a round function F, a *linear trail* [25] is defined as a particular sequence of linear approximations of the round function ($\alpha = \alpha_0, \alpha_1, \ldots, \alpha_r = \beta$). The correlation of the approximation for a given key is the sum of the *correlation contributions* of all its linear trails.

$$\mathrm{cor}_K(\alpha, \beta) = (-1)^{\langle \alpha_0, K_0 \rangle \oplus \cdots \oplus \langle \alpha_r, K_r \rangle} \prod_{i=1}^{r} \widehat{F}(\alpha_{i-1}, \alpha_i).$$

For some keys, the signs of these contributions cancel each other, and for others they add up to a larger value. Under some key schedule assumptions [40],

$$\mathrm{ELP}(\alpha, \beta) = \sum_{\alpha_1 \in \mathbb{F}_2^n} \cdots \sum_{\alpha_{r-1} \in \mathbb{F}_2^n} \prod_{i=1}^{r} \widehat{F}(\alpha_{i-1}, \alpha_i)^2.$$

We note that finding a collection of high-correlation trails is often enough to obtain an accurate lower bound for the ELP. A noise component 2^{-n} which accounts for any unknown trails [14] is often included too.

2.5   Key Recovery Linear Attack Scenario

Since this work focuses on the key recovery step of linear attacks, we focus on the functions which relate the plaintext, the ciphertext, the key guess, and the value of a linear approximation through the following abstraction:

Definition 1 (Attack scenario). *Consider that as part of a linear key recovery attack, the adversary has to compute the experimental correlation of a linear approximation for a given number of key guesses. Let $x \in \mathbb{F}_2^l$ denote the concatenation of the segments of the plaintext and ciphertext which influence the value of this linear approximation. We also consider that there is an external key guess*

$k_{\text{ext}} \in \mathbb{F}_2^l$ which is xored to this text segment, and an internal key guess k_{int} which is not. Let $f_0(x)$ be a separate plaintext-and-ciphertext-only term which is not influenced by the key. The linear approximation can be written as

$$\nu(p, c, k_{\text{ext}}, k_{\text{int}}) = f_0(p, c) \cdot f(x \oplus k_{\text{ext}}, k_{\text{int}}). \tag{1}$$

The first and last round subkey guess is represented by k_{ext}, while the rest is represented by k_{int}. f_0 is an arbitrary term which is independent of the key. This function is called the key recovery map. The attacker is given a list $\mathcal{D}$ of N plaintext-ciphertext pairs $(p, c = E_K(p))$ which are generated with a secret key K. By examining the key schedule, the attacker can construct a list $\mathcal{K}$ of L valid key guesses $(k_{\text{int}}, k_{\text{ext}})$, and a list $\mathcal{K}_{\text{int}}$ of size L_{int} with the permitted values of k_{int}. The aim of the attacker is to compute the experimental correlations

$$\widetilde{\text{cor}}(k_{\text{ext}}, k_{\text{int}}) = \frac{1}{N} \sum_{(p,c) \in \mathcal{D}} f_0(p, c) \cdot f(x(p, c) \oplus k_{\text{ext}}, k_{\text{int}}) \tag{2}$$

for all $(k_{\text{ext}}, k_{\text{int}}) \in \mathcal{K}$, which can either be used directly or processed further.

There are several algorithms which compute the experimental correlations.

Matsui's Algorithm 2 [35]. Initialise an array which will store $\widetilde{\text{cor}}$ to zero. Then, for each plaintext-ciphertext pair, each of the entries is either incremented or decremented individually. The total time complexity is thus $\mathcal{O}(NL)$.

Algorithm 2 with distillation [36]. Algorithm 2 evaluates f multiple times for the same input. Matsui proposed an improved version with two stages:

1. **Distillation phase:** A table $\mathbf{a}$ of size 2^l is initialised to zero. For each plaintext-ciphertext pair, we increment or decrement one position to obtain

$$\mathbf{a}[x] = \sum_{\substack{(p,c) \in \mathcal{D} \\ x(p,c)=x}} f_0(p, c).$$

   The distillation table contains all the relevant information about the data sample, and can be constructed in $\mathcal{O}(N)$ time.

2. **Analysis phase:** For each key guess $(k_{\text{ext}}, k_{\text{int}}) \in \mathcal{K}$, we have:

$$\widetilde{\text{cor}}(k_{\text{ext}}, k_{\text{int}}) = \frac{1}{N} \sum_{x \in \mathbb{F}_2^l} f(x + k_{\text{ext}}, k_{\text{int}}) \cdot \mathbf{a}[x].$$

   Each key guess takes 2^l operations, so the total cost is $\mathcal{O}(2^l L)$.

The total time complexity is $\mathcal{O}(N) + \mathcal{O}(2^l L)$.

Fast Walsh transform attack [23]. A further attack algorithm was introduced by Collard et al.. We first note that the array $\mathbf{a}$ can be interpreted as a function $\mathbf{a} : \mathbb{F}_2^l \longrightarrow \mathbb{R}$. We momentarily fix the value of k_{int}, and define $\widetilde{\text{cor}}_{k_{\text{int}}} : \mathbb{F}_2^l \longrightarrow \mathbb{R}$

as $\widetilde{\mathrm{cor}}_{k_{\mathrm{int}}}(k_{\mathrm{ext}}) = \widetilde{\mathrm{cor}}(k_{\mathrm{ext}}, k_{\mathrm{int}})$ and $f_{k_{\mathrm{int}}} : \mathbb{F}_2^l \longrightarrow \mathbb{R}$ as $f_{k_{\mathrm{int}}}(x) = f(x, k_{\mathrm{int}})$. Under this notation, $\widetilde{\mathrm{cor}}_{k_{\mathrm{int}}}$ is the convolution of $f_{k_{\mathrm{int}}}$ and $\mathbf{a}$:

$$\widetilde{\mathrm{cor}}_{k_{\mathrm{int}}}(k_{\mathrm{ext}}) = \frac{1}{N} \sum_{x \in \mathbb{F}_2^l} f_{k_{\mathrm{int}}}(x + k_{\mathrm{ext}}) \cdot \mathbf{a}[x] = \frac{1}{N} \left(f_{k_{\mathrm{int}}} * \mathbf{a} \right)(k_{\mathrm{ext}}).$$

This suggests that it can be evaluated efficiently using the convolution theorem:

1. Construct the distillation table $\mathbf{a}$ as in the previous attack algorithm.
2. Evaluate $\widehat{f_{k_{\mathrm{int}}}}$ and $\widehat{\mathbf{a}}$ using the fast Walsh transform algorithm [24].
3. Multiply the previous vectors component-wise.
4. Apply the fast Walsh transform again to obtain $N2^{-l}\widetilde{\mathrm{cor}}_{k_{\mathrm{int}}}$.

Except for the computation of $\widehat{\mathbf{a}}$, each of the steps 2 to 4 has to be repeated for each of the L_{int} guesses of k_{int}. The cost of each fast Walsh transform is $l2^l$ additions. The time complexity of the attack is thus $\mathcal{O}(N) + \mathcal{O}\left(L_{\mathrm{int}}l2^l\right)$.

Pruning-Based Attacks. Several improvements to this algorithm make use of pruning techniques on the fast Walsh transform [27,28], that is, of optimised Walsh transform algorithms which can be used when the nonzero inputs or the desired outputs are restricted. A brief description of the attack algorithm of [27] can be found in [29]. In summary, it was shown that when the support of the Walsh spectrum $\widehat{f_{k_{\mathrm{int}}}}$ is covered by an affine subspace of dimension d, the complexity can be reduced to $\mathcal{O}(N) + \mathcal{O}\left(L_{\mathrm{int}}d2^d\right)$. By using the linearity of the convolution, this technique can also be applied when the Walsh spectrum lies on the union of T such subspaces, at a cost of $\mathcal{O}(TN) + \mathcal{O}\left(\sum_i L_{\mathrm{int},i}d_i2^{d_i}\right) + \mathcal{O}(TL)$. Since the pruned fast Walsh transform can accommodate restrictions in both the input and the output, this complexity can be enhanced further by also accounting for the structure of the plaintext material and the key guesses.

2.6 Distribution of the Experimental Correlation

The probability of success of a linear key recovery attack depends on the statistical distribution of the key recovery statistic for both correct and incorrect key guesses. This paper follows the framework which is described in [15]. A sampling correction coefficient B is considered, which is 1 in the classical known plaintext scenario and $\frac{2^n-N}{2^n-1}$ if the plaintexts are assumed to be distinct.

The wrong key recovery statistic is normally distributed (Theorem 2 in [15]):

$$\widetilde{\mathrm{cor}}_W \sim \mathcal{N}\left(0, \frac{B}{N} + 2^{-n}\right). \tag{3}$$

We assume that these are statistically independent for different wrong key guesses.

For the right key recovery statistic, we consider two possibilities:

– If the approximation has no dominant linear trails, its correlation follows a normal distribution (usually with mean $c = 0$). Per Theorem 5 in [15]:

$$\widetilde{\text{cor}}_R \sim \mathcal{N}\left(c, \frac{B}{N} + \text{ELP} - c^2\right). \tag{4}$$

– If there is a single dominant trail, the keyspace can be separated into two disjoint parts of equal size so that (Theorem 4 in [15]):

$$\widetilde{\text{cor}}_R \sim \mathcal{N}\left(\pm c, \frac{B}{N} + \text{ELP} - c^2\right), \tag{5}$$

in each of the subsets ($+c$ in one and $-c$ in the other). The overall distribution of the statistic is thus a bimodal distribution with two peaks.

These distributions can be used to deduce the probability of success of the attack (see Sect. 2 of [15]). For the purposes of this paper, we instead focus on how to compensate the data complexity of a modified linear attack so that the resulting probability distributions match those of the original attack.

3 Approximating the Key Recovery Map

There are several examples in the literature in which the key recovery map f is substituted for another map g which "approximates" it in such a way that the impact on the data complexity can be predicted. For example, f may be substituted for another Boolean function g which is highly correlated with f (as in [2,5,11] and others), and the correlation is incorporated into the correlation of the distinguisher and used to determine the new data complexity. We can also consider that g is a copy of f which rejects some specific inputs (as in [17,27, 37]), which amounts to sieving the plaintexts for each key guess. Assuming the correlation of the linear approximation is the same within the remaining pairs, the data complexity is compensated by the inverse of the proportion of rejected plaintexts. In all of these applications, g is chosen so that the key recovery becomes less costly, for example by having a smaller effective input space.

In [27], the rejected inputs are chosen specifically with the aim of reducing the dimension of the support of the Walsh spectrum. However, in order to nullify one coefficient of the Walsh spectrum, the whole spectrum has to be modified. In particular, forcing several Walsh coefficients to be zero often means rejecting all the inputs. This is the motivation for the question of whether it is possible to modify the Walsh spectrum directly, even if the resulting key recovery map is not a Boolean function in the traditional sense.

We introduce a generalisation of these existing techniques in which f is replaced by an arbitrary approximation g, as well as a statistical analysis of the effect on the attack's data complexity. One specific instance is *Walsh spectrum puncturing*, which consists of removing "inconvenient" coefficients from the Walsh spectrum of f to obtain g. This is motivated by the fact that the attack complexity of [27] is highly dependent on the structure of the support of $\widehat{f}$.

3.1   Effect on the Data Complexity

Let $f : \mathbb{F}_2^l \longrightarrow \mathbb{F}_2$ be the key recovery map of a linear attack for a specific internal key guess (more generally, f can be real-valued). We also consider the approximating pseudoboolean function $g : \mathbb{F}_2^l \longrightarrow \mathbb{R}$. For simplicity, we assume that both f and g are balanced, that is, $\mathrm{E}[f(x)] = \widehat{f}(0) = \mathrm{E}[g(x)] = \widehat{g}(0) = 0$. By projecting g orthogonally onto f, we obtain the following decomposition:

$$g = \frac{\langle f, g \rangle}{\|f\|_2^2} f + g^\perp, \tag{6}$$

where $g^\perp$ is orthogonal to f, that is, both components are uncorrelated as random variables. We note that the orthogonality of both components also means that

$$\|g\|_2^2 = \frac{\langle f, g \rangle^2}{\|f\|_2^2} + \|g^\perp\|_2^2,$$

from which we deduce that the variance of $g^\perp$ is $\|g^\perp\|_2^2 = \|g\|_2^2 - \langle f, g \rangle^2 / \|f\|_2^2$.

We denote the alternative key recovery statistic which uses g instead of f by $\widetilde{\mathrm{cor}}^g(k)$. This statistic can also be separated into two orthogonal components, one of which is a scaled copy of the original key recovery statistic:

$$\widetilde{\mathrm{cor}}^g(k) = \frac{1}{N} \sum_{(p,c) \in \mathcal{D}} g(x(p,c) \oplus k) = \frac{\langle f, g \rangle}{\|f\|_2^2} \widetilde{\mathrm{cor}}^f(k) + \widetilde{\mathrm{cor}}^{g^\perp}(k).$$

Assuming the statistical distribution of $g^\perp$ under the attack sample is the same as for a uniformly-distributed input, we can prove the following:

Theorem 2. *the distributions of the right-key and wrong-key key recovery statistics using the approximation g of the key recovery map f (both assumed balanced) can be approximated by the normal distributions*

$$\widetilde{\mathrm{cor}}_R^g \sim \mathcal{N} \left(\frac{\langle f, g \rangle}{\|f\|_2^2} c, \|g\|_2^2 \frac{B}{N} + \frac{\langle f, g \rangle^2}{\|f\|_2^2} (\mathrm{ELP} - c^2) \right), \tag{7}$$

$$\widetilde{\mathrm{cor}}_W^g \sim \mathcal{N} \left(0, \|g\|_2^2 \frac{B}{N} + \frac{\langle f, g \rangle^2}{\|f\|_2^2} 2^{-n} \right). \tag{8}$$

Proof. Since the experimental correlation statistic is a (scaled) sum of equally-distributed independent random variables, we can assume that it is normally distributed, and we only have to determine its expected value and variance:

$$\mathrm{E}_{\mathcal{D},K} \left[\widetilde{\mathrm{cor}}_R^g \right] = \mathrm{E}_{\mathcal{D},K} \left[\frac{\langle f, g \rangle}{\|f\|_2^2} \widetilde{\mathrm{cor}}_R^f \right] + \mathrm{E}_{\mathcal{D},K} \left[\widetilde{\mathrm{cor}}_R^{g^\perp} \right]$$

$$\simeq \frac{\langle f, g \rangle}{\|f\|_2^2} c + \mathrm{E}_K \left[\mathrm{E}_{\mathcal{D}} \left[\widetilde{\mathrm{cor}}_R^{g^\perp} \right] \right] = \frac{\langle f, g \rangle}{\|f\|_2^2} c,$$

assuming that $\mathrm{E}_{\mathcal{D}} \left[\widetilde{\mathrm{cor}}_R^{g^\perp} \right] = \mathrm{E} \left[g^\perp(x) \right] = 0$.

$$\text{Var}_{\mathcal{D},K}\left(\widetilde{\text{cor}}_R^g\right) = \text{Var}_{\mathcal{D},K}\left(\frac{\langle f,g\rangle}{\|f\|_2^2}\widetilde{\text{cor}}_R^f\right) + \text{Var}_K\left(\text{E}_{\mathcal{D}}\left[\widetilde{\text{cor}}_R^{g^\perp}\right]\right)$$

$$+ \text{E}_K\left[\text{Var}_{\mathcal{D}}\left(\widetilde{\text{cor}}_R^{g^\perp}\right)\right] - 2\text{Cov}_{\mathcal{D},K}\left(\frac{\langle f,g\rangle}{\|f\|_2^2}\widetilde{\text{cor}}_R^f, \widetilde{\text{cor}}_R^{g^\perp}\right)$$

$$\simeq \frac{\langle f,g\rangle^2}{\|f\|_2^2}\left(\frac{B}{N} + \text{ELP} - c^2\right) + \|g^\perp\|_2^2\frac{B}{N}$$

$$= \|g\|_2^2\frac{B}{N} + \frac{\langle f,g\rangle^2}{\|f\|_2^2}(\text{ELP} - c^2),$$

assuming $\text{Cov}_{\mathcal{D},K}\left(\widetilde{\text{cor}}_R^f, \widetilde{\text{cor}}_R^{g^\perp}\right) = \text{Cov}\left(f(x), g^\perp(x)\right) = 0$. To deduce $\text{Var}_{\mathcal{D},K}\left(\widetilde{\text{cor}}_R^f\right) = \|f\|_2^2\left(B/N + \text{ELP} - c^2\right)$ and $\text{Var}_{\mathcal{D}}\left(\widetilde{\text{cor}}_R^{g^\perp}\right) = \|g^\perp\|_2^2\frac{B}{N}$, we require a similar assumption and the central limit theorem (in the distinct known plaintext case, we need to use a variant of the central limit theorem which accounts for sampling without replacement in finite populations, which is discussed in [29].

The wrong key case can be treated similarly:

$$\text{E}_{\mathcal{D},K}\left[\widetilde{\text{cor}}_W^g\right] \simeq \frac{\langle f,g\rangle}{\|f\|_2^2}\text{E}_{\mathcal{D},K}\left[\widetilde{\text{cor}}_W\right] + \text{E}_K\left[\text{E}_{\mathcal{D}}\left[\widetilde{\text{cor}}_W^{g^\perp}\right]\right] = 0.$$

$$\text{Var}_{\mathcal{D},K}\left(\widetilde{\text{cor}}_W^g\right) \simeq \frac{\langle f,g\rangle^2}{\|f\|_2^2}\left(\frac{B}{N} + 2^{-n}\right) + \|g^\perp\|_2^2\frac{B}{N} = \|g\|_2^2\frac{B}{N} + \frac{\langle f,g\rangle^2}{\|f\|_2^2}2^{-n}.$$

$\square$

We believe the assumption that $\widetilde{\text{cor}}^{g^\perp}$ behaves the same in the data as for a uniform input sample is reasonable because in a realistic attack scenario, as the odds of a random balanced Boolean function being biased in the data are low, the only exception being the key recovery maps of linear approximations. However, we could theoretically find g which approximates the key recovery maps of more than one approximation. Describing this scenario and how it may be exploited in cryptanalysis remains an open problem.

This result can be applied directly in the formulas in Sect. 2 of [15]. However, there is a handy way of *compensating* the data complexity:

Corollary 3. *The success probability of a linear attack which substitutes the balanced key recovery map f for the balanced approximation g remains the same as long as the corrected data sample size N/B is increased by a factor $1/\rho^2$, where*

$$\rho = \frac{|\langle f,g\rangle|}{\|f\|_2 \cdot \|g\|_2} = \frac{|\text{Cov}(f(x), g(x))|}{\sqrt{\text{Var}(f(x))}\sqrt{\text{Var}(g(x))}}, \tag{9}$$

which is the Pearson correlation coefficient of $f(x)$ and $g(x)$.

Proof. We first consider the case in which the correlation of the linear approximation is normally distributed over the keyspace. Let N/B be the corrected sample size for the base attack. The expected value of $\widetilde{\text{cor}}^f$ is c, and its variance is $\|f\|_2^2(B/N + \mathrm{ELP} - c^2)$ for the right key case. For the wrong key case the mean is 0 and the variance is $\|f\|_2^2(B/N + 2^{-n})$. Let N^*/B^* be the corrected sample for the attack using g. The expected value and variance of $\widetilde{\mathrm{cor}}^g$ are $\frac{\langle f,g\rangle}{\|f\|_2^2}c$ and $\|g\|_2^2\frac{B^*}{N^*} + \frac{\langle f,g\rangle^2}{\|f\|_2^2}(\mathrm{ELP} - c^2)$ for the right key case and 0 and $\|g\|_2^2\frac{B^*}{N^*} + \frac{\langle f,g\rangle^2}{\|f\|_2^2}2^{-n}$ in the wrong key case. If we take $N^*/B^* = (N/B)/\rho^2$, this variance is $\frac{\langle f,g\rangle^2}{\|f\|_2^2}(B/N + \mathrm{ELP} - c^2)$ for the right key case and $\frac{\langle f,g\rangle^2}{\|f\|_2^2}(B/N + 2^{-n})$ for the wrong key. This means $\widetilde{\mathrm{cor}}^g$ has the same distribution as $\frac{\langle f,g\rangle}{\|f\|_2^2}\widetilde{\mathrm{cor}}^f$ in both the right and wrong key cases. Since substituting the key recovery statistic for a multiple has no effect on the success probability, we conclude that it is the same for both attacks.

The case in which a single dominant trail exists and the correlation distribution is bimodal remains. The keyspace consists of two disjoint parts, and the right key experimental correlation statistic is normally distributed in both. By swapping the sign in one of the parts, both distributions become identical. The squared statistic is thus distributed as if both parts were identical, and the previous reasoning still applies. We note that the case in which a small number of dominant trails exists is not covered by these arguments.   □

In the known plaintext scenario, the data complexity N just increases by $1/\rho^2$. In the distinct known plaintext scenario, we must consider that B decreases with N. In order to compensate by increasing the data complexity, the original data complexity N must be increased to N^* so that

$$\frac{(2^n - N^*)N}{(2^n - N)N^*} = \rho^2.$$

We can confirm that Corollary 3 generalises existing techniques:

Boolean Function Substitution. If g is also a Boolean function, then $\|f\|_2 = \|g\|_2 = 1$, which means that $\rho^2 = \langle f,g\rangle^2 = \mathrm{cor}(f,g)^2$, and the data complexity must be increased by a factor equal to the square of the correlation of f and g.

Plaintext Rejection. If g is a copy of f which rejects some of the inputs (that is, $g(x) \in \{f(x),0\}$ for all x), then $\langle f,g\rangle = \|g\|_2^2 = \frac{1}{2^l}\left|x \in \mathbb{F}_2^l : g(x) \neq 0\right|$, and the increase in data complexity $1/\rho^2$ is the inverse of the fraction of inputs of f which are not rejected by g.

We now provide a brief additional justification for the result using the generalised linear cryptanalysis framework of [6]. The functions f and g define one-dimensional subspaces $U = \mathrm{span}\,\{f\}, V = \mathrm{span}\,\{g\}$ of $\mathbb{F}_2^n$. They define a linear approximation map over the identity $\langle V,U\rangle_{\mathrm{id}}$, whose principal correlation is ρ. When this map is appended to the original approximation using the piling-up lemma, a new approximation for the full cipher is obtained whose correlation is multiplied by ρ, and the data complexity has to be increased by $1/\rho^2$.

3.2   Walsh Spectrum Puncturing

In [27], it is shown that the structure of the support the Walsh spectrum of the key recovery map plays a key role in the time complexity. This suggests a simple way to construct an approximation g of f: take some nonzero Walsh coefficients of f, corresponding to a subset $\mathscr{P} \subseteq \mathbb{F}_2^n$, and set them to zero to obtain g:

Definition 4 (Walsh spectrum puncturing). *Let $f : \mathbb{F}_2^l \longrightarrow \mathbb{F}_2$ be a boolean function and $\widehat{f}$ its Walsh spectrum. A puncture set is any subset $\mathscr{P} \subseteq \mathbb{F}_2^l$. To simplify the analysis, we assume that f is balanced ($\widehat{f}(0) = 0$), and $0 \notin \mathscr{P}$. We define the punctured function of f according to $\mathscr{P}$ as the pseudoboolean function $g = f - \sum_{u \in \mathscr{P}} \widehat{f}(u) \mathbf{h}_u$. The puncture coefficient ε is defined as*

$$\varepsilon = \mathrm{Var}(f - g) = \|f - g\|_2^2 = \sum_{u \in \mathscr{P}} \widehat{f}(u)^2. \tag{10}$$

The proportion of f which remains, $1 - \varepsilon$, is called puncturing correlation*:*

$$1 - \varepsilon = \sum_{u \notin \mathscr{P}} \widehat{f}(u)^2 = \langle f, g \rangle = \mathrm{cor}(f, g).$$

We note that, since $\widehat{f}(0) = 0$, we also have $\widehat{g}(0) = 0$, so g is also balanced.

Corollary 5. *Let $f : \mathbb{F}_2^l \longrightarrow \mathbb{F}_2$ be the balanced key recovery map of a linear attack, and let g be a punctured version with puncture coefficient ε. Substituting f for g in the attack and increasing the (corrected) data sample by a factor $\frac{1}{1-\varepsilon}$ yields an attack with the same success probability and advantage.*

Proof. According to Corollary 3, the data complexity must be increased by

$$\frac{1}{\rho^2} = \frac{\|f\|_2^2 \cdot \|g\|_2^2}{\langle f, g \rangle^2} = \frac{1 \cdot (1 - \varepsilon)}{(1 - \varepsilon)^2} = \frac{1}{1 - \varepsilon}.$$

$\square$

We note that the increase in data complexity is inversely proportional to the puncturing correlation instead of its square, as may be suggested by intuition.

3.3   Experimental Verification

We perform some experiments to verify the accuracy of the assumptions.

Normally Distributed Correlation. We consider an attack on 8-round PRESENT (a figure is included in [29]) using a 6-round linear approximation between rounds 1 and 6. The input mask (before SboxLayer in round 1) is 00000000 00A00000, and that the output mask (before Sboxlayer in round 7) is 00000000 00200020. It is known that many similar linear trails exist [28], so the approximation's correlation is normally-distributed and centered at zero. Several scenarios with puncture coefficients $\varepsilon = 0.25$ and 0.5 were considered, where the spectrum of one of the four active Sboxes is punctured. They included restricting the spectrum to a hyperplane, removing a single coefficient, or removing a random subset.

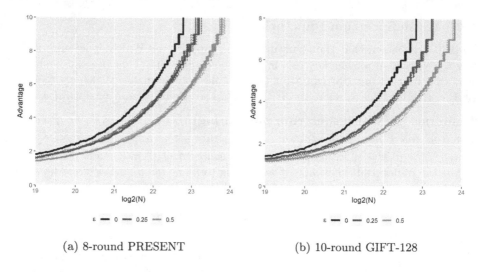

(a) 8-round PRESENT   (b) 10-round GIFT-128

Fig. 1. The results of the puncturing experiments

Bimodal Correlation. We consider 10-round GIFT-128 (a figure is included in [29]) and a 5-round linear trail with correlation 2^{-10} extracted from Fig. 4 of [43]. The trail covers rounds 3 to 7 and has input mask 00000000 00000000 00000000 11000000 and output mask 00000000 05000000 00000000 05000000. There are no additional high-correlation trails. We consider three key recovery rounds on the input side and two on the output side, and puncture the spectra of the four active Sboxes in the inner key recovery rounds 2 and 8.

The attacks were performed for data sample sizes between 2^{19} and 2^{24}, and the experimental correlation of the correct key was compared with that of 2^{10} random wrong keys (2^8 for the GIFT-128 attacks), thus detecting advantage ([42]) values of up to 10 or 8 bits. Each of the punctured attacks was run 5000 times at each data complexity value. The median of the achieved advantages approximates the probability 50% advantage. The advantages are plotted against the data complexity in Fig. 1. The black line represents the base attack without puncturing. The dotted blue lines represent the $\varepsilon = 0.25$ experiments and the dotted green lines represent the $\varepsilon = 0.5$ experiments. The predictions corresponding to a data complexity increase from the base case by $1/(1 - \varepsilon)$ are shown as continuous lines.

The results indicate that although there is some variability between the results of different scenarios at a given ε, they all follow the model predictions closely. The variability can be attributed to several factors, the most likely of which is the fact that a punctured key recovery map may approximate the key recovery maps of additional linear approximations.

3.4   Relationship to Multiple and Multidimensional Attacks

This subsection briefly discusses how puncturing the Walsh spectrum of the key recovery map compares to other techniques which appear superficially similar, specifically multiple [13] and multidimensional [30–32] linear cryptanalysis. This is motivated by the observation that puncturing the spectrum of the key recovery map to a single coefficient $\widehat{f}(u)$ essentially amounts to appending one round to the approximation with masks β and u. Although the effective key guess collapses to dimension zero, the key recovery statistic can still be used to distinguish the cipher from a random permutation. Since the expected increase in data complexity is inversely proportional to $\widehat{f}(u)^2$, the data complexity is the same that is predicted by the piling-up lemma. This suggests (punctured) key recovery attacks can be interpreted as using several linear approximations at the same time, each one corresponding to a single coefficient of the Walsh spectrum.

Multiple Linear Cryptanalysis. Multiple linear cryptanalysis [13,33], it can use an arbitrary set of linear approximations, and can be applied in both Algorithm 1 and Algorithm 2-type attacks, with Algorithm 2 being the most common. Unlike puncturing, it uses a χ^2 statistic which is not optimised to the joint distribution of the correlations. As a result, the expected data complexity is around $\sqrt{l}/C$ [31], where l is the number of approximations and C is the sum of their squared correlations. It also requires the assumption that the approximations are statistically independent. If the approximations match a punctured key recovery attack, the data complexity of that attack attack would be around $1/C$.

Multidimensional Linear Cryptanalysis. Introduced by Hermelin et al. [30–32], a multidimensional approximation is a vector space of classical linear approximations, which are not assumed to be independent. In addition to the χ^2 statistic with around $\sqrt{l}/C$ data complexity, the LLR statistic is available, with data complexity $1/C$. It takes the joint distribution and sign of the correlations into account, and the data complexity is similar to a punctured key recovery attack. Since the joint correlation distribution has to be known, in many cases it requires key guessing to determine this distribution. This suggests that puncturing may be interpreted as a hybrid approach in which *some* key material is guessed to determine some partial information about the correlation distribution. We note that in many cases, the way multidimensional approximations are constructed consists of selecting subspaces of the Walsh spectrum of the round function (see for example [21]), which is similar to puncturing. However, multidimensional linear cryptanalysis is limited to vector spaces of linear approximations, while in puncturing the choice of remaining coefficients is arbitrary.

4   Puncturing Walsh Spectra

In the previous section, a theoretical framework which predicts the effect of Walsh spectrum puncturing on the data complexity of a key recovery linear attack has been laid out. This section deals with the puncturing step itself. Subsection 4.1 provides some intuitive results about puncturing common operations such as the composition and the XOR of Boolean functions. Detailed proofs can be found in [29]. Subsection 4.2 features a discussion of several ways of puncturing the spectrum for typical cipher designs.

4.1   Some Useful Results

We first focus on puncturing a composition of functions, which corresponds to a key recovery scenario covering multiple rounds. When puncturing the last function of the composition, the same ρ^2 applies to the whole composition.

Proposition 6. *Let* $f_1 : \mathbb{F}_2^l \longrightarrow \mathbb{F}_2^r$ *and* $f_2 : \mathbb{F}_2^r \longrightarrow \mathbb{R}$ *be two Boolean functions, and let* $f = f_2 \circ f_1$ *be their composition. We also assume that the components of* f_1 *are all balanced. Let* $g_2 : \mathbb{F}_2^r \longrightarrow \mathbb{R}$ *be a map which approximates* f_2 *with Pearson correlation coefficient* ρ. *Then* $g = g_2 \circ f_1$ *is an approximation of* f, *and the Pearson correlation coefficient is also* ρ.

Remark. Puncturing the components of f_1 is also possible, but it requires an abstract definition of the composition of vectorial pseudoboolean functions as the inverse Walsh transform of the matrix product of their Walsh spectra.

Next, we look at puncturing the XOR of several functions (product of real-valued functions). We prove the result in the case in which both functions have the same input domain because it requires the most strict assumptions, but it also holds when the functions have (partially) disjoint input domains.

Proposition 7. *Let* $f_1, f_2 : \mathbb{F}_2^l \longrightarrow \mathbb{R}$ *be two balanced pseudoboolean functions, and let* $f : \mathbb{F}_2^l \longrightarrow \mathbb{F}_2, f = f_1 \cdot f_2$. *Let* $g_1, g_2 : \mathbb{F}_2^l \longrightarrow \mathbb{R}$ *be balanced functions which approximate* f_1 *and* f_2 *with correlation coefficients* ρ_1 *and* ρ_2, *respectively. Then* $g : \mathbb{F}_2^l \longrightarrow \mathbb{R}, g = g_1 \cdot g_2$ *is an approximation of* f, *and the compensation factor is* $\rho_1 \rho_2$, *under the assumption that*

$$\mathrm{Cov}(f_1(x), f_2(x)) = \mathrm{Cov}(f_1^2(x), f_2^2(x)) = \mathrm{Cov}(g_1(x), g_2(x))$$
$$=\mathrm{Cov}(g_1^2(x), g_2^2(x)) = \mathrm{Cov}(f_1(x), g_2(x)) = \mathrm{Cov}(f_2(x), g_1(x)) = 0.$$

We would also like a more general result which permits "step-by-step approximation" which would permit starting from the key recovery map f and taking successive approximations $g_1, g_2, \ldots$ where each function approximates the previous one. Unfortunately, the correlation is not a distance. Indeed, taking $f, g, h : \mathbb{F}_2 \to \mathbb{R}$ with $f = (1, 1)$, $g = (1, 0)$, and $h = (1, -1)$, the Pearson correlation coefficient between f and g and between g and h is $1/\sqrt{2}$, but f and h are uncorrelated. However, in the scope of normal applications, there are many instances in which the puncturing coefficients can be multiplied, such as in Proposition 7. This means that we can often puncture the whole key recovery map by puncturing the spectra of its components, such as Sboxes.

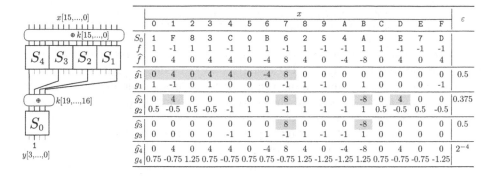

Fig. 2. Example of puncturing (the coefficients are multiplied by 16 for clarity).

4.2 Puncturing Strategies

Generic Hyperplane Puncturing. Given a Walsh transform-based linear attack with data complexity $N \leq 2^{n-1}$ and a key recovery input space of dimension l (so the complexity of the transforms is $l2^l$ additions), we can choose any hyperplane of $\mathbb{F}_2^l$ and puncture the spectrum of f to either the hyperplane itself or its complement. Since the sum of the puncture coefficients of both options is 1, one must be equal to or smaller than $1/2$. This means it's always possible to construct a pruned transform attack with data complexity at most $2N$ with complexity $\mathcal{O}\left((l-1)2^{l-1}\right)$. This is a generic technique which can be used to rapidly create time-data trade-offs in a wide range of attacks.

Bit Puncturing. Puncturing can be used to find optimal ways to model the cost of ignoring parts of the key recovery map input space. For example, forcefully making one input bit of an Sbox inactive to exclude part of the key guess means forcing a hyperplane of its Walsh spectrum to be zero. It is clear that simply puncturing these coefficients gives the optimal approximation of the Sbox, and the data complexity impact is easy to compute.

Example 1. Consider the key recovery map depicted in Fig. 2. The key recovery map to compute y_2 requires all of x and a 20-bit key guess. In the FWT-based procedure, we compute the Walsh transform for every 4-bit internal key guess. The complexity of a Walsh transform attack is thus proportional to $2^4 \times 16 \times 2^{16}$.

We focus on S_0 and let f denote $f(x) = (-1)^{\langle 4, S_0(x) \rangle}$, and $\widehat{f}$ its Walsh spectrum. Using bit puncturing, we exclude the MSB of the input of S_0. We obtain the punctured spectrum $\widehat{g_1}$, and we can compute the associated function g_1. We observe that the MSB is indeed irrelevant, as $g_1(x) = g_1(x \oplus 8)$ for all x. In this case g_1 can be described as a traditional Boolean function which rejects some inputs, but this is not always the case. The puncture coefficient is $\varepsilon = 4 \times 2^{-4} + 2^{-2} = 2^{-1}$, i.e. the data must be doubled. We obtain a better time complexity than hyperplane puncturing because it effectively makes S_4 inactive, thus making the key bits k_{15}, k_{14}, k_{13}, k_{12} and k_{19} unnecessary, and reducing the complexity of the Walsh transforms to $2^3 \times 12 \times 2^{12}$.

More advanced bit puncturing is also possible in the case of ciphers with more complicated linear layers. For example, we may decide that one Sbox will become inactive, and transforming this condition through the linear layer leads to restrictions on the spectra of the Sboxes of the next round. This technique is used in the Serpent attacks of Sect. 5. In the GIFT attacks of Sect. 6, the spectrum of the GIFT super Sbox is punctured instead of the spectrum of the Sbox itself. In this case, we don't obtain a traditional Boolean function which rejects some inputs, but a function taking multiple different real values.

LAT Subspace Puncturing. When applying hyperplane puncturing, it is often possible to choose a hyperplane for which ε will be significantly smaller than $1/2$, or to choose a subspace of smaller dimension with $\varepsilon = 1/2$. Quite often, these subspaces can be found by examining the Walsh spectra of the Sbox(es). For example, with 4-bit Sboxes, there often exists an affine subspace of dimension 1 (that is, two coefficients) which concentrates half of the 2-norm of the map.

Example 2. We return to Fig. 2. First, we consider puncturing the coefficients in the positions $\{3, 4, 6, 8, A, F\}$ to obtain $\widehat{g_2}$ and the corresponding function g_2. The puncture coefficient is $\varepsilon = 6 \times 2^{-4} = 6/16$, so the data complexity is increased by a factor of $1/(1 - 6/16) = 1.6$. All remaining nonzero coefficients lie in the affine subspace $1 + \text{span}\{6, A\}$. Since the dimension is 2, only a 2-bit internal key guess is enough. Thus, the complexity of the Walsh transforms is reduced to $2^2 \times 16 \times 2^{16}$.

Example 3. Puncturing all coefficients of value $\pm 2^{-2}$, we obtain $\widehat{g_3}$ with puncture coefficient $\varepsilon = 8 \times 2^{-4} = 2^{-1}$, which doubles the data. The remaining nonzero coefficients are positions 7 and B, which form an affine subspace of dimension 1, i.e., $7 + \text{span}\{C\}$. The complexity of the Walsh transforms is $2^1 \times 16 \times 2^{16}$.

To explain the reduction of the internal key guess, we show why using g_3 reduces it to 1 bit. Let $a = (a_3, a_2, a_1, a_0)$ be the input to S_0 before xoring the key $k = (k_{19}, k_{18}, k_{17}, k_{16})$. We guess the bit $\langle C, k \rangle$. When $\langle C, a \oplus k \rangle = 0$, the input of S_0 can be $00**$ or $11**$, where $*$ are arbitrary. Looking at g_3, the outputs are always 0, so this data is rejected. When $\langle C, a \oplus k \rangle = 1$, the input of S_0 can be $10**$ or $01**$, and we have $g_3 = (-1)^{\langle 7, a \oplus k \rangle}$. In other words, $\langle 7, k \rangle$ just flips the sign of the correlation, which is unnecessary in many attacks.

We can use LAT subspace puncturing more generally than bit puncturing because it doesn't require taking the outermost key recovery map into consideration. This technique is used in the Serpent attacks of Sect. 5.

Hamming Weight Puncturing. The plaintext-ciphertext pair rejection technique of [27] is used in cases in which the key recovery map is of the form

$$f(x_0, x_1, \ldots, x_d) = f_2(f_{10}(x_0), f_{11}(x_1), \ldots, f_{1d}(x_d)),$$

which is frequent on attacks on Sbox-based ciphers with bit permutations as linear layers. A subset of inputs of f_2 is selected so that the function which rejects these inputs, f_2^*, verifies $\widehat{f_2^*}(\texttt{11...1}) = 0$. As a result, the support of the Walsh spectrum of the modified key recovery map can be covered with d subspaces of smaller dimension. However, rejecting these inputs of f_2 modifies its whole Walsh spectrum. Using puncturing, we can simply remove the coefficient $\widehat{f_2}(\texttt{11...1})$, which has a smaller impact on the data complexity. Furthermore, additional Walsh coefficients can be targeted, such as the ones of Hamming weight $d - 1$, to cover the Walsh spectrum with even smaller subspaces. An example of this strategy is the attack on the DES of Sect. 7.

Example 4. We puncture the coefficient of Hamming weight four (mask F) to obtain $\widehat{g_4}$. The corresponding pseudoboolean function is g_4. The puncture coefficient ε is 2^{-4}, and as a result the data complexity increases by a factor of $1/0.9375$. The key recovery map then decomposes into four components with supports of dimension 12. Therefore, the complexity of the Walsh transforms is reduced to $4 \times 2^3 \times 12 \times 2^{12}$.

Generic Puncturing. Finally, it is possible to study the possible propagation of the input and output masks of the linear approximation to obtain a list of the Walsh coefficients of the key recovery map which are larger than a bigger threshold. Then, which Walsh coefficients will be used in the attack can be decided as an optimization problem (for example, trying to obtain the largest possible ρ while keeping the number of active key bits below a certain threshold). This is the approach used in the NOEKEON attack of Sect. 8.

5 Application to Serpent

Serpent is a 128-bit block cipher and one of the AES competition finalists [7,8]. The full specification is included in [29]. It is the subject of substantial cryptanalysis, such as linear [9,10,22,23], multidimensional-linear [30,32,39], and differential-linear [10,17,34] attacks, which are summarised in Table 1.

On the Key Recovery Attack Against 11-Round Serpent-128. Before describing the 12-round attack, we start with an 11-round attack. Figure 3 shows the high-level structure, which uses the 9-round linear trail with correlation 2^{-57} reported in [22] (see [29]). We also searched for other linear trails with the same input/output mask to evaluate the ELP, but found no such trails with correlation higher than 2^{-64}. Therefore, we estimate the ELP as $2^{-114} + 2^{-128}$, where 2^{-128} is the noise component.

We append one key recovery round to both the plaintext and ciphertext sides, leading to a $1 + 9 + 1 = 11$-round attack. 15 Sboxes and 12 Sboxes are active in the first and last rounds, respectively. This attack structure is identical to the previous attack [23], where the Walsh transform complexity was 108×2^{108}.

```
X₀  |  -*XY---Y------***-*-***--**-*--X  |
Y₀  |  08E100010000002B40B046300C70D00E  |  ⟩S₂

              ↓ c = 2⁻⁵⁷                        X={2,3,A,B}=2+{1,8}

X₁₀|  40006000040280C00008000050B02C03  |      Y={A,B,E,F}=A+{1,4}
Y₁₀ |  *---*----*-**-*----*----*-Z-**-*  |  ⟩S₄   Z={4,5,8,9}=4+{1,C}
```

Fig. 3. Key recovery attack against 11-round Serpent

We first apply Walsh transform pruning [27]. The spectra of $\langle E, S_2\rangle$, $\langle 1, S_2\rangle$ and $\langle B, S_4^{-1}\rangle$ contain only four nonzero coefficients, and they lie in subspaces of dimension 2. The spectrum therefore occupies an $(52 + 46) = 98$-dimensional affine space[1]. The complexity of the Walsh transforms is reduced to 98×2^{98}.

Puncturing Walsh coefficients of the first or last-round Sboxes can reduce the time complexity in return for a slight data increase. However, the dominant complexity of the 11-round attack is the data collection. Therefore, we must reduce the data complexity to improve the 11-round attack. It is possible by switching some active Sboxes of the approximation to punctured key recovery. We adopt such an approach in the application to GIFT and NOEKEON. Here, we focus on a simpler and more attractive case with a longer key length.

5.1 Improved Key Recovery Attack Against 12-Round Serpent-256

To attack 12-round Serpent-256, we add an additional round of key recovery to the ciphertext side of the 11-round attack. Figure 4 shows these last two key recovery rounds. On the left is the original key recovery map. Since the 11th Sbox in the 12th round is not involved, $128 - 4 = 124$ ciphertext bits are used. Similarly to the 11-round attack, 52 plaintext bits, 52 first-round subkey bits and 46 11th-round subkey bits are involved in the key recovery.

On the right of Fig. 4, we use bit puncturing. First, we focus on Sbox 19 at round 11. The input mask is 8, and the Walsh spectrum of $\langle 8, S_4^{-1}\rangle$ is

$$(0, 0, 0, 8, 4, -4, 4, 4, 0, 0, 0, -8, 4, -4, 4, 4).$$

When the MSB is ignored, via the linear layer, Sbox 26 in the last round becomes inactive. Therefore, we puncture the five coefficients which involve the MSB. The key guess is reduced by 5 bits, and the data complexity is doubled. Next, we try to exclude the 6th Sbox in the 12th round from the key recovery map. To do it, we puncture the following coefficients in the 11th round: five coefficients whose mask LSB is 1 in the 20th Sbox, four coefficients whose mask MSB is 0 in the 31st Sbox, and four coefficients whose 2nd mask MSB is 0 in the 3rd Sbox.

---

[1] The authors of [38] make a similar observation and decrease the number of recovered bits from 108 to 98. However, without pruning techniques [27], the complexity of the transforms of their attack is still 108×2^{108}.

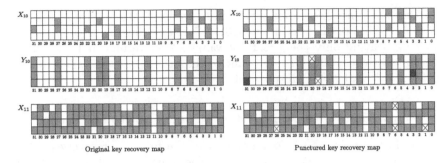

Fig. 4. Ciphertext side of the key recovery attack against 12-round Serpent

The puncturing correlations are 2^{-1}, $3/4$ and $3/4$. Therefore, the key guess is reduced by 7 bits at $2 \times 4/3 \times 4/3 \approx 2^{1.83}$ higher data.

In summary, puncturing reduces the number of active ciphertext bits from 124 to 116 and the key guess by 12 bits. On the other hand, the data complexity is increased by a factor $\rho^{-2} = 2^{2.83}$.

Attack Procedure. We have the following attack procedure using the FWT.

1. Store N known plaintext-ciphertext pairs.
2. Guess the 52 active subkey bits in the 1st round.
   (a) Prepare a distillation table, $\mathbf{a}$, of 2^{116} elements.
   (b) Compute the input parity of the 9-round linear approximation. According to the input parity, we increment or decrement the entry of the distillation table $\mathbf{a}$ indexed by the 116-bit truncated ciphertext.
   (c) Evaluate $\hat{\mathbf{a}}$ using the FWT.
   (d) Guess the $4 \times 7 + 3 \times 4 + 2 = 42$-bit internal key.
      i. Compute the (punctured) key recovery map $g_{k_{\text{int}}} : \mathbb{F}_2^{112} \longrightarrow \mathbb{R}$.
      ii. Evaluate $\widehat{g_{k_{\text{int}}}}$ by using the FWT.
      iii. Multiply $\hat{\mathbf{a}}$ with $\widehat{g_{k_{\text{int}}}}$ component-wise.
      iv. Apply the FWT to the resulting table.

The attack procedure above evaluates the experimental correlation of every $52 + 42 + 116 = 210$-bit key guess with a time complexity of

$$N + 2^{52} \cdot \left(N + 116 \cdot 2^{116} \texttt{ADD} + 2^{42} \cdot \left(2^{116} \texttt{PD} + 116 \cdot 2^{116} \texttt{ADD} + 2^{116} \texttt{MUL} + 116 \cdot 2^{116} \texttt{ADD}\right)\right),$$

where PD, ADD, and MUL denote the costs of a 2-round decryption, an addition, and a multiplication, respectively.

With $N\rho^2 = 2^{122.33}$, the success probability with advantage $a = 210$ is higher than 81%. Therefore, we use $N = 2^{125.16}$ known plaintexts. The correct guess ranks among the few highest correlations, and auxiliary techniques recover the rest of the key bits. Assuming that ADD and MUL are faster than one round function and one encryption, respectively, the time complexity is at most $\frac{2}{12}2^{210} + \frac{116}{12}2^{210} + 2^{210} + \frac{116}{12}2^{210} \approx 2^{214.36}$. The dominant part of the memory complexity is storing the data, $2^{125.16}$.

Further puncturing results in a time-data trade-off. The above attack punctures four coefficients in the 3rd and 31st Sboxes. Puncturing a further four coefficients, leaving only coefficients of value $\pm 2^{-1}$, results in LAT subspace puncturing with $\rho^2 = 2^{-4}$. This variant of the attack has time and data complexities $2^{210.36}$ and $2^{126.30}$, respectively.

5.2   Improved Key Recovery Attack Against 12-Round Serpent-192

We next show, to the best of our knowledge, the first key recovery attack on 12-round Serpent-192. Overall it's is almost the same as the attack on 12-round Serpent-256, but we use LAT subspace puncturing to reduce the time complexity further. Returning to the right part of Fig. 4, there are 12 active Sboxes in the 11th round. The 5th Sbox is special because a 2-bit guess is enough to determine the parity. We use the same puncturing as above for the 19th and 20th Sbox because it reduces the size of involved ciphertext bits. For the other 9 Sboxes, we puncture all Walsh coefficients with $\pm 2^{-2}$. As a result, we can reduce the number of involved ciphertext bits from 124 to 116, and the $1+1+3\times 9+8 = 37$-bit guess by increasing the data by a factor of 2^{11}. The new attack procedure evaluates the correlation of every $52 + 17 + 116 = 185$-bit guess with a time complexity of

$$N + 2^{52} \times \left(N + 116 \times 2^{116} \text{ADD} \quad + 2^{17} \times (2^{116} \text{PD} \quad + 116 \times 2^{116} \text{ADD} \quad + 2^{116} \text{MUL} \quad + 116 \times 2^{116} \text{ADD}) \right).$$

To save some more time, we can use $2^{17+116} = 2^{133}$ memory registers and precompute $g_{k_{\text{int}}}$ and $\widehat{g_{k_{\text{int}}}}$ before guessing the first round subkey. This precomputation reduces the time complexity to around $2^{185} + \frac{116}{12} \times 2^{185} \approx 2^{188.42}$.

With $N = 2^{127.5}$ known plaintexts, the success probability with advantage $a = 3.00$ is higher than 80%. This means that we must keep 2^{185-3} candidates for the 185-bit subkey. If, like [17], we assume that an a-bit advantage on the key guess leads to a an a-bit advantage on the master key without any complexity overhead, the final attack complexity is $2^{188.42} + 2^{189} \approx 2^{189.74}$. In reality, such a conversion is nontrivial due to the nonlinear key schedule. We analyzed the key schedule and found how to convert the partially recovered key to the full master key, although the memory complexity is 2^{185-3}. We show the technique in [29].

6   Application to GIFT-128

GIFT is a lightweight block cipher introduced in [4] by Banik et al. There are two versions of GIFT, and we focus on the 128-bit block version, GIFT-128. Please refer to [29] for a detailed specification. Similarly to existing attacks [43–45], we discuss attacks in the general and COFB [3, 20] settings. Please note that we use a more traditional step-by-step key recovery algorithm instead of the FWT. The reason is that the GIFT-128 state is 128 bits, but the round subkey is only 64 bits, which makes step-by-step guessing a better fit.

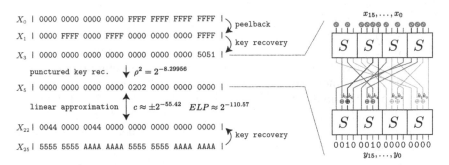

X_0 | 0000 0000 0000 0000 FFFF FFFF FFFF FFFF |⟩ peelback

X_1 | 0000 FFFF 0000 FFFF 0000 0000 0000 FFFF |⟩ key recovery

X_3 | 0000 0000 0000 0000 0000 0000 0000 5051 | -----

punctured key rec. ↓ $\rho^2 = 2^{-8.29956}$

X_5 | 0000 0000 0000 0000 0202 0000 0000 0000 | -----

linear approximation ↑ $c \approx \pm 2^{-55.42}$ $ELP \approx 2^{-110.57}$

X_{22} | 0044 0000 0044 0000 0000 0000 0000 0000 |

X_{25} | 5555 5555 AAAA AAAA 5555 5555 AAAA AAAA |⟩ key recovery

Fig. 5. Overview of the 25-round attack

Table 2. Punctured Walsh spectrum, where each value is multiplied by 2^{16}.

$k_7 \| k_5 \| k_4$	type	Non-zero coefficients of the spectrum						ρ^2
		1011	1051	4011	4051	5011	5051	
000	A	512	512	2048	2048	−1536	−1536	$2^{-8.30}$
001	B	−1536	−1536	−2048	−2048	512	512	$2^{-8.30}$
010	B	1536	1536	2048	2048	−512	−512	$2^{-8.30}$
011	A	−512	−512	−2048	−2048	1536	1536	$2^{-8.30}$
100	A	−512	−512	−2048	−2048	1536	1536	$2^{-8.30}$
101	B	1536	1536	2048	2048	−512	−512	$2^{-8.30}$
110	B	−1536	−1536	−2048	−2048	512	512	$2^{-8.30}$
111	A	512	512	2048	2048	−1536	−1536	$2^{-8.30}$

6.1 Application to GIFT-128 in the General Setting

Linear cryptanalysis of GIFT-128 has been discussed in [43–45]. To the best of our knowledge, the best results were reported in [44], which attacks 25 rounds using a 19-round linear approximation.

We propose an improved version with lower data complexity, a high-level overview of which is shown in Fig. 5. We switch an active super Sbox of the approximation (between X_3 and X_5) to key recovery and apply bit puncturing on it. Since there is no whitening key before the first Sbox layer, we peel back X_0 to X_1. The key recovery involves 48 bits of X_1 and 64 bits of X_{25}.

Correlation and ELP of the 17-Round Linear Approximation. The correlation of the (shortened) 17-round linear trail is 2^{-56}. We find another linear trail with the same input and output masks and correlation 2^{-57}. However, it involves exactly the same secret key bits so that the correlations of both trails always have the same sign. Considering this situation, we estimated that $ELP \approx 2^{-110.57}$. Furthermore, the correlation distribution is bimodal with peaks at $c \approx \pm 2^{-55.42}$. Please refer to [29] for details.

Punctured Super Sbox. We puncture the super Sbox to approximate the parity at X_5 from X_3. The right of Fig. 5 represents the active super Sbox. For simplicity, we use $(x_{15}, \ldots, x_0)$, $(y_{15}, \ldots, y_0)$, and $(k_7, \ldots, k_0)$ as the input, output and key of this super Sbox, respectively. The initial goal is to compute $y_{13} \oplus y_9$. To make adding three more key recovery rounds feasible, we use bit puncturing and remove the 11 input bits indexed by $\{15, 13, 11, 10, 9, 8, 7, 5, 3, 2, 1\}$, which also excludes k_6. Table 2 summarizes the Walsh spectrum after puncturing. The puncturing correlation ρ^2 generally depends on the internal key, but here it takes the same value for all key guesses. Moreover, up to a sign swap, there are only two different Walsh spectra, A and B in the Table. The same spectrum always returns the same absolute experimental correlation. Therefore, guessing $k_4 \oplus k_5$ instead of the three bits is enough. In summary, the puncturing increases the data complexity by $2^{8.30}$, but the number of active input bits is reduced from 16 to 5, and the internal key guess is reduced from 4 to 1 bits.

Overview of Results. We use a step-by-step key recovery procedure on the top and bottom three rounds. We first collect the data and prepare a distillation table. Step-by-step round subkey guesses are used to slowly reduce the size of the distillation tables, until a table indexed by the 5-bit input of the punctured super Sbox for each key guess is obtained. The (approximate) experimental correlation is obtained after guessing an additional keybit internal to the super Sbox. Refer to [29] for the detailed procedure.

The time complexity of the main attack procedure is $N + 2^{117.40}$. When $N\rho^2 = 2^{114.72}$ with $a = 4.98$-bit advantage, the success probability is higher than 80%. Then, the required data complexity is $N = 2^{114.72} \times 2^{8.30} = 2^{123.02}$ known plaintexts. The total time complexity is $2^{123.02} + (2^{123.02} + 2^{117.40}) + 2^{128-4.98} \approx 2^{124.61}$. The attack requires 2^{112} memory.

6.2   Application to GIFT-128 on the COFB Setting

Linear cryptanalysis is not the best attack strategy against GIFT-128, as differential attacks cover more rounds [45]. Nevertheless, we believe improving linear attacks is meaningful because of the weaker assumption, i.e., known plaintext instead of chosen plaintext. In practice, in many modes of operation it is impossible to choose the input of the underlying block cipher. Linear cryptanalysis is applicable even if GIFT-128 is used on such modes [43–45].

We consider the COFB setting, where the collectable data is up to the birthday bound. Moreover, we cannot observe the top half of the plaintext because a secret block-dependent mask is XORed. The best existing attack targets 16 rounds using a 10-round linear approximation with 2^{-29} correlation [44].

We improve the attack from 16 to 17 rounds. We first construct an 11-round linear trail, but its correlation is 2^{-34}, which makes it inapplicable because of the birthday bound on the data complexity. Therefore, we switch the first and the last two rounds of the linear approximation to key recovery and apply bit puncturing on these rounds. Unlike in the 25-round attack on the general setting, bit puncturing is used in both the plaintext and ciphertext sides. The puncturing

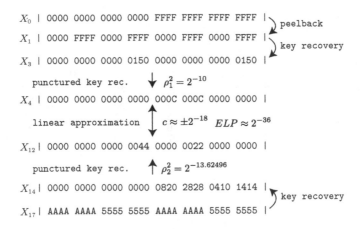

$$X_0 \mid \texttt{0000 0000 0000 0000 FFFF FFFF FFFF FFFF} \mid$$ peelback

$$X_1 \mid \texttt{0000 FFFF 0000 FFFF 0000 FFFF 0000 FFFF} \mid$$ key recovery

$$X_3 \mid \texttt{0000 0000 0000 0150 0000 0000 0000 0150} \mid$$

punctured key rec. $\quad\downarrow\quad \rho_1^2 = 2^{-10}$

$$X_4 \mid \texttt{0000 0000 0000 0000 000C 000C 0000 0000} \mid$$

linear approximation $\quad\uparrow\quad c \approx \pm 2^{-18} \quad ELP \approx 2^{-36}$

$$X_{12} \mid \texttt{0000 0000 0000 0044 0000 0022 0000 0000} \mid$$

punctured key rec. $\quad\uparrow\quad \rho_2^2 = 2^{-13.62496}$

$$X_{14} \mid \texttt{0000 0000 0000 0000 0820 2828 0410 1414} \mid$$ key recovery

$$X_{17} \mid \texttt{AAAA AAAA 5555 5555 AAAA AAAA 5555 5555} \mid$$

Fig. 6. Overview of the 17-round attack against GIFT-128 on the COFB setting

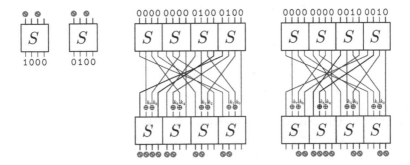

Fig. 7. Puncturing for the attack against GIFT-128 on the COFB setting

correlations are $\rho_1^2 = 2^{-10}$ and $\rho_2^2 = 2^{-13.62}$ for the plaintext and ciphertext sides, respectively. Figure 6 shows a high-level overview, and Fig. 7 shows the behaviour of the bit puncturing. Refer to [29] for a detailed analysis.

The time complexity of the main attack procedure is $N \times 2^{58} + 2^{115.09}$. Using $2^{62.10}$ known plaintexts (the same data complexity as the existing 16-round attack), and with $a = 2.96$-bit advantage, the success probability is higher than 80%. The total time complexity is $2^{62.10} + (2^{62.10+58} + 2^{115.09}) + 2^{128-2.96} \approx 2^{125.09}$. The main analysis requires a table of size 2^{50}, but since we must store the N plaintext-ciphertext pairs, the memory complexity is N.

7 Application to the Data Encryption Standard

This section describes a variant of the attack on the DES [1] of [27], which uses a 13-round linear approximation which is extended by one key recovery round on the plaintext side and two on the ciphertext side. In rounds 1 and 15, only S_5 is active, while there are six active Sboxes in round 16. It leverages several

Table 3. Part of the Walsh spectrum of S_5, $\widehat{S_5}(\cdot, F)$, highlighting the entries which cover the spectrum in [27] as well as the ones used in the punctured version.

00	0	08	8	10	-40	18	-8	20	0	28	0	30	8	38	0
01	0	09	-8	11	8	19	-8	21	0	29	0	31	8	39	0
02	-8	0A	0	12	0	1A	0	22	-24	2A	8	32	0	3A	-8
03	-8	0B	0	13	0	1B	0	23	-8	2B	8	33	0	3B	8
04	0	0C	-8	14	0	1C	0	24	0	2C	0	34	0	3C	8
05	8	0D	0	15	8	1D	8	25	-8	2D	-8	35	8	3D	0
06	0	0E	-8	16	0	1E	0	26	0	2E	0	36	0	3E	8
07	-8	0F	0	17	8	1F	-8	27	-8	2F	-8	37	-8	3F	0

properties to improve the complexity, such as the bits which are duplicated by the expansion function and the key schedule.

The Walsh spectrum of S_5 in round 15 is studied carefully, as shown in Table 3. The Walsh coefficient associated to the all-ones mask 3F is zero. The key recovery map is thus the (arithmetic) sum of five components, each one corresponding to one of the nonzero coefficients with mask of Hamming weight 5. In each component, one of the six active Sboxes in round 16 becomes effectively inactive. The correlation calculation is also separated into five parts where this inactive Sbox can be used to reduce the complexity.

In our variant, the coefficients corresponding to input masks of Hamming weight 5 are punctured. According to Proposition 6, the resulting puncturing coefficient is $\varepsilon = 0.0781$, and the data complexity increases by a factor of $1.085 \simeq 2^{0.117}$ to $2^{41.62}$. The remaining nonzero coefficients are covered by eight masks of Hamming weight 4 and one mask of Hamming weight 3. For each one of these masks, we now have two instead of one inactive Sbox in round 16. The time and memory complexities are obtained in [29], and are $2^{41.76}$ equivalent encryptions and $2^{34.54}$ registers.

We note that through a very small increase in data complexity by a factor of $2^{0.12}$, we are able to reduce the memory complexity by a much larger factor of $2^{4.21}$. This is especially interesting because the memory complexity decreases from 3.3TB to 186.1GB, which makes the attack significantly more practical.

8   Application to NOEKEON

This section describes an improvement on the linear attack on 12-round NOEKEON in [18]. The idea is to exclude the first and last rounds from the known 9-round linear approximation. We then apply the puncturing technique to these excluded rounds. The following is a summary of our attack structure.

Round 0	Round 1	Round 2		Round 9	Round 10	Round 11
$\theta\ \pi_1\ \gamma\ \pi_2$	$\theta\ \pi_1\ \gamma\ \pi_2$	$\theta\ \pi_1\ \gamma\ \pi_2$	$\ldots$	$\theta\ \pi_1\ \gamma\ \pi_2$	$\theta\ \pi_1\ \gamma\ \pi_2$	$\theta\ \pi_1\ \gamma\ \pi_2$
Key rec.	Puncture	Linear approximation		Puncture	Key rec.	Peelback

The linear approximation determines the input mask to γ (the nonlinear layer) in Round 9. We enumerated the Walsh spectrum coefficients of γ which activate at most 12 columns on the peeled-back ciphertext. There are only two such coefficients, and the puncture correlation is $1 - \varepsilon = 2^{-9.68}$. There may be up to $12 \times 4 = 48$ active ciphertext bits, but the dimension of the support is 35.

We next focus on γ in Round 1. We adopted a computer-aided *generic puncturing*. We enumerated all non-zero Walsh spectrum coefficients for which the size of the active plaintext bits is reasonably small. Specifically, we use 460 (out of 10^5) non-zero Walsh spectrum coefficients and puncture the rest. As a result, the puncture correlation is $\rho_1^2 = 2^{-6}$, and it involves $20 \times 4 = 80$ bits of plaintext.

The key recovery is performed using the algorithm of [27]. As a result, the cost of the analysis phase is $2^{118.52}$ for the distillation phase, $2^{116.38}$ for the first FWT, and $2^{112.33}$ for the second FWT. For further detail, refer to [29].

When $N\rho^2 = 2^{103.86}$ with a 8.45-bit advantage, the success probability is higher than 80%. Therefore, the required data complexity is $N = 2^{103.86} \times 2^6 \times 2^{9.68} = 2^{119.54}$. The final time complexity is

$$2^{119.55} + 0.2 \cdot (2^{118.52} + 2^{116.38} + 2^{112.33}) + 2^{128-8.45} \approx 2^{120.63},$$

where we inherit the same constant factor 0.2 as the cost of ADD from [18]. The memory complexity is dominated by the distillation table of 2^{115} registers.

9 Conclusion

We have introduced a model which successfully generalises all previous techniques of key recovery map approximation, and which provides a simple formula which describes the data complexity of the modified linear attack. This new model can be applied to Walsh spectrum puncturing, which allows for larger time complexity improvements at a lower data complexity penalty than the existing techniques. Puncturing can be applied in a variety of scenarios, as shown by the applications to Serpent, GIFT-128, the DES and NOEKEON. In particular, we have described, to the best of our knowledge, the first attack on 12-round Serpent with 192-bit key. We consider the following open problems:

- *Simultaneous puncturing:* Developing a generalisation of the model so that the new key recovery map can approximate the value of more than one linear approximation may lead to more accurate results, as well as enabling more powerful key recovery attacks.
- *Relationship to distinguishers:* Understanding the relationship between punctured key recovery and known distinguishers such as multidimensional linear cryptanalysis with LLR may deepen our understanding of both puncturing as well as these techniques.
- *Finding the optimal key recovery procedure with puncturing:* For each application, we found an adequate puncturing strategy by hand. Since there is a wide variety of puncturing strategies, we may not have found the optimal strategy. Whether we can develop an automatic tool that can handle this variety is an open problem.

References

1. Data Encryption Standard (DES). Federal Information Processing Standards Publication 46-3, U.S. Department of Commerce, National Institute of Standards and Technology (1977, reaffirmed 1988, 1993, 1999, withdrawn 2005)
2. Aumasson, J.-P., Fischer, S., Khazaei, S., Meier, W., Rechberger, C.: New features of Latin dances: analysis of Salsa, ChaCha, and Rumba. In: Nyberg, K. (ed.) FSE 2008. LNCS, vol. 5086, pp. 470–488. Springer, Heidelberg (2008). https://doi.org/10.1007/978-3-540-71039-4_30
3. Banik, S., et al.: GIFT-COFB. IACR Cryptol. ePrint Arch. p. 738 (2020). https://eprint.iacr.org/2020/738
4. Banik, S., Pandey, S.K., Peyrin, T., Sasaki, Yu., Sim, S.M., Todo, Y.: GIFT: a small present. In: Fischer, W., Homma, N. (eds.) CHES 2017. LNCS, vol. 10529, pp. 321–345. Springer, Cham (2017). https://doi.org/10.1007/978-3-319-66787-4_16
5. Beierle, C., et al.: Improved differential-linear attacks with applications to ARX ciphers. J. Cryptol. $35(4)$, 29 (2022)
6. Beyne, T.: A geometric approach to linear cryptanalysis. In: Tibouchi, M., Wang, H. (eds.) ASIACRYPT 2021. LNCS, vol. 13090, pp. 36–66. Springer, Cham (2021). https://doi.org/10.1007/978-3-030-92062-3_2
7. Biham, E., Anderson, R., Knudsen, L.: Serpent: a new block cipher proposal. In: Vaudenay, S. (ed.) FSE 1998. LNCS, vol. 1372, pp. 222–238. Springer, Heidelberg (1998). https://doi.org/10.1007/3-540-69710-1_15
8. Biham, E., Anderson, R.J., Knudsen, L.R.: Serpent: A proposal for the Advanced Encryption Standard. AES Competition (1998)
9. Biham, E., Dunkelman, O., Keller, N.: Linear cryptanalysis of reduced round serpent. In: Matsui, M. (ed.) FSE 2001. LNCS, vol. 2355, pp. 16–27. Springer, Heidelberg (2002). https://doi.org/10.1007/3-540-45473-X_2
10. Biham, E., Dunkelman, O., Keller, N.: Differential-linear cryptanalysis of serpent. In: Johansson, T. (ed.) FSE 2003. LNCS, vol. 2887, pp. 9–21. Springer, Heidelberg (2003). https://doi.org/10.1007/978-3-540-39887-5_2
11. Biham, E., Perle, S.: Conditional linear cryptanalysis - cryptanalysis of DES with less than 2^{42} complexity. IACR Trans. Symmetric Cryptology **2018**(3), 215–264 (2018)
12. Biham, E., Shamir, A.: Differential cryptanalysis of the full 16-round DES. In: Brickell, E.F. (ed.) CRYPTO 1992. LNCS, vol. 740, pp. 487–496. Springer, Heidelberg (1993). https://doi.org/10.1007/3-540-48071-4_34
13. Biryukov, A., De Cannière, C., Quisquater, M.: On multiple linear approximations. In: Franklin, M. (ed.) CRYPTO 2004. LNCS, vol. 3152, pp. 1–22. Springer, Heidelberg (2004). https://doi.org/10.1007/978-3-540-28628-8_1
14. Blondeau, C., Nyberg, K.: Improved parameter estimates for correlation and capacity deviates in linear cryptanalysis. IACR Trans. Symmetric Cryptology **2016**(2), 162–191 (2016)
15. Blondeau, C., Nyberg, K.: Joint data and key distribution of simple, multiple, and multidimensional linear cryptanalysis test statistic and its impact to data complexity. Des. Codes Crypt. **82**(1–2), 319–349 (2017)
16. Bogdanov, A., Vejre, P.S.: Linear cryptanalysis of DES with asymmetries. In: Takagi, T., Peyrin, T. (eds.) ASIACRYPT 2017. LNCS, vol. 10624, pp. 187–216. Springer, Cham (2017). https://doi.org/10.1007/978-3-319-70694-8_7
17. Broll, M., et al.: New attacks from old distinguishers improved attacks on serpent. In: Galbraith, S.D. (ed.) CT-RSA 2022. LNCS, vol. 13161, pp. 484–510. Springer, Cham (2022). https://doi.org/10.1007/978-3-030-95312-6_20

18. Broll, M., Canale, F., Flórez-Gutiérrez, A., Leander, G., Naya-Plasencia, M.: Generic framework for key-guessing improvements. In: Tibouchi, M., Wang, H. (eds.) ASIACRYPT 2021. LNCS, vol. 13090, pp. 453–483. Springer, Cham (2021). https://doi.org/10.1007/978-3-030-92062-3_16

19. Carlet, C.: Boolean Functions for Cryptography and Coding Theory. Cambridge University Press, Cambridge (2021)

20. Chakraborti, A., Iwata, T., Minematsu, K., Nandi, M.: Blockcipher-based authenticated encryption: how small can we go? In: Fischer, W., Homma, N. (eds.) CHES 2017. LNCS, vol. 10529, pp. 277–298. Springer, Cham (2017). https://doi.org/10.1007/978-3-319-66787-4_14

21. Cho, J.Y.: Linear cryptanalysis of reduced-round PRESENT. In: Pieprzyk, J. (ed.) CT-RSA 2010. LNCS, vol. 5985, pp. 302–317. Springer, Heidelberg (2010). https://doi.org/10.1007/978-3-642-11925-5_21

22. Collard, B., Standaert, F.-X., Quisquater, J.-J.: Improved and multiple linear cryptanalysis of reduced round serpent. In: Pei, D., Yung, M., Lin, D., Wu, C. (eds.) Inscrypt 2007. LNCS, vol. 4990, pp. 51–65. Springer, Heidelberg (2008). https://doi.org/10.1007/978-3-540-79499-8_6

23. Collard, B., Standaert, F.-X., Quisquater, J.-J.: Improving the time complexity of Matsui's linear cryptanalysis. In: Nam, K.-H., Rhee, G. (eds.) ICISC 2007. LNCS, vol. 4817, pp. 77–88. Springer, Heidelberg (2007). https://doi.org/10.1007/978-3-540-76788-6_7

24. Cooley, J., Tukey, J.: An algorithm for the machine calculation of complex Fourier series. Math. Comput. 19, 297–301 (1965)

25. Daemen, J., Govaerts, R., Vandewalle, J.: Correlation matrices. In: Preneel, B. (ed.) FSE 1994. LNCS, vol. 1008, pp. 275–285. Springer, Heidelberg (1995). https://doi.org/10.1007/3-540-60590-8_21

26. Daemen, J., Peeters, M., Van Assche, G., Rijmen, V.: The NOEKEON block cipher. Proposal to the NESSIE Project (2000)

27. Flórez-Gutiérrez, A.: Optimising linear key recovery attacks with affine Walsh transform pruning. In: Agrawal, S., Lin, D. (eds.) Advances in Cryptology – ASIACRYPT 2022. ASIACRYPT 2022. LNCS, vol. 13794. Springer, Cham (2022). https://doi.org/10.1007/978-3-031-22972-5_16

28. Flórez-Gutiérrez, A., Naya-Plasencia, M.: Improving key-recovery in linear attacks: application to 28-round PRESENT. In: Canteaut, A., Ishai, Y. (eds.) EUROCRYPT 2020. LNCS, vol. 12105, pp. 221–249. Springer, Cham (2020). https://doi.org/10.1007/978-3-030-45721-1_9

29. Flórez-Gutiérrez, A., Todo, Y.: Improving linear key recovery attacks using Walsh spectrum puncturing. IACR Cryptology ePrint Archive p. 151 (2024). https://eprint.iacr.org/2024/151

30. Hermelin, M., Cho, J.Y., Nyberg, K.: Multidimensional linear cryptanalysis of reduced round Serpent. In: Australasian Conference on Information Security and Privacy, ACISP 2008, Proceedings, pp. 203–215 (2008)

31. Hermelin, M., Cho, J.Y., Nyberg, K.: Multidimensional extension of Matsui's algorithm 2. In: Dunkelman, O. (ed.) FSE 2009. LNCS, vol. 5665, pp. 209–227. Springer, Heidelberg (2009). https://doi.org/10.1007/978-3-642-03317-9_13

32. Hermelin, M., Cho, J.Y., Nyberg, K.: Multidimensional linear cryptanalysis. J. Cryptol. 32(1), 1–34 (2019)

33. Kaliski, B.S., Robshaw, M.J.B.: Linear cryptanalysis using multiple approximations. In: Desmedt, Y.G. (ed.) CRYPTO 1994. LNCS, vol. 839, pp. 26–39. Springer, Heidelberg (1994). https://doi.org/10.1007/3-540-48658-5_4

34. Liu, M., Lu, X., Lin, D.: Differential-linear cryptanalysis from an algebraic perspective. In: Malkin, T., Peikert, C. (eds.) CRYPTO 2021. LNCS, vol. 12827, pp. 247–277. Springer, Cham (2021). https://doi.org/10.1007/978-3-030-84252-9_9
35. Matsui, M.: Linear cryptanalysis method for DES cipher. In: Helleseth, T. (ed.) EUROCRYPT 1993. LNCS, vol. 765, pp. 386–397. Springer, Heidelberg (1994). https://doi.org/10.1007/3-540-48285-7_33
36. Matsui, M.: The first experimental cryptanalysis of the data encryption standard. In: Desmedt, Y.G. (ed.) CRYPTO 1994. LNCS, vol. 839, pp. 1–11. Springer, Heidelberg (1994). https://doi.org/10.1007/3-540-48658-5_1
37. Matsui, M., Yamagishi, A.: A new method for known plaintext attack of FEAL cipher. In: Rueppel, R.A. (ed.) EUROCRYPT 1992. LNCS, vol. 658, pp. 81–91. Springer, Heidelberg (1993). https://doi.org/10.1007/3-540-47555-9_7
38. McLaughlin, J., Clark, J.A.: Filtered nonlinear cryptanalysis of reduced-round serpent, and the wrong-key randomization hypothesis. In: Stam, M. (ed.) IMACC 2013. LNCS, vol. 8308, pp. 120–140. Springer, Heidelberg (2013). https://doi.org/10.1007/978-3-642-45239-0_8
39. Nguyen, P.H., Wu, H., Wang, H.: Improving the algorithm 2 in multidimensional linear cryptanalysis. In: Parampalli, U., Hawkes, P. (eds.) ACISP 2011. LNCS, vol. 6812, pp. 61–74. Springer, Heidelberg (2011). https://doi.org/10.1007/978-3-642-22497-3_5
40. Nyberg, K.: Linear approximation of block ciphers. In: De Santis, A. (ed.) EUROCRYPT 1994. LNCS, vol. 950, pp. 439–444. Springer, Heidelberg (1995). https://doi.org/10.1007/BFb0053460
41. O'Donnell, R.: Analysis of Boolean Functions. Cambridge University Press, Cambridge (2014)
42. Selçuk, A.A.: On probability of success in linear and differential cryptanalysis. J. Cryptol. 21(1), 131–147 (2008)
43. Sun, L., Wang, W., Wang, M.: Linear cryptanalyses of three AEADs with GIFT-128 as underlying primitives. IACR Trans. Symmetric Cryptology 2021(2), 199–221 (2021)
44. Sun, L., Wang, W., Wang, M.: Addendum to linear cryptanalyses of three AEADs with GIFT-128 as underlying primitives. IACR Trans. Symmetric Cryptology 2022(1), 212–219 (2022)
45. Zong, R., Dong, X., Chen, H., Luo, Y., Wang, S., Li, Z.: Towards key-recovery-attack friendly distinguishers: application to GIFT-128. IACR Trans. Symmetric Cryptology 2021(1), 156–184 (2021)

A Generic Algorithm for Efficient Key Recovery in Differential Attacks – and its Associated Tool

Christina Boura[1(✉)], Nicolas David[2], Patrick Derbez[3], Rachelle Heim Boissier[1], and María Naya-Plasencia[2]

[1] Université Paris-Saclay, UVSQ, CNRS, Laboratoire de mathématiques de Versailles, 78000 Versailles, France
`{christina.boura,rachelle.heim}@uvsq.fr`
[2] Inria, Paris, France
`{nicolas.david,maria.naya-plasencia}@inria.fr`
[3] Univ Rennes, Inria, CNRS, IRISA, Rennes, France
`patrick.derbez@irisa.fr`

Abstract. Differential cryptanalysis is an old and powerful attack against block ciphers. While different techniques have been introduced throughout the years to improve the complexity of this attack, the key recovery phase remains a tedious and error-prone procedure. In this work, we propose a new algorithm and its associated tool that permits, given a distinguisher, to output an efficient key guessing strategy. Our tool can be applied to SPN ciphers whose linear layer consists of a bit-permutation and whose key schedule is linear or almost linear. It can be used not only to help cryptanalysts find the best differential attack on a given cipher but also to assist designers in their security analysis. We applied our tool to four targets: `RECTANGLE`, `PRESENT-80`, `SPEEDY-7-192` and `GIFT-64`. We extend the previous best attack on `RECTANGLE-128` by one round and the previous best differential attack against `PRESENT-80` by 2 rounds. We improve a previous key recovery step in an attack against `SPEEDY` and present more efficient key recovery strategies for `RECTANGLE-80` and `GIFT`. Our tool outputs the results in only a second for most targets.

Keywords: differential cryptanalysis · key recovery · automatic tool · SPEEDY · GIFT · PRESENT · RECTANGLE

1 Introduction

Differential cryptanalysis is an old and powerful technique introduced in 1990 by Biham and Shamir [5]. Soon after its discovery this technique allowed to successfully break some of the most important block ciphers and hash functions of that time, such as `FEAL` [6], `Snefru`, `Khafre`, `LOKI` [7] and `DES` [8], to cite just a few. The success of this attack against the cryptosystems of the 70s and 80s, forced the designers of the succeeding ciphers to develop strategies to ensure the resistance of the new designs against this attack. This is how Daemen and Rijmen proposed the *wide-trail strategy* [16] and used it to design the `AES` or why Vaudenay invented the *decorrelation theory* [35].

© International Association for Cryptologic Research 2024
M. Joye and G. Leander (Eds.): EUROCRYPT 2024, LNCS 14651, pp. 217–248, 2024.
https://doi.org/10.1007/978-3-031-58716-0_8

Differential attacks are based on the existence of a high-probability differential, that is an input difference that propagates after some rounds to an output difference with a probability much higher than what would be expected for a random permutation. In the case of block ciphers, the existence of one or more such differentials can usually be exploited to recover the secret key through a key recovery procedure. A differential attack against a block cipher can thus be seen as a two-step approach. First, a high-probability differential must be exhibited. Then, this differential is extended to some rounds to permit to recover the secret key or parts of it. The first part of the attack has been, and continues to be, extensively studied and many interesting algorithms and approaches have been proposed. One can cite for example the dynamic programming approach of [21] to find good differential characteristics for AES-128 in the related-key setting, the MILP-based approach of [33] for bit-oriented block ciphers, the constraint programming (CP)-based method of [31] for all versions of Rijndael or the SAT-based method of [32] applicable to many ciphers. It can be seen that this step of differential attacks can be automatized and almost all the approaches that have been proposed lately are based on automatic tools.

All of the above cited algorithms and tools to find good differential distinguishers are exclusively dedicated to this step and there have not been approaches to optimize both steps at the same time. This would be beneficial, as it is not always the best distinguisher that leads to the best attack. There have been efforts in this direction for other families of cryptanalysis, e.g., impossible differential, zero-correlation, integral, meet-in-the-middle, boomerang and rectangle attacks, where tools combining both steps have been proposed [10,17,22,30,39]. However, most of these approaches use heuristics for the key recovery part, by providing for example a rough estimation for the number of involved key bits, and are not guaranteed to lead to the most optimal attack. To build a complete tool for differential cryptanalysis, the key recovery process of these attacks must be well understood. Yet, this step is very technical and error-prone, see for example [34]. Moreover, it is very difficult to come up with an optimal key recovery procedure, as demonstrated by differential attacks published against block ciphers, whose key recovery step was improved by following works. Such examples include attacks against the block ciphers GIFT [32] and RECTANGLE [38] whose key recovery was later improved in [14] and [13] respectively.

Throughout the years, a series of techniques have been proposed to improve the key recovery step of differential attacks. These techniques and improvements, some of which were introduced for other related attacks but are still applicable to differential cryptanalysis, include the early abort technique [25] to gradually reduce the number of plaintext/ciphertext pairs, the conditional differential cryptanalysis [23], the dynamic key-guessing technique [29,37], other key-guessing strategies [18] or techniques to avoid unnecessary key guesses [2]. Another idea, proposed in [13] for S-box-based designs, was to take advantage of the structure of the S-box in order to reduce the number of necessary key guesses. However, despite the existence of these techniques a global treatment of the key recovery step is still missing and it remains very difficult to combine the different techniques together to end with a generic efficient procedure.

The lack of a generic and optimal procedure for the key recovery has direct consequences on the design of new ciphers. While most of the newly proposed designs come with claims on the resistance against differential attacks, this is usually done by applying branch-and-bound arguments to determine the highest number of rounds covered by a differential and then, the key recovery added by the designers, if any, is rarely optimal. This can lead then to an erroneous estimation of the security margin and to the choice of a too small number of rounds for the design. This happened recently with the block cipher SPEEDY-7-192 [24] that provided a wrong estimation of the number of rounds on which key recovery was possible [12].

The main problem one has to solve during the key recovery phase of a differential attack is finding the best key guessing order. This is a difficult combinatorial problem and doing this step by hand is time consuming and there is no guarantee that the followed process is optimal, or even error-free. The existence of a fully automated procedure for this step would be of great help for cryptanalysts but also for designers. Indeed, the existence of such a tool could assist designers in choosing a well suited number of rounds. A first attempt for building such a tool was made by Nageler in [26] and permitted to improve a differential attack on 5-round MANTIS. However, this approach had several limitations, as it could only handle bit-permutation key schedules and output basic key recoveries.

Our Contributions. We propose in this paper the first generic algorithm to find efficient key recovery strategies in differential attacks under some reasonable assumptions, as well as an automatic tool that implements it. Our algorithm captures an efficient key recovery strategy by taking into account many possible optimizations. This algorithm is then transformed into an automated tool that we implemented in C++. Our tool takes as input a very simple description of the cipher and a given differential and outputs an efficient order for the key guesses together with the associated time complexity. For each execution of the tool, the user must indicate the number of key recovery rounds to add on both sides. By gradually increasing the number of rounds, the user can get a more precise estimation of the longest valid differential attack that a concrete distinguisher can lead to. This can notably allow designers to choose the best suited number of rounds for their primitive. For this, we focused on SPN ciphers with a bit-permutation as linear layer. We applied our tool to RECTANGLE, PRESENT-80 and SPEEDY-7-192 in the single-key model and to GIFT-64 in the related-key model by using differential distinguishers that have been previously given in the literature. Note that we have not verified the validity of the characteristics ourselves as this is out of scope for our work. The correctness of the attacks depends on the validity of these underlying characteristics. Under the assumption that the given characteristic is correct, we improve the best known attack on RECTANGLE-128 by one round. Further, we slightly improve the best previous key recovery on SPEEDY. As for PRESENT-80, we extend the best previous differential attack by 2 rounds. Last but not least, we obtain efficient key recovery strategies for GIFT-64 (in the related-key model) and RECTANGLE-80, but do not manage to improve the best previous differential attacks as our tool does not incorporate yet techniques such as the "tree-based graphs" or the "key-absorption" technique used in [13] or [14]. We however beat all previous key recovery procedures that do not use these techniques, such as the attack of [38] on RECTANGLE-80 and the attack of [32] on GIFT-64. We refer to Table 1 for a summary of our results. Furthermore, the tool is easy to use, as only a very basic description of the cipher is needed. It is also fast as, for most of the attacks, the results were outputted in one second. The code of our tool can be found here:

https://gitlab.inria.fr/capsule/kyrydi

The rest of the paper is organized as follows. Section 2 describes the key recovery procedure in differential attacks. Section 3 introduces our modelization of the problem and discusses important optimizations and features we have taken into account, taking as example a toy cipher. Then, Sect. 4 introduces our new algorithm and describes the related tool. Finally, Sect. 5 presents our applications to RECTANGLE, PRESENT-80, SPEEDY-7-192 and GIFT-64.

2   The Key Recovery Problem in Differential Cryptanalysis

We start this section by introducing differential attacks and the key recovery process. We also describe the type of primitives we will consider in our work, and describe a toy cipher that will be useful to illustrate our algorithm.

2.1   Differential Cryptanalysis

As for most cryptanalysis techniques against symmetric primitives, building a differential attack requires two separated, though non-independent, steps. First, an attacker must be able to exhibit a property of the cipher that allows him to distinguish E_K, for any K, from a permutation chosen uniformly at random. In differential cryptanalysis, the distinguisher consists of a pair of differences $(\delta_{in}, \delta_{out}) \in \mathbb{F}_2^n \times \mathbb{F}_2^n$ such that the difference δ_{in} propagates to the difference δ_{out} through a reduced number of rounds with probability strictly higher than 2^{-n}. In a second step, the attacker extends the differential by some rounds, usually to both directions. The appended rounds are called the key recovery rounds. They permit to determine which (partial) keys allow a high number of plaintext pairs and their corresponding ciphertext pairs to follow the differential. An overview of a classical differential attack against a block cipher is depicted in Fig. 1. As can be seen in this figure, an attacker first finds a differential $(\delta_{in}, \delta_{out})$ over $r_\delta < r$ rounds of the block cipher E that has probability $2^{-p} > 2^{-n}$. The difference δ_{in} (resp. δ_{out}) propagates with probability 1 to a difference in a set D_{in}, r_{in} rounds before (resp. D_{out}, r_{out} rounds after). The attack can be symmetrically done in both directions. However, without loss of generality, we focus here on the case where the attacker makes calls to an encryption oracle.

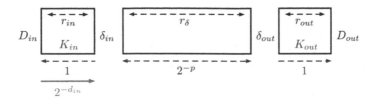

Fig. 1. A differential attack against a block cipher.

Number of Needed Plaintext Pairs. A classical method to efficiently build the plaintext pairs in differential and other related attacks is to use *structures*. This technique, introduced in [8], permits to reduce the data complexity. A structure is a set of plaintexts that have a fixed value on the inactive bits of D_{in}. Each structure has size $|D_{in}| = 2^{d_{in}}$, and thus allows to build $2^{2d_{in}-1}$ pairs. For the attack to work, the attacker must be able to generate 2^p pairs that have difference δ_{in} after r_{in} rounds. Since each pair in D_{in} satisfies $n - d_{in}$ necessary conditions, we approximate the probability that a pair in D_{in} has difference δ_{in} after r_{in} rounds by $2^{-d_{in}}$. Thus, we need to build $2^{p+d_{in}}$ pairs to get one satisfying the differential with a reasonable probability. This can be done by using $2^s = 2^{p-d_{in}+1}$ structures, corresponding to a data of $\mathcal{D} = 2^{p+1}$.

Key Recovery. The goal of this step is to find, for each pair, the possible keys that would partially encrypt the pair to the difference δ_{in} and partially decrypt it to the difference δ_{out}. However, some of the pairs cannot satisfy the differential, independently of the key, e.g., pairs such that their ciphertext difference does not belong to D_{out}. To only work with plaintext pairs whose ciphertext difference belongs to D_{out}, the data of each structure is stored in a hash table indexed by the $n - d_{out}$ inactive bits on the ciphertext. The attacker then looks for collisions on this inactive part. At the end, we can thus build $N = 2^{p+d_{in}-n+d_{out}}$ pairs with a time complexity of $\max(2^{p+1}, 2^{p+d_{in}-n+d_{out}})$ simple operations and a memory complexity of $2^{d_{in}}$ plaintext/ciphertext pairs. For each of these N pairs, we associate the candidate values for the key material involved in the attack and thus generate candidate triplets (P, P', k), where $k \in K_{in} \cup K_{out}$, with K_{in} (resp. K_{out}) being the part of the key to be guessed in the first (resp. last) key recovery rounds. We introduce the parameter C_S to denote the average cost of this step per triplet. At the end of this procedure, if the total number of triplet candidates is smaller than the number of involved key bits, then the attack is considered as successful. Indeed, we can then test the remaining key candidates by completing the missing key bits for a lower cost than that of the exhaustive search. On the other hand, if the number of triplets is higher than the number of involved key bits, we have to consider more data so that the right key will be the one that appears the highest number of times. In this case, one has to take a vector for storing the number of times each candidate key appears, but this makes no difference for the key recovery algorithm we are going to propose.

Alternatively, one can also use rounds inside the differential distinguisher to get additional filtering.

As shown in [12], the time ($\mathcal{T}$), data ($\mathcal{D}$), and memory ($\mathcal{M}$) complexities of the attack can be computed in the following way:

$$\mathcal{T} = \left(2^{p+1} + 2^{p+1}\frac{C_S}{C_E} + 2^{p-n+d_{in}+d_{out}}\frac{C_{KR}}{C_E}\right)C_E, \quad \mathcal{D} = 2^{p+1}, \quad \mathcal{M} = 2^{d_{in}},$$

where C_E is the cost of one encryption and C_{KR} is the average cost of the key recovery step per pair. In the time complexity, the first term corresponds to the cost of generating the N pairs, the second term is the complexity of the sieving step and the last term is the complexity of the key recovery step on the remaining $2^{p-n+d_{in}+d_{out}}$ pairs. This last term is the one we want to optimize in this work.

2.2   Efficient Key Recovery

The key recovery step of a differential attack is traditionally solved by tedious and error-prone procedures. This step is often done by hand and can lead to non-optimal complexities, e.g., [32,36,38]. In this paper, we propose an algorithm that allows to optimize the key recovery step, together with an associated tool. To present our algorithm, we first need to detail further how to perform the key recovery, that is, how to build candidate triplets (P, P', k), with $k \in K_{in} \cup K_{out}$, as described in the previous section. We must also define what it means for an attack to be efficient. We do so in the rest of this section.

To obtain triplets (P, P', k), the attacker must consider each active S-box of the key recovery rounds, and take into account the differential constraints of this S-box. For each pair, the attacker must determine whether this pair *can* respect the differential constraints, and, if yes, under which conditions on the key. Under what we denote by *solving* this S-box, the attacker obtains a list of triplets containing the kept pairs and a partially determined key, with fixed values on the key bits corresponding to this S-box, *i.e.* the key bits added before (resp. after) the S-box on the plaintext (resp. ciphertext) side. The goal of the attack is thus to efficiently reduce as early as possible the number of pairs considered whilst maximizing the number of key bits of $K_{in} \cup K_{out}$ that are fixed.

An attack is optimal when it has the lowest time complexity.[1] What determines the complexity of the key recovery is threefold. First, the order in which each S-box is solved impacts the complexity. For example, if an S-box allows to reduce significantly the number of pairs whilst fixing all key bits, it is often better to solve this S-box early to reduce the overall time complexity. Second, it is possible to *solve* several S-boxes at the same time, which can also help reduce the overall time complexity. Last but not least, S-boxes and sets of S-boxes can be solved in parallel, as described later on. It comes that finding an efficient key recovery procedure consists in choosing an efficient partition of the S-boxes with

---

[1] The attack must also have a reasonable memory complexity, but we will detail how we take this into account later.

an associated order on each element of the partition. We will detail these three techniques further in Sect. 3.

Note that we can exhibit a natural upper bound for the complexity of the key recovery step. This bound is $\min(2^\kappa, N \cdot 2^{|K_{in} \cup K_{out}|})$, where κ is the bit-size of the secret key. This corresponds to the naïve procedure for which an attacker would guess for each pair (P, P') all the key bits in $K_{in} \cup K_{out}$ to see which pairs and associated key guess lead to the differential. On the other hand, we can also show a lower bound for the key recovery procedure. This lower bound is $N + N \cdot 2^{|K_{in} \cup K_{out}|-d_{in}-d_{out}}$, where $N \cdot 2^{|K_{in} \cup K_{out}|-d_{in}-d_{out}}$ corresponds to the number of expected solutions, $i.e.$ the number of pairs and associated partial keys that are obtained at the end of the key recovery procedure. An efficient key recovery algorithm allows us to reach a time complexity for this step as close as possible to this lower bound.

2.3 Considered Ciphers

As determining an efficient key recovery procedure is a complex combinatorial problem, it is difficult to solve it once and for all types of symmetric primitives. For this reason, we decided to start with analyzing this problem for the simplest type of SPN constructions, that is, block ciphers such that their round function is composed of an XOR with the round key, a non-linear layer composed of the parallel application of an S-box and a bit-permutation playing the role of the linear layer. This is already a complex case with many applications and will serve as basis for future extensions. Furthermore, we focused on ciphers with linear or almost linear key schedules. Examples of block ciphers that belong to this category are notably PRESENT [9], RECTANGLE [38] and GIFT [1]. Furthermore, we can add to this category ciphers with more complex linear layers as long as this operation is not involved in the key recovery rounds. This is the case of the SPEEDY block cipher [24], whose 7-round variant was broken by a differential attack [12] where only 1.5 round was added to the distinguisher and this 1.5 round did not include the complex linear operation, due to the particular construction of the round function.

Toy Cipher. We now describe a toy cipher whose design is inspired by GIFT [1], and that belongs to the above category. We will use this toy cipher throughout the paper to explain the way our algorithm and its associated tool work. The structure of the cipher together with the description of a differential attack on it can be seen in Fig. 2. The block and key length of the toy cipher are 16 and 80 bits respectively. There are 7 rounds, and each round is composed of a bit-wise key addition, an S-box layer, and a permutation layer. The S-box is the one of GIFT:

x	0	1	2	3	4	5	6	7	8	9	10	11	12	13	14	15
$S(x)$	1	10	4	12	6	15	3	9	2	13	11	7	5	0	8	14

and the linear layer P is a bit-permutation given as:

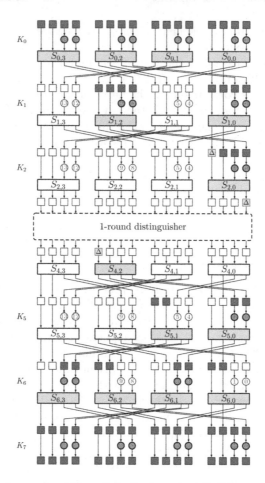

Fig. 2. Our toy cipher and a differential attack against it. S-boxes in green are active. Bits with a difference Δ are active bits, while bits in blue are bits with an unknown difference (0 or 1). Bits in a circle correspond to key bits. Those in blue, are the ones that need to be guessed during the attack. (Color figure online)

i	0	1	2	3	4	5	6	7	8	9	10	11	12	13	14	15
$P(i)$	4	5	2	3	12	13	10	11	0	1	6	7	8	9	14	15

We consider the bit 0, i.e. the least significant bit, to be on the right for both the state and the round keys. Furthermore, and similarly to GIFT, we consider the key addition to be partial and only applied to the two rightmost bits before each S-box. Last, we suppose that there is no key schedule and we treat all round keys as independent. For this toy cipher, we consider the input difference $\delta_{in} = \texttt{0x0001}$ that propagates after 1 extended round (permutation, addition of K_3, S-box layer, permutation, addition of K_4) to the output difference $\delta_{out} = \texttt{0x0800}$ as depicted in Fig. 2. The difference δ_{in} can be propagated three rounds backwards with probability one to give $\Delta_{in} = \mathbb{F}_2^{16}$. Similarly, the difference δ_{out} can be propagated three rounds forwards with probability one to give $\Delta_{out} = \mathbb{F}_2^{16}$. The active S-boxes, i.e. the ones which have a non-zero input difference, are colored in green.

Our goal is to determine an efficient algorithm to determine in which order and manner we have to guess these subkey bits, as described in Sect. 2.2.

3   Modeling the Key Recovery Problem

In this section, we present how we model the key recovery problem. A good modeling plays a crucial role in finding an algorithm to solve the problem in the most efficient way. We also describe three techniques that are used in our tool to obtain an improved key recovery strategy: the S-box sieving technique, the precomputation of partial solutions and the use of parallel computations.

3.1   Our Modelization

To model the problem of finding an efficient key recovery for a given differential, we use a directed graph. On this graph, each node represents an active S-box. The graph is then constructed as follows. On the plaintext side, a vertex goes from an S-box S_A at round r to an S-box S_B at round $r+1$ if the input bits of S_B depend on the output bits of S_A. Similarly, for the key recovery rounds on the ciphertext side, a vertex goes from an S-box S_A at round r to an S-box S_B at round $r-1$ if the output bits of S_B depend on the input bits of S_A. An example of such a graph, built to model the toy cipher of Fig. 2, is represented in Fig. 3. We can see in this graph that the number of vertices going to an internal node is always two, as the four output bits of any S-box affect only two S-boxes in the following round, and as all round keys are considered independent.

Once the graph is built, the key recovery problem corresponds to choosing a specific partition of the nodes together with an associated order. A partition of the nodes divides the original graph into subgraphs and the order indicates in which order the different subgraphs must be treated. A graph representing a key recovery strategy for the toy cipher of Fig. 2, can be visualized in Fig. 3. Each S-box of the same color belongs to the same subgraph, and the order is represented by a number of the same color. Each partition implies certain subsets of partial solutions and a cost for merging them to obtain the final global solution. The goal is to come up with an algorithm that will output the partition associated with the lowest possible cost.

In the next section, we describe some classical techniques in differential cryptanalysis that impact the modelization of the key recovery problem. Before doing so, we will need some definitions that we introduce below.

Definitions. Let S be an S-box in the key recovery rounds that must satisfy the differential constraint $\nu_{in} \rightarrow \nu_{out}$. We call *solution* to S any tuple $(x, x', S(x), S(x'))$ such that $x \oplus x' = \nu_{in}$ and $S(x) \oplus S(x') = \nu_{out}$. We denote by *input solutions* (resp. *output solutions*) any pair of values (x, x') (resp. (y, y')) such that $(x, x', S(x), S(x'))$ (resp. $(S^{-1}(y), S^{-1}(y'), y, y')$) is a solution. When it is clear from the context, we sometimes use the term *solutions* to denote input or output solutions.

This definition can be generalized to a subgraph in the following manner. A *solution* to a subgraph is a tuple containing:

- a solution to an S-box in the subgraph that is situated in the first or last key recovery round, i.e. that takes as input a part of the plaintext or the ciphertext.
- a partial solution to an S-box linked to an S-box outside the subgraph. The term partial means that we only consider the bits linked to an external S-box.

For example, a solution to the blue subgraph in Fig. 3, is a tuple containing a solution to $S_{0,1}$, a solution to $S_{0,3}$ and a solution to $S_{2,0}$, truncated to its two leftmost bits.

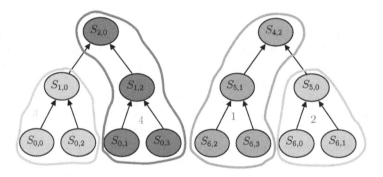

Fig. 3. Graph example and associated partitions of a key recovery strategy for an attack on the toy cipher represented in Fig. 2.

3.2   Sieving of the Pairs Using the Differential Constraints of the S-Boxes

Let N be the number of pairs that the attacker is using for the key recovery. Although N impacts the complexity of the key recovery as this number is multiplied by C_{KR} (i.e. average cost of the key recovery step per pair), the choice of an optimal key recovery strategy does *not* depend on the value of N.[2]

To keep C_{KR} as low as possible, it is smart to try to reduce the number of pairs/triplets as quickly as possible. A very classical technique in differential cryptanalysis is to perform a sieving (or filtering) step on the initial N pairs,

---

[2] This is assuming N is reasonably big, as we work using average values. We remind the reader that $N = 2^{p+d_{in}-n+d_{out}}$..

using the differential constraints of the S-boxes of the first and last round. This sieving step, that we will call *pre-sieving* allows the attacker to further keep only the pairs that *can* satisfy the differential constraints, and to discard those that cannot, as early on as possible. If N' is the number of pairs remaining after the pre-sieving ($N' \leq N$), the attacker performs the rest of the key recovery on those N' pairs.

To perform the pre-sieving, the attacker typically precomputes the *solutions* to each S-box of the external rounds. However, the attacker does not necessarily store all the solutions. Instead, he builds offline a *sieving list* in the following way: on the bits where a key addition is applied, only the difference is stored; on the bits where there is no key addition, the value of each element in the pair is stored. For instance, if the key is XORed to the whole state, only the differences that satisfy the transition are stored. During the online phase, this sieving step consists, for each pair and each S-box, of checking whether the pair is consistent with the sieving list. The filter of the sieving step for that S-box is then computed as the size of the sieving list divided by the total number of possible differences/pairs of values. Note that for this second sieving step we only consider S-boxes that reduce the size of N.

We give an example of this step on the toy cipher of Fig. 2. We consider the first S-box of the first round, namely $S_{0,0}$. The differential constraints for this S-box are of the form: $(* * * *) \rightarrow (* * 0\ 0)$ and only the first two input bits to this S-box have key bits XORed to them. Thus, for any solution $(x_3 x_2 x_1 x_0, x'_3 x'_2 x'_1 x'_0)$ that satisfies this differential transition, we store the corresponding 6-bit word $(x_3 x'_3 x_2 x'_2 || x_1 \oplus x'_1 || x_0 \oplus x'_0)$ in a list $L_{0,0}$. After building $L_{0,0}$, one can see that for this particular S-box this list has length 36. On the other hand, a 6-bit word can take up to 2^6 values. This provides then a filter of $36/2^6 = 2^{-0.83}$ for this S-box. Using the same reasoning, we obtain the same filter for $S_{0,1}$, as well as a filter $2^{-0.48}$ for $S_{0,3}$ and $S_{0,2}$. On the ciphertext side, the filter for $S_{6,0}$ and $S_{6,2}$ is of $2^{-0.83}$ and it is of $2^{-0.68}$ for the S-boxes $S_{6,1}$ and $S_{6,3}$. In conclusion for this example, the pre-sieving step allows to work with $N' = 2^{-5.63} \cdot N$ pairs instead of N.

Compensation of Pre-sieving. One important point is that the pre-sieving described in the above paragraph and performed in the initial steps must be taken into account later on in the key recovery procedure. Take for instance the example of the S-box $S_{0,0}$ of the toy cipher. This S-box has 2^6 solutions, and each solution fixes a value on the two leftmost bits, and a difference on the two rightmost bits (because of the key addition). On the other hand, an online pair can take 2^4 values on the two leftmost bits, and 2^2 differences on the two rightmost bits. An online pair thus has probability $2^6/2^6 = 1$ to match a solution. Since each solution is a pair of values, a match on a solution fixes the key bits. On the other hand, with the pre-sieving, we initially filter out $2^{-0.83}$ of the pairs, but when determining the key bit values we will get $2^{0.83}$ possibilities per pair on average, thus canceling locally out the gain of the pre-sieving. This example shows that sieving on a single S-box and solving this S-box immediately after is not a good strategy. Nevertheless, there is often a significant advantage when the pre-sieving is applied to all the S-boxes very early on: as the compensation is gradual, the time complexity is overly reduced. Indeed, the attacker will still work with less pairs during the different steps than if no pre-sieving was applied. For example, if we apply the pre-sieving step to all S-boxes but $S_{0,0}$ in the toy cipher, we start by working with $2^{0.83} \cdot N' = 2^{-4.8} \cdot N$ pairs, the cost of solving $S_{0,0}$ is $2^{-4.8} \cdot N$, and we keep only $2^{-4.8} \cdot N$ pairs after solving $S_{0,0}$.

Generalization to Any Active S-Box. Note that it is also possible to sieve later by using S-boxes of other key recovery rounds, as long as we have reached a point in the key recovery procedure where the input of these S-boxes is fixed. This sieving must not be confused with the pre-sieving that only applies to the external key recovery rounds.

3.3   Precomputing Partial Solutions

Besides the pre-sieving method described above, an attacker can also apply another technique to reduce the time complexity. The idea of this technique is to precompute the partial solutions to some subgraph(s). However, such pre-computations can impact the memory complexity of the attack and increase the offline time of the attack. Thus, the optimal key recovery strategy depends on how much memory and offline time are allowed. For this, we introduce a parameter M which corresponds to the maximum memory complexity (aside from storing the pairs) and the maximum allowed precomputation time complexity. The result obtained will directly depend on this parameter. We give an example of such a precomputation phase on the toy cipher of Fig. 2.

Precomputing the Solutions to $S_{0,0}$, $S_{0,2}$ and $S_{1,0}$. We compute the number of solutions to a subgraph containing as nodes the S-boxes $S_{0,0}$, $S_{0,2}$ and $S_{1,0}$. The differential constraints of $S_{1,0}$ are as follows: $(* * * *) \rightarrow (1 * 0 0)$. There are $2^5 (= 2^{2\times4-3})$ output solutions to this S-box, and thus 2^5 input solutions. Looking at the input *before the key addition*, each input solution determines the value of the pair on the two leftmost input bits and the difference on the two rightmost ones, i.e. the ones concerned by the key addition.

We now consider a fixed input solution to $S_{1,0}$, and look at $S_{0,0}$. Two output bits of $S_{0,0}$ are fixed by this solution. However, the two rightmost bits, which have the only constraint of having a zero difference, can take up to 2^2 values. This means that for a solution to $S_{1,0}$, there are 2^2 possibilities at the output of $S_{0,0}$, and thus 2^2 solutions at its input. For each solution, the information at the input of $S_{0,0}$ is fixed in value on the two leftmost bits, and in difference on the two rightmost bits because of the key addition.

Still using a fixed solution to $S_{1,0}$, we investigate $S_{0,2}$. The two rightmost output bits have their difference fixed by the solution to $S_{1,0}$, whilst the two leftmost output bits have a 0-difference by propagation of the differential. There are therefore 2^4 possibilities for the output pairs for this S-box, and thus 2^4 input solutions. Note that each solution fixes the bits added at the input of $S_{1,0}$. As for the previous S-box, each solution completely fixes the value of the two leftmost input bits (where there is no key addition), and the difference on the other two.

In total we have $2^5 \cdot 2^2 \cdot 2^4 = 2^{11}$ solutions at the input of $S_{0,0}$ and $S_{0,2}$. Each solution is a fixed pair of values after the first key addition. Thus, when considering an online pair, for this pair to be kept whilst solving $S_{0,0}$, $S_{0,2}$ and $S_{1,0}$, it must match a solution in value on the two leftmost bits of each S-box (which can take $2^{2 \cdot 2 \cdot 2} = 2^8$ values), and in difference on the two rightmost bits (which can take $2^{2 \cdot 2} = 2^4$ differences). The average probability of a match is thus $2^{11}/2^{12} = 2^{-1}$. Since a match fixes the solution, and thus the value after key addition, each match fixes the key bits at the input of $S_{0,0}$, $S_{0,2}$ and $S_{1,0}$.

This represents a filter of 2^{-1} on the online pairs. By letting N'' to be the number of solutions before this subgraph, the number of pairs remaining after solving it is $2^{-1} \cdot N''$. If we have already applied a pre-sieving on $S_{0,0}$ and $S_{0,2}$, then this sieving must be compensated. Thus, the number of remaining pairs is $2^{1.3} \cdot 2^{-1} \cdot N'' = 2^{0.3} \cdot N''$. Further, each of the $N'' \cdot 2^{0.3}$ new triplets has a fixed value on the key bits at the input of $S_{0,0}$, $S_{0,2}$ and $S_{1,0}$. *Testing* each of the N'' pairs, that is, checking whether each pair belongs to the pre-computed table of solutions, can be done with a time complexity of $N'' \cdot 2^{0.3}$ using hash tables.[3] In this example, the precomputation is not too costly as it requires 2^{11} applications of the S-box, and the storage of 2^{11} pairs of length $4 \cdot 2 \cdot 2 + 2 \cdot 3 = 22$ bits (the pairs of input values of $S_{0,0}$ and $S_{0,1}$, as well as all the key bits).

We can compare the use of the precomputation technique here to the use of a sequential solving. In this example, we suppose that among the N'' pairs, a pre-sieving on $S_{0,0}$ and $S_{0,2}$ has already been applied. If we want to advance sequentially further in the graph, we need to determine the key bits of $S_{0,0}$ and $S_{0,2}$ before solving $S_{1,0}$. Determining those key bits costs $2^{1.3} N''$, whilst the 2^{-1} filter from $S_{1,0}$ is only applied in a second step. On the other hand, if we use the precomputed list of solutions, we can directly compute the $N'' \cdot 2^{1.3} \cdot 2^{-1} = N'' \cdot 2^{0.3}$ solutions for a cost of $N'' \cdot 2^{0.3} < N'' \cdot 2^{1.3}$.

This example shows how the amount of memory complexity allowed can impact the complexity of the key recovery step. We invite the reader to use our tool on the toy cipher using different memory/offline time complexity constraints and to compare the results.

3.4   Computing in Parallel

An attacker can perform certain steps in parallel to improve the complexity of the attack. We give an example using the first step of the key recovery on the toy cipher. We consider the problem of solving in parallel $S_{6,2}$, $S_{6,3}$, $S_{5,1}$ and $S_{4,2}$ on one hand, and $S_{6,0}$, $S_{6,1}$ and $S_{5,0}$ on the other hand. This corresponds to the purple and green subgraphs in Fig. 3 respectively. Further, we consider that we have started our key recovery procedure by applying a pre-sieving on all S-boxes of the first and last round, leaving us with $N' = 2^{-5.63} \cdot N$ pairs.

---

[3] In fact, once divided by the cost of the toy cipher, the time complexity is smaller than $N'' \cdot 2^{0.3}$.

The Purple Subgraph. We begin by computing the remaining number of pairs after solving the S-boxes of the purple group. There are 2^6 solutions to $S_{6,2}$. Taking into account the sieving step, the number of triplets remaining after solving this S-box is thus $(2^{6+0.83}/2^6) \cdot N' = 2^{0.83} \cdot N' = 2^{-4.8} \cdot N$, and each triplet has a fixed value on the bits added at the input of $S_{6,2}$. Using the same reasoning, it follows that the number of pairs remaining after solving $S_{6,3}$ and $S_{5,1}$ is $2^{0.83+0.68} \cdot N'' = 2^{-4.12} \cdot N$. There are 2^4 solutions to $S_{4,2}$. After solving $S_{5,1}$, only 2 bits are fixed, and there are 2^4 possibilities for the remaining 2 bits. The filter obtained by solving $S_{4,2}$ is thus $(2^{4+4}/2^8) \cdot N = 1$. The number of solutions after solving the purple is thus $2^{-4.12} \cdot N$. This step can be done at a cost $2^{-4.12} \cdot N$ using precomputations using a memory 2^{16}.

The Green Subgraph. Using a similar reasoning, the number of pairs remaining after solving $S_{6,0}$ and $S_{6,1}$ is $2^{-4.12}N$. This fixes the 4 input bits to $S_{5,0}$, and thus the number of solutions remaining after solving $S_{5,0}$ is also $2^{-4.12} \cdot N$. Solving these S-boxes can also be done at a cost of $2^{-4.12} \cdot N$ using precomputations with a memory of 2^{12}.

Merging the Two Subgraphs. We now merge the solutions of the green group with those of the purple group. Solving the green group has fixed two output bits of $S_{5,0}$, whilst solving the purple group has fixed the same two input bits of $S_{4,2}$, but *after* the key addition. Thus, the probability that a solution of the purple group is also a solution to the green group is the probability that the difference on these two bits is equal. This probability is thus 2^{-2}. Further, each newly computed solution fixes the key bits. Thus, after merging the two subgraphs, the number of pairs remaining is $2^{-2+2\cdot0.83+2\cdot0.68} \cdot N' = 2^{-4.61} \cdot N$. This can be done at a cost of $2 \cdot 2^{-4.12} \cdot N$ (the size of each subgraph), by for example starting by solving the purple subgraph using pre-computed partial solutions to that subgraph and then merging the result with the pre-computed partial solutions of the green subgraph.

Using a sequential attack would have been less efficient here. For example, if one would have first solved $S_{6,0}$, $S_{6,1}$, $S_{6,2}$, $S_{6,3}$, $S_{5,0}$ and $S_{5,1}$ before solving $S_{4,2}$, then the cost of solving $S_{4,2}$ would have been about $2^{2\cdot0.83+2\cdot0.68} \cdot N'' = 2^{3.02} \cdot N' = 2^{-2.61} \cdot N$ (the number of solutions remaining after solving those S-boxes), which is strictly greater than the cost using parallelization.

4   Algorithm and Its Associated Tool

We provide in this section a description of our tool which captures an efficient key recovery strategy. We begin by presenting the algorithm, on which the tool is based, in a high-level manner. Then, we describe how we incorporate the techniques of Sect. 3. Finally, we give the parameters of the tool and discuss the limitations of our algorithm.

4.1   High-Level Description of Our Algorithm

Using the modelization described in Sect. 3.1 it is quite straightforward to describe an algorithm ready to be implemented. Given a distinguisher and a number of key recovery rounds, we start by identifying all active S-boxes involved in the key recovery. As they correspond to the nodes of the graph, we will sometimes denote them by *nodes* in this section. For each S-box, we compute its solutions, and compute the resulting filter as described in Sect. 3.2.

Then, our algorithm considers what we call *strategies*. Given a subgraph X, a strategy $\mathcal{S}_X$ for the subgraph X is a divide-and-conquer procedure that allows to enumerate all the possible values that the S-boxes of X can take under the differential constraints imposed by the distinguisher. The most important parameters of a strategy $\mathcal{S}_X$ are

- its *number of solutions*, which in fact does not depend on the strategy itself but only on the subgraph X;
- its *online time complexity*, that is, the average time complexity it takes to check whether an online pair is consistent with the differential constraints of the subgraph .

A strategy can be further refined with extra information such as the memory complexity and the offline time complexity needed to attain the online time complexity.

The output of the tool is an efficient *graph strategy*, *i.e.* a strategy for the whole graph. This strategy corresponds to an efficient algorithm associating to each online pair the key values that partially encrypt/decrypt this pair to the distinguisher differences. It is built using *basic strategies*, that is strategies for a single S-box. Given those basic strategies, and by incorporating the techniques of Sect. 3 as described in Sect. 4.2, the tool finds the most efficient order in which to combine all basic subgraphs, aiming to minimize the complexity of the resulting strategy. The algorithm is schematically described in Algorithm 1.

Comparing Strategies. To look for the best strategy, our tool must be able to compare them. It only makes sense to compare strategies for a common subgraph, at least initially. Considering a subgraph X, and two strategies $\mathcal{S}_X^1$ and $\mathcal{S}_X^2$ for X, these strategies necessarily possess the same number of solutions. To compare them, we thus compare their second parameter, that is, their time complexity. Of course, the best strategy has the lowest complexity. When taking into account the memory complexity, if two strategies have the same online time complexity, then the strategy with the lowest memory complexity is considered to be the best.

Merging Strategies. To build a global strategy from the basic ones, we must precisely define what is the complexity of the strategy $\mathcal{S}_{X \cup Y}$ obtained by merging together two strategies $\mathcal{S}_X$ and $\mathcal{S}_Y$. As the number of solutions of a subgraph strategy depends only on the subgraph, the number of solutions of $\mathcal{S}_{X \cup Y}$ only depends on $X \cup Y$. We evaluate this number of solutions by summing (assuming a logarithmic representation) the number of solutions of each node from $X \cup Y$, and by subtracting the number of bit-relations between these nodes, including relations obtained from the key schedule. Note that we restricted ourselves to linear key schedules and thus computing the relations between the round key bits involved in a strategy is as simple as computing the dimension of some vector space. The time and memory complexity are easily computed as follows:

- Time online/offline: $T(\mathcal{S}_{X \cup Y}) \approx \max(T(\mathcal{S}_X), T(\mathcal{S}_Y), Sol(\mathcal{S}_{X \cup Y}))$
- Memory: $M(\mathcal{S}_{X \cup Y}) \approx \max(M(\mathcal{S}_X), M(\mathcal{S}_Y), \min(Sol(\mathcal{S}_X), Sol(\mathcal{S}_Y)))$

This is because the actual procedure behind the combination of two strategies is to first run the one with the smallest number of solutions, store these solutions in a hash table indexed by the bit relations between the two subgraphs, run the second one, and look for matches into the hash table. Note that the *real* complexities of a strategy have to be multiplied by the number of S-boxes it enumerates, and thus the real formula we use is $T(\mathcal{S}_{X \cup Y}) \times |X \cup Y| \approx \max(T(\mathcal{S}_X) \times |X|, T(\mathcal{S}_Y) \times |Y|, Sol(\mathcal{S}_{X \cup Y}) \times |X \cup Y|)$. This formula is quite accurate since most often, optimal strategies are built from disjoint sub-strategies.

It is important at this point to notice that the online time complexity of a strategy resulting from a merge only depends on the time complexities of the two merging strategies. It comes that an optimal strategy can always be obtained by merging two optimal strategies: if a strategy for X (resp. Y) has the lowest online time complexity possible, then necessarily the maximum of these two values is also the lowest possible. Thus, the strategy for $X \cup Y$ obtained by merging these two strategies is necessarily the most efficient. This justifies using a bottom-up approach, merging first the strategies with the smallest time complexity to reach a graph strategy with a minimal time complexity. We can rely on dynamic programming-related techniques to ensure that, for any subgraph X, we only keep one optimal strategy to enumerate it. Furthermore, note that we can extend the cases in which two strategies can be compared. Indeed, if X contains Y and if the number of solutions of X is not higher than the number of solutions of Y, then we can freely replace any strategy for Y by a strategy for X as long as it has a better or similar time complexity.

While this reduces a lot the number of merges to perform, there are still, assuming n nodes, $\sum_{i=2}^{n} \binom{n}{i} \sum_{j=1}^{i-1} \binom{i}{j}$ merge combinations to try for, which is intractable. Thus, to limit the number of allowed merges, our tool only considers merges for which there is at least one bit relation between the two subgraphs. Graphically, this corresponds to the existence of at least one vertex between two nodes of the subgraph, or a common S-box. For instance, looking at Fig. 3, our tool does not allow the merge of $S_{1,0}$ together with $S_{0,1}$ since these two S-boxes are not related.

4.2   Taking into Account the Techniques of Section 3

It can be easily seen that the algorithm as described above already outputs strategies taking parallel computations into account. However, other techniques such as pre-sieving and precomputations require some adaptation.

Algorithm 1. Key recovery algorithm

$L_{done} \leftarrow \emptyset$
$L_{current} \leftarrow$ basic strategy for each node of the graph
while $L_{current} \neq \emptyset$ **do**
    Let S be the strategy from $L_{current}$ with the smallest time complexity
    for every S' in L_{done} allowed to be merged with S **do**
        Let S'' be the merge between S and S'
        if no strategy from L_{done} nor $L_{current}$ is similar or better than S'' **then**
            Update S'' for free (by merging with basic strategies)
            Remove from both L_{done} and $L_{current}$ all strategies worst than S''
            Add S'' to $L_{current}$
        end if
    end for
    Remove S from $L_{current}$ and add it to L_{done}
end while

Sieving. To take into account the sieving, the tool uses in practice a modelization that is slightly more complex than the one described so far where each S-box was seen as a single node. In this modelization, each S-box is fully described by *two* nodes. The first node corresponds to the sieving step on this S-box (it contains the sieving list defined in Sect. 3.2), whilst the second node contains the full S-box (i.e. all the solutions). Thus, a subgraph containing the sieving node but not the second node describes a step in the key recovery in which the attacker has performed a sieving on this S-box but does not want to enumerate its actual values to avoid increasing the number of solutions at this step of the key recovery. Note that to merge the second node to a subgraph, we require the sieving node to belong to this subgraph.

Precomputations. Our algorithm distinguishes between online and offline strategies. Online strategies depend on the data (their online time complexity is expressed as a coefficient that multiplies N), while offline ones do not (in fact, they do not possess an online time complexity). This attribute has one main effect regarding the merge of two strategies and slightly modifies the formula used to compute the inner complexities of the resulting one. Let S_X and S_Y be respectively an online and an offline strategy. The complexities of the strategy obtained by merging both of them, i.e. $S_{X \cup Y}$, are defined as follows:

- Time online: $T_{on}(S_{X \cup Y}) \approx \max(T_{on}(S_X), Sol(S_{X \cup Y}))$
- Time offline: $T_{off}(S_{X \cup Y}) \approx \max(T_{off}(S_X), T_{off}(S_Y))$
- Memory: $M(S_{X \cup Y}) \approx \max(M(S_X), M(S_Y), Sol(S_Y))$

In other words, in this particular scenario, the offline strategy is selected to be the one stored into the hash table while the solutions of the online strategy will be generated on the fly.

    The user can set an upper bound on the time spent offline and this bound can be higher than the bound for the online time (a feature that could be useful depending on the attack scenario the key recovery is a part of).

Restricting Merges. To decrease the number of merges to consider, we add an additional restriction on the allowed merges. Our idea is to force that a non-filtering node can be merged with an online strategy if and only if either the node is obtained for free (i.e. it does not increase the current number of solutions of the strategy) or it is computed by partially encrypting/decrypting the data. For instance, if $S_{1,2}$ was not filtering then we would not allow to merge $S_{0,1}$ with it, and only a strategy enumerating both $S_{0,1}$ and $S_{0,3}$ would be allowed to do so.

4.3   Parameters and Limitations

To provide the best key recovery strategy, our tool must take as input a description of the cipher and the distinguisher.

The Block Cipher. To describe the block cipher, the user must provide the specification of the S-box S, the bit-permutation P, the number of rounds n_R and the key schedule. Note that for now, only linear key schedules are allowed. For non-linear key schedules, the user can either replace $S(k)$ by a new variable (i.e. omitting the relation between k and $S(k)$) or replace it by $L(k)$ for a random invertible linear function L. These two options give the user an upper and a lower bound respectively on the complexity of the key recovery.

The Distinguisher. To specify the distinguisher, the user must provide the input difference δ_{in} and the output difference δ_{out} of the distinguisher, the number of key recovery rounds nr_p to prepend to the differential (plaintext side) and the number of key recovery rounds nr_c to append to the differential (ciphertext side). Note that for our tool, a round corresponds to the XOR of the round key to the state, the S-box layer and then the permutation layer, always taken in this exact order. Last but not least, if the attack is in the related-key model, the attacker must specify the difference on each round key.

An Option to Control the Propagation. The user can optionally specify some differential constraints on the last S-box transition preceding the distinguisher. This can be done by specifying a difference on some or all bits at the input of the last S-box application before entering the distinguisher. Similarly, the user can optionally specify a difference on some or all bits at the output of the first S-box after the distinguisher. This is a way for the attacker to be able to control part of the propagation if they wish to do so.

The above parameters are given as input to the program in the form of a .txt file containing a very simple description of the above parameters.

Constraints on the Precomputation. Finally, the program allows for optional constraints on the memory complexity and on the offline time complexity in a precomputation phase. This is done thanks to options specified during the execution, as described in the README.md file that can be found in the git repository of our tool.

An Option to Accelerate the Search. Our tool can be used either to find the most efficient key recovery strategy using the maximum amount of memory and or precomputation specified by the user or simply to find a key recovery strategy that has complexity under a given security parameter, to verify whether there is an attack that exists. While the tool is in general very efficient, in some cases, when several key recovery rounds are appended, the running time could be too high. In this case, using a particular option specified in the above mentioned README.md file, permits the user to quickly check whether an attack exists, without asking the tool to find the most efficient key recovery strategy.

Minimizing the Memory Complexity. We have described up to now only parallel merges, in which the memory depends on the smallest number of solutions between the two strategies involved in the combination. However, let X, Y and Z be 3 subgraphs and assume we have access to a strategy for each of them. If the optimal strategy, in terms of time complexity, to enumerate $X \cup Y \cup Z$ requires to merge $S_{X \cup Y}$ and $S_{X \cup Z}$, it might be interesting to construct both of them with *sequential* merges to minimize the memory complexity. In other words, we would like to first enumerate all the possible values for X and then, for each of them, compute the possible values for both Y and Z in parallel and after that look for matches. This might be very efficient to reduce the memory complexity of the final strategy. However, doing so makes the search for the best strategy much harder, especially since the order in which merges were performed inside a strategy does matter for future merges, forbidding to use an approach based on dynamic programming. Thus we do not optimize on the memory complexity and only keep at most one strategy per subgraph. Still, among the strategies constructed during the search procedure, we will always keep the ones minimizing the memory complexity.

Parallel Matching Algorithms. In several key recovery procedure, like in [14] and in [12], a complex algorithm for efficiently matching partial solutions that were computed in parallel is used: the parallel matching [15,27] permits to find with an efficient complexity the total number of solutions with respect to non-linear relations. Actually, this technique can be seen as a merge of three strategies in one step while we only described how to merge two strategies. We did not take this technique into account for two reasons. First, it would make the search space much bigger since the number of possible combinations increases exponentially. Second, when the third strategy is composed of two sub-strategies (which is the case for all of them but the basic ones enumerating a single S-box), we experimentally found that merging them 2 by 2 always led to the same overall time complexity (though usually to higher memory needs). Additionally, in the remaining case of a third strategy enumerating a single S-box or its associated filter, the gain over our merging process is marginal, due to both the small number of solutions enumerated and the small filter that basic strategies offer. Still, it would be a nice future work to identify precisely the cases in which we should switch to the parallel matching technique instead of the simple merge procedure.

Accuracy of the Complexity. In order to evaluate the complexity of a given strategy, we need to be able to compute the number of solutions outputted by each sub-strategy it is composed of. This is a difficult problem in general as it corresponds to the evaluation of the number of solutions of a complex polynomial system over $\mathbb{F}_2$. Thus we use the common assumption that a system of n linearly independent polynomial equations involving m variables on $\mathbb{F}_2$ has approximately 2^{m-n} solutions. Taking into account that the non-linear part of the polynomial equations all come from the S-boxes involved in the target cipher, that all the S-boxes are permutations and that the number of pairs on which is performed the key recovery is most often much higher than the size of the S-boxes, this assumption should hold in most scenario. Actually the same one was for instance used in [10] in which the authors verified its accuracy on some examples involving the AES S-box.

We provide a comparison with previous works in the full version of our article [11].

5 Applications

We describe the application of our tool to four block ciphers: RECTANGLE, GIFT-64, PRESENT-80 and SPEEDY-7-192. The three first ones have a bit-permutation as linear layer, whilst SPEEDY has two types of linear operations: a bit-permutation and a more complex one, represented by a matrix multiplication. However, this second operation is not involved in the key recovery rounds of the attack we are going to analyze. Thus, our tool can still be applied to it. SPEEDY and GIFT, have a linear key schedule, whilst PRESENT and RECTANGLE do not. Since our tool does not handle non-linear schedules, we apply it to PRESENT by replacing the S-box involved in the key schedule by a randomly generated matrix. Then, we verified by hand that the proposed attack still worked with the original key schedule of PRESENT as there is only a single S-box application per round. For RECTANGLE, as the key schedule is more complex, we consider that all round keys are independent.

The four applications we considered demonstrate the applicability of our tool to primitives with different characteristics. Once a differential distinguisher is provided, it is very easy to determine the highest number of rounds that can be attacked by trying different configurations for the key recovery rounds. This allowed us to mount a 19-round differential attack on RECTANGLE-128 with a differential distinguisher provided by the designers [38], while designers as well as cryptanalysts who improved this same attack [13] missed this possible extension and stopped at 18 rounds. While it has been shown in [4] that the underlying differential distinguisher is only valid for half of the keys, our application still demonstrates the facility of our tool to check for the existence of attacks on any number of rounds once a differential distinguisher is given. It will be easily applied if better valid distinguishers are provided in the future for this cipher. For PRESENT, differential attacks are not the best existing attacks. On the other hand, the differential attack of Wang [36] on 16-round PRESENT-80 has been known for more than 15 years now and has not been significantly improved since. We show here that using the same differential distinguisher with an improved efficient key recovery strategy, one can mount an attack on two extra rounds. This result was very easy to find by simply applying our tool for all relevant configurations of the key recovery rounds. The particular case of GIFT is very interesting, and a comparison with previous attacks will be described in detail. Finally, for SPEEDY we slightly improve the complexity of the key-recovery part of the attack in [12] by launching the tool on this cipher and analyzing the produced key recovery graph. This only took one second to the tool, while the authors of [12] found the key recovery strategy by hand through a very tedious procedure.

For each application, we briefly provide the specification of the cipher as well as the previous best known differential attack on it. In each case, we keep the same differential distinguisher as the one given in the original cryptanalysis papers. Indeed, our goal is not to improve the differential search step, but to ameliorate the key recovery procedure (or at least to find an equivalent one effortlessly). We will present our different applications. The graph produced for each attack can be visualized on the Git repository we provide. The complexity of the key recovery step for each analyzed cipher is summarized in Table 1.

Table 1. Summary of the previous best attacks, and of how our results impact them, on RECTANGLE, PRESENT-80, SPEEDY-7-192 and GIFT-64. C_{KR} corresponds to the cost of the key recovery, while T represents the total time complexity of the attack. *The complexities in the attack on SPEEDY are given with the cost of one encryption as unit, that is estimated to 2^7. We use the same unit here. †These attacks are in the related-key model.

Cipher	# Rounds	N	$N \times C_{KR}$	T	Ref
RECTANGLE-80	18	$2^{50.83}$	$N \cdot 2^{27.84}$	$2^{78.67}$	[38]
RECTANGLE-80	18	$2^{50.83}$	$N \cdot 2^{13.27}$	2^{64}	[13]
RECTANGLE-80	18	$2^{50.83}$	$N \cdot 2^{19}$	$2^{69.83}$	Section 5.2
RECTANGLE-128	19	$2^{78.83}$	$N \cdot 2^{43}$	$2^{121.83}$	Section 5.2
PRESENT-80	16	2^{28}	N	2^{65}	[36]
PRESENT-80	18	2^{58}	$N \cdot 2$	2^{59}	Section 5.3
SPEEDY-7-192*	7	$2^{190.32}$	$N \cdot 2^{2.83}$	$2^{187.84}$	[12]
SPEEDY-7-192*	7	$2^{190.32}$	N	$2^{187.38}$	Section 5.5
GIFT-64†	26	$2^{115.96}$	$N \cdot 2^{7.27}$	$2^{123.23}$	[32]
GIFT-64†	26	$2^{115.96}$	N	$2^{115.96}$	Section 5.4

5.1 Validity and Experiments

We applied our tool to differential distinguishers that have been described in the literature for the different ciphers to show how much our tool can improve previous key recoveries. We also verified by hand the key recovery of the new attacks given in Table 1. More precisely, we checked that the strategies outputted by our tool are coherent (e.g. no missing nodes, realistic costs, ...) and then we computed by hand the number of solutions at each step of the process as we did in Sect. 3 for the toy example. For concision reasons, we do not include these descriptions in this work.

We also emphasize that we did not check whether the theoretical probabilities of the distinguishers match the experimental ones as this was out of scope for the current work. Therefore, our attacks (and actually all differential attacks in the literature) can be considered as valid only under the assumption that the underlying distinguishers are valid themselves. In particular, Beyne and Rijmen showed that the differential characteristic used in the attack against RECTANGLE-80 only holds for at most half of the keys [4]. The recent work of Peyrin and Tan [28] also suggests that the differential characteristics used in other lightweight ciphers should be carefully checked.

5.2   RECTANGLE

RECTANGLE is a block cipher designed by Zhang, Bao, Lin, Rijmen, Yang and Verbauwhede in 2015 [38]. It is based on an SPN construction and uses a state of 64 bits. The state can be seen as a concatenation of 16 nibbles. The round function consists of an XOR with the round key, the application of a 4-bit S-box in parallel to each nibble of the state and a bit-permutation that plays the role of the linear layer. The round function is iterated 25 times. The key of RECTANGLE can be 80-bit or 128-bit long. We do not describe the key schedule here as we consider all subkeys to be independent.

The Differential Attack of [38]. The designers of RECTANGLE described a differential attack on 18-round RECTANGLE for both versions of the cipher. This attack is based on a 14-round differential distinguisher of probability $2^{-62.83}$. Two key recovery rounds are added on both sides (see Fig. 2 for the propagation of the differences). This attack has a data complexity of 2^{64}, a time complexity of $2^{78.67}$ and a memory complexity of 2^{72} key counters. An improvement of the time complexity of the original attack was however later given in [13]. In this last article, the authors used several advanced techniques, such as the "tree-based graphs" and the key-absorption technique, which allowed them to improve the time complexity to 2^{64} in a non-automated, very technical and hard to verify way. While we would have liked to reach the same complexity, this example shows that our tool can only be beaten by using very sophisticated techniques and permit to researchers to focus on them. Note however, that Beyne and Rijmen showed in [4] that the distinguisher on which both the attacks of [38] and [13] are based is valid for at most half of the keys only.

Application of Our Tool. We applied our tool to RECTANGLE by adding 2 key recovery rounds in both directions as done in the original attack of [38]. As the probability of the distinguisher is $2^{-p} = 2^{-62.83}$, the data complexity of the

Table 2. Differential attack on $(14+x)$-round `RECTANGLE` based on the 14-round distinguisher from [38], where $x \in 4, 5$. ΔI_r and ΔO_r are respectively the states before and after the S-box layer of round r. The symbol '.' stands for a non-active bit, '1' for an active bit, and '*' stands for a bit with an unknown difference. Finally, '0' corresponds to a bit with 0 difference but whose value needs to be known for the key-recovery.

S-box	15	14	13	12	11	10	9	8	7	6	5	4	3	2	1	0
ΔI_{r-3}	****	****	****	****	****	****	****		****	****	*11*	0000	****	****		****
ΔO_{r-3}	**0*	***.	*...	...*	.***	*1**	*.*.	....	...*	..**	..1.	.0..	0*..	*...	....	.*.0
ΔI_{r-2}	****			****	****	****			****	*11*						0000
ΔO_{r-2}	*			...*	.1*	*			...*	..1						.0
ΔI_{r-1}				*0**					*11*							
ΔO_{r-1}				.11					..1							
ΔI_r			..1					.11								
14-round distinguisher																
ΔI_{r+14}				.1											..1	
ΔO_{r+14}				**11											****	
ΔI_{r+15}		*	.*1	...1			*	.*					.*		...*	
ΔO_{r+15}		****	****	**1*			****	****					****		****	
ΔI_{r+16}	*.*	****	.*1*	...*	..*	*.**	****	.*.*		*	*.*	*	..*	.**	...*	
ΔO_{r+16}	****	****	****	****	****	****	****	****		****	****	****	****	****	****	

attack is $\mathcal{D} = 2^{p+1} = 2^{63.83}$. The number of pairs can be computed based on the related spaces D_{in} and D_{out} (see Sect. 2). For the 18-round attack, $d_{in} = 24$ and $d_{out} = 28$. Thus, by using the encryption oracle, we can form $2^{p+d_{in}} = 2^{86.83}$ pairs, and among them $N = 2^{p+d_{in}-(n-d_{out})} = 2^{50.83}$ should survive the filtering by the ciphertext difference. Our tool outputted a complexity for the key recovery phase equal to $N \cdot 2^{19} = 2^{69.83}$. This is the dominant term in the complexity of our attack, yet, it is much lower than the complexity of the key recovery in the original attack of [38]. As the execution of the tool for the above instance was very fast, we decided to test whether this distinguisher could be extended to more rounds in each direction. Thus, we tried to prepend one more round at the beginning or to append one more round at the end, or both. The propagation of the differences is shown in Table 2. In this table, round r is the round on which the differential starts. For the attack of [38] with 2 prepended rounds $r = 2$, while if we prepend 3 rounds then $r = 3$.

Table 3 summarizes the results. The best configuration for a concrete total number of rounds is shown in blue. We see for example, that when adding 2 key recovery rounds at the beginning and 3 at the end, it is possible to obtain a valid attack on `RECTANGLE-128`. Indeed, in this case $d_{in} = 52$, $d_{out} = 28$, so $N = 2^{p+d_{in}-(n-d_{out})} = 2^{78.83}$. For this configuration, the tool returned a key recovery complexity of 2^{43}. This complexity is optimal in the sense that it corresponds to the number of expected solutions. This gives an attack with time complexity $2^{78.83+43} = 2^{121.83}$, which is smaller than the exhaustive search for the 128-bit key version. This would lead to the first attack on `RECTANGLE-128` reaching 19 rounds in the single-key setting if there would have been no problem with the differential distinguisher. As can be seen from Table 3 we also launched the tool with three added key recovery rounds in both directions, but the returned complexity of 2^{70} was too high to lead to a valid attack.

Table 3. Summary of the results on RECTANGLE. The column C_{KR} corresponds to the cost of the key recovery given by our tool and should be multiplied by the number of pairs N. If $(N \cdot C_{KR}) < 80$ then we get a valid attack against both versions of RECTANGLE. If furthermore $(N \cdot C_{KR}) < 128$, then we obtain a valid attack against RECTANGLE-128. Best attacks are highlighted in blue.

Cipher	nr_p	nr_c	#Rounds $(14 + nr_p + nr_c)$	d_{in}	d_{out}	N $(2^{p+d_{in}+d_{out}-n})$	C_{KR} $(\cdot N)$	Valid attack
RECTANGLE-80	2	2	18	24	28	$2^{50.83}$	2^{19}	✓
RECTANGLE-128	2	3	19	24	56	$2^{78.83}$	2^{46}	✓
RECTANGLE-128	3	2	19	52	28	$2^{78.83}$	2^{43}	✓
RECTANGLE-128	3	3	20	52	56	$2^{106.83}$	2^{70}	✗

5.3   PRESENT

The PRESENT block cipher was designed by Bogdanov, Knudsen, Leander, Paar, Poschmann, Robshaw, Seurin and Vikkelsoe in 2007 [9]. Similar to RECTANGLE, it uses a 64-bit state where the state can be seen as a concatenation of 16 nibbles. Its round function also consists of an XOR with the round key, the application of a 4-bit S-box in parallel to the state and a bit-permutation. The round function is iterated 31 times with a final whitening subkey. PRESENT supports keys of 80 or 128 bits. We provide the key schedule of PRESENT-80 together with the description of the other components of the cipher in [11].

The best attacks on PRESENT are linear attacks reaching 28 rounds [20] and 29 rounds [19] on the 80-bit and 128-bit versions respectively. To illustrate the efficiency of our tool, we consider here the best known differential attacks. Indeed, PRESENT is a very interesting example as it shows that our tool can be efficient with not only linear but almost linear key schedules. To analyze PRESENT, we considered an alternative linear key schedule. We replaced the S-box by a matrix multiplication with a randomly generated non-singular matrix in $\mathcal{M}_4(\mathbb{F}_2)$. Once the tool found an efficient key recovery strategy, we adapted the attack to the real key schedule of PRESENT, and verified our result by hand.

The Differential Attack of [36]. In 2007, Wang presented a differential attack against 16-round PRESENT-80. This attack was based on the 14-round differential distinguisher

$$0700\ 0000\ 0000\ 0700 \longrightarrow_{14r} 0000\ 0009\ 0000\ 0009,$$

of probability 2^{-62}. Two rounds were appended to this distinguisher on the ciphertext side. This led to an attack with data complexity 2^{64} and time complexity of 2^{65} (measured in number of memory accesses).[4]

We applied our tool to PRESENT-80 with this distinguisher and tried different configurations for the key recovery rounds. More precisely, we tried to append up to 4 rounds to the end and to prepend at most 4 rounds in the beginning. The propagation of the differences is shown in Fig. 4. As before, in this table, r is the round number on which the differential starts. For the original attack of Wang with 0 prepended rounds $r = 0$, while if we prepend 1 round (resp. 2 or 3 rounds), $r = 1$ (resp. $r = 2, 3$). The state before the S-boxes application of round r is denoted by ΔI_r, while that after the S-boxes and before the linear layer is denoted by ΔO_r.

Table 4. Differential attack on $(14 + x)$-round PRESENT based on the 14-round distinguisher from [36]. ΔI_r and ΔO_r are respectively the states before the S-box layer of round r. The symbol '.' stands for a non-active bit, '1' for an active bit, and '*' stands for a bit with an unknown difference (active of inactive). Finally, '0' corresponds to a bit with 0 difference but whose value needs to be known for the key recovery.

S-box	15	14	13	12	11	10	9	8	7	6	5	4	3	2	1	0
ΔI_{r-4}	****	****	****	****	****	****	****	****	****	****	****	****	****	****	****	****
ΔO_{r-4}	****	****	****	****	****	****	****	****	****	****	****	****	****	****	****	****
ΔI_{r-3}	****	****	****	****	****	****	****	****	****	****	****	****	****	****	****	****
ΔO_{r-3}	.***	.***	.***	.***	.***	.***	.***	.***	.***	.***	.***	.***	.***	.***	.***	.***
ΔI_{r-2}					****	****	****	****	****	****	****	****	****	****	****	****
ΔO_{r-2}					*	*	*	*	*	*	*	*	*	*	*	*
ΔI_{r-1}					****	****	****									
ΔO_{r-1}					1..1	1..1	1..1									
ΔI_r		.111												.111		
14-round distinguisher																
ΔI_{r+14}							1..1									1..1
ΔO_{r+14}							***0									***0
ΔI_{r+15}		...*		...*		...*		...*		...*		...*		...0		...0
ΔO_{r+15}		****		****		****		****		****		****		0000		0000
ΔI_{r+16}	.*.*	.*.*	.*.*	.0.0	.*.*	.*.*	.*.*	.0.0	.*.*	.*.*	.*.*	.0.0	.*.*	.*.*	.*.*	.0.0
ΔO_{r+16}	****	****	****	0000	****	****	****	0000	****	****	****	0000	****	****	****	0000
ΔI_{r+17}	***0	***0	***0	***0	***0	***0	***0	***0	***0	***0	***0	***0	***0	***0	***0	***0
ΔO_{r+17}	****	****	****	****	****	****	****	****	****	****	****	****	****	****	****	****
ΔI_{r+18}	****	****	****	****	****	****	****	****	****	****	****	****	****	****	****	****
ΔO_{r+18}	****	****	****	****	****	****	****	****	****	****	****	****	****	****	****	****

For all the relevant configurations we first computed the number of pairs based on the related spaces D_{in} and D_{out} (see Sect. 2). Then, we launched the

---

[4] Tezcan claimed later in [34] that there were errors in the key recovery procedure, providing a corrected attack for the same number of rounds with the same distinguisher.

tool with this number of pairs to see if a solution was found. As for most of the configurations the execution took a few seconds only, it was easy to automatically test all the attack scenarios. For the configuration with $nr_p = 4$ and $nr_c = 0$ the execution was slow so we ran the tool with the option - time x, for x the smallest value such that $\log_2(N) + x \geq 80$. This option allows to search only for attacks with time complexity $\leq N \cdot 2^x$ and greatly accelerates the research. This permitted us to check that there was no valid attack in this setting. We also checked all configurations that would permit to reach an attack on 19 rounds of PRESENT-80 for this distinguisher and confirmed that it is not possible to obtain a valid attack on this number of rounds.

Parameters and Complexities of the Attacks. For all the attacks, as the probability of the distinguisher is $2^{-p} = 2^{-62}$, the data complexity is $2^{p+1} = 2^{63}$ according to the formulas of Sect. 2. For each configuration (number of nr_p prepended rounds and nr_c appended rounds), we determine the number of initial pairs N the attack should start with and provide the complexity given by the tool. For the notation of the parameters, we refer to Sect. 2.

Our results against PRESENT-80 are summarized in Table 5.

Table 5. Summary of the results on PRESENT-80. The column C_{KR} corresponds to the cost of the key recovery given by our tool and should be multiplied by the number of pairs N. An attack against PRESENT-80 is valid if the complexity of the key recovery is lower than 2^{80}. The best attacks are highlighted in blue.

Cipher	nr_p	nr_c	#Rounds $(14 + nr_p + nr_c)$	d_{in}	d_{out}	N $(2^{p+d_{in}+d_{out}-n})$	C_{KR} $(\cdot N)$	Valid attack
PRESENT-80	0	2	16	6	24	2^{28}	1	✓
PRESENT-80	0	3	17	6	48	2^{52}	1	✓
PRESENT-80	1	2	17	12	24	2^{34}	2^4	✓
PRESENT-80	2	1	17	48	6	2^{52}	2^8	✓
PRESENT-80	3	0	17	64	4	2^{62}	$2^{10.62}$	✓
PRESENT-80	0	4	18	6	64	2^{68}	$> 2^{12}$	✗
PRESENT-80	1	3	18	12	48	2^{58}	2^1	✓
PRESENT-80	2	2	18	48	24	2^{70}	1	✓
PRESENT-80	3	1	18	64	6	2^{68}	2^9	✓
PRESENT-80	4	0	18	64	4	2^{66}	$> 2^{14}$	✗

As can be seen from Table 5 we managed to extend the previous best differential attack on PRESENT-80 by 2 rounds. Notably for 18 rounds, the complexity of the key recovery stage given by our tool is $C_{KR} = 2^{59}$. In this case, as only 1 round is appended in the beginning, and as the 3 active input S-boxes are continuous, the attack applies directly to the real key schedule, so to PRESENT-80 with

18 rounds. By guessing one extra key bit, that then gets canceled out before the bottleneck of the process, we manage to recover all the key bits with the non-linear key schedule.

5.4 GIFT-64

GIFT-64 is a member of the GIFT family of lightweight block ciphers designed by Banik, Pandey, Peyrin, Sasaki, Sim and Todo [1]. It is a 64-bit block cipher with a 128-bit key and is composed of 28 rounds. It is a classical SPN cipher whose state can be divided into 16 nibbles. First, the round key is XORed to the state. A particularity of GIFT is that the key is only added to half of the state, and more precisely to all bits at position b such that $b = 0 \pmod 4$ or $b = 1 \pmod 4$. Then, a 4-bit S-box is applied in parallel to all nibbles of the state and this application is followed by a bit-permutation. The key schedule consists in a bit-permutation of the master key and is described together with the other components of the cipher in the long version of this article [11].

The Related-Key Differential Attack of [32]. Sun et al. provided a differential attack on 26 rounds of GIFT-64 in the related-key setting. This attack was based on a 18-round related-key differential distinguisher of probability $2^{-p} = 2^{-58}$:

$$0000\ 6000\ 0000\ 0600 \longrightarrow_{18r} 0000\ 0014\ 0000\ 0041.$$

The difference on the 128-bit master key is taken to be as follows:[5]

$$0000\ 1400\ 0000\ 0000\ 0000\ 0000\ 0000\ 0000.$$

The authors prepended 3 key recovery rounds in the beginning and appended 5 key recovery rounds at the end to mount an attack with data, time and memory complexities equal to $\mathcal{D} = 2^{60.96}, \mathcal{T} = 2^{123.23}, \mathcal{M} = 2^{102.86}$. The differential propagation on the key recovery rounds can be visualized in Table 6.

Application of Our Tool and Comparison with the Attack of [32]. Using the same distinguisher and attack parameters as in [32], our tool outputted a key recovery strategy of complexity $N = 2^{115.96}$, that is also the global complexity of the attack. This strategy improved thus the attack of [32] by a factor of $2^{7.27}$. Based on the same setup, the work of [14] improved the complexity of the attack of [32] with a very tedious procedure. It is important to note that while this attack uses refined techniques such as tree-based key recovery techniques and key absorption from [13], our tool was able to derive a more efficient procedure.

---

[5] Note that in [32] the least significant bit (LSB) was taken on the left, contrary to the original cipher's description [1]. Here, we stick to the original notation and place the LSB on the right.

Table 6. Differential attack on 26-round `GIFT-24` based on the 18-round related-key distinguisher from [32].

S-box	15	14	13	12	11	10	9	8	7	6	5	4	3	2	1	0
ΔI_0	****	****	****	****	****	****	****	****	****	****	****	****	****	****	****	****
ΔO_0	****	****	****	****	1***	11**	*1**	****	*1**	****	1***	11**	****	****	****	****
ΔI_1	****	****	11	****	****	****	11	****	****	11	****	****	****	11	****	****
ΔO_1	...*	1	.1	..*	...*	*	.1	..*	1	.1	..*	...*	*	.1	..*	...*
ΔI_2									11**	*1**					11**	*1**
ΔO_2									.1	..1					.1	..1
ΔI_3			.11									.11				
18-round related-key differential distinguisher																
ΔI_{21}	...1	.1							.1	...1						
ΔO_{21}	****	***1							***1	****						
ΔI_{22}	.**		.**		..*1		..**		*..*		*..1		**		**	
ΔO_{22}	****		****		****		****		****		****		****		****	
ΔI_{23}	.*.*	.*.*	.*.*	.*.*	.*.*	.*.*	.*.*	.*.*	.*.*	.*.*	.*.*	.*.*	.*.*	.*.*	.*.*	.*.*
ΔO_{23}	****	****	****	****	****	****	****	****	****	****	****	****	****	****	****	****
ΔI_{24}	****	****	****	****	****	****	****	****	****	****	****	****	****	****	****	****
ΔO_{24}	****	****	****	****	****	****	****	****	****	****	****	****	****	****	****	****
ΔI_{25}	****	****	****	****	****	****	****	****	****	****	****	****	****	****	****	****
ΔO_{25}	****	****	****	****	****	****	****	****	****	****	****	****	****	****	****	****

5.5   Application to SPEEDY-7-192

SPEEDY-7-192 is a member of the `SPEEDY` family of low-latency block ciphers introduced by Leander, Moos, Moradi and Rasoolzadeh at CHES 2021 [24]. Last year, a differential attack on the full version of `SPEEDY-7-192` was published [12]. This attack exploited a 5.5-round differential of probability $2^{-p} = 2^{-183.59}$ that was extended to one round backwards and half a round forwards. The key recovery in [12] was done by hand, requiring a particularly tedious procedure. We decided to launch our tool on this cipher, keeping the same parameters as in [12], in order to show the applicability of our tool on a different cipher and to see if the key recovery complexity could be improved. Note however that in a very recent note [3], subsequent to ours, the authors claim that the distinguisher used is not valid due to the existence of quasidifferentials cancelling the probability. Our tool outputted a complexity for the key recovery phase equal to N improving thus by a factor of $2^{2.83}$ the key recovery complexity of [12]. As this term was not the bottleneck of the attack, the improvement in the overall time complexity is small: $2^{0.5}$. This application shows however that our tool can complete in a few seconds a procedure that would be extremely long by hand. Our tool will be automatically applicable to any new and valid differential distinguisher that gets presented for this cipher in the future. More details can be found in the long version of our article [11].

6   Conclusion and Open Problems

In this paper, we have proposed a new algorithm (and an automatic tool that implements it) to find efficient key recovery strategies in differential attacks. This permitted us to find efficient key recovery strategies for the attacks on many ciphers. We believe that our tool, which will be publicly available, will be of great help to cryptanalysts, but also to designers, as it will assist them in mounting attacks and in choosing optimal parameters for their construction.

We believe that the proposed tool is the first step towards a fully automated treatment of differential attacks. Many extensions and improvements can be considered. Indeed, our tool can for the moment only handle block ciphers with a bit-permutation linear layer and a linear or almost-linear key schedule. A natural extension is to adapt the tool such that it applies to ciphers with more complex linear layers, based for example on an MDS multiplication. Another improvement would be to adapt the tool to ciphers with non-linear key schedules as currently, our tool needs the user to either linearise non-linear key schedules or replace non-linear equations with new variables. Another interesting direction is to adapt the tool to take into account tree-based key recovery techniques by exploiting the structure of the involved S-boxes, as those proposed in [13].

Finally, the ultimate goal would be to combine this tool with algorithms that search for differential distinguishers to propose a complete tool for differential cryptanalysis that would produce attacks based on differential distinguishers that are the best adapted for the key recovery. This is a challenging but particularly important task, as it is known that the best distinguisher does not always lead to the best attack.

Acknowledgements. This research is partially supported through the France 2030 program under grant agreement No. ANR-22-PECY-0010, by the French Agence Nationale de la Recherche through the OREO project under Contract ANR-22-CE39-0015 and the SWAP project under Contract ANR-21-CE39-0012 and it has been partially funded by the European Union (ERC-2023-COG, SoBaSyC, 101125450). Views and opinions expressed are however those of the author(s) only and do not necessarily reflect those of the European Union or the European Research Council Executive Agency. Neither the European Union nor the granting authority can be held responsible for them.

References

1. Banik, S., Pandey, S.K., Peyrin, T., Sasaki, Yu., Sim, S.M., Todo, Y.: GIFT: a small present - towards reaching the limit of lightweight encryption. In: Fischer, W., Homma, N. (eds.) CHES 2017. LNCS, vol. 10529, pp. 321–345. Springer, Cham (2017). https://doi.org/10.1007/978-3-319-66787-4_16
2. Beierle, C., et al.: Improved differential-linear attacks with applications to ARX ciphers. J. Cryptol. **35**(4), 29 (2022)
3. Beyne, T., Neyt, A.: Note on the cryptanalysis of speedy. Cryptology ePrint Archive, Paper 2024/262 (2024). https://eprint.iacr.org/2024/262

4. Beyne, T., Rijmen, V.: Differential cryptanalysis in the fixed-key model. In: Dodis, Y., Shrimpton, T. (eds.) CRYPTO 2022, Part III. LNCS, vol. 13509, pp. 687–716. Springer, Cham (2022). https://doi.org/10.1007/978-3-031-15982-4_23

5. Biham, E., Shamir, A.: Differential cryptanalysis of DES-like cryptosystems. In: Menezes, A.J., Vanstone, S.A. (eds.) CRYPTO 1990. LNCS, vol. 537, pp. 2–21. Springer, Heidelberg (1991). https://doi.org/10.1007/3-540-38424-3_1

6. Biham, E., Shamir, A.: Differential cryptanalysis of feal and N-hash. In: Davies, D.W. (ed.) EUROCRYPT 1991. LNCS, vol. 547, pp. 1–16. Springer, Heidelberg (1991). https://doi.org/10.1007/3-540-46416-6_1

7. Biham, E., Shamir, A.: Differential cryptanalysis of Snefru, Khafre, REDOC-II, LOKI and Lucifer. In: Feigenbaum, J. (ed.) CRYPTO 1991. LNCS, vol. 576, pp. 156–171. Springer, Heidelberg (1992). https://doi.org/10.1007/3-540-46766-1_11

8. Biham, E., Shamir, A.: Differential cryptanalysis of the full 16-round DES. In: Brickell, E.F. (ed.) CRYPTO 1992. LNCS, vol. 740, pp. 487–496. Springer, Heidelberg (1993). https://doi.org/10.1007/3-540-48071-4_34

9. Bogdanov, A., et al.: PRESENT: an ultra-lightweight block cipher. In: Paillier, P., Verbauwhede, I. (eds.) CHES 2007. LNCS, vol. 4727, pp. 450–466. Springer, Heidelberg (2007). https://doi.org/10.1007/978-3-540-74735-2_31

10. Bouillaguet, C., Derbez, P., Fouque, P.-A.: Automatic search of attacks on round-reduced AES and applications. In: Rogaway, P. (ed.) CRYPTO 2011. LNCS, vol. 6841, pp. 169–187. Springer, Heidelberg (2011). https://doi.org/10.1007/978-3-642-22792-9_10

11. Boura, C., David, N., Derbez, P., Heim Boissier, R., Naya-Plasencia, M.: A generic algorithm for efficient key recovery in differential attacks - and its associated tool. Cryptology ePrint Archive, Paper 2024/288 (2024). https://eprint.iacr.org/2024/288

12. Boura, C., David, N., Heim Boissier, R., Naya-Plasencia, M.: Better steady than speedy: full break of SPEEDY-7-192. In: Hazay, C., Stam, M. (eds.) EUROCRYPT 2023, Part IV. LNCS, vol. 14007, pp. 36–66. Springer, Cham (2023). https://doi.org/10.1007/978-3-031-30634-1_2

13. Broll, M., Canale, F., Flórez-Gutiérrez, A., Leander, G., Naya-Plasencia, M.: Generic framework for key-guessing improvements. In: Tibouchi, M., Wang, H. (eds.) ASIACRYPT 2021. LNCS, vol. 13090, pp. 453–483. Springer, Cham (2021). https://doi.org/10.1007/978-3-030-92062-3_16

14. Canale, F., Naya-Plasencia, M.: Guessing less and better: improved attacks on GIFT-64. IACR Cryptology ePrint Archibe p. 354 (2023)

15. Canteaut, A., Naya-Plasencia, M., Vayssière, B.: Sieve-in-the-middle: improved MITM attacks. In: Canetti, R., Garay, J.A. (eds.) CRYPTO 2013. LNCS, vol. 8042, pp. 222–240. Springer, Heidelberg (2013). https://doi.org/10.1007/978-3-642-40041-4_13

16. Daemen, J., Rijmen, V.: The wide trail design strategy. In: Honary, B. (ed.) Cryptography and Coding 2001. LNCS, vol. 2260, pp. 222–238. Springer, Heidelberg (2001). https://doi.org/10.1007/3-540-45325-3_20

17. Derbez, P., Euler, M., Fouque, P., Nguyen, P.H.: Revisiting related-key boomerang attacks on AES using computer-aided tool. In: Agrawal, S., Lin, D. (eds.) ASIACRYPT 2022, Part III. LNCS, vol. 13793, pp. 68–88. Springer, Cham (2022). https://doi.org/10.1007/978-3-031-22969-5_3

18. Dong, X., Qin, L., Sun, S., Wang, X.: Key guessing strategies for linear key-schedule algorithms in rectangle attacks. In: Dunkelman, O., Dziembowski, S. (eds.) EUROCRYPT 2022, Part III. LNCS, vol. 13277, pp. 3–33. Springer, Cham (2022). https://doi.org/10.1007/978-3-031-07082-2_1

19. Flórez-Gutiérrez, A.: Optimising linear key recovery attacks with affine Walsh transform pruning. In: Agrawal, S., Lin, D. (eds.) ASIACRYPT 2022, Part IV. LNCS, vol. 13794, pp. 447–476. Springer, Cham (2022). https://doi.org/10.1007/978-3-031-22972-5_16

20. Flórez-Gutiérrez, A., Naya-Plasencia, M.: Improving key-recovery in linear attacks: application to 28-round PRESENT. In: Canteaut, A., Ishai, Y. (eds.) EURO-CRYPT 2020, Part I. LNCS, vol. 12105, pp. 221–249. Springer, Cham (2020). https://doi.org/10.1007/978-3-030-45721-1_9

21. Fouque, P.-A., Jean, J., Peyrin, T.: [Structural evaluation of , and chosen-key distinguisher of 9-round AES-128. In: Canetti, R., Garay, J.A. (eds.) CRYPTO 2013, Part I. LNCS, vol. 8042, pp. 183–203. Springer, Heidelberg (2013). https://doi.org/10.1007/978-3-642-40041-4_11

22. Hadipour, H., Sadeghi, S., Eichlseder, M.: Finding the impossible: automated search for full impossible-differential, zero-correlation, and integral attacks. In: Hazay, C., Stam, M. (eds.) EUROCRYPT 2023, Part IV. LNCS, vol. 14007, pp. 128–157. Springer, Cham (2023). https://doi.org/10.1007/978-3-031-30634-1_5

23. Knellwolf, S., Meier, W., Naya-Plasencia, M.: Conditional differential cryptanalysis of NLFSR-based cryptosystems. In: Abe, M. (ed.) ASIACRYPT 2010. LNCS, vol. 6477, pp. 130–145. Springer, Heidelberg (2010). https://doi.org/10.1007/978-3-642-17373-8_8

24. Leander, G., Moos, T., Moradi, A., Rasoolzadeh, S.: The SPEEDY family of block ciphers engineering an ultra low-latency cipher from gate level for secure processor architectures. IACR Trans. Cryptogr. Hardw. Embed. Syst. 2021(4), 510–545 (2021)

25. Lu, J., Kim, J., Keller, N., Dunkelman, O.: Improving the efficiency of impossible differential cryptanalysis of reduced camellia and MISTY1. In: Malkin, T. (ed.) CT-RSA 2008. LNCS, vol. 4964, pp. 370–386. Springer, Heidelberg (2008). https://doi.org/10.1007/978-3-540-79263-5_24

26. Nageler, M.: Automatic cryptanlysis of block ciphers: finding efficient key-recovery attacks. Master's thesis, Graz University of Technology (2022). https://doi.org/10.3217/n8ehm-dgj71

27. Naya-Plasencia, M.: How to improve rebound attacks. In: Rogaway, P. (ed.) CRYPTO 2011. LNCS, vol. 6841, pp. 188–205. Springer, Heidelberg (2011). https://doi.org/10.1007/978-3-642-22792-9_11

28. Peyrin, T., Tan, Q.Q.: Mind your path: on (key) dependencies in differential characteristics. IACR Trans. Symmetric Cryptol. 2022(4), 179–207 (2022)

29. Qiao, K., Hu, L., Sun, S.: Differential security evaluation of Simeck with dynamic key-guessing techniques. In: Camp, O., Furnell, S., Mori, P. (eds.) ICISSP 2016, pp. 74–84. SciTePress (2016)

30. Qin, L., Dong, X., Wang, X., Jia, K., Liu, Y.: Automated search oriented to key recovery on ciphers with linear key schedule applications to boomerangs in SKINNY and ForkSkinny. IACR Trans. Symmetric Cryptol. 2021(2), 249–291 (2021)

31. Rouquette, L., Gérault, D., Minier, M., Solnon, C.: And Rijndael?: Automatic related-key differential analysis of Rijndael. In: Batina, L., Daemen, J. (eds.) AFRICACRYPT 2022. LNCS, vol. 13503, pp. 150–175. Springer, Cham (2022). https://doi.org/10.1007/978-3-031-17433-9_7

32. Sun, L., Wang, W., Wang, M.: Accelerating the search of differential and linear characteristics with the SAT method. IACR Trans. Symmetric Cryptol. 2021(1), 269–315 (2021)

33. Sun, S., Hu, L., Wang, P., Qiao, K., Ma, X., Song, L.: Automatic security evaluation and (related-key) differential characteristic search: application to SIMON, PRESENT, LBlock, DES(L) and other bit-oriented block ciphers. In: Sarkar, P., Iwata, T. (eds.) ASIACRYPT 2014, Part I. LNCS, vol. 8873, pp. 158–178. Springer, Heidelberg (2014). https://doi.org/10.1007/978-3-662-45611-8_9

34. Tezcan, C.: Differential factors revisited: corrected attacks on PRESENT and SERPENT. In: Güneysu, T., Leander, G., Moradi, A. (eds.) LightSec 2015. LNCS, vol. 9542, pp. 21–33. Springer, Cham (2016). https://doi.org/10.1007/978-3-319-29078-2_2

35. Vaudenay, S.: Decorrelation: a theory for block cipher security. J. Cryptol. **16**(4), 249–286 (2003)

36. Wang, M.: Differential cryptanalysis of reduced-round PRESENT. In: Vaudenay, S. (ed.) AFRICACRYPT 2008. LNCS, vol. 5023, pp. 40–49. Springer, Heidelberg (2008). https://doi.org/10.1007/978-3-540-68164-9_4

37. Wang, N., Wang, X., Jia, K., Zhao, J.: Differential attacks on reduced SIMON versions with dynamic key-guessing techniques. Sci. China Inf. Sci. **61**(9), 098103:1–098103:3 (2018)

38. Zhang, W., Bao, Z., Lin, D., Rijmen, V., Yang, B., Verbauwhede, I.: RECTANGLE: a bit-slice lightweight block cipher suitable for multiple platforms. Sci. China Inf. Sci. **58**(12), 1–15 (2015)

39. Zhao, B., Dong, X., Jia, K.: New related-tweakey boomerang and rectangle attacks on Deoxys-BC including BDT effect. IACR Trans. Symmetric Cryptol. **2019**(3), 121–151 (2019)

Tight Security of TNT and Beyond
Attacks, Proofs and Possibilities for the Cascaded LRW Paradigm

Ashwin Jha[1,2](✉) ⓘ, Mustafa Khairallah[3,4](✉) ⓘ, Mridul Nandi[5](✉) ⓘ,
and Abishanka Saha[5](✉) ⓘ

[1] Ruhr-Universität Bochum, Bochum, Germany
ashwin.jha@rub.de
[2] CISPA Helmholtz Center for Information Security, Saarbrücken, Germany
[3] Seagate Research Group, Singapore, Singapore
khairallah@ieee.org
[4] Lund University, Lund, Sweden
[5] Indian Statistical Institute, Kolkata, India
mridul.nandi@gmail.com, sahaa.1993@gmail.com

Abstract. Liskov, Rivest and Wagner laid the theoretical foundations for tweakable block ciphers (TBC). In a seminal paper, they proposed two (up to) birthday-bound secure design strategies — LRW1 and LRW2 — to convert any block cipher into a TBC. Several of the follow-up works consider cascading of LRW-type TBCs to construct beyond-the-birthday bound (BBB) secure TBCs. Landecker et al. demonstrated that just two-round cascading of LRW2 can already give a BBB security. Bao et al. undertook a similar exercise in context of LRW1 with TNT — a three-round cascading of LRW1 — that has been shown to achieve BBB security as well. In this paper, we present a CCA distinguisher on TNT that achieves a non-negligible advantage with $O(2^{n/2})$ queries, directly contradicting the security claims made by the designers. We provide a rigorous and complete advantage calculation coupled with experimental verification that further support our claim. Next, we provide new and simple proofs of birthday-bound CCA security for both TNT and its single-key variant, which confirm the tightness of our attack. Furthering on to a more positive note, we show that adding just one more block cipher call, referred as 4-LRW1, does not just re-establish the BBB security, but also amplifies it up to $2^{3n/4}$ queries. As a side-effect of this endeavour, we propose a new abstraction of the cascaded LRW-design philosophy, referred to as the LRW+ paradigm, comprising two block cipher calls sandwiched between a pair of tweakable universal hashes. This helps us to provide a modular proof covering all cascaded LRW constructions with at least 2 rounds, including 4-LRW1, and its more established relative, the well-known CLRW2, or more aptly, 2-LRW2.

Keywords: TNT · LRW1 · 4-LRW1 · CLRW2 · birthday-bound attack

© International Association for Cryptologic Research 2024
M. Joye and G. Leander (Eds.): EUROCRYPT 2024, LNCS 14651, pp. 249–279, 2024.
https://doi.org/10.1007/978-3-031-58716-0_9

1   Introduction

Tweakable Block Cipher or TBC is a highly versatile symmetric-key primitive that has found applications in almost all verticals of modern information security, including encryption schemes [8], message authentication codes [21], authenticated encryption [29,38], and even leakage resilience [42]. The popularity of TBCs is largely credited to the simplicity of TBC-based constructions, and more importantly, comparatively simpler proofs of beyond-the-birthday bound (BBB) security.

In a seminal paper [32] at CRYPTO 2002, Liskov, Rivest, and Wagner (LRW) formalized the notion of tweakable block ciphers (TBCs), although the high-level idea already appeared in some AES candidates such as Hasty Pudding [41] and Misty [13]. Over the years, the design landscape of TBCs has changed progressively. The design of a TBC mainly falls into one of the two categories: ad hoc designs based on well-established primitive design paradigms, or provably secure designs based on block ciphers or cryptographic permutations. In recent years, the popularity of ad-hoc designs has gained momentum with the advent of the TWEAKEY framework [22], its chief example being Deoxys-TBC [23], Skinny [6] and Qarma [2]. These designs are built from scratch, and their security mainly depends on cryptanalysis. On the other hand, the security of provably secure designs is directly linked to the security of the underlying primitives, such as a block cipher, a permutation, or a pseudorandom function. Some prominent examples include LRW's original constructions [32] LRW1 and LRW2, XEX [40] by Rogaway, and its extensions by Chakraborty and Sarkar [9], Minematsu [35], and Granger et al. [16]. Note that all these schemes are inherently birthday bound secure due to detectable internal collisions.

CASCADING LRW2: Landecker et al. were the first to notice [31] that a cascading of two independent instances of LRW2 results in a BBB secure TBC construction. They proved that 2-round cascaded LRW2 is secure up to approx. $2^{2n/3}$ CCA queries, where n denotes the block size in bits. The initial proof was flawed [39], and superseded by a corrected proof by both Landecker et al. and Procter [39]. The construction was later found [26,34] to be tightly secure up to $2^{3n/4}$ CCA queries. For any arbitrary $r \geq 2$-round independent cascading of LRW2, denoted r-LRW2, Lampe and Seurin proved [30] CCA security up to approx. $2^{\frac{rn}{r+2}}$ queries.

CASCADING LRW1: The idea to cascade LRW1 came quite later in [4], where Bao et al. showed that 3-round cascading of LRW1, referred as TNT, is CCA secure up to $2^{2n/3}$ queries. The design is highly appreciated in the community for its simple design and high provable security guarantee. In fact, the CPA security was later improved to $2^{3n/4}$ queries, essentially matching the bound for 2-round LRW2. Since this later result, it is widely believed that the CPA improvement carries over to the CCA setting, as well. For the more general case of arbitrary $r \geq 3$, denoted r-LRW1, Zhang et al. proved [43] CCA security up to approx. $2^{\frac{r-1}{r+1}n}$ queries.

We remark that the aforementioned LRW-based constructions are all studied under the standard assumption on the pseudorandomness of the underlying block ciphers. However, several good constructions are also based on cryptographic permutations [11,12] and even rekeying[1] of block ciphers [25,33,35]. We skip a detailed discussion on these ideal model constructions since the focus here is specific to the LRW design paradigm. We encourage the readers to see [26,34] for a more inclusive discussion on ideal model constructions.

1.1 Motivation

The primary motivation behind this work is a peculiar non-random behavior exhibited by TNT in the CCA setting.

Suppose π_1, π_2, π_3 are three independent random permutations of $\{0,1\}^n$. The TNT construction (see Fig. 1) based on π_1, π_2, π_3 is a TBC with n-bit tweak and n-bit block input, defined by the mapping

$$(t, m) \xrightarrow{\text{TNT}} \pi_3(t \oplus \pi_2(t \oplus \pi_1(m))).$$

As can be noticed by the definition of TNT, it has a peculiar property, that

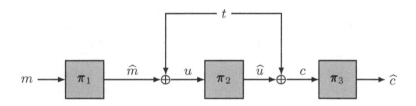

Fig. 1. The TNT construction [4].

we refer as the *final-block cancellation* property. Specifically, suppose we have a triple $(t, m, \widehat{c})$ such that $\text{TNT}(t, m) = \widehat{c}$. Then, it is easy to see that any inverse query of the form $(t', \widehat{c})$ would result in a cancellation of the call to π_3, and this is independent of the tweak values t and $t' = t \oplus \delta$. Essentially, the construction boils down to the one in Fig. 2. Let's call it $\text{TNT}_{\delta,m}$ for some fixed $\delta \neq 0^n$ and $m \in \{0,1\}^n$. For a fixed m, we have $u_1 \oplus u_2 = t_1 \oplus t_2$. Now, suppose the adversary can find a pair of tweaks (t_1, t_2) such that there is a collision at the output, i.e.,

$$(m_1' = m_2') \iff (\widehat{m}_1' = \widehat{m}_2') \iff (u_1' \oplus u_2' = t_1 \oplus t_2)$$

So, an output collision happens if and only if $u_1' \oplus u_2' = u_1 \oplus u_2$. Interestingly, for $\text{TNT}_{\delta,m}$, we have the following property:

$$(\widehat{u}_1 \oplus \widehat{u}_2 = \delta) \implies (u_1' \oplus u_2' = u_1 \oplus u_2),$$

---

[1] These constructions are generally analyzed in the ideal cipher model.

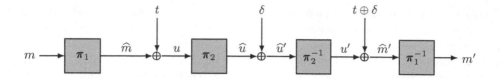

Fig. 2. TNT with final-block cancellation.

which implies that there are two sources of collisions in $\mathsf{TNT}_{\delta,m}$. A collision happens whenever $\widehat{u}_1 \oplus \widehat{u}_2 = \delta$, or $\widehat{u}_1 \oplus \widehat{u}_2 \neq \delta$ and $u'_1 \oplus u'_2 = u_1 \oplus u_2$. This indicates that one can expect more number of collisions (roughly double) in $\mathsf{TNT}_{\delta,m}$ as compared to a random function.

1.2 Contributions

Our contributions are threefold:

1. BIRTHDAY-BOUND CCA ATTACK ON TNT: In Sect. 3, we start by formalizing the aforementioned non-random behavior of TNT. We show (see Sect. 3.1) that the expected number of output collisions for $\mathsf{TNT}_{\delta,m}$ is approximately twice the expected number for $\widetilde{\pi}_{\delta,m}$, where $\widetilde{\pi}$ is an n-bit uniform random permutation with n-bit tweaks. Our analysis strongly indicates a global non-random phenomenon that can be detected in roughly $O(2^{n/2})$ CCA queries. We establish this assertion by giving a fully scalable CCA distinguisher. We provide a rigorous analysis for the query complexity and advantage of our distinguisher, which shows that the distinguisher has an advantage expression of $1 - O(2^n/q^2)$, where q denotes the number of CCA queries. We provide details (see Sect. 3.3) for efficient implementation and verification of our attacks, including results for an attack on TNT-GIFT-64, the TNT instantiation using GIFT-64 block cipher.

   Since the attack clearly contradicts the security claims of the designers of TNT, we study their security proof in Sect. 4 and identify a bug, where a random variable is erroneously assumed to have a uniform distribution, leading to an overestimation of the security.

   See [28] and [27] for two alternative analyses of the attack. The former employs random permutations statistics to estimate the number of collisions and the latter directly bounds the probability of collisions in the two worlds. The analysis in this paper is more comprehensive and leads to a scalable advantage, but all three analyses come to the same conclusion: TNT can be broken in birthday bound queries!

2. BIRTHDAY-BOUND CCA SECURITY OF TNT: In Sect. 5, we provide a simple proof of birthday-bound CCA security for TNT. Note that the CCA security bound also follows from the results in [43]. Nevertheless, given the flaws in TNT's original analysis, we believe that multiple security proofs using different techniques will lead to greater confidence in the revised security claim.

In addition to the original TNT, we also analyze the single-keyed variant of TNT, and show that it retains the same level of CCA security as well.

3. A Generalization of Cascaded LRW Paradigm: In a more abstract direction, in Sect. 6, we present a generalized view of the cascaded LRW design strategy for any arbitrary number of rounds $r \geq 2$, called the LRW+ construction. It consists of two block cipher calls sandwiched between a pair of tweakable universal hashes. We show that as long as the tweakable hashes are sufficiently[2] universal, the LRW+ construction is CCA secure up to $2^{3n/4}$ queries. Note that LRW+ encompasses both 2-LRW2 and 4-LRW1. Thus, as a direct side-effect of our analysis, in Sect. 6.2, we show that 2-LRW2 and 4-LRW1 are CCA secure up to $2^{3n/4}$ queries. In case of 2-LRW2, our bound matches the tight analysis in [26], and in case of 4-LRW1, our bound matches a concurrent result [15] by Datta et al.

Note that the result on LRW+ directly shows that r-LRW1 is at least $3n/4$-bit secure for any $r \geq 4$, improving on the results for $r \leq 8$. Similarly, for r-LRW2 it shows at least $3n/4$-bit security for any $r \geq 2$, improving on the results for $r \leq 6$. See Table 1 for a summary of the state-of-the-art on the security of cascaded LRW constructions.

Comparison with [15]: Concurrently, Datta et al. also proposed [15] an improved bound for 4-LRW1 that matches our $2^{3n/4}$ bound. Both the proofs follow the proof strategy [26] used for 2-LRW2 by Jha and Nandi, although ours is in a more general form (analyzing LRW+) that applies to all the cascaded LRW constructions with two or more block cipher calls.

1.3 Impact of Our Birthday-Bound Attack

As mentioned before, the authors of [4] claimed the CCA security of TNT to be $2n/3$ bits. In Asiacrypt 2020, the authors of [18] conjectured that the CCA security of TNT is probably $3n/4$ bits. In [43], the authors have stated:

A natural open problem is the exact security of r-LRW1. Unlike r-LRW2, the exact security of r-LRW1 for $r = 3$ already appears challenging, and might require new proof approaches.

We believe this work answers a critical research question of both practical and theoretical implications. On one hand, it studies the exact security of an efficient construction that has several practical applications. On the other hand, it offers another cautionary tale on how to use statistical proof techniques such as the χ^2 method.[3]

Additionally, the attack applies to practical instances of TNT: TNT-AES in [4] and TNT-SM4-128 in [19]. The authors of [19] also introduced TNT-SM4-32, where the tweak size is limited to 32 bits. Our distinguisher requires $O(2^{n/2})$

---

[2] Having approx. 2^{-n}-AU bound.

[3] Refer to [7] for another example of erroneously estimated distributions.

Table 1. Summary of security bounds for LRW-based construction. We have assumed all hash functions to be 2^{-n}-(XOR) universal. The bottom four rows present our results. LRW+ generalizes both 2-LRW2 and 4-LRW1. So the bound on LRW+ implies similar bounds for 2-LRW2 and 4-LRW1.

Construction	BC calls	Hash calls	Security bound	Tightness
LRW1 [32]	1	0	$2^{n/2}$ (CPA) [32]	✓
LRW2 [32]	1	1	$2^{n/2}$ [32]	✓
3-LRW1 (TNT [18])	3	0	$2^{2n/3}$ [18]	(flawed)
4-LRW1	4	0	$2^{3n/4}$ [15]	–
2-LRW2 (CLRW2 [31])	2	2	$2^{3n/4}$ [26]	✓ [34]
r-LRW1 [43]	r odd	0	$2^{\frac{r-1}{r+1}n}$ [43]	–
	r even		$2^{\frac{r-2}{r}n}$	–
r-LRW2 [30]	r odd	r	$2^{\frac{r-1}{r+1}n}$ [30]	–
	r even		$2^{\frac{r}{r+2}n}$	–
3-LRW1 (TNT)	3	0	$2^{n/2}$	✓
1k-TNT	3	0	$2^{n/2}$	✓
LRW+	2	2	$2^{3n/4}$	–
4-LRW1	4	0	$2^{3n/4}$	–

tweaks, where $n = 128$ in case of TNT-SM4. Hence, the distinguisher directly applies to TNT-SM4-128, which has a tweak size of 128 bits. It does not directly apply to TNT-SM4-32, since the tweak space is too small. However, since our distinguisher breaks the BBB security proof in [4], the exact security of TNT-SM4-32 and whether it has BBB security is an open question.

We note that in Eurocrypt 2023, a full-round distinguisher on TNT-AES using truncated boomerang attacks was presented in [5]. However, the attack is particular to TNT-AES and requires almost 2^n queries. Our attack applied to any 128-bit instantiation of TNT, including TNT-AES, requires $\leq 2^{69}$ queries to have an almost 100% success rate, making it the best-known distinguisher for any 128-bit TNT variant, without relying on the properties of the underlying block cipher. We sum up all known distinguishers on TNT-AES in Table 2, which indicates that our distinguisher is not only theoretical but outperforms all cryptanalytic efforts on TNT, so far.

2   Preliminaries

NOTATIONAL SETUP: For $n \in \mathbb{N}$, $[n]$ denotes the set $\{1, 2, \ldots, n\}$, $\{0,1\}^n$ denotes the set of bit strings of length n, and $\mathsf{Perm}(n)$ denotes the set of all permutations over $\{0,1\}^n$. For $\tau, n \in \mathbb{N}$, $\widetilde{\mathsf{Perm}}(\tau, n)$ denotes the set of all families of permu-

Table 2. Known distinguishers against TNT-AES. CCA stands for adaptive Chosen Ciphertext Adversary. NCPA stands for Non-adaptive Chosen Plaintext Adversary. **Rounds** is the number of AES rounds in π_1, π_2 and π_3, respectively. $\star$ means any number of rounds. Generic attacks do not rely on any AES properties and apply to TNT instantiated with any 128-bit block cipher. 2^{69} is the complexity for which our attack is expected to have almost 100% success rate, while 2^{68} is expected to have 99% success rate.

Ref.	Type	Data	Time	Adversary	Rounds
[4]	Boomerang	2^{126}	2^{126}	CCA	$\star - 5 - \star$
[18]	Impossible Differential	$2^{113.6}$	$2^{113.6}$	NCPA	$5 - \star - \star$
[18]	Generic	$2^{99.5}$	$2^{99.5}$	NCPA	$\star - \star - \star$
[5]	Truncated Boomerang	2^{76}	2^{76}	CCA	$\star - 5 - \star$
[5]	Truncated Boomerang	2^{87}	2^{87}	CCA	$5 - 5 - \star$
[5]	Truncated Boomerang	$2^{127.8}$	$2^{127.8}$	CCA	$\star - 6 - \star$
This paper	Generic	$\leq 2^{69}$	$\leq 2^{69}$	CCA	$\star - \star - \star$

tations $\pi_t := \pi(t, \cdot) \in \mathsf{Perm}(n)$, indexed by $t \in \{0,1\}^\tau$. Any $\widetilde{\pi} \in \widetilde{\mathsf{Perm}}(\tau, n)$ is referred as a (τ, n)-tweakable permutation.

For $n, r \in \mathbb{N}$, such that $n \geq r$, we define the falling factorial $(n)_r := n!/(n - r)! = n(n-1)\cdots(n-r+1)$, and define $(n)_0 := 1$.

For $q \in \mathbb{N}$, x^q denotes the q-tuple $(x_1, x_2, \ldots, x_q)$, and in this context, $\mathsf{M}(x^q)$ and $\mathsf{S}(x^q)$ respectively denote the multiset and set corresponding to $\{x_i : i \in [q]\}$. For a set $\mathcal{I} \subseteq [q]$ and a q-tuple x^q, $x^\mathcal{I}$ denotes the tuple $(x_i)_{i \in \mathcal{I}}$. For a pair of tuples x^q and y^q, (x^q, y^q) denotes the 2-ary q-tuple $((x_1, y_1), \ldots, (x_q, y_q))$. An n-ary q-tuple is defined analogously. For $q \in \mathbb{N}$, for any set $\mathcal{X}$, $(\mathcal{X})_q$ denotes the set of all q-tuples with distinct elements from $\mathcal{X}$. For $q \in \mathbb{N}$, a 2-ary tuple (x^q, y^q) is called permutation compatible, denoted $x^q \leftrightsquigarrow y^q$, if $x_i = x_j \iff y_i = y_j$. Extending notations, a 3-ary tuple (t^q, x^q, y^q) is called tweakable permutation compatible, denoted by $(t^q, x^q) \leftrightsquigarrow (t^q, y^q)$, if $(t_i, x_i) = (t_j, x_j) \iff (t_i, y_i) = (t_j, y_j)$. For any tuple $x^q \in \mathcal{X}^q$, and for any function $f : \mathcal{X} \to \mathcal{Y}$, $f(x^q)$ denotes the tuple $(f(x_1), \ldots, f(x_q))$. We use shorthand notation $\exists^*$ to represent the phrase "there exists distinct".

Unless stated otherwise, upper and lower case letters denote variables and values, respectively, and Serif font letters are used to denote random variables. For a finite set $\mathcal{X}$, $\mathsf{X} \leftarrow_\$ \mathcal{X}$ denotes the uniform and random sampling of X from $\mathcal{X}$. We write $\mathsf{X}^q \xleftarrow{\mathrm{wor}} \mathcal{X}$ to denote WOR (without replacement sampling) of a q-tuple X^q from the set $\mathcal{X}$, where $|\mathcal{X}| \geq q$ is obvious. More precisely, $\mathsf{X}^q \leftarrow_\$ (\mathcal{X})_q$.

We will use the following proposition, which is a slight variation of [17, Lemma 6].

Proposition 2.1. *Let* R_0 *and* R_1 *be two random variables with variances* σ_0^2 *and* σ_1^2, *respectively, and suppose their expectations follow the relation* $\mathsf{Ex}(\mathsf{R}_0) \geq$

$\mu_0 \geq \mu_1 \geq \mathsf{Ex}(\mathsf{R}_1)$, *for some* $\mu_0 \geq \mu_1 \geq 0$. *Then, for* $\mu = (\mu_0 + \mu_1)/2$, *we have*

$$|\mathsf{Pr}(\mathsf{R}_0 > \mu) - \mathsf{Pr}(\mathsf{R}_1 > \mu)| \geq 1 - \frac{4(\sigma_0^2 + \sigma_1^2)}{(\mu_0 - \mu_1)^2}.$$

When $\mathsf{Ex}(\mathsf{R}_0) = \mu_0$ and $\mathsf{Ex}(\mathsf{R}_1) = \mu_1$, we get back [17, Lemma 6]. A proof of this proposition can be derived using a similar approach as used in the proof of [17, Lemma 6]. We provide a short alternate proof in the full version of this paper [24] by using the Bienaymé-Chebyshev inequality.

2.1 (Tweakable) Block Ciphers and Random Permutations

A (κ, n)-block cipher with key size κ and block size n is a family of permutations $E \in \widetilde{\mathsf{Perm}}(\kappa, n)$. For $k \in \{0, 1\}^\kappa$, we denote $E_k(\cdot) := E(k, \cdot)$, and $E_k^{-1}(\cdot) := E^{-1}(k, \cdot)$. A (κ, τ, n)tweakable block cipher with key size κ, tweak size τ and block size n is a family of permutations $\widetilde{E} \in \widetilde{\mathsf{Perm}}((\kappa, \tau), n)$. For $k \in \{0, 1\}^\kappa$ and $t \in \{0, 1\}^\tau$, we denote $\widetilde{E}_k(t, \cdot) := \widetilde{E}(k, t, \cdot)$, and $\widetilde{E}_k^{-1}(t, \cdot) := \widetilde{E}^{-1}(k, t, \cdot)$. Throughout this paper, we fix $\kappa, \tau, n \in \mathbb{N}$ as the key size, tweak size, and block size, respectively, of the given (tweakable) block cipher.

We say that π is an (ideal) random permutation on block space $\{0, 1\}^n$ to indicate that $\pi \leftarrow_\$ \mathsf{Perm}(n)$. Similarly, we say that $\widetilde{\pi}$ is an (ideal) tweakable random permutation on tweak space $\{0, 1\}^\tau$ and block space $\{0, 1\}^n$ to indicate that $\widetilde{\pi} \leftarrow_\$ \widetilde{\mathsf{Perm}}(\tau, n)$.

2.2 Security Definition

In this paper, we assume that the distinguisher is non-trivial, i.e. it never makes a duplicate query, and it never makes a query for which the response is already known due to some previous query. Let $\mathbb{A}(q, t)$ be the class of all non-trivial distinguishers limited to q oracle queries, and t computations.

In our analyses, especially security proofs, it will be convenient to work in the information-theoretic setting. Accordingly, we always skip the boilerplate hybrid steps and often assume that the adversary is computationally unbounded, i.e., $t = \infty$, and deterministic. A computational equivalent of all our security proofs can be easily obtained by a simple hybrid argument.

IND-CCA SECURITY: The IND-CCA advantage of distinguisher $\mathbf{A}$ against $\widetilde{E}$ instantiated with a key $\mathsf{K} \leftarrow_\$ \{0, 1\}^\kappa$ is defined as

$$\mathbf{Adv}_{\widetilde{E}}^{\mathsf{ind\text{-}cca}}(\mathbf{A}) = \mathbf{Adv}_{\widetilde{E}^\pm; \widetilde{\pi}^\pm}(\mathbf{A}) := \left| \mathsf{Pr}\left(\mathbf{A}(\widetilde{E}_\mathsf{K}^\pm) = 1\right) - \mathsf{Pr}\left(\mathbf{A}(\widetilde{\pi}^\pm) = 1\right) \right|. \quad (1)$$

The IND-CCA security of $\widetilde{E}$ is defined as

$$\mathbf{Adv}_{\widetilde{E}}^{\mathsf{ind\text{-}cca}}(q, t) := \max_{\mathbf{A} \in \mathbb{A}(q, t)} \mathbf{Adv}_{\widetilde{E}}^{\mathsf{ind\text{-}cca}}(\mathbf{A}).$$

2.3   The Expectation Method

Let $\mathbf{A}$ be a computationally unbounded and deterministic distinguisher that tries to distinguish between two oracles $\mathcal{O}_0$ and $\mathcal{O}_1$ via black box interaction with one of them. We denote the query-response tuple of $\mathbf{A}$'s interaction with its oracle by a transcript ω. This may also include any additional information the oracle chooses to reveal to the distinguisher at the end of the query-response phase of the game. We denote by Θ_1 (res. Θ_0) the random transcript variable when $\mathbf{A}$ interacts with $\mathcal{O}_1$ (res. $\mathcal{O}_0$). The probability of realizing a given transcript ω in the security game with an oracle $\mathcal{O}$ is known as the *interpolation probability* of ω with respect to $\mathcal{O}$. Since $\mathbf{A}$ is deterministic, this probability depends only on the oracle $\mathcal{O}$ and the transcript ω. A transcript ω is said to be *attainable* if $\Pr(\Theta_0 = \omega) > 0$. The expectation method [20] (stated below) is a generalization of Patarin's H-coefficients technique [36], which is quite useful in obtaining improved bounds in many cases [20, 26].

Lemma 2.1 (Expectation Method [20]). *Let Ω be the set of all transcripts. For some $\epsilon_{\mathsf{bad}} \geq 0$ and a non-negative function $\epsilon_{\mathsf{ratio}} : \Omega \to [0, \infty)$, suppose there is a set $\Omega_{\mathsf{bad}} \subseteq \Omega$ satisfying the following:*

- $\Pr(\Theta_0 \in \Omega_{\mathsf{bad}}) \leq \epsilon_{\mathsf{bad}}$;
- *For any $\omega \notin \Omega_{\mathsf{bad}}$, ω is attainable and $\dfrac{\Pr(\Theta_1 = \omega)}{\Pr(\Theta_0 = \omega)} \geq 1 - \epsilon_{\mathsf{ratio}}(\omega)$.*

Then for any distinguisher $\mathbf{A}$ trying to distinguish between $\mathcal{O}_1$ and $\mathcal{O}_0$, we have the following bound on its distinguishing advantage:

$$\mathbf{Adv}_{\mathcal{O}_1;\mathcal{O}_0}(\mathbf{A}) \leq \epsilon_{\mathsf{bad}} + \mathsf{Ex}\left(\epsilon_{\mathsf{ratio}}(\Theta_0)\right).$$

When $\epsilon_{\mathsf{ratio}}$ is a constant function, we get the H-coefficients technique.

3   Birthday-Bound Attack on TNT

We consider the TNT construction in an information-theoretic setting. Accordingly, we instantiate TNT based on three independent uniform random permutations π_1, π_2, and π_3 of $\{0,1\}^n$. Recall that, the TNT construction is defined by the mapping

$$(t, m) \xmapsto{\text{TNT}} \pi_3(t \oplus \pi_2(t \oplus \pi_1(m))), \tag{2}$$

For some non-zero $\delta \in \{0,1\}^n$ and $m \in \{0,1\}^n$, consider the function $\mathcal{O}_{\delta,m} : \{0,1\}^n \to \{0,1\}^n$, associated to each n-bit tweakable permutation $\mathcal{O}$ with n-bit tweak, defined by the mapping

$$t \xmapsto{\mathcal{O}_{\delta,m}} \mathcal{O}^{-1}(t \oplus \delta, \ \mathcal{O}(t, \ m)). \tag{3}$$

We are only interested in $\widetilde{\pi}_{\delta,m}$ and $\text{TNT}_{\delta,m}$ where $\widetilde{\pi}$ is a tweakable uniform random permutation of $\{0,1\}^n$ with n-bit tweaks.

Suppose $\widetilde{\pi}_{\delta,m}$ is executed over q distinct inputs $(t_1, \ldots, t_q)$. Observe that, for any valid choice of $(t_1, \ldots, t_q)$, $\widetilde{\pi}$ is executed at most twice for any tweak t_i. Thus, one can expect $\widetilde{\pi}_{\delta,m}(\cdot)$ to be almost uniform and independent, and thus, indistinguishable from a uniform random function $\rho : \{0,1\}^n \to \{0,1\}^n$ for a large range of q. In fact, as long as

$$\widetilde{\pi}(t_i, m) \neq \widetilde{\pi}(t_j, m) \text{ for all } i \neq j \text{ such that } t_j = t_i \oplus \delta,$$

$\widetilde{\pi}_{\delta,m}$ can be shown to be indistinguishable from ρ up to $O(2^n)$ queries. More importantly, as we show in the following discussion, one can easily show that the $\widetilde{\pi}_{\delta,m}$ is almost identical to ρ in terms of the number of output collisions.

TNT$_{\delta,m}$, on the other hand, exhibits a rather peculiar and interesting property. Apparently, TNT$_{\delta,m}$ is more prone to collisions as compared to $\widetilde{\pi}_{\delta,m}$, which results in a direct IND-CCA distinguisher for TNT. A formal distinguisher with complete advantage calculation appears later in Sect. 3.2. We first demonstrate the biased behavior by comparing the number of output collisions for TNT$_{\delta,m}$ and $\widetilde{\pi}_{\delta,m}$.

3.1   Comparing the Number of Collision Pairs in $\widetilde{\pi}_{\delta,m}$ and TNT$_{\delta,m}$

Fix some non-negative integer $q \leq 2^n$. Fix a set $\mathcal{T} = \{t_1, \ldots, t_q\} \subseteq \{0,1\}^n$ of size q, an $m \in \{0,1\}^n$, and a non-zero $\delta \in \{0,1\}^n$. Let $\mathcal{O}$ be a tweakable permutation (which is either $\widetilde{\pi}$ in the ideal world or TNT in the real world). We compute $\mathsf{M}_i' = \mathcal{O}_{\delta,m}(t_i)$ by making a forward query $\mathcal{O}(t_i, m) := \widehat{\mathsf{C}}_i$, followed by a backward query $\mathsf{M}_i' = \mathcal{O}^{-1}(t_i \oplus \delta, \widehat{\mathsf{C}}_i)$. We write $\mathsf{COLL}(\mathcal{O}_{\delta,m})$ to denote the number of pairs (i, j), $i < j$ such that $\mathsf{M}_i' = \mathsf{M}_j'$.

ANALYZING $\mathsf{coll}_{\mathsf{id}} := \mathsf{COLL}(\widetilde{\pi}_{\delta,m})$: For any $i \neq j \in [q]$, let $\mathbb{1}_{i,j}$ denote the indicator random variable corresponding to the event: $\mathsf{M}_j' = \mathsf{M}_i'$. Then, using linearity of expectation, we have

$$\mathsf{Ex}\left(\mathsf{coll}_{\mathsf{id}}\right) = \sum_{i<j \in [q]} \mathsf{Ex}\left(\mathbb{1}_{i,j}\right) = \sum_{i<j \in [q]} \mathsf{Pr}\left(\mathbb{1}_{i,j}\right), \qquad (4)$$

where we abused the notation slightly to use $\mathbb{1}_{i,j}$ to denote the event $\mathbb{1}_{i,j} = 1$. Let $\sim$ be a relation on $[q]$, such that for all $i \neq j \in [q]$, $i \sim j$ if and only if $t_i = t_j \oplus \delta$. Note that $\sim$ is symmetric. Suppose there are ν pairs (t_i, t_j), $i < j$ such that $t_i \sim t_j$. Clearly, $\nu \leq q/2$. Now, we can split the right-hand side of (4) as follows:

$$\sum_{i<j \in [q]} \mathsf{Pr}\left(\mathbb{1}_{i,j}\right) = \sum_{\substack{i<j \in [q] \\ i \sim j}} \mathsf{Pr}\left(\mathbb{1}_{i,j}\right) + \sum_{\substack{i<j \in [q] \\ i \not\sim j}} \mathsf{Pr}\left(\mathbb{1}_{i,j}\right) \qquad (5)$$

Case $i \not\sim j$: We must have $\{t_i, t_j\} \cap \{t_i \oplus \delta, t_j \oplus \delta\} = \emptyset$. Thus, the two calls to $\widetilde{\pi}_{\delta,m}$ corresponding to the i-th and j-th queries result in exactly 2 calls to $\widetilde{\pi}$

and 2 calls $\widetilde{\pi}^{-1}$, each with a distinct tweak than others. Hence, the outputs of $\widetilde{\pi}_{\delta,m}$ on inputs t_i and t_j are mutually independent and uniformly distributed in $\{0,1\}^n$. Thus, for any $i \not\sim j$, we have

$$\mathsf{Pr}\left(\mathbb{1}_{i,j}\right) = \frac{1}{2^n}, \tag{6}$$

which results in

$$\sum_{\substack{i<j\in[q]\\i\not\sim j}} \mathsf{Pr}\left(\mathbb{1}_{i,j}\right) = \left(\binom{q}{2} - \nu\right)\frac{1}{2^n}, \tag{7}$$

Case $i \sim j$: In this case we have $t_i = t_j \oplus \delta$. Let $\mathsf{F}_{i,j}$ be the event that $\widetilde{\pi}(t_i, m) = \widetilde{\pi}(t_j, m)$. Then, we have $\mathsf{M}'_i = \mathsf{M}'_j = m$. Since, $t_i \neq t_j$, $\mathsf{Pr}\left(\mathsf{F}_{i,j}\right) = 2^{-n}$. So, for any $i \sim j$, we have

$$\begin{aligned}
\mathsf{Pr}\left(\mathbb{1}_{i,j}\right) &= \mathsf{Pr}\left(\mathbb{1}_{i,j} \wedge \mathsf{F}_{i,j}\right) + \mathsf{Pr}\left(\mathbb{1}_{i,j} \wedge \neg\mathsf{F}_{i,j}\right) \\
&= \mathsf{Pr}\left(\mathsf{F}_{i,j}\right) + \mathsf{Pr}\left(\mathbb{1}_{i,j} \wedge \neg\mathsf{F}_{i,j}\right) \\
&= \frac{1}{2^n} + \mathsf{Pr}\left(\mathbb{1}_{i,j} \wedge \neg\mathsf{F}_{i,j}\right),
\end{aligned}$$

which immediately gives

$$\frac{1}{2^n} \le \mathsf{Pr}\left(\mathbb{1}_{i,j}\right) \le \frac{1}{2^n} + \mathsf{Pr}\left(\mathbb{1}_{i,j} \mid \neg\mathsf{F}_{i,j}\right) \le \frac{1}{2^n} + \frac{1}{2^n - 1}. \tag{8}$$

Note that the last inequality follows from the observation that given $\neg\mathsf{F}_{i,j}$, outputs of $\widetilde{\pi}^{-1}(t_i \oplus \delta)$ and $\widetilde{\pi}^{-1}(t_j \oplus \delta)$ are sampled independently from a set of size exactly $2^n - 1$. This further results in

$$\frac{\nu}{2^n} \le \sum_{\substack{i<j\in[q]\\i\sim j}} \mathsf{Pr}\left(\mathbb{1}_{i,j}\right) \le \nu\left(\frac{1}{2^n} + \frac{1}{2^n - 1}\right). \tag{9}$$

Using (4), (5), (7), (9), and $\nu \le q/2$ we have

$$\binom{q}{2}\frac{1}{2^n} \le \mathsf{Ex}\left(\mathsf{coll}_{\mathsf{id}}\right) \le \binom{q}{2}\frac{1}{2^n} + \frac{q}{2^n}. \tag{10}$$

ANALYZING $\mathsf{coll}_{\mathsf{re}} := \mathsf{COLL}(\mathsf{TNT}_{\delta,m})$: The analysis of $\mathsf{COLL}(\mathsf{TNT}_{\delta,m})$ is a bit more subtle and interesting. Figure 3 gives a pictorial view of the i-th execution of $\mathsf{TNT}_{\delta,m}$. Clearly, the respective calls to π_3 and its inverse cancel out each other, resulting in the compressed view illustrated in Fig. 4.

Note that for any $i, j \in [q]$, $\mathsf{U}_i \oplus \mathsf{U}_j = t_i \oplus t_j$. Now, fix a pair of inputs (t_i, t_j) such that there is a collision at the output, i.e.,

$$(\mathsf{M}'_i = \mathsf{M}'_j) \iff (\widehat{\mathsf{M}}'_i = \widehat{\mathsf{M}}'_j) \iff (\mathsf{U}'_i \oplus \mathsf{U}'_j = t_i \oplus t_j) \iff (\mathsf{U}'_i \oplus \mathsf{U}'_j = \mathsf{U}_i \oplus \mathsf{U}_j),$$

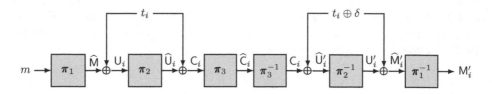

Fig. 3. The execution trace for $\mathsf{TNT}_{\delta,m}$ on input t_i.

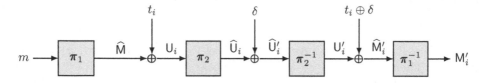

Fig. 4. The effective execution trace for $\mathsf{TNT}_{\delta,m}$ on input t_i.

and let $\mathbb{1}_{i,j}$ denote the corresponding indicator random variable. Observe that $\mathsf{TNT}_{\delta,m}$, has the following interesting property:

$$(\widehat{\mathsf{U}}_i \oplus \widehat{\mathsf{U}}_j = \delta) \implies (\mathsf{U}'_i \oplus \mathsf{U}'_j = \mathsf{U}_i \oplus \mathsf{U}_j = t_i \oplus t_j),$$

which implies that there are two sources of collisions in $\mathsf{TNT}_{\delta,m}$. A collision happens whenever

1. $\widehat{\mathsf{U}}_i \oplus \widehat{\mathsf{U}}_j = \delta$, or
2. $\widehat{\mathsf{U}}_i \oplus \widehat{\mathsf{U}}_j \neq \delta$ and $\mathsf{U}'_i \oplus \mathsf{U}'_j = t_i \oplus t_j$.

From this one can easily get a good upper and lower bound on the expected number of collisions in the real world. Using linearity of expectation, we have

$$\mathsf{Ex}\,(\mathsf{coll}_{\mathrm{re}}) = \sum_{i<j\in[q]} \mathsf{Ex}\,(\mathbb{1}_{i,j}) = \sum_{i<j\in[q]} \mathsf{Pr}\,(\mathbb{1}_{i,j}) \tag{11}$$

Further, from the above discussion, we have

$$\begin{aligned}
\mathsf{Pr}\,(\mathbb{1}_{i,j}) &= \mathsf{Pr}\left(\mathbb{1}_{i,j} \wedge \widehat{\mathsf{U}}_i \oplus \widehat{\mathsf{U}}_j = \delta\right) + \mathsf{Pr}\left(\mathbb{1}_{i,j} \wedge \widehat{\mathsf{U}}_i \oplus \widehat{\mathsf{U}}_j \neq \delta\right) \\
&= \mathsf{Pr}\left(\widehat{\mathsf{U}}_i \oplus \widehat{\mathsf{U}}_j = \delta\right) + \mathsf{Pr}\left(\widehat{\mathsf{U}}_i \oplus \widehat{\mathsf{U}}_j \neq \delta\right) \\
&\qquad\qquad \times \mathsf{Pr}\left(\mathsf{U}'_i \oplus \mathsf{U}'_j = t_i \oplus t_j \mid \widehat{\mathsf{U}}_i \oplus \widehat{\mathsf{U}}_j \neq \delta\right) \\
&= \frac{1}{2^n - 1} + \left(1 - \frac{1}{2^n - 1}\right) \\
&\qquad\qquad \times \mathsf{Pr}\left(\mathsf{U}'_i \oplus \mathsf{U}'_j = t_i \oplus t_j \mid \widehat{\mathsf{U}}_i \oplus \widehat{\mathsf{U}}_j \neq \delta\right),
\end{aligned} \tag{12}$$

Note that $\widehat{U}_i \oplus \widehat{U}_j \neq \delta$ implies that $U'_i, U'_j \notin \{U_i, U_j\}$. Now, fix a valid choice for $(U_i, U_j, \widehat{U}_i, \widehat{U}_j)$, say $(u_i, u_j, \widehat{u}_i, \widehat{u}_j)$. Then, the number of valid choices for (U'_i, U'_j) that satisfy the equation $U'_i \oplus U'_j = t_i \oplus t_j$, are all $(x, x \oplus t_i \oplus t_j)$ pairs such that

$$x \in \{0,1\}^n \setminus (\{u_i, u_j\} \cup \{u_i \oplus t_i \oplus t_j, u_j \oplus t_i \oplus t_j\})$$

But, observe that $\{u_i, u_j\} = \{u_i \oplus t_i \oplus t_j, u_j \oplus t_i \oplus t_j\}$ by definition, for any valid choice of (u_i, u_j). Therefore, the number of valid $(x, x \oplus t_i \oplus t_j)$ is exactly $2^n - 2$. Furthermore, this counting is independent of the choice of $(u_i, u_j, \widehat{u}_i, \widehat{u}_j)$, whence it holds unconditionally. Now, each such choice for (U'_i, U'_j) occurs with at most $1/(2^n - 2)(2^n - 3)$ probability, as they are sampled from $\{0,1\}^n \setminus \{U_i, U_j\}$ in a WOR (without replacement) manner. Then, using (12), we have

$$\begin{aligned}
\Pr(\mathbb{1}_{i,j}) &= \frac{1}{2^n - 1} + \left(1 - \frac{1}{2^n - 1}\right) \times \frac{1}{2^n - 3} \\
&= \frac{1}{2^n - 1} + \frac{1}{2^n - 3} - \frac{1}{(2^n - 1)(2^n - 3)} \\
&= \frac{2}{2^n} + \frac{1}{2^n(2^n - 1)} + \frac{3}{2^n(2^n - 3)} - \frac{1}{(2^n - 1)(2^n - 3)}
\end{aligned}$$

Using (11), we immediately have

$$\mathsf{Ex}(\mathsf{coll}_{re}) = \binom{q}{2}\left(\frac{1}{2^n - 1} + \frac{1}{2^n - 3} - \frac{1}{(2^n - 1)(2^n - 3)}\right) \geq \binom{q}{2}\frac{2}{2^n}, \quad (13)$$

and on comparing this with (10), we can conclude that

$$\mathsf{Ex}(\mathsf{coll}_{re}) \approx 2\mathsf{Ex}(\mathsf{coll}_{id}).$$

This clearly indicates that the occurrence of collisions in $\mathsf{TNT}_{\delta,m}$ is approximately twice that of $\widetilde{\pi}_{\delta,m}$.

3.2 The Collision Counting Distinguisher

Based on the observations from the preceding section, we now present a formal distinguisher, called $\mathbf{A}^*$, in Algorithm 1.

Fix a message $m \in \{0,1\}^n$, a set $\mathcal{T} = \{t_1, \ldots, t_q\} \subseteq \{0,1\}^n$ of size q, and a $\delta \neq 0^n$. Let $\theta(q,n)$ be some non-negative function of q and n, which will be defined later in the course of analysis.

Let $\mathcal{O}^\pm$ be the oracle $\mathbf{A}^*$ is interacting with. Then, $\mathbf{A}^*$ works by collecting $\mathsf{M}'_i = \mathcal{O}_{\delta,m}(t_i)$ for all $t_i \in \mathcal{T}$ in a multiset $\mathcal{M}$. As shown in the preceding section and Algorithm 1, this can be easily done by a pair of encryption-decryption queries for each $i \in [q]$. After this, $\mathbf{A}^*$ counts the number of collisions in $\mathcal{M}$ using the function collCount. If the number of collisions is greater than $\theta(q,n)$, the distinguisher returns 1, otherwise, it returns 0.

Algorithm 1. Algorithmic description of $\mathbf{A}^*(\mathcal{O}^{\pm})$. Note that `collCount` is an abstract function that counts the number of collisions in a multiset.

1: $m \leftarrow 0^n$ ▷ m can be initialized to any constant
2: $\delta \leftarrow 1^n$ ▷ δ can be initialized to any non-zero constant
3: $\mathcal{T} \leftarrow \{t_1, \ldots, t_q\}$ ▷ a set of q fixed but distinct tweaks
4: $\mathcal{M} \leftarrow \emptyset$ ▷ an empty multiset
5: **for** $i = 1 \ldots q$ **do**
6:     $\widehat{C}_i \leftarrow \mathcal{O}(t_i, m)$
7:     $\mathsf{M}'_i \leftarrow \mathcal{O}^{-1}(t_i \oplus \delta, \widehat{C}_i)$ ▷ ln. 6 and 7 together give $\mathcal{O}_{\delta,m}(t_i)$
8:     $\mathcal{M} \leftarrow \mathcal{M} \cup \{\mathsf{M}'_i\}$
9: $\mathsf{COLL}(\mathcal{O}_{\delta,m}) \leftarrow \mathtt{collCount}(\mathcal{M})$
10: **if** $\mathsf{COLL}(\mathcal{O}_{\delta,m}) > \theta(q, n)$ **then**
11:     **return** 1
12: **else**
13:     **return** 0

Note that the exact implementation of `collCount` is not relevant for the forthcoming advantage calculation. So, we postpone a discussion on its implementation and resulting time and space complexity analysis to Sect. 3.3, where we also provide experimental verification for $\mathbf{A}^*$.

However, it is amply evident that the space complexity of the attack is $O(q)$, i.e., dominated by the query complexity. Further, looking ahead momentarily, one can implement `collCount` in such a way that it runs in time $O(q \log_2 q)$. Other than this, $\mathbf{A}^*$ only makes $2q$ calls to $\mathcal{O}$, thus the overall time complexity is also in $O(q \log_2 q)$.

Define

$$\mu_{\mathrm{re}} := \binom{q}{2}\frac{2}{2^n} \qquad\qquad \mu_{\mathrm{id}} := \binom{q}{2}\frac{1}{2^n} + \frac{q}{2^n}.$$

Then, from (10) and (13), we have that $\mathsf{Ex}\,(\mathsf{COLL}(\mathsf{TNT}_{\delta,m})) \geq \mu_{\mathrm{re}} \geq \mu_{\mathrm{id}} \geq \mathsf{Ex}\,(\mathsf{COLL}(\widetilde{\pi}_{\delta,m}))$, whenever $q \geq 3$.

Theorem 3.1. *For $n \geq 4$, $10 \leq q \leq 2^n$, and $\theta(q,n) = (\mu_{\mathrm{re}} + \mu_{\mathrm{id}})/2$, we have*

$$\mathbf{Adv}_{TNT}^{\mathrm{ind\text{-}cca}}(\mathbf{A}^*) \geq 1 - 371\frac{2^n}{q^2}.$$

Specifically, for $q \geq 28 \times 2^{\frac{n}{2}}$, $\mathbf{Adv}_{TNT}^{\mathrm{ind\text{-}cca}}(\mathbf{A}^*) \geq 0.5$.

Proof. Recall that $\mathsf{coll}_{\mathrm{id}} = \mathsf{COLL}(\widetilde{\pi}_{\delta,m})$ and $\mathsf{coll}_{\mathrm{re}} = \mathsf{COLL}(\widetilde{\pi}_{\delta,m})$. Let $\sigma_s^2 := \mathsf{Var}\,(\mathsf{coll}_s)$, for all $s \in \{\mathrm{id}, \mathrm{re}\}$. In addition, whenever necessary, we also reuse the notations and definitions from the expectation calculation given in Sect. 3.1.

Now, we have

$$\mathbf{Adv}_{\mathsf{TNT}}^{\mathsf{ind\text{-}cca}}(\mathbf{A}^*) = |\Pr\left(\mathbf{A}^*(\mathsf{TNT}_{\delta,m}) = 1\right) - \Pr\left(\mathbf{A}^*(\widetilde{\pi}_{\delta,m}) = 1\right)|$$
$$= |\Pr\left(\mathsf{coll}_{\mathsf{re}} > \theta(q,n)\right) - \Pr\left(\mathsf{coll}_{\mathsf{id}} > \theta(q,n)\right)|$$
$$\geq 1 - \frac{4(\sigma_{\mathsf{re}}^2 + \sigma_{\mathsf{id}}^2)}{(\mu_{\mathsf{re}} - \mu_{\mathsf{id}})^2}. \tag{14}$$

where the last inequality follows from Proposition 2.1. We make the following claim on σ_{re}^2 and σ_{id}^2.

Claim 3.1. For $n \geq 4$, $10 \leq q \leq 2^n$, we have

$$\sigma_{\mathsf{id}}^2 \leq \frac{4q^2}{2^n} \qquad \sigma_{\mathsf{re}}^2 \leq \frac{11q^2}{2^n}$$

A proof of this claim is available in the full version of this paper [24]. Next, from (10) and (13), we have

$$(\mu_{\mathsf{re}} - \mu_{\mathsf{id}})^2 \geq \left(\binom{q}{2}\frac{2}{2^n} - \binom{q}{2}\frac{1}{2^n} - \frac{q}{2^n}\right)^2$$
$$\geq \binom{q}{2}^2 \frac{1}{2^{2n}} \left(1 - \frac{1}{q}\right)^2 \geq 0.162 \frac{q^4}{2^{2n}} \tag{15}$$

where the last inequality follows from $q \geq 10$. The result then follows from (14), Claim 3.1, and (15). $\qquad \square$

Remark 3.1. Note that the constant in Theorem 3.1 is a bit loose for the sake of simplicity. It is likely that this constant can be improved by a more tighter estimation or a more sophisticated concentration inequality. Indeed, in the next section, we show that in practical applications the advantage might already be close to 0.8 when the number of queries is close to $4 \times 2^{\frac{n}{2}}$.

With that being said, it's important to highlight that our attack demonstrates full scalability. In other words, as the value of q approaches 2^n, the advantage becomes close to 1.

3.3 Experimental Verification

We have implemented the collision counting Algorithm 1 for different values for n. We have implemented two variants of the collCount function of the algorithm, which include various optimizations to make the attack practical. The first variant is an adversary without space complexity and with time complexity $O(q)$, and is given in Algorithm 2. The second is for a space-optimized adversary, with space complexity $O(q)$ and time complexity $O(q \log_2(q))$, described in Algorithm 3. For the underlying random permutations, we used generated using Python NumPy's shuffle and argsort functions, to generate and invert a permutation, respectively. We generated permutations of sizes 16, 20, 24, 28 and 32 bits and performed the distinguishing attack on each generated permutation. Results where taken over an average of $1,000 \sim 10,000$ random generations (each consisting of 3 independent permutations). In the ideal world, random values are sampled, since the tweaks are never repeated and lazy sampling can be used. Table 3 includes the average number of collisions for $n = 16$ and $n = 20$. The distinguisher reaches 16 expected collisions in the real world 4× faster than the distinguisher in [18] for $n = 16$ and 16× faster for $n = 20$.

Algorithm 1 is expected to have twice as many collisions in the real world as in the ideal world. $\theta(q, n)$ is set to:

$$\theta(q, n) = 2^{2d-1} + 2^{2d-2}$$

when $q = 2^{n/2+d}$, which is roughly 1.5 times the expected number of collisions in the ideal case.

Algorithm 2. An implementation of collCount($\mathcal{M}$) from Algorithm 1 with no memory limitations. Here, $\mathcal{M}$ (the multiset of outputs) is assumed to be an array of size q.

```
1: for x ∈ {0,1}ⁿ do
2:     L[x] ← 0
3: coll ← 0
4: for i ∈ {1,...,q − 1} do
5:     x ← M[i]
6:     coll ← coll + L[x]
7:     L[x] ← L[x] + 1
```

Algorithm 3. An implementation of collCount($\mathcal{M}$) from Algorithm 1 with memory limited to $O(q)$. Here, $\mathcal{M}$ (the multiset of outputs) is assumed to be an array of size q.

```
1: M ← sort(M)
2: rep ← 1
3: coll ← 0
4: x ← M[1]
5: for i ∈ {2,...,q} do
6:     if x = M[i] then
7:         coll ← coll + rep
8:         rep ← rep + 1
9:     else
10:        rep ← 1
11:        x ← M[i]
```

Table 3. Average number of collisions using random permutations.

n	16					
$\log_2(q)$	6	7	8	9	10	11
real	0.06	0.27	0.96	3.72	15.62	63.59
ideal	0.023	0.12	0.48	1.98	7.91	31.17
n	20					
$\log_2(q)$	8	9	10	11	12	13
real	0.073	0.203	1.02	4.01	15.69	63.63
ideal	0.023	0.11	0.47	1.94	7.92	32.57

We also calculated the success rate, which is the number of successful distinguishing attempts over the total number of attempts, for different values of q

and $\theta(q,n)$. This is equivalent to the advantage in Theorem 3.1. Table 4 shows the success rate for the different parameters. The distinguisher reaches $\geq 85\%$ with $q = 2^{n/2+2}$ and 99% success rate with $q = 2^{n/2+3}$. The attack complexities are $2^{n/2+3}$ and $2^{n/2+4}$, respectively, since each iteration includes two queries to the construction. For large n, the factors 2^3 and 2^4 are small. With complexity $2^{n/2+5}$, we get a success rate of almost 100%, and an attack that breaks the security claim for In practice, $n \geq 64$. The complexity of the distinguisher is compared to known TNT distinguishers with $n = 128$ in Table 2.

Note that our experimental estimations closely match the advantage curve obtained through theoretical analysis, up to a change in constant. In fact, we get a more optimistic constant in experimental results. In particular, we estimate that the advantage is around

$$1 - 2\frac{2^n}{q^2},$$

but the discrepancy is expected since the theoretical advantage is more conservative and bound to be a bit loose for the sake of simplicity.

We also calculated the success rate, which is the number of successful distinguishing attempts over the total number of attempts, for different values of q and $\theta(q,n)$. Table 4 shows the success rate for the different parameters. The distinguisher reaches $\geq 85\%$ with $q = 2^{n/2+2}$ and 99% success rate with $q = 2^{n/2+3}$. The attack complexities are $2^{n/2+3}$ and $2^{n/2+4}$, respectively, since each iteration includes two queries to the construction. For large n, the factors 2^3 and 2^4 are small. With complexity $2^{n/2+5}$, we get a success rate of almost 100%, and an attack that breaks the security claim for In practice, $n \geq 64$. The complexity of the distinguisher is compared to known TNT distinguishers with $n = 128$ in Table 2.

Table 4. The success rate achieved for different values of n and q.

n	q	$\theta(q,n)$	Success Rate	q	$\theta(q,n)$	Success Rate
16	10	12	87.2%	11	48	99%
20	12	12	86.6%	13	48	99%
24	14	12	90%	15	48	99%
28	16	12	85%	17	48	99%
32	18	12	87.5%	19	48	99%

On the Time-Memory Trade-Off. Algorithm 2 runs in time $O(q)$, with space complexity $O(2^n)$. This is sufficient and provides optimal time complexity for information-theoretic (unbounded) adversaries. On the other hand, Algorithm 3 is more geared towards linear space complexity. Its time complexity is dominated by the sort function, which can be executed with time complexity $O(q \log_2(q))$

using merge-sort. The space complexity is dominated by the size of the list L which is $O(q)$.

In practice, while we assume that the cost of applying encryption is constant, executing q encryptions are decryptions is more costly than sort a list with q entries. However, the adversary will not actually execute the encryptions and decryptions themselves, but will request them from the challenger, and in that case, the time complexity of Algorithm 2 is indeed superior to that of Algorithm 3, since the former will be able to terminate shortly after all the queries are executed, while the later needs to execute the costly sorting operation. However, the exponential space complexity of Algorithm 2 makes it unsuitable for attacking practical instances of TNT. In Table 2, we provide the parameters for attacking TNT-AES using Algorithm 3, bounding both time and memory by $2^{n/2+5} = 2^{69}$. We ignore the $\log_2$ term in the time complexity since this is concerning the practical and not asymptotic performance, which is dominated by the encryptions and decryptions.

Attacking TNT-GIFT-64. We have implemented this variant to attack TNT instantiated with GIFT-64 [3]. We used the implementation of GIFT-64 described in [1] which can encrypt 2 blocks at the same time. We implemented the attack over 16 cores on an Intel Xeon E5-2630 CPU, each doing 2^{31} encryption calls and 2^{31} decryption calls (2^{30} calls $\times$ 2 blocks), generating 2^{35} blocks in total. This process took two hours (32 core-hours). In practice, the adversary is unlikely to be able to parallelize the queries, since that depends on the challenger.

Counting the collisions cannot be parallelized. It requires 40 min to count collisions in a set of 2^{32} blocks and 1 h, 20 min in a set of 2^{33} blocks, generating on average 1 collision and 4 collisions, respectively. These results are reported in details in Table 5. We note that for $q \geq 2^{34}$, the attack uses less memory and significantly more time than the other cases. This is due to memory limitations, since the platform is limited by 256 GB, so the collision counting phase had to be optimized towards memory consumption, leading to a significant slow down. The time in Table 5 seems (at first glance) dominated by collision counting, which is contradictory to the statement we made earlier. However, it is to be noted that the collision counting part is serial in nature, while the TNT queries have been parallelized. For instance, performing the attack with 2^{35} complexity needs 68 core-hour, while counting needs 36 core-hour on a limited memory machine, but can be faster on a machine with more memory. In particular, we estimate that with memory of about 384 GB and 768 GB, we can run the attacks with 2^{34} and 2^{35} complexities in slightly more than 20 and 40 core-hours, respectively.

Table 5. Results for an attack on TNT-GIFT-64.

n	64			
$\log_2(q)$	32	33	34	35
Average Number of Collisions	1	4	16	61
Time	3 h	3 h 40 mins	12 h 15 mins	20 h
CPU Time	5 h	10 h	28 h 15 mins	72 h
Number of Cores	2	4	8	16
RAM	96 GB	192 GB	128 GB	192 GB
Disk Space	73 GB	146 GB	292 GB	583 GB

4   Spotting the Flaw in the BBB Security Proof of TNT

In [4], Bao et al. presented an IND-CCA security proof for TNT that contradicts our attack. This proof employs the χ^2 technique [14] — a relatively new proof technique — due to Dai et al.

In this section, we carefully revisit the security proof with the distinguisher $\mathcal{A}^*$, and identify an issue that involves a subtle, yet fundamental, case analysis. We temporarily switch to the notation of [4] to follow their proof approach. Namely, the random variable corresponding to plaintext is referred to as X. The random variable corresponding to ciphertext is referred to as Y and the random variable corresponding to the tweak is referred to as T. The rest of the random variables are related to the internal values of TNT and relate to the first three variables as: $S = \pi_1(M)$, $U = T \oplus S$, $V = \pi_2(U)$, $W = T \oplus V$ and $Y = \pi_3(W)$. For the lth query to the construction, we define a set $\mathcal{Q}_l$ as the set of the first l queries $\{(T_1, X_1, Y_1), \ldots, (T_l, X_l, Y_l)\}$. We follow a slight abuse of notation utilized in [4]: we say $X \in \mathcal{Q}_l$ to mean $\exists (T, X, Y) \in \mathcal{Q}_l$, and similarly for Y. We define a random variable Inter as the vector of internal values in the first $l - 1$ queries:

$$((S_1, \ldots, S_{l-1}), (U_1, \ldots, U_{l-1}), (V_1, \ldots, V_{l-1}), (W_1, \ldots, W_{l-1})).$$

The main technique of the proof, from a high level point of view, works as follows:

- A deterministic distinguisher observes the first $l - 1$ queries and selects whether the next query is a forward or inverse query as well as the tweak T_l and the plaintext X_l or ciphertext Y_l (M_l and C_l using our notations, respectively).
- Find the probability distribution of all the internal values of the construction given the first $l - 1$ query. We call a set of possible vectors of internal values Inter.
- For each possible Inter, estimate the probability distribution of each possible response to query l.

The authors then analyze different possible cases and apply the χ^2 method on the resulting distribution.

In order to better understand the issue, we analyze our distinguisher in the flow of the security proof. Our distinguisher works as follows:

- If l is odd, it makes a forward query $(X_0, T_{l-2} + 1)$.
- If l is even, it makes a backward query $(Y_{l-1}, T_{l-1} \oplus \delta)$.

Let (S_o, U_o, V_o) are the output of π_1, input of π_2 and output of π_2 in the last (odd) query $l - 1$, and we estimate the probability, for a given $X_i \in \mathcal{Q}_l$ where i is even, $\Pr[X_l = X_i]$.

Let (S_i, U_i, V_i) and (S_e, U_e, V_e) are the corresponding internal values of X_i and X_l, respectively. Then, we know that $V_o \oplus V_e = \delta$ and

$$\Pr[X_l = X_i] = \Pr[S_e = S_i] = \Pr[U_e \oplus T_{l-1} \oplus \delta = U_i \oplus T_{i-1} \oplus \delta]$$
$$= \Pr[U_e \oplus U_i = T_{l-1} \oplus T_{i-1}]$$

Since X_0 is fixed for all odd queries, so is S_o. Thus, $U_o \oplus T_{l-1} = U_{i-1} \oplus T_{i-1}$. Therefore,

$$\Pr[U_e \oplus U_i = T_{l-1} \oplus T_{i-1}] = \Pr[U_e \oplus U_o = U_i \oplus U_{i-1}] \approx \frac{c}{2^n},$$

where c is a small positive integer constant. The security proof considers two possible cases such collisions may occur. The first is when U_e has appeared before in one of the previous queries, and the second is when it has never appeared before. They dubbed these two cases as class $\mathcal{A}$ and class $\mathcal{B}$ respectively. The collision can occur in either class $\mathcal{A}$ or class $\mathcal{B}$, which the proof bounds the probability of their probability for the lth query by $4l/2^{2n}$ and $1/(2^n - l)$, respectively. Thus, our analysis deviates from the distribution assumed in [4]. In terms of the proof presented in [4], the event we are discussing belongs to case 5 (case 1 if we swap all the forward and backward queries). In this case, the authors claim [4, (9)]).

$$\Pr[X_l = X_i] \leq \frac{4l}{2^{2n}} + \frac{1}{2^n - l}$$

We argue that the distribution assumed for case 5/case 1 - class $\mathcal{A}$ erroneously underestimates the probability of certain bad events, and by changing the distribution to account for these bad events, the proof argumentation falls apart. Besides, it is not clear how to do so in the existing proof framework using the χ^2 method.

In particular, we look at the term $4l/2^{2n}$. The term stems from the following argument in [4]:

It remains to bound $\Pr[\mathsf{Inter} \in \mathcal{A}|\mathcal{Q}_{l-1}]$. For this, note that once the values in Inter except for $(\mathsf{S}_l, \mathsf{W}_l)$ have been fixed, the number of choices for $(\mathsf{S}_l, \mathsf{W}_l)$ is at least $(2^n - \alpha(\mathcal{Q}_{l-1}))(2^n - \gamma(\mathcal{Q}_{l-1})) \geq 2^{2n}/4$, where $\alpha(\mathcal{Q}_{l-1}) \geq q \geq 2^n/2$ and $\gamma(\mathcal{Q}_{l-1}) \geq q \geq 2^n/2$ are the number of distinct values in $(\mathsf{S}_1, \dots \mathsf{S}_{l-1})$ and $(\mathsf{W}_1, \dots \mathsf{W}_{l-1})$. Out of these $\geq 2^{2n}/4$ choices, the number of choices that ensure the desired property TNT $(\mathsf{T}_l, \mathsf{X}_l) = \mathsf{Y}_l$ is at most $l - 1$, which results from the following selection process: we first pick a pair of input-output $(\mathsf{U}_i, \mathsf{V}_i)$ with $i \leq l - 1$, and then set $\mathsf{S}_l = \mathsf{T}_l \oplus \mathsf{U}_i$ and $\mathsf{W}_l = \mathsf{T}_l \oplus \mathsf{V}_i$. Therefore, $\Pr[\mathsf{Inter} \in \mathcal{A}|\mathcal{Q}_{l-1}] \leq 4l/2^{2n}$, and thus the upper bound in this case is

$$\frac{4l}{2^{2n}} + \frac{1}{2^n - l}.$$

Consider the first case of the collision in Fig. 5. We note that if the triplet $(\alpha, \mathsf{S}_o, \mathsf{U}_o)$ is known, then the collision happens with probability 1, which puts it in class $\mathcal{A}$. Then, what remains is to calculate what is the probability that the adversary can force this collision, i.e.,

$$\Pr[\mathsf{Inter} \in \mathcal{A}|\mathcal{Q}_{l-1}] = \Pr[\mathsf{U}_e \oplus \mathsf{U}_o = \mathsf{T}_{l-1} \oplus \mathsf{T}_{i-1}|\mathcal{Q}_{l-1}],$$

where $\mathsf{T}_{l-1} = t_{l/2}$ and $\mathsf{T}_{i-1} = t_{i/2}$ are determined by the adversary during previous queries. This means than once U_o and all other values of U except U_e in Inter are fixed (both U_o and U_e belong to queries $i, j < l$), U_e has at most $2^n - \alpha(\mathcal{Q}_{l-1})$ choices where $\alpha(\mathcal{Q}_{l-1}) \leq q \leq 2^{n-1}$ is the number of distinct values in $\{\mathsf{U}_1, \dots \mathsf{U}_l\} \setminus \{\mathsf{U}_e\}$, and at most 1 of them ($\mathsf{U}_e = \mathsf{U}_o \oplus \alpha$) enforces the collision. In other words,

$$\Pr[\mathsf{Inter} \in \mathcal{A}|\mathcal{Q}_{l-1}] = \Pr[\mathsf{U}_e \oplus \mathsf{U}_o = \mathsf{T}_{l-1} \oplus \mathsf{T}_{i-1}|\mathcal{Q}_{l-1}] \geq \frac{1}{2^n - \alpha(\mathcal{Q}_{l-1})}$$

$$\geq \frac{1}{2^n} \gg \frac{4l}{2^{2n}},$$

when $l \ll q$, contradicting [4, (9)]. This reflects in the final analysis of case 1 as follows: In [4, (11)], we take the maximum of two expressions. One is on the form $al/2^{2n}$ for a small constant a, and one is on the form $4l/2^{2n} + O(l/2^{2n})$. The term $4l/2^{2n}$ comes from [4, (9)]. However, if the term is on the form $O(1/2^n)$ instead of $4l/2^{2n}$, as suggested by our attack, then the maximum function in [4, (11)] would return $O(1/2^n) + O(l/2^{2n})$. Thus, the squared difference used in the χ^2 statistic becomes one the form

$$\left(\frac{1}{2^n - \alpha(\mathcal{Q}_{l-1})} - \frac{1}{2^n - \mu_l} + \frac{1}{2^n - l} \right)^2$$

or

$$\left(\frac{A2^n + B2^{2n}}{2^{3n}} \right)^2$$

for some constants A and B. Note that $\alpha(\mathcal{Q}_{l-1})$ is based on the probabilistic behaviour of the transcript, while μ_l is fully controlled by the adversary, and we cannot ensure that $\mu_l = \alpha(\mathcal{Q}_{l-1})$. Thus, the squared difference cannot be bounded tighter than $O(1/2^{2n})$. Besides,

$$\frac{1}{2^n - \alpha(\mathcal{Q}_{l-1})}$$

is a lower bound. The χ^2 statistic then becomes on the form

$$\sum \frac{O(1/2^{2n})}{O(1/2^n)} \approx \sum O(1/2^n) \approx 2^n \dot{O}(1/2^n) \approx O(1)$$

not leading to any meaningful security.

Note that the values of V_i and W_i for $i < l$ did not affect the behaviour of the collision or the probability that Inter is in class $\mathcal{A}$. It seems the ambiguity may stem from applying the χ^2 method to a primitive with two dependent functions ($\tilde{\pi}$ and its inverse). By cascading forward and backward queries, we managed to eliminate W_i for all $1 \leq i \leq q$ and the values of W_l do not matter for the attack. Similarly, by fixing the difference between V_o and V_e to a constant δ, we minimize the effect of their exact values on the attack.

5   Birthday-Bound Security of **TNT** and Its Variant

In light of the above discussion, it is clear that the security of TNT is in limbo. One can rely on the IND-CCA bound by Zhang et al. to demonstrate the tightness of the proposed attacks. However, we observe that the generic bound in [43]

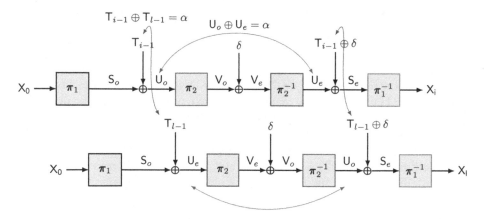

Fig. 5. A class $\mathcal{A}$ collision occurring in Algorithm 1. If the collision occurs, then permutation calls with the same color compute the same permutation point. Curved arrows represent difference relations (if the collision occurs with these internal values, each two connected nodes differ by α).

introduces some constant factors, and in general, an independent security proof, using a different proof technique, will instill greater confidence in the revised security claims of TNT.

Theorem 5.1. *Let* π_1, π_2, *and* π_3 *be three independent random permutations of* $\{0,1\}^n$. *Then, for all* $q \geq 1$, *we have*

$$\mathbf{Adv}_{TNT}^{\text{ind-cca}}(q) \leq \frac{q^2}{2^n}.$$

In fact, we intend to prove a stronger version of Theorem 5.1, as stated in Theorem 5.2 below. Particularly, we show that even the single-keyed TNT, which we denote as 1k-TNT, is sufficient to achieve birthday-bound security. A proof of Theorem 5.1 is available in the full version of this paper [24], for the sake of completeness.

Theorem 5.2. *Let* $\pi_1 = \pi_2 = \pi_3 = \pi$, *where* π *is a uniform random permutation of* $\{0,1\}^n$. *Then, for all* $q \geq 1$, *we have*

$$\mathbf{Adv}_{1k\text{-}TNT}^{\text{ind-cca}}(q) \leq \frac{8q^2}{2^n}.$$

Proof. The statement is vacuously true for $q \geq 2^{n/2}$. We will use the Expectation method (see Lemma 2.1) to prove the statement for $1 \leq q < 2^{n/2}$.

Let $\mathcal{O}_1$ and $\mathcal{O}_0$ be the oracles corresponding to 1k-TNT and a tweakable random permutation $\widetilde{\pi}$, respectively. If $(\mathsf{T}_i, \mathsf{M}_i)$ is the encryption query with a tweak T_i we write the response as $\widehat{\mathsf{C}}_i$. Similarly, if $(\mathsf{T}_i, \widehat{\mathsf{C}}_i)$ is the decryption query with a tweak T_i we write the response as M_i. After all queries have been made, the two oracles release some additional data to the adversary, who is obviously free to ignore this additional information, $\widehat{\mathsf{M}}^q$ and C^q.

In the real world, $\widehat{\mathsf{M}}^q$ and C^q correspond to the output of the first permutation and input of the third permutation, respectively, and thus they are well defined from the definition of 1k-TNT. The real-world transcript is thus defined as the tuple

$$\Theta_1 := (\mathsf{T}^q, \mathsf{M}^q, \widehat{\mathsf{C}}^q, \widehat{\mathsf{M}}^q, \mathsf{C}^q).$$

In the ideal system $\widetilde{\pi}$, we sample $\widehat{\mathsf{M}}^q, \mathsf{C}^q$ as follows: For every $i \in [q]$,

1. $\widehat{\mathsf{M}}_i = \widehat{\mathsf{M}}_j$ whenever $\mathsf{M}_i = \mathsf{M}_j$ for $j < i$. Otherwise (for all $j < i$, $\mathsf{M}_j \neq \mathsf{M}_i$), we sample

$$\widehat{\mathsf{M}}_i \xleftarrow{\$} \{0,1\}^n \setminus \mathsf{S}(\widehat{\mathsf{M}}^{[i-1]}).$$

2. $\mathsf{C}_i = \mathsf{C}_j$ whenever $\widehat{\mathsf{C}}_j = \widehat{\mathsf{C}}_i$ for $j < i$. Otherwise (for all $j < i$, $\widehat{\mathsf{C}}_j \neq \widehat{\mathsf{C}}_i$), we sample

$$\mathsf{C}_i \xleftarrow{\$} \{0,1\}^n \setminus \mathsf{S}(\mathsf{C}^{[i-1]}).$$

The ideal world transcript is defined as

$$\Theta_0 := (\mathsf{T}^q, \mathsf{M}^q, \widehat{\mathsf{C}}^q, \widehat{\mathsf{M}}^q, \mathsf{C}^q).$$

Note that we use the same notation to denote the random variables in both worlds. However, their probability distributions will be unambiguously determined at the time of probability computations.

BAD TRANSCRIPT AND ITS ANALYSIS: Let $u^q := \widehat{m}^q \oplus t^q$, and $\widehat{u}^q := c^q \oplus t^q$. A transcript $(t^q, m^q, \widehat{c}^q, \widehat{m}^q, c^q)$ is called *bad* if and only if any of the following bad events occur:

bad_{1a}: $\exists i \neq j \in [q]$ such that $\widehat{m}_i = \widehat{c}_j$.
bad_{1b}: $\exists i \neq j \in [q]$ such that $c_i = m_j$.
bad_{2a}: $\exists i < j \in [q]$ such that $u_i = u_j$.
bad_{2b}: $\exists i < j \in [q]$ such that $\widehat{u}_i = \widehat{u}_j$.
bad_{3a}: $\exists i \neq j \in [q]$ such that $u_i = m_j$.
bad_{3b}: $\exists i \neq j \in [q]$ such that $\widehat{u}_i = \widehat{c}_j$.
bad_{4a}: $\exists i \neq j \in [q]$ such that $u_i = c_j$.
bad_{4b}: $\exists i \neq j \in [q]$ such that $\widehat{u}_i = \widehat{m}_j$.

Let Ω_{bad} denote the set of all bad transcripts. Then, using union bound, we have

$$\Pr\left(\Theta_0 \in \Omega_{\text{bad}}\right) \leq \sum_{\substack{i \in [4] \\ s \in \{a,b\}}} \Pr\left(\text{bad}_{is}\right) \tag{16}$$

On the right-hand side, we bound the probability for bad_{ia} for all $i \in [4]$. The $s = b$ cases can be bounded analogously.

- $\Pr\left(\text{bad}_{1a}\right) \leq \frac{q^2}{2^n}$. This follows from union bound: For a fixed choice of i and j, bad_{1a} happens with 2^{-n} probability, and there are q^2 such (i, j) pairs.
- $\Pr\left(\text{bad}_{2a}\right) \leq \sum_{i<j} \Pr\left(\widehat{M}_i + T_i = \widehat{M}_j + T_j\right) \leq q^2/2^n$. This can be argued as follows: For fixed i and j, $\Pr\left(\widehat{M}_i + T_i = \widehat{M}_j + T_j\right) \leq 1/2^{n-1} \leq 2^{1-n}$, and there are $\binom{q}{2}$ such (i, j) pairs.
- $\Pr\left(\text{bad}_{3a}\right) \leq \frac{q^2}{2^n}$. The argumentation is similar to the one for bad_{1a}.
- $\Pr\left(\text{bad}_{4a}\right) \leq \frac{q^2}{2^n}$. This can be argued as follows: For any fixed i and j, bad_{4a} happens with at most 2^{-n} probability, and there are at most q^2 such (i, j) pairs.

Thus, on combining everything in (16), we have

$$\Pr\left(\Theta_0 \in \Omega_{\text{bad}}\right) \leq \frac{8q^2}{2^n}.$$

ANALYSIS OF GOOD TRANSCRIPTS: For a good transcript $\tau = (t^q, m^q, \widehat{c}^q, \widehat{m}^q, c^q)$, we know that $(m^q, \widehat{m}^q)$, $(c^q, \widehat{c}^q)$, and $(u^q, \widehat{u}^q)$ are permutation consistent non-overlapping input-output pairs and hence for the real world we have

$$\Pr(\Theta_1 = \omega) = \Pr(\boldsymbol{\pi}(m^q) = \widehat{m}^q) \times \Pr(\boldsymbol{\pi}(u^q) = \widehat{u}^q) \times \Pr(\boldsymbol{\pi}(c^q) = \widehat{c}^q)$$

$$= \frac{1}{(2^n)_{r+q+s}}$$

where r and s denote the size of $S(m^q)$ and $S(\widehat{c}^q)$ respectively. In the ideal world, we have,

$$\Pr(\Theta_0 = \omega) = \Pr(\widetilde{\pi}(t^q, m^q) = \widehat{c}^q) \times \frac{1}{(2^n)_r} \times \frac{1}{(2^n)_s} \leq \frac{1}{(2^n)_q} \times \frac{1}{(2^n)_r} \times \frac{1}{(2^n)_s},$$

where the final inequality follows from the fact that $\Pr(\widetilde{\pi}(t^q, m^q) = \widehat{c}^q)$ maximizes when $t_i = t_j$ for all $1 \leq i < j \leq q$. Thus

$$\frac{\Pr(\Theta_1 = \omega)}{\Pr(\Theta_0 = \omega)} \geq \frac{(2^n)_q \times (2^n)_r \times (2^n)_s}{(2^n)_{q+r+s}} \geq 1$$

Now the result follows from the Expectation method by setting ϵ_{ratio} to be a zero function.

6   The Generalized LRW Paradigm

In this section, we propose a generalized view of the cascaded LRW design that encompasses both cascaded LRW1 and cascaded LRW2 constructions. In addition, we identify some necessary properties to guarantee IND-CCA security up to $2^{3n/4}$ queries.

ALMOST XOR UNIVERSAL HASH FUNCTION: A (τ, n)-hash function family $\mathcal{H}$, is a family of functions $\{h : \{0,1\}^\tau \rightarrow \{0,1\}^n\}$, keyed implicitly by the choice of h. A (τ, n)-hash function family $\mathcal{H}$ is called an ϵ-almost XOR universal hash family (AXUHF) if for all $t \neq t' \in \{0,1\}^\tau$, and $\delta \in \{0,1\}^n$, we have

$$\Pr(H \leftarrow_\$ \mathcal{H} : H(t) \oplus H(t') = \delta) \leq \epsilon. \tag{17}$$

For the special case of $\delta = 0^n$, $\mathcal{H}$ is referred as an ϵ-AUHF.

THE LRW+ CONSTRUCTION: Let $\widetilde{\mathcal{H}}$ be a family of (τ, n)-tweakable permutations, and $\mathcal{H}$ be a (τ, n)-hash function family. Let $\widehat{\mathcal{H}} = (\widetilde{\mathcal{H}}^2 \times \mathcal{H})$, $(\widetilde{H}_1, \widetilde{H}_2, H) \leftarrow KG(\widehat{\mathcal{H}})$, and $(\boldsymbol{\pi}_1, \boldsymbol{\pi}_2) \leftarrow_\$ \text{Perm}(n)$, where $KG(\widehat{\mathcal{H}})$ is an efficient probabilistic algorithm that returns a random triple from $\widehat{\mathcal{H}}$.

The LRW+ construction is a (τ, n)- tweakable permutation family, defined by the following mapping (see Fig. 6 for an illustration):

$$(t, m) \mapsto \widetilde{H}_2^{-1}\left(t, \boldsymbol{\pi}_2\left(H(t) \oplus \boldsymbol{\pi}_1\left(\widetilde{H}_1(t, m)\right)\right)\right). \tag{18}$$

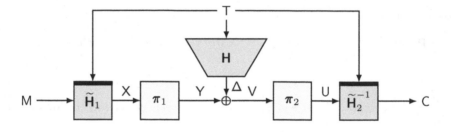

Fig. 6. The LRW+ construction.

6.1   Security of LRW+

We say that $\mathsf{KG}\left(\widehat{\mathcal{H}}\right)$ is a pairwise independent sampling mechanism or PISM, if $(\widetilde{\mathsf{H}}_1, \widetilde{\mathsf{H}}_2, \mathsf{H}) \leftarrow \mathsf{KG}\left(\widehat{\mathcal{H}}\right)$ is a pairwise independent tuple.

We say that $\widetilde{\mathcal{H}}$ is an ϵ-almost universal tweakable permutation family (AUTPF) if and only if for all distinct $(t, m), (t', m') \in \{0, 1\}^\tau \times \{0, 1\}^n$,

$$\Pr\left(\widetilde{\mathsf{H}} \leftarrow_\$ \widetilde{\mathcal{H}} \ : \ \widetilde{\mathsf{H}}(t, m) = \widetilde{\mathsf{H}}(t', m')\right) \leq \epsilon.$$

Theorem 6.1. *Let* $\tau, n \in \mathbb{N}$, *and* $\epsilon_1, \epsilon_2 \in [0, 1]$. *If* $\widetilde{\mathcal{H}}$ *and* $\mathcal{H}$ *are respectively* ϵ_1-*AUTPF and* ϵ_2-*AUHF, and* $\mathsf{KG}\left(\widehat{\mathcal{H}}\right)$ *is a PISM, then, for* $q \leq 2^{n-2}$, *we have*

$$\mathbf{Adv}^{\mathsf{ind\text{-}cca}}_{LRW+}(q) \leq \epsilon(q, n),$$

where

$$\epsilon(q, n) = 2q^2 \epsilon_1^{1.5} + \frac{4q^4 \epsilon_1^2}{2^n} + \frac{32q^4 \epsilon_1}{2^{2n}} + \frac{13q^4}{2^{3n}} + q^2 \epsilon_1^2 + q^2 \epsilon_1 \epsilon_2 + \frac{2q^2}{2^{2n}}. \tag{19}$$

A proof of this theorem follows from a simple generalization of Jha and Nandi's (JN) proof [26] for 2-LRW2. In particular, the exact same strategy of using the expectation method with the JN adaptation of mirror theory [10, 37] in the tweakable permutation settings works here as well. For the sake of completeness, we give the complete proof in the full version of this paper [24].

Remark 6.1. The proof presented in [26] appears to have overlooked the analysis of a specific subset of transcripts, which in hindsight of our generalized analysis seems to be a minor issue. Indeed, our proof demonstrates that this omission does not impact the overall bound significantly, with any potential effects being limited to a small constant factor.

6.2   Instantiating LRW+

We show that any cascaded LRW construction with $r \geq 2$ rounds can be viewed as an instance of LRW+. Thus, they can be proven secure up to $2^{3n/4}$ queries provided the derived hash functions are close to 2^{-n}-universal. Note that it would be sufficient to define $\widetilde{H}_1, \widetilde{H}_2, H, \pi_1$ and π_2 for each construction. In the following discussion, let $\pi'^r \leftarrow_\$ \mathsf{Perm}(n)$ and $H'^r \leftarrow_\$ \mathcal{H}^r$, where $\mathcal{H}$ is an ϵ-AXUHF.

Cascaded LRW1. For $r \geq 2$, the r-LRW1$[\pi^r]$ construction takes as input $(t, m) \in \{0,1\}^n \times \{0,1\}^n$ and returns $c \in \{0,1\}^n$, which is defined as follows: Let $y_0 = t \oplus m$ and for all $i \in [r]$:

$$x_i := t \oplus y_{i-1} \qquad \text{and} \qquad y_i := \pi'_i(x_i),$$

and finally $c := y_r$. The inverse of r-LRW1 is analogously defined.

CASCADED LRW1 AS AN INSTANCE OF LRW+: For some $r \geq 2$, $r' := \lfloor r/2 \rfloor$, and any (t, m) such that $r\text{-LRW1}(t, m) = c$, define $\widetilde{H}_1(t, m) := x_{r'}$, $H(t) := t$, $\widetilde{H}_2(t, c) := y_{r'+1}$, $\pi_1 := \pi'_{r'}$, and $\pi_2 := \pi'^{-1}_{r'+1}$.

Clearly, the LRW+ instance so defined is same as r-LRW1. We have the following corollary on the security of cascaded LRW1.

Corollary 6.1. *For $r \geq 4$, we have*

$$\mathbf{Adv}^{\mathsf{ind\text{-}cca}}_{r\text{-}LRW1}(q) \leq \frac{2q^2}{(2^n - 1)^{1.5n}} + \frac{49q^4}{(2^n - 1)^3} + \frac{3q^2}{(2^n - 1)^2}.$$

In particular, for $r = 4$, we have proved CCA security for 4-LRW1 up to $2^{3n/4}$ queries. A proof of this corollary is available in the full version of this paper [24].

Cascaded LRW2. For $r \geq 1$, the r-LRW2$[\pi^r, H'^r]$ construction takes as input $(t, m) \in \{0,1\}^\tau \times \{0,1\}^n$ and returns $c \in \{0,1\}^n$, which is defined as follows: Let $y_0 = m$, H'_0 be a constant function that returns 0^n, and for all $i \in [r]$:

$$x_i := H'_{i-1}(t) \oplus H'_i(t) \oplus y_{i-1} \qquad \text{and} \qquad y_i := \pi'_i(x_i),$$

and finally $c := H'_r(t) \oplus y_r$. The inverse of r-LRW2 is analogously defined.

CASCADED LRW2 AS AN INSTANCE OF LRW+: For some $r \geq 2$, $r' = \lfloor r/2 \rfloor$, and any (t, k, m) such that $r\text{-LRW2}(t, m) = c$, define $\widetilde{H}_1(t, m) := x_{r'}$, $H(t) := H'_{r'}(t) \oplus H'_{r'+1}(t)$, $\widetilde{H}_2(t, c) := y_{r'+1}$, $\pi_1 := \pi'_{r'}$, $\pi_2 := \pi'^{-1}_{r'+1}$.

Clearly, the LRW+ instance so defined is same as r-LRW2. We have the following corollary on the security of cascaded LRW2.

Corollary 6.2. *For $r \geq 2$, we have*

$$\mathbf{Adv}^{\mathsf{ind\text{-}cca}}_{r\text{-}LRW2}(q) \leq 2q^2\epsilon^{1.5} + \frac{4q^4\epsilon^2}{2^n} + \frac{32q^4\epsilon}{2^{2n}} + \frac{13q^4}{2^{3n}} + 2q^2\epsilon^2 + \frac{2q^2}{2^{2n}}.$$

In particular, for $r = 2$, assuming $\epsilon = O\left(2^{-n}\right)$, we have reproved[4] the CCA security for 2-LRW2 up to $2^{3n/4}$ queries. A proof of this corollary is available in the full version of this paper [24].

---

[4] The proof in [26] also has a minor issue, that leads to a slightly worse constant.

7　Conclusion and Future Directions

In this paper, we gave a birthday-bound CCA distinguisher on TNT, thereby completely invalidating its beyond-the-birthday bound security claims. Further, we showed that our attack is tight by reestablishing a birthday bound security for TNT and its single-keyed variant.

In addition, we showed that by adding just one more block cipher call, the security can be amplified to $3n/4$-bit even in the CCA setting. We note that our generalization of the cascaded LRW constructions could be of independent interest.

OPEN PROBLEMS: This work opens several new research avenues in (block cipher-based) TBC constructions. Some prominent problems that are worth exploring include:

1. OPTIMAL LRW CONSTRUCTION FOR BBB SECURITY: 4-LRW1 employs 4 calls of block cipher. Similarly, 2-LRW2 with block cipher based hash functions also requires 4 calls. This raises a natural question regarding their optimality. In other words, are 4 block cipher calls necessary for BBB security?
2. REDUCED-KEY VERSION OF 4-LRW1: 4-LRW1 needs 4 independent keys. Is it possible to reduce the number of keys from 4 to 3, or 2?
3. EXACT SECURITY OF 4-LRW1: We do not have an attack against 4-LRW1. Neither Mennink's $O(\sqrt{n}2^{3n/4})$-distinguisher, nor any variant of our $O(2^{n/2})$-distinguisher seem to work. The additional permutation calls seem to help in avoiding these attack strategies. It would be interesting to see if there exists an attack that matches our bound, or if the construction is beyond $3n/4$-bit secure?
4. SECURITY OF SHORT-TWEAK TNT: Our attack requires a tweak space of size roughly $2^{n/2}$. So it is natural to ask if TNT is still BBB secure when the tweak space size is much less than $2^{n/2}$?
5. SECURITY OF LONGER CASCADES OF LRW: This is a long standing problem even for the more analyzed case of r-LRW2, for $r \geq 3$. The best bounds [11,43] that we have in this case are coupling-based. It is clear from our bound for LRW+ that these bounds are rather loose. It would be interesting to explore the possibility of better security bounds for the general case with a dedicated and more tighter analysis.

Acknowledgments. The authors would like to thank Chun Guo for his comments on the attacks presented on TNT. This work was partially supported by the German Research Foundation (DFG) within the framework of the Excellence Strategy of the Federal Government and the States – EXC 2092 CASA – 39078197. Additionally, a part of this work was carried out under the framework of the French-German-Center for Cybersecurity, a collaboration of CISPA and LORIA, while Ashwin Jha was employed at the CISPA Helmholtz Center for Information Security. Mustafa Khairallah performed this work as part of the Seagate Research Group.

References

1. Adomnicai, A., Najm, Z., Peyrin, T.: Fixslicing: a new GIFT representation fast constant-time implementations of GIFT and GIFT-COFB on ARM cortex-m. IACR Trans. Cryptogr. Hardw. Embed. Syst. **2020**(3), 402–427 (2020)
2. Avanzi, R.: The QARMA block cipher family. almost MDS matrices over rings with zero divisors, nearly symmetric even-mansour constructions with non-involutory central rounds, and search heuristics for low-latency s-boxes. IACR Trans. Symmetric Cryptol. **2017**(1), 4–44 (2017)
3. Banik, S., Pandey, S.K., Peyrin, T., Sasaki, Y., Sim, S.M., Todo, Y.: GIFT: A small present - towards reaching the limit of lightweight encryption. In: Cryptographic Hardware and Embedded Systems - CHES 2017, Proceedings, pp. 321–345 (2017)
4. Bao, Z., Guo, C., Guo, J., Song, L.: TNT: how to tweak a block cipher. In: Advances in Cryptology - EUROCRYPT 2020, Proceedings, Part II, pp. 641–673 (2020)
5. Bariant, A., Leurent, G.: Truncated boomerang attacks and application to aes-based ciphers. In: Advances in Cryptology - EUROCRYPT 2023, Proceedings, Part IV, pp. 3–35 (2023). https://doi.org/10.1007/978-3-031-30634-1_1
6. Beierle, C., Jean, J., Kölbl, S., Leander, G., Moradi, A., Peyrin, T., Sasaki, Yu., Sasdrich, P., Sim, S.M.: The SKINNY family of block ciphers and its low-latency variant MANTIS. In: Robshaw, M., Katz, J. (eds.) CRYPTO 2016. LNCS, vol. 9815, pp. 123–153. Springer, Heidelberg (2016). https://doi.org/10.1007/978-3-662-53008-5_5
7. Bhattacharya, S., Nandi, M.: A note on the chi-square method: a tool for proving cryptographic security. Cryptogr. Commun. **10**(5), 935–957 (2018)
8. Bhaumik, R., List, E., Nandi, M.: ZCZ - Achieving n-bit SPRP Security with a Minimal Number of Tweakable-Block-Cipher Calls. In: Advances in Cryptology - ASIACRYPT 2018, Proceedings, Part I. pp. 336–366 (2018)
9. Chakraborty, D., Sarkar, P.: A General Construction of Tweakable Block Ciphers and Different Modes of Operations. IEEE Trans. Information Theory **54**(5), 1991–2006 (2008)
10. Cogliati, B., Dutta, A., Nandi, M., Patarin, J., Saha, A.: Proof of mirror theory for a wide range of ξ_max. In: Advances in Cryptology - EUROCRYPT 2023, Proceedings, Part IV, pp. 470–501 (2023). https://doi.org/10.1007/978-3-031-30634-1_16
11. Cogliati, B., Lampe, R., Seurin, Y.: Tweaking even-mansour ciphers. In: Advances in Cryptology - CRYPTO 2015, Proceedings, Part I. pp. 189–208 (2015). https://doi.org/10.1007/978-3-662-47989-6_9
12. Cogliati, B., Seurin, Y.: Beyond-birthday-bound security for tweakable even-mansour ciphers with linear tweak and key mixing. In: Advances in Cryptology - ASIACRYPT 2015, Proceedings, Part II, pp. 134–158 (2015).https://doi.org/10.1007/978-3-662-48800-3_6
13. Crowley, P.: Mercy: A Fast Large Block Cipher for Disk Sector Encryption. In: Fast Software Encryption - FSE 2000, Proceedings, pp. 49–63 (2000)
14. Dai, W., Hoang, V.T., Tessaro, S.: Information-theoretic indistinguishability via the chi-squared method. In: Katz, J., Shacham, H. (eds.) CRYPTO 2017. LNCS, vol. 10403, pp. 497–523. Springer, Cham (2017). https://doi.org/10.1007/978-3-319-63697-9_17
15. Datta, N., Dey, S., Dutta, A., Mondal, S.: Cascading Four Round LRW1 is Beyond Birthday Bound Secure. IACR Cryptol. ePrint Arch, p. 1242 (2023). https://eprint.iacr.org/2023/1242

16. Granger, R., Jovanovic, P., Mennink, B., Neves, S.: Improved masking for tweakable blockciphers with applications to authenticated encryption. In: Fischlin, M., Coron, J.-S. (eds.) EUROCRYPT 2016. LNCS, vol. 9665, pp. 263–293. Springer, Heidelberg (2016). https://doi.org/10.1007/978-3-662-49890-3_11

17. Gunsing, A., Bhaumik, R., Jha, A., Mennink, B., Shen, Y.: Revisiting the indifferentiability of the sum of permutations. IACR Cryptol. ePrint Arch., p. 840 (2023)

18. Guo, C., Guo, J., List, E., Song, L.: Towards closing the security gap of Tweak-aNd-Tweak (TNT). In: Moriai, S., Wang, H. (eds.) ASIACRYPT 2020. LNCS, vol. 12491, pp. 567–597. Springer, Cham (2020). https://doi.org/10.1007/978-3-030-64837-4_19

19. Guo, Z., Wang, G., Dunkelman, O., Pan, Y., Liu, S.: Tweakable SM4: how to tweak SM4 into tweakable block ciphers? J. Inf. Secur. Appl. **72**, 103406 (2023)

20. Hoang, V.T., Tessaro, S.: Key-alternating ciphers and key-length extension: exact bounds and multi-user security. In: Robshaw, M., Katz, J. (eds.) CRYPTO 2016. LNCS, vol. 9814, pp. 3–32. Springer, Heidelberg (2016). https://doi.org/10.1007/978-3-662-53018-4_1

21. Iwata, T., Minematsu, K., Peyrin, T., Seurin, Y.: ZMAC: a fast tweakable block cipher mode for highly secure message authentication. In: Katz, J., Shacham, H. (eds.) CRYPTO 2017. LNCS, vol. 10403, pp. 34–65. Springer, Cham (2017). https://doi.org/10.1007/978-3-319-63697-9_2

22. Jean, J., Nikolić, I., Peyrin, T.: Tweaks and keys for block ciphers: the TWEAKEY framework. In: Sarkar, P., Iwata, T. (eds.) ASIACRYPT 2014. LNCS, vol. 8874, pp. 274–288. Springer, Heidelberg (2014). https://doi.org/10.1007/978-3-662-45608-8_15

23. Jean, J., Nikolic, I., Peyrin, T., Seurin, Y.: The deoxys AEAD family. J. Cryptol. **34**(3), 31 (2021)

24. Jha, A., Khairallah, M., Nandi, M., Saha, A.: Tight security of TNT and beyond: Attacks, proofs and possibilities for the cascaded LRW paradigm. IACR Cryptol. ePrint Arch., p. 1272 (2023)

25. Jha, A., List, E., Minematsu, K., Mishra, S., Nandi, M.: XHX – a framework for optimally secure tweakable block ciphers from classical block ciphers and universal hashing. In: Lange, T., Dunkelman, O. (eds.) LATINCRYPT 2017. LNCS, vol. 11368, pp. 207–227. Springer, Cham (2019). https://doi.org/10.1007/978-3-030-25283-0_12

26. Jha, A., Nandi, M.: Tight security of cascaded LRW2. J. Cryptol. **33**(3), 1272–1317 (2020)

27. Jha, A., Nandi, M., Saha, A.: Tight security of TNT: reinforcing Khairallah's birthday-bound attack. IACR Cryptol. ePrint Arch., p. 1233 (2023)

28. Khairallah, M.: CLRW1^3 is not Secure Beyond the Birthday Bound Breaking TNT with $O(2^{n/2})$ Queries. IACR Cryptol. ePrint Arch., p. 1212 (2023)

29. Krovetz, T., Rogaway, P.: The software performance of authenticated-encryption modes. In: Fast Software Encryption - FSE 2011. Revised Selected Papers, pp. 306–327 (2011)

30. Lampe, R., Seurin, Y.: Tweakable blockciphers with asymptotically optimal security. In: Fast Software Encryption - FSE 2013, Revised Selected Papers, pp. 133–151 (2013)

31. Landecker, W., Shrimpton, T., Terashima, R.S.: Tweakable blockciphers with beyond birthday-bound security. In: Safavi-Naini, R., Canetti, R. (eds.) CRYPTO 2012. LNCS, vol. 7417, pp. 14–30. Springer, Heidelberg (2012). https://doi.org/10.1007/978-3-642-32009-5_2

32. Liskov, M., Rivest, R.L., Wagner, D.: Tweakable block ciphers. In: Yung, M. (ed.) CRYPTO 2002. LNCS, vol. 2442, pp. 31–46. Springer, Heidelberg (2002). https:// doi.org/10.1007/3-540-45708-9_3

33. Mennink, B.: Optimally secure tweakable blockciphers. In: Fast Software Encryption - FSE 2015, Revised Selected Papers, pp. 428–448 (2015)

34. Mennink, B.: Towards tight security of cascaded LRW2. In: Beimel, A., Dziembowski, S. (eds.) TCC 2018. LNCS, vol. 11240, pp. 192–222. Springer, Cham (2018). https://doi.org/10.1007/978-3-030-03810-6_8

35. Minematsu, K.: Improved security analysis of XEX and LRW modes. In: Selected Areas in Cryptography - SAC 2006, Revised Selected Papers, pp. 96–113 (2006)

36. Patarin, J.: The "Coefficients H" technique. In: Selected Areas in Cryptography - SAC 2008, Revised Selected Papers, pp. 328–345 (2008)

37. Patarin, J.: Introduction to Mirror Theory: Analysis of Systems of Linear Equalities and Linear Non Equalities for Cryptography. IACR Cryptol. ePrint Arch., p. 287 (2010)

38. Peyrin, T., Seurin, Y.: Counter-in-tweak: authenticated encryption modes for tweakable block ciphers. In: Robshaw, M., Katz, J. (eds.) CRYPTO 2016. LNCS, vol. 9814, pp. 33–63. Springer, Heidelberg (2016). https://doi.org/10.1007/978-3-662-53018-4_2

39. Procter, G.: A note on the CLRW2 tweakable block cipher construction. IACR Cryptology ePrint Archive **2014**, 111 (2014)

40. Rogaway, P.: Efficient instantiations of tweakable blockciphers and refinements to modes OCB and PMAC. In: Lee, P.J. (ed.) ASIACRYPT 2004. LNCS, vol. 3329, pp. 16–31. Springer, Heidelberg (2004). https://doi.org/10.1007/978-3-540-30539-2_2

41. Schroeppel, R., Orman, H.: The Hasty Pudding Cipher. AES candidate submitted to NIST (1998). https://www.princeton.edu/~rblee/HPC/index.htm

42. Shen, Y., Peters, T., Standaert, F., Cassiers, G., Verhamme, C.: Triplex: an efficient and one-pass leakage-resistant mode of operation. IACR Trans. Cryptogr. Hardw. Embed. Syst. **2022**(4), 135–162 (2022)

43. Zhang, Z., Qin, Z., Guo, C.: Just tweak! asymptotically optimal security for the cascaded LRW1 tweakable blockcipher. Des. Codes Cryptogr. **91**(3), 1035–1052 (2023)

Improved Differential Meet-in-the-Middle Cryptanalysis

Zahra Ahmadian[1]([✉]), Akram Khalesi[1], Dounia M'Foukh[2], Hossein Moghimi[1], and María Naya-Plasencia[2]

[1] Shahid Beheshti University, Tehran, Iran
{z_ahmadian,a_khalesi}@sbu.ac.ir, h.moghimi@mail.sbu.ac.ir
[2] Inria, Paris, France
{dounia.mfoukh,maria.naya_plasencia}@inria.fr

Abstract. In this paper, we extend the applicability of differential meet-in-the-middle attacks, proposed at Crypto 2023, to truncated differentials, and in addition, we introduce three new ideas to improve this type of attack: we show how to add longer structures than the original paper, we show how to improve the key recovery steps by introducing some probability in them, and we combine this type of attacks with the state-test technique, that was introduced in the context of impossible differential attacks. Furthermore, we have developed a MILP-based tool to automate the search for a truncated differential-MITM attack with optimized overall complexity, incorporating some of the proposed improvements. Thanks to this, we can build the best known attacks on the cipher CRAFT, reaching 23 rounds against 21 previously; we provide a new attack on 23-round SKINNY-64-192, and we improve the best attacks on SKINNY-128-384.

Keywords: differential meet-in-the-middle cryptanalysis · truncated cryptanalysis · parallel partitioning · state-test technique · tool · SKINNY · CRAFT

1 Introduction

Symmetric cryptanalysis is crucial for trusting symmetric primitives: the more we cryptanalyze a primitive without success, the more confidence we will have in it. It is essential for determining the security margin of the cryptographic constructions and being able to anticipate problems. Many different cryptanalysis families exist, like differential attacks [9], linear attacks [25], meet-in-the-middle attacks [13], invariant sub-space attacks [23], integral attacks [21]. Often new techniques and variants are proposed to augment these attacks, but proposing new families is less common.

In [11] a new cryptanalysis was proposed: the differential meet-in-the-middle (MITM) attack. It combines ideas from differential and MITM attacks, allowing to build the best known attack on the cipher SKINNY-128-384 in the single-tweak setting [11]. As described by the authors, these attacks could be seen in

© International Association for Cryptologic Research 2024
M. Joye and G. Leander (Eds.): EUROCRYPT 2024, LNCS 14651, pp. 280–309, 2024.
https://doi.org/10.1007/978-3-031-58716-0_10

part as a new way of performing the key recovery in differential attacks, or as MITM ones where instead of looking for a partial collision at some middle state, we look for states that verify, with certain probability, a differential relation. The authors proposed in the SKINNY-128-384 scenario, a way of extending the attack using parallel partitioning to gain one round, techniques usually applied in MITM attacks [2,3,10], but not applicable during classical differential attacks. Some questions were left unsolved in the original paper, such as whether these attacks could be seen as just a new way of performing the key recovery part, but were in essence differential attacks. Another interesting question was if they could be combined with truncated differential attacks – as the probability in both directions of a truncated path is often not symmetric, it seemed at first counter-intuitive to apply it. We have considered and answered these two questions, and in addition proposed two additional improvements to the technique: allowing some probability in the key-guessing part, and combining it with the state-test technique, introduced in [12] in the context of impossible differential attacks.

We have applied our new techniques to CRAFT [8], SKINNY-128-384 [7] and SKINNY-64-192 [7], providing the best known attacks in the two first cases, and an attack reaching the highest number of rounds as the best attack for the third. These attacks can be seen in Table 1.

This paper is organized as follows: Sect. 2 presents the previous framework of differential MITM attacks. Section 3 describes our proposition of combining this attack with truncated differentials and Sect. 4 the newly proposed improvements. Section 5 presents our new tool that finds the distinguishers providing the best overall attacks, considering in addition most of the new improvements on the external rounds, and Sect. 6 and Sect. 7 describe the new applications. The paper is ended with a conclusion.

2 Preliminaries: Differential Meet-in-the-Middle

The differential meet-in-the-middle (MITM) technique, introduced in [11], represents a novel approach for the cryptanalysis of symmetric primitives. This attack combines two significant families of symmetric cryptanalysis attacks: the meet-in-the-middle attack and the differential attack. In [11], it is described as both an extension of classical MITM attacks and as a new key recovery method to apply in differential cryptanalysis.

This new technique was successfully applied to SKINNY-128-384, the 128-bit block cipher variant with a 384-bit tweakey, breaking 25 out of the 56 rounds in the single-tweakey setting [11]. This application highlights the attack's efficiency by surpassing the best known attack on this cipher by two rounds. Furthermore, another instance provided in [11], involved AES-256, where this technique managed to break 12 rounds of the cipher in the related-key model. This attack requires only 2 related keys while the previous attacks with the same number of related keys achieve a maximum of 10 rounds.

In this section, we will provide an overview of how differential MITM attacks are constructed, along with the original improvements introduced in [11]. One

Table 1. Summary of the best known cryptanalysis on CRAFT, SKINNY-64-192 and SKINNY-128-384 in the single tweak setting (related tweak the strongest setting).

Cipher	Rounds	Time	Data	Memory	Attack	Setting/Model	Ref
CRAFT	18	$2^{101.7}$	$2^{60.92}$	2^{84}	Rectangle	STK	[17]
	19	$2^{114.68}$	2^{56}	2^{109}	DS-MITM	STK,CP	[24]
	19	$2^{112.61}$	$2^{60.92}$	2^{72}	Rectangle	SK	[30]
	20	$2^{126.96}$	2^{56}	2^{109}	DS-MITM	STK,CP	[24]
	21	$2^{106.53}$	$2^{60.99}$	2^{100}	ID	STK,CP	[18]
	21	$\mathbf{2^{116}}$	$\mathbf{2^{56}}$	$\mathbf{2^{68}}$	**Tr-Diff-MITM**	**STK**	Sect. 6
	22	$\mathbf{2^{125}}$	$\mathbf{2^{58}}$	$\mathbf{2^{72}}$	**Tr-Diff-MITM**	**STK**	Sect. 6
	23	$\mathbf{2^{125}}$	$\mathbf{2^{60}}$	$\mathbf{2^{68}}$	**Tr-Diff-MITM**	**STK**	Sect. 6
SKINNY-64-192	21	$2^{180.01}$	2^{44}	$2^{191.55}$	DS-MITM	STK	[29]
	21	$2^{174.42}$	$2^{62.43}$	2^{168}	ID	STK/CP	[18]
	22	$2^{183.97}$	$2^{47.84}$	$2^{74.84}$	ID	STK	[31]
	23	2^{188}	2^{52}	2^{4}	MITM	STK	[14]
	23	2^{184}	2^{60}	2^{8}	MITM	STK	[6]
	23	2^{188}	2^{28}	2^{4}	MITM	STK	[6]
	23	$\mathbf{2^{188}}$	$\mathbf{2^{56}}$	$\mathbf{2^{104}}$	**Tr-Diff-MITM**	**STK**	Sect. 7.1
SKINNY-128-384	23	2^{376}	2^{104}	2^{8}	MITM	STK	[14]
	23	2^{372}	2^{96}	$2^{352.46}$	DS-MITM	STK	[29]
	23	$2^{361.9}$	2^{117}	$2^{118.5}$	Diff-MITM	STK	[11]
	24	$2^{361.9}$	2^{117}	2^{183}	Diff-MITM	STK	[11]
	24	$2^{372.5}$	$2^{122.3}$	$2^{123.8}$	Diff-MITM	STK	[11]
	25	$2^{372.5}$	$2^{122.3}$	$2^{188.3}$	Diff-MITM	STK	[11]
	25	$\mathbf{2^{378.9}}$	$\mathbf{2^{117}}$	$\mathbf{2^{165}}$	**Diff-MITM**	**STK**	Sect. 7.2
	25	$\mathbf{2^{366}}$	$\mathbf{2^{122.3}}$	$\mathbf{2^{188.3}}$	**Diff-MITM**	**STK**	Sect. 7.2

MITM: Meet In The Middle	ID: Impossible Differential
CP: Chosen Plaintext	DS-MITM: Demirci-Selcuk
Diff-MITM: Differential MITM	Tr-Diff-MITM: Truncated Differential MITM
STK: Single-Tweak/Tweakey	SK: Single Key

improvement, achieved through a parallel treatment of data partitions, extends the attack for one round more, mostly at no cost, particularly when the key was exclusively added to half of the internal state. Another one is a technique designed to reduce data complexity in the originally full code-book attack scenario.

2.1   Framework of the Differential MITM Attack

Consider an n-bit cipher E decomposed into three sub-ciphers $E_{out} \circ E_m \circ E_{in}$ of r_{in}, r_m and r_{out} rounds respectively, as depicted in Fig. 1. Finally, suppose that the efficient differential $(\alpha \rightarrow \beta)$, covering the r_m middle rounds, with probability 2^{-p} is a distinguisher for E_m. The core idea of the attack involves employing the MITM approach. In other words, given a pair of plaintext/ciphertext (P, C), we independently compute the candidate plaintexts and ciphertexts $\tilde{P}$ and $\tilde{C}$ such that they follow the differential characteristic as summarized on Fig. 1. $\tilde{P}$ is computed from the plaintext P and the difference α for each possible value of the associated key k_{in}, and $\tilde{C}$ from the ciphertext C and the difference β for each possible value of the associated key k_{out}.

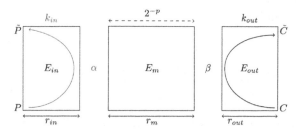

Fig. 1. Framework of the differential meet-in-the-middle attack.

Thus the aim of the following procedure is to find a pair of plaintext/ciphertext (P, C) and $(\tilde{P}, \tilde{C})$ such that:

$$\begin{cases} E_{in}(P) \oplus E_{in}(\tilde{P}) = \alpha \\ E_{out}^{-1}(C) \oplus E_{out}^{-1}(\tilde{C}) = \beta. \end{cases} \tag{1}$$

Procedure. First, we randomly pick a plaintext P and ask the encryption oracle for its ciphertext C.

- *Upper Part:* From P, α and some key information, we aim to compute $\tilde{P}$ such that $E_{in}(P) \oplus E_{in}(\tilde{P}) = \alpha$, if the key guess is correct. Thus, we want to minimize the amount of key information, denoted by k_{in}, needed. For each possible value i of k_{in}, we have a different candidate $\tilde{P}^i$. Thus, we have $2^{|k_{in}|}$ candidates at the end of this step. For each $\tilde{P}^i$, we ask the oracle for its encryption $\hat{C}^i$, and store them in a hash table.
- *Lower Part:* Similarly, given C, β and a minimized amount of key information, denoted by k_{out}, we can compute $\tilde{C}^j$ such that $E_{out}^{-1}(C) \oplus E_{out}^{-1}(\tilde{C}^j) = \beta$, if the key guess is correct. We have $2^{|k_{out}|}$ candidates for $\tilde{C}^j$.

Actually, during the procedure before the upper and lower parts, we can first guess the subkey bits of k_{in} and k_{out} in common thanks to the possible linear relations between k_{in} and k_{out} given by the key schedule.

Furthermore, given that $P(\alpha \to \beta) = 2^{-p}$, we have to repeat the procedure 2^p times using 2^p different plaintext/ciphertexts pairs (P_l, C_l) to have a good pair $(P_l, \tilde{P}_l^i)$ and $(C_l, \tilde{C}_l^j)$, satisfying the distinguisher. When this is the case, we will get a collision between a $\hat{C}^i = E(\tilde{P}^i)$ of the upper part and a $\tilde{C}^j$ of the lower part. Each collision (i, j) yields a candidate key.

For each P_l, we initially have $2^{|k_{in}|+|k_{out}|}$ candidate pairs $(\hat{C}_l^i, i)$ and $(\tilde{C}_l^j, j)$ in search of a collision. After matching through the relation $\hat{C}_l^i = \tilde{C}_l^j$, we are left with $2^{|k_{in}|+|k_{out}|-n}$ candidates. Thus, in the end, for each P_l, the number of expected collisions would be $2^{|k_{in}|+|k_{out}|-n-|k_{in}\cap k_{out}|}$.

Complexity. The time complexity for the computations in the upper and lower parts of the procedure is $2^{|k_{in}|+p}$ and $2^{|k_{out}|+p}$, respectively. And as explained above, the number of expected candidate keys is $2^{|k_{in}|+|k_{out}|-n-|k_{in}\cap k_{out}|+p}$.

Thus, the time complexity is:

$$2^p \times 2^{|k_{in} \cap k_{out}|} (2^{|k_{in}| - |k_{in} \cap k_{out}|} + 2^{|k_{out}| - |k_{in} \cap k_{out}|} + 2^{|k_{in}| + |k_{out}| - n - 2|k_{in} \cap k_{out}|}).$$

With this, we recover $k_{in} \cup k_{out}$. So, if we expect fewer key candidates than the whole key space $\mathcal{K}$ of size 2^k, then we can guess the remaining bits of the master key and test the guess with additional pairs. Thus, we recover the whole key with a complexity smaller than the cost of an exhaustive key search, and the additional cost of $2^{k - |k_{in} \cup k_{out}|} \times \max(1, 2^{|k_{in}| + |k_{out}| - n - |k_{in} \cap k_{out}| + p})$ to be added to the time complexity $\mathcal{T}$. In the case that we need to guess the remaining bits of the master key, specifically if $|k_{in}| + |k_{out}| - n - |k_{in} \cap k_{out}| + p > 0$, the total time complexity would be:

$$\mathcal{T} = 2^{p + |k_{in} \cap k_{out}|} (2^{|k_{in}| - |k_{in} \cap k_{out}|} + 2^{|k_{out}| - |k_{in} \cap k_{out}|} + 2^{|k_{in}| + |k_{out}| - n - 2|k_{in} \cap k_{out}|})$$
$$+ 2^{k - n + p}. \tag{2}$$

The data complexity is $\mathcal{D} = \min(2^n, 2^{p + \min(|k_{in}|, |k_{out}|)})$, and the memory complexity is $\mathcal{M} = 2^{\min(|k_{in}| - |k_{in} \cap k_{out}|, |k_{out}| - |k_{in} \cap k_{out}|)}$.

2.2   Improvement: Parallel Partitions for Layers with Partial Subkeys

In [11], two methods for improving the original differential MITM attack are proposed. The first method, elaborated upon below, focuses on adding an extra round at the beginning or the end of the attack, in some specific cases.

In the cases where the round key addition only affects a part of the state, as is the case with SKINNY [7] or GIFT [5] block ciphers, the differential MITM attack can be extended by one round. Suppose $m < n$ bits of the state are affected by the round key addition. The framework of the improvement is given in Fig. 2, where one round is added at the end of the attack covering $r - 1$ rounds of the cipher and we have eliminated all the transformations after the round key addition of round r, if any. Let A and B denote the states before and after adding K_r, respectively. The main idea of the improvement is to only keep the ciphertexts that satisfy the following condition: we fix the $n - m$ bits that are not affected by the key addition in A and B, and compute all the 2^m possible values for A and B. Now, we will repeat the procedure 2^{p-m} times. So, we can apply this improvement without increasing the time complexity, if $p > m$.

Then, from all the 2^m possible values for A, we can proceed with the lower part of the differential MITM attack. We get $2^{|k_{out}| + m}$ possible candidates $(A, \tilde{A}, j)$. In parallel, we do the same for each of the 2^m possible values for B, and we proceed with the upper part of differential MITM attack and we get $2^{|k_{in}| + m}$ possible candidates $(B, \tilde{B}, i)$; hence $2^{|k_{in}| + |k_{out}| + 2m}$ total candidates which is a factor 2^m higher than before, as we are comparing this to performing the attack without structures 2^m times. Nevertheless, note that we have to match A and B and their associated pairs $\tilde{A}$ and $\tilde{B}$ through the relation $A \oplus B = \tilde{A} \oplus \tilde{B}$. This also yields the value of K_r, already determined by k_{in} and k_{out}, usually.

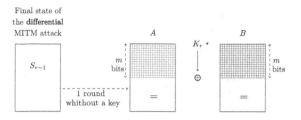

Fig. 2. Framework of the parallel partitioning improvement.

So, the number of expected collisions does not increase: in total, we need to collide on $n - m$ bits of the key-free parts of $\tilde{A}$ and $\tilde{B}$; and we have to collide for both pairs in the m bits once the key is added, providing a total filtering of $(n - m) + 2m = n + m$. As we now have 2^m additional potential candidates, but a 2^{m+n} filter, we expect a total proportion of remaining candidates of 2^{-n}, as in the attack without parallel partitions. In [11], they applied this technique to reach one more round of SKINNY-128-384 without increasing the time complexity and thus mounting the best known attack on this cipher in the single tweak setting.

2.3   Reducing Data Needed with Imposed Conditions

The idea is to fix x bits of the plaintext P and of the associated plaintext $\tilde{P}$ to a specific value, thereby restricting them to a set of 2^{n-x} plaintexts instead of the whole codebook. We can choose the plaintext P as desired but the probability to get a $\tilde{P}$ with the fixed x bits is 2^{-x}. Then, the probability of the attack decreases by 2^x as we have to repeat the procedure 2^x times to get a pair that satisfies the differential characteristic along with this new condition. On the other hand, it means that during the upper and lower part of the attack, we will discard a proportion of 2^x tuples of $(P, \tilde{P}, i)$ and $(C, \tilde{C}, j)$, the ones that do not satisfy the conditions. Thus the data and memory complexities will decrease by 2^x.

Furthermore, considering the attributes of the differential MITM attack, we can derive the following two bounds on the number of fixed bits x:

$$p + x \leq n - x \text{ and } 2^{p+x}(2^{|k_{in}|} + 2^{|k_{out}|}) < 2^k.$$

This technique particularly applies when the whole codebook would be needed, as it is in the differential MITM attack on SKINNY-128-384 presented in [11].

3   Truncated Differential Meet-in-the-Middle Attack

Truncated differential cryptanalysis was introduced at FSE in 1994 [20] by Knudsen as an extension of differential cryptanalysis and has proven its efficacy by successfully attacking several ciphers which seemed to be secure against differential attacks. It is the case with the KLEIN block cipher, for which its security against bit-wise differential attack had been proved but was broken by some truncated differential attacks [22, 27]. Thus the main extension of the differential MITM attack that we will explain in this section is the truncated differential MITM attack. A challenge of building this extension is that since the probability of a truncated differential characteristic is not the same in both directions, then it was not clear how to properly take this propriety into account in the truncated differential MITM extension.

The main idea of truncated differential-MITM attacks is to use, instead of a differential path, a truncated differential path as the underlying distinguisher of the attack. As stated in Appendix A of the longer version of this paper [1], a truncated differential operates based on sets of input and output differences rather than concrete ones. It considers whether a word (typically of the S-box size in the cipher) has a non-zero difference or not, regardless of its concrete value. One advantage of the truncated differential attack is that during the key recovery step, we do not need to know the concrete values of the states just before and after the distinguisher. Consequently, we may need to guess fewer subkey words, potentially allowing us to reach more rounds. Additionally, for certain ciphers, truncated differential distinguishers can reach more rounds than concrete differentials (as in [26]). Finally, the search space for truncated differentials is much smaller than that of concrete differentials, making it easier to deal with an automated method [26].

3.1   Framework of the Truncated Differential MITM Attack

Similar to the differential MITM attack, consider the n-bit cipher E decomposed into three sub-ciphers: $E_{out} \circ E_m \circ E_{in}$, of r_{in}, r_m and r_{out} rounds respectively, as depicted in Fig. 3. Finally, suppose that $(\Delta_{in} \xrightarrow{E_m} \Delta_{out})$ is a truncated distinguisher for E_m with the probability of 2^{-p}, where $|\Delta_{in}| = 2^{\delta_{in}}$ and $|\Delta_{out}| = 2^{\delta_{out}}$. So $(\Delta_{in} \xrightarrow{E_m} \Delta_{out})$ is an efficient differential if $p < n - \delta_{out}$.

We randomly pick a pair of plaintext/ciphertext pair (P, C), and try to generate appropriate candidates for $(\tilde{P}, \tilde{C})$ such that the difference of these two data ensures the truncated difference Δ_{in} at round r_{in}, i.e. $E_{in}(P) \oplus E_{in}(\tilde{P}) \in \Delta_{in}$, and the truncated difference Δ_{out} at round $r_{in} + r_m$, i.e. $E_{out}^{-1}(C) \oplus E_{out}^{-1}(\tilde{C}) \in \Delta_{out}$. The procedures of the upper and lower parts of the attack are as follows.

Upper Part: To generate $\tilde{P}$, we guess some key material, denoted by k_{in}. For each P, and each guess i of k_{in}, there are $2^{\delta_{in}}$ distinct candidates $\tilde{P}_l^i$, each corresponding to an input difference $l \in \Delta_{in}$. All the $2^{|k_{in}| + \delta_{in}}$ ciphertexts $\hat{C}_l^i = E_K(\tilde{P}_l^i)$, along with its associated key material i are stored in a hash table.

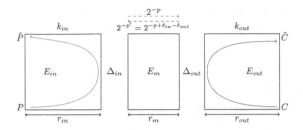

Fig. 3. Framework of the truncated differential meet-in-the-middle attack. The probability of the distinguisher in the forward (backward) direction is 2^{-p} ($2^{-p'}$).

Lower Part: In the ciphertext side, given C, for each guess j of k_{out}, we compute all the $2^{\delta_{out}}$ ciphertexts corresponding to the $2^{\delta_{out}}$ possible differences $m \in \Delta_{out}$. So, there would be in total $2^{|k_{out}|} \times 2^{\delta_{out}}$ values for $\tilde{C}^j_m$.

Number of Pairs: For the correct key guess, the transition $(\Delta_{in} \xrightarrow{E_m} \Delta_{out})$ will happen with probability 2^{-p}. So, a number of 2^p pairs of data is expected to be tested to find the correct key. For each P and a fixed key material i, we can provide $2^{\delta_{in}}$ differential pairs $(P, \tilde{P})$, each of which corresponds to a specific value of Δ_{in}. So, it is required to repeat the upper and lower parts of the attack for a number of $2^{p-\delta_{in}}$ plaintexts P. On the other hand, despite the concrete differential-MITM attack, the output difference Δ_{out} does not have a specific single value, but it belongs to a set of size $2^{\delta_{out}}$, whole of which should be checked to certainly determine if the event $(\Delta_{in} \xrightarrow{E_m} \Delta_{out})$ has occurred or not.

3.2 Attack Complexities

As done in the differential MITM attack, we first guess the possible linear relations between k_{in} and k_{out}, i.e. $k_{in} \cap k_{out}$. During the upper part of the attack, for each guess of $k_{in} - k_{in} \cap k_{out}$, we get $2^{\delta_{in}}$ candidates $\tilde{P}^i_l$ hence $2^{|k_{in}|+\delta_{in}-|k_{in} \cap k_{out}|}$ candidates for $(P, \tilde{P}, i)$. Similarly, in the lower part, we have $2^{|k_{out}|+\delta_{out}-|k_{in} \cap k_{out}|}$ candidates triplets for $(C, \tilde{C}, j)$. So, there is $2^{|k_{in}|+\delta_{in}+|k_{out}|+\delta_{out}-2|k_{in} \cap k_{out}|}$ candidates for (i, j). Let's denote $\hat{C} = E(\tilde{P})$. The matching of $\hat{C}^i_l$ with $\tilde{C}^j_m$ leaves us with $2^{|k_{in}|+\delta_{in}+|k_{out}|+\delta_{out}-2|k_{in} \cap k_{out}|-n}$ candidates. Moreover, similar to the original differential-MITM attack, we can guess the remaining bits of the master key and test the guess with additional pairs. Thus, the time complexity of the attack is:

$$\mathcal{T} = 2^{p-\delta_{in}} \times 2^{|k_{in} \cap k_{out}|} \left(2^{|k_{in}|+\delta_{in}-|k_{in} \cap k_{out}|} + 2^{|k_{out}|+\delta_{out}-|k_{in} \cap k_{out}|}\right)$$
$$+ 2^{p-\delta_{in}} \times 2^{|k_{in} \cap k_{out}|} \left(2^{|k_{in}|+\delta_{in}+|k_{out}|+\delta_{out}-2|k_{in} \cap k_{out}|-n}\right) \tag{3}$$

The data and memory complexities are similar to the differential MITM ones.

$$\mathcal{D} = \min(2^n, 2^{p-\delta_{in}+\min(|k_{in}|+\delta_{in}, |k_{out}|+\delta_{out})}), \tag{4}$$
$$\mathcal{M} = \min(2^{|k_{in}|+\delta_{in}-|k_{in} \cap k_{out}|}, 2^{|k_{out}|+\delta_{out}-|k_{in} \cap k_{out}|}). \tag{5}$$

The second line of (3) refers to the number of candidates for $k_{in} \cup k_{out}$ to be tested, which should be less than the whole set $k_{in} \cup k_{out}$. This holds if $p + |k_{in}| + |k_{out}| - |k_{in} \cap k_{out}| - n + \delta_{out} < |k_{in} \cup k_{out}|$, implying that $p < n - \delta_{out}$, which is ensured by an efficient distinguisher.

Remark 1. It holds for the reverse transition that $P(\Delta_{out} \xrightarrow{E_m^{-1}} \Delta_{in}) = 2^{-p'}$, where $p' = p + \delta_{out} - \delta_{in}$. Using this equality, one can infer that all the complexities of the reverse attack (the chosen ciphertext scenario) are equivalent to that of the forward attack: Eqs. (3), (4), (5).

4   New Improvements to Differential MITM Attacks

We present in this section three new improvements that can be incorporated into either the truncated or the original variants of differential MITM attacks. These improvements include an extension of the parallel partitioning technique, the state-test technique, and the probabilistic key recovery technique. The extended parallel partitioning technique, built upon the concept initially proposed in [11] (also reviewed in Sect. 2.2 of this paper), expands its range of applicability. The other two techniques focus on minimizing the information needed to be guessed during the key guessing step, which has a direct impact on the complexity. Specifically, the state-test technique, adopted from the impossible differential attacks [12], guesses a word of the state instead of a larger-size key material, thereby decreasing the total information that needs to be guessed. The probabilistic key recovery technique introduces a probability into the key-guessing step to reduce the number of active words in the key recovery parts of the attack, and consequently, the keybits involved.

4.1   Improving the Parallel Partitioning

As explained in Sect. 2.2, the original parallel partitioning method proposed in [11] effectively extends the attack for one round, in situations where the round key addition impacts only a portion of the cipher's state. This extension has no additional cost in time or data complexities if certain specific conditions are met. In this section, inspired by the structures commonly employed in MITM attacks like initial structures [4] and bicliques [19], we explain how the applicability range can be extended, specifically in two directions: One round extension, in the case of SPN ciphers with a whole-state key addition (applied to CRAFT in Sect. 6 of this paper). Additionally, more than one round extension, in the case of SPN ciphers with a partial-state key addition (applied in Sect. 7 of this paper). *The General Idea.* Without loss of generality, we explain the procedure for the round(s) extensions at the end of the cipher. A general view is shown in Fig. 4. Suppose that the cipher state is formed of W words of size s bits ($n = Ws$). Let A be the final state of the (truncated) differential-MITM attack, and B be the ciphertext, typically one or two rounds after A. Without any extra conditions, there are 2^{Ws} possibilities for A and B values, each. A set of F words,

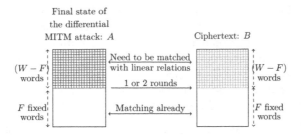

Fig. 4. High-level representation of the proposed structures when added at the end of the attack. They could also be added at the input without loss of generality.

representing independent conditions, enforced at any point within the internal states of the added rounds, would reduce the number of possibilities for each of A and B to $2^{(W-F)s}$. The whole set of these possible values for A and B is called a pair of initial structures of size $2^{(W-F)s}$. These conditions typically involve forcing some words within the internal state into fixed values or imposing linear relationships on specific internal state words. This set of conditions of size Fs bits are selected so that having them, along with k_{in} (resp. k_{out}), allows one to uniquely determine an equivalent of Fs information bits of B (resp. A). Therefore, it makes sense to consider the Fs-bit internal state condition as the starting point for the structures.

As in the previous parallel partitioning method, we next perform the upper and lower procedures for both structures of size $2^{(W-F)s}$ in parallel, generating lists of $(B, \tilde{B}, i)$ and $(A, \tilde{A}, j)$. Therefore, we need to repeat the modified attack $2^{p-(W-F)s}$ times, while the first two terms of time complexity in (2) and (3), would be increased by a factor of $2^{(W-F)s}$, and the third term by a factor of $2^{2(W-F)s}$. So it is required to have efficient sieving on the candidates when merging the two partial lists of solutions, to retain a number well below the exhaustive search. The sieving over the candidate solutions is done in two ways: Firstly, a 2^{-Fs} sieving over $\tilde{B}$ and $\tilde{A}$, in the words involved in the starting point. These words computed from the both sides, (i.e. from the Fs information bits of $\tilde{A}$ and $\tilde{B}$ possibly with the aid of the associated k_{out} and k_{in}, respectively) should return the same values. Secondly, an L-bit sieving by new linear relations between A and B (similarly, $\tilde{A}$ and $\tilde{B}$) independent from those Fs-bit matching over the starting point. To profit from the whole sieving potential, we would need to discover $2(W-F)s$ linear relations between the pairs A and B, as well as between $\tilde{A}$ and $\tilde{B}$. The accurate value of L, upper bounded by $2(W-F)s$, depends on the particular cases. Finally, as far as $(W-F)s \leq p$, this technique imposes no additional costs to the time complexity of the original attack, besides the possible increase in the size of k_{in} and k_{out} if more bits are needed to check the linear relations.

The time complexity of the truncated differential-MITM is then:

$$\mathcal{T} = 2^{p-(W-F)s-\delta_{in}+|k_{in}\cap k_{out}|} \times (2^{(W-F)s} \times 2^{|k_{in}|+\delta_{in}-|k_{in}\cap k_{out}|}$$

$$+2^{(W-F)s} \times 2^{|k_{out}|+\delta_{out}-|k_{in}\cap k_{out}|} + 2^{|k_{in}|+\delta_{in}+|k_{out}|+\delta_{out}+2(W-F)s-Fs-L-2|k_{in}\cap k_{out}|}).$$

A positive side effect of this improvement is that thanks to the linear relations checked in the second sieving, we recover most of the time the whole values of the last subkey bits, which increases the size of the number of bits recovered, as we will see in the applications.

In the following, we provide a brief description of two specific examples illustrating how this technique is applicable for more than one round (for SKINNY), or even when the key is added to the entire state (for CRAFT).

The Case of SKINNY. In Sect. 7.1, we add two rounds at the end of our truncated differential MITM attack on SKINNY-64-192 as shown in Fig. 10. For the cipher SKINNY, knowing the first key row of the first added key allows checking of all the linear equations needed to profit from the whole sieving potential. In our attack, we construct structures of size 2^{40}, thus to profit from the whole sieving potential, we want to find 10 linear relations between the pairs A and B, as well as between $\tilde{A}$ and $\tilde{B}$. In our case, we guessed 3 subkey bits of the first key row of the first key which gives us 8 linear equations out of the 10 linear equations we want. And we guess the 2 subkey bits of the third column of the second key to find the 2 remaining linear relations. A similar idea is applied in our improvements of the SKINNY-128-384 attacks of Sect. 7.2.

The Case of CRAFT. In our attack of CRAFT in Sect. 6, we can check less than all the linear equations as we have a bigger margin - we do not need to use all the potentially available sieving. Thus we get our linear equation by checking the relation $MC(A) \oplus B = MC(\tilde{A}) \oplus \tilde{B}$ for all the non-fixed words, which erases the unknown key bits. Since we fixed 5 words in A and B, we get 11 linear relations on 4 bits each.

4.2 Probabilistic Key Recovery Technique

Usually, in the key recovery step of the differential attacks, we extend with probability one the differential characteristic for some rounds in both sides. Our second idea for improvement is to force one or more transitions to have zero difference, paying some probability. Thus the number of active words will decrease and fewer key bits will need to be guessed.

Suppose we are in the case of a differential attack. In the classical case, we propagate Δ_{in} and Δ_{out} with probability 1 for r_{in} rounds backward and r_{out} rounds forward respectively, determining the truncated differences that pairs of plaintexts/ciphertexts should verify. Then we will test the pairs verifying this truncated differential and the possible keys that would lead to this differential.

Here instead of extending Δ_{in} and Δ_{out} for r_{in} and r_{out} rounds with probability 1, we allow these transitions to happen with probability $2^{-p_{in}}$ and $2^{-p_{out}}$. Thus the overall probability for a random pair to follow the differential path is now $2^{-p-p_{in}-p_{out}}$. Therefore we have to repeat the attack $2^{p_{in}+p_{out}}$ more times. However, the number of pairs we keep for each side decreases by $2^{p_{in}}$ for the upper part and of $2^{p_{out}}$ for the lower part, so this is often compensated in the final time complexity. On the other hand, this technique restricts the large diffusion of active nibbles in the upper and lower sides, resulting in smaller sets of

k_{in} and k_{out}. We will show an application of this improvement in our attack on CRAFT in Sect. 6.

Comparison with Differential Attacks. In differential attacks, the complexity of the key recovery step is usually quite low, thanks to early abort techniques, and therefore the improvement of using probabilistic key recovery thechnique might be less advantageous, though it could still be applied. Here the number of involved keybits is directly associated to the final complexity.

4.3   Applying the State-Test Technique

The state-test technique was introduced in [12,15] in the context of impossible differential and MITM attacks respectively, to reduce the amounts of bits guessed in the key guessing step. The main idea is to test a part of the internal state that will uniquely define a partition of the involved key bits instead of guessing these keybits, reducing, therefore, the complexity of the guess.

During the key guessing part, some internal state words needed for computing $\tilde{P}$ or $\tilde{C}$ are smaller than the key materials that affect them. Thus guessing the state words instead of the key bits involved decreases the time complexity. Indeed, if l key or subkey bits are only needed to compute s bits of internal state with no differences but required to compute some internal state with differences. In such cases, we can guess s bits instead of the l key bits as P (or C) is fixed and this will define a disjoint partition of the involved keybits. Thus the time complexity of this part decreases of 2^{l-s}. We use this technique in both applications of Sect. 6 and Sect. 7.

This idea can be easily applied to differential-MITM attacks, unlike to classical differential attacks, as the plaintext for which we guess the keys is fixed, therefore defining a disjoint partition of the involved keybits.

Analysis of the Secret Information Recovered. As instead of recovering direct bits from the key we can recover non-linear equations, we have to be careful when computing the overall complexity that the number of recovered keybits of the actual key is bigger than the number of candidates for the triplets $(P, \tilde{P}, |k_{in} \cup k_{out}|)$ so that we do not have to deal with counters. We will see how to deal with particular cases in the applications.

5   MILP Modeling of the Truncated Differential-MITM Attack

In this section, we describe the automatic MILP-aided method for searching the truncated differential-MITM attack. We first introduce the modeling of the basic attack. Then, we explain how the state-test and probabilistic key recovery techniques can be incorporated into the model. We leave the inclusion of the parallel partitioning method as an open problem for future work. All source codes are available at https://github.com/CraftSkinny.

5.1   MILP Model of the Basic Attack

The set of constraints used in our model can be divided into three parts: constraints describing the distinguisher, constraints associated to k_{in} and k_{out}, and constraints describing the objective function.

Constraints Associated with the Distinguisher. This set of constraints is derived according to the method given in [26]. Once the model is solved, the approximated values of transition probabilities will be replaced by the accurate ones, given in the Branching Property Tables (BPT) described in Appendix D of [1]. To be more conservative, we can examine the accurate method given in [16], which computes the exact value of the probability for a given path. Moreover, we develop a distinguisher-only model with an accurate DBT, to compute the clustering effect on the differential probability, by summing up the probabilities of all the paths with $(\Delta_{in}, \Delta_{out})$ fixed to that of the optimum solution.

Constraints Determining k_{in} and k_{out}. We explain the method for the identification of the set k_{out}. A similar scenario holds for k_{in}, as well. The set k_{out} is determined by two factors: First, all the subkeys involved in the *differential propagation* of Δ_{out} to the ciphertext, and second, all the subkeys involved in the *value determination* of active words of Δ_{out} from the ciphertext. These two concepts have been previously used and modeled in other works such as automation of MITM attacks [28]. In Appendix B of [1], the two given theorems unify the description of the MILP modeling of the differential propagation and value determination through the linear layer of a given matrix $\mathbf{M}$ with input and output $\mathbf{a}$ and $\mathbf{b}$, respectively.

These two concepts have been denoted in Fig. 5, where the differential propagation and value determination of active words are indicated by $\{D_i\}$ and $\{V_i\}$ chains, respectively. The active words in round r, i.e. D_r only depend on the active words in D_{r-1}, however, the words whose values should be determined in round r, i.e. V_r, depend on both D_{r-1} and V_{r-1}, i.e. on $D_{r-1} \vee V_{r-1}$.

There is a nuanced aspect at the starting point of chain $\{V_i\}$. Note that since the truncated differential attack is not dependent on the concrete values of differences, the attacker avoids the need to guess the subkeys required for value determination just before and after the distinguisher. Moreover, this property may partially overspread to the next rounds. For instance, consider a differential output of a distinguisher for Skinny-64-192, denoted by $\Delta_{out} = (a, b, 0, c)$, propagating to $(a + c, a, b, a)$ after the MixColumn operation. It's important to note that we do not have to determine the values of all four active words; rather, we only need to determine the values of the second and fourth words, while the other two can remain undetermined. This is because the differences in the second and fourth words are independent of the others, allowing them to have any non-zero value, thanks to the truncated nature of the attack.

Finally, we have specified the active words as well as the words whose values need to be determined over all states of the first r_{in} and the last r_{out} rounds. With this information, determining k_{in} and k_{out} becomes straightforward, as it

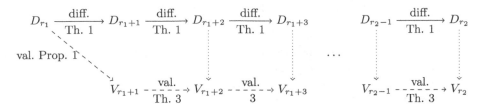

Fig. 5. Differential propagation and value determination in the lower part, where $r_1 = r_{in} + r_m$ and $r_2 = r_{in} + r_m + r_{out}$. The solid arrows show the differential propagation, the dashed ones show the value determination trace and the dotted arrows show the update of V_i by $V_i \vee D_i$, for $r_1 + 2 \leq i \leq r_2$. D_{r_1} corresponds to Δ_{out}. We refer to [1] for the Theorems and Propositions used.

equates to $D \vee V$ at the internal states where the round keys are introduced. All details of the MILP parameters for the two cases studied in this paper, i.e. CRAFT and Skinny-64-192, are given in Tables 2 and 3, where D_i is the input differential state of round $r_1 \leq i \leq r_2$, $D_{r_{in}} = \Delta_{in}$, $D_{r_{in}+r_m} = \Delta_{out}$, $V_{r_{in}} = V_{r_{in}+r_m} = 0$, and $T_i = D_i \vee V_i$. Finally, $T_i[R_j]$ denotes the jth row of state T_i.

Constraints Associated with the Objective Function. The model should minimize the time complexity given in (3) while preserving the efficient distinguisher constraint. Let the time complexity be dominated by the integer-valued variable u. The set of constraints associated to these parameters would be defined as follows.

$$\begin{aligned}
&\min \ u \\
&s.t. \ p < n - \delta_{out} \\
&\quad p + |k_{in}| < u \\
&\quad p + |k_{out}| + \delta_{out} - \delta_{in} < u \\
&\quad |k_{in} \cup k_{out}| + p + \delta_{out} - n < u
\end{aligned} \tag{6}$$

5.2 MILP Model of the Improved Attack

State-Test Enhanced Attack. In this section, we propose a general method for MILP modeling of the state-test technique introduced in Sect. 4.3, for reducing the guessed key material on each side. This technique specifically influences the constraints related to the value determination, in such a way that if a word of the internal state is preferred to be guessed, the value-determination trace corresponding only to this specific word should be aborted, then. To MILP model this event, for each state word whose value is supposed to be determined, we define a new binary variable s, indicating whether the corresponding word should undergo the state-test ($s = 1$) or not ($s = 0$). Then, the value-determination

Table 2. Skinny-64-192 MILP parameters.

	Lower Part		Upper Part	
	Parameters	Description	Parameters	Description
Rounds	r_1	$r_{in} + r_m$	r_1	0
$(r_1 \leq i \leq r_2)$	r_2	$r_{in} + r_m + r_{out} - 1$	r_2	r_{in}
Differential	M	MC	M	Inverse MC
Propagation	a	$SR(D_i)$	a	D_i
	b	D_{i+1}	b	$SR(D_{i-1})$
Value	M	Inverse MC	M	MC
Determination	a	V_{i+1}	a	$SR(V_{i-1})$
	b	$SR(T_i)$	b	T_i
Involved Subkeys	$\lvert k_{out}\rvert$	$\displaystyle\sum_{i=r_1+1}^{r_2} T_i[R_0, R_1]$	$\lvert k_{in}\rvert$	$\displaystyle\sum_{i=r_1}^{r_2-2} T_i[2] + (\bigvee_{j\neq 2} T_i[R_j])$

Table 3. CRAFT MILP parameters.

	Lower Part		Upper Part	
	Parameters	Description	Parameters	Description
Rounds	r_1	$r_{in} + r_m$	r_1	0
$(r_1 \leq i \leq r_2)$	r_2	$r_{in} + r_m + r_{out} - 1$	r_2	r_{in}
Differential	M	MC	M	Inverse MC
Propagation	a	D_i	a	$P^{-1}(D_i)$
	b	$P^{-1}(D_{i+1})$	b	D_{i-1}
Value	M	Inverse MC	M	MC
Determination	a	$P^{-1}(V_{i+1})$	a	V_{i-1}
	b	T_i	b	$P^{-1}(T_i)$
Involved subkeys	$\lvert k_{out}\rvert$	$\displaystyle\sum_{\substack{i=r_1+1 \\ i\ even}}^{r_2} (\bigvee P^{-1}(T_i)) + \sum_{\substack{i=r_1+1 \\ i\ odd}}^{r_2} (\bigvee P^{-1}(T_i))$	$\lvert k_{in}\rvert$	$\displaystyle\sum_{\substack{i=r_1 \\ i\ even}}^{r_2-2} (\bigvee (T_i)) + \sum_{\substack{i=r_1 \\ i\ odd}}^{r_2-2} (\bigvee (T_i))$

constraints would be as regular if $s = 0$ or aborted if $s = 1$. Theorem 3 from [1] identifies the required constraints corresponding to the value-determination for state-test enhanced attack.

Finally, in the objective function constraints (6), $\lvert k_{in}\rvert$ should be replaced by $\lvert k_{in}\rvert + s_{in}$ where $s_{in} = \sum_{0 \leq i \leq r_{in}-2} Hw(\mathbf{s}_i)$, and $\lvert k_{out}\rvert$ should be replaced by $\lvert k_{out}\rvert + s_{out}$ where $s_{out} = \sum_{r_{in}+r_m+1 \leq i \leq r_{in}+r_m+r_{out}-1} Hw(\mathbf{s}_i)$.

Probabilistic Key Recovery Ehanced Attack. In order to incorporate this technique into the model, it suffices to replace the differential propagation constraints generated according to Theorem 1 from [1] by the MILP model of the probabilistic truncated differential propagation given in [26]. In the upper part, this model is used for the inverse of MixColumn matrix as $\mathbf{M}$, and in the lower part, with MixColumn matrix. Then, the constraint $p + \lvert k_{in}\rvert < u$ of (6) should be modified as $p + p_{out} + |k_{in}| < u$, and $p + |k_{out}| + \delta_{out} - \delta_{in} < u$ should be modified to $p + p_{in} + |k_{out}| + \delta_{out} - \delta_{in} < u$.

6   Application on 23-Round CRAFT

CRAFT is a lightweight, tweakable block cipher designed with the goal of protecting implementations against differential fault analysis while also providing strong security guarantees within the related-tweak model. The specification of this cipher is provided in the long version of this paper [1].

Security Claim. In [8], the authors presented optimum differentials for 13 and 14 rounds of CRAFT and claimed that using those differentials the attacker cannot have a successful single-tweak differential attack on 22 rounds. The best previous known attack on CRAFT [18] is a 21-round impossible differential attack with time complexity of $2^{106.53}$, data complexity of $2^{60.99}$ and memory complexity of 2^{100}.

Using truncated differential-MITM, enhanced with parallel partitioning for whole-state key addition ciphers, probabilistic key guessing, and the state-test techniques we managed to provide the best attack on CRAFT [8], improving by 2 rounds the best known attack, as detailed in Table 1.

6.1   An Attack on 23 Rounds of CRAFT

The truncated differential-MITM attack proposed in this section is composed of a 22-round core attack followed by one additional round using the parallel partitioning method. We conducted an automatic search for the optimum 22-round core attack on CRAFT, enhanced with the state-test and probabilistic key guessing techniques, based on the MILP method proposed in Sect. 5. We set $r_m = 11$, $r_{in} = 6$, and $r_{out} = 5$. The 11-round distinguisher and the core 22-round attack are represented in Figs. 6 and 7 respectively, with the following parameters:

p	p_{in}	p_{out}	s_{in}	s_{out}	δ_{in}	δ_{out}	$|k_{in}|$	$|k_{out}|$
44	16	12	16	12	16	16	32	32

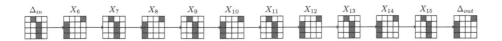

Fig. 6. CRAFT 11-round truncated differential distinguisher with $p = 44$

where s_{in} and s_{out} is the number of state-test bits to guess. The clustering effect was also examined which has a negligible impact. Since the matrix M used in

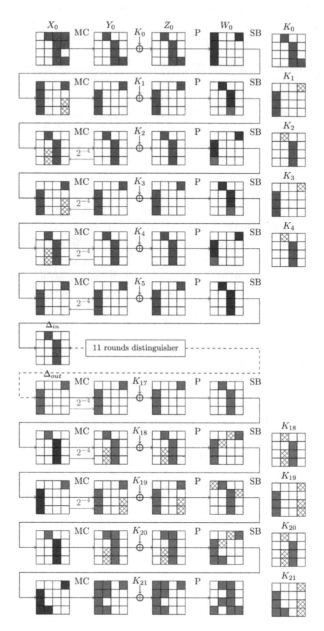

Fig. 7. The 22-round core part of the 23-round attack on CRAFT not including the structures. Differential propagation in the upper (lower) part has been shown in red (blue). The state-test nibble is shown in orange. The gray-striped nibbles are whose values are no longer required thanks to the state-tests, except K_{21} that the XOR of gray-striped nibbles are required. (Color figure online)

Table 4. Subkey nibbles guessed during the 23-round attack of CRAFT.

Subkey	k_{in}	k_{out}	$|k_{in} \cap k_{out}|$
Even	$K_0[1,6,10,14,15]$	$K_0[6,10,14]$	3 nibbles
Odd	$K_1[4,8,12]$	$K_1[4,8,12,13,3 \oplus 11 \oplus 15]$	3 nibbles

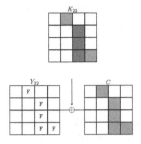

Fig. 8. The last round of the 23-round attack on CRAFT, using parallel partitioning technique. The red nibbles are known or can be computed from the fixed values and k_{in} in the upper part of the attack and the blue nibbles are known or can be computed from the fixed values in the lower part of the attack as $Y_{22} = \text{MC}(\text{SB}(W_{21}))$. The purple subkey nibbles are known in both the upper and lower parts.

the MixColumn operation is involutory, and the input and output differences of the distinguisher are the same, the propagation of active nibbles in the upper and lower parts is very similar. Thus, as shown in Table 4, the subkey words needed on both parts have many words in common thanks to the key schedule and the position of the odd and even subkeys, which allows us to efficiently apply the parallel partitioning technique. The parallel key guessing steps of this attack benefit from the state-test technique from Sect. 4.3 and the probabilistic key recovery technique of Sect. 4.2.

Probabilistic Key Recovery Technique. It is imposed that the difference during the MixColumn transition on nibbles $X_2[2], X_3[0], X_4[2], X_5[0], Y_{17}[0], Y_{18}[2]$ and $Y_{19}[0]$ is null. This decreases the overall probability by a factor of $2^{p_{in}+p_{out}} = 2^{16+12}$, but the number of active words, and consequently $|k_{in}|$ and $|k_{out}|$, also decreases dramatically. This attack is easy to adapt to 21 rounds, as we will show in Sec 6.2.

State-Test Technique. We use the state-test technique to guess four and three nibbles of the internal state in the upper and lower parts respectively: $W_1[14]$, $W_2[12], W_3[14], W_4[12], X_{20}[1], X_{19}[3], X_{18}[1]$ (detailed equations in [1]).

Parallel Guessing Step. From a pair (P, Y_{22}), we need to know the values of the active nibbles before the S-boxes, in green in Fig. 7, to be able to compute the associated value of $\tilde{P}$ for each k_{in} and of $\tilde{Y}_{22}$ for each k_{out}. We will first describe the procedure over the 22 first rounds, and then show how to deal with the last round with parallel partitions.

1. We first guess the $6 \times 4 = 24$ subkey bits of $(k_{in} \cap k_{out})$ given in Table 4. We then fix $F = 5$ nibbles $Y_{22}[1, 6, 10, 14, 15]$, the words denoted by F in Fig. 8 and since we know the subkey nibbles $K_{22}[6, 10, 14]$ for both the upper and lower parts, and of $K_{22}[1, 15]$ for the upper part, then we also have the fixed values of the ciphertext $C[1, 6, 10, 14, 15]$.

2. As 5 nibbles from C and Y_{22} are fixed, we can build a pair of structures of size $2^{4(16-5)} = 2^{44}$ for Y_{22} and for the ciphertext C. We decrypt the 2^{44} ciphertexts C_s and we obtain the associated plaintexts P_s.

3. For each of the $2^{|k_{in} - k_{in} \cap k_{out}|} \times 2^{s_{in}} = 2^{8+16} = 2^{24}$ possible values i of k_{in} and the state-test relations, and each of the 2^{44} P_s from the structure defined at the previous step, compute all possible tuples $(P_s, \tilde{P}_s, i)$ such that they generate Δ_{in} after 6 rounds and they follow the probabilistic differential transitions in the first rounds. There are 2^{24} possible values for k_{in}, and it needs to be done for each $2^{\delta_{in}} = 2^{16}$ possible differences in Δ_{in}, but we expect only a proportion of $2^{-p_{in}} = 2^{-16}$ to verify the upward path, so the expected number of total solutions per P_s will be $2^{24+16-16}$, and if we use rebound-like techniques as shown in the original paper [11] the cost of this step would be equal to the number of solutions: $2^{44+24} = 2^{68}$. We store them in a hash table.

4. Similarly, for each of the $2^{|k_{out} - k_{in} \cap k_{out}|} \times 2^{s_{out}} = 2^{8+12} = 2^{20}$ possible values j of k_{out} and the state-test relations, and each of the 2^{44} states $Y_{22,s}$, compute all possible tuples $(Y_{22}, \tilde{Y}_{22}, j)$ such that there is the Δ_{out} difference on the state before the 17th S-box layer. It needs to be done for each $2^{\delta_{out}} = 2^{16}$ possible difference in Δ_{out} but we expect only a proportion of $2^{-p_{out}} = 2^{-12}$ to verify the downward path, so the expected number of total solutions per $Y_{22,s}$ will be $2^{20+16-12}$. As the previous step, we expect a cost and a number of solutions of $2^{44+24} = 2^{68}$. For each solution, check for possible matches on the hash table. The match is performed on two quantities:
   - The values of $\tilde{Y}_{22}[1, 6, 10, 14, 15]$ can be fully computed from $\tilde{C}[1, 6, 10, 14, 15]$ and the guessed k_{in}: 20-bit filter;
   - The linear relations between Y_{22} and C and between $\tilde{Y}_{22}$ and $\tilde{C}$, i.e. $Y_{22} \oplus C = \tilde{Y}_{22} \oplus \tilde{C}$, excluding the nibbles we could fully compute as they were already used in the 20 bit filter: 44-bit filter (11 equations on 4 bits each);

5. Repeat from Step 1 until the right key is retrieved: as the structures check 2^{44} plaintexts, we need to repeat all this procedure $2^{44-16+16+12-44} = 2^{12}$, to expect having a pair of data that verifies the middle distinguisher and the external transitions 2^{-56}.

The data complexity of the attack is 2^{64} as we ask the whole codebook to the oracle. But, applying the improved data technique from [11], we can fix $\frac{64-56}{2} = 4$ bits of the ciphertexts to reduce the data needed without increasing the time complexity, hence the data complexity will become $\mathcal{D} = 2^{60}$.

The memory complexity is determined by Step 3 where 2^{68} words of $64 \times 2 + 16 + 8 = 152$ bits each are stored in the hash table, so $\mathcal{M} = 2^{68}$.

The time complexity so far is

$$2^{12}2^{24} \left(2^{44}2^{24}2^{16-16} + 2^{44}2^{20}2^{16-12} + 2^{68+68-20-44} \right) = 2^{108}.$$

But the attack is not yet finished. Indeed, we have recovered $5 \times 4 = 20$ bits of K_1, as well as 64 bits of K_0, as the unguessed bits of $K_0 = K_{22}$ would be revealed as a side effect of the second sieving, explained in Step. 4. In addition, we recover $7 \times 4 = 28$ bits of information in key bits due to the 7 nibbles of state-tests, so $64 + 20 + 28 = 112$ information-bits of the key in total, which is bigger than the number of candidates, i.e. 108. The big question now is how to determine the whole key from each candidate because of the complex form of the state test equations.

How to Recover the Whole Key. The whole key K_0 is known. Considering this and rewriting the state-test equations given in Appendix E of [1], we recover the following values and relations. From the first equation we can derive the value of $K_1[3]$, giving us $K_1[11] \oplus K_1[15]$ from the guesses, and we choose to write $K_1[15]$ as a function of $K_1[11]$. Then we rewrite the equations given on rounds 4 and 18 as a function of some variables $x_1, \ldots, x_{24}$ which depend only on the plaintext, the ciphertext, the guessed values of the state tests, the nibbles of K_0 and those nibbles of K_1 from k_{in} and k_{out}. We obtain the following equations:

Equation 4 : $SB(K_1[2] \oplus SB(SB(K_1[0] \oplus x_1) \oplus SB(K_1[14] \oplus x_2) \oplus SB(K_1[7]$
$\oplus x_3) \oplus x_4) \oplus SB(SB(K_1[1] \oplus x_5) \oplus SB(K_1[10] \oplus x_6) \oplus x_7)$
$\oplus SB(SB(K_1[2] \oplus x_8) \oplus x_9)) \oplus SB(K_1[5] \oplus SB(SB(K_1[5] \oplus x_{10})$
$\oplus x_{11}) \oplus x_{12}) \oplus x_{13} = 0,$

Equation 18 : $SB(K_1[2] \oplus K_1[10] \oplus K_1[14] \oplus SB(SB(K_1[7] \oplus K_1[11]) \oplus x_{14})$
$\oplus SB(SB(K_1[0] \oplus x_{15}) \oplus SB(K_1[14] \oplus x_{16}) \oplus x_{17})) \oplus SB(SB(K_1[1] \oplus K_1[9]$
$\oplus x_{18}) \oplus SB(K_1[10] \oplus x_{19}) \oplus x_{20}) \oplus SB(SB(K_1[2] \oplus K_1[10] \oplus K_1[14]$
$\oplus x_{21}) \oplus x_9) \oplus SB(K_1[5] \oplus SB(SB(K_1[5] \oplus x_{22}) \oplus x_{11}) \oplus x_{23}) \oplus x_{24} = 0.$

During the attack procedure, we stock the candidates we find after the matching in a table of size 2^s with $s \geq 100$, and sort this table based on $x_1, \ldots, x_{24}$. We will have 2^{96} groups of candidates of size $2^x = 2^{s-96}$ with the same variables. Since $x_1, \cdots, x_{24}$ define Eqs. 4 and 18, each candidate in one group will have the same set of solutions for those two equations. Thus, for each group, we can calculate and store the list of the 2^{20} solutions for Eq. 4 and 18. And in parallel, for each of the 2^x candidates in the group, we calculate the 2^{16} possible solutions of Eqs. 3 and 19. For each of these 2^{16} solutions, we get one match with the stored list of 2^{20} solutions from Eq. 4 and 18 with respect to the nibbles $K_1[0, 1, 9, 11, 14]$. Thus, for each element in the group, we can find 2^{16} possibilities for $K_1[0, 1, 2, 5, 6, 7, 9, 10, 11, 14, 15]$ giving us the whole key. Finally, the overall time cost of this will be:

$$\mathcal{T} = 2^{108-s}2^{96} \left(2^{20} + 2^x 2^{16}\right),$$

which equals to 2^{124} if $x > 4$ and if $x = 4$ it equals to 2^{125} of small computations for recovering the whole key, which is lower than exhaustive search. And the memory complexity is 2^s as we stock the candidates in a table of size 2^s. For $s = 101$, we get a time complexity of $2^{124.58}$, and many trade-offs are possible.

6.2   Other Attacks on CRAFT and Conclusion

The attack described above can be applied to fewer than 23 rounds straightforwardly by subsequently removing one round from each side and adapting the structures to the known key nibbles. These results can be seen in Table 1. In this case, the data will be smaller, as we can apply the data reduction idea from [11].

It is worth pointing out that the authors did not expect differential attacks to reach 22 rounds with the best paths they found. Given that these paths reached 13 rounds, and the distinguisher used in our attack reaches 11 (two less rounds), it makes us deduce that truncated MITM attacks seem to be much more performant on CRAFT than differential attacks, and the most performant attack, to the best of our knowledge. We believe this is the case because of its alternated key schedule and the existence of iterative truncated paths, both with period two. The number of rounds reached is still far from the full version, but we expect further attacks with these techniques and better dealing with the state-test relations to reach more rounds.

7   Applications: SKINNY-64-192 and SKINNY-128-384

In this section, we provide two applications on two variants of SKINNY. Using a truncated path, state-test technique and the enhanced parallel partitioning method over two rounds, we provide a new attack on 23-round SKINNY-64-192, with slightly better time and lower data than the best known attack. In order to illustrate the importance of our improved parallel partitioning method, we have improved the previous differential MITM attack on SKINNY-128-384, that provided the best attacks on the single tweakey setting, and we have managed to slightly reduce their time or data complexity thanks to the structures, providing the best current attack on SKINNY-128-384 in the single tweakey setting. The specification of this cipher is given in the long version of this paper [1]. In the proposed attacks, we use the modified round key addition in the upper part where $U_r = \text{MC}(\text{SR}(K_r))$ is Xored to the output state of the MixColumn operation. This shows the fact that (truncated) differential MITM attacks work well on reduced-round variants of the SKINNY constructions. As further work, we plan to automatize the tool including more evolved structures, as the ones used in the MITM attacks from [2,3,10], and we expect we might be able to reach more rounds in both variants.

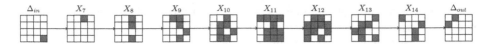

Fig. 9. 9-round truncated differential characteristic of probability 2^{52} for SKINNY-64-192.

7.1   Attack on 23-Round SKINNY-64-192

Since SKINNY key schedule is linear, it would be an efficient approach to guess some subkey bits and retrieve the whole key after guessing enough independent round key bits. Moreover, the key schedule makes the evaluation of the dimension of any set of round key nibbles easy since a round key nibble depends on exactly three master key nibbles, $\mathbf{TK1}[i]$, $\mathbf{TK2}[i]$, and $\mathbf{TK3}[i]$, for a specific $i \in \{0, \ldots, 15\}$.

An Attack on SKINNY-64-192 Without Parallel Partitioning. We first propose a 21-round truncated differential-MITM attack which is followed by two additional rounds using the parallel partitioning method, resulting in a 23-round attack. We conducted an automatic search for the optimum 21-round core attack on SKINNY-64-192, enhanced with the state-test key guessing technique, based on the MILP method proposed in Sect. 5. We set $r_m = 9$, $r_{in} = 6$, and $r_{out} = 6$. The core attack is represented in Fig. 14 in Appendix F of the longer version of this paper [1], with the following parameters:

Rounds	p	s_{in}	s_{out}	δ_{in}	δ_{out}	$|k_{in}|$	$|k_{out}|$
22	52	4	4	4	8	128	116

The clustering effect increases p to 51.78, which is not very significant. Although we have included the probabilistic key recovery method in our search, the optimum solution returned $p_{in} = p_{out} = 0$, meaning that a deterministic key guessing is more efficient for SKINNY-64-192.

Table 9 in Appendix F of [1] describes all the subkey nibbles of k_{in} and k_{out} needed in the 21-round attack of SKINNY-64-192 which are also reflected in Fig. 14 from [1] (that also includes this information in the needed key nibbles for the 23-round full attack in Table 10). It also indicates which nibble of the master key each subkey nibble of k_{in} and k_{out} depends on, and presents the total number of linear relations in each nibble of the master key, given k_{in} and k_{out}. In this way, we can determine the number of common linear relations, i.e. the size of the intersection $|k_{in} \cap k_{out}|$ which is $15 \times 4 = 60$ bits.

State-Test Ttechnique. We could use the state-test technique to reduce $|k_{in}|$ and $|k_{out}|$ by testing the 3 and 2 respective nibbles of Table 5, instead of guessing the 5 and 4 respective subkeys nibbles described on the table. Thanks to this technique, the number of bits in k_{in} could be reduced by 8 bits, and the number of bits in k_{out} could also be reduced by 8 bits. The optimal time complexity is nevertheless reached when we only consider one state-test technique for each part (the non-crossed ones in Table 5).

Table 5. Non-linear relations available in the state-test technique on the 21 and 23 rounds of SKINNY-64-192. The crossed cells will not be used in the 23-round attack.

Wanted nibble	RoundKey nibbles involved	Nibbles needed from the precedent state
~~$X_4[2]$~~	$K_3[2], K_2[7]$	$K_3[2] \oplus \text{SC}(X_3[2]) \oplus \text{SC}(X_3[15]) \oplus \text{SC}(K_2[7] \oplus \text{SC}(X_2[7]) \oplus \text{SC}(X_2[10]))$
~~$X_4[10]$~~	$K_3[5], K_2[7]$	$K_3[5] \oplus \text{SC}(X_3[5]) \oplus \text{SC}(K_2[7] \oplus \text{SC}(X_2[7]) \oplus \text{SC}(X_2[10]))$
$X_5[9]$	$K_4[4], K_3[6]$	$K_4[4] \oplus \text{SC}(X_4[4]) \oplus \text{SC}(K_3[6] \oplus \text{SC}(X_3[6]) \oplus \text{SC}(X_3[9]))$
~~$X_{17}[5]$~~	$K_{17}[5], K_{18}[6]$	$K_{17}[5] \oplus \text{SC}^{-1}(X_{18}[10]) \oplus \text{SC}^{-1}(X_{18}[14]) \oplus \text{SC}^{-1}(K_{18}[6] \oplus \text{SC}^{-1}(X_{19}[7]) \oplus \text{SC}^{-1}(X_{19}[11]) \oplus \text{SC}^{-1}(X_{19}[15]))$
$X_{16}[5]$	$K_{16}[5], K_{17}[6]$	$K_{16}[5] \oplus \text{SC}^{-1}(X_{17}[10]) \oplus \text{SC}^{-1}(X_{17}[14]) \oplus \text{SC}^{-1}(K_{17}[6] \oplus \text{SC}^{-1}(X_{18}[7]) \oplus \text{SC}^{-1}(X_{18}[11]) \oplus \text{SC}^{-1}(X_{18}[15]))$

Attack Steps. We describe now the core attack on 21 rounds of SKINNY-64-192. The guesses needed for this attack are summarized in Table 9 from [1] and the state test equations to guess are given in Table 5.

1. Ask for the encryption of the whole codebook (we will explain later how to apply the data reduction of Sect. 2.3 to this case).
2. Pick one plaintext/ciphertext pair (P, C).
3. First we guess the 44 subkey bit common relations shared between k_{in} and k_{out}.
4. Compute all possible tuples $(P, \tilde{P}, i)$ for each value i of the remaining 84 bits of k_{in} such that the difference after the 6th S-box layer is according to Δ_{in} of Fig. 9. At the end of this step, we have 2^{84+4} possible candidates. For all $\tilde{P}$, compute $E(\tilde{P}) = \hat{C}$ and store them in a hash table.
5. Similarly, for each value j of the remaining 72 bits of k_{out}, compute all possible tuples $(C, \tilde{C}, j)$ so that the difference on the state before the 15th S-box layer is according to Δ_{out} of Fig. 9. At the end of this step, we have 2^{72+8} possible candidates for the tuples $(C, \tilde{C}, j)$. And check for possible matches on the hash table. The match is performed on both the new ciphertext $\hat{C}$ and $\tilde{C}$ so that $(\tilde{P}, \tilde{C})$ is a valid plaintext/ciphertext pair.
6. Repeat from Step 1 until the right key is retrieved.

Adjustment for the Number of Candidate Triplets. If we consider what complexity such an attack would have, we obtain:

$$2^{52-4}2^{44}\left(2^{128-44+4} + 2^{116-44+8} + 2^{168-64}\right) = 2^{196},$$

that exceeds the exhaustive search.

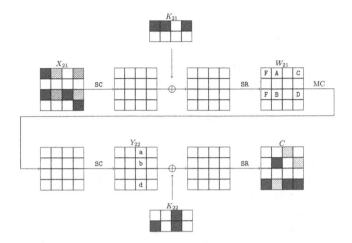

Fig. 10. The two last rounds of the 23-round attack on SKINNY-64-192, using parallel partitioning with fixed values for $X[1]\oplus X[11]$, $X[3]\oplus X[9]$, $Y[2]\oplus Y[13]$ and $Y[7]\oplus Y[13]$.

This is a possible side effect of the state test technique, that allows less sieving regarding the keybits. To compensate this, we will consider less state-test equations: we will guess in addition $K_2[7]$, that will determine because of the two first state-test equations $K_3[2]$ and $K_3[5]$; and also $K_{18}[6]$ and $K_{17}[6]$ that will determine because of the fourth and fifth state test equations $K_{17}[5]$ and $K_{16}[5]$. These three words guesses provide an additional sieving of 6 words, so 2^{-24}. The complexity will then be below exhaustive search:

$$2^{52-4}2^{68}\left(2^{128+4-68+4}+2^{116+8-68+8}+2^{132-64}\right)=2^{184}.$$

Attack on 23-Round of SKINNY-64-192 Now we will explain how to extend for two rounds this 21-round attack thanks to the improvement with the parallel partitioning method. In addition to the 21-round attack, we guess words $K_{22}[6]$, $K_{21}[0]$, $K_{21}[3]$ and $K_{21}[1]$, as they will be needed to sieve with respect to all the available potential during the parallel partitioning. In Fig. 10, we give the scheme of the two last rounds of the attack. We represent in red the internal state and the subkey words that we will use to build the parallel partitions and compute the upper part of the attack. Similarly, we represent in blue the internal state and the subkey words used to build the initial structure and compute the lower part of the attack. The remaining attack procedure of the 23-round attack is similar to the 21-round one:

1. We fix the values of the words F, $A\oplus B$ and $C\oplus D$ of W_{21} in Fig. 10, and of the words $a\oplus d$ and $b\oplus d$ of Y_{22} in Fig. 10.
2. We guess the 76 bits of common linear relations of $(k_{in}\cap k_{out})$, detailed in Table 10 in [1].
3. Then for each value i of the remaining 56+4=60 bits of $(k_{in}-k_{in}\cap k_{out})$, we can compute from the values of step 1, the fixed nibbles $C[5,12,14,15]$,

$C[2] \oplus C[13]$ and $C[7] \oplus C[13]$ as shown in Fig. 10. Then we have 2^{40} possible states for C as we have imposed the values of 6 nibbles thus there are 10 nibbles that can take all possible values. For all the possible values for C, we compute the ciphertext and get the corresponding plaintext P.

4. Compute all possible tuples $(P, \tilde{P}, i)$ for each $2^{|k_{in} - k_{in} \cap k_{out}|} \times 2^{s_{in}} = 2^{56+4}$ values i of $k_{in} - |k_{in} \cap k_{out}|$ and the state test relation, and each P from the structure defined at the previous step, such that they generate Δ_{in} after six rounds. At the end of this step, we have $2^{40} \times 2^{60+4} = 2^{104}$ possible candidates, and store them in a hash table.

5. Similarly, for each of the $2^{|k_{out} - k_{in} \cap k_{out}|} \times 2^{s_{out}} = 2^{52+4}$ possible values j of $(k_{out} - k_{in} \cap k_{out})$ and state-test relations, we can compute from the values of step 1, the fixed values $X_{21}[0, 8, 10, 15]$, $X_{21}[1] \oplus X_{21}[11]$ and $X_{21}[3] \oplus X_{21}[9]$, in blue in Fig. 10. We then pick all the 2^{40} possible states of X_{21} and we compute the 2^{40} possible $W_{20} = \text{MC}^{-1}(X_{21})$.

6. For each $2^{52+4} = 2^{56}$ values j of $(k_{out} - k_{in} \cap k_{out})$ and state-test relation and for each value of state W_{20}, compute all possible tuples $(W_{20}, \tilde{W}_{20}, j)$ so that there is a difference on the state before the 15th S-box layer on both nibbles. At the end of this step we have $2^{40} \times 2^{56+8} = 2^{104}$ possible candidates for the tuples $(W_{20}, \tilde{W}_{20}, j)$.

7. Check for possible matches on the hash table. The match is performed on two quantities:
   - The values of the nibbles $\tilde{X}_{21}[8]$ and $\tilde{X}_{21}[15]$ can be fully computed from $\tilde{C}[2] \oplus \tilde{C}[13], \tilde{C}[7] \oplus \tilde{C}[13]$ and the guessed k_{in} and similarly the values of the nibbles $\tilde{C}[5], \tilde{C}[12], \tilde{C}[14]$ and $\tilde{C}[15]$ can be fully computed from $\tilde{X}_{21}[0], \tilde{X}_{21}[10], \tilde{X}_{21}[1] \oplus \tilde{X}_{21}[11], \tilde{X}_{21}[3] \oplus \tilde{X}_{21}[9]$ and the guessed k_{out}: a $6 \times 4 = 24$ bit filter;
   - The linear relations between X_{21} and C, and $\tilde{X}_{21}$ and $\tilde{C}$: a 80-bit filter (10×2 equations on 4 bits each), summarized in Table 11 from [1].

8. Repeat from Step 1 with different values for the fixed nibbles until the right key is retrieved.

Linear Relations to Match with the Parallel Partitioning Improvement. At the end of the attack procedure we have to match X_{21} and C and their associated pair $\tilde{X}_{21}$ and $\tilde{C}$. After two rounds of SKINNY-64-192, if we know the 4 first subkey nibbles then the relations between the words of X_{21} and C and $\tilde{X}_{21}$ and $\tilde{C}$, of Fig. 10, are linear. In our application, we have guessed the subkey nibbles $K_{21}[0], K_{21}[1]$ and $K_{21}[3]$. We do not know the subkey nibble $K_{21}[2]$ but we have guessed the subkey nibbles $K_{22}[2]$ and $K_{22}[6]$ and thus we obtain the linear relations of Column 3. To match both sides of the equations when the subkey word is not completely determined, we add on each side the subkey information known by each side, respectively. Thus the relations are linear as we can compute each side of the equations independently. The linear relations (given for the pair (X_{21}, C), but that are also true for $(\tilde{X}_{21}, \tilde{C})$) to match are given in Table 11 of

Appendix F in [1]. The time complexity of this step will be:

$$\mathcal{T} = 2^{52-4-40} 2^{76} \left(2^{56+4+4} 2^{40} + 2^{52+4+8} 2^{40} + 2^{104+104-24-40-40} \right) = 2^{188}.$$

To reduce the data complexity of our attack, we use the improvement of [11] to impose the value of $\frac{64-48}{2} = 8$ bits of the ciphertexts. Thus we fix the nibbles $C[6]$, $C[1] \oplus C[13]$, $\tilde{C}[6]$ and $\tilde{C}[1] \oplus \tilde{C}[13]$, which is a 8 bits condition. Moreover, we compute and build a stored table with the data needed to perform the attack to avoid doing the decryption during the upper part of the attack. Finally the data complexity of this attack is $\mathcal{D} = 2^{64-8} = 2^{56}$. The memory complexity is determined by Step 6 storing $\mathcal{M} = 2^{104}$ words of $64 + 64 = 128$.

Thanks to the truncated differential, we manage to extend the characteristic for more rounds than if it was a concrete differential characteristic since the subkeys around the characteristic are not needed in the attack. Moreover in the case of SKINNY, we can use, with little cost, the parallel partitioning improvement to reach two more rounds and thus reach the same best number of rounds in the single tweak setting as the best known attack.

7.2 Improved Attacks on 25-Round SKINNY-128-384

We consider the 24-round and the 25-round attack given in [11] in Sect. 3.4 and 3.5 respectively. Each uses a different differential. By considering the core attack on 23 rounds that is extended by one round in the paper, we will apply our improved structure with a two-round extension, reducing the data complexity of the best known attacks, that cover 25 rounds. By considering the 25-round attack also considered in the paper, and including the last key recovery round in the final structure, reaching now 2 rounds instead of 1, we are able to reduce the overall time complexity, as we have fewer key bits to guess, providing the 25-round SKINNY-128-384 attacks with the lowest complexity. These results are shown in Table 1, compared to all the previous results.

Reducing the Data Needed. The application is quite straightforward given the previous attack, so we will omit the details and refer to the original paper [11]. We consider exactly the same core over 23 rounds, but we will add two rounds instead of one. For this, we will additionally guess nibbles 5, 2, and 4 from K_{24} in k_{in}, and nibbles 14 and 11 from K_{23} in K_{out}. All these guesses add equations in the common part of the key to guess. This will allow us to build structures of size 2^{64}, with 2 fixed words from the first and the last columns, 3 from the second, and one from the third – see Fig. 15 from [1]. The full filtering can be applied as we can rewrite all equations as linear ones in the unknown parts of the key. The time complexity becomes:

$$\mathcal{T} = 2^{105.9-64} 2^{120+40} \left(2^{128-16} 2^{64} + 2^{136-24} 2^{64} + 2^{128-16+64+136-24+64-128-64} \right)$$

So we have $\mathcal{T} = 2^{201.9} \left(2^{176} + 2^{176} + 2^{160} \right) = 2^{378.9}$, and the memory complexity, with $x = (128 - 105.9)/2 = 11.05$ becomes $2^{170-11.05} = 2^{165}$, and data

$\mathcal{D} = 2^{128-11.05} = 2^{117}$, providing the best data complexity for a 25-round attack, as can be seen in Table 1.

Reducing the Time. We consider the attack from [11] on 25 rounds, which added 4 rounds at the top and 5 rounds at the bottom of a 15-round distinguisher, plus one added through a structure. As the bottleneck term is the five rounds at the lower part, where we guess 8 more keybits than the upper part, we propose our attack with a 2-round structure, yielding a configuration of 4+15+4+2 rounds. As we are guessing 1 less word from k_{out} (all but the word 12 from K_{23}) than before, as we add 7 words needed in order to verify linearly the equations in the structure and to build small structures, all the complexities stay the same, but the time reduces of about a factor of 2^8 as shown in Table 1. We can build now 4 fixed relations between the input and the output of the structure, given by equations A_1+C_1, A_2+C_2, A_3+C_3, A_4+C_4, B_1+C_1, B_2+C_2, B_3+C_3 from Fig. 16 from [1], and the structures will have a size of 2^{72}. We do not guess the word 12 from round K_{23} anymore, which reduces by 1 word the lower guess and leaves the number of common keybits the same. The time complexity becomes:

$$\mathcal{T} = 2^{116.5-72}2^{120} \left(2^{128+72} + 2^{136-64+56+72} + 2^{128+72+136-64+56+72-72-128} \right),$$

giving $\mathcal{T} = 2^{164.5} \left(2^{200} + 2^{200} + 2^{200} \right) = 2^{366}$, while previous best time was $2^{372.5}$. Applying the same idea as in the previous attack for reducing the data and memory needed, we obtain, without modifying the time and memory complexities a data of also $2^{128-x} = 2^{122.25}$, as $x = \frac{128-116.5}{2} = 5.75$, with a memory complexity of $2^{194.25}$, that stays the same.

8   Conclusion

We have implemented a tool, based on MILP modeling, that finds the distinguishers that produce the best overall attack complexities when considering the key-guessing rounds and their two related improvements. The inclusion of the structures is left as an open problem for the future.

We have been able to apply the variety of results to CRAFT, SKINNY-64-192 and SKINNY-128-384. For CRAFT we managed to improve by two rounds the previous attacks with a truncated version of differential MTIM. For SKINNY-128-384 we managed to improve the complexities of the best known attacks in the single tweak setting, and for SKINNY-64-192 we matched the same number of rounds while the time stays comparable and the memory and data are worse.

We have in particular shown that differential MITM attacks have a different nature than differential attacks that allow them to be combined with MITM-related techniques that can not be combined with differential attacks, like the parallel partitions that are closely related to initial structures and bicliques.

Actually, we leave as an open problem to produce a tool that will combine differential MITM attacks with parallel partitioning technique [4] and bicliques [19] over more rounds, as the one in [14].

In addition, we showed that differential MITM attacks can be easily combined with the state-test technique, thanks to the fact that each key is tested for a fixed data. In differentials attacks it would be much harder to apply.

Acknowledgements. This research has been partially funded by the European Union (ERC-2023-COG, SoBaSyC, 101125450).

References

1. Ahmadian, Z., Khalesi, A., M'foukh, D., Moghimi, H., Naya-Plasencia, M.: Improved differential meet-in-the-middle cryptanalysis. Cryptology ePrint Archive, Paper 2024/351 (2024). https://eprint.iacr.org/2024/351
2. Aoki, K., Sasaki, Y.: Preimage attacks on one-block MD4, 63-step MD5 and more. In: Avanzi, R.M., Keliher, L., Sica, F. (eds.) Selected Areas in Cryptography. LNCS, vol. 5381, pp. 103–119. Springer, Heidelberg (2009). https://doi.org/10.1007/978-3-642-04159-4_7
3. Aoki, K., Sasaki, Y.: Meet-in-the-middle preimage attacks against reduced SHA-0 and SHA-1. In: Halevi, S. (ed.) Advances in Cryptology. CRYPTO 2009. LNCS, vol. 5677, pp. 70–89. Springer, Heidelberg (2009). https://doi.org/10.1007/978-3-642-03356-8_5
4. Aoki, K., Sasaki, Y.: Meet-in-the-middle preimage attacks against reduced SHA-0 and SHA-1. In: Halevi, S. (ed.) Advances in Cryptology. CRYPTO 2009. LNCS, vol. 5677, pp. 70–89. Springer, Heidelberg (2009). https://doi.org/10.1007/978-3-642-03356-8_5
5. Banik, S., Pandey, S.K., Peyrin, T., Sasaki, Y., Sim, S.M., Todo, Y.: GIFT: a small present: towards reaching the limit of lightweight encryption. In: Fischer, W., Homma, N. (eds.) Cryptographic Hardware and Embedded Systems. CHES 2017. LNCS, vol. 10529, pp. 321–345. Springer, Cham (2017). https://doi.org/10.1007/978-3-319-66787-4_16
6. Bao, Z., Guo, J., Shi, D., Tu, Y.: Superposition meet-in-the-middle attacks: updates on fundamental security of AES-like hashing. In: Dodis, Y., Shrimpton, T. (eds.) Advances in Cryptology. CRYPTO 2022. LNCS, vol. 13507, pp. 64–93. Springer, Cham (2022). https://doi.org/10.1007/978-3-031-15802-5_3
7. Beierle, C., et al.: The SKINNY family of block ciphers and its low-latency variant MANTIS. In: Robshaw, M., Katz, J. (eds.) Advances in Cryptology. CRYPTO 2016. LNCS, vol. 9815, pp. 123–153. Springer, Heidelberg (2016). https://doi.org/10.1007/978-3-662-53008-5_5
8. Beierle, C., Leander, G., Moradi, A., Rasoolzadeh, S.: CRAFT: lightweight tweakable block cipher with efficient protection against DFA attacks. IACR Trans. Symmet. Cryptol. **2019**(1), 5–45 (2019)
9. Biham, E., Shamir, A.: Diffcrential cryptanalysis of des-like cryptosystems. In: Menezes, A., Vanstone, S.A. (eds.) Advances in Cryptology. CRYPTO 1990. LNCS, vol. 537, pp. 2–21. Springer, Heidelberg (1990). https://doi.org/10.1007/3-540-38424-3_1

10. Bogdanov, A., Khovratovich, D., Rechberger, C.: Biclique cryptanalysis of the full AES. In: Lee, D.H., Wang, X. (eds.) Advances in Cryptology. ASIACRYPT 2011. LNCS, vol. 7073, pp. 344–371. Springer, Heidelberg (2011). https://doi.org/10.1007/978-3-642-25385-0_19

11. Boura, C., David, N., Derbez, P., Leander, G., Naya-Plasencia, M.: Differential meet-in-the-middle cryptanalysis. In: Handschuh, H., Lysyanskaya, A. (eds.) Advances in Cryptology. CRYPTO 2023. LNCS, vol. 14083, pp. 240–272. Springer, Cham (2023). https://doi.org/10.1007/978-3-031-38548-3_9

12. Boura, C., Naya-Plasencia, M., Suder, V.: Scrutinizing and improving impossible differential attacks: applications to clefia, camellia, lblock and simon. In: Sarkar, P., Iwata, T. (eds.) Advances in Cryptology. ASIACRYPT 2014. LNCS, vol. 8873, pp. 179–199. Springer, Heidelberg (2014). https://doi.org/10.1007/978-3-662-45611-8_10

13. Diffie, W., Hellman, M.E.: Special feature exhaustive cryptanalysis of the NBS data encryption standard. Computer 10(6), 74–84 (1977)

14. Dong, X., Hua, J., Sun, S., Li, Z., Wang, X., Hu, L.: Meet-in-the-middle attacks revisited: key-recovery, collision, and preimage attacks. In: Malkin, T., Peikert, C. (eds.) Advances in Cryptology. CRYPTO 2021. LNCS, vol. 12827, pp. 278–308. Springer, Cham (2021). https://doi.org/10.1007/978-3-030-84252-9_10

15. Dunkelman, O., Sekar, G., Preneel, B.: Improved meet-in-the-middle attacks on reduced-round DES. In: Srinathan, K., Rangan, C.P., Yung, M. (eds.) Progress in Cryptology. INDOCRYPT 2007. LNCS, vol. 4859, pp. 86–100. Springer, Heidelberg (2007). https://doi.org/10.1007/978-3-540-77026-8_8

16. Eichlseder, M., Leander, G., Rasoolzadeh, S.: Computing expected differential probability of (truncated) differentials and expected linear potential of (multidimensional) linear hulls in SPN block ciphers. In: Progress in Cryptology. INDOCRYPT 2020, pp. 345–369. Springer (2020)

17. Hadipour, H., Bagheri, N., Song, L.: Improved rectangle attacks on SKINNY and CRAFT. IACR Trans. Symmetric Cryptol. 2021(2), 140–198 (2021)

18. Hadipour, H., Sadeghi, S., Eichlseder, M.: Finding the impossible: automated search for full impossible-differential, zero-correlation, and integral attacks. In: Hazay, C., Stam, M. (eds.) Advances in Cryptology. EUROCRYPT 2023. LNCS, vol. 14007, pp. 128–157. Springer, Cham (2023). https://doi.org/10.1007/978-3-031-30634-1_5

19. Khovratovich, D., Rechberger, C., Savelieva, A.: Bicliques for preimages: attacks on skein-512 and the SHA-2 family. In: Canteaut, A. (ed.) Fast Software Encryption. FSE 2012. LNCS, vol. 7549, pp. 244–263. Springer, Heidelberg (2012). https://doi.org/10.1007/978-3-642-34047-5_15

20. Knudsen, L.R.: Truncated and higher order differentials. In: Preneel, B. (ed.) Fast Software Encryption: Second International Workshop. LNCS, vol. 1008, pp. 196–211. Springer, Heidelberg (1994). https://doi.org/10.1007/3-540-60590-8_16

21. Knudsen, L.R., Wagner, D.A.: Integral cryptanalysis. In: Daemen, J., Rijmen, V. (eds.) Fast Software Encryption. FSE 2002. LNCS, vol. 2365, pp. 112–127. Springer, Heidelberg (2002). https://doi.org/10.1007/3-540-45661-9_9

22. Lallemand, V., Naya-Plasencia, M.: Cryptanalysis of KLEIN. In: Cid, C., Rechberger, C. (eds.) Fast Software Encryption. FSE 2014. LNCS, vol. 8540, pp. 451–470. Springer, Heidelberg (2014). https://doi.org/10.1007/978-3-662-46706-0_23

23. Leander, G., Abdelraheem, M.A., AlKhzaimi, H., Zenner, E.: A cryptanalysis of printcipher: the invariant subspace attack. In: Rogaway, P. (ed.) Advances in Cryptology. CRYPTO 2011. LNCS, vol. 6841, pp. 206–221. Springer, Heidelberg (2011). https://doi.org/10.1007/978-3-642-22792-9_12

24. Ma, Z., Li, M., Chen, S.: Meet-in-the-middle attacks on round-reduced CRAFT based on automatic search. IET Inf. Secur. **17**(3), 534–543 (2023)
25. Matsui, M.: Linear cryptanalysis method for DES cipher. In: Helleseth, T. (ed.) Advances in Cryptology. EUROCRYPT 1993. LNCS, vol. 765, pp. 386–397. Springer, Heidelberg (1993). https://doi.org/10.1007/3-540-48285-7_33
26. Moghaddam, A.E., Ahmadian, Z.: New automatic search method for truncated-differential characteristics application to midori. SKINNY and CRAFT. Comput. J. **63**(12), 1813–1825 (2020)
27. Rasoolzadeh, S., Ahmadian, Z., Salmasizadeh, M., Aref, M.R.: An improved truncated differential cryptanalysis of KLEIN. Tatra Mount. Math. Publ. **67**(1), 135–147 (2016)
28. Shi, D., Sun, S., Derbez, P., Todo, Y., Sun, B., Hu, L.: Programming the demirci-selçuk meet-in-the-middle attack with constraints. In: Peyrin, T., Galbraith, S.D. (eds.) Advances in Cryptology. ASIACRYPT 2018. LNCS, vol. 11273, pp. 3–34. Springer, Cham (2018). https://doi.org/10.1007/978-3-030-03329-3_1
29. Shi, D., Sun, S., Song, L., Hu, L., Yang, Q.: Exploiting non-full key additions: full-fledged automatic demirci-selçuk meet-in-the-middle cryptanalysis of SKINNY. In: Hazay, C., Stam, M. (eds.) Advances in Cryptology. EUROCRYPT 2023. LNCS, vol. 14007, pp. 67–97. Springer, Cham (2023). https://doi.org/10.1007/978-3-031-30634-1_3
30. Song, L., et al.: Optimizing rectangle attacks: a unified and generic framework for key recovery. In: Agrawal, S., Lin, D. (eds.) Advances in Cryptology. ASIACRYPT 2022. LNCS, vol. 13791, pp. 410–440. Springer, Cham (2022). https://doi.org/10.1007/978-3-031-22963-3_14
31. Tolba, M., Abdelkhalek, A., Youssef, A.M.: Impossible differential cryptanalysis of reduced-round SKINNY. In: Joye, M., Nitaj, A. (eds.) Progress in Cryptology. AFRICACRYPT 2017. LNCS, vol. 10239, pp. 117–134. Springer, Cham (2017). https://doi.org/10.1007/978-3-319-57339-7_7

Post-quantum Security of Tweakable Even-Mansour, and Applications

Gorjan Alagic[1,2]($\boxtimes$), Chen Bai[1], Jonathan Katz[3], Christian Majenz[4], and Patrick Struck[5]

[1] University of Maryland, College Park, USA
{galagic,cbai1}@umd.edu
[2] NIST,Gaithersburg, USA
[3] Google, Washington DC, USA
[4] Technical University of Denmark, Kongens Lyngby, Denmark
chmaj@dtu.dk
[5] University of Konstanz, Konstanz, Germany
patrick.struck@uni.kn

Abstract. The tweakable Even-Mansour construction yields a tweakable block cipher from a public random permutation. We prove post-quantum security of tweakable Even-Mansour when attackers have *quantum* access to the random permutation but only *classical* access to the secretly-keyed construction, the relevant setting for most real-world applications. We then use our results to prove post-quantum security— in the same model—of the symmetric-key schemes Chaskey (an ISO-standardized MAC), Elephant (an AEAD finalist of NIST's lightweight cryptography standardization effort), and a variant of Minalpher (an AEAD second-round candidate of the CAESAR competition).

1 Introduction

The development of large-scale quantum computers would have a significant impact on cryptography. For symmetric-key cryptosystems—even ideal ciphers—one must at least double the key length in order to achieve the same security against quantum attackers as is enjoyed against classical adversaries, due to the possibility of using Grover's search algorithm [8] to carry out a key-recovery attack. In general, however, doubling the key length may not be sufficient [4,13, 14], and it is therefore critical to understand the security of various symmetric-key constructions against quantum attackers.

One can consider two models of quantum attacks [3]. In the so-called Q2 model, the attacker is given quantum access to any underlying public primitives (e.g., a block cipher) as well as the secretly keyed construction itself. In contrast, the Q1 model assumes the adversary has quantum access to all *public* primitives but only classical access to the secretly keyed scheme. The distinction between

---

J. Katz—Work done in part while at the University of Maryland.

M. Joye and G. Leander (Eds.): EUROCRYPT 2024, LNCS 14651, pp. 310–338, 2024.
https://doi.org/10.1007/978-3-031-58716-0_11

Q1 and Q2 is significant: for many symmetric-key constructions, polynomial-query attacks are known in the Q2 model but not in the Q1 model [12–14]. At the same time, the Q2 model appears to be highly unrealistic, particularly for real-world applications where the honest parties only run the construction on classical inputs, and do not expose any quantum interface to an attacker (which is necessarily the case when the honest devices implementing the construction are entirely classical). The Q1 model is thus a much better fit for realistic quantum attacks, and several recent works [1, 4, 11] have focused on that model. From here on, by "post-quantum security" we will mean the Q1 model by default.

Proving security in the Q1 model is challenging since it requires reasoning about a combination of (related) classical and quantum oracles. Additional complications arise when reasoning about permutations (rather than functions), particularly when their inverse may also be queried, as in the random-permutation and ideal-cipher models. Indeed, most results in a "hybrid" classical-/quantum-query setting (e.g., [5, 9, 16]) deal with oracles for functions, and there are only a few existing results in the Q1 model that deal with random permutations. Jaeger et al. [11] gave positive results for security of the FX construction (a mechanism for key-length extension of an ideal cipher); their work also implies security for the Even-Mansour construction either for non-adaptive adversaries or for a variant of the construction based on a public random function. Subsequent work by Alagic et al. [1] showed post-quantum security of the full Even-Mansour construction (i.e., based on a random permutation) against adaptive adversaries.

1.1 Our Results

We show post-quantum security of the *tweakable* Even-Mansour construction, a tweakable block cipher constructed from a public random permutation. We then use this result to establish post-quantum security of several symmetric-key schemes. We stress that post-quantum security of tweakable Even-Mansour does not follow from post-quantum security of Even-Mansour. Indeed, the tweak must be incorporated in a way that satisfies several technical conditions; in addition, incorporating both tweaks and possible key expansion introduces dependencies and requires significant technical work to analyze. In all of our results, adversaries can make adaptive queries to any permutations to which they have access (whether quantum or classical, as appropriate) in both the forward and inverse directions. We now summarize our results.

Tweakable Even-Mansour. Let $P : \{0,1\}^n \to \{0,1\}^n$ be a permutation. The tweakable Even-Mansour scheme $\mathsf{TEM}^{f_1,f_2}[P] : \{0,1\}^n \times \mathcal{T} \times \{0,1\}^n \to \{0,1\}^n$ is defined as

$$\mathsf{TEM}_k^{f_1,f_2}[P](t,x) = P(x \oplus f_1(t,k)) \oplus f_2(t,k),$$

where the key k is of length n, the set $\mathcal{T}$ is a tweak space, and f_1, f_2 are functions satisfying some technical conditions we omit here. We also consider a variant $\mathsf{TEM\text{-}KX}^{f_1,f_2}[P] : \{0,1\}^\kappa \times \mathcal{T} \times \{0,1\}^n \to \{0,1\}^n$ (where $\kappa \leq n$) that combines tweakable Even-Mansour with key expansion, and is defined as

$$\mathsf{TEM\text{-}KX}_k^{f_1,f_2}[P](t,x) = P(x \oplus f_1(t, P(k\|0^{n-\kappa}))) \oplus f_2(t, P(k\|0^{n-\kappa})).$$

Our main result is that both the above are secure (post-quantum) tweakable block ciphers when P is modeled as a random permutation.

Theorem 1 (informal). *An adaptive adversary making q_C classical queries to* TEM-KX$_k^{f_1,f_2}[P]$ *(for uniform $k \in \{0,1\}^\kappa$) and q_Q quantum queries to a random permutation P can distinguish the former from a uniform tweakable block cipher with probability at most* $\mathcal{O}\big(2^{-\kappa/2} \cdot (q_C\sqrt{q_Q} + q_Q\sqrt{q_C})\big)$.

(The above is stated formally as Theorem 3 and proved in Sect. 4.1.) Setting $\kappa = n$ implies security of TEM as a corollary (since $P(k)$ is uniform when $k \in \{0,1\}^n$ is uniform, for any permutation P). It follows that any post-quantum attack against TEM requires $q_C^2 \cdot q_Q + q_Q^2 \cdot q_C \approx 2^n$; hence $\Omega(2^{n/3})$ queries are necessary for constant success probability, matching known attacks [3,10].

We also consider an alternative method of performing key expansion in which a key $k \in \{0,1\}^\kappa$ is expanded to an "effective key" of length n by computing $F_P(k) = P(k\|0^{n-\kappa}) \oplus k\|0^{n-\kappa}$. This gives rise to another variant of tweakable Even-Mansour, defined as

$$\text{TEM-KX1}_k^{f_1,f_2}[P](t,x) = P(x \oplus f_1(t, F_P(k))) \oplus f_2(t, F_P(k)).$$

We show that the key-expansion function F_P is a pseudorandom generator (even for adversaries having quantum access to P). Using this fact, we are able to prove a tighter security bound for TEM-KX1 than what we show for TEM-KX (see Theorem 5 in Sect. 4.2 for a formal statement):

Theorem 2 (informal). *An adaptive adversary making q_C classical queries to* TEM-KX1$_k^{f_1,f_2}[P]$ *(for uniform $k \in \{0,1\}^\kappa$) and q_Q quantum queries to a random permutation P can distinguish the former from a uniform tweakable block cipher with probability at most* $\mathcal{O}\big(2^{-\kappa/2} \cdot (q_C + q_Q) + 2^{-n/2} \cdot (q_C\sqrt{q_Q} + q_Q\sqrt{q_C})\big)$.

A New Resampling Lemma. As a key technical tool used in our results, we prove a generalization of existing "resampling lemmas" [1,7] sufficient to handle tweakable block ciphers, something we believe to be of independent interest. A resampling lemma controls the success probability of a quantum-query adversary $\mathcal{D}$ in an experiment of the following form:

1. $\mathcal{D}$ receives quantum oracle access to a random permutation P;
2. two inputs s_0, s_1 are sampled from some distribution;
3. $\mathcal{D}$ receives quantum oracle access to either P, or P with inputs s_0 and s_1 "swapped"; it succeeds if it can correctly guess which is the case.

Prior work considered only the uniform distribution on s_0, s_1. We give a new resampling lemma that handles a wider class of (adversarially influenced) distributions, and even allows the distribution to depend on information $\mathcal{D}$ learns about P during step 1 of the above experiment (cf. Lemma 3 in Sect. 3):

Lemma 1 (informal). *In the above experiment, for any $\mathcal{D}$ making at most q quantum queries to P in step 1,* $\Pr[\mathcal{D} \text{ succeeds}] \leq 1/2 + \mathcal{O}(\sqrt{q\varepsilon})$, *where ε is the min-entropy of s_0, s_1.*

To prove the lemma, we develop a novel permutation variant of the stateful simulation technique for quantum-accessible random oracles [19] (i.e., the *superposition oracle* technique). In this context, *some* information about the input-output pairs learned by the adversary via quantum queries can be read directly from the oracle's internal quantum register. In the original superposition oracle technique [19], this useful feature is a consequence of the statistical independence of the function values of a random oracle. Existing generalizations to invertible random permutations [1] lack this feature.

Applications. In Sect. 5 we use our results to derive corollaries regarding the post-quantum security of various symmetric-key schemes when modeling the underlying permutations on which they are based as ideal permutations. In each case, security is established in two stages. First, we choose the tweak space $\mathcal{T}$ and the tweak functions f_1 and f_2 appropriately, and apply our theorems above to prove security for a certain block cipher construction. Then, we invoke existing results to reduce security of the overall cryptographic scheme (in the appropriate sense) to security of this cipher. Specifically:

1. We show how to specialize TEM so it captures the three pseudorandom permutations used by Chaskey [15], an ISO-standardized lightweight MAC. We can thus prove post-quantum security of Chaskey using Theorem 1.
2. We show how to specialize TEM-KX to the tweakable block cipher at the core of Elephant [2], an authenticated encryption scheme that was a finalist of NIST's lightweight standardization effort [18]. Theorem 1 then implies post-quantum security for Elephant. Using Theorem 2, we can prove a tighter security bound for a variant of Elephant that uses a slightly different key-expansion step.
3. We show how to specialize TEM-KX1 to the tweakable block cipher used by (a variant of) Minalpher [17], an authenticated encryption scheme that was a second-round candidate of the CAESAR competition. Theorem 2 then implies post-quantum security for this variant.

To our knowledge, these are the first proofs of post-quantum security for any versions of Chaskey, Elephant, or Minalpher.

2 Preliminaries

Notation and Basic Definitions. We let $\mathcal{P}(n)$ denote the set of all permutations on $\{0,1\}^n$. In the *public-permutation model* (or random-permutation model), a uniform permutation $P \leftarrow \mathcal{P}(n)$ is sampled and then provided as an oracle (in both the forward and inverse directions) to all parties.

A block cipher $E : \{0,1\}^\kappa \times \{0,1\}^n \to \{0,1\}^n$ is a keyed permutation, i.e., $E_k(\cdot) = E(k, \cdot)$ is a permutation of $\{0,1\}^n$ for all $k \in \{0,1\}^\kappa$. We say E is a *pseudorandom permutation* if E_k (for uniform $k \in \{0,1\}^\kappa$) is indistinguishable from a uniform permutation in $\mathcal{P}(n)$ even for adversaries who may query their oracle in both the forward and inverse directions.

For a set $\mathcal{T}$, let $\mathcal{E}(\mathcal{T}, n)$ be the set of all functions $E : \mathcal{T} \times \{0,1\}^n \to \{0,1\}^n$ such that $E(t, \cdot)$ is a permutation on $\{0,1\}^n$ for all $t \in \mathcal{T}$. A tweakable block cipher $\tilde{E} : \{0,1\}^\kappa \times \mathcal{T} \times \{0,1\}^n \to \{0,1\}^n$ is a family of permutations indexed by both a key $k \in \{0,1\}^\kappa$ and a tweak $t \in \mathcal{T}$, i.e., we now require that $\tilde{E}_k(t, \cdot) = \tilde{E}(k, t, \cdot)$ is a permutation of $\{0,1\}^n$ for all $k \in \{0,1\}^\kappa$ and $t \in \mathcal{T}$. Tweakable block cipher $\tilde{E}_k$ is *secure* if $\tilde{E}_k$ (for uniform choice of $k \in \{0,1\}^\kappa$) is indistinguishable from a uniform $\tilde{E} \leftarrow \mathcal{E}(\mathcal{T}, n)$.

In all the security notions mentioned above we consider algorithms having only classical access to secretly keyed primitives. When we consider constructions of keyed primitives (e.g., a tweakable block cipher) from public primitives (e.g., a random permutation), however, we provide the distinguisher with *quantum* oracle access to the public primitive. Thus, for example, a quantum distinguisher in the public-permutation model can apply the unitary operators

$$|x\rangle|y\rangle \mapsto |x\rangle|y \oplus P(x)\rangle$$
$$|x\rangle|y\rangle \mapsto |x\rangle|y \oplus P^{-1}(x)\rangle$$

to quantum registers of the adversary's choice. (We emphasize that this includes evaluating P/P^{-1} on arbitrary superpositions of inputs.) This is well-motivated, as in practice P would be instantiated by a publicly known permutation; adversaries with quantum computers would thus be able to coherently execute the reversible circuit for computing P/P^{-1}. On the other hand, secretly keyed primitives would be implemented by honest parties; if honest parties only evaluate the primitive on classical inputs then the attacker has no way to obtain quantum access to that keyed primitive.

A Reprogramming Lemma. We recall here a reprogramming lemma from prior work [1] that applies to the following experiment. A distinguisher $\mathcal{D}$ chooses an arbitrary function F along with a randomized process $\mathcal{B}$ for determining a set of points B at which F should (potentially) be reprogrammed to some known value. $\mathcal{D}$ is then given quantum access to either F or a reprogrammed version of F; when it is done making its oracle queries, $\mathcal{D}$ is given B. Roughly, the lemma says that $\mathcal{D}$ cannot determine whether it was interacting with F or the reprogrammed version of F as long as no point is reprogrammed with high probability.

Formally, for a function $F : \{0,1\}^m \to \{0,1\}^n$ and a set $B \subset \{0,1\}^m \times \{0,1\}^n$ such that each $x \in \{0,1\}^m$ is the first element of at most one tuple in B, define

$$F^{(B)}(x) := \begin{cases} y & \text{if } (x,y) \in B \\ F(x) & \text{otherwise.} \end{cases}$$

The following is taken verbatim from [1, Lemma 3]:

Lemma 2. *Let $\mathcal{D}$ be a quantum distinguisher in the following experiment:*

Phase 1: *$\mathcal{D}$ outputs descriptions of a function $F_0 = F : \{0,1\}^m \to \{0,1\}^n$ and a randomized algorithm $\mathcal{B}$ whose output is a set $B \subset \{0,1\}^m \times \{0,1\}^n$*

where each $x \in \{0,1\}^m$ is the first element of at most one tuple in B. Let $B_1 = \{x \mid \exists y : (x,y) \in B\}$ and $\varepsilon = \max_{x \in \{0,1\}^m} \{\Pr_{B \leftarrow \mathcal{B}}[x \in B_1]\}$.

Phase 2: $\mathcal{B}$ is run to obtain B. Let $F_1 = F^{(B)}$. A uniform bit b is chosen, and $\mathcal{D}$ is given quantum access to F_b.

Phase 3: $\mathcal{D}$ loses access to F_b, and receives the randomness r used to invoke $\mathcal{B}$ in phase 2. Then $\mathcal{D}$ outputs a guess b'.

For any $\mathcal{D}$ making q queries in expectation when its oracle is F_0, it holds that

$$|\Pr[\mathcal{D} \text{ outputs } 1 \mid b = 1] - \Pr[\mathcal{D} \text{ outputs } 1 \mid b = 0]| \leq 2q \cdot \sqrt{\varepsilon}.$$

3   A New Resampling Lemma

In this section, we describe a new resampling lemma for random permutations that generalizes earlier results [1,7]. We consider a two-phase experiment in which a distinguisher $\mathcal{D}$ is first given quantum oracle access to a uniform permutation $P : \{0,1\}^n \to \{0,1\}^n$. Then, a point $s_0 \in \{0,1\}^n$ is chosen in a manner specified by the distinguisher and a uniform point $s_1 \in \{0,1\}^n$ is also chosen; in a second phase $\mathcal{D}$ is given access either to the original permutation $P^{(0)} = P$ or a modified permutation $P^{(1)}$ that is the same as P except that the values of $P(s_0)$ and $P(s_1)$ are swapped. (See below for details.) We show, roughly speaking, that so long as the distribution of s_0 has high min-entropy and $\mathcal{D}$ makes only a bounded number of queries in the first phase of the experiment, $\mathcal{D}$ cannot distinguish those possibilities.

Compared to prior work of Alagic et al. [1], our result is more general in the following ways:

- it allows for more general distributions of s_0;
- it allows for the distribution of s_0 to be *adaptively* chosen by $\mathcal{D}$, after $\mathcal{D}$ makes queries to P in the first phase;
- it furthermore allows $\mathcal{D}$ to select a sampling algorithm for s_0 that will itself make a query to P.

In order to achieve these improvements, we use a different proof technique from that of Alagic et al. [1]. Our approach is closer in spirit to an earlier technique of Grilo et al. [7], which was previously only applied to random functions.

We now state our new resampling lemma. For $s_0, s_1 \in \{0,1\}^n$, define

$$\mathsf{swap}_{s_0, s_1}(x) = \begin{cases} s_1 & \text{if } x = s_0 \\ s_0 & \text{if } x = s_1 \\ x & \text{otherwise.} \end{cases}$$

Lemma 3. *Let $F \subset \mathcal{P}(n)$. Consider the following experiment involving a quantum distinguisher $\mathcal{D}$:*

Phase 1: *Choose uniform $P \in \mathcal{P}(n)$, and give $\mathcal{D}$ quantum access to P. $\mathcal{D}$ outputs (D, τ), where D is a distribution on $\{0,1\}^n$ and $\tau \in F$.*

Phase 2: *Sample* $\hat{s} \leftarrow D$, *set* $s_0 = \tau \circ P(\hat{s})$, *and choose* $s_1 \leftarrow \{0,1\}^n$. *Let* $P^{(0)} = P$ *and define* $P^{(1)} = P \circ \mathsf{swap}_{s_0, s_1}$. *A uniform bit* $b \in \{0,1\}$ *is chosen, and* D *is given* $\hat{s}$ *and quantum access to* $P^{(b)}$. *Then* D *outputs a guess* b'.

Let $\varepsilon = 2 \cdot \mathbb{E}_{(D,\tau) \leftarrow D^P} \left[\max_{x \in \{0,1\}^n} \Pr_{x' \leftarrow D}[x' = x] \right]$. For any D making at most q queries to P in phase 1,

$$|\Pr[D \text{ outputs } 1 \mid b = 1] - \Pr[D \text{ outputs } 1 \mid b = 0]|$$

$$\leq \sqrt{\varepsilon} \cdot \left(1 + \sqrt{q + \log\left(\frac{11 \cdot |F|}{\sqrt{\varepsilon}}\right)} \right).$$

The proof of Lemma 3 is given in Appendix A.

4   Post-quantum Security of Tweakable Even-Mansour

We use the result of the previous section to prove the post-quantum security of three different variants of the tweakable Even-Mansour construction. In Sect. 4.1, we prove security of TEM-KX; we then prove security of TEM as a corollary. In Sect. 4.2, we prove security of TEM-KX1 by showing that its key-expansion function is a pseudorandom generator.

4.1   Security of **TEM-KX** and **TEM**

Let $P \in \mathcal{P}(n)$ be a permutation and $\mathcal{T}$ a finite set, and fix two functions $f_1, f_2 \colon \mathcal{T} \times \{0,1\}^n \to \{0,1\}^n$. We consider a key-expanding version of the tweakable Even-Mansour scheme $\mathsf{TEM\text{-}KX}^{f_1, f_2}[P] : \{0,1\}^\kappa \times \mathcal{T} \times \{0,1\}^n \to \{0,1\}^n$ defined as

$$\mathsf{TEM}_k^{f_1, f_2}[P](t, x) = P(x \oplus f_1(t, P(k\|0^{n-\kappa}))) \oplus f_2(t, P(k\|0^{n-\kappa})).$$

We assume the tweak functions f_1, f_2 satisfy some structural properties.

Definition 1. *A function* $f : \mathcal{T} \times \{0,1\}^n \to \{0,1\}^n$ *is* **proper** *(with respect to* $\mathcal{T}$*) if it satisfies the following two properties:*

Uniformity: *For all* $t \in \mathcal{T}$, *the function* $f(t, \cdot)$ *is a permutation.*
XOR-universality: *For all distinct* $t, t' \in \mathcal{T}$ *and all* $y \in \{0,1\}^n$,

$$\Pr_{k \leftarrow \{0,1\}^n}[f(t, k) \oplus f(t', k) = y] \leq 2^{-n}.$$

Theorem 3. *Let* TEM-KX *be as above, and let* $\mathcal{A}$ *be an adversary making* q_C *classical queries to its first oracle and* $q_Q \geq \max\{n, \log(11 \cdot |\mathcal{T}|)\}$ *quantum queries[1] to its second oracle. If* f_1, f_2 *are proper with respect to* $\mathcal{T}$, *then*

---

[1] The mild assumption on q_Q can be avoided at the expense of an additive term of $\mathcal{O}(q_C \cdot 2^{-\kappa/2} \cdot (n + \log|\mathcal{T}|))$ in the bound.

$$\left| \Pr_{\substack{k \leftarrow \{0,1\}^{\kappa}; \\ P \leftarrow \mathcal{P}(n)}} \left[\mathcal{A}^{\mathsf{TEM\text{-}KX}_k^{f_1,f_2}[P],P} = 1 \right] - \Pr_{\substack{\tilde{E} \leftarrow \mathcal{E}(\mathcal{T},n); \\ P \leftarrow \mathcal{P}(n)}} \left[\mathcal{A}^{\tilde{E},P} = 1 \right] \right|$$

$$\leq 7 \cdot 2^{-\kappa/2} \left(q_C \sqrt{q_Q} + q_Q \sqrt{q_C} \right).$$

Proof. The high-level structure of our proof is similar to the proof of security for the Even-Mansour construction by Alagic et al. [1], though here relying heavily on our new resampling lemma. For that reason, we copy some portions of their proof (with appropriate updates for our setting).

Without loss of generality, we assume $\mathcal{A}$ never makes a redundant classical query; that is, once it learns a triple (t, x, y) of tweak, input, and output by making a query to its classical oracle, it never again submits a query (t, x) (resp., (t, y)) to that oracle in the forward (resp., inverse) direction. We divide an execution of $\mathcal{A}$ into $q_C + 1$ stages $0, \ldots, q_C$, where the jth stage corresponds to the time between the jth and $(j + 1)$st classical queries of $\mathcal{A}$. (The 0th stage is the period of time before $\mathcal{A}$ makes its first classical query, and the q_Cth stage is the period of time after $\mathcal{A}$ makes its last classical query.) $\mathcal{A}$ may adaptively[2] distribute its q_Q quantum queries between these stages arbitrarily, and we let $q_{Q,j}$ be the expected number of quantum queries that $\mathcal{A}^{\tilde{E},P}$ makes in the jth stage, where the expectation is taken over $\tilde{E} \leftarrow \mathcal{E}(\mathcal{T}, n)$ and $P \leftarrow \mathcal{P}(n)$ and any internal randomness/measurements of $\mathcal{A}$. Note that $\sum_{j=0}^{q_C} q_{Q,j} = q_Q$.

Fixing f_1, f_2, we write $\mathsf{TEM\text{-}KX}_k$ for $\mathsf{TEM\text{-}KX}_k^{f_1,f_2}$. In a given execution of $\mathcal{A}$, we denote its jth classical query by (t_j, x_j, y_j, b_j), where $t_j \in \mathcal{T}$ is a tweak, $(x_j, y_j) \in \{0,1\}^n \times \{0,1\}^n$ is an input/output pair, and $b_j \in \{0,1\}$ indicates the query direction, i.e., $b_j = 0$ (resp., $b_j = 1$) means that the jth classical query was in the forward (resp., inverse) direction. We let $T_j = \big((t_1, x_1, y_1, b_1), \ldots, (t_j, x_j, y_j, b_j)\big)$ be the ordered list of the first j classical queries of $\mathcal{A}$.

Our proof involves a sequence of experiments in which $\mathcal{A}$'s oracles are modified based on the classical queries made by $\mathcal{A}$ thus far. We first establish the appropriate notation. We use the product symbol $\prod$ to denote sequential composition of operations, i.e., $\prod_{i=1}^n f_i = f_1 \circ \cdots \circ f_n$. Note that order matters, since function composition is not commutative in general. We use the notation $\prod_{i=n}^1 f_i = f_n \circ \cdots \circ f_1$ to denote the composition in reverse order. For a permutation P, a key k, and a list $T_j = \big((t_1, x_1, y_1, b_1), \ldots, (t_j, x_j, y_j, b_j)\big)$ as above, define the operators

---

[2] Alternatively, the techniques of [6] can be used to turn the adversary into one that uses a fixed query schedule; the overall bound would be unchanged.

$$\overrightarrow{S}_{T_j,P,k} = \prod_{i=1}^{j} \mathsf{swap}^{1-b_i}_{P(x_i \oplus f_1(t_i, P(k||0^{n-\kappa}))),\, y_i \oplus f_2(t_i, P(k||0^{n-\kappa}))}$$

$$\overrightarrow{Q}_{T_j,P,k} = \prod_{i=1}^{j} \mathsf{swap}^{1-b_i}_{x_i \oplus f_1(t_i, P(k||0^{n-\kappa})),\, P^{-1}(y_i \oplus f_2(t_i, P(k||0^{n-\kappa})))}$$

$$\overleftarrow{S}_{T_j,P,k} = \prod_{i=j}^{1} \mathsf{swap}^{b_i}_{P(x_i \oplus f_1(t_i, P(k||0^{0-\kappa}))),\, y_i \oplus f_2(t_i, P(k||0^{n-\kappa}))}$$

$$\overleftarrow{Q}_{T_j,P,k} = \prod_{i=j}^{1} \mathsf{swap}^{b_i}_{x_i \oplus f_1(t_i, P(k||0^{n-\kappa})),\, P^{-1}(y_i \oplus f_2(t_i, P(k||0^{n-\kappa})))}$$

where, as usual, f^0 is the identity map and $f^1 = f$ for any function f. We define the modified permutation $P^{T_j,k}$ as

$$P^{T_j,k}(x) = \overleftarrow{S}_{T_j,P,k} \circ \overrightarrow{S}_{T_j,P,k} \circ P(x).$$

Since $P \circ \mathsf{swap}_{x,y} = \mathsf{swap}_{P(x),P(y)} \circ P$ for all x, y, we have

$$\overleftarrow{S}_{j,P,k} \circ \overrightarrow{S}_{T_j,P,k} \circ P = \overleftarrow{S}_{T_j,P,k} \circ P \circ \overrightarrow{Q}_{T_j,P,k} = P \circ \overleftarrow{Q}_{T_j,P,k} \circ \overrightarrow{Q}_{T_j,P,k}.$$

Roughly speaking, $P^{T_j,k}$ is the minimal modification of P that is consistent with the forward ($\rightarrow$) and inverse ($\leftarrow$) queries from the transcript T_j when post-composed (S) or pre-composed (Q) with P. For compactness we occasionally write P^j in place of $P^{T_j,k}$ when T_j and k are understood from the context.

We now define a sequence of hybrid experiments $\mathbf{H}_j$, for $j = 0, \ldots, q_C$.

Experiment $\mathbf{H}_j$. Sample uniform $\tilde{E} \in \mathcal{E}(\mathcal{T}, n)$ and $P \in \mathcal{P}(n)$, and a uniform key $k \in \{0,1\}^\kappa$. Then:

1. Run $\mathcal{A}$, answering its classical queries using $\tilde{E}$ and its quantum queries using P, stopping immediately *before* its $(j+1)$st classical query. Let $T_j = \big((t_1, x_1, y_1, b_1), \ldots, (t_j, x_j, y_j, b_j)\big)$ be the list of classical queries so far.
2. For the remainder of the execution of $\mathcal{A}$, answer its classical queries using $\mathsf{TEM\text{-}KX}_k[P^{T_j,k}]$ and its quantum queries using $P^{T_j,k}$.

We can compactly represent $\mathbf{H}_j$ as the experiment in which $\mathcal{A}$'s queries are answered using the oracle sequence

$$\underbrace{P, \tilde{E}, P, \cdots, \tilde{E}, P,}_{j \text{ classical queries}} \underbrace{\mathsf{TEM\text{-}KX}_k[P^j], P^j, \cdots, \mathsf{TEM\text{-}KX}_k[P^j], P^j}_{q_C - j \text{ classical queries}}.$$

Each instance of $\tilde{E}$ or $\mathsf{TEM\text{-}KX}_k[P^j]$ represents a single classical query, while each instance of P or P^j represents a stage during which $\mathcal{A}$ makes multiple quantum queries to that oracle but no queries to its classical oracle. Observe that $\mathbf{H}_0$ corresponds to the execution of $\mathcal{A}$ in the real world, i.e., $\mathcal{A}^{\mathsf{TEM\text{-}KX}_k[P],P}$, and $\mathbf{H}_{q_C}$ is the execution of $\mathcal{A}$ in the ideal world, i.e., $\mathcal{A}^{\tilde{E},P}$.

For $j = 0, \ldots, q_C - 1$, we introduce additional experiments $\mathbf{H}'_j$:

Experiment $\mathbf{H}'_j$. Sample uniform $\tilde{E} \in \mathcal{E}(\mathcal{T}, n)$ and $P \in \mathcal{P}(n)$, and uniform $k \in \{0, 1\}^\kappa$. Then:

1. Run $\mathcal{A}$, answering its classical queries using $\tilde{E}$ and its quantum queries using P, stopping immediately *after* its $(j + 1)$st classical query. Let $T_{j+1} = ((t_1, x_1, y_1, b_1), \ldots, (t_{j+1}, x_{j+1}, y_{j+1}, b_{j+1}))$ be the classical queries so far.
2. For the remainder of the execution of $\mathcal{A}$, answer its classical queries using TEM-KX$_k[P^{T_{j+1},k}]$ and its quantum queries using $P^{T_{j+1},k}$.

Thus, $\mathbf{H}'_j$ corresponds to running $\mathcal{A}$ using the oracle sequence

$$\underbrace{P, \tilde{E}, P, \cdots, \tilde{E}, P,}_{j \text{ classical queries}} \tilde{E}, P^{j+1}, \underbrace{\text{TEM-KX}_k[P^{j+1}], P^{j+1} \cdots, \text{TEM-KX}_k[P^{j+1}], P^{j+1}}_{q_C - j - 1 \text{ classical queries}}.$$

In Lemma 4 and Lemma 5, we establish the following bounds on the distinguishability of $\mathbf{H}'_j$ and $\mathbf{H}_{j+1}$, as well as $\mathbf{H}_j$ and $\mathbf{H}'_j$, for $0 \le j < q_C$:

$$\left| \Pr[\mathcal{A}(\mathbf{H}'_j) = 1] - \Pr[\mathcal{A}(\mathbf{H}_{j+1}) = 1] \right| \le 2^{-\kappa/2} \cdot 2 \cdot q_{Q,j+1} \sqrt{2 \cdot (j+1)}$$

and

$$\left| \Pr[\mathcal{A}(\mathbf{H}_j) = 1] - \Pr[\mathcal{A}(\mathbf{H}'_j) = 1] \right|$$
$$\le 2^{-\kappa/2} \left(1 + \sqrt{q_Q + \log(11 |\mathcal{T}|) + n + \kappa/2} \right) + \frac{4j}{2^\kappa}.$$

Using the above, we have

$$\left| \Pr[\mathcal{A}(\mathbf{H}_0) = 1] - \Pr[\mathcal{A}(\mathbf{H}_{q_C}) = 1] \right|$$
$$\le \sum_{j=0}^{q_C-1} \left(2^{-\kappa/2} \left(1 + \sqrt{q_Q + \log(11 |\mathcal{T}|) + n + \kappa/2} + 2q_{Q,j+1}\sqrt{2(j+1)} \right) + \frac{4j}{2^\kappa} \right)$$
$$\le \frac{4q_C^2}{2^\kappa} + \sum_{j=0}^{q_C-1} 2^{-\kappa/2} \left(1 + \sqrt{q_Q + \log(11 |\mathcal{T}|) + n + \kappa/2} + 2 \cdot q_{Q,j+1}\sqrt{2q_C} \right)$$
$$\le \frac{4q_C^2}{2^\kappa} + 2^{-\kappa/2} \left(q_C + q_C\sqrt{q_Q + \log(11 |\mathcal{T}|) + n + \kappa/2} + 2\sqrt{2}q_Q\sqrt{q_C} \right).$$

The above bound can be simplified. By assumption, $q_Q \ge \log(11 \cdot |\mathcal{T}|)$ and $q_Q \ge n \ge \kappa$. So $\sqrt{q_Q + \log(11 \cdot |\mathcal{T}|) + n + \kappa/2} \le \sqrt{7q_Q/2}$. We may also assume $q_C \le 2^{\kappa/2}$ since otherwise the bound is larger than 1. Under these assumptions, we have $4q_C^2 \cdot 2^{-\kappa} \le 4q_C \cdot 2^{-\kappa/2} \le 4q_C \sqrt{q_Q} \cdot 2^{-\kappa/2}$ and so

$$\frac{4q_C^2}{2^\kappa} + 2^{-\kappa/2} \cdot \left(q_C + q_C \sqrt{q_Q + \log(11 \cdot |\mathcal{T}|) + n + \kappa/2} + 2\sqrt{2}q_Q\sqrt{q_C} \right)$$

$$\le 2^{-\kappa/2} \cdot \left(5q_C + q_C\sqrt{7q_Q/2} + 2\sqrt{2}q_Q\sqrt{q_C} \right)$$

$$\le 2^{-\kappa/2} \cdot \left(\left(5 + \sqrt{\frac{7}{2}}\right) q_C \sqrt{q_Q} + 2\sqrt{2}q_Q\sqrt{q_C} \right)$$

$$\le 2^{-\kappa/2} \cdot \left(7q_C\sqrt{q_Q} + 2\sqrt{2}q_Q\sqrt{q_C} \right) \le 7 \cdot 2^{-\kappa/2} \cdot \left(q_C\sqrt{q_Q} + q_Q\sqrt{q_C} \right),$$

as claimed.

We now prove Lemma 4 and Lemma 5.

Lemma 4. *For $j = 0, \ldots, q_C - 1$,*

$$\Pr[\mathcal{A}(\mathbf{H}_j') = 1] - \Pr[\mathcal{A}(\mathbf{H}_{j+1}) = 1]| \le 2 \cdot q_{Q,j+1}\sqrt{2 \cdot (j+1)/2^\kappa},$$

where $q_{Q,j+1}$ is the expected number of queries $\mathcal{A}$ makes to P in the $(j+1)$st stage in the ideal world (i.e., in $\mathbf{H}_{q_C}$).

Proof. Let $\mathcal{A}$ be a distinguisher between $\mathbf{H}_j'$ and $\mathbf{H}_{j+1}$. We construct a distinguisher $\mathcal{D}$ for the experiment from Lemma 2:

Phase 1: $\mathcal{D}$ samples uniform $\tilde{E} \in \mathcal{E}(\mathcal{T}, n)$ and $P \in \mathcal{P}(n)$. It then runs $\mathcal{A}$, answering its quantum queries using P and its classical queries using $\tilde{E}$, until after it responds to $\mathcal{A}$'s $(j+1)$st classical query. Let $T_{j+1} = ((t_1, x_1, y_1, b_1), \ldots, (t_{j+1}, x_{j+1}, y_{j+1}, b_{j+1}))$ be the list of classical queries by $\mathcal{A}$ thus far. $\mathcal{D}$ defines $F(a, x) := P^a(x)$ for $a \in \{1, -1\}$.

It also defines the following randomized algorithm $\mathcal{B}$: sample $k \leftarrow \{0,1\}^\kappa$ and then compute the set B of input/output pairs to be reprogrammed so that $F^{(B)}(a, x) = (P^{T_{j+1},k})^a(x)$ for all a, x. Finally, $\mathcal{D}$ outputs $(F, \mathcal{B})$.

Phase 2: $\mathcal{B}$ is run to generate B, and $\mathcal{D}$ is given quantum access to an oracle F_b. $\mathcal{D}$ resumes running $\mathcal{A}$, answering its quantum queries using F_b. Phase 2 ends before $\mathcal{A}$ makes its next (i.e., $(j+2)$nd) classical query.

Phase 3: $\mathcal{D}$ is given k. It resumes running $\mathcal{A}$, answering its classical queries using $\mathsf{TEM\text{-}KX}_k[P^{T_{j+1},k}]$ and its quantum queries using $P^{T_{j+1},k}$. Finally, it outputs whatever $\mathcal{A}$ outputs.

It is immediate that if $b = 0$ (i.e., $\mathcal{D}$'s oracle in phase 2 is $F_0 = F$), then $\mathcal{A}$'s output is identically distributed to its output in $\mathbf{H}_{j+1}$, whereas if $b = 1$ (i.e., $\mathcal{D}$'s oracle in phase 2 is $F_1 = F^{(B)}$), then $\mathcal{A}$'s output is identically distributed to its output in $\mathbf{H}_j'$. It follows that $|\Pr[\mathcal{A}(\mathbf{H}_j') = 1] - \Pr[\mathcal{A}(\mathbf{H}_{j+1}) = 1]|$ is equal to the distinguishing advantage of $\mathcal{D}$ in the reprogramming experiment of Lemma 2. To bound this quantity, we bound the parameter ε and the expected number of queries made by $\mathcal{D}$ in phase 2 (when $F = F_0$).

The value of ε can be bounded using the definition of $P^{T_{j+1},k}$ and the fact that $F^{(B)}(a, x) = (P^{T_{j+1},k})^a(x)$. Fixing P and T_{j+1}, the probability that any particular input (a, x) is reprogrammed is at most the probability (over k) that it lies in the set

$$\left\{ \begin{matrix} (1, x_i \oplus f_1(t_i, P(k||0^{n-\kappa}))), & (1, P^{-1}(y_i \oplus f_2(t_i, P(k||0^{n-\kappa})))), \\ (-1, P(x_i \oplus f_1(t_i, P(k||0^{n-\kappa})))), & (-1, y_i \oplus f_2(t_i, P(k||0^{n-\kappa}))) \end{matrix} \right\}_{i=1}^{j+1}.$$

We compute the probability that $(a, x) = (1, x_i \oplus f_1(t_i, P(k||0^{n-\kappa})))$ for some fixed i. P is a permutation, and so is $f_1(t_i, \cdot)$. As k is uniform,

$$\Pr_k[(a, x) = (1, x_i \oplus f_1(t_i, P(k||0^{n-\kappa})))] = \begin{cases} 2^{-\kappa} & a = 1 \\ 0 & a = -1 \end{cases}.$$

A similar bound holds for the other possibilities. By distinguishing the cases $a = 1$ and $a = -1$ and applying a union bound, we get $\varepsilon \le 2(j+1)/2^\kappa$.

The expected number of queries made by $\mathcal{D}$ in phase 2 when $F = F_0$ is equal to the expected number of queries made by $\mathcal{A}$ in its $(j+1)$st stage in $\mathbf{H}_{j+1}$. Since $\mathbf{H}_{j+1}$ and $\mathbf{H}_{q_E}$ are identical until after the $(j+1)$st stage is complete, this is precisely $q_{Q,j+1}$. □

Lemma 5. For $j = 0, \ldots, q_C$,

$$\left| \Pr[\mathcal{A}(\mathbf{H}_j) = 1] - \Pr[\mathcal{A}(\mathbf{H}'_j) = 1] \right|$$
$$\le \frac{1}{2^{\kappa/2}} \left(1 + \sqrt{q_Q + \log(11 |\mathcal{T}|) + n + \kappa/2} \right) + \frac{4j}{2^\kappa}.$$

Proof. We introduce additional experiments $\mathbf{H}_j^*$ and $\mathbf{H}_j^{**}$.

Experiment $\mathbf{H}_j^*$. Sample uniform $\tilde{E} \in \mathcal{E}(\mathcal{T}, n)$, $P \in \mathcal{P}(n)$, and $k \in \{0,1\}^\kappa$. Then

1. Run $\mathcal{A}$, answering its classical queries using $\tilde{E}$ and its quantum queries using P, until $\mathcal{A}$ makes its $(j + 1)$st classical query $(t_{j+1}, x_{j+1}, b_{j+1} = 0)$, which we assume for concreteness to be in the forward direction.[3]
2. Define $s_0 = f_1(t_{j+1}, P(k||0^{n-\kappa})) \oplus x_{j+1}$ and sample uniform $s_1 \in \{0,1\}^n$. Define $P^{(1)}$ as $P^{(1)}(x) = (P \circ \mathsf{swap}_{s_0, s_1})(x)$. Then continue running $\mathcal{A}$, answering its remaining classical queries (including the $(j + 1)$st) using TEM-KX$_k[(P^{(1)})^{T_j,k}]$, and its quantum queries using $(P^{(1)})^{T_j,k}$.

Experiment $\mathbf{H}_j^{**}$ is the same as $\mathbf{H}_j^*$, except that the $(j + 1)$st query is answered using $\tilde{E}$ to obtain $y_{j+1} = \tilde{E}(t_{j+1}, x_{j+1})$, and then we define $s_1 = (P^{T_j,k})^{-1}(y_{j+1} \oplus f_2(t_{j+1}, P(k||0^{n-\kappa})))$. We have

$$\left| \Pr[\mathcal{A}(\mathbf{H}_j) = 1] - \Pr[\mathcal{A}(\mathbf{H}'_j) = 1] \right| \le \left| \Pr[\mathcal{A}(\mathbf{H}_j) = 1] - \Pr[\mathcal{A}(\mathbf{H}_j^*) = 1] \right|$$
$$+ \left| \Pr[\mathcal{A}(\mathbf{H}_j^*) = 1] - \Pr[\mathcal{A}(\mathbf{H}_j^{**}) = 1] \right|$$
$$+ \left| \Pr[\mathcal{A}(\mathbf{H}_j^{**}) = 1] - \Pr[\mathcal{A}(\mathbf{H}'_j) = 1] \right|.$$

---

[3] As in [1], the case of an inverse query is entirely symmetric.

We now bound the three differences on the right-hand side.

Let $\mathcal{A}$ be a distinguisher between $\mathbf{H}_j$ and $\mathbf{H}_j^*$. We construct a distinguisher $\mathcal{D}$ for the experiment of Lemma 3, where $F = \{f_1(t, \cdot) \oplus x\}_{t \in \mathcal{T}, x \in \{0,1\}^n}$.

Phase 1: $\mathcal{D}$ is given quantum access to a uniform permutation P. It samples uniform $\tilde{E} \leftarrow \mathcal{E}(\mathcal{T}, n)$ and then runs $\mathcal{A}$, answering its quantum queries using P and its classical queries using $\tilde{E}$ (in the appropriate directions), until $\mathcal{A}$ submits its $(j+1)$st classical query $(t_{j+1}, x_{j+1}, b_{j+1} = 0)$. At that point, $\mathcal{D}$ has a list $T_j = ((t_1, x_1, y_1, b_1), \ldots, (t_j, x_j, y_j, b_j))$ of the queries $\mathcal{A}$ has made to its classical oracle thus far. $\mathcal{D}$ lets $\tau \in F$ be such that $\tau(\cdot) = f_1(t_{j+1}, \cdot) \oplus x_{j+1}$, and defines the distribution D on $\{0,1\}^n$ that chooses uniform $k \in \{0,1\}^\kappa$ and outputs $k \| 0^{n-\kappa}$. Finally, $\mathcal{D}$ outputs (D, τ).

Phase 2: The challenger samples $\hat{s} \leftarrow D$ with $\hat{s} = k \| 0^{n-\kappa}$. Then $\mathcal{D}$ is given $\hat{s}$ and quantum oracle access to the permutation $P^{(b)}$. It continues running $\mathcal{A}$, answering its remaining classical queries—including the $(j+1)$st—using TEM-KX$_k[(P^{(b)})^{T_j,k}]$, and its remaining quantum queries using $(P^{(b)})^{T_j,k}$. $\mathcal{D}$ outputs whatever $\mathcal{A}$ does.

In phase 1, distinguisher $\mathcal{D}$ perfectly simulates experiments $\mathbf{H}_j$ and $\mathbf{H}_j^*$ for $\mathcal{A}$ until the point where $\mathcal{A}$ makes its $(j+1)$st classical query. If $b = 0$, $\mathcal{D}$ gets access to $P^{(0)} = P$ in phase 2. Since $\mathcal{D}$ answers all quantum queries using $(P^{(0)})^{T_j,k}$ and all classical queries using TEM-KX$_k[(P^{(0)})^{T_j,k}]$, we see that $\mathcal{D}$ perfectly simulates $\mathbf{H}_j$ for $\mathcal{A}$ in that case. If, on the other hand, $b = 1$ in phase 2, then $\mathcal{D}$ gets access to $P^{(1)}$, where $P^{(1)}(x) = P \circ \mathsf{swap}_{s_0, s_1}(x)$. In this case $\mathcal{D}$ perfectly simulates $\mathbf{H}_j^*$ for $\mathcal{A}$. Applying Lemma 3 thus gives

$$\left| \Pr[\mathcal{A}(\mathbf{H}_j) = 1] - \Pr[\mathcal{A}(\mathbf{H}_j^*) = 1] \right| \le \sqrt{\varepsilon} \left(1 + \sqrt{q_Q + \log\left(\frac{11 |F|}{\sqrt{\varepsilon}} \right)} \right)$$

$$= \frac{1}{2^{\kappa/2}} \left(1 + \sqrt{q_Q + \log\left(\frac{11 |\mathcal{T}| 2^n}{2^{-\kappa/2}} \right)} \right). \quad (1)$$

Next, we bound the distinguishability of $\mathbf{H}_j^*$ and $\mathbf{H}_j^{**}$. Recall that in $\mathbf{H}_j^*$ the answer to the $(j+1)$st classical query is $y_{j+1} = \mathsf{TEM\text{-}KX}_k[(P^{(1)})^{T_j,k}](t_{j+1}, x_{j+1})$, whereas in $\mathbf{H}_j^{**}$ the response is $y_{j+1} = \tilde{E}_{t_{j+1}}(x_{j+1})$. In $\mathbf{H}_j^*$, we have

$$y_{j+1} \stackrel{\text{def}}{=} \mathsf{TEM\text{-}KX}_k[(P^{(1)})^{T_j,k}](t_{j+1}, x_{j+1})$$
$$= (P^{(1)})^{T_j,k}(s_0) \oplus f_2(t_{j+1}, P(k\|0^{n-\kappa}))$$
$$= P^{T_j,k}(s_1) \oplus f_2(t_{j+1}, P(k\|0^{n-\kappa})).$$

Since s_1 is uniform and $P^{T_j,k}(\cdot) \oplus f_2(t_{j+1}, P(k\|0^{n-\kappa}))$ is a permutation, we conclude that y_{j+1} is uniform. This is not identical to the distribution of y_{j+1} in $\mathbf{H}_j^{**}$, which is uniform subject to the constraint that $\tilde{E}_{t_{j+1}}$ is a permutation. Define the set $\mathcal{Y}_{j+1} = \{y_i \mid t_i = t_{j+1}\}$, i.e., these are the outputs of $\tilde{E}$ that $\mathcal{A}$ learned from queries with the same tweak t_{j+1} used in the $(j+1)$st query.

Bounding the probability that $y_{j+1} \in \mathcal{Y}_{j+1}$ when y_{j+1} is uniform gives an upper bound on the probability that $\mathcal{A}$ can distinguish $\mathbf{H}_j^*$ and $\mathbf{H}_j^{**}$. Thus,

$$\left| \Pr[\mathcal{A}(\mathbf{H}_j^*) = 1] - \Pr[\mathcal{A}(\mathbf{H}_j^{**}) = 1] \right| \leq \frac{|\mathcal{Y}_{j+1}|}{2^n} \leq \frac{j}{2^n} \leq \frac{j}{2^\kappa}. \qquad (2)$$

Finally, we bound the distinguishability of $\mathbf{H}_j^{**}$ and $\mathbf{H}_j'$. Recall that the difference between these experiments is that from the $(j+1)$st query onward the former uses $(P^{(1)})^{T_j,k}$ while the latter uses $P^{T_{j+1},k}$ (both for the quantum queries of $\mathcal{A}$ and to instantiate TEM-KX for the classical queries of $\mathcal{A}$). Thus, the two experiments are identical if $(P^{(1)})^{T_j,k}$ and $P^{T_{j+1},k}$ are equal. In what follows we upper bound the probability that they are not equal.

Both $(P^{(1)})^{T_j,k}$ and $P^{T_{j+1},k}$ involve $j+1$ swaps: $(P^{(1)})^{T_j,k}$ involves j swaps from the first j queries plus the extra swap by the definition of $P^{(1)}$, whereas $P^{T_{j+1},k}$ involves $j+1$ swaps from the first $j+1$ queries. Since the $(j+1)$st query is a forward query, we have

$$\left(P^{(1)}\right)^{T_j,k}(x) = \overleftarrow{S}_{T_j,P^{(1)},k} \circ \overrightarrow{S}_{T_j,P^{(1)},k} \circ P^{(1)}(x)$$

and

$$\left(P\right)^{T_{j+1},k}(x) = \overleftarrow{S}_{T_{j+1},P,k} \circ \overrightarrow{S}_{T_{j+1},P,k} \circ P(x).$$

Let $\mathcal{X} = \{x_1 \oplus f_1(t_1, P(k||0^{n-\kappa})), \ldots, x_j \oplus f_1(t_j, P(k||0^{n-\kappa}))\}$, i.e., $\mathcal{X}$ contains the inputs to P from the first j classical queries of $\mathcal{A}$. Let Bad_0 be the event that $x_{j+1} \oplus f_1(t_{j+1}, P(k||0^{n-\kappa})) \in \mathcal{X}$ and Bad_1 be the event that $s_1 \in \mathcal{X}$. We upper bound the probabilities of Bad_0, Bad_1, and then show that $(P^{(1)})^{T_j,k} = P^{T_{j+1},k}$ when neither Bad_0 nor Bad_1 occurs.

Since s_1 is $\frac{j}{2^n}$-close to uniform by (2), $\Pr[\mathsf{Bad}_1] \leq \frac{2j}{2^n}$. Bounding the probability of Bad_0 is more complex since we have to consider the tweaks from the first j queries of $\mathcal{A}$. Intuitively, for queries whose tweak was the same as t_{j+1}, we rely on the assumption that $\mathcal{A}$ does not repeat queries; for queries where the tweaks are different, we use the XOR-universality of f_1, f_2. Define

$$\mathcal{X}^= = \{x_i \oplus f_1(t_i, P(k||0^{n-\kappa})) \mid 1 \leq i \leq j, \ t_i = t_{j+1}\}$$
$$\mathcal{X}^{\neq} = \{x_i \oplus f_1(t_i, P(k||0^{n-\kappa})) \mid 1 \leq i \leq j, \ t_i \neq t_{j+1}\}.$$

These sets partition $\mathcal{X}$ into those inputs using the same tweak as in the $(j+1)$st query ($\mathcal{X}^=$) and those using different tweaks ($\mathcal{X}^{\neq}$). Hence,

$$\Pr[\mathsf{Bad}_0] = \Pr[\mathsf{Bad}_0^=] + \Pr[\mathsf{Bad}_0^{\neq}],$$

where $\mathsf{Bad}_0^=$ is the event that $x_{j+1} \oplus f_1(t_{j+1}, P(k||0^{n-\kappa})) \in \mathcal{X}^=$ and $\mathsf{Bad}_0^{\neq}$ is the event that $x_{j+1} \oplus f_1(t_{j+1}, P(k||0^{n-\kappa})) \in \mathcal{X}^{\neq}$. For $\mathsf{Bad}_0^=$, we have

$$x_{j+1} \oplus f_1(t_{j+1}, P(k||0^{n-\kappa})) \in \{x_i \oplus f_1(t_i, P(k||0^{n-\kappa})) \mid t_i = t_{j+1}\}$$
$$\Leftrightarrow x_{j+1} \in \{x_i \mid t_i = t_{j+1}\}.$$

Since $\mathcal{A}$ does not repeat queries, this means $\Pr[\mathsf{Bad}_0^=] = 0$.

For $\mathsf{Bad}_0^{\neq}$, rewriting yields

$$x_{j+1} \oplus f_1(t_{j+1}, P(k||0^{n-\kappa})) \in \{x_i \oplus f_1(t_i, P(k||0^{n-\kappa})) \,|\, t_i \neq t_{j+1}\}$$
$$\Leftrightarrow x_{j+1} \in \{x_i \oplus f_1(t_i, P(k||0^{n-\kappa})) \oplus f_1(t_{j+1}, P(k||0^{n-\kappa})) \,|\, t_i \neq t_{j+1}\}.$$

XOR-universality of f_1, together with the fact that $f_1(t, \cdot)$ is a permutation for all t, implies that the mapping $g_{t,t'} : x \mapsto f_1(t, x) \oplus f_1(t', x)$ is a permutation whenever $t \neq t'$. Thus $g_{t_i, t_{j+1}} \circ P$ preserves the min-entropy of $k||0^{n-\kappa}$ and $\Pr[\mathsf{Bad}_0^{\neq}] \leq |\mathcal{X}^{\neq}|/2^\kappa \leq j/2^\kappa$. Summarizing,

$$\Pr[\mathsf{Bad}_0] = \Pr[\mathsf{Bad}_0^{=}] + \Pr[\mathsf{Bad}_0^{\neq}] \leq 0 + \frac{|\mathcal{X}^{\neq}|}{2^\kappa} \leq \frac{j}{2^\kappa}.$$

If neither Bad_0 or Bad_1 happens, we have $P^{(1)}(x_i \oplus f_1(t_i, P(k||0^{n-\kappa}))) = P(x_i \oplus f_1(t_i, P(k||0^{n-\kappa})))$ for all $1 \leq i \leq j$; furthermore, $P^{T_j,k}(s_1) = P(s_1)$ or, in other words, $P(s_1) = y_{j+1} \oplus f_2(t_{j+1}, P(k||0^{n-\kappa}))$. Therefore,

$$\overrightarrow{S}_{T_j, P^{(1)}, k} = \prod_{i=1}^{j} \mathsf{swap}^{1-b_i}_{P^{(1)}(x_i \oplus f_1(t_i, P(k||0^{n-\kappa}))), \, y_i \oplus f_2(t_i, P(k||0^{n-\kappa}))}$$
$$= \prod_{i=1}^{j} \mathsf{swap}^{1-b_i}_{P(x_i \oplus f_1(t_i, P(k||0^{n-\kappa}))), \, y_i \oplus f_2(t_i, P(k||0^{n-\kappa}))} = \overrightarrow{S}_{T_j, P, k}$$

and

$$\overleftarrow{S}_{T_j, P^{(1)}, k} = \prod_{i=j}^{1} \mathsf{swap}^{b_i}_{P^{(1)}(x_i \oplus f_1(t_i, P(k||0^{n-\kappa}))), \, y_i \oplus f_2(t_i, P(k||0^{n-\kappa}))}$$
$$= \prod_{i=j}^{1} \mathsf{swap}^{b_i}_{\overline{P(x_i \oplus f_1(t_i, P(k||0^{n-\kappa}))), \, y_i \oplus f_2(t_i, P(k||0^{n-\kappa}))}} = \overleftarrow{S}_{T_j, P, k},$$

and so

$$(P^{(1)})^{T_j, k}(x) = \overleftarrow{S}_{j, P^{(1)}, k} \circ \overrightarrow{S}_{j, P^{(1)}, k} \circ P^{(1)}(x)$$
$$= \overleftarrow{S}_{j, P, k} \circ \overrightarrow{S}_{j, P, k}$$
$$\quad \circ \mathsf{swap}_{P(f_1(t_{j+1}, P(k||0^{n-\kappa})) \oplus x_{j+1}), \, y_{j+1} \oplus f_2(t_{j+1}, P(k||0^{n-\kappa}))} \circ P(x)$$
$$= \overleftarrow{S}_{j+1, P, k} \circ \overrightarrow{S}_{j+1, P, k} \circ P(x) = P^{T_{j+1}, k}.$$

Putting everything together, we conclude that

$$\left| \Pr[\mathcal{A}(\mathbf{H}_j^{**}) = 1] - \Pr[\mathcal{A}(\mathbf{H}_j') = 1] \right| \leq \Pr[\mathsf{Bad}_0] + \Pr[\mathsf{Bad}_1] \leq \frac{3j}{2^\kappa}.$$

Combining the above with (1) and (2) concludes the proof of Lemma 5, and hence the proof of Theorem 3. □

Tweakable Even-Mansour. Recall that the tweakable Even-Mansour construction TEM is defined as

$$\mathsf{TEM}_k^{f_1,f_2}[P](t,x) = P(x \oplus f_1(t,k)) \oplus f_2(t,k).$$

Setting $\kappa = n$ and noting that $P(k)$ is uniform when k is uniform (since P is a permutation), Theorem 3 yields the following as an easy corollary:

Theorem 4. *Let $\mathcal{A}$ be an adversary making q_C classical queries to its first oracle and $q_Q \geq 1$ quantum queries to its second oracle. If f_1, f_2 are proper with respect to $\mathcal{T}$, then*

$$\left| \Pr_{\substack{k \leftarrow \{0,1\}^n; \\ P \leftarrow \mathcal{P}(n)}} \left[\mathcal{A}^{\mathsf{TEM}_k^{f_1,f_2}[P],P} = 1 \right] - \Pr_{\substack{\tilde{E} \leftarrow \mathcal{E}(\mathcal{T},n); \\ P \leftarrow \mathcal{P}(n)}} \left[\mathcal{A}^{\tilde{E},P} = 1 \right] \right|$$
$$\leq 7 \cdot 2^{-n/2} \cdot \left(q_C \sqrt{q_Q} + q_Q \sqrt{q_C} \right).$$

(Note: Theorem 4 is a corollary of Theorem 3 only for $q_Q \geq \max\{n, \log(11 \cdot |\mathcal{T}|)\}$. While small values of q_Q are not particularly interesting, Theorem 4 can be shown to hold for $q_Q \geq 1$ by a dedicated analysis that we omit here).

4.2   Security of TEM-KX1

We also consider an alternate method of expanding a key $k \in \{0,1\}^\kappa$ to an effective key of length n, in which we compute $F_P(k) = P(k\|0^{n-\kappa}) \oplus k\|0^{n-\kappa}$. This gives rise to TEM-KX1, a variant of tweakable Even-Mansour defined as

$$\mathsf{TEM\text{-}KX1}_k^{f_1,f_2}[P](t,x) = P(x \oplus f_1(t, F_P(k))) \oplus f_2(t, F_P(k)).$$

We obtain a tighter security bound for this variant than for TEM-KX; this allows us to give a tighter bound for Elephant in Sect. 5.2.

We first show that F_P is a pseudorandom generator, even against adversaries with quantum oracle access to P and P^{-1}.

Lemma 6. *For any quantum algorithm $\mathcal{A}$ making q_Q quantum queries,*

$$\left| \Pr_{\substack{r \leftarrow \{0,1\}^n \\ P \leftarrow \mathcal{P}(n)}} \left[\mathcal{A}^P(r) = 1 \right] - \Pr_{\substack{k \leftarrow \{0,1\}^\kappa \\ P \leftarrow \mathcal{P}(n)}} \left[\mathcal{A}^P(P(k\|0^{n-\kappa}) \oplus k\|0^{n-\kappa}) = 1 \right] \right| \leq \frac{4 \cdot q_Q}{2^{\kappa/2}}.$$

Proof. Given an adversary $\mathcal{A}$, we construct a distinguisher $\mathcal{D}$ for the reprogramming experiment from Lemma 2:

Phase 1: $\mathcal{D}$ samples uniform $P \in \mathcal{P}_n$ and $r \in \{0,1\}^n$, and defines a randomized algorithm $\mathcal{B}$ that proceeds as follows:
   1. sample uniform $k \in \{0,1\}^\kappa$;

2. output a set of reprogramming pairs B so that P blinded with B is
$$P^{(B)}(x) = P \circ \mathsf{swap}_{P^{-1}((k||0^{n-\kappa})\oplus r),\, k||0^{n-\kappa}}.$$
Then $\mathcal{D}$ outputs P and B.

Phase 2: $\mathcal{B}$ is run with a uniform $k \in \{0,1\}^\kappa$ to compute B. Let $P_0 = P$ and $P_1 = P^{(B)}$. A uniform $b \in \{0,1\}$ is chosen and $\mathcal{D}$ is given access to P_b (in the forward and inverse directions). $\mathcal{D}$ runs $\mathcal{A}$ with input r and oracle P_b. This phase ends when $\mathcal{A}$ has made its last query and outputs its guess.

Phase 3: $\mathcal{D}$ outputs what $\mathcal{A}$ outputs.

Note that there are at most four reprogrammed points. By construction, it holds that $\Pr_{k \leftarrow \{0,1\}^\kappa}[x \in B_1] \leq 4 \cdot 2^{-\kappa}$. By Lemma 2,

$$|\Pr[\mathcal{D} \text{ outputs } 1 \mid b = 0] - \Pr[\mathcal{D} \text{ outputs } 1 \mid b = 1]| \leq 4q_Q \cdot 2^{-\kappa/2}. \qquad (3)$$

When $b = 0$, $\mathcal{D}$ runs $\mathcal{A}^P(r)$ for uniform and independent P, r. When $b = 1$, $\mathcal{D}$ runs $\mathcal{A}^{P_1}(r)$ where P_1 and r are each uniform but are not independent. Indeed,

$$P_1(k||0^{n-\kappa}) \oplus k||0^{n-\kappa} = P(P^{-1}((k||0^{n-\kappa}) \oplus r)) \oplus k||0^{n-\kappa}$$
$$= k||0^{n-\kappa} \oplus r \oplus k||0^{n-\kappa} = r.$$

We prove that P_1 is uniform subject to that constraint. Let $\ell = 2^n - 1$, and let $x_1, \ldots, x_\ell$ and $y_1, \ldots, y_\ell$ be arbitrary enumerations of $X = \{0,1\}^n \setminus \{k||0^{n-\kappa}\}$ and $Y = \{0,1\}^n \setminus \{r \oplus k||0^{n-\kappa}\}$, respectively. We show that

$$\Pr[\forall i = 1, \ldots, \ell : P_1(x_i) = y_i] = \frac{1}{(2^n - 1)!}.$$

Letting

$$\mathbf{A} = \Pr[P^{-1}((k||0^{n-\kappa}) \oplus r) \notin X]$$
$$\cdot \Pr[\forall i = 1, \ldots, \ell : P_1(x_1) = y_i \mid P^{-1}((k||0^{n-\kappa}) \oplus r) \notin X]$$
$$= 2^{-n} \cdot \frac{1}{(2^n - 1)!} = \frac{1}{2^n!}$$

and

$$\mathbf{B} = \sum_{j=1}^{\ell} \Pr[P^{-1}((k||0^{n-\kappa}) \oplus r) = x_j]$$
$$\cdot \Pr[\forall i \neq j : P(k||0^{n-\kappa}) = y_j \wedge P_1(x_i) = y_i \mid P^{-1}((k||0^{n-\kappa}) \oplus r) = x_j]$$
$$= \sum_{j=1}^{\ell} 2^{-n} \cdot \frac{1}{(2^n - 1)!} = \frac{\ell}{2^n!} = \frac{2^n - 1}{2^n!},$$

we have

$$\Pr[\forall i = 1, \ldots, \ell : P_1(x_i) = y_i] = \mathbf{A} + \mathbf{B} = \frac{1}{(2^n - 1)!},$$

as desired. The claimed result thus follows from (3). $\qquad\square$

The following is an immediate corollary of Theorem 4 and Lemma 6.

Theorem 5. *Let $\mathcal{A}$ be an adversary making q_C classical queries to its first oracle and $q_Q \geq 1$ quantum queries to its second oracle. If f_1, f_2 are proper with respect to $\mathcal{T}$, then*

$$
\left| \Pr_{\substack{k \leftarrow \{0,1\}^{\kappa}; \\ P \leftarrow \mathcal{P}(n)}} \left[\mathcal{A}^{\mathsf{TEM\text{-}KX1}_k^{f_1,f_2}[P],P} = 1 \right] - \Pr_{\substack{\tilde{E} \leftarrow \mathcal{E}(\mathcal{T},n) \\ P \leftarrow \mathcal{P}(n)}} \left[\mathcal{A}^{\tilde{E},P} = 1 \right] \right|
$$

$$
\leq 4 \cdot q_Q 2^{-\kappa/2} + 7 \cdot 2^{-n/2} \left(q_C \sqrt{q_Q} + q_Q \sqrt{q_C} \right).
$$

5 Applications

In this section we use our results of Sect. 4 to show post-quantum security of the lightweight symmetric-key schemes Chaskey [15], Elephant [2], and a variant of Minalpher [17]. Note that our proofs of security hold when some public permutation at the core of each scheme is modeled as a random permutation; we do not analyze the public permutations themselves.

5.1 Chaskey

Chaskey [15] is an ISO-standardized lightweight MAC whose construction is based on a specific permutation P that we model as a random permutation. Define $\mathsf{F}_{k,k'}^P(x) = P(x \oplus k) \oplus k'$, i.e., the Even-Mansour cipher based on P. Evaluating Chaskey using key k involves evaluating $\mathsf{F}_{k,k}^P$, $\mathsf{F}_{k \oplus k_1, k_1}^P$, and $\mathsf{F}_{k \oplus k_2, k_2}^P$, where $k_1 = 2k$, $k_2 = 4k$, and multiplication is in the field $GF(2^n)$ with respect to a particular representation of field elements as n-bit strings. Prior work [15] shows that Chaskey is a secure MAC if these three instances of F^P are indistinguishable from three independent random permutations—a notion called *3PRP security*—and also proves 3PRP security of F when P is modeled as a public random permutation. Although this prior work considered classical adversaries only, it is not hard to verify that the proofs carry through to imply security of Chaskey against quantum adversaries making classical MAC queries, so long as 3PRP security of F holds against adversaries making classical queries to the secretly keyed ciphers and quantum queries to P.

As we now show, Theorem 4 readily implies 3PRP security of F in the post-quantum setting.

Theorem 6. *Let $\mathcal{A}$ be a quantum algorithm making q_C classical queries to its first three oracles and $q_Q \geq 1$ quantum queries to its fourth oracle. Then*

$$
\left| \Pr_{\substack{k \leftarrow \{0,1\}^n, \\ P \leftarrow \mathcal{P}(n)}} \left[\mathcal{A}^{\mathsf{F}_{k,k}^P, \mathsf{F}_{k \oplus k_1, k_1}^P, \mathsf{F}_{k \oplus k_2, k_2}^P, P} = 1 \right] - \Pr_{R_1, R_2, R_3, P \leftarrow \mathcal{P}(n)} \left[\mathcal{A}^{R_1, R_2, R_3, P} = 1 \right] \right|
$$

$$
\leq 7 \cdot 2^{-n/2} \left(q_C \sqrt{q_Q} + q_Q \sqrt{q_C} \right),
$$

where $k_1 = 2k$ and $k_2 = 4k$.

Proof. Letting $\mathcal{T} = \{0, 1, 2\} \subset GF(2^n)$ and defining $f_1(t, k) = k \oplus (2tk)$ and $f_2(t, k) = 2^t \cdot k$, we see that

$$\mathsf{TEM}_k^{f_1, f_2}[P](0, x) = P(x \oplus k) \oplus k = \mathsf{F}_{k,k}(x)$$
$$\mathsf{TEM}_k^{f_1, f_2}[P](1, x) = P(x \oplus k \oplus 2k) \oplus 2k = \mathsf{F}_{k \oplus k_1, k_1}(x)$$
$$\mathsf{TEM}_k^{f_1, f_2}[P](2, x) = P(x \oplus k \oplus 4k) \oplus 4k = \mathsf{F}_{k \oplus k_2, k_2}(x).$$

The theorem thus follows from Theorem 4 once we verify that f_1, f_2 are proper. Uniformity of f_1 and f_2 follows readily from invertibility of non-zero elements in $GF(2^n)$. Finally, note that

$$f_1(t, k) \oplus f_1(t', k) = 2 \cdot (t \oplus t') \cdot k \text{ and } f_2(t, k) \oplus f_2(t', k) = (2^t \oplus 2^{t'}) \cdot k,$$

with $t \oplus t'$ and $2^t \oplus 2^{t'}$ non-zero for distinct t, t'; XOR-universality follows. This concludes the proof of the theorem. □

As discussed earlier, the above theorem in combination with prior results [15] imply post-quantum security (in the random-permutation model) of Chaskey. Below we state a simple version of the theorem, leaving out some details and parameters. We formulate MAC unforgeability in terms of a distinguishing experiment in which the adversary is equipped with the Mac_k oracle, and must distinguish the oracle implementing Ver_k from the oracle (denoted by $\bot$) that always rejects. (To exclude trivial attacks, the adversary cannot forward a message/tag pair obtained from the first oracle to the second oracle).

Theorem 7. *Let* (Mac, Ver) *be the* Chaskey *MAC, and let* $\mathcal{A}$ *be a quantum algorithm making* q_C *classical queries to its first two oracles and* q_Q *quantum queries to its third oracle. Then*

$$\left| \Pr_{\substack{k \leftarrow \{0,1\}^n; \\ P \leftarrow \mathcal{P}(n)}} \left[\mathcal{A}^{\mathsf{Mac}_k, \mathsf{Ver}_k, P} = 1 \right] - \Pr_{\substack{k \leftarrow \{0,1\}^n \\ P \leftarrow \mathcal{P}(n)}} \left[\mathcal{A}^{\mathsf{Mac}_k, \bot, P} = 1 \right] \right|$$
$$\leq \mathcal{O}(2^{-n} \cdot q_C) + 7 \cdot 2^{-n/2} \left(q_C \sqrt{q_Q} + q_Q \sqrt{q_C} \right).$$

5.2   Elephant

Elephant [2] is a lightweight authenticated encryption scheme with associated data (AEAD) that was a finalist in the NIST lightweight cryptography standardization effort [18]. It is based on a tweakable block cipher we call ELE, which is constructed from a specific permutation P. Prior work [2] proves—in the purely classical setting—that Elephant is secure if ELE is a secure tweakable block cipher, and that ELE is a secure tweakable block cipher if P is modeled as a public random permutation. As with Chaskey, it is straightforward to verify that the former result carries over to the setting of quantum adversaries with classical access to Elephant if ELE is post-quantum secure.

The tweakable block cipher $\mathsf{ELE}[P] : \{0,1\}^{n-s} \times \mathcal{T} \times \{0,1\}^n \to \{0,1\}^n$ used by Elephant is defined as

$$\mathsf{ELE}[P]_k(t, x) = P(x \oplus f(t, P(k\|0^s))) \oplus f(t, P(k\|0^s)), \tag{4}$$

where $f : \mathcal{T} \times \{0,1\}^n \to \{0,1\}^n$ is a function that is proper with respect to $\mathcal{T}$. (The particular structure of f and $\mathcal{T}$ is not relevant here.) Since ELE is a special case of TEM-KX where $f_1 = f_2 = f$, post-quantum security of ELE follows directly from Theorem 3.

Theorem 8. *Let* ELE *be as above and let* $\mathcal{A}$ *be an adversary making* q_C *classical queries to its first oracle and* $q_Q \geq \max\{n, \log(11 \cdot |\mathcal{T}|)\}$ *quantum queries to its second oracle. Then*

$$\left| \Pr_{\substack{k \leftarrow \{0,1\}^n; \\ P \leftarrow \mathcal{P}(n)}} \left[\mathcal{A}^{\mathsf{ELE}[P]_k, P} = 1 \right] - \Pr_{\substack{\tilde{E} \leftarrow \mathcal{E}(\mathcal{T}, n); \\ P \leftarrow \mathcal{P}(n)}} \left[\mathcal{A}^{\tilde{E}, P} = 1 \right] \right|$$
$$\leq 7 \cdot 2^{-n/2} \left(q_C \sqrt{q_Q} + q_Q \sqrt{q_C} \right).$$

As discussed earlier, the above theorem in combination with [2, Theorem B.3] implies post-quantum security (in the random-permutation model) of Elephant. Recall that in the authenticated encryption security experiment the adversary is tasked with distinguishing the oracles $(\mathsf{Enc}_k, \mathsf{Dec}_k)$ from the pair of oracles in which the first (denoted \$) outputs random ciphertexts and the second (denoted $\perp$) always rejects. (Typical restrictions have to be imposed on the adversary to avoid trivial attacks; we do not state these here explicitly.) A fully flexible security theorem for Elephant involves many parameters; for simplicity, we record only a simple version below.

Theorem 9. *Let* $(\mathsf{Enc}, \mathsf{Dec})$ *be the* Elephant *AEAD scheme, and let* $\mathcal{A}$ *be a quantum adversary making a total of* q_C *classical queries to its first two oracles and* $q_Q \geq \max\{n, \log(11 \cdot |\mathcal{T}|)\}$ *quantum queries to its third oracle. Then*

$$\left| \Pr_{\substack{k \leftarrow \{0,1\}^n; \\ P \leftarrow \mathcal{P}(n)}} \left[\mathcal{A}^{\mathsf{Enc}_k, \mathsf{Dec}_k, P} = 1 \right] - \Pr_{P \leftarrow \mathcal{P}(n)} \left[\mathcal{A}^{\$, \perp, P} = 1 \right] \right|$$
$$\leq \mathcal{O}(2^{-n} \cdot q_C) + 7 \cdot 2^{-n/2} \left(q_C \sqrt{q_Q} + q_Q \sqrt{q_C} \right).$$

A Variant with a Tighter Security Bound. Next, we consider a slight variant of Elephant for which we can give a tighter security bound. Recall that ELE expands the key via $k\|0^s \mapsto P(k\|0^s)$. Here we instead expand the key via $k \mapsto k\|0^s \oplus P(k\|0^s)$. The tweakable block cipher then becomes

$$\mathsf{ELE\text{-}KX1}[P]_k(t, x) = P(x \oplus f(t, P(k\|0^s) \oplus k\|0^s)) \oplus f(t, P(k\|0^s) \oplus k\|0^s). \tag{5}$$

Security of the above is then a direct consequence of Theorem 5.

Theorem 10. *Let* ELE-KX1 *be as above and let* $\mathcal{A}$ *be an adversary making* q_C *classical queries to its first oracle and* $q_Q \geq 1$ *quantum queries to its second oracle. Then*

$$\left| \Pr_{\substack{k \leftarrow \{0,1\}^{n-s}; \\ P \leftarrow \mathcal{P}(n)}} \left[\mathcal{A}^{\mathsf{ELE\text{-}KX1}[P]_k, P} = 1 \right] - \Pr_{\substack{\tilde{E} \leftarrow \mathcal{E}(\mathcal{T},n); \\ P \leftarrow \mathcal{P}(n)}} \left[\mathcal{A}^{\tilde{E}, P} = 1 \right] \right|$$

$$\leq 2(q_Q + q_C) \cdot \sqrt{2/2^{n-s}} + 7 \cdot 2^{-n/2} \left(q_C \sqrt{q_Q} + q_Q \sqrt{q_C} \right).$$

The above implies post-quantum security of the variant of Elephant constructed from the cipher in (5) (in place of the cipher from (4)).

5.3 (A Variant of) Minalpher

Minalpher [17] is an AEAD scheme[4] that was a second-round candidate in the CAESAR competition. Minalpher is based on a single-round tweakable Even-Mansour cipher that we call MA, which is constructed from a specific permutation P. Prior work in the purely classical setting [17] first proves that MA is a secure tweakable block cipher when P is modeled as a random permutation and then proves, as a consequence, that Minalpher is a secure AEAD scheme. Just as with Elephant and Chaskey, the latter step easily translates to the post-quantum setting if MA is secure in that setting.

We specify MA in more detail. The tweak space $\mathcal{T}$ contains tweaks of the form (flag, N, i, j), where flag is an s-bit string that takes two possible values, $N \in \{0,1\}^{n/2-s}$, and i, j are non-negative integers with $i < 2^\ell$ giving an upper bound on the message length and $j \in \{0,1,2\}$. The tweakable block cipher MA : $\{0,1\}^{n/2} \times \mathcal{T} \times \{0,1\}^n \to \{0,1\}^n$ used by Minalpher is then given by

$$\mathsf{MA}_k(t,x) = P(x \oplus L(t,k))) \oplus L(t,k),$$

where

$$L((\mathsf{flag}, N, i, j), k) = y^i(y+1)^j \cdot (P(k||\mathsf{flag}||N) \oplus (k||\mathsf{flag}||N))$$

with y some fixed element of $GF(2^n)$. Note that Minalpher pads the key with part of the tweak (in contrast to Elephant which just pads the key with 0s), which prevents us from using Theorem 3 to analyze MA. We thus consider a variant of Minalpher based on a different tweakable block cipher MA' in which the key is padded with 0s. Specifically, we set $s = 1$ so that flag is simply a bit, encode j using two bits, and then fix the lengths of N and i so their combined length is $n - 3$ bits. We then define

$$\mathsf{MA}'_k(t,x) = P(x \oplus f(t,k)) \oplus f(t,k),$$

where

$$f(t,k) = (\mathsf{flag}||N||i||j) \cdot \left(P(k||0^{n/2}) \oplus (k||0^{n/2}) \right).$$

Since f is proper, Theorem 5 implies:

---

[4] Minalpher can also be used as a MAC, but here we focus on the AEAD scheme.

Theorem 11. *Let* MA′ *be as above and let* $\mathcal{A}$ *be an adversary making* q_C *classical queries to its first oracle and* q_Q *quantum queries to its second oracle. Then*

$$\left| \Pr_{\substack{k \leftarrow \{0,1\}^{n/2}; \\ P \leftarrow \mathcal{P}(n)}} \left[\mathcal{A}^{\mathsf{MA}'_k, P} = 1 \right] - \Pr_{\substack{\tilde{E} \leftarrow \mathcal{E}(\mathcal{T}, n); \\ P \leftarrow \mathcal{P}(n)}} \left[\mathcal{A}^{\tilde{E}, P} = 1 \right] \right|$$
$$\leq 2(q_Q + q_C) \cdot \sqrt{2/2^{n/2}} + 7 \cdot 2^{-n/2} \left(q_C \sqrt{q_Q} + q_Q \sqrt{q_C} \right).$$

Let Minalpher′ be the variant of Minalpher constructed by using MA′ in place of MA. We can combine the above with classical results about the security of Minalpher [17] to prove post-quantum security of Minalpher′.

Theorem 12. *Let* (Enc, Dec) *be the* Minalpher′ *AEAD scheme, and let* $\mathcal{A}$ *be a quantum adversary making a total of* q_C *classical queries to its first two oracles and* q_Q *quantum queries to its third oracle. Then*

$$\left| \Pr_{\substack{k \leftarrow \{0,1\}^{n/2}; \\ P \leftarrow \mathcal{P}(n)}} \left[\mathcal{A}^{\mathsf{Enc}_k, \mathsf{Dec}_k, P} = 1 \right] - \Pr_{P \leftarrow \mathcal{P}(n)} \left[\mathcal{A}^{\$, \perp, P} = 1 \right] \right|$$
$$\leq \mathcal{O}(2^{-n/2} \cdot q_C) + 2(q_Q + q_C) \cdot \sqrt{2/2^{n/2}} + 7 \cdot 2^{-n/2} \left(q_C \sqrt{q_Q} + q_Q \sqrt{q_C} \right).$$

Acknowledgments. Work of Gorjan Alagic, Chen Bai, and Jonathan Katz was supported in part by NSF award CNS-2154705. Gorjan Alagic also acknowledges support from the U.S. Army Research Office under Grant Number W911NF-20-1-0015, the U.S. Department of Energy under Award Number DE-SC0020312, and the AFOSR under Award Number FA9550-20-1-0108. Work of Christian Majenz was funded by an NWO VENI grant (Project No. VI.Veni.192.159) and a DFF Sapere Aude grant "IM-3PQC" (Grant Id. 10.46540/2064-00034B). Work of Patrick Struck was funded by the Bavarian State Ministry of Science and the Arts in the framework of the bidt Graduate Center for Postdocs (while working at University of Regensburg) and the Hector Foundation II.

Gorjan would like to thank Yu Sasaki for suggesting to analyze Minalpher using the results of this paper.

A   Proof of New Resampling Lemma

We now restate and prove Lemma 3.

Lemma 7. *Let* $F \subset \mathcal{P}(n)$. *Consider the following experiment involving a quantum distinguisher* $\mathcal{D}$:

Phase 1: *Choose uniform* $P \in \mathcal{P}(n)$, *and give* $\mathcal{D}$ *quantum access to* P. $\mathcal{D}$ *outputs* (D, τ), *where* D *is a distribution on* $\{0,1\}^n$ *and* $\tau \in F$.
Phase 2: *Sample* $\hat{s} \leftarrow D$, *set* $s_0 = \tau \circ P(\hat{s})$, *and choose* $s_1 \leftarrow \{0,1\}^n$. *Let* $P^{(0)} = P$ *and define* $P^{(1)} = P \circ \mathsf{swap}_{s_0, s_1}$.

Let $\varepsilon = 2 \cdot \mathbb{E}_{(D,\tau) \leftarrow \mathcal{D}^P} \left[\max_{x \in \{0,1\}^n} \Pr_{x' \leftarrow D}[x' = x] \right]$. For any $\mathcal{D}$ making at most q queries to P in phase 1,

$$|\Pr[\mathcal{D} \text{ outputs } 1 \mid b = 1] - \Pr[\mathcal{D} \text{ outputs } 1 \mid b = 0]|$$

$$\leq \sqrt{\varepsilon} \cdot \left(1 + \sqrt{q + \log \left(\frac{11 |F|}{\sqrt{\varepsilon}} \right)} \right).$$

Proof. Note that $s_1 = s_0$ then $P^{(0)} = P^{(1)}$. Thus, the distinguishing advantage of $\mathcal{D}$ is upper bounded by its distinguishing advantage conditioned on $s_1 \neq s_0$, and this is what we analyze in the rest of the proof.

Given $s_1 \neq s_0$, let $H \subset \{0,1\}^n$ be a set of size 2^{n-1} containing s_0 but not s_1, and let M be a bijection between H and $\{0,1\}^n \setminus H$ that maps s_0 to s_1. Define

$$\langle x \rangle = \begin{cases} \{x, M(x)\} & \text{if } x \in H \\ \{x, M^{-1}(x)\} & \text{if } x \notin H \end{cases}.$$

We use the plain superposition oracle for permutations as defined, e.g., by Alagic et al. [1] to simulate the permutation P. The resampling experiment with a superposition in place of P acts on quantum registers X (query input), Y (query output), E (adversary memory), and F (the oracle simulation's internal register). The oracle register F is partitioned into 2^n registers F_x, indexed by permutation inputs x. The initial state is

$$|\eta\rangle_F = (2^n!)^{-1/2} \sum_{\pi \in \mathcal{P}(n)} |\pi\rangle_F,$$

where $|\pi\rangle_F = \bigotimes_x |\pi(x)\rangle_{F_x}$.

We begin by defining a basis B_M of $\mathbb{C}\mathcal{P}(n) = \text{span}\{|\pi\rangle : \pi \in \mathcal{P}(n)\}$. Define the relation $R_M \subset \mathcal{P}(n) \times \mathcal{P}(n)$ such that

$$(\pi, \sigma) \in R_M \Leftrightarrow \{\pi(x), \pi(M(x))\} = \{\sigma(x), \sigma(M(x))\} \text{ for all } x \in H,$$

with the corresponding equivalence classes

$$[\pi]_M = \{\sigma \in \mathcal{P}(n) : (\pi, \sigma) \in R_M\}.$$

We denote the set of all equivalence classes by $\mathcal{P}(n)/R_M$. For any $x, x' \in \{0,1\}^n$ and $c \in \{0,1\}$, define the quantum state

$$|\Psi_{x,x'}^c\rangle = \frac{1}{\sqrt{2}} (|x\rangle|x'\rangle + (-1)^c |x'\rangle|x\rangle).$$

Define $\Gamma_M = \mathcal{P}(n)/R_M \times \{0,1\}^H$. Although Γ_M and the equivalence classes $[\pi]_M$ depend on M, we will sometimes suppress this in the notation.

For each pair $([\pi], y) \in \Gamma$ we define a vector $|([\pi], y)\rangle_F$ as follows. Let π be such that $\pi(x) > \pi(M(x))$ for all $x \in H$, where "$<$" denotes lexicographic order; we call this π the canonical representative of $[\pi]$. Define

$$|([\pi], y)\rangle_F := \bigotimes_{x \in H} \left| \Psi_{\pi(x), \pi(M(x))}^{y_x} \right\rangle_{F_x F_{M(x)}}.$$

Observe that if $[\pi] = [\sigma]$ and $y = y'$ then $\langle ([\pi], y) \mid ([\sigma], y') \rangle = 1$, and otherwise $\langle ([\pi], y) \mid ([\sigma], y') \rangle = 0$. The set

$$B_M = \{ |([\pi], y)\rangle : ([\pi], y) \in \Gamma \}$$

is thus an orthonormal set. To see that it forms a basis of $\mathbb{C}\mathcal{P}(n)$, observe that $|B_M| = |\mathcal{P}(n)|$. It follows that any state $|\varphi\rangle_{XYEF}$ can be decomposed as

$$|\varphi\rangle_{XYEF} = \sum_{([\pi], y) \in \Gamma} |\varphi([\pi], y)\rangle_{XYE} \otimes |([\pi], y)\rangle_F,$$

where $|\varphi([\pi], y)\rangle$ are subnormalized such that

$$\sum_{([\pi], y) \in \Gamma} \| |\varphi([\pi], y)\rangle \|^2 = 1.$$

Define $\Gamma_j = \{ ([\pi], y) \in \Gamma : |y| \leq j \}$, where $|y|$ denotes Hamming weight.

Claim. Let $|\phi_q\rangle_{XYEF}$ be the global state after the (unitary part of the) distinguisher has made q queries in phase 1 to a superposition oracle initialized in any state $|\tilde{\tau}\rangle$ such that $\langle ([\pi], y) \mid \tilde{\tau} \rangle = 0$ for all $y \neq 0$. Then for all y with $|y| > q$, we have $| \phi_q([\pi]_M, y) \rangle = 0$.

Proof. We prove the claim by induction on q. The base case $q = 0$ holds by assumption. For the inductive step, say the claim holds for $q - 1$, and recall that

$$|\phi_q\rangle_{XYEF} = U_{XYE} O_{XYF} |\phi_{q-1}\rangle_{XYEF}.$$

By the induction hypothesis we can decompose

$$|\phi_{q-1}\rangle_{XYEF} = \sum_{([\pi], y) \in \Gamma_{q-1}} |\psi_{q-1}([\pi], y)\rangle_{XYE} \otimes |([\pi], y)\rangle_F.$$

Using this decomposition and a linearity argument, it suffices to show that for $|y| \leq q - 1$, the state $O_{XYF} |x\rangle_X |y\rangle_Y |([\pi], y)\rangle_F$ is supported on basis vectors $|([\pi'], y')\rangle_F$ with $|y'| \leq q$. This follows from the fact that

$$O_{XYF} |x\rangle_X = |x\rangle_X \otimes O^{(x)}_{YF_x}.$$

for some operator $O^{(x)}$. This establishes the claim. $\qquad\square$

Next, define the projector

$$\Pi_F^{\leq q} := \sum_{([\pi], y) \in \Gamma_q} |([\pi], y)\rangle \langle ([\pi], y)|_F$$

and let $\Pi^{\pm} = \frac{1}{2}(\mathbb{1} \pm \mathsf{Swap})$ be the projectors onto the symmetric and antisymmetric subspaces of $\mathbb{C}^{2^n} \otimes \mathbb{C}^{2^n}$.

We will rely on the following claim:

Claim. For any $m \in \mathbb{N}$ we have

$$\Pr_{\sigma \leftarrow \mathcal{P}(n)} [\exists \tau \in F, S \subset \{0,1\}^n \; \forall x \in S : |S| = m \wedge \tau \circ \sigma(x) \in \langle x \rangle] \leq 11 \cdot 2^{-m} \cdot |F|,$$

Proof. For fixed $\tau \in F$ and $S \subset \{0,1\}^n$ of size m, the number of permutations P for which $P(x) \in \langle x \rangle$ for all $x \in S$ is at most $2^m \cdot (2^n - m)!$. Thus,

$$\Pr_{\sigma \leftarrow \mathcal{P}(n)} [\forall x \in S : \tau \circ \sigma(x) \in \langle x \rangle] \leq 2^m \frac{(2^n - m)!}{2^n!}.$$

A union bound over all τ and S yields

$$\Pr_{\sigma \leftarrow \mathcal{P}(n)} [\exists \tau \in F, S \subset \{0,1\}^n \text{ with } |S| = m \; \forall x \in S : \tau \circ \sigma(x) \in \langle x \rangle] \leq \frac{|F| 2^m}{m!}.$$

Using $11m! \geq 4^m$ proves the claim. □

We now return to the proof of Lemma 3. Let $\Sigma_{\overline{F}}^{\leq m}$ be the projector onto the subspace of $\mathbb{C}\mathcal{P}(n)$ spanned by the permutations π such that

$$|\{x \in \{0,1\}^n \mid \forall \tau \in F : \tau \circ \pi(x) \in \langle x \rangle\}| \leq m.$$

The claim implies

$$\left\| |\eta\rangle - \frac{1}{\sqrt{\|\Sigma_{\overline{F}}^{\leq m}|\eta\rangle\|}} \Sigma_{\overline{F}}^{\leq m} |\eta\rangle \right\| \leq 2 \cdot \sqrt{11 \cdot 2^{-m} |F|}.$$

Note that $\Pi^{\leq 0} \Sigma^{\leq m} |\eta\rangle = \Sigma^{\leq m} |\eta\rangle$. We analyze the resampling experiment where the random permutation is replaced by a superposition oracle initialized with $\frac{1}{\sqrt{\|\Sigma_{\overline{F}}^{\leq m}|\eta\rangle\|}} \Sigma_{\overline{F}}^{\leq m} |\eta\rangle_F$.

Let $|\psi\rangle_{XYEF}$ denote the global state after phase 1, conditioned on a particular pair (D, τ) output by the distinguisher. As in [7], we can relax the task of the distinguisher as follows: instead of merely providing access to an oracle interface acting on $|\psi\rangle_{XYEF}$ for $b = 0$ and $\mathsf{Swap}_{F_{s_0} F_{s_1}} |\psi\rangle_{XYEF}$ for $b = 1$, we give the distinguisher arbitrary access to all registers; the distinguisher's task is then to distinguish those quantum states.

For $x \in \{0,1\}^n$, define the projector $Q^{\langle x \rangle} = \sum_{y \in \langle x \rangle} |y\rangle\langle y|$. In the following, z is a variable that corresponds to the result of measuring $F_{\hat{s}}$, i.e., $\tau(z) = s_0$. Setting

$$\Pi_{\psi, \hat{s}, z} = \frac{1}{\||z\rangle\langle z|_{F_{\hat{s}}} |\psi\rangle_{XYEF}\|^2} |z\rangle\langle z|_{F_{\hat{s}}} |\psi\rangle\langle\psi|_{XYEF} |z\rangle\langle z|_{F_{\hat{s}}},$$

it follows that

$$2\Pr[b = b' \mid (D, H, M), s_0] - 1$$

$$\leq \frac{1}{2} \left\| \Pi_{\psi, \hat{s}, z} - \mathsf{Swap}_{F_{\langle \tau(z) \rangle}} \, \Pi_{\psi, \hat{s}, z} \mathsf{Swap}_{F_{\langle \tau(z) \rangle}} \right\|_1$$

$$= \frac{1}{2} \left\| \Pi_{\psi, \hat{s}, z} (\mathbb{1} - \mathsf{Swap})_{F_{\langle \tau(z) \rangle}} + (\mathbb{1} - \mathsf{Swap})_{F_{\langle \tau(z) \rangle}} \, \Pi_{\psi, \hat{s}, z} \mathsf{Swap}_{F_{\langle \tau(z) \rangle}} \right\|_1$$

$$\leq \left\| \Pi_{\psi, \hat{s}, z} \Pi_{F_{\langle \tau(z) \rangle}}^{-} \right\|_1 + \left\| \Pi_{F_{\langle \tau(z) \rangle}}^{-} \, \Pi_{\psi, \hat{s}, z} \mathsf{Swap}_{F_{\langle \tau(z) \rangle}} \right\|_1$$

$$= \frac{2}{\left\| |z\rangle \langle z|_{F_{\hat{s}}} |\psi\rangle_{XYEF} \right\|} \left\| \Pi_{F_{\langle \tau(z) \rangle}}^{-} |z\rangle \langle z|_{F_{\hat{s}}} |\psi\rangle_{XYEF} \right\|_2.$$

(The second inequality is the triangle inequality.) Taking the expectation over $\hat{s} \leftarrow D$ and z, we get

$$2\Pr[b = b' \mid (D, H, M)] - 1$$

$$\leq 2 \mathbb{E}_{\hat{s}, z} \frac{1}{\left\| |z\rangle \langle z|_{F_{\hat{s}}} |\psi\rangle_{XYEF} \right\|} \left\| \Pi_{F_{\langle \tau(z) \rangle}}^{-} |z\rangle \langle z|_{F_{\hat{s}}} |\psi\rangle_{XYEF} \right\|_2$$

$$\leq 2 \sqrt{ \mathbb{E}_{\hat{s}, z} \frac{1}{\left\| |z\rangle \langle z|_{F_{\hat{s}}} |\psi\rangle_{XYEF} \right\|} \left\| \Pi_{F_{\langle \tau(z) \rangle}}^{-} |z\rangle \langle z|_{F_{\hat{s}}} |\psi\rangle_{XYEF} \right\|^2 }$$

$$= 2 \sqrt{ \sum_{\hat{s}, z} D(\hat{s}) \left\| \Pi_{F_{\langle \tau(z) \rangle}}^{-} |z\rangle \langle z|_{F_{\hat{s}}} |\psi\rangle_{XYEF} \right\|^2 }, \tag{6}$$

where the first inequality is Jensen's inequality.

It remains to prove the following claim:

Claim. For any pair (D, τ) and any normalized state $|\varphi\rangle_{XYEF}$ such that

$$\Pi_{F}^{\leq q} |\varphi\rangle_{XYEF} = |\varphi\rangle_{XYEF} \quad \text{and} \quad \Sigma_{F}^{\leq m} |\varphi\rangle_{XYEF} = |\varphi\rangle_{XYEF},$$

we have

$$\sum_{\hat{s}, z} D(\hat{s}) \left\| \Pi_{F_{\langle \tau(z) \rangle}}^{-} |z\rangle \langle z|_{F_{\hat{s}}} |\psi\rangle_{XYEF} \right\|^2 \leq (m + q)\varepsilon_D.$$

Proof. Observe that

$$\Pi^{-} \left| \Psi_{\pi(x), \pi(M(x))}^{0} \right\rangle = 0 \quad \text{and} \quad \Pi^{-} \left| \Psi_{\pi(x), \pi(M(x))}^{1} \right\rangle = \left| \Psi_{\pi(x), \pi(M(x))}^{1} \right\rangle$$

for all x and all canonical representatives π. It follows that

$$\Pi_{F_{s_0} F_{s_1}}^{-} |\varphi\rangle_{XYEF} = \sum_{\substack{([\pi], y) \in \Gamma_q: \\ y_{s_0} = 1}} |\varphi([\pi], y)\rangle_{XYE} \otimes |([\pi], y)\rangle_F.$$

We can now bound

$$\sum_{\hat{s},z} D(\hat{s}) \left\| \Pi^-_{F_{\langle \tau(z) \rangle}} |z\rangle\langle z|_{F_{\hat{s}}} |\psi\rangle_{XYEF} \right\|^2$$

$$\leq \sum_{\hat{s}} \sum_{z:\hat{s}\in\langle\hat{\tau}(z)\rangle} D(\hat{s}) \left\| |z\rangle\langle z|_{F_{\hat{s}}} |\psi\rangle_{XYEF} \right\|^2$$

$$+ \sum_{\hat{s}} \sum_{z:\hat{s}\notin\langle\hat{\tau}(z)\rangle} D(\hat{s}) \left\| \left(\Pi^-_{F_{\langle\tau(z)\rangle}} \otimes |z\rangle\langle z|_{F_{\hat{s}}} \right) |\psi\rangle_{XYEF} \right\|^2.$$

We bound the two terms separately, beginning with the second. We decompose

$$|\psi\rangle_{XYEF} = \sum_{([\pi],y)\in\Gamma_q} |\psi([\pi],y)\rangle_{XYE} \otimes |([\pi],y)\rangle_F$$

and denote the only element of $\langle x \rangle \cap H$ by $\tilde{x}$. We have

$$\sum_{\hat{s}} \sum_{z:\hat{s}\notin\langle\hat{\tau}(z)\rangle} D(\hat{s}) \left\| \left(\Pi^-_{F_{\langle\tau(z)\rangle}} \otimes |z\rangle\langle z|_{F_{\hat{s}}} \right) |\psi\rangle_{XYEF} \right\|^2$$

$$= \sum_{\hat{s}} \sum_{z:\hat{s}\notin\langle\hat{\tau}(z)\rangle} D(\hat{s}) \sum_{([\pi],y)\in\Gamma_q} \left\| \left(\Pi^-_{F_{\langle\tau(z)\rangle}} \otimes |z\rangle\langle z|_{F_{\hat{s}}} \right) |\psi([\pi],y)\rangle_{XYE} \otimes |([\pi],y)\rangle_F \right\|^2$$

$$= \sum_{\substack{([\pi],y)\in\Gamma_q}} \sum_{\substack{\hat{s}\notin\langle\tau\circ\pi(x)\rangle:\\ y_{\pi(x)}=1}} D(\hat{s}) \left\| |\psi([\pi],y)\rangle_{XYE} \right\|^2$$

$$\leq \sum_{([\pi],y)\in\Gamma_q} q\varepsilon_D \left\| |\psi([\pi],y)\rangle_{XYE} \right\|^2 = q\cdot\varepsilon_D.$$

For the first term, we have $\Sigma_F^{\leq m}|\varphi\rangle_{XYEF} = |\varphi\rangle_{XYEF}$, i.e., for any permutation π in the support of this state there are at most m values x such that $\tau\circ\pi(x)\in\langle x\rangle$. For the second term, we have $\Sigma_{\bar{F}}^{\leq m}|\varphi\rangle_{XYEF} = |\varphi\rangle_{XYEF}$, i.e., $|\varphi\rangle$ is supported on basis states $|[\pi],y\rangle$ where π has at most m fixed points. Using essentially the same chain of inequalities as for the second term, we get

$$\sum_{\hat{s}} \sum_{z:\hat{s}\in\langle\hat{\tau}(z)\rangle} D(\hat{s}) \left\| |z\rangle\langle z|_{F_{\hat{s}}} |\psi\rangle_{XYEF} \right\|^2 \leq m\varepsilon_D.$$

This completes the proof.   □

Combining the above claim with (6), taking the expectation over (D,τ), and applying Jensen's inequality one more time results in the bound

$$|\Pr[\mathcal{D} \text{ outputs } 1 \mid b=1] - \Pr[\mathcal{D} \text{ outputs } 1 \mid b=0]| \leq \sqrt{(q+m)\varepsilon}$$

for the modified resampling experiment and thus

$$|\Pr[\mathcal{D} \text{ outputs } 1 \mid b=1] - \Pr[\mathcal{D} \text{ outputs } 1 \mid b=0]| \leq \sqrt{(q+m)\varepsilon} + 11\cdot 2^{-m}|F|.$$

Setting $m = \log\left(\frac{11|F|}{\sqrt{\varepsilon}}\right)$ we get

$$|\Pr[\mathcal{D} \text{ outputs } 1 \mid b = 1] - \Pr[\mathcal{D} \text{ outputs } 1 \mid b = 0]|$$

$$\leq \sqrt{\varepsilon}\left(1 + \sqrt{q + \log\left(11\frac{|F|}{\sqrt{\varepsilon}}\right)}\right),$$

matching the lemma. □

References

1. Alagic, G., Bai, C., Katz, J., Majenz, C.: Post-quantum security of the Even-Mansour cipher. In: Dunkelman, O., Dziembowski, S. (eds.) Advances in Cryptology – EUROCRYPT 2022. EUROCRYPT 2022, Part III. LNCS, vol. 13277, pp. 458–487. Springer, Cham (2022). https://doi.org/10.1007/978-3-031-07082-2_17

2. Beyne, T., Chen, Y.L., Dobraunig, C., Mennink, B.: Elephant v2. Technical report, NIST (2021). https://csrc.nist.gov/CSRC/media/Projects/lightweight-cryptography/documents/finalist-round/updated-spec-doc/elephant-spec-final.pdf

3. Bonnetain, X., Hosoyamada, A., Naya-Plasencia, M., Sasaki, Yu., Schrottenloher, A.: Quantum attacks without superposition queries: the offline Simon's algorithm. In: Galbraith, S.D., Moriai, S. (eds.) ASIACRYPT 2019, Part I. LNCS, vol. 11921, pp. 552–583. Springer, Cham (2019). https://doi.org/10.1007/978-3-030-34578-5_20

4. Bonnctain, X., Schrottenloher, A., Sibleyras, F.: Beyond quadratic speedups in quantum attacks on symmetric schemes. In: Dunkelman, O., Dziembowski, S. (eds.) Advances in Cryptology—Eurocrypt 2022, Part III. LNCS, vol. 13277, pp. 315–344. Springer, Cham (2022). https://doi.org/10.1007/978-3-031-07082-2_12

5. Cojocaru, A., Garay, J., Song, F.: Generalized hybrid search and applications (2023). https://ia.cr/2023/798

6. Don, J., Fehr, S., Huang, Y.-H.: Adaptive versus static multi-oracle algorithms, and quantum security of a split-key PRF. In: Kiltz, E., Vaikuntanathan, V. (eds.) 20th Theory of Cryptography Conference—TCC 2022, Part I. LNCS, vol. 13747, pp. 33–51. Springer, Cham (2022). https://doi.org/10.1007/978-3-031-22318-1_2

7. Grilo, A.B., Hövelmanns, K., Hülsing, A., Majenz, C.: Tight adaptive reprogramming in the QROM. In: Tibouchi, M., Wang, H. (eds.) Advances in Cryptology—2021, Part I. LNCS, vol. 13090, pp. 637–667. Springer, Cham (2021). https://doi.org/10.1007/978-3-030-92062-3_22, https://eprint.iacr.org/2020/1361

8. Grover, L.K.: A fast quantum mechanical algorithm for database search. In: 28th Annual ACM Symposium on Theory of Computing (STOC), pp. 212–219. ACM Press (1996)

9. Hamoudi, Y., Liu, Q., Sinha, M.: Quantum-classical tradeoffs in the random oracle model (2022). https://arxiv.org/abs/2211.12954

10. Hosoyamada, A., Sasaki, Y.: Cryptanalysis against symmetric-key schemes with online classical queries and offline quantum computations. In: Smart, N. (eds.) Topics in Cryptology—Cryptographers' Track at the RSA Conference (CT-RSA) 2018, vol. 10808, pp. 198–218. LNCS. Springer, Cham (2018). https://doi.org/10.1007/978-3-319-76953-0_11

11. Jaeger, J., Song, F., Tessaro, S.: Quantum key-length extension. In: Nissim, K., Waters, B. (eds.) TCC 2021, Part I. LNCS, vol. 13042, pp. 209–239. Springer, Cham (2021). https://doi.org/10.1007/978-3-030-90459-3_8

12. Kaplan, M., Leurent, G., Leverrier, A., Naya-Plasencia, M.: Breaking symmetric cryptosystems using quantum period finding. In: Robshaw, M., Katz, J. (eds.) CRYPTO 2016, Part II. LNCS, vol. 9815, pp. 207–237. Springer, Heidelberg (2016). https://doi.org/10.1007/978-3-662-53008-5_8

13. Kuwakado, H., Morii, M.: Quantum distinguisher between the 3-round Feistel cipher and the random permutation. In: Proceedings of IEEE International Symposium on Information Theory, pp. 2682–2685. IEEE (2010)

14. Kuwakado, H., Morii, M.: Security on the quantum-type Even-Mansour cipher. In: Proceedings of International Symposium on Information Theory and its Applications, pp. 312–316. IEEE (2012)

15. Mouha, N., Mennink, B., Van Herrewege, A., Watanabe, D., Preneel, B., Verbauwhede, I.: Chaskey: an efficient MAC algorithm for 32-bit microcontrollers. In: Joux, A., Youssef, A. (eds.) SAC 2014. LNCS, vol. 8781, pp. 306–323. Springer, Cham (2014). https://doi.org/10.1007/978-3-319-13051-4_19

16. Rosmanis, A.: Hybrid quantum-classical search algorithms (2022). https://arxiv.org/abs/2202.11443

17. Sasaki, Y., et al.: Minalpher v1.1 (2015). https://competitions.cr.yp.to/caesar-submissions.html

18. Turan, M.S., et al.: Status report on the second round of the NIST lightweight cryptography standardization process. NIST IR 8369 (2021)

19. Zhandry, M.: How to record quantum queries, and applications to quantum indifferentiability. In: Boldyreva, A., Micciancio, D. (eds.) CRYPTO 2019, Part II. LNCS, vol. 11693, pp. 239–268. Springer, Cham (2019). https://doi.org/10.1007/978-3-030-26951-7_9

Probabilistic Extensions: A One-Step Framework for Finding Rectangle Attacks and Beyond

Ling Song[2,3], Qianqian Yang[1,5(✉)], Yincen Chen[2,3], Lei Hu[1,5], and Jian Weng[2,3,4]

[1] Key Laboratory of Cyberspace Security Defense, Institute of Information Engineering, Chinese Academy of Sciences, Beijing, China
{yangqianqian,hulei}@iie.ac.cn
[2] College of Cyber Security, Jinan University, Guangzhou, China
[3] National Joint Engineering Research Center of Network Security Detection and Protection Technology, Jinan University, Guangzhou, China
[4] Guangdong Key Laboratory of Data Security and Privacy Preserving, Jinan University, Guangzhou, China
[5] School of Cyber Security, University of Chinese Academy of Sciences, Beijing, China

Abstract. In differential-like attacks, the process typically involves extending a distinguisher forward and backward with probability 1 for some rounds and recovering the key involved in the extended part. Particularly in rectangle attacks, a holistic key recovery strategy can be employed to yield the most efficient attacks tailored to a given distinguisher. In this paper, we treat the distinguisher and the extended part as an integrated entity and give a one-step framework for finding rectangle attacks with the purpose of reducing the overall complexity or attacking more rounds. In this framework, we propose to allow probabilistic differential propagations in the extended part and incorporate the holistic recovery strategy. Additionally, we introduce the "split-and-bunch technique" to further reduce the time complexity. Beyond rectangle attacks, we extend these foundational concepts to encompass differential attacks as well. To demonstrate the efficiency of our framework, we apply it to Deoxys-BC-384, SKINNY, ForkSkinny, and CRAFT, achieving a series of refined and improved rectangle attacks and differential attacks. Notably, we obtain the first 15-round attack on Deoxys-BC-384, narrowing its security margin to only one round. Furthermore, our differential attack on CRAFT extends to 23 rounds, covering two more rounds than the previous best attacks.

Keywords: Rectangle attack · Differential attack · Key recovery attack · Deoxys-BC · SKINNY · ForkSkinny · CRAFT

1 Introduction

Differential cryptanalysis, proposed by Biham and Shamir [BS91] in 1991, is one of the most efficient and powerful cryptanalysis for symmetric ciphers. In

© International Association for Cryptologic Research 2024
M. Joye and G. Leander (Eds.): EUROCRYPT 2024, LNCS 14651, pp. 339–367, 2024.
https://doi.org/10.1007/978-3-031-58716-0_12

differential cryptanalysis, the adversary aims to discover the in-homogeneity in high-probability occurrences of plaintext and ciphertext differences, *i.e.*, high-probability differentials. For a certain block cipher, if an r-round high-probability differential is found, one could add some outer rounds and extract the information of the key in the outer rounds using the differential.

However, it is a challenging task to find a long differential trail with high probability for most ciphers. To this, Wanger proposed the boomerang attack [Wag99] in 1999 as an extension of differential cryptanalysis. In a boomerang attack, two short differential trails are combined to form a long one. The basic boomerang attack requires adaptive chosen plaintexts and ciphertexts. In [KKS00], Kelsey *et al.* converted it into a chosen-plaintext variant, which was named the amplified boomerang attack. Later, Biham *et al.* [BDK01] made further improvements on the amplified boomerang attack by proposing the rectangle attack, which takes into account as many differences as possible in the middle of the distinguisher to estimate the probability more accurately. Since then, the boomerang and rectangle attacks have been extensively studied and applied to many block ciphers. For example, boomerang attacks on full AES-192 and AES-256 in the related-key setting were proposed in [BK09, DEFN22]; the best cryptanalysis results so far on Deoxys [BL23], SKINNY [SZY+22], and GIFT [DQSW22] were all based on boomerang attacks or rectangle attacks.

In either differential attacks or rectangle attacks, it is common to take two steps to mount key recovery attacks. The first step is to find a high-probability distinguisher covering a large number of rounds. To this end, many approaches have been proposed in the literature [Mat94, MP13, SHW+14, HBS21, DDV21]. Once a high-probability distinguisher is obtained, then in the second step, the distinguisher is extended backward and forward over some rounds with probability 1 for the key recovery attack. In recent years, many studies focused on achieving key recovery attacks as efficiently as possible for a given distinguisher. For differential attacks, Boura *et al.* [BDD+23] introduced a novel method that recovers the key in a meet-in-the-middle manner, which brought out improved results on block ciphers SKINNY-128-384 and AES-256. For rectangle attacks, various algorithms have been proposed for the key recovery [BDK01, BDK02, ZDJ19, DQSW21, SZY+22], each of which follows a different strategy for guessing the key. Among them, the unified key recovery algorithm proposed in [SZY+22] supports any strategy for guessing the key and covers all the previous algorithms. Most notably, this algorithm is able to produce the most efficient key recovery attack for a given distinguisher. As a result, it led to the state-of-the-art results of rectangle key recovery attack on Serpent [ABK98], CRAFT [BLMR19], SKINNY [BJK+16] and Deoxys [JNPS16].

However, prior research has demonstrated that the best distinguisher does not necessarily yield the most effective key recovery attack [LGS17, ZDC+21, QDW+21]. This phenomenon is even not limited to differential attacks and rectangle attacks [SSD+18, HSE23]. These studies have revealed that distinguishers are more conducive to key recovery attacks when their input and output differences exhibit sparsity and slow diffusion in the extended rounds. In [ZDC+21], the authors specifically sought differentials that were more favorable for key recovery, while [QDW+21] incorporated both the rectangle distinguisher and the extended part in their modeling to find better attacks.

Motivation. Previous research offers valuable insights that inform our work.

- The effectiveness of a key recovery attack hinges not only on the probability of the distinguisher but also on the differential propagation in the outer rounds. Slower diffusion of differences in the outer rounds tends to yield better results.
- The key recovery is likely to be more efficient when the outer rounds involve fewer key bits.
- The choice of key guessing strategy significantly influences the complexity of the key recovery attack.

Despite the key recovery algorithm in [SZY+22] offering the best rectangle attacks for a given distinguisher, we are prompted to explore whether there is room for improving rectangle attacks further when we treat the distinguisher and the extended part as a whole and meanwhile incorporate the lessons mentioned above. Additionally, we are curious whether similar advancements can be applied to differential attacks.

Our Contributions. In this work, we treat the distinguisher and the extended part as a whole and present a one-step framework for finding rectangle attacks. Instead of extending the distinguisher forward and backward with probability 1, we introduce probabilistic differential propagations in the extended part. Traditionally, the extended part only contained deterministic truncated differentials, but now it can include probabilistic (truncated) differential propagations as well. Since the probability of the extended part may be smaller than 1, we refer to the part relevant to the key recovery phase as the *outer part* and the remaining part as the *inner part*.

The effects of probabilistic extensions are multifaceted

- Probabilistic extensions help make differences in the outer part sparse, which potentially reduces the time complexity or covers more rounds.
- The boundaries separating the inner part and the outer part are no longer predefined and not necessarily well-aligned. Instead, they are dynamically determined in conjunction with the probabilistic extensions
- The data complexity is then determined by the overall probability.

To further optimize the time complexity, we propose the *split-and-bunch technique*. When probabilistic extensions are used, differences in the outer part become sparse and certain key bits may form intricate connections with the inner part. In cases where we can identify a compressed representation of these connections, we can isolate and replace these key bits with this compressed version. As a result, the actual number of involved key bits decreases, leading to reduced time complexity.

Table 1. Summary of the cryptanalytic results. Rect./ D/ ZC/ ID = rectangle, differential, zero-correlation, impossible differential. RTK/ SK/ ST/ WK/ WT=related-tweakey, single key, single tweak, weak-key, weak-tweak.

Cipher	Rounds	Data	Memory	Time	Approach	Setting	Ref.
Deoxys-BC-384	14	$2^{125.2}$	2^{140}	2^{260}	Rect.	RTK	[DQSW22]
	14	$2^{115.7}$	2^{160}	$2^{260.59}$	Rect.	RTK	Sect. 4.1
	14	$2^{115.7}$	2^{128}	$2^{242.7}$	Rect.	RTK	Sect. 4.1
	15	$2^{115.7}$	2^{128}	$2^{371.7}$	Rect.	RTK	Sect. 4.1
SKINNY-128-256	26	$2^{126.53}$	$2^{128.44}$	$2^{254.4}$	Rect.	RTK	[DQSW22]
	26	$2^{126.53}$	2^{136}	$2^{241.38}$	Rect.	RTK	[SZY+22]
	26	$2^{121.93}$	2^{136}	$2^{219.93}$	Rect.	RTK	Full Ver
ForkSkinny	28	$2^{118.88}$	$2^{118.88}$	$2^{224.76}$	Rect.	RTK	[DQSW22]
-128-256	28	$2^{123.89}$	$2^{123.89}$	$2^{212.89}$	Rect.	RTK	Full Ver.
CRAFT	23	2^{74}	2^{51}	2^{94}	D	WK&ST	[LR22]
	26	2^{73}	2^{60}	2^{105}	D	WK&WT	[LR22]
	20	$2^{62.89}$	2^{49}	$2^{120.43}$	ZC	SK&ST	[HSE23]
	21	$2^{60.99}$	2^{100}	$2^{106.53}$	ID	SK&ST	[HSE23]
	19	$2^{60.99}$	2^{68}	$2^{94.59}$	D	SK&WT	[GSS+20]
	21	$2^{60.99}$	2^{92}	$2^{87.60}$	D	SK&WT	Sect. 4.2
	23	$2^{60.99}$	2^{120}	$2^{111.46}$	D	SK&WT	Sect. 4.2

Moreover, our framework incorporates the holistic key recovery strategy, *i.e.*, the method of finding the best key recovery attack by choosing a proper key guessing strategy.

The main ideas of this framework are not limited to rectangle attacks but can also be applied to differential attacks. We apply the framework to several block ciphers and obtain the following results, which are summarized in Table 1.

– We provide improved 14-round rectangle attacks on Deoxys-BC-384 and introduce the first attack on 15 rounds, reducing the security margin to just one round.
– The data and time complexities of the 26-round rectangle attack on SKINNY-128-256 are reduced. Similar improvements can be made on the 28-round attack on ForkSkinny-128-256. The details can refer to the full version [SYC+24] of the paper.
– We propose differential attacks on CRAFT with up to 23 rounds in the single-key setting, which is two rounds more than the previous best attacks.

Organization. The rest of the paper is organized as follows. In Sect. 2, we review differential attacks, rectangle attacks, and the key recovery algorithms. In Sect. 3, probabilistic extensions will be introduced via examples, and the one-step framework will be given. In Sect. 4, we apply our framework to several block ciphers. We conclude this paper in Sect. 5.

2   Preliminaries

2.1   Differential Attacks

Differential cryptanalysis [BS91] is a technique used to analyze the propagation of difference through a cipher $E : \mathbb{F}_2^n \to \mathbb{F}_2^n$. Typically, an attacker aims to find a differential $(\alpha, \delta) \in \mathbb{F}_2^n \times \mathbb{F}_2^n$ such that the probability $Pr(\alpha \to \delta) = Pr\left[E(x) \oplus E(x \oplus \alpha) = \delta\right]$ is high. Since E is a permutation, it follows that $Pr(\alpha \to \delta) = Pr(\alpha \leftarrow \delta)$. A truncated differential [Knu95] is characterized by a set of input differences $\mathcal{D}_i$ and a set of output differences $\mathcal{D}_o$ and the probability $Pr(\mathcal{D}_i \to \mathcal{D}_o)$ is defined as $\mathrm{Avg}_{\alpha \in \mathcal{D}_i} Pr\left[E(x) \oplus E(x \oplus \alpha) \in \mathcal{D}_o\right]$. Note that $Pr(\mathcal{D}_i \to \mathcal{D}_o)$ and $Pr(\mathcal{D}_i \leftarrow \mathcal{D}_o)$ are usually not equal. Typical sets for truncated differentials often involve patterns where some bits can take on all possible values, while others are constrained to be zero.

In differential-like attacks, a distinguisher is extended backward and forward with probability 1 over some rounds. The goal of these attacks is to recover the key used in the extended rounds. Essentially, the differential in the extended rounds is actually truncated differentials with probability 1. These types of attacks are designed to understand how differences propagate with a high degree of certainty, allowing for the identification of key bits used in those rounds.

Key Recovery Attacks. Suppose a differential $\alpha \to \delta$ over E_d is of high probability P. Suppose E_b and E_f are added around E_d, as shown in Fig. 1.

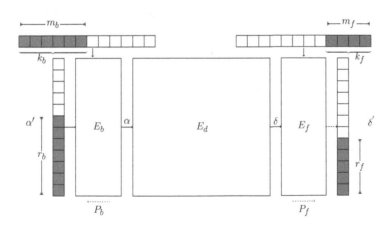

Fig. 1. Outline of the key recovery attack

The input difference of E_d α propagates back over E_b^{-1} with probability $P_b = 1$ to α'. Let V_b be the space spanned by all possible α' where $r_b = \log_2 |V_b|$. The output difference δ of E_d propagates forward over E_f with probability $P_f = 1$ to δ'. Let V_f be the space spanned by all possible δ' where $r_f = \log_2 |V_f|$. Let k_b

be the subset of subkey bits that are employed in E_b and affect the propagation $\alpha' \to \alpha$. Let k_f be the subset of subkey bits which are employed in E_f and affect the propagation $\delta \leftarrow \delta'$. Let $m_b = |k_b|$ and $m_f = |k_f|$ be the number of the bits in k_b and k_f.

In a key recovery attack, some key bits may be guessed in advance to sieve the data faster. Suppose a part of k_b and k_f, denoted by k'_b, k'_f, is guessed at first. Let $m'_b = |k'_b|$ and $m'_f = |k'_f|$ and $0 \leq m'_b \leq m_b, 0 \leq m'_f \leq m_f$. Suppose under the guessed subkey bits a r'_b-bit condition on the top and a r'_f-bit condition on the bottom can be verified. Finally, let $r^*_b = r_b - r'_b$ and $r^*_f = r_f - r'_f$. Note that the other parameters are determined when k'_b, k'_f are chosen.

In [SYL23], a unified key recovery algorithm for differential attack was proposed and the details can refer to Appendix A.1 in the full version [SYC+24] of the paper. With k'_b, k'_f being guessed at first, the complexities of the differential attack are as follows.

Complexities. A plaintext structure takes all possible values for the r_b bits and chooses a constant for the remaining $n - r_b$ bits. For one structure, there are 2^{2r_b-1} pairs of plaintext and 2^{r_b-1} of them satisfy α difference by meeting the r_b-bit condition. Suppose the number of the structures needed is y which y structures can constitute $y \cdot 2^{r_b-1}$ pairs that satisfy α difference. Set s to be the number of right pairs, then $y \cdot 2^{r_b-1} = s \cdot P^{-1}$ and the data complexity $D = y \cdot 2^{r_b} = 2s \cdot P^{-1}$. The memory complexity is $M = \max\{D, 2^{t+m_b+m_f-m'_b-m'_f}\}$ for storing the data and key counters where $0 \leq t \leq m'_b + m'_f$.

The time complexity of the differential attack contains four parts:

- $T_0 = 2^{m'_b+m'_f} \times D$ for partial encryption and decryption under the guessed key bits;
- $T_1 = 2^{m'_b+m'_f} \times D \times 2^{r_b-1+r_f-n-r'_b-r'_f}$ for getting the pairs that satisfy some filtering conditions;
- $T_2 = D \cdot 2^{m_b+m_f-n-1} \cdot \epsilon, \epsilon \geq 1$ for extracting all the $D \cdot 2^{m_b+m_f-n-1}$ key candidates where ϵ depends on the concrete situation;
- $T_3 = 2^{k-h}$, where $h \leq t + m_b + m_f - m'_b - m'_f$ for the exhaustive search.

2.2 Rectangle Attacks

In a boomerang attack, the target cipher is treated as a composition of two subciphers E_0 and E_1, i.e., $E = E_1 \circ E_0$. As illustrated in Fig. 2, the differential trail $\alpha \to \beta$ travels in E_0 with probability p, and the differential trail $\gamma \to \delta$ travels in E_1 with probability q, respectively. Then the probability of the boomerang distinguisher is

$$\Pr\left[E^{-1}\big(E(x) \oplus \delta\big) \oplus E^{-1}\big(E(x \oplus \alpha) \oplus \delta\big) = \alpha\right] = p^2 q^2.$$

The basic boomerang attack requires adaptive chosen plaintexts and ciphertexts. As a refinement of the boomerang attack, the rectangle attack requires only chosen plaintexts and considers as many differences as possible in the middle.

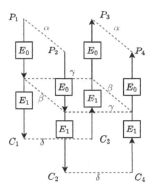

Fig. 2. Boomerang distinguisher

Since the boomerang attack was proposed, a series of studies have emerged focusing on the analysis of the connection probability. The probability p^2q^2 of a boomerang distinguisher is obtained under the assumption that the two differentials are independent. However, the probability may deviate from p^2q^2 on some concrete ciphers [BK09, Mur11], which demonstrates the dependency between the two differentials for boomerang attack. Instead of splitting the target cipher into two sub-ciphers, Dunkelman et al. [DKS10, DKS14] proposed to split it into three sub-ciphers and estimate the probability as p^2q^2r where r is the exact probability of the middle part, i.e., the connection probability. That is also known as the sandwich attack. Later in [CHP+18], the dependency issue in boomerang distinguishers was revisited, and a tool named Boomerang Connectivity Table (BCT) was proposed. Immediately after, a generalized framework of BCT is given in [SQH19], which allows the probability r to be calculated systematically.

2.3   Key Recovery of Rectangle Attacks

The key recovery of rectangle attacks has been extensively studied in [BDK01, BDK02, ZDM+20]. Each of these works proposed its own key recovery algorithm that uses a fixed strategy for guessing key bits and the performance varies from cipher to cipher.

Recently in [SZY+22], a unified framework was put forward for finding the best rectangle attack for a given distinguisher. It contains a generic key recovery algorithm and a strategy for finding the best attack. The algorithm covers all the previous key recovery algorithms, as it supports any strategies for guessing key bits or utilizing the filters. Among all the strategies, there will be a certain one leading to an optimal attack. We call this method of finding the best key recovery attack by choosing a proper strategy the *holistic key recovery strategy*.

Suppose we treat a target cipher as $E = E_f \circ E_d \circ E_b$, where there is a boomerang distinguisher over E_d of probability P^2. As in differential attacks, a part of k_b and k_f, denoted by k'_b, k'_f, is guessed at first, and $m'_b = |k'_b|$ and $m'_f = |k'_f|$. Similarly, with the guessed subkey bits, a r'_b-bit condition on the top and a r'_f-bit condition on the bottom can be verified. Following the generic key recovery algorithm, which can refer to Appendix A.2 in the full version of the paper, the complexities of the rectangle attack are as follows.

Complexities. The data complexity is $D = \sqrt{s}2^{n/2+1}/P$ where s is the expected number of right quartets. The memory complexity is $M = f_M(D, k'_b, k'_f) = D + min\{D \cdot 2^{r^*_b-1}, D^2 \cdot 2^{r^*_f-n-1}\} + 2^{t+m_b+m_f-m'_b-m'_f}$ for storing the data, the pairs and the key counters, where $0 \leq t \leq m'_b + m'_f$. The time complexity $T = f_T(D, k'_b, k'_f)$ is composed of four parts. The time complexity of collecting data is $T_0 = D$, the time complexity of doing partial encryption and decryption under guessed key bits is

$$T_1 = 2^{m'_b+m'_f} \cdot D,$$

the time complexity of generating pairs is

$$T_2 = 2^{m'_b+m'_f} \cdot D \cdot min\{2^{r^*_b-1}, D \cdot 2^{r^*_f-n-1}\},$$

the time complexity of generating and processing quartet candidates is

$$T_3 = 2^{m'_b+m'_f} \cdot D^2 \cdot 2^{2r^*_b} \cdot 2^{2r^*_f} \cdot 2^{-2n-2} \cdot \epsilon,$$

where ϵ is a factor that depends on the cipher, and the time complexity of the exhaustive search is $T_4 = 2^{k-h}$, where $h \leq t + m_b + m_f - m'_b - m'_f$.

Remark. In essence, the holistic key recovery strategy is to find a proper choice for k'_b, k'_f such that the four parts of the time complexity are balanced and that the overall time complexity is minimized under constraints for data and memory.

3   A One-Step Framework for Finding Rectangle Attacks

In this section, we present our one-step framework for finding rectangle attacks. To begin, we use some examples from a toy cipher to convey the essential notions of the probabilistic extensions and the split-and-bunch technique. Subsequently, we provide a concise overview of the holistic key recovery strategy. By leveraging these concepts, we present a one-step framework for rectangle attacks, which is likewise applicable to differential attacks.

3.1   Probabilistic Extensions

In a classical differential key recovery attack, some rounds are added around the differential distinguisher $\alpha \to \delta$, as shown in Fig. 1. The α difference propagates to α' via E_b^{-1} with probability 1, and the δ difference propagates to δ' via E_f with probability 1. It is natural to consider what occurs when difference propagates probabilistically in the outer parts. The following are examples to illustrate the impact of probabilistic extensions on the data and time complexities. For simplicity, none of the key bits are guessed in advance and the analysis of the memory complexity is omitted in the examples.

We suppose that the round function of the 128-bit toy cipher is the same as AES and the key schedule is rather simple. Each round uses the 128-bit master key K as the round key RK_i. The ordering of the bytes in the state matrix is as follows.

$$\begin{pmatrix} 0 & 4 & 8 & 12 \\ 1 & 5 & 9 & 13 \\ 2 & 6 & 10 & 14 \\ 3 & 7 & 11 & 15 \end{pmatrix}$$

Example 1. Suppose the probability of the inner part is P_d, and append 3 rounds. These three rounds are depicted in Fig. 3. The parameters of the attack are $n = 128, k = 128, m_b = r_b = 0, m_f = r_f = 128$.

According to Sect. 2.1, the data complexity is $D = 2s \cdot P_d^{-1}$. From D plaintexts, there are $D \cdot 2^{r_b + r_f - n - 1}$ pairs satisfying the plaintext difference and ciphertext difference. Thus the time complexity for constructing pairs is $T_1 = 2^{-1} \cdot D$. As there will be $2^{-1} \cdot D \cdot 2^{m_f - r_f} = 2^{-1} \cdot D$ suggestions for k_f in total, the time complexity for extracting key candidates is $T_2 = D \cdot 2^{-1} \cdot \epsilon$. We precompute several tables as illustrated in Table 2, so that ϵ is equivalent to about 2^{24} memory accesses. As the time complexity for the exhaustive search is flexible, we assume it is not dominant. Therefore, the overall time complexity is $T = T_2 = 2^{-1} \cdot D \cdot 2^{24} = 2^{24} \cdot s \cdot P_d^{-1}$ memory accesses.

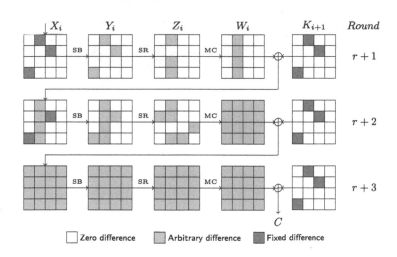

Fig. 3. The toy example of differential attack in the related-key model

Example 2. Different from Example 1, in this example the δ difference propagates to δ' via E_f with probability $P_f = 2^{-16}$. As shown in Fig. 4, the probability comes from two inactive bytes of W_{r+1}, *i.e.*, $W_{r+1}[6, 7]$. The effect is that fewer bytes are activated afterward. The parameters of the attack are $n = 128, k = 128, m_b = r_b = 0, m_f = 128, r_f = 72$.

Table 2. Precomputation tables for Example 1 where $eqk = \mathtt{SR}^{-1} \circ \mathtt{MC}^{-1}(K)$

Tables	Involved key	Filters	Remaining pairs
1	$eqk[4,5,6,7]$	$\Delta Z_{r+2}[6] = 0$	$2^{24} \cdot 2^{-1} \cdot D$
2	$eqk[3,9]$	$\Delta X_{r+2}[3,9] = \Delta K_{r+1}[3,9]$	$2^{24} \cdot 2^{-1} \cdot D$
3	$eqk[0,1,2]$	$\Delta Z_{r+2}[0,2,3] = 0$	$2^{24} \cdot 2^{-1} \cdot D$
4	$eqk[8,10,11]$	$\Delta Z_{r+2}[8,9,10] = 0$	$2^{24} \cdot 2^{-1} \cdot D$
5	$eqk[12,13,14,15]$	$\Delta Z_{r+2}[12,13,15] =$ $\Delta Z_{r+1}[5] = 0$ $\Delta X_{r+1}[3,4,9]$	$2^{-1} \cdot D$

The data complexity is $D = 2s \cdot (P_d P_f)^{-1}$. The time complexities are $T_1 = D \cdot 2^{0+72-128-1} = 2^{-57} \cdot D$, $T_2 = D \cdot 2^{-57} \cdot \epsilon$. We pre-compute several tables as illustrated in Table 3, so that ϵ is equivalent to about 2^{40} memory accesses. The overall time complexity is $T_2 = 2^{-57} \cdot D \cdot 2^{40} = s \cdot P_d^{-1}$ memory accesses.

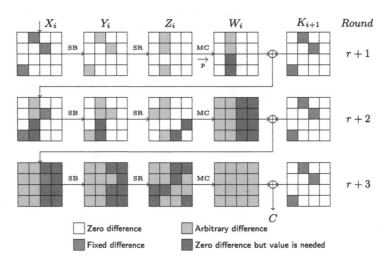

Fig. 4. The toy example of differential attack in the related-key model with probabilistic extension

Comparison Between Example 1 and Example 2. Example 1 uses traditional deterministic extensions in which the δ difference propagates to δ' via E_f with probability 1. On the contrary, Example 2 uses probabilistic extensions in which the δ difference propagates to δ' via E_f with probability $P_f = 2^{-16}$.

Increasing the Data Complexity. The data complexity for the case with probabilistic extensions is $P_f^{-1} = 2^{16}$ times the data complexity with deterministic

Table 3. Precomputation tables for Example 2 where $eqk = \text{SR}^{-1} \circ \text{MC}^{-1}(K)$

Tables	Involved key	Filters	Remaining pairs
1	$eqk[9]$	$\Delta X_{r+3}[9] = \Delta K_{r+2}[9]$	$2^{-57} \cdot D$
2	$eqk[0,1,2,3]$	$\Delta Z_{r+2}[0,2,3] = 0$	$2^{-49} \cdot D$
3	$eqk[4,5,6,7]$	$\Delta Z_{r+2}[6] = \Delta Z_{r+1}[6] = 0$ $\Delta X_{r+2}[3,9] = \Delta K_{r+1}[3,9]$	$2^{-49} \cdot D$
4	$eqk[8, 10 \sim 15]$	$\Delta X_{r+1}[3,4,9]$	$2^{-17} \cdot D$

extensions. In other words, the data complexity of the attack is determined by the overall probability $P_d P_f$ rather than by the probability P_d only.

Decreasing the Time Complexity. The time complexity of Example 1 is $2^{24} \cdot s \cdot P_d^{-1}$ and it is $s \cdot P_d^{-1}$ for Example 2. By using the probabilistic extensions, the time complexity is reduced by a factor of 2^{24}. Thus, probabilistic extensions are a technique that not only trades off data against time but may also have a gain as $2^{24} > 2^{16}$.

Flexible Boundaries. Different from the classical attack in which the boundaries between the inner and outer parts are fixed and well-aligned, the boundaries are flexible when probabilistic extensions are allowed. For a specified round, it is possible that some S-boxes belong to the inner part while others belong to the outer part. More interestingly, probabilistic differential transitions and deterministic differential transitions may occur simultaneously in the outer part and they may be even interleaved, the attack on SKINNY-128-256 can refer to Sect. 4.2 in the full version of the paper. Thus, there are no predefined boundaries. The boundaries will depend on differential transitions.

Increasing the Number of Filters and Earlier Usage. On one hand, the utilization of probabilistic extensions leads to an expansion of the total number of filter bits, growing from n to $n + \log_2 P_f^{-1}$. On the other hand, the filters appear earlier than before in the key recovery attack. The ability to employ filters at an earlier stage significantly enhances the efficiency of key candidate extraction, providing a reduction in the time complexity.

Remarks. Allowing probabilistic extensions essentially enables probabilistic differential propagations in the outer parts, which is the focus of key recovery.

- It is clear that the data complexity is related to the overall probability. Probabilistic extensions can strike a harmonious balance between data complexity and time complexity. However, it is important to note that probabilistic extensions do not necessarily increase data complexity in the search for a globally optimal attack, as exemplified by the attack on Deoxys-BC-384 in Sect. 4.1.

– Employing probabilistic extensions has the potential to reduce the density of active cells in the outer parts while simultaneously increasing the number of available filters. Notably, the probabilistic differential transitions are flexibly distributed in the outer parts and they do not have to connect to the differential trail over the inner part directly. This flexibility facilitates the adaptable selection of filters, ultimately resulting in improved time complexity.
– These extensions can be applied to E_b as well. Setting $P_b \geq 1$, $P_f \geq 1$ makes the probabilistic extensions cover the traditional deterministic extensions. Different extensions lead to different placements of filters. Among all possible extensions, there may be some that lead to more efficient key recovery attacks, in terms of time complexity or the number of rounds that can be attacked, compared to what deterministic extensions can achieve. Our applications to concrete ciphers will confirm this. Importantly, although our examples in this section primarily pertain to differential attacks, these same principles are applicable to rectangle attacks as well.

3.2   The Split-and-Bunch Technique

From Example 2, it is known that using probabilistic extensions brings the filters closer to the ciphertext, but the involved keys are the same. In this example, the last step is to verify $\Delta X_{r+1}[3, 4, 9]$. To compute this 3-byte difference, one has to know the values of $W_{r+1}[6, 7]$. However, another 56 key bits, i.e., $eqtk[8, 10 \sim 15]$ are required to compute $W_{r+1}[6, 7]$ from the ciphertext. In other words, the 56-bit key brings the final 24-bit filter. Therefore, the remaining pairs expand by a factor of 2^{32} as shown in Table 3. A question arises: Does the 56-bit key have to be traversed? To answer this question, we start with an observation on Example 2.

Observation 1. *Let $k_f = k_f^1 \| k_f^2$ with $m_f^1 = 72$ and $m_f^2 = 56$. For one pair of ciphertexts, if we traverse all possible values of the 16-bit $W_{r+1}[6, 7]$ without trying all possible values of the 56-bit k_f^2, we can find that:*

– *For the right k_f^1, when a right pair takes the right values in the two bytes, it makes the counter plus one. Traversal must cause the right value to be taken, so the number of suggestions for the right subkey is the same.*
– *For a wrong pair, the number of suggestions for the wrong key is equal to expanding the number of pairs by a factor of 2^{16}.*

We call this technique a split-and-bunch technique. Let e be the average number of suggestions for a wrong key k_f when the split-and-bunch technique is not used. When it is used, the number of suggestions for a wrong k_f^1 is expanded by a factor of $2^{m_e} = 2^{16}$ from e, i.e., it is $e \cdot 2^{m_e}$, while the number of suggestions for the right k_f^1 is $s + e \cdot 2^{m_e} = s + e \cdot 2^{16}$.

In Example 2, the whole key is involved in E_f, i.e., $m_f = 128$. In total we will get $D \cdot 2^{m_f - n - 1} = D \cdot 2^{-1}$ suggestions for 128-bit k_f. On average, the number of suggestions for a wrong subkey is $e = D \cdot 2^{-129} = P_d^{-1} \cdot s \cdot 2^{-128} \leq 1$, while it is $s + e$ for the right subkey.

When we use the split-and-bunch technique and set counters only for the $m_f^1 = 72$ key bits, we will get $D \cdot 2^{-57} \cdot 2^{16} = D \cdot 2^{-41}$ suggestions for 72-bit k_f. Thus the number of suggestions for a wrong k_f^1 is $e' = 2^{-41-72} \cdot D = P_d^{-1} \cdot s \cdot 2^{-112}$, while it is $s + e'$ for the right k_f^1, where $e' = 2^{m_e} \cdot e$. Thus, $m_e = 16$ is called the number of expansion bits. When e and e' are enough small, one could use the split-and-bunch technique to decrease the time complexity. The following example gives a better illustration.

Example 3. we use the split-and-bunch technique for this attack, as shown in Fig. 4. The number m_f of the involved key k_f in E_f is 72. The other parameters are $n = 128, k = 128, m_b = r_b = 0, r_f = 72, m_e = 16$.

The data complexity is $D = 2s \cdot (P_d P_f)^{-1}$. The time complexities are $T_1 = D \cdot 2^{72-128-1} = 2^{-57} \cdot D$, $T_2 = D \cdot 2^{-57} \cdot \epsilon$. We pre-compute several tables as illustrated in Table 4, so that ϵ is equivalent to about 2^8 memory accesses. The overall time complexity is $T = T_2 = 2^{-49} \cdot D = 2^{-32} \cdot s \cdot P_d^{-1}$ memory accesses.

Table 4. Precomputation tables for Example 3 where $eqk = \mathtt{SR}^{-1} \circ \mathtt{MC}^{-1}(K)$

Tables	Involved key	Filters	Remaining pairs
1	$eqk[9]$	$\Delta X_{r+3}[9] = \Delta K_{r+2}[9]$	$2^{-57} \cdot D$
2	$eqk[0, 1, 2, 3]$	$\Delta Z_{r+2}[0, 2, 3] = 0$	$2^{-49} \cdot D$
3	$eqk[4, 5, 6, 7]$	$\Delta Z_{r+2}[6] = \Delta Z_{r+1}[6] = 0$ $\Delta X_{r+2}[3, 9] = \Delta K_{r+1}[3, 9]$	$2^{-49} \cdot D$
4	$W_{r+1}[6, 7]$	$\Delta X_{r+1}[3, 4, 9]$	$2^{-57} \cdot D$

Comparisons Between Example 2 and Example 3. Example 3 uses the split-and-bunch technique and the time complexity is $T = 2^{-49} \cdot D = 2^{-32} \cdot s \cdot P_d^{-1}$, which reduces the time complexity of Example 2 by a factor 2^{-32}.

Decreasing the Time Complexity. The split-and-bunch technique reduces the time complexity further. This technique splits the key bits into two distinct categories: friendly key bits and unfriendly key bits. The former facilitates the efficient application of filters, while the latter, albeit intricately connected to some filters, can map to values comprising only a limited number of bits (i.e., m_e bits). Rather than directly trying all possibilities of the unfriendly key bits themselves, we streamline the process by traversing the m_e-bit value, ensuring that the correct key is not overlooked. Consequently, the split-and-bunch technique results in an expansion of the counter value for incorrect keys but simultaneously reduces the overall number of key suggestions. This deliberate trade-off effectively minimizes the overall time complexity.

When Counters are Not Used. Differential attacks are possible without using counters in some cases, for example, using enumeration [Din14]. The split-and-bunch can also be used and may provide an improvement. Suppose we split at an m_e-bit state, after which key extraction becomes two parts. If the complexity of key extraction for each part is reduced by more than 2^{m_e}, then split-and-bunch can provide an improvement.

3.3 Holistic Key Recovery Strategy

Probabilistic extensions fit well with the unified key recovery algorithm from [SZY+22]. However, the situation for the holistic key recovery strategy is different. Previously, the holistic key recovery strategy was considered in cases where a boomerang distinguisher was given. Hence, the boundaries between the inner and outer parts are clear and well-aligned. The only task is to find a proper set of key bits to be guessed in advance so that the overall time complexity is optimized.

On the contrary, the boundaries are not predetermined when probabilistic extensions are allowed. Instead, the boundaries and the set of guessed key bits should be determined together. That is, the situation for the holistic key recovery strategy is more generic in the presence of probabilistic extensions. To apply the holistic key recovery strategy, one needs to determine the involved key bits k_b, k_f from the boundaries, the guessed key bits k_b', k_f', and other parameters affected by k_b', k_f', including the obtained filters.

3.4 The Framework for Rectangle Attacks

Previously, one looked for the best rectangle attack for a given distinguisher. In this subsection, we present the one-step framework for rectangle attacks where the distinguisher and the extended part are considered together as a whole. The framework has four components: the unified key recovery algorithm, the holistic key recovery strategy, the core part, and the probabilistic extensions. In practice, we search for a cell-wise active pattern with the overall time complexity of the attack as the objective function and then instantiate it. As the treatment of the core part remains as in previous rectangle attacks, we focus on the upper and lower parts where probabilistic extensions occur and the determination of the boundaries is needed. Next, we present a constraint programming model for these parts.

Suppose the boomerang distinguisher $\alpha \rightarrow \delta$ over the middle part E_d has probability P_d^2. Suppose α propagates backward to α' with probability $P_b \leq 1$ and δ propagates backward to δ' with probability $P_f \leq 1$. The data complexity depends on these probabilities. Besides the probabilities, another important factor is the boundaries between the inner and outer parts since they mark the positions the key recovery phase has to reach and also determine the involved keys k_b, k_f.

Data Complexity. The probability for the whole attack is $P^2 = P_b^2 P_d^2 P_f^2$. We will show the formula for the data complexity remains as $D = \sqrt{s} 2^{n/2+1}/P$. Each plaintext structure takes all possible values for the r_b bits and chooses a constant for the remaining $n - r_b$ bits. For each structure, there are $2^{2r_b - 1}$ pairs of plaintext with difference in V_b and $P_b \cdot 2^{r_b - 1}$ of them satisfy α difference. That is equal to a $(\log_2 P_b^{-1} + r_b)$-bit condition. The distinguisher over the inner part has probability P_d^2, the number of quartets satisfying the input difference α should be at least $s P_d^{-2} 2^n$ for a rectangle attack, where s is the expected number of right quartets. Suppose the number of structures needed is y. These structures can constitute $2 \cdot \binom{y \cdot P_b \cdot 2^{r_b - 1}}{2}$ quartets that satisfy α difference. Due to the output difference of E_d δ propagating forward over E_f with probability P_f to δ', a right quartet propagates forward over E_f with probability P_f^2. Thus we get $2 \cdot \binom{y \cdot P_b \cdot 2^{r_b - 1}}{2} \cdot P_f^2 = s P_d^{-2} 2^n$. Then $y = \sqrt{s} 2^{n/2 - r_b + 1}/P$ and the data complexity is $D = y \cdot 2^{r_b} = \sqrt{s} 2^{n/2+1}/P$.

Labels. Due to the probabilistic extensions, there is a mix of concrete differences and truncated differences in the extended parts. For each cell of the internal state, we use two labels to describe its difference: $(x, y) \in \{(0,0), (1,0), (1,1)\}$, where

- inactive, denoted by $(x, y) = (0, 0)$ or □;
- active with a fixed non-zero difference, denoted by $(x, y) = (1, 0)$, or ■;
- active with an arbitrary (truncated) difference, denoted by $(x, y) = (1, 1)$ or ■.

Additionally, we use a label v to denote if the value of the cell is needed to verify the distinguisher. If it is, we denote by $v = 1$ and $v = 0$ otherwise. Then the labels will help to identify the boundaries as well as the probabilities P_b, P_f of the extension.

Boundaries and P_b, P_f. We take the forward extension as an example. The same techniques apply to the backward extension but in a reverse direction. There are several cases that happen with a probability.

- For the S-box layer, the probabilistic extension involves two cases: ■ → ■ and ■ → ■. The number of such cases can be computed by

$$\sum_i (O_i.x - O_i.y), \tag{1}$$

where $O_i.x, O_i.y$ are labels for the output cells of the S-box layer.
If the transition is ■ → ■, then the output of the S-box is needed for the verification, *i.e.*, $O.v = 1$ for the output. Besides, $O.v = I.v$. Meanwhile, the fixed input difference acts as a one-cell filter.
- For the linear layer, where each output cell is a linear combination of some input cells, the probabilistic extension happens when truncated differences exist in the input but the output is a fixed difference. This fixed difference

happens with a probability. Let $T = 1$ if some $I_i.y = 1$ and $T = 0$ if all $I_i.y = 0$. The number of such cases can be obtained by

$$\sum (T - O.y). \tag{2}$$

Conversely, each input cell is a linear combination of some output cells. If $v = 1$ for the input cell, then the values for the involved output cells are also needed.

Now P_b, P_f can be computed (or estimated) by considering Eqs. (1) and (2) together. The outer parts are composed of those internal state cells with label $v = 1$ as well as the operations and functions on them. This implies the boundaries. Then k_b, k_f are those key bits that are needed for determining the internal state cell with label $v = 1$.

Guessing the Key and Filters. The holistic key recovery strategy uses the guess-and-determine logic, which can be modeled as follows. For each key addition, if the key is guessed (a key cell in k_f) and the output is known, then the input can be determined. Therefore, we introduce another label d for each state cell to denote if it is determined. For each key cell, we introduce a label g to denote if it is guessed. We then have $I.d = 1$ when $(K.g = 1) \wedge (O.d = 1)$ for $I \oplus K = O$. Then the determination can proceed backward naturally. For a linear operation, a filter is reached under the following conditions: (1) its output contains truncated cells, (2) the difference of an input cell can be determined, and (3) this input difference has a fixed difference. For the S-box, if the input can be determined and the input difference is fixed, then we have a filter. Finally, the number of filters r'_f can be computed by recording such cases and the number of guessed keys k'_f can be computed by counting distinct key cells with $g = 1$.

Constraints for the Complexities. The constraints for the data and memory complexities can be added, such as $D < 2^n$. The objective is to minimize the overall time complexity as described in Sect. 2.3. The source codes for the constraint programmind model are available here.

3.5   The Framework for Differential Attacks

Similar to the framework for rectangle attacks, a framework for differential attacks can be built, because the basic ideas and all the involved parameters are the same. The only difference lies in the computation of complexities.

4   Applications

In this section, we apply our new framework to Deoxys-BC-384, SKINNY-128-256, and CRAFT block ciphers. For Deoxys-BC-384, using the one-step framework for rectangle attacks obtains a 15-round rectangle attack for the first time, containing a 10-round inner part rather than the longest 11-round one. For SKINNY-128-256, we get a new 26-round rectangle attack with reduced data and time complexities. For CRAFT, we obtain a 21-round differential attack and a 23-round differential attack by the new framework.

4.1   Application to Deoxys-BC-384

Specification. Deoxys-BC is an AES-based tweakable block cipher [JNPS16], based on the tweakey framework [JNP14]. The Deoxys authenticated encryption scheme makes use of two versions of the cipher as its internal primitive: Deoxys-BC-256 and Deoxys-BC-384. Both versions are ad-hoc 128-bit tweakable block ciphers which besides the two standard inputs, a plaintext P (or a ciphertext C) and a key K, also take an additional input called a *tweak* T. The concatenation of the key and tweak states is called the *tweakey* state. For Deoxys-BC-384, the tweakey size is 384 bits.

Deoxys-BC is an AES-like design, *i.e.*, it is an iterative substitution-permutation network (SPN) that transforms the initial plaintext (viewed as a 4×4 matrix of bytes) using the AES round function, with the main differences with AES being the number of rounds and the round subkeys that are used every round. Deoxys-BC-384 has 16 rounds.

Similarly to the AES, one round of Deoxys-BC has the following four transformations applied to the internal state in the order specified below:

- AddRoundTweakey – XOR the 128-bit round subtweakey to the internal state.
- SubBytes – Apply the 8-bit AES S-box to each of the 16 bytes of the internal state.
- ShiftRows – Rotate the 4-byte i-th row left by $\rho[i]$ positions, where $\rho = (0, 1, 2, 3)$.
- MixColumns – Multiply the internal state by the 4×4 constant MDS matrix of AES.

After the last round, a final AddRoundTweakey operation is performed to produce the ciphertext.

We denote the concatenation of the key K and the tweak T as KT, *i.e.*, $KT = K\|T$. For Deoxys-BC-384, the size of KT is 384 bits, and we denote the first, second and third 128-bit words of KT by W_3, W_2 and W_1, respectively. Finally, we denote by STK_i the 128-bit *subtweakey* that is added to the state at round i during the AddRoundTweakey operation. For Deoxys-BC-384, a subtweakey is defined as $STK_i = TK_i^1 \oplus TK_i^2 \oplus TK_i^3 \oplus RC_i$. The tweakey schedule algorithm is defined as $TK_{i+1}^1 = h(TK_i^1)$, $TK_{i+1}^2 = h(LFSR_2(TK_i^2))$ and $TK_{i+1}^3 = h(LFSR_3(TK_i^3))$, where the byte permutation h is defined as

$$\begin{pmatrix} 0 & 1 & 2 & 3 & 4 & 5 & 6 & 7 & 8 & 9 & 10 & 11 & 12 & 13 & 14 & 15 \\ 1 & 6 & 11 & 12 & 5 & 10 & 15 & 0 & 9 & 14 & 3 & 4 & 13 & 2 & 7 & 8 \end{pmatrix},$$

with the 16 bytes of a tweakey word numbered by the usual AES byte ordering.

14-Round Rectangle Attack on Deoxys-BC-384. By our new one-step framework, we get a 14-round rectangle attack on Deoxys-BC-384 with a 10-round inner part in E_d, 1-round in E_b and 3-round in E_f, as shown in Fig. 5. Detailed of the 10-round inner part refers to Fig. 11 in the full version of the paper. The probability of E_b is 1, the probability of E_d is $P_d^2 = 2^{-14 \times 2 - 11.4 - 7 \times 2 - 14 \times 2} = 2^{-81.4}$

and the probability of E_f is $P_f^2 = 2^{-8 \times 2}$. Thus the probability of the whole rectangle attack is $P^2 = P_b^2 P_d^2 P_f^2 = 2^{-97.4}$, and other parameters of the attack are: $n = 128, k = 384, m_b = r_b = 80, m_f = 8 \times (16 + 7 + 3) = 208$ and $r_f = 8 \times 13 = 104$.

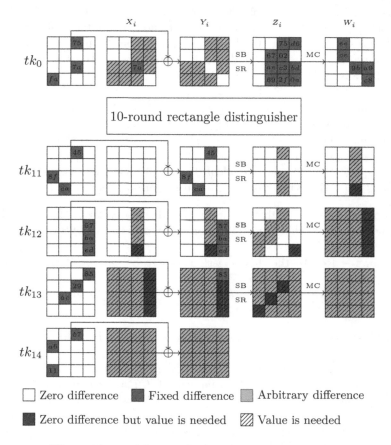

Fig. 5. 14-round Rectangle Attack on Deoxys-BC-384

The best guessing parameters are $m_b' = 8 \times 10 = 80, r_b' = 8 \times 10 = 80$, $m_f' = 8 \times (5 + 1) = 48, r_f' = 32$, $r_b^* = 0$ and $r_f^* = 72$, which means guessing 10 bytes of k_b and 6 bytes of k_f. The 6 bytes of k_f are $eqtk_{14}[8, 9, 10, 11, 12]$ and $eqtk_{13}[13]$ respectively. The complexities of our new attack are as follows[1].

- The data complexity is $D_R = 4 \cdot D = 4 \cdot y \cdot 2^{r_b} = 4 \cdot \sqrt{s} \cdot 2^{n/2}/P = 4 \cdot \sqrt{s} \cdot 2^{48.7+64} = \sqrt{s} \cdot 2^{114.7}$.
- The memory complexity is $M_R = D_R + D \cdot 2^{r_b*} + 2^{t+m_b+m_f-m_b'-m_f'} = \sqrt{s} \cdot 2^{114.7} + \sqrt{s} \cdot 2^{112.7} + 2^{t+160}$.

---

[1] We use a variant of formulas from Sect. 2.3 in the related-key setting for ciphers with a linear key schedule.

- The time complexity $T_1 = 2^{m'_b + m'_f} \cdot D_R = \sqrt{s} \cdot 2^{128+114.7} = \sqrt{s} \cdot 2^{242.7}$;
- $T_2 = 2^{m'_b + m'_f} \cdot D = \sqrt{s} \cdot 2^{128+112.7} = \sqrt{s} \cdot 2^{240.7}$;
- $T_3 = 2^{m'_b + m'_f} \cdot D^2 \cdot 2^{2r_b^*} \cdot 2^{2r_f^*} \cdot 2^{-2n} \cdot \epsilon = s \cdot 2^{128+112.7 \times 2 + 72 \times 2 - 2 \times 128} \cdot \epsilon = s \cdot 2^{241.4} \cdot \epsilon$;
- $T_4 = 2^{m'_b + m'_f - t} \cdot 2^{k+t-m'_b-m'_f-h} = 2^{k-h}$.

Processing a candidate quartet to retrieve the rest k_f can be realized by looking up tables. We pre-compute several tables as illustrated in Table 5, detailed refers to [SZY+22], so that ϵ is equivalent to about 2^{25} memory accesses which is around $2^{25} \times \frac{1}{14} \times \frac{1}{16} = 2^{17.19}$ encryption. The time complexity and memory complexity of the tables are related to the involved state bits, the involved subkeys and the filters. The time complexity and memory complexity of the tables are all 2^{128}. If we set $s = 4, t = 0$, then the data, memory, and time complexities of our attack are $2^{115.7}$, 2^{160} and $2^{260.59}$ respectively.

Table 5. Precomputation tables for the 14-round attack on **Deoxys-BC-384** where $eqtk_i = \mathrm{SR}^{-1} \circ \mathrm{MC}^{-1}(\mathrm{tk}_i)$ (let $Q = s \cdot 2^{241.4}$)

Tables	Involved key	Filters	Remaining quartets
1	$eqtk_{14}[0, 1, 2, 3]$	$\Delta Z_{12}[0, 1] = 0$	Q
2	$eqtk_{13}[15]$	$\Delta Y_{12}[15] = 0xed$	$Q \cdot 2^{-8}$
3	$eqtk_{14}[4, 5, 6, 7]$	$\Delta Z_{12}[4, 7] = 0$	$Q \cdot 2^{-8}$
4	$eqtk_{13}[14]$	$\Delta Y_{12}[14] = 0xba$	$Q \cdot 2^{-16}$
5	$eqtk_{13}[8, 9, 10]$	$\Delta Z_{11}[10] = 0$	$Q \cdot 2^{-8}$
6	$eqtk_{14}[13, 14, 15], eqtk_{13}[11]$	-	$Q \cdot 2^{24}$
7	$eqtk_{12}[2, 7, 8]$	$\Delta Y_{12}[2, 7, 8] = 0x8f, 0xca, 0x45$	Q

Improved 14-Round Rectangle Attack by the Split-and-bunch Technique. From the time complexity of the 14-round rectangle attack above, we can find that in subtable 6 there are 4 bytes involved subkeys and 0 filter. The number of quartets in this subtable reaches the maximum, making the time complexity of this step dominant.

With the same guessing strategy, by using the split-and-bunch technique, the number of the involved subkeys bits in E_f is $m_f = 8 \times (13+6+3) = 176$. And the number of the counts for a wrong key is $e = D^2 \cdot 2^{m_e - 2n - 16} = s \cdot 2^{225.4 + 8 - 272} = s \cdot 2^{-38.6} \ll s$. We get the new ϵ as illustrated in Table 6. The time complexity and memory complexity of the tables are 2^{128}. It is shown ϵ is equivalent to about 2 memory accesses which is around $2 \times \frac{1}{14} \times \frac{1}{16} = 2^{-6.81}$ encryption. The memory complexity is $\sqrt{s} \cdot 2^{114.7} + \sqrt{s} \cdot 2^{112.7} + 2^{t+(176+80)-80-48}$. If we set $s = 4, t = 0$, then the data, memory and time complexities of our attack are $2^{115.7}$, 2^{128} and $2^{243.7}$ respectively.

Table 6. Precomputation tables for the improved 14-round attack on `Deoxys-BC-384` where $eqtk_i = \mathtt{SR}^{-1} \circ \mathtt{MC}^{-1}(\mathtt{tk}_i)$ (let $Q = s \cdot 2^{241.4}$)

Tables	Involved key	Filters	Remaining quartets
1	$eqtk_{14}[0,1,2,3]$	$\Delta Z_{12}[0,1] = 0$	Q
2	$eqtk_{13}[15]$	$\Delta Y_{12}[15] = 0xed$	$Q \cdot 2^{-8}$
3	$eqtk_{14}[4,5,6,7]$	$\Delta Z_{12}[4,7] = 0$	$Q \cdot 2^{-8}$
4	$eqtk_{13}[14]$	$\Delta Y_{12}[14] = 0xba$	$Q \cdot 2^{-16}$
5	$eqtk_{13}[8,9,10]$	$\Delta Z_{11}[10] = 0$	$Q \cdot 2^{-8}$
6	$eqtk_{12}[2,7,8], W_{11}[11]$	$\Delta Y_{12}[2,7,8] = 0x8f, 0xca, 0x45$	$Q \cdot 2^{-24}$

15-Round Rectangle Attack on `Deoxys-BC-384`. Using our new framework, we get a 15-round rectangle attack which is equal to add one round after the 14-round rectangle attack, as shown in Fig. 6.

In order to get an effective attack, we also use the split-and-bunch technique in the 15-round rectangle attack. The parameters of the attack are: $m_b = r_b = 80, m_f = 8 \times (16+13+6+3) = 304$ and $r_f = 128$. Due to the key schedule, $k_b \cup k_f$ contains 376 information bits. The best guessing parameters are $m'_b = 80, r'_b = 80$ and $m'_f = 8 \times (16 + 5 + 1) = 176, r'_f = 8 \times (4 + 3) = 56$, which means guessing the whole subkey of k_b, 16 bytes of tk_{15}, 5 bytes of the equivalent subkey $eqtk_{14}$ and 1 bytes of the equivalent subkey $eqtk_{13}$. The complexities of our 15-round attack are as follows:

- The data complexity is $D_R = 4 \cdot D = 4 \cdot y \cdot 2^{r_b} = 4 \cdot \sqrt{s} \cdot 2^{n/2}/\tilde{P} = 4 \cdot \sqrt{s} \cdot 2^{48.7+64} = \sqrt{s} \cdot 2^{114.7}$.
- The memory complexity is $M_R = D_R + D \cdot 2^{r_b*} + 2^{t+m_b+m_f-m'_b-m'_f} = \sqrt{s} \cdot 2^{114.7} + \sqrt{s} \cdot 2^{112.7} + 2^{t+120}$.
- The time complexity $T_1 = 2^{m'_b+m'_f} \cdot D_R = \sqrt{s} \cdot 2^{256+114.7} = \sqrt{s} \cdot 2^{370.7}$;
- $T_2 = 2^{m'_b+m'_f} \cdot D = \sqrt{s} \cdot 2^{256+112.7} = \sqrt{s} \cdot 2^{368.7}$;
- $T_3 = 2^{m'_b+m'_f} \cdot D^2 \cdot 2^{2r_b^*} \cdot 2^{2r_f^*} \cdot 2^{-2n} \cdot \epsilon = s \cdot 2^{256+112.7 \times 2+72 \times 2-2 \times 128} \cdot \epsilon = s \cdot 2^{369.4} \cdot \epsilon$;
- $T_4 = 2^{m'_b+m'_f-t} \cdot 2^{k+t-m'_b-m'_f-h} = 2^{k-h}$.

Similar to the improved rectangle attack on 14-round `Deoxys-BC-384`, for $s \cdot 2^{369.4}$ quartets, ϵ is equivalent to about 2 memory accesses which is around $2 \times \frac{1}{14} \times \frac{1}{16} = 2^{-6.81}$ encryption. The time complexity and memory complexity of the tables both are 2^{128}. If we set $s = 4, t = 0$ then the data, memory, and time complexities are $2^{115.7}$, 2^{128} and $2^{371.7}$, respectively.

Comparison. The comparison with the previous rectangle attacks is presented in Table 7. A note on how the new attacks are obtained is as follows. We search for the active patterns of the whole attack with the total time complexity of the attack as the objective function in one step and then instantiate these patterns. In order to balance the time complexity and data complexity, we impose some restrictions on the data complexity in the model.

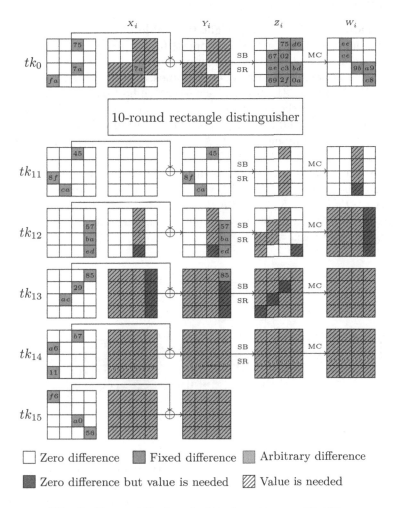

Fig. 6. 15-round Rectangle Attack on `Deoxys-BC-384`

Table 7. Comparisons of rectangle attacks on `Deoxys-BC-384`

P^2	Rounds	m_b, m_f	m'_b, m'_f	Data	Memory	Time	Reference
$2^{-118.4}$	14	88, 168	88, 24	$2^{125.2}$	2^{140}	2^{260}	[DQSW22]
$2^{-97.4}$	14	80, 208	80, 48	$2^{115.7}$	2^{160}	$2^{260.59}$	This
$2^{-97.4}$	14	80, 176	80, 48	$2^{115.7}$	2^{128}	$2^{243.7}$	This
$2^{-97.4}$	15	80, 304	80, 176	$2^{115.7}$	2^{128}	$2^{371.7}$	This

4.2   Application to CRAFT

Specification. CRAFT is a lightweight tweakable block cipher that was introduced by Beierle *et al.* [BLMR19]. It supports 64-bit plaintexts, 128-bit keys, and 64-bit tweaks. Its round function is composed of involutory building blocks. The 64-bit input is arranged as a state of 4×4 nibbles. The state is then going through 32 rounds $\mathcal{R}_i, i \in 0, \cdots, 31$, to generate a 64-bit ciphertext. As depicted in Fig. 7, each round, excluding the last round, has five functions, *i.e.*, MixColumn (MC), AddRoundConstants (ARC), AddTweakey (ATK), PermuteNibbles (PN), and S-box (SB). The last round only includes MC, ARC and ATK, *i.e.*, $\mathcal{R}_{31} = \text{ATK}_{31} \circ \text{ARC}_{31} \circ \text{MC}$, while for any $0 \le i \le 30$, $\mathcal{R}_i = \text{SB} \circ \text{PN} \circ \text{ATK}_i \circ \text{ARC}_i \circ \text{MC}$.

The tweakey schedule of CRAFT is rather simple. Given the secret key $K = K_0 \| K_1$ and the tweak $T \in \{0,1\}^{64}$, where $K_i \in \{0,1\}^{64}$, four round tweakeys $TK_0 = K_0 \oplus T$, $TK_1 = K_1 \oplus T$, $TK_2 = K_0 \oplus Q(T)$ and $TK_3 = K_1 \oplus Q(T)$ are generated, where Q is a nibble-wise permutation. Then at the round $\mathcal{R}_i$, $TK_{i\%4}$ is used as the subtweakey.

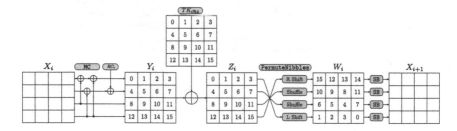

Fig. 7. A round of CRAFT

21-Round Differential Attack on CRAFT. By using our new framework, we obtain a 21-round differential attack on CRAFT, as depicted in Fig. 8, which contains a 14-round inner part, 3-round in E_b and 4-round in E_f. The input difference is $0a00000000a000a0$ and the output difference is $0a0000?000x000x0$. The probability of the inner part is $P = 2^{-54}$ and for a random permutation, the probability is 2^{-56}. This inner part uses a 2-round invariant property of CRAFT proposed in [GSS+20] when the tweak T satisfies the conditions $T[6] \oplus K[12] \in \{0x0, 0xa\}$ and $T[12] \oplus K[12] \in \{0x0, 0xa\}$ the difference $0xa$ propagates 2-round to $0xa$ with probability 1, detailed can refer to Appendix C in the full version of the paper. This is a single-key model with some conditions in tweak T.

In this attack, we build 2^x structures for each value of $T[6]$ with the tweak T satisfying $T[6] = T[12]$. For each $T[6]$, we perform the following steps.

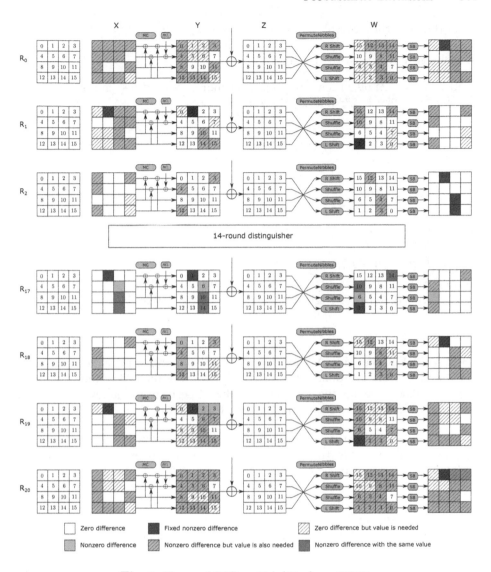

Fig. 8. 21-round Differential Attack on CRAFT

1. We build 2^x structures that $Y_0[0, 3, 4, 8, 11, 12, 13, 14]$ traverse all possible values while the other cells are fixed to some random constants. The data complexity is $D_0 = 2^{x+32}$. By using 2^{x+32} plaintexts, there are $N_0 = 2^x \cdot 2^{32 \times 2 - 1} = 2^{x+63}$ pairs of plaintexts. The expected number of the remaining pairs of ciphertexts are $N_1 = N_0 \cdot 2^{-4 \times 8} = 2^{x+31}$. The time complexity of this step is $T_0 = D = 2^{x+32}$.

2. For each of $N_1 = 2^{x+31}$ pairs, determine the key candidates and increase the corresponding counters. We pre-compute several tables as shown in Table 8,

so that the time complexity of this step is $T_1 = 2^{36} \cdot N_1 = 2^{x+67}$ which is about $2^{x+67} \times \frac{1}{21} \times \frac{1}{16} \approx 2^{x+58.61}$ encryption.

3. Exhaustively search the remaining keys.

Set $x = 24.99$, then the data, memory, and time complexities are $2^{4+24.99+32} = 2^{60.99}$, 2^{92} and $2^{87.60}$, respectively.

Table 8. Precomputation tables for the 21-round attack on CRAFT.

Tables	Involved key	Filters	Remaining pairs
1	$K_0[12] = T[12]$	$\Delta X_1[1] = \Delta W_{19}[12] = a$	$2^{-8} \cdot N_1$
2	$K_0[0, 8, 11, 14]$	$\Delta Y_1[3, 7] = \Delta X_{19}[3, 7] = 0$	$2^{-8} \cdot N_1$
3	$K_0[13, 4, 3, 15]$	$\Delta Y_1[2, 6] = \Delta X_{19}[2] = 0$	$2^{-4} \cdot N_1$
4	$K_0[1, 2, 5, 6, 9, 10]$	-	$2^{20} \cdot N_1$
5	$K_1[1], K_1[9] \oplus K_1[13]$	-	$2^{28} \cdot N_1$
6	$K_1[6, 14, 10, 15]$	$\Delta X_2[0] = \Delta X_{18}[0] = 0, \Delta X_3[10] = a$	$2^{32} \cdot N_1$
7	$K_1[0, 7], K_1[8] \oplus K_1[12]$	$\Delta X_3[14] = a, \Delta W_{17}[3] = \Delta W_{17}[4]$	$2^{36} \cdot N_1$

23-Round Differential Attack on CRAFT. Expending one round before and one round after the 21-round differential attack, we obtain a 23-round differential attack on CRAFT. As for the 21-round attack, we perform the following steps for each $T[6]$. For 23-round attack, $K_1[12] = T[6] = T[12]$.

1. We build 2^x structures that $Y_0[2, 3, 6, 7, 8, 9, 10, 12, 13, 14, 15]$ traverse all possible values while the other cells are fixed to some random constants. The data complexity is $D_0 = 2^{x+44}$. By using 2^{x+44} plaintexts, there are $N_0 = 2^x \cdot 2^{44 \times 2 - 1} = 2^{x+87}$ pairs of plaintexts. The expected number of the remaining pairs of ciphertexts are $N_1 = N_0 \cdot 2^{-4 \times 5} = 2^{x+67}$ pairs. The time complexity of this step is $T_0 = D = 2^{x+44}$.
2. For each of $N_1 = 2^{x+87}$ pairs, determine the key candidates and increase the corresponding counters. We pre-compute several tables as shown in Table 9, so that the time complexity of this step is $T_1 = 2^{40} \cdot N_1 = 2^{x+107}$ which is about $2^{x+107} \times \frac{1}{23} \times \frac{1}{16} \approx 2^{x+98.47}$ encryption.
3. Exhaustively the remaining keys (Fig. 9).

Set $x = 12.99$, then the data, memory, and time complexities are $2^{4+12.99+44} = 2^{60.99}$, 2^{120} and $2^{111.46}$, respectively. The comparison with the previous attacks is presented in Table 10.

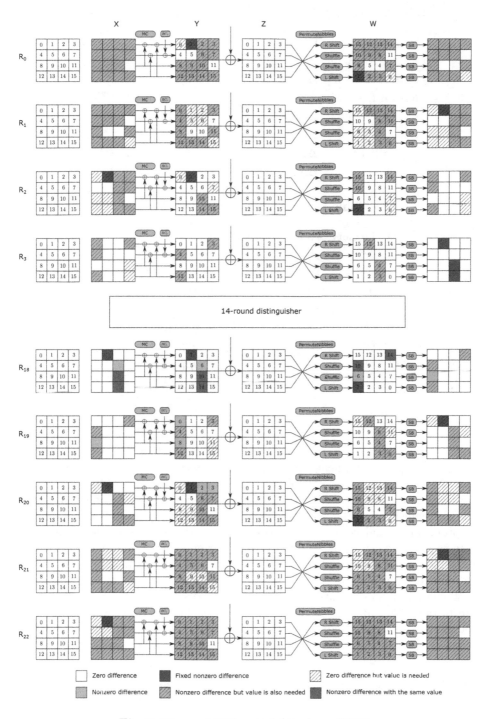

Fig. 9. 23-round Differential Attack on CRAFT

Table 9. Precomputation tables for the 23-round attack on CRAFT.

Tables	Involved keys	Filters	Remaining pairs
1	$K_0[9,2,10,14,12]$	$\Delta X_{21}[1,5] = \Delta Y_1[1,5] = 0$	$2^4 \cdot N_1$
2	$K_0[8,13,3,11,15]$	$\Delta X_{21}[2,6] = \Delta Y_1[2,6] = 0$	$2^8 \cdot N_1$
3	$K_0[0,1,4,5,6,7]$	-	$2^{32} \cdot N_1$
4	$K_1[0,8,11,14]$	$\Delta Y_2[3,7] = \Delta X_{20}[3,7] = 0$	$2^{32} \cdot N_1$
5	$K_1[13,4,3,15]$	$\Delta Y_2[2,6] = \Delta X_{20}[2] = 0$	$2^{36} \cdot N_1$
6	$K_1[2,5,9,10]$	$\Delta Y_3[1] = \Delta X_{19}[0] = 0, \Delta X_4[10] = a$	$2^{40} \cdot N_1$
7	$K_1[1,6]$	$\Delta X_4[14] = a, \Delta W_{18}[3] = \Delta W_{18}[4]$	$2^{40} \cdot N_1$

Table 10. Comparison of attacks on CRAFT

Rounds	Data	Memory	Time	Attack	Setting	Reference
23	2^{74}	2^{51}	2^{94}	D	WK(16-bit) & ST	[LR22]
26	2^{73}	2^{60}	2^{105}	D	WK(20-bit) & WT(12-bit)	[LR22]
20	$2^{62.89}$	2^{49}	$2^{120.43}$	ZC	SK & ST	[HSE23]
21	$2^{60.99}$	2^{100}	$2^{106.53}$	ID	SK & ST	[HSE23]
19	$2^{60.99}$	2^{68}	$2^{94.59}$	D	SK & WT(4-bit)	[GSS+20]
21	$2^{60.99}$	2^{92}	$2^{87.60}$	D	SK & WT(4-bit)	This
23	$2^{60.99}$	2^{120}	$2^{111.46}$	D	SK & WT(4-bit)	This

5   Conclusion

In this paper, we propose a one-step framework for finding the rectangle attacks with the purpose of reducing the overall complexities or attacking more rounds. Instead of extending the distinguisher forward and backward with probability 1, we propose to allow probabilistic propagations in the extended part. We treat the distinguisher and the extended part as a whole with a more flexible selection of propagation and involved keys to get better attacks. Moreover, we incorporate the holistic key recovery strategy into our one-step framework. Further, we introduce a technique, which is called the split-and-bunch technique, to reduce the time complexity. Applying our framework to Deoxys-BC-384, we obtain the first 15-round rectangle attack for Deoxys-BC-384, narrowing its security margin to only one round. Applying to SKINNY and ForkSkinny, we obtain a new rectangle attack with reduced data and time complexities. We also apply the main ideas of the framework to differential attacks on CRAFT block cipher, which achieves 2 more rounds than the previous best attacks.

Further Works. In this paper, we only apply the new framework to rectangle attacks and differential attacks. It would be a potential future work to explore the application of these ideas to other attacks.

Acknowledgement. The authors would like to thank anonymous reviewers for their helpful comments and suggestions and Ye Luo for preparing some figures. The work of this paper was supported by the National Key Research and Development Program (No. 2018YFA0704704) and the National Natural Science Foundation of China (Grants 62202460, 62372213, 62132008, 62022036). Jian Weng is supported by the National Natural Science Foundation of China under Grant Nos. 61825203, 62332007, and U22B2028, Science and Technology Major Project of Tibetan Autonomous Region of China under Grant No. XZ202201ZD0006G, National Joint Engineering Research Center of Network Security Detection and Protection Technology, Guangdong Key Laboratory of Data Security and Privacy Preserving, Guangdong Hong Kong Joint Laboratory for Data Security and Privacy Protection, and Engineering Research Center of Trustworthy AI, Ministry of Education.

References

ABK98. Anderson, R., Biham, E., Knudsen, L.: Serpent: a proposal for the advanced encryption standard. NIST AES Proposal **174**, 1–23 (1998)

BDD+23. Boura, C., David, N., Derbez, P., Leander, G., Naya-Plasencia, M.: Differential meet-in-the-middle cryptanalysis. In: Handschuh, H., Lysyanskaya, A. (eds.) CRYPTO 2023, Part III. LNCS, vol. 14083, pp. 240–272. Springer, Cham (2023). https://doi.org/10.1007/978-3-031-38548-3_9

BDK01. Biham, E., Dunkelman, O., Keller, N.: The rectangle attack — rectangling the serpent. In: Pfitzmann, B. (ed.) EUROCRYPT 2001. LNCS, vol. 2045, pp. 340–357. Springer, Heidelberg (2001). https://doi.org/10.1007/3-540-44987-6_21

BDK02. Biham, E., Dunkelman, O., Keller, N.: New results on boomerang and rectangle attacks. In: Daemen, J., Rijmen, V. (eds.) FSE 2002. LNCS, vol. 2365, pp. 1–16. Springer, Heidelberg (2002). https://doi.org/10.1007/3-540-45661-9_1

BJK+16. Beierle, C., et al.: The SKINNY family of block ciphers and its low-latency variant MANTIS. In: Robshaw, M., Katz, J. (eds.) CRYPTO 2016, Part II. LNCS, vol. 9815, pp. 123–153. Springer, Heidelberg (2016). https://doi.org/10.1007/978-3-662-53008-5_5

BK09. Biryukov, A., Khovratovich, D.: Related-key cryptanalysis of the full AES-192 and AES-256. In: Matsui, M. (ed.) ASIACRYPT 2009. LNCS, vol. 5912, pp. 1–18. Springer, Heidelberg (2009). https://doi.org/10.1007/978-3-642-10366-7_1

BL23. Bariant, A., Leurent, G.: Truncated boomerang attacks and application to AES-based ciphers. In: Hazay, C., Stam, M. (eds.) EUROCRYPT 2023, Part IV. LNCS, vol. 14007, pp. 3–35. Springer, Cham (2023). https://doi.org/10.1007/978-3-031-30634-1_1

BLMR19. Beierle, C., Leander, G., Moradi, A., Rasoolzadeh, S.: CRAFT: lightweight tweakable block cipher with efficient protection against DFA attacks. IACR Trans. Symmetric Cryptol. **2019**(1), 5–45 (2019)

BS91. Biham, E., Shamir, A.: Differential cryptanalysis of DES-like cryptosystems. J. Cryptol. **4**(1), 3–72 (1991)

CHP+18. Cid, C., Huang, T., Peyrin, T., Sasaki, Yu., Song, L.: Boomerang connectivity table: a new cryptanalysis tool. In: Nielsen, J.B., Rijmen, V. (eds.) EUROCRYPT 2018. LNCS, vol. 10821, pp. 683–714. Springer, Cham (2018). https://doi.org/10.1007/978-3-319-78375-8_22

DDV21. Delaune, S., Derbez, P., Vavrille, M.: Catching the fastest boomerangs - application to SKINNY. IACR Cryptology ePrint Archive, p. 20 (2021)

DEFN22. Derbez, P., Euler, M., Fouque, P.A., Nguyen, P.H.: Revisiting related-key boomerang attacks on AES using computer-aided tool. In: Agrawal, S., Lin, D. (eds.) ASIACRYPT 2022, Part III. LNCS, vol. 13793, pp. 68–88. Springer, Cham (2022). https://doi.org/10.1007/978-3-031-22969-5_3

Din14. Dinur, I.: Improved differential cryptanalysis of round-reduced speck. In: Joux, A., Youssef, A. (eds.) SAC 2014. LNCS, vol. 8781, pp. 147–164. Springer, Cham (2014). https://doi.org/10.1007/978-3-319-13051-4_9

DKS10. Dunkelman, O., Keller, N., Shamir, A.: A practical-time related-key attack on the Kasumi cryptosystem used in GSM and 3G telephony. In: Rabin, T. (ed.) CRYPTO 2010. LNCS, vol. 6223, pp. 393–410. Springer, Heidelberg (2010). https://doi.org/10.1007/978-3-642-14623-7_21

DKS14. Dunkelman, O., Keller, N., Shamir, A.: A practical-time related-key attack on the KASUMI cryptosystem used in GSM and 3G telephony. J. Cryptol. **27**(4), 824–849 (2014)

DQSW21. Dong, X., Qin, L., Sun, S., Wang, X.: Key guessing strategies for linear key-schedule algorithms in rectangle attacks. IACR Cryptology ePrint Archive, p. 856 (2021)

DQSW22. Dong, X., Qin, L., Sun, S., Wang, X.: Key guessing strategies for linear key-schedule algorithms in rectangle attacks. In: Dunkelman, O., Dziembowski, S. (eds.) EUROCRYPT 2022, Part III. LNCS, vol. 13277, pp. 3–33. Springer, Cham (2022). https://doi.org/10.1007/978-3-031-07082-2_1

GSS+20. Guo, H., et al.: Differential attacks on CRAFT exploiting the involutory s-boxes and tweak additions. IACR Trans. Symmetric Cryptol. **2020**(3), 119–151 (2020)

HBS21. Hadipour, H., Bagheri, N., Song, L.: Improved rectangle attacks on SKINNY and CRAFT. IACR Trans. Symmetric Cryptol. **2021**(2), 140–198 (2021)

HSE23. Hadipour, H., Sadeghi, S., Eichlseder, M.: Finding the impossible: automated search for full impossible-differential, zero-correlation, and integral attacks. In: Hazay, C., Stam, M. (eds.) EUROCRYPT 2023. LNCS, vol. 14007, pp. 128–157. Springer, Cham (2023). https://doi.org/10.1007/978-3-031-30634-1_5

JNP14. Jean, J., Nikolić, I., Peyrin, T.: Tweaks and keys for block ciphers: the TWEAKEY framework. In: Sarkar, P., Iwata, T. (eds.) ASIACRYPT 2014, Part II. LNCS, vol. 8874, pp. 274–288. Springer, Heidelberg (2014). https://doi.org/10.1007/978-3-662-45608-8_15

JNPS16. Jean, J., Nikolic, I., Peyrin, T., Seurin, Y.: Deoxys v1. 41. In: Submitted to CAESAR, vol. 124 (2016)

KKS00. Kelsey, J., Kohno, T., Schneier, B.: Amplified boomerang attacks against reduced-round MARS and serpent. In: Goos, G., Hartmanis, J., van Leeuwen, J., Schneier, B. (eds.) FSE 2000. LNCS, vol. 1978, pp. 75–93. Springer, Heidelberg (2001). https://doi.org/10.1007/3-540-44706-7_6

Knu95. Knudsen, L.R.: Truncated and higher order differentials. In: Preneel, B. (ed.) FSE 1994. LNCS, vol. 1008, pp. 196–211. Springer, Heidelberg (1995). https://doi.org/10.1007/3-540-60590-8_16

LGS17. Liu, G., Ghosh, M., Song, L.: Security analysis of SKINNY under related-TWEAKEY settings. IACR Trans. Symmetric Cryptol. **2017**(3), 37–72 (2017)

LR22. Leander, G., Rasoolzadeh, S.: Weak tweak-keys for the CRAFT block cipher. IACR Trans. Symmetric Cryptol. **2022**(1), 38–63 (2022)

Mat94. Matsui, M.: On correlation between the order of S-boxes and the strength of DES. In: De Santis, A. (ed.) EUROCRYPT 1994. LNCS, vol. 950, pp. 366–375. Springer, Heidelberg (1995). https://doi.org/10.1007/BFb0053451

MP13. Mouha, N., Preneel, B.: A proof that the ARX cipher Salsa20 is secure against differential cryptanalysis. IACR Cryptology ePrint Archive, p. 328 (2013)

Mur11. Murphy, S.: The return of the cryptographic boomerang. IEEE Trans. Inf. Theory **57**(4), 2517–2521 (2011)

QDW+21. Qin, L., Dong, X., Wang, X., Jia, K., Liu, Y.: Automated search oriented to key recovery on ciphers with linear key schedule applications to boomerangs in SKINNY and FORKSKINNY. IACR Trans. Symmetric Cryptol. **2021**(2), 249–291 (2021)

SHW+14. Sun, S., Hu, L., Wang, P., Qiao, K., Ma, X., Song, L.: Automatic security evaluation and (related-key) differential characteristic search: application to SIMON, PRESENT, LBlock, DES(L) and other bit-oriented block ciphers. In: Sarkar, P., Iwata, T. (eds.) ASIACRYPT 2014, Part I. LNCS, vol. 8873, pp. 158–178. Springer, Heidelberg (2014). https://doi.org/10.1007/978-3-662-45611-8_9

SQH19. Song, L., Qin, X., Lei, H.: Boomerang connectivity table revisited: application to SKINNY and AES. IACR Trans. Symmetric Cryptol. **2019**(1), 118–141 (2019)

SSD+18. Shi, D., Sun, S., Derbez, P., Todo, Y., Sun, B., Hu, L.: Programming the Demirci-Selçuk meet-in-the-middle attack with constraints. In: Peyrin, T., Galbraith, S. (eds.) ASIACRYPT 2018, Part II. LNCS, vol. 11273, pp. 3–34. Springer, Cham (2018). https://doi.org/10.1007/978-3-030-03329-3_1

SYC+24. Song, L., Yang, Q., Chen, Y., Hu, L., Weng, J.: Probabilistic extensions: a one-step framework for finding rectangle attacks and beyond. Cryptology ePrint Archive, Paper 2024/344 (2024). https://eprint.iacr.org/2024/344

SYL23. Song, L., Yang, Q., Liu, H.: Revisiting the differential meet-in-the-middle cryptanalysis. IACR Cryptology ePrint Archive, p. 1302 (2023)

SZY+22. Song, L., et al.: Optimizing rectangle attacks: a unified and generic framework for key recovery. In: Agrawal, S., Lin, D. (eds.) ASIACRYPT 2022, Part I. Lecture Notes in Computer Science, vol. 13791, pp. 410–440. Springer, Cham (2022). https://doi.org/10.1007/978-3-031-22963-3_14

Wag99. Wagner, D.: The boomerang attack. In: Knudsen, L. (ed.) FSE 1999. LNCS, vol. 1636, pp. 156–170. Springer, Heidelberg (1999). https://doi.org/10.1007/3-540-48519-8_12

ZDC+21. Zong, R., Dong, X., Chen, H., Luo, Y., Wang, S., Li, Z.: Towards key-recovery-attack friendly distinguishers: application to GIFT-128. IACR Trans. Symmetric Cryptol. **2021**(1), 156–184 (2021)

ZDJ19. Zhao, B., Dong, X., Jia, K.: New related-TWEAKEY boomerang and rectangle attacks on Deoxys-BC including BDT effect. IACR Trans. Symmetric Cryptol. pp. 121–151 (2019)

ZDM+20. Zhao, B., Dong, X., Meier, W., Jia, K., Wang, G.: Generalized related-key rectangle attacks on block ciphers with linear key schedule: applications to SKINNY and GIFT. Des. Codes Crypt. **88**(6), 1103–1126 (2020)

Massive Superpoly Recovery
with a Meet-in-the-Middle Framework
Improved Cube Attacks on TRIVIUM and Kreyvium

Jiahui He[1,3], Kai Hu[1,3,4], Hao Lei[1,3], and Meiqin Wang[1,2,3(✉)]

[1] School of Cyber Science and Technology, Shandong University, Qingdao, Shandong, China
{hejiahui2020,leihao}@mail.sdu.edu.cn, {kai.hu,mqwang}@sdu.edu.cn
[2] Quan Cheng Shandong Laboratory, Jinan, China
[3] Key Laboratory of Cryptologic Technology and Information Security, Ministry of Education, Shandong University, Jinan, China
[4] School of Physical and Mathematical Sciences, Nanyang Technological University, Singapore, Singapore

Abstract. The cube attack extracts the information of secret key bits by recovering the coefficient called superpoly in the output bit with respect to a subset of plaintexts/IV, which is called a cube. While the division property provides an efficient way to detect the structure of the superpoly, superpoly recovery could still be prohibitively costly if the number of rounds is sufficiently high. In particular, Core Monomial Prediction (CMP) was proposed at ASIACRYPT 2022 as a scaled-down version of Monomial Prediction (MP), which sacrifices accuracy for efficiency but ultimately gets stuck at 848 rounds of TRIVIUM.

In this paper, we provide new insights into CMP by elucidating the algebraic meaning to the core monomial trails. We prove that it is sufficient to recover the superpoly by extracting all the core monomial trails, an approach based solely on CMP, thus demonstrating that CMP can achieve perfect accuracy as MP does. We further reveal that CMP is still MP in essence, but with variable substitutions on the target function. Inspired by the divide-and-conquer strategy that has been widely used in previous literature, we design a meet-in-the-middle (MITM) framework, in which the CMP-based approach can be embedded to achieve a speedup.

To illustrate the power of these new techniques, we apply the MITM framework to TRIVIUM, Grain-128AEAD and Kreyvium. As a result, not only can the previous computational cost of superpoly recovery be reduced (e.g., 5x faster for superpoly recovery on 192-round Grain-128AEAD), but we also succeed in recovering superpolies for up to 851 rounds of TRIVIUM and up to 899 rounds of Kreyvium. This surpasses the previous best results by respectively 3 and 4 rounds. Using the memory-efficient Möbius transform proposed at EUROCRYPT 2021, we can perform key recovery attacks on target ciphers, even though the superpoly

---

Due to page limits, all appendixes and some tables of this paper are provided in our full version [21].

M. Joye and G. Leander (Eds.): EUROCRYPT 2024, LNCS 14651, pp. 368–397, 2024.
https://doi.org/10.1007/978-3-031-58716-0_13

may contain over 2^{40} monomials. This leads to the best cube attacks on the target ciphers.

Keywords: Cube Attack · Superpoly · TRIVIUM · Grain-128AEAD · Kreyvium · Division Property · Monomial Prediction · Core Monomial Prediction

1   Introduction

Cube Attack. Cube attack was proposed by Dinar and Shamir [13] at EURO-CRYPT 2009 and has become one of the general cryptanalytic techniques against symmetric ciphers. Since its proposal, it has been applied to analyze various symmetric ciphers [4,12,14,17,25,27,30,34,36]. In particular, against the Ascon cipher [15] that is selected by NIST for future standardization of the lightweight cryptography, the cube attack shows outstanding effectiveness [5,28,32,33]. The cube attack exploits the fact that each output bit of a cipher can be expressed as a Boolean function of the key bits and plaintext/IV bits. For a randomly chosen set I of indices of the plaintext/IV bits, we can form a monomial t_I as the product of the bits indexed by I. After fixing the plaintext/IV bits outside of I to constant values, we attempt to recover the polynomial related to key bits, called *superpoly*, that is multiplied by t_I in the output bit. If the superpoly is obtained, the value of the superpoly can be computed by summing over a structure called *cube*, denoted by C_I, which consists of all possible combinations of values that those plaintext/IV bits indexed by I can take. Subsequently, the information of key bits may be deduced by solving the equation built from the value of the superpoly.

Division Property. The original division property was proposed at EURO-CRYPT 2015 [42] as a generalization of the integral property. By tracking the integral characteristics more accurately with the division property, the long-standing cipher MISTY1 was broken theoretically for the first time [41]. At FSE 2016, the word-based division property was refined into bit-based division property [44], with which the experimentally discovered integral characteristics for bit-based block cipher SIMON32 and SIMECK32 are proved for the first time. The corresponding MILP model for deducing the division property was proposed by Xiang et al. [50] at ASIACRYPT 2016, where the propagation rules of basic operations are encoded as linear equalities. This MILP method has been used to improve the integral attack against many other ciphers [18,37,38,47].

Exact Superpoly Recovery. Initially, the cube attack treats the target cipher as a black box [13,17,31], and the structure of the superpoly can only be detected by experimental tests, thus limiting the superpoly to simple forms (e.g., linear or quadratic). Later, the Conventional Bit-based Division Property [44] was introduced into the cube attack [43], so that those secret variables that are not involved in the superpoly could be efficiently identified. In the same year, Liu et al. [29] discovered constant superpolies with the numeric mapping technique.

When determining whether a monomial exists in the superpoly, however, the bit-based division property may produce false positives, so a further series of work was carried out to improve its accuracy. In [48], Wang et al. took the cancellation of constant 1 bits into account and proposed the flag technique to improve the precision of the bit-based division property. At ASIACRYPT 2019, Wang et al. [49] recovered the exact superpoly for the first time with the pruning technique combined with the three-subset division property. However, this technique is limited by its assumption that almost all elements in the 1-subset can be pruned. The inaccuracy problem was finally resolved by Hao et al. in [20], where the unknown subset was discarded and the cancellation of the 1-subset vectors was transformed into the parity of the number of division trails. This new variant of division property is called three-subset division property without unknown subset (3SDPwoU), which is interpreted as the so-called monomial prediction (MP) from a purely algebraic viewpoint [24]. The MILP model of MP can be further optimized if we represent the propagation of MP as a directed graph [10]. Both the MP and 3SDPwoU will encounter a bottleneck if the number of division trails exceeds the upper limit of the number of solutions that can be enumerated by an MILP solver. To this end, Hu et al. [23] proposed an improved framework called *nested monomial prediction* to recover massive superpolies, which can be viewed as a recursive application of the divide-and-conquer strategy. Recently, He et al. [22] proposed the core monomial prediction (CMP), which is claimed to sacrifice accuracy for efficiency compared to MP, thus significantly reducing the computational cost of superpoly recovery.

Motivation. MP can achieve perfect accuracy because we can determine whether a monomial appears in the output bit by evaluating the parity of the number of monomial trails, but what information beyond the existence can be brought to the table by core monomial trails remains unknown. Even in [22], the authors only exploit the existence of a core monomial trail, but do not show how we can benefit from all core monomial trails. Also, we notice that the definition of CMP naturally lends itself to forward propagations, i.e., derivation from round 0 to higher rounds, while recovering the superpoly with MP does not have such a property, because it does not impose any constraints on the secret variables. Forward propagation often implies the possibility of improving accuracy and efficiency, as in the pruning technique [49] where the division property was propagated and filtered from the bottom up round by round.

Our Contributions. This paper aims to recover superpolies for more initialization rounds of stream ciphers, for which we propose purely CMP-based approach and framework to improve the efficiency of superpoly recovery.

- *Refinement of CMP theory: new CMP-based approach.* It was believed in previous works that CMP is a scaled-down version of MP that sacrifices accuracy for efficiency. However, in this paper, we prove that CMP is also perfectly accurate, as the three-subset division property without unknown subset and monomial prediction, which refines the division property family. After investigating how each core monomial trail contributes to the composition of the superpoly, we demonstrate that it is sufficient to recover the exact superpoly by extracting all core monomial trails.

– *Meet-in-the-middle (MITM) framework.* Inspired by the divide-and-conquer strategy, we show that it is possible to split a complex problem of superpoly recovery into multiple simpler problems of superpoly recovery, by performing forward or backward propagation of CMP. By using these two types of propagation interchangeably and recursively, we can embed our CMP-based approach into an MITM framework to further achieve a speedup.

Since it has been shown in [22] that the MILP model for CMP is simpler than that for MP, we claim that our purely CMP-based approach and framework perform better than the method in [22] that combines CMP and MP. The most intuitive evidence for this is that we can reproduce previous superpolies at a much smaller computational cost. For TRIVIUM, we halve the time it took to recover the superpolies (see [21, Table 6]); for 192-round Grain-128AEAD, we reduce the time of superpoly recovery to about $\frac{1}{5}$ of the original (see Sect. 5.2).

Notably, our MITM framework enables us to extend the number of initialization rounds of superpoly recovery for several prominent ciphers, including TRIVIUM (ISO/IEC standard [1,3]) and Kreyvium (designed for Fully Homomorphic Encryption [8]). Ultimately, we succeed in recovering the superpolies for up to 851-round TRIVIUM and up to 899-round Kreyvium, extending the previous best results by 3 and 4 rounds, respectively. With the help of the memory-efficient Möbius transform proposed at EUROCRYPT 2021 [11], we can utilize the recovered superpolies to perform key recovery at a complexity lower than exhaustive search, leading to the best results of cube attacks against target ciphers.

The summary of our cube attack results are provided in Table 1. The source codes for superpoly recovery, as well as some recovered superpolies, can be found in our anonymous git repository

$$\text{https://github.com/viocently/sdfkjxu192lc78-s0}.$$

2   Cube Attack and Monomial Prediction

2.1   Notations and Definitions

In this paper, we use bold italic or Greek letters to represent binary vectors. For a binary vector $x \in \mathbb{F}_2^m$, its ith bit is represented by $x[i]$; the Hamming weight of x is calculated as $wt(x) = \sum_{i=0}^{m-1} x[i]$; the indices of ones in x are represented by the set $\text{Ind}[x] = \{i \mid x[i] = 1\}$. Given two binary vectors $x \in \mathbb{F}_2^m$ and $u \in \mathbb{F}_2^m$, we use x^u to represent $\prod_{i=0}^{m-1} x[i]^{u[i]}$; $x[u] = \left(x[i_0], \ldots, x[i_{wt(u)-1}]\right) \in \mathbb{F}_2^{wt(u)}$ denotes a sub-vector of x with respect to u, where $i_0, \ldots, i_{wt(u)-1}$ are elements of $\text{Ind}[u]$ in ascending order. We define $x \succeq u$ (resp. $x \succ u$) if $x[i] \geq u[i]$ (resp. $x[i] > u[i]$) for all i and $x \preceq u$ (resp. $x \prec u$) if $x[i] \leq u[i]$ (resp. $x[i] < u[i]$) for all i. The concatenation of x and u is denoted by $x\|u$. The bitwise operations AND,OR,XOR,NOT are denoted by $\wedge, \vee, \oplus, \neg$ respectively and can be applied

Table 1. Summary of the key recovery attacks on TRIVIUM and Kreyvium

Cipher	Rounds	#Cube*	Cube size	Attack type	Data	Time	Reference
TRIVIUM	672	63	12	Cube	$2^{18.6}$	2^{17}	[13]
	709	80	22–23	Cube	2^{23}	$2^{29.14}$	[31]
	767	35	28–31	Cube	2^{31}	2^{45}	[13]
	784	42	30–33	Cube	2^{33}	2^{39}	[17]
	799	18	32–37	Cube	2^{38}	2^{62}	[17]
	802	8	34–37	Cube	2^{37}	2^{72}	[51]
	805	42	32–38	Cube	2^{38}	$2^{41.4}$	[52]
	805	28	28	Correlation Cube	2^{28}	2^{73}	[30]
	806	16	34–37	Cube	$2^{38.64}$	2^{64}	[52]
	806	29	34–37	Cube	2^{39}	2^{39}	[40]
	808	37	39–41	Cube	2^{44}	$2^{44.58}$	[40]
	810	39	40–42	Cube	2^{44}	$2^{44.17}$	[26]
	815	35	44–46	Cube	2^{47}	$2^{47.32}$	[9]
	820	30	48–51	Cube	2^{53}	$2^{53.17}$	[9]
	820†	2^{13}	38	Correlation Cube	2^{51}	2^{60}	[45]
	825	31	49–52	Cube	2^{53}	$2^{53.09}$	[26]
	825†	2^{12}	41	Correlation Cube	2^{53}	2^{60}	[45]
	830†	2^{13}	41	Correlation Cube	2^{54}	2^{60}	[45]
	832	1	72	Cube	2^{72}	2^{79}	[43, 49]
	835	41	35	Correlation Cube	2^{35}	2^{75}	[30]
	840	1	78	Cube	2^{78}	$2^{79.6}$	[20]
	840	3	75	Cube	$2^{76.6}$	$2^{77.8}$	[24]
	840	6	47–62	Cube	2^{62}	$2^{76.32}$	[23]
	841	1	78	Cube	2^{78}	$2^{79.6}$	[20]
	841	2	76	Cube	2^{77}	$2^{78.6}$	[24]
	841	3	56–76	Cube	2^{76}	2^{78}	[23]
	842	1	78	Cube	2^{78}	$2^{79.6}$	[20]
	842	2	76	Cube	2^{77}	$2^{78.6}$	[24]
	842	3	56–76	Cube	2^{76}	2^{78}	[23]
	843	2	78	Cube	2^{78}	$2^{79.6}$	[40]
	843	5	56–76	Cube	2^{56}	2^{77}	[23]
	844	2	54–55	Cube	2^{56}	2^{78}	[23]
	845	2	54–55	Cube	2^{56}	2^{78}	[23]
	846	6	51–54	Cube	2^{51}	2^{79}	[22]
	847	2	52–53	Cube	2^{52}	2^{79}	[22]
	848	1	52	Cube	2^{52}	2^{79}	[22]
	849	**2**	**44**	**Cube**	$\mathbf{2^{44}}$	$\mathbf{2^{79}}$	**Sect. 5.1**
	850	**1**	**44**	**Cube**	$\mathbf{2^{44}}$	$\mathbf{2^{79}}$	**Sect. 5.1**
	851	**1**	**44**	**Cube**	$\mathbf{2^{44}}$	$\mathbf{2^{79}}$	**Sect. 5.1**
Kreyvium	≤ 893	-	≤ 119	Cube	$\le 2^{119}$	$\le 2^{127}$	[19, 20, 40, 43, 48]
	894	1	119	Cube	2^{119}	2^{127}	[23]
	895	1	120	Cube	2^{120}	2^{127}	[22]
	896	**2**	**123–124**	**Cube**	$\mathbf{2^{123}}$	$\mathbf{2^{127}}$	**Sect. 5.3**
	897	**1**	**124**	**Cube**	$\mathbf{2^{124}}$	$\mathbf{2^{127}}$	**Sect. 5.3**
	898*	2	126	Cube	2^{127}	$2^{127.58}$	[16]
	898	**1**	**124**	**Cube**	$\mathbf{2^{124}}$	$\mathbf{2^{127}}$	**Sect. 5.3**
	899*	1	126	Cube	2^{126}	$2^{127.58}$	[16]
	899	**1**	**124**	**Cube**	$\mathbf{2^{124}}$	$\mathbf{2^{127}}$	**Sect. 5.3**
	900*	1	126	Cube	2^{126}	$2^{127.58}$	[16]

* #Cube represents the number of cubes whose superpolies are recovered, but this may not be equal to the number of cubes eventually used in the key recovery attack.
† The 820-, 825- and 830-round attacks in [45] work for only $2^{79.8}$, $2^{79.7}$ and $2^{79.3}$ of the keys in the key space, respectively.
* We notice that after our submission, the superpolies of up to 900 rounds of Kreyvium have been recovered in [16], where the complexity analysis is based on the concept of implementation dependency. This leads to the cube attacks against up to 900 rounds of Kreyvium.

to bits or binary vectors. As a special case, we use $\mathbf{0}$ and $\mathbf{1}$ to refer to the all-zero vector and the all-one vector, respectively.

We add subscripts to distinguish n binary vectors that use the same letter (e.g., $\boldsymbol{x}_0, \ldots, \boldsymbol{x}_{n-1}$) and superscripts to represent the binary vectors associated with a specific number of rounds (e.g., $\boldsymbol{x}^i$ is a binary vector at round i). For clarity, we will use $\pi(\boldsymbol{x}, \boldsymbol{u})$ instead of $\boldsymbol{x}^{\boldsymbol{u}}$ when both $\boldsymbol{x}$ and $\boldsymbol{u}$ have superscripts or subscripts.

When introducing a concrete MILP model, we use regular italic letters to represent MILP variables, and similarly we add superscripts to denote the number of rounds if they correspond to a certain round and add subscripts to distinguish them if they use a same letter.

Let $f : \mathbb{F}_2^n \to \mathbb{F}_2$ be a Boolean function whose *algebraic normal form* (ANF) is represented as $f(\boldsymbol{x}) = \bigoplus_{\boldsymbol{u} \in \mathbb{F}_2^n} a_{\boldsymbol{u}} \boldsymbol{x}^{\boldsymbol{u}}$, where $a_{\boldsymbol{u}} \in \mathbb{F}_2$ and $\boldsymbol{x} \in \mathbb{F}_2^n$. $\boldsymbol{x}^{\boldsymbol{u}}$ is called a monomial. We say a monomial $\boldsymbol{x}^{\boldsymbol{u}}$ appears in f, if the coefficient of $\boldsymbol{x}^{\boldsymbol{u}}$ in f is 1, i.e., $a_{\boldsymbol{u}} = 1$, and we denote this case by $\boldsymbol{x}^{\boldsymbol{u}} \to f$; otherwise, we denote the absence of $\boldsymbol{x}^{\boldsymbol{u}}$ in f by $\boldsymbol{x}^{\boldsymbol{u}} \nrightarrow f$.

Let $\boldsymbol{f} : \mathbb{F}_2^n \to \mathbb{F}_2^m$ be a vectorial Boolean function with $\boldsymbol{x}$ and $\boldsymbol{y}$ being the input and output, respectively. Given a monomial $\boldsymbol{y}^{\boldsymbol{v}}$ of $\boldsymbol{y}$, we can derive a Boolean function g of $\boldsymbol{x}$ by taking $\boldsymbol{y}^{\boldsymbol{v}}$ as the output of g. In the remainder of the paper, notations of the form $\boldsymbol{y}^{\boldsymbol{v}}$ may represent either a monomial of $\boldsymbol{y}$ or the Boolean function g derived from it, depending on the context. We then write $\boldsymbol{x}^{\boldsymbol{u}} \to \boldsymbol{y}^{\boldsymbol{v}}$ if $\boldsymbol{x}^{\boldsymbol{u}} \to g$; otherwise we write $\boldsymbol{x}^{\boldsymbol{u}} \nrightarrow \boldsymbol{y}^{\boldsymbol{v}}$. The ANF of g is denoted by $\mathsf{Expr}\,\langle \boldsymbol{y}^{\boldsymbol{v}}, \boldsymbol{x} \rangle$, which represents a Boolean polynomial of $\boldsymbol{x}$ determined by $\boldsymbol{y}^{\boldsymbol{v}}$. For a polynomial p of $\boldsymbol{y}$, $\mathsf{Expr}\,\langle p, \boldsymbol{x} \rangle$ is defined as the summation of $\mathsf{Expr}\,\langle \boldsymbol{y}^{\boldsymbol{v}}, \boldsymbol{x} \rangle$ over all monomials $\boldsymbol{y}^{\boldsymbol{v}}$ appearing in p. We would like to point out that when we use above notations, we may not give $\boldsymbol{f}$ explicitly, so the readers should be able to derive $\boldsymbol{f}$ from the context on their own.

2.2 Cube Attack

The cube attack was proposed by Dinur and Shamir at EUROCRYPT 2009 [13] as an extension of the higher-order differential attack. Given a cipher with secret variables $\boldsymbol{k} \in \mathbb{F}_2^n$ and public variables $\boldsymbol{v} \in \mathbb{F}_2^m$ being the input, any output bit can be represented as a Boolean function of $\boldsymbol{k}$ and $\boldsymbol{v}$, denoted by $f(\boldsymbol{k}, \boldsymbol{v})$.

Given $I \subseteq \{0, \ldots, m-1\}$ as a set of indices of the public variables, we can uniquely express $f(\boldsymbol{k}, \boldsymbol{v})$ as

$$f(\boldsymbol{k}, \boldsymbol{v}) = p(\boldsymbol{k}, \boldsymbol{v}) \cdot t_I + q(\boldsymbol{k}, \boldsymbol{v}),$$

where $t_I = \prod_{i \in I} v[i]$, $p(\boldsymbol{k}, \boldsymbol{v})$ only relates to $v[s]$'s ($s \notin I$) and the secret variables $\boldsymbol{k}$, and each monomial appearing in $q(\boldsymbol{k}, \boldsymbol{v})$ misses at least one variable from $\{v[i] \mid i \in I\}$. I is called *cube indices*, whose size is denoted by $|I|$. If we assign all the possible combinations of 0/1 values to $v[j]$'s ($j \in I$) and leave $v[s]$'s ($s \notin I$) undetermined, we can determine a set C_I from I, which is called *cube*. The coefficient $p(\boldsymbol{k}, \boldsymbol{v})$ is called the *superpoly* of the cube C_I or the cube indices

I, which can be computed by summing the output bit $f(\boldsymbol{k}, \boldsymbol{v})$ over the cube, namely

$$p(\boldsymbol{k}, \boldsymbol{v}) = \sum_{\boldsymbol{v} \in C_I} f(\boldsymbol{k}, \boldsymbol{v}).$$

If we set the non-cube variables $v[s]$'s ($s \notin I$) to constants, the coefficient $p(\boldsymbol{k}, \boldsymbol{v})$ reduces to a polynomial that only relates to $\boldsymbol{k}$, which we denote by $\mathsf{Coe}\langle f, t_I \rangle$.

The typical process for carrying out a cube attack can be summarized as follows:

- In the offline phase, the attacker recovers superpolies for selected cubes of the cipher without knowledge of the secret key.
- In the online phase, the attacker exploits the output bits generated under the unknown key to evaluate the recovered superpolies. This allows building a system of equations in the key bits.
- Solving this system of equations recovers part of the key. The remaining key bits can be obtained through an exhaustive search.

The core idea is that the successful recovery of superpolies allows to construct a solvable system of equations that leak key bits, which can break the security of the cipher by facilitating full key recovery.

2.3   Monomial Prediction (MP)

Let $\boldsymbol{f} : \mathbb{F}_2^{n_0} \rightarrow \mathbb{F}_2^{n_r}$ be a composite vectorial Boolean function built by composition from a sequence of vectorial Boolean functions $\boldsymbol{f}^i : \mathbb{F}_2^{n_i} \rightarrow \mathbb{F}_2^{n_{i+1}}, 0 \leq i \leq r-1$, i.e.,

$$\boldsymbol{f} = \boldsymbol{f}^{r-1} \circ \boldsymbol{f}^{r-2} \circ \cdots \circ \boldsymbol{f}^0,$$

where $\boldsymbol{x}^i \in \mathbb{F}_2^{n_i}$ and $\boldsymbol{x}^{i+1} \in \mathbb{F}_2^{n_{i+1}}$ are the input and output of $\boldsymbol{f}^i$, respectively.

Given a starting number r_s and an ending number r_e with $0 \leq r_s < r_e \leq r$, let $r' = r_e - r_s$. Given $r' + 1$ monomials $\pi(\boldsymbol{x}^{r_s}, \boldsymbol{u}^{r_s}), \cdots, \pi(\boldsymbol{x}^{r_e}, \boldsymbol{u}^{r_e})$, if for each $j, r_s \leq j \leq r_e - 1$ we have $\pi(\boldsymbol{x}^j, \boldsymbol{u}^j) \rightarrow \pi(\boldsymbol{x}^{j+1}, \boldsymbol{u}^{j+1})$, we write the connection of these transitions as

$$\pi(\boldsymbol{x}^{r_s}, \boldsymbol{u}^{r_s}) \rightarrow \pi(\boldsymbol{x}^{r_s+1}, \boldsymbol{u}^{r_s+1}) \rightarrow \cdots \rightarrow \pi(\boldsymbol{x}^{r_e}, \boldsymbol{u}^{r_e}),$$

which is called an r'-round *monomial trail*. If there exists at least one monomial trail from $\pi(\boldsymbol{x}^{r_s}, \boldsymbol{u}^{r_s})$ to $\pi(\boldsymbol{x}^{r_e}, \boldsymbol{u}^{r_e})$, we write $\pi(\boldsymbol{x}^{r_s}, \boldsymbol{u}^{r_s}) \rightsquigarrow \pi(\boldsymbol{x}^{r_e}, \boldsymbol{u}^{r_e})$. The set containing all the monomial trails from $\pi(\boldsymbol{x}^{r_s}, \boldsymbol{u}^{r_s})$ to $\pi(\boldsymbol{x}^{r_e}, \boldsymbol{u}^{r_e})$ is denoted by $\pi(\boldsymbol{x}^{r_s}, \boldsymbol{u}^{r_s}) \bowtie \pi(\boldsymbol{x}^{r_e}, \boldsymbol{u}^{r_e})$, whose size is represented as $|\pi(\boldsymbol{x}^{r_s}, \boldsymbol{u}^{r_s}) \bowtie \pi(\boldsymbol{x}^{r_e}, \boldsymbol{u}^{r_e})|$. If there is no trail from $\pi(\boldsymbol{x}^{r_s}, \boldsymbol{u}^{r_s})$ to $\pi(\boldsymbol{x}^{r_e}, \boldsymbol{u}^{r_e})$, we denote it by $\pi(\boldsymbol{x}^{r_s}, \boldsymbol{u}^{r_s}) \not\rightsquigarrow \pi(\boldsymbol{x}^{r_e}, \boldsymbol{u}^{r_e})$ and accordingly we have $|\pi(\boldsymbol{x}^{r_s}, \boldsymbol{u}^{r_s}) \bowtie \pi(\boldsymbol{x}^{r_e}, \boldsymbol{u}^{r_e})| = 0$.

The monomial prediction focuses on how to determine accurately whether $\pi(\boldsymbol{x}^{r_s}, \boldsymbol{u}^{r_s}) \rightarrow \pi(\boldsymbol{x}^{r_e}, \boldsymbol{u}^{r_e})$ for two given monomials $\pi(\boldsymbol{x}^{r_s}, \boldsymbol{u}^{r_s})$ and $\pi(\boldsymbol{x}^{r_e}, \boldsymbol{u}^{r_e})$, and the following theorem relates this problem to the number of monomial trails.

Theorem 1 ([24, **Proposition 1**]). *Use the notations defined above. We have* $\pi(\boldsymbol{x}^{r_s}, \boldsymbol{u}^{r_s}) \rightarrow \pi(\boldsymbol{x}^{r_e}, \boldsymbol{u}^{r_e})$ *if and only if*

$$|\pi(\boldsymbol{x}^{r_s}, \boldsymbol{u}^{r_s}) \bowtie \pi(\boldsymbol{x}^{r_e}, \boldsymbol{u}^{r_e})| \equiv 1 \pmod{2}.$$

Theorem 2 (Superpoly Recovery [24]). *Let f be the output bit of a cipher represented as a monomial of the output state, which is generated from the secret variables $\boldsymbol{k}$ and the public variables $\boldsymbol{x}$ through a series of round functions. Given the cube indices I and $t_I = \prod_{i \in I} v[i]$, set the non-cube variables $v[s]$'s ($s \notin I$) to 0, then*

$$\mathsf{Coe}\langle f, t_I \rangle = \sum_{|\boldsymbol{k}^w t_I \bowtie f| \equiv 1 \pmod{2}} \boldsymbol{k}^w,$$

where $\boldsymbol{k}^w t_I \bowtie f$ is the set of monomial trails that propagate $\boldsymbol{k}^w t_I$ to f through the round functions.

Propagation Rules and MILP Models. Since any symmetric primitive can be constructed from basic operations like XOR, AND and COPY, it is sufficient to define propagation rules for these basic functions. By listing all input-output pairs that exhibit monomial prediction, and encoding these pairs as linear inequalities [6,35,39], we can model the propagation of monomial prediction in a way that is amenable to efficient MILP solving. We provide the concrete propagation rules and MILP models in [21, Sup.Mat. A]. In this paper, we choose the state-of-the-art commercial MILP solver, Gurobi [2], to solve our MILP models.

3 Recalling Core Monomial Prediction (CMP)

This paper targets an r-round cipher represented by a parameterized vectorial Boolean function $\boldsymbol{f}(\boldsymbol{k}, \boldsymbol{v})$ with secret variables $\boldsymbol{k}$ and public variables $\boldsymbol{v}$ being the input. $\boldsymbol{f}$ can be written as the composition of a sequence of simple round functions whose ANFs are known, i.e.,

$$\boldsymbol{f}(\boldsymbol{k}, \boldsymbol{v}) = \boldsymbol{f}^{r-1} \circ \boldsymbol{f}^{r-2} \circ \cdots \circ \boldsymbol{f}^0, \tag{1}$$

where $\boldsymbol{f}^i, 0 \leq i \leq r - 1$, represents the round function at round i, with input variables $\boldsymbol{x}^i \in \mathbb{F}_2^{n_i}$ and output variables $\boldsymbol{x}^{i+1} \in \mathbb{F}_2^{n_{i+1}}$. The initial state $\boldsymbol{x}^0$ is loaded with $\boldsymbol{k}$, $\boldsymbol{v}$, constant 1 bits and constant 0 bits. The output bit z of the cipher is defined as the sum of several monomials of $\boldsymbol{x}^r$. After choosing the cube indices I and setting the non-cube variables to constants (not necessarily constant 0), we aim to efficiently compute $\mathsf{Coe}\langle z, t_I \rangle$, where $t_I = \prod_{i \in I} v[i]$. We first recall some details about the core monomial prediction proposed in [22].

Superpoly Recovery Method in [22]. Since z is the sum of several monomials of $\boldsymbol{x}^r$, we consider computing $\mathsf{Coe}\langle \pi(\boldsymbol{x}^r, \boldsymbol{u}^r), t_I \rangle$ for each $\pi(\boldsymbol{x}^r, \boldsymbol{u}^r)$ satisfying $\pi(\boldsymbol{x}^r, \boldsymbol{u}^r) \rightarrow z$. There are two steps for computing $\mathsf{Coe}\langle \pi(\boldsymbol{x}^r, \boldsymbol{u}^r), t_I \rangle$ in [22]. In the first step, the authors choose a fixed middle round r_m and recover all $\pi(\boldsymbol{x}^{r_m}, \boldsymbol{u}^{r_m})$'s that satisfy: (A) $\pi(\boldsymbol{x}^{r_m}, \boldsymbol{u}^{r_m}) \rightarrow \pi(\boldsymbol{x}^r, \boldsymbol{u}^r)$, (B) $\exists \boldsymbol{w}$ such that

$k^w t_I \rightsquigarrow \pi(\boldsymbol{x}^{r_m}, \boldsymbol{u}^{r_m})$. In the second step, compute $\mathsf{Coe}\langle \pi(\boldsymbol{x}^{r_m}, \boldsymbol{u}^{r_m}), t_I \rangle$ by MP. The sum of all $\mathsf{Coe}\langle \pi(\boldsymbol{x}^{r_m}, \boldsymbol{u}^{r_m}), t_I \rangle$'s is exactly $\mathsf{Coe}\langle \pi(\boldsymbol{x}^r, \boldsymbol{u}^r), t_I \rangle$. In [22], Condition B was characterized by a focus on those bits in $\pi(\boldsymbol{x}^{r_m}, \boldsymbol{u}^{r_m})$ that relate to cube variables, thus leading to the flag technique.

Flag Technique for CMP [22]. Let b be one bit of an intermediate state $\boldsymbol{x}^i$, b can have three types of flags:

1. If b is 0, denote its flag by $b.F = 0_c$;
2. Otherwise, express b as the polynomial of $\boldsymbol{k}$ and cube variables, if none of cube bits appear in b, denote its flag by $b.F = 1_c$;
3. Otherwise, denote its flag by $b.F = \delta$.

The flags of all bits in $\boldsymbol{x}^i$ are denoted by a vector $\boldsymbol{x}^i.F = (x^i[0].F, \ldots, x^i[n_i - 1].F)$, which can be calculated from $\boldsymbol{x}^0.F$ by the following operation rules:

$$1_c \times x = x \times 1_c = x \qquad 1_c \oplus 1_c = 1_c \qquad 0_c \oplus x = x \oplus 0_c = x$$
$$0_c \times x = x \times 0_c = 0_c \qquad \delta \oplus x = x \oplus \delta = \delta \qquad \delta \times \delta = \delta$$

where x can be any of $\{0_c, 1_c, \delta\}$.

Remark 1. Note that the flag technique for CMP is essentially different from the one for the two-subset division property used in [48]. The most significant difference lies in how to process the secret key bits. In the flag technique for CMP, the secret key bits are regarded as 1_c bits and it is an unalienable part of the CMP technique, whereas in [48], the secret keys are treated as free variables and the flag technique is only a skill to improve the precision and efficiency of the division property.

Definition of Core Monomial Trail [22]. Let $\mathsf{Ind}[\boldsymbol{M}^{i,\delta}] = \{j \mid x^i[j].F = \delta\}$; $\mathsf{Ind}[\boldsymbol{M}^{i,1_c}] = \{j \mid x^i[j].F = 1_c\}$; $\mathsf{Ind}[\boldsymbol{M}^{i,0_c}] = \{j \mid x^i[j].F = 0_c\}$. The vectors $\boldsymbol{M}^{i,\delta}, \boldsymbol{M}^{i,1_c}, \boldsymbol{M}^{i,0_c}$ are called *flag masks*. Given two monomials $\pi(\boldsymbol{x}^{r_s}, \boldsymbol{t}^{r_s})$ and $\pi(\boldsymbol{x}^{r_e}, \boldsymbol{t}^{r_e})$ for $0 \le r_s < r_e \le r$, with $\boldsymbol{t}^{r_s} \preceq \boldsymbol{M}^{r_s,\delta}$ and $\boldsymbol{t}^{r_e} \preceq \boldsymbol{M}^{r_e,\delta}$, if there exists a monomial $\pi(\boldsymbol{x}^{r_s}, \boldsymbol{u}^{r_s})$ such that $\boldsymbol{u}^{r_s} \wedge \boldsymbol{M}^{r_s,\delta} = \boldsymbol{t}^{r_s}$, $\boldsymbol{u}^{r_s} \wedge \boldsymbol{M}^{r_s,0_c} = \boldsymbol{0}$ and $\pi(\boldsymbol{x}^{r_s}, \boldsymbol{u}^{r_s}) \to \pi(\boldsymbol{x}^{r_e}, \boldsymbol{t}^{r_e})$, then we say $\pi(\boldsymbol{x}^{r_s}, \boldsymbol{t}^{r_s})$ can propagate to $\pi(\boldsymbol{x}^{r_e}, \boldsymbol{t}^{r_e})$ under the *core monomial prediction*, denoted by $\pi(\boldsymbol{x}^{r_s}, \boldsymbol{t}^{r_s}) \xrightarrow{\mathcal{C}} \pi(\boldsymbol{x}^{r_e}, \boldsymbol{t}^{r_e})$; otherwise we denote it by $\pi(\boldsymbol{x}^{r_s}, \boldsymbol{t}^{r_s}) \xnrightarrow{\mathcal{C}} \pi(\boldsymbol{x}^{r_e}, \boldsymbol{t}^{r_e})$.

Let $r' = r_e - r_s$. We call the connection of r' transitions $\pi(\boldsymbol{x}^{r_s}, \boldsymbol{t}^{r_s}) \xrightarrow{\mathcal{C}} \pi(\boldsymbol{x}^{r_s+1}, \boldsymbol{t}^{r_s+1}) \xrightarrow{\mathcal{C}} \cdots \xrightarrow{\mathcal{C}} \pi(\boldsymbol{x}^{r_e}, \boldsymbol{t}^{r_e})$ an r'-round *core monomial trail*. If there is at least one r'-round core monomial trail from $\pi(\boldsymbol{x}^{r_s}, \boldsymbol{t}^{r_s})$ to $\pi(\boldsymbol{x}^{r_e}, \boldsymbol{t}^{r_e})$, we denote it by $\pi(\boldsymbol{x}^{r_s}, \boldsymbol{t}^{r_s}) \xrightsquigarrow{\mathcal{C}} \pi(\boldsymbol{x}^{r_e}, \boldsymbol{t}^{r_e})$; otherwise we write $\pi(\boldsymbol{x}^{r_s}, \boldsymbol{t}^{r_s}) \xnrightsquigarrow{\mathcal{C}} \pi(\boldsymbol{x}^{r_e}, \boldsymbol{t}^{r_e})$. The set containing all the trails from $\pi(\boldsymbol{x}^{r_s}, \boldsymbol{t}^{r_s})$ to $\pi(\boldsymbol{x}^{r_e}, \boldsymbol{t}^{r_e})$ is denoted by $\pi(\boldsymbol{x}^{r_s}, \boldsymbol{t}^{r_s}) \xbowtie{\mathcal{C}} \pi(\boldsymbol{x}^{r_e}, \boldsymbol{t}^{r_e})$. The propagation rules and MILP models of CMP are provided in [21, Sup.Mat. B]. In the propagation of CMP, the 0_c bits are excluded, the 1_c bits are treated as constants that can be ignored, thus only the δ bits are tracked.

Limitations of the CMP Theory in [22]. In [22], only the existence property of a core monomial trail was used in theory, and the CMP technique was considered as a compromised version of MP which sacrificed accuracy for efficiency. However, we observe that more information has been associated with a core monomial trail besides the existence property, which was ignored by [22]. When considering these information, CMP can be as precise as MP. To intuitively show this, let us consider a simple example.

Example 1. Consider a simple cipher $\boldsymbol{f} = \boldsymbol{f}^2 \circ \boldsymbol{f}^1 \circ \boldsymbol{f}^0$ where

$$\boldsymbol{x}^0 = (v[0], v[1], v[2], k[0], k[1], k[2], 0, 1),$$
$$\boldsymbol{x}^1 = \boldsymbol{f}^0(\boldsymbol{x}^0) = (x^0[0]x^0[1] + x^0[1]x^0[2] + x^0[1]x^0[4],$$
$$x^0[0]x^0[3] + x^0[3], x^0[4] + x^0[5], x^0[7] + x^0[6]),$$
$$\boldsymbol{x}^2 = \boldsymbol{f}^1(\boldsymbol{x}^1) = (x^1[0]x^1[2] + x^1[0]x^1[1], x^1[2], x^1[3]),$$
$$\boldsymbol{x}^3 = \boldsymbol{f}^2(\boldsymbol{x}^2) = (x^2[0]x^2[1] + x^2[0]x^2[2]).$$

Assume $t_I = v[0]v[1], v[2] = 1$ and we want to compute $\mathsf{Coe}\langle x^3[0], t_I \rangle$.

We first compute $\boldsymbol{x}^0.F = (\delta, \delta, 1_c, 1_c, 1_c, 1_c, 0_c, 1_c), \boldsymbol{x}^1.F = (\delta, \delta, 1_c, 1_c)$, $\boldsymbol{x}^2.F = (\delta, 1_c, 1_c)$ and $\boldsymbol{x}^3.F = (\delta)$. Then, we expand $x^3[0]$ into a polynomial of $\boldsymbol{x}^2$ and combine the monomials according to δ bits.

$$x^3[0] = (x^2[1] + x^2[2]) \cdot x^2[0]$$

Note that $x^2[1].F = x^2[2].F = 1.c$, we derive

$$x^3[0] = (x^2[1] + x^2[2]) \cdot x^2[0] = (1 + k[1] + k[2]) \cdot x^2[0].$$

Similarly, for $x^2[0]$ we have

$$x^2[0] = (x^1[2]) \cdot x^1[0] + x^1[0]x^1[1] = (k[1] + k[2]) \cdot x^1[0] + x^1[0]x^1[1],$$

and further for $x^1[0]$ and $x^1[0]x^1[1]$ we have

$$x^1[0] = (x^0[2] + x^0[4]) \cdot x^0[1] + x^0[0]x^0[1] = (1 + k[1]) \cdot x^0[1] + x^0[0]x^0[1],$$
$$x^1[0]x^1[1] = (x^0[2]x^0[3] + x^0[3]x^0[4]) \cdot x^0[0]x^0[1] + (x^0[2]x^0[3] + x^0[3]x^0[4]) \cdot x^0[1]$$
$$= (k[0] + k[0]k[1]) \cdot x^0[0]x^0[1] + (k[0] + k[0]k[1]) \cdot x^0[1].$$

Thus, there are two core monomial trails

$$x^0[0]x^0[1] \xrightarrow{\mathcal{C}} x^1[0] \xrightarrow{\mathcal{C}} x^2[0] \xrightarrow{\mathcal{C}} x^3[0],$$
$$x^0[0]x^0[1] \xrightarrow{\mathcal{C}} x^1[0]x^1[1] \xrightarrow{\mathcal{C}} x^2[0] \xrightarrow{\mathcal{C}} x^3[0],$$

Multiply the coefficients of each core monomial trail. We take the first core monomial trail as an example. From $x^0[0]x^0[1] \xrightarrow{\mathcal{C}} x^1[0]$, the corresponding coefficient of $x^0[0]x^0[1]$ is 1; from $x^1[0] \xrightarrow{\mathcal{C}} x^2[0]$, the corresponding coefficient of $x^1[0]$ is $k[1] + k[2]$; from $x^2[0] \xrightarrow{\mathcal{C}} x^3[0]$, the corresponding coefficient of $x^2[0]$ is $1 + k[1] + k[2]$. Thus, the first core monomial trail leads to $(1 + k[1] + k[2])(k[1] + k[2])$. Similarly, the second core monomial trail leads to $(1 + k[1] + k[2])(k[0] + k[0]k[1])$. It is easy to verify that $\mathsf{Coe}\langle x^3[0], t_I \rangle$ is just $(1 + k[1] + k[2])(k[1] + k[2]) + (1 + k[1] + k[2])(k[0] + k[0]k[1])$.

In [22], all possible concatenations of a core monomial trail of the first r_m rounds and a monomial trail of the subsequent $r - r_m$ rounds are enumerated when solving the MILP model in practice. However, the above example reveals that it is sufficient to compute $\mathsf{Coe}\langle \pi(\boldsymbol{x}^r, \boldsymbol{u}^r), t_I \rangle$ by computing all core monomial trails of the r rounds and then extracting the coefficients from each core monomial trail, where the latter step is a fully offline process independently from the MILP solver. Hence, the new method is surely more efficient than the method in [22].

4   Beyond Existence: Refinement of CMP Theory

In this section, we prove that CMP can reach perfect accuracy as MP does by developing a purely CMP-based approach for the superpoly recovery, thus addressing the limitations of the CMP theory. On this basis, we further design an MITM framework to enhance the CMP-based approach.

4.1   Extending CMP Theory Using SR Problem

In order to study the CMP theory independently from a specific cryptographic context, we start by breaking the association between flags and cube indices.

Indeterminate Flags. While the flag technique presented in Sect. 3 is defined based on the chosen cube indices I, the definition and propagation of CMP are independent of how the flags are defined. Therefore, in the rest of the paper, we drop the previous definition of flags based on cube variables, which is to say, the flag of a bit b is no longer based on representing b as a Boolean polynomial of $\boldsymbol{k}$ and cube variables. Instead, we consider flags as variables that can take values δ, 1_c and 0_c, which are referred to as *indeterminate flags*, but the operation rules remain unchanged. As a result, the flag masks become variables as well, but for $0 \le i \le r$, the requirement that $\mathsf{Ind}[\boldsymbol{M}^{i,\delta}]$, $\mathsf{Ind}[\boldsymbol{M}^{i,1_c}]$ and $\mathsf{Ind}[\boldsymbol{M}^{i,0_c}]$ form a partition of $\{0, \ldots, n_i - 1\}$ still holds.

Note that different values assigned to the flag masks can result in different propagation of CMP. Therefore, when we discuss the propagation of CMP from round r_s to round r_e for $0 \le r_s < r_e \le r$, if the values of $\boldsymbol{M}^{r_s, \delta}, \boldsymbol{M}^{r_s, 1_c}, \boldsymbol{M}^{r_s, 0_c}$ are not clear from the context, we will give specific values for $\boldsymbol{M}^{r_s, \delta}, \boldsymbol{M}^{r_s, 1_c}, \boldsymbol{M}^{r_s, 0_c}$, and implicitly assume that the values of $\boldsymbol{M}^{j, \delta}, \boldsymbol{M}^{j, 1_c}, \boldsymbol{M}^{j, 0_c}, r_s < j \le r_e$ are calculated from round r_s according to operation rules.

Extending CMP Theory with SR Problem. In the context of indeterminate flags, we analyze the reasons why the previous CMP theory is considered inaccurate. Assume the flag masks $M^{r_s,\delta}, M^{r_s,1_c}, M^{r_s,0_c}$ take the values $\alpha^{r_s,\delta}, \alpha^{r_s,1_c}, \alpha^{r_s,0_c} = \neg(\alpha^{r_s,\delta} \vee \alpha^{r_s,1_c})$. By the definition of CMP, the transition $\pi(\boldsymbol{x}^{r_s}, \boldsymbol{t}^{r_s}) \xrightarrow{\mathcal{C}} \pi(\boldsymbol{x}^{r_e}, \boldsymbol{t}^{r_e})$ emphasizes the existence of a $\boldsymbol{w} \preceq \alpha^{r_s,1_c}$ such that $\pi(\boldsymbol{x}^{r_s}, \boldsymbol{w}) \cdot \pi(\boldsymbol{x}^{r_s}, \boldsymbol{t}^{r_s}) \rightarrow \pi(\boldsymbol{x}^{r_e}, \boldsymbol{t}^{r_e})$, but does not provide explicit information about the exact value of $\boldsymbol{w}$. In other words, the definition of CMP does not give any precise information related to the exact expressions of the monomials appearing in $\mathsf{Expr}\,\langle\pi(\boldsymbol{x}^{r_e}, \boldsymbol{t}^{r_e}), \boldsymbol{x}^{r_s}\rangle$. Consequently, it may give the impression that the previous CMP theory is inaccurate.

In order to refine the CMP theory to be precise, it is necessary to capture all $\boldsymbol{w}$'s that satisfy $\boldsymbol{w} \preceq \alpha^{r_s,1_c}$ and $\pi(\boldsymbol{x}^{r_s}, \boldsymbol{w}) \cdot \pi(\boldsymbol{x}^{r_s}, \boldsymbol{t}^{r_s}) \rightarrow \pi(\boldsymbol{x}^{r_e}, \boldsymbol{t}^{r_e})$. This can be easily achieved if we can obtain the concrete expression of $\mathsf{Expr}\,\langle\pi(\boldsymbol{x}^{r_e}, \boldsymbol{t}^{r_e}), \boldsymbol{x}^{r_s}\rangle$ (e.g., when the vectorial Boolean function mapping $\boldsymbol{x}^{r_s}$ to $\boldsymbol{x}^{r_e}$ is simple). However, when $\mathsf{Expr}\,\langle\pi(\boldsymbol{x}^{r_e}, \boldsymbol{t}^{r_e}), \boldsymbol{x}^{r_s}\rangle$ is not available, the situation becomes much more complicated, which deserves further investigation, thus we formalize it as the following SR problem.

Definition 1 (SR Problem). *Let the target cipher $\boldsymbol{f}$ be as defined in Eq. (1). Given $r_s, r_e, 0 \le r_s < r_e \le r$ and the values $\alpha^{r_s,\delta}, \alpha^{r_s,1_c}, \alpha^{r_s,0_c} = \neg(\alpha^{r_s,\delta} \vee \alpha^{r_s,1_c})$ assigned to the flag masks $M^{r_s,\delta}, M^{r_s,1_c}, M^{r_s,0_c}$, for each $j, r_s < j \le r_e$, let $M^{j,\delta}, M^{j,1_c}, M^{j,0_c}$ take the values $\alpha^{j,\delta}, \alpha^{j,1_c}, \alpha^{j,0_c}$ that are calculated from $\alpha^{r_s,\delta}, \alpha^{r_s,1_c}, \alpha^{r_s,0_c}$ according to the operation rules of flags. Given two monomials $\pi(\boldsymbol{x}^{r_s}, \boldsymbol{t}^{r_s})$ and $\pi(\boldsymbol{x}^{r_e}, \boldsymbol{t}^{r_e})$ that satisfy $\boldsymbol{t}^{r_s} \preceq \alpha^{r_s,\delta}$ and $\boldsymbol{t}^{r_e} \preceq \alpha^{r_e,\delta}$, we can uniquely and symbolically express $\pi(\boldsymbol{x}^{r_e}, \boldsymbol{u}^{r_e})$ as a polynomial of $\boldsymbol{x}^{r_s}$, i.e.,*

$$\mathsf{Expr}\,\langle\pi(\boldsymbol{x}^{r_e}, \boldsymbol{t}^{r_e}), \boldsymbol{x}^{r_s}\rangle = p(\boldsymbol{x}^{r_s}[\alpha^{r_s,1_c} \vee \alpha^{r_s,0_c}]) \cdot \pi(\boldsymbol{x}^{r_s}, \boldsymbol{t}^{r_s}) + q(\boldsymbol{x}^{r_s}), \quad (2)$$

where each monomial $\pi(\boldsymbol{x}^{r_s}, \boldsymbol{u}^{r_s})$ appearing in $q(\boldsymbol{x}^{r_s})$ satisfies $\boldsymbol{u}^{r_s} \wedge \alpha^{r_s,\delta} \ne \boldsymbol{t}^{r_s}$. If we set $\boldsymbol{x}^{r_s}[\alpha^{r_s,0_c}]$ to $\boldsymbol{0}$, then the coefficient $p(\boldsymbol{x}^{r_s}[\alpha^{r_s,1_c} \vee \alpha^{r_s,0_c}])$ reduces to a polynomial that only relates to $\boldsymbol{x}^{r_s}[\alpha^{r_s,1_c}]$. The question is, what is the exact expression of this polynomial?

We use $\mathsf{SR}_{\alpha^{r_s,\delta}, \alpha^{r_s,1_c}}\langle\boldsymbol{t}^{r_e}, \boldsymbol{t}^{r_s}\rangle$ to denote a concrete instance of the SR problem, which is uniquely determined by six parameters, namely the numbers r_s, r_e of rounds, the values $\alpha^{r_s,\delta}, \alpha^{r_s,1_c}$ assigned to $M^{r_s,\delta}, M^{r_s,1_c}$ and the vectors $\boldsymbol{t}^{r_s}, \boldsymbol{t}^{r_e}$ corresponding to the monomials $\pi(\boldsymbol{x}^{r_s}, \boldsymbol{t}^{r_s}), \pi(\boldsymbol{x}^{r_e}, \boldsymbol{t}^{r_e})$. The solution of this instance, denoted by $\mathsf{Sol}_{\alpha^{r_s,\delta}, \alpha^{r_s,1_c}}\langle\boldsymbol{t}^{r_e}, \boldsymbol{t}^{r_s}\rangle$, is the coefficient $p(\boldsymbol{x}^{r_s}[\alpha^{r_s,1_c} \vee \alpha^{r_s,0_c}])$ in Eq. (2) after setting $\boldsymbol{x}^{r_s}[\alpha^{r_s,0_c}]$ to $\boldsymbol{0}$. When $\alpha^{r_s,\delta}, \alpha^{r_s,1_c}$ can be inferred from the context without ambiguity, we write $\mathsf{SR}\langle\boldsymbol{t}^{r_e}, \boldsymbol{t}^{r_s}\rangle$ and $\mathsf{Sol}\langle\boldsymbol{t}^{r_e}, \boldsymbol{t}^{r_s}\rangle$ for simplicity. Each instance $\mathsf{SR}_{\alpha^{r_s,\delta}, \alpha^{r_s,1_c}}\langle\boldsymbol{t}^{r_e}, \boldsymbol{t}^{r_s}\rangle$ uniquely corresponds to a CMP transition $\pi(\boldsymbol{x}^{r_s}, \boldsymbol{t}^{r_s}) \xrightarrow{\mathcal{C}} \pi(\boldsymbol{x}^{r_e}, \boldsymbol{t}^{r_e})$. In particular, $\mathsf{Sol}_{\alpha^{r_s,\delta}, \alpha^{r_s,1_c}}\langle\boldsymbol{t}^{r_e}, \boldsymbol{t}^{r_s}\rangle$ is exactly the sum of all $\boldsymbol{w} \preceq \alpha^{r_s,1_c}$ that satisfy $\pi(\boldsymbol{x}^{r_s}, \boldsymbol{w}) \cdot \pi(\boldsymbol{x}^{r_s}, \boldsymbol{t}^{r_s}) \rightarrow \pi(\boldsymbol{x}^{r_e}, \boldsymbol{t}^{r_e})$. When $\mathsf{Sol}_{\alpha^{r_s,\delta}, \alpha^{r_s,1_c}}\langle\boldsymbol{t}^{r_e}, \boldsymbol{t}^{r_s}\rangle$ is available, the transition $\pi(\boldsymbol{x}^{r_s}, \boldsymbol{t}^{r_s}) \xrightarrow{\mathcal{C}} \pi(\boldsymbol{x}^{r_e}, \boldsymbol{t}^{r_e})$ is considered accurate.

The SR problem can be considered as an extension of the CMP theory used to specify the precise algebraic information implied by a CMP transition. Hence, the solution of an instance $\mathsf{SR}_{\alpha^{r_s,\delta},\alpha^{r_s,1_c}}\langle t^{r_e}, t^{r_s}\rangle$ not only uniquely determines a CMP transition, but also reflects the information of exact monomials in the algebraic composition of $\mathsf{Expr}\,\langle\pi(x^{r_e}, t^{r_e}), x^{r_s}\rangle$, as stated in Lemma 1 and Lemma 2. Since these two lemmas are direct consequences of Definition 1, we omit the proofs of them here.

Lemma 1. *Letting* $\alpha^{r_s,\delta}, \alpha^{r_s,1_c}$ *be any values assigned to* $M^{r_s,\delta}, M^{r_s,1_c}$ *and* $M^{r_s,0_c} = \neg(\alpha^{r_s,\delta} \vee \alpha^{r_s,1_c})$, *for each* $j, r_s < j \leq r_e$ *we calculate the values of* $M^{j,\delta}, M^{j,1_c}, M^{j,0_c}$ *as* $\alpha^{j,\delta}, \alpha^{j,1_c}, \alpha^{j,0_c}$. *Then,* $\mathsf{Sol}\langle t^{r_e}, t^{r_s}\rangle$ *is not equal to 0 if and only if* $\pi(x^{r_s}, t^{r_s}) \xrightarrow{\mathcal{C}} \pi(x^{r_e}, t^{r_e})$.

Lemma 2. *Let the values of flag masks be defined as in Lemma 1. Given any monomial* $\pi(x^{r_e}, t^{r_e})$ *satisfying* $t^{r_e} \preceq \alpha^{r_e,\delta}$, *after setting* $x^{r_s}[\alpha^{r_s,0_c}]$ *to* $\mathbf{0}$, *if* $\mathsf{Expr}\,\langle\pi(x^{r_e}, t^{r_e}), x^{r_s}\rangle \neq 0$, *then we can uniquely express* $\pi(x^{r_e}, t^{r_e})$ *as*

$$\mathsf{Expr}\,\langle\pi(x^{r_e}, t^{r_e}), x^{r_s}\rangle = \sum_{\pi(x^{r_s}, t^{r_s}) \xrightarrow{\mathcal{C}} \pi(x^{r_e}, t^{r_e})} \mathsf{Sol}\langle t^{r_e}, t^{r_s}\rangle \cdot \pi(x^{r_s}, t^{r_s}),$$

where the summation is over all t^{r_s} *'s that satisfy* $\pi(x^{r_s}, t^{r_s}) \xrightarrow{\mathcal{C}} \pi(x^{r_e}, t^{r_e})$.

We would also like to point out that both the SR problem and MP are concerned with the presence of specific monomials in the polynomial expanded from a higher-round monomial; the only difference is that MP is concerned with whether a single monomial exists in the polynomial, whereas the SR problem is concerned with the existence of several monomials of the same form in the polynomial. For example, the instance $\mathsf{SR}_{\alpha^{r_s,\delta},\alpha^{r_s,1_c}}\langle t^{r_e}, t^{r_s}\rangle$ is concerned with whether monomials of the form $\pi(x^{r_s}, w) \cdot \pi(x^{r_s}, t^{r_s})$ appear in the polynomial $\mathsf{Expr}\,\langle\pi(x^{r_e}, t^{r_e}), x^{r_s}\rangle$, where $\pi(x^{r_s}, w)$ is a monomial in $\mathsf{Sol}_{\alpha^{r_s,\delta},\alpha^{r_s,1_c}}\langle t^{r_e}, t^{r_s}\rangle$.

Relationships Between Superpoly Recovery and SR Problem. Since the SR problem is accurate as an extension of CMP, we can utilize it to compute the exact superpoly.

Proposition 1 (Reducing Superpoly Recovery to Solving SR Problem). *Recall that the initial state* x^0 *is loaded with* k, v, *constant 1 bits and constant 0 bits. Let* $M^{0,\delta}, M^{0,1_c}$ *and* $M^{0,0_c}$ *take the particular values* $\gamma^{0,\delta}, \gamma^{0,1_c}$ *and* $\gamma^{0,0_c}$ *respectively, where*

$\mathsf{Ind}[\gamma^{0,\delta}] = \{i \mid x^{(0)}[i] \text{ is loaded with a cube variable}\}$,

$\mathsf{Ind}[\gamma^{0,0_c}] = \{i \mid x^{(0)}[i] \text{ is loaded with a non-cube variable that is set to constant } 0\}$

$\qquad \bigcup\{i \mid x^{(0)}[i] \text{ is loaded with constant } 0\}$,

$$\gamma^{0,1_c} = \neg\left(\gamma^{0,\delta} \vee \gamma^{0,0_c}\right). \tag{3}$$

For each $j, 0 < j \leq r$, *let* $\gamma^{j,\delta}, \gamma^{j,1_c}, \gamma^{j,0_c}$ *be calculated from* $\gamma^{0,\delta}, \gamma^{0,1_c}, \gamma^{0,0_c}$ *according to the operation rules of flags. For* $t_I = \prod_{i \in I} v[i]$ *and the output bit* z *as the sum of monomials of* x^r, *we define two sets* $S^0 = \{t^0 \mid t^0 \preceq$

$\gamma^{0,\delta}$, $\mathsf{Expr}\,\langle \pi(\boldsymbol{x}^0, \boldsymbol{t}^0), \boldsymbol{v}\rangle = t_I\}$ and $S^r = \{\boldsymbol{u}^r \mid \pi(\boldsymbol{x}^r, \boldsymbol{u}^r) \to z, \boldsymbol{u}^r \wedge \gamma^{r,0_c} = \mathbf{0}\}$.
Then, either $|S^r| = 0$, which is easy to verify and indicates that $\mathsf{Coe}\langle z, t_I\rangle = 0$,
or we can compute $\mathsf{Coe}\langle z, t_I\rangle$ as

$$\mathsf{Coe}\langle z, t_I\rangle = \sum_{\boldsymbol{u}^r \in S^r}\left(\sum_{\boldsymbol{t}^0 \in S^0} \mathsf{Expr}\,\Big\langle \mathsf{Sol}\langle \boldsymbol{u}^r \wedge \gamma^{r,\delta}, \boldsymbol{t}^0\rangle, \boldsymbol{k}\Big\rangle \cdot \mathsf{Expr}\,\Big\langle \pi(\boldsymbol{x}^r, \boldsymbol{u}^r \wedge \gamma^{r,1_c}), \boldsymbol{k}\Big\rangle\right). \tag{4}$$

Proof. Due to page limits, the proof of this proposition is provided in [21, Sect. 4.1]. □

In Eq. (4), it is assumed that $\mathsf{Expr}\,\big\langle \pi(\boldsymbol{x}^r, \boldsymbol{u}^r \wedge \gamma^{r,1_c}), \boldsymbol{k}\big\rangle$ can be calculated quickly based on the round functions. In practice, due to the diffusion of round functions, usually the state bits of round r (e.g., $r = 850$ for TRIVIUM) are all δ bits, resulting in $\mathsf{Expr}\,\big\langle \pi(\boldsymbol{x}^r, \boldsymbol{u}^r \wedge \gamma^{r,1_c}), \boldsymbol{k}\big\rangle$ being 1. Therefore, computing $\mathsf{Coe}\langle z, t_I\rangle$ naturally reduces to the problem of seeking solutions for instances of the form $\mathsf{Sol}_{\gamma^{0,\delta},\gamma^{0,1_c}}\langle \boldsymbol{t}^r, \boldsymbol{t}^0\rangle$, where the values of flag masks are given as in Proposition 1 and $\boldsymbol{t}^r, \boldsymbol{t}^0$ can be any vectors that satisfy $\boldsymbol{t}^0 \in S^0, \boldsymbol{t}^r \preceq \gamma^{r,\delta}$.

4.2 Solving SR Problem with CMP

A CMP transition can be refined to be precise if the instance of the SR problem corresponding to this transition can be solved. Unfortunately, this is not always achievable for a complex instance. To address this problem, it would be necessary to study how to split a high-round instance into multiple instances of lower round, so that we can compute the solution of a complex instance from the solutions of simpler instances. With a little derivation, we immediately have the following lemma.

Lemma 3. *Assuming $r_s + 1 < r_e$, let the values of flag masks be defined as in Lemma 1. Given a monomial $\pi(\boldsymbol{x}^{r_e}, \boldsymbol{t}^{r_e})$ satisfying $\boldsymbol{t}^{r_e} \preceq \boldsymbol{\alpha}^{r_e,\delta}$, after setting $\boldsymbol{x}^{r_s}[\boldsymbol{\alpha}^{r_s,0_c}]$ to $\mathbf{0}$, then for any $j, r_s < j < r_e$, either $\mathsf{Expr}\,\big\langle \pi(\boldsymbol{x}^{r_e}, \boldsymbol{t}^{r_e}), \boldsymbol{x}^j\big\rangle = 0$ or we can calculate $\mathsf{Sol}\langle \boldsymbol{t}^{r_e}, \boldsymbol{t}^{r_s}\rangle$ as*

$$\mathsf{Sol}\langle \boldsymbol{t}^{r_e}, \boldsymbol{t}^{r_s}\rangle = \sum_{\pi(\boldsymbol{x}^j, \boldsymbol{t}^j)\xrightarrow{\mathcal{C}}\pi(\boldsymbol{x}^{r_e}, \boldsymbol{t}^{r_e})} \mathsf{Expr}\,\big\langle \mathsf{Sol}\langle \boldsymbol{t}^{r_e}, \boldsymbol{t}^j\rangle, \boldsymbol{x}^{r_s}\big\rangle \cdot \mathsf{Sol}\langle \boldsymbol{t}^j, \boldsymbol{t}^{r_s}\rangle, \tag{5}$$

where the summation is over all $\boldsymbol{t}^j$'s that satisfy $\pi(\boldsymbol{x}^j, \boldsymbol{t}^j) \xrightarrow{\mathcal{C}} \pi(\boldsymbol{x}^{r_e}, \boldsymbol{t}^{r_e})$.

Proof. After setting $\boldsymbol{x}^{r_s}[\boldsymbol{\alpha}^{r_s,0_c}]$ to $\mathbf{0}$, $\boldsymbol{x}^j[\boldsymbol{\alpha}^{j,0_c}]$ is also set to $\mathbf{0}$ according to operation rules. According to Lemma 2, either $\mathsf{Expr}\,\big\langle \pi(\boldsymbol{x}^{r_e}, \boldsymbol{t}^{r_e}), \boldsymbol{x}^j\big\rangle = 0$ or we can express $\pi(\boldsymbol{x}^{r_e}, \boldsymbol{t}^{r_e})$ as

$$\mathsf{Expr}\,\big\langle \pi(\boldsymbol{x}^{r_e}, \boldsymbol{t}^{r_e}), \boldsymbol{x}^j\big\rangle = \sum_{\pi(\boldsymbol{x}^j, \boldsymbol{t}^j)\xrightarrow{\mathcal{C}}\pi(\boldsymbol{x}^{r_e}, \boldsymbol{t}^{r_e})} \mathsf{Sol}\langle \boldsymbol{t}^{r_e}, \boldsymbol{t}^j\rangle \cdot \pi(\boldsymbol{x}^j, \boldsymbol{t}^j).$$

Notice that for each $\pi(\boldsymbol{x}^j, \boldsymbol{t}^j)$ satisfying $\pi(\boldsymbol{x}^j, \boldsymbol{t}^j) \xrightarrow{\mathcal{C}} \pi(\boldsymbol{x}^{r_e}, \boldsymbol{t}^{r_e})$, $\mathsf{Sol}\langle \boldsymbol{t}^{r_e}, \boldsymbol{t}^j \rangle$ only relates to $\boldsymbol{x}^j[\boldsymbol{\alpha}^{j,1_c}]$ and can be expressed as polynomial of $\boldsymbol{x}^{r_s}[\boldsymbol{\alpha}^{r_s,1_c}]$, so it suffices to calculate $\mathsf{Sol}\langle \boldsymbol{t}^j, \boldsymbol{t}^{r_s} \rangle$, thus proving the lemma.   □

According to Lemma 3, we can calculate $\mathsf{Sol}\langle \boldsymbol{t}^{r_e}, \boldsymbol{t}^{r_s} \rangle$ as

$$\mathsf{Sol}\langle \boldsymbol{t}^{r_e}, \boldsymbol{t}^{r_s} \rangle = \sum_{\boldsymbol{t}^{r_e-1}} \mathsf{Expr} \left\langle \mathsf{Sol}\langle \boldsymbol{t}^{r_e}, \boldsymbol{t}^{r_e-1} \rangle, \boldsymbol{x}^{r_s} \right\rangle \cdot \mathsf{Sol}\langle \boldsymbol{t}^{r_e-1}, \boldsymbol{t}^{r_s} \rangle,$$

where the summation of over all $\boldsymbol{t}^{r_e-1}$'s that satisfy $\pi(\boldsymbol{x}^{r_e-1}, \boldsymbol{t}^{r_e-1}) \xrightarrow{\mathcal{C}} \pi(\boldsymbol{x}^{r_e}, \boldsymbol{t}^{r_e})$. By applying Lemma 3 to each $\mathsf{Sol}\langle \boldsymbol{t}^{r_e-1}, \boldsymbol{t}^{r_s} \rangle$ again, we have

$$\mathsf{Sol}\langle \boldsymbol{t}^{r_e}, \boldsymbol{t}^{r_s} \rangle = \sum_{\boldsymbol{t}^{r_e-2}, \boldsymbol{t}^{r_e-1}} \mathsf{Expr} \left\langle \mathsf{Sol}\langle \boldsymbol{t}^{r_e}, \boldsymbol{t}^{r_e-1} \rangle \cdot \mathsf{Sol}\langle \boldsymbol{t}^{r_e-1}, \boldsymbol{t}^{r_e-2} \rangle, \boldsymbol{x}^{r_s} \right\rangle \cdot \mathsf{Sol}\langle \boldsymbol{t}^{r_e-2}, \boldsymbol{t}^{r_s} \rangle,$$

where the summation is over all $\boldsymbol{t}^{r_e-2}, \boldsymbol{t}^{r_e-1}$'s that satisfy $\pi(\boldsymbol{x}^{r_e-2}, \boldsymbol{t}^{r_e-2}) \xrightarrow{\mathcal{C}} \pi(\boldsymbol{x}^{r_e-1}, \boldsymbol{t}^{r_e-1}) \xrightarrow{\mathcal{C}} \pi(\boldsymbol{x}^{r_e}, \boldsymbol{t}^{r_e})$. This process can be repeated round by round until we arrive at round r_s, namely

$$\mathsf{Sol}\langle \boldsymbol{t}^{r_e}, \boldsymbol{t}^{r_s} \rangle = \sum_{\boldsymbol{t}^{r_s+1}, \ldots, \boldsymbol{t}^{r_e-1}} \mathsf{Expr} \left\langle \prod_{j=r_s}^{r_e-1} \mathsf{Sol}\langle \boldsymbol{t}^{j+1}, \boldsymbol{t}^j \rangle, \boldsymbol{x}^{r_s} \right\rangle \cdot \mathsf{Sol}\langle \boldsymbol{t}^{r_s}, \boldsymbol{t}^{r_s} \rangle,$$

where the summation is over all $\boldsymbol{t}^{r_s+1}, \ldots, \boldsymbol{t}^{r_e-1}$'s that satisfy $\pi(\boldsymbol{x}^{r_s}, \boldsymbol{t}^{r_s}) \xrightarrow{\mathcal{C}} \pi(\boldsymbol{x}^{r_s+1}, \boldsymbol{t}^{r_s+1}) \xrightarrow{\mathcal{C}} \cdots \xrightarrow{\mathcal{C}} \pi(\boldsymbol{x}^{r_e-1}, \boldsymbol{t}^{r_e-1}) \xrightarrow{\mathcal{C}} \pi(\boldsymbol{x}^{r_e}, \boldsymbol{t}^{r_e})$. Note that $\mathsf{Sol}\langle \boldsymbol{t}^{r_s}, \boldsymbol{t}^{r_s} \rangle$ is trivially 1, so we actually get an approach to compute $\mathsf{Sol}\langle \boldsymbol{t}^{r_e}, \boldsymbol{t}^{r_s} \rangle$ based on core monomial trails. We next formalize this approach as a theory, where the role of each core monomial trail is explicitly specified.

Definition 2 (Contribution of Core Monomial Trail). *Let the values of flag masks be defined as in Lemma 1. For any core monomial trail ℓ written as*

$$\pi(\boldsymbol{x}^{r_s}, \boldsymbol{t}^{r_s}) \xrightarrow{\mathcal{C}} \pi(\boldsymbol{x}^{r_s+1}, \boldsymbol{t}^{r_s+1}) \xrightarrow{\mathcal{C}} \cdots \xrightarrow{\mathcal{C}} \pi(\boldsymbol{x}^{r_e}, \boldsymbol{t}^{r_e}),$$

we define the contribution of this trail as

$$\mathsf{Contr}_{\boldsymbol{\alpha}^{r_s,\delta}, \boldsymbol{\alpha}^{r_s,1_c}} \langle l \rangle = \prod_{j=r_s}^{r_e-1} \mathsf{Sol}_{\boldsymbol{\alpha}^{j,\delta}, \boldsymbol{\alpha}^{j,1_c}} \langle \boldsymbol{t}^{j+1}, \boldsymbol{t}^j \rangle.$$

If $\boldsymbol{\alpha}^{r_s,\delta}, \boldsymbol{\alpha}^{r_s,1_c}$ are clear from the context, we write $\mathsf{Contr}\langle l \rangle$ for simplicity.

The contribution of a core monomial trail specifies the algebraic information carried by the trail. Collecting the contributions of all core monomial trails enables us to solve a complex instance efficiently. More precisely,

Proposition 2 (Solving SR Problem by Core Monomial Trails). *Let the values of flag masks be defined as in Lemma 1. Given an instance of the SR problem denoted by* $\mathsf{SR}\langle t^{r_e}, t^{r_s}\rangle$, *if* $\pi(\boldsymbol{x}^{r_s}, t^{r_s}) \overset{\mathcal{C}}{\not\rightsquigarrow} \pi(\boldsymbol{x}^{r_e}, t^{r_e})$, *the solution of this instance is 0; otherwise, we can calculate the solution of this instance by*

$$\mathsf{Sol}\langle t^{r_e}, t^{r_s}\rangle = \sum_{\ell \in \pi(\boldsymbol{x}^{r_s}, t^{r_s}) \overset{\mathcal{C}}{\bowtie} \pi(\boldsymbol{x}^{r_e}, t^{r_e})} \mathsf{Expr}\langle \mathsf{Contr}\langle \ell \rangle, \boldsymbol{x}^{r_s}\rangle.$$

Proof. We prove this proposition by fixing r_s and performing induction on r_e. When $r_e = r_s + 1$, the proposition clearly holds according to Definition 2 and Lemma 2. Assuming the proposition holds for $r_e < m$, we are going to prove that it also holds for $r_e = m$.

If $\pi(\boldsymbol{x}^{r_s}, t^{r_s}) \overset{\mathcal{C}}{\not\rightsquigarrow} \pi(\boldsymbol{x}^m, t^m)$, then either $\mathsf{Expr}\langle \pi(\boldsymbol{x}^m, t^m), \boldsymbol{x}^{m-1}\rangle = 0$, meaning that $\mathsf{Sol}\langle t^m, t^{r_s}\rangle = 0$, or $\pi(\boldsymbol{x}^{r_s}, t^{r_s}) \overset{\mathcal{C}}{\not\rightsquigarrow} \pi(\boldsymbol{x}^{m-1}, t^{m-1})$ for each $\pi(\boldsymbol{x}^{m-1}, t^{m-1})$ satisfy $\pi(\boldsymbol{x}^{m-1}, t^{m-1}) \overset{\mathcal{C}}{\rightarrow} \pi(\boldsymbol{x}^m, t^m)$. For the latter case, we set $\boldsymbol{x}^{r_s}[\boldsymbol{\alpha}^{r_s, 0_c}]$ to $\boldsymbol{0}$ and calculate $\mathsf{Sol}\langle t^m, t^{r_s}\rangle$ according to Lemma 3 as

$$\mathsf{Sol}\langle t^m, t^{r_s}\rangle = \sum_{\pi(\boldsymbol{x}^{m-1}, t^{m-1}) \overset{\mathcal{C}}{\rightarrow} \pi(\boldsymbol{x}^m, t^m)} \mathsf{Expr}\langle \mathsf{Sol}\langle t^m, t^{m-1}\rangle, \boldsymbol{x}^{r_s}\rangle \cdot \mathsf{Sol}\langle t^{m-1}, t^{r_s}\rangle. \tag{6}$$

According to the induction hypothesis, $\pi(\boldsymbol{x}^{r_s}, t^{r_s}) \overset{\mathcal{C}}{\not\rightsquigarrow} \pi(\boldsymbol{x}^{m-1}, t^{m-1})$ leads to $\mathsf{Sol}\langle t^{m-1}, t^{r_s}\rangle = 0$, thus for the latter case we also have $\mathsf{Sol}\langle t^m, t^{r_s}\rangle = 0$.

If $\pi(\boldsymbol{x}^{r_s}, t^{r_s}) \overset{\mathcal{C}}{\rightsquigarrow} \pi(\boldsymbol{x}^{r_e}, t^{r_e})$, similarly we set $\boldsymbol{x}^{r_s}[\boldsymbol{\alpha}^{r_s, 0_c}]$ to $\boldsymbol{0}$ and obtain Eq. (6). According to the induction hypothesis we made at the beginning,

$$\mathsf{Sol}\langle t^{m-1}, t^{r_s}\rangle = \sum_{\ell \in \pi(\boldsymbol{x}^{r_s}, t^{r_s}) \overset{\mathcal{C}}{\bowtie} \pi(\boldsymbol{x}^{m-1}, t^{m-1})} \mathsf{Expr}\langle \mathsf{Contr}\langle \ell \rangle, \boldsymbol{x}^{r_s}\rangle. \tag{7}$$

Define the set S as

$$S = \{(t^{m-1}, \ell) \mid \pi(\boldsymbol{x}^{m-1}, t^{m-1}) \overset{\mathcal{C}}{\rightarrow} \pi(\boldsymbol{x}^m, t^m), \ell \in \pi(\boldsymbol{x}^{r_s}, t^{r_s}) \overset{\mathcal{C}}{\bowtie} \pi(\boldsymbol{x}^{m-1}, t^{m-1})\}.$$

Combining Eqs. (6) and (7), we have

$$\mathsf{Sol}\langle t^m, t^{r_s}\rangle = \sum_{(t^{m-1}, \ell) \in S} \mathsf{Expr}\langle \mathsf{Sol}\langle t^m, t^{m-1}\rangle \cdot \mathsf{Contr}\langle \ell \rangle, \boldsymbol{x}^{r_s}\rangle, \tag{8}$$

where the summation is over all the pairs $(t^{m-1}, \ell) \in S$. Notice that Eqn (8) is equivalent to

$$\mathsf{Sol}\langle t^m, t^{r_s}\rangle = \sum_{\ell' \in \pi(\boldsymbol{x}^{r_s}, t^{r_s}) \overset{\mathcal{C}}{\bowtie} \pi(\boldsymbol{x}^m, t^m)} \mathsf{Expr}\langle \mathsf{Contr}\langle \ell' \rangle, \boldsymbol{x}^{r_s}\rangle,$$

which proves the proposition. $\qquad\square$

Corollary 1. *Let the values of flag masks be defined as in Lemma 1. Then,* $\pi(\boldsymbol{x}^{r_s}, t^{r_s}) \overset{\mathcal{C}}{\rightsquigarrow} \pi(\boldsymbol{x}^{r_e}, t^{r_e})$ *if* $\pi(\boldsymbol{x}^{r_s}, t^{r_s}) \overset{\mathcal{C}}{\rightarrow} \pi(\boldsymbol{x}^{r_e}, t^{r_e})$.

Algorithm 1: Iterative variable substitutions

---

1 **Procedure** VariableSubstitution($\mathsf{SR}_{\alpha^{r_s,\delta},\alpha^{r_s,1c}}\langle t^{r_e},t^{r_s}\rangle$):
2   Initialize an integer $j = r_s$ and an empty hash table T
3   Initialize $r_e - r_s$ empty vectors $c^{r_s}, c^{r_s+1}, \ldots, c^{r_e-1}$ of variables
4   **while** $j < r_e$ **do**
5   **for** *each possible pair (t^j, t^{j+1}) satisfying* $\pi(x^j, t^j) \overset{\mathcal{C}}{\to} \pi(x^{j+1}, t^{j+1})$ **do**
6   Calculate $\mathsf{Sol}\langle t^{j+1}, t^j\rangle$
7   Substitute $\mathsf{Sol}\langle t^{j+1}, t^j\rangle$ by a new variable c such that
                $c \cdot \pi(x^j, t^j) \to \pi(x^{j+1}, t^{j+1})$
8   Add c to the end of c^j, and store the substitution by letting
                $T[c] = \mathsf{Sol}\langle t^{j+1}, t^j\rangle$
9   Increment j by one   // $j = j+1$
10   **return** $c^{r_s}, c^{r_s+1}, \ldots, c^{r_e-1}, T$

Proof. We prove the contrapositive of this corollary. Since $\pi(x^{r_s}, t^{r_s}) \overset{\mathcal{C}}{\nrightarrow} \pi(x^{r_e}, t^{r_e})$, $|\pi(x^{r_s}, t^{r_s}) \overset{\mathcal{C}}{\bowtie} \pi(x^{r_e}, t^{r_e})| = 0$. According to Proposition 2, $\mathsf{Sol}\langle t^{r_e}, t^{r_s}\rangle = 0$. As stated by Lemma 1, this holds if and only if $\pi(x^{r_s}, t^{r_s}) \overset{\mathcal{C}}{\nrightarrow} \pi(x^{r_e}, t^{r_e})$.   □

As mentioned earlier, each round function $f^j, 0 \le j \le r$ in Eq. (1) performs a simple transformation and its ANF has been determined, which means we can calculate the contribution of a core monomial trail efficiently. Hence, Proposition 2 provides a feasible CMP-based way to solve $\mathsf{SR}_{\alpha^{r_s,\delta},\alpha^{r_s,1c}}\langle t^{r_e}, t^{r_s}\rangle$ even if the concrete expression of $\mathsf{Expr}\langle \pi(x^{r_e}, t^{r_e}), x^{r_s}\rangle$ is not available, thus completing the refinement of the CMP theory.

Since both the SR problem and MP are concerned with the presence of monomials, it would be necessary to investigate the relationship between the CMP-based approach in Proposition 2 and the usual MP-based method in Theorem 2. In fact, we can equivalently relate CMP and MP by means of variable substitution.

Equivalence Between CMP and MP. Let the values of flag masks be defined as in Lemma 1. We set $x^{r_s}[\alpha^{r_s,0c}]$ to $\mathbf{0}$. Given an instance $\mathsf{SR}_{\alpha^{r_s,\delta},\alpha^{r_s,1c}}\langle t^{r_e}, t^{r_s}\rangle$, we illustrate how to solve this instance based on MP. First, theoretically we can perform iterative variable substitutions following Algorithm 1. The basic idea behind Algorithm 1 is, if we regard $\mathsf{Sol}_{\alpha^{j,\delta},\alpha^{j,1c}}\langle t^{j+1}, t^j\rangle$ as a single bit c for the transition $\pi(x^j, t^j) \to \pi(x^{j+1}, t^{j+1})$, then we have $c \cdot \pi(x^j, t^j) \to \pi(x^{j+1}, t^{j+1})$, thus establishing the equivalence between CMP and MP.

In Line 5–8, we describe a generic approach to perform variable substitution for a round function f^j, but this may not always be practical to directly implement as it requires enumerating an exponential number of monomials. Corresponding to the propagation rules of CMP, we propose several rules to replace Line 5–8 to optimize the substitution process.

Algorithm 2: Perform variable substitution on $\boldsymbol{f}^j$ that consists of multiple S-boxes

---

1 **for** *each S-box* $S_i, 0 \le i < m$ **do**
2   **for** *each possible pair* $(\boldsymbol{t}^j, \boldsymbol{t}^{j+1})$ *satisfying that* $\pi(\boldsymbol{x}^j, \boldsymbol{t}^j)$ *only relates to the input δ bits of S_i,* $\pi(\boldsymbol{x}^{j+1}, \boldsymbol{t}^{j+1})$ *only relates to the output δ bits of S_i,* *and* $\pi(\boldsymbol{x}^j, \boldsymbol{t}^j) \overset{\mathcal{C}}{\to} \pi(\boldsymbol{x}^{j+1}, \boldsymbol{t}^{j+1})$ **do**
3   Calculate $\mathsf{Sol}\langle \boldsymbol{t}^{j+1}, \boldsymbol{t}^j \rangle$
4   Substitute $\mathsf{Sol}\langle \boldsymbol{t}^{j+1}, \boldsymbol{t}^j \rangle$ by a new variable c such that
             $c \cdot \pi(\boldsymbol{x}^j, \boldsymbol{t}^j) \to \pi(\boldsymbol{x}^{j+1}, \boldsymbol{t}^{j+1})$
5   Add c to the end of $\boldsymbol{c}^j$, and store the substitution by letting
             $T[c] = \mathsf{Sol}\langle \boldsymbol{t}^{j+1}, \boldsymbol{t}^j \rangle$

Rule 1 (COPY) *Assume the round function* $\boldsymbol{f}^j$ *is the basic operation* COPY *with* $x^j[0] \xrightarrow{COPY} (x^{j+1}[0], \ldots, x^{j+1}[m-1])$. *We do not need to perform variable substitution because* $\mathsf{Sol}\langle \boldsymbol{t}^{j+1}, \boldsymbol{t}^j \rangle = 1$ *if* $\pi(\boldsymbol{x}^j, \boldsymbol{t}^j) \overset{\mathcal{C}}{\to} \pi(\boldsymbol{x}^{j+1}, \boldsymbol{t}^{j+1})$.

Rule 2 (AND) *Assume the round function* $\boldsymbol{f}^j$ *is the basic operation* AND *with* $(x^j[0], x^j[1], \ldots, x^j[m-1]) \xrightarrow{AND} x^{j+1}[0]$. *If* $\{1_c, \delta\} \subseteq \{x^j[0].F, x^j[1].F, \ldots, x^j[m-1].F\}$ *and* $x^{j+1}[0].F = \delta$, *we substitute a new variable c for* $\prod_{\substack{0 \le i < m \\ x^j[i].F = 1_c}} x^j[i]$, *add c to the end of* $\boldsymbol{c}^j$, *and store the substitution by letting* $T[c] = \prod_{\substack{0 \le i < m \\ x^j[i].F = 1_c}} x^j[i]$; *otherwise we do not perform variable substitution.*

Rule 3 (XOR) *Assume the round function* $\boldsymbol{f}^j$ *is the basic operation* XOR *with* $(x^j[0], x^j[1], \ldots, x^j[m-1]) \xrightarrow{XOR} x^{j+1}[0]$. *If* $\{1_c, \delta\} \subseteq \{x^j[0].F, x^j[1].F, \ldots, x^j[m-1].F\}$, *we substitute a new variable c for* $\sum_{\substack{0 \le i < m \\ x^j[i].F = 1_c}} x^j[i]$, *add c to the end of* $\boldsymbol{c}^j$, *and store the substitution by letting* $T[c] = \sum_{\substack{0 \le i < m \\ x^j[i].F = 1_c}} x^j[i]$; *otherwise we do not perform variable substitution.*

Rule 4 (S-boxes) *Let* $\boldsymbol{f}^j$ *be a function that consists of m S-boxes, denoted by* $S_0, \ldots, S_{m-1}$. *We can set* $\boldsymbol{c}^j$ *and* T *following Algorithm 2.*

Utilizing the new variables $\boldsymbol{c}^{r_s}, \boldsymbol{c}^{r_s+1}, \ldots, \boldsymbol{c}^{r_e-1}, T$ returned by Algorithm 1, we are able to establish a one-to-one correspondence between core monomial trails and monomial trails.

Proposition 3. *There is a core monomial trail written as*

$$\pi(\boldsymbol{x}^{r_s}, \boldsymbol{t}^{r_s}) \overset{\mathcal{C}}{\to} \pi(\boldsymbol{x}^{r_s+1}, \boldsymbol{t}^{r_s+1}) \overset{\mathcal{C}}{\to} \cdots \overset{\mathcal{C}}{\to} \pi(\boldsymbol{x}^{r_e}, \boldsymbol{t}^{r_e})$$

if and only if there is a monomial trail written as

$$\pi(c^{r_s}\|\cdots\|c^{r_e-1}\|x^{r_s}, w^{r_s}\|\cdots\|w^{r_e-1}\|t^{r_s})$$
$$\rightarrow \pi(c^{r_s+1}\|\cdots\|c^{r_e-1}\|x^{r_s+1}, w^{r_s+1}\|\cdots\|w^{r_e-1}\|t^{r_s+1})$$
$$\rightarrow \cdots$$
$$\rightarrow \pi(c^{r_e-1}\|x^{r_e-1}, w^{r_e-1}\|t^{r_e-1})$$
$$\rightarrow \pi(x^{r_e}, t^{r_e}). \tag{9}$$

Moreover, by substituting each variable c in $c^j, r_s \leq j < r_e$ back with $T[c]$, we can get a polynomial of $x^{r_s}, \ldots, x^{r_e-1}$ from $\pi(c^{r_s}\|\cdots\|c^{r_e-1}, w^{r_s}\|\cdots\|w^{r_e-1})$, which is exactly the contribution of the core monomial trail.

Proof. For each $j, r_s \leq j < r_e$, according to the process of iterative variable substitutions, $\pi(x^j, t^j) \xrightarrow{\mathcal{C}} \pi(x^{j+1}, t^{j+1})$ if and only if there is an unique w^j such that $\pi(c^j\|x^j, w^j\|t^j) \rightarrow \pi(x^{j+1}, t^{j+1})$. Combining all these MP transitions $\pi(c^{r_s}\|x^{r_s}, w^{r_s}\|t^{r_s}) \rightarrow \pi(x^{r_s+1}, t^{r_s+1}), \pi(c^{r_s+1}\|x^{r_s+1}, w^{r_s+1}\|t^{r_s+1}) \rightarrow \pi(x^{r_s+2}, t^{r_s+2}), \ldots, \pi(c^{r_e-1}\|x^{r_e-1}, w^{r_e-1}\|t^{r_e-1}) \rightarrow \pi(x^{r_e}, t^{r_e})$ yields an equivalent monomial trail described in the proposition. □

We can therefore also solve $\mathsf{SR}_{\alpha^{r_s,\delta},\alpha^{r_s,1c}}\langle t^{r_e}, t^{r_s}\rangle$ by extracting all monomials trails of the form (9) after performing the iterative variable substitutions, which gives an equivalent MP-based interpretation for the CMP-based approach in Proposition 2. For ease of understanding, we give a concrete example in [21, Sup. Mat. D].

4.3   MITM Framework

At this point, we have a complete process for computing the superpoly $\mathsf{Coe}\langle z, t_I\rangle$, i.e., we first reduce the superpoly recovery to the instances of the SR problem using Proposition 1 and then solve the instances by the CMP-based approach in Proposition 2. The remaining question is how to further improve the efficiency of this process. A similar issue has been also encountered in previous work related to MP [23,24], and it is resolved by a divide-and-conquer strategy, which can be further used in a nested fashion. Inspired by this, we have also tailored a nested divide-and-conquer framework for solving the SR problem.

Divide-and-Conquer: Forward Expansion and Backward Expansion. As a natural corollary of Proposition 2, Eq. (5) in Lemma 3 can be enhanced to

$$\mathsf{Sol}\langle t^{r_e}, t^{r_s}\rangle = \sum_{t^j} \mathsf{Expr}\left\langle \mathsf{Sol}\langle t^{r_e}, t^j\rangle, x^{r_s}\right\rangle \cdot \mathsf{Sol}\langle t^j, t^{r_s}\rangle,$$

where the summation is over all t^j's that satisfy both $\pi(x^{r_s}, t^{r_s}) \xrightarrow{\mathcal{C}} \pi(x^j, t^j)$ and $\pi(x^j, t^j) \xrightarrow{\mathcal{C}} \pi(x^{r_e}, t^{r_e})$. This reveals the following two perspectives for computing $\mathsf{Sol}\langle t^{r_e}, t^{r_s}\rangle$ by the divide-and-conquer strategy:

- *Forward expansion*: We choose a j between r_s and r_e, and determine all $\pi(\boldsymbol{x}^j, \boldsymbol{t}^j)$'s that satisfy $\pi(\boldsymbol{x}^{r_s}, \boldsymbol{t}^{r_s}) \overset{\mathcal{C}}{\rightsquigarrow} \pi(\boldsymbol{x}^j, \boldsymbol{t}^j)$. For each such $\pi(\boldsymbol{x}^j, \boldsymbol{t}^j)$, we precompute $\mathsf{Sol}\langle \boldsymbol{t}^j, \boldsymbol{t}^{r_s} \rangle$. If $\mathsf{Sol}\langle \boldsymbol{t}^j, \boldsymbol{t}^{r_s} \rangle$ is not 0 (i.e., $\pi(\boldsymbol{x}^{r_s}, \boldsymbol{t}^{r_s}) \overset{\mathcal{C}}{\rightarrow} \pi(\boldsymbol{x}^j, \boldsymbol{t}^j)$), we store $\mathsf{Sol}\langle \boldsymbol{t}^j, \boldsymbol{t}^{r_s} \rangle$ and then focus on computing $\mathsf{Sol}\langle \boldsymbol{t}^{r_e}, \boldsymbol{t}^j \rangle$.
- *Backward expansion*: We choose a j between r_s and r_e, and determine all $\pi(\boldsymbol{x}^j, \boldsymbol{t}^j)$'s that satisfy $\pi(\boldsymbol{x}^j, \boldsymbol{t}^j) \overset{\mathcal{C}}{\rightsquigarrow} \pi(\boldsymbol{x}^{r_e}, \boldsymbol{t}^{r_e})$. For each such $\pi(\boldsymbol{x}^j, \boldsymbol{t}^j)$, we precompute $\mathsf{Sol}\langle \boldsymbol{t}^{r_e}, \boldsymbol{t}^j \rangle$. If $\mathsf{Sol}\langle \boldsymbol{t}^{r_e}, \boldsymbol{t}^j \rangle$ is not 0 (i.e., $\pi(\boldsymbol{x}^j, \boldsymbol{t}^j) \overset{\mathcal{C}}{\rightarrow} \pi(\boldsymbol{x}^{r_e}, \boldsymbol{t}^{r_e})$), we store $\mathsf{Sol}\langle \boldsymbol{t}^{r_e}, \boldsymbol{t}^j \rangle$ and then focus on computing $\mathsf{Sol}\langle \boldsymbol{t}^j, \boldsymbol{t}^{r_s} \rangle$.

Typically, we will choose j close to r_e in the backward expansion and j close to r_s in the forward expansion, so that the precomputation takes only a small amount of time.

One obvious advantage of these two expansions is that both of them split a complex instance into multiple simpler instances that are easier to deal with. Furthermore, if not using any expansion, solving $\mathsf{SR}\langle \boldsymbol{t}^{r_e}, \boldsymbol{t}^{r_s} \rangle$ would require enumerating $|\pi(\boldsymbol{x}^{r_s}, \boldsymbol{t}^{r_s}) \overset{\mathcal{C}}{\bowtie} \pi(\boldsymbol{x}^{r_e}, \boldsymbol{t}^{r_e})|$ core monomial trails, but with backward expansion the total number of enumerated core monomial trails will be (ignoring the core monomial trails needed for the precomputation)

$$\sum_{\pi(\boldsymbol{x}^j, \boldsymbol{t}^j) \overset{\mathcal{C}}{\rightarrow} \pi(\boldsymbol{x}^{r_e}, \boldsymbol{t}^{r_e})} |\pi(\boldsymbol{x}^{r_s}, \boldsymbol{t}^{r_s}) \overset{\mathcal{C}}{\bowtie} \pi(\boldsymbol{x}^j, \boldsymbol{t}^j)|,$$

which is not larger than $|\pi(\boldsymbol{x}^{r_s}, \boldsymbol{t}^{r_s}) \overset{\mathcal{C}}{\bowtie} \pi(\boldsymbol{x}^{r_e}, \boldsymbol{t}^{r_e})|$, so the backward expansion reduces the number of required core monomial trails, and the same is also true for forward expansion.

Forward and Backward Overlaps. We further discuss the rationale behind the forward and backward expansion. Now consider that we want to solve two instances denoted by $\mathsf{SR}\langle \boldsymbol{t}_0^{r_e}, \boldsymbol{t}^{r_s} \rangle$ and $\mathsf{SR}\langle \boldsymbol{t}_1^{r_e}, \boldsymbol{t}^{r_s} \rangle$ simultaneously with the flag masks taking the same values as in Lemma 3. If we use the backward expansion from round r_e to round j separately on the two instances, the total number of enumerated core monomial trails will be

$$\sum_{\pi(\boldsymbol{x}^j, \boldsymbol{t}^j) \overset{\mathcal{C}}{\rightarrow} \pi(\boldsymbol{x}^{r_e}, \boldsymbol{t}_0^{r_e})} |\pi(\boldsymbol{x}^{r_s}, \boldsymbol{t}^{r_s}) \overset{\mathcal{C}}{\bowtie} \pi(\boldsymbol{x}^j, \boldsymbol{t}^j)| + \sum_{\pi(\boldsymbol{x}^j, \boldsymbol{t}^j) \overset{\mathcal{C}}{\rightarrow} \pi(\boldsymbol{x}^{r_e}, \boldsymbol{t}_1^{r_e})} |\pi(\boldsymbol{x}^{r_s}, \boldsymbol{t}^{r_s}) \overset{\mathcal{C}}{\bowtie} \pi(\boldsymbol{x}^j, \boldsymbol{t}^j)|,$$

where the left summation is for $\mathsf{SR}\langle \boldsymbol{t}_0^{r_e}, \boldsymbol{t}^{r_s} \rangle$ and the right summation is for $\mathsf{SR}\langle \boldsymbol{t}_1^{r_e}, \boldsymbol{t}^{r_s} \rangle$. However, if there exists a $\pi(\boldsymbol{x}^j, \boldsymbol{t}^j)$ satisfying both $\pi(\boldsymbol{x}^j, \boldsymbol{t}^j) \overset{\mathcal{C}}{\rightarrow} \pi(\boldsymbol{x}^{r_e}, \boldsymbol{t}_0^{r_e})$ and $\pi(\boldsymbol{x}^j, \boldsymbol{t}^j) \overset{\mathcal{C}}{\rightarrow} \pi(\boldsymbol{x}^{r_e}, \boldsymbol{t}_1^{r_e})$, we can observe that the core monomial trails in $\pi(\boldsymbol{x}^{r_s}, \boldsymbol{t}^{r_s}) \overset{\mathcal{C}}{\bowtie} \pi(\boldsymbol{x}^j, \boldsymbol{t}^j)$ can only be enumerated once for both $\mathsf{SR}\langle \boldsymbol{t}_0^{r_e}, \boldsymbol{t}^{r_s} \rangle$ and $\mathsf{SR}\langle \boldsymbol{t}_1^{r_e}, \boldsymbol{t}^{r_s} \rangle$, and we say that $\mathsf{SR}\langle \boldsymbol{t}_0^{r_e}, \boldsymbol{t}^{r_s} \rangle$ and $\mathsf{SR}\langle \boldsymbol{t}_1^{r_e}, \boldsymbol{t}^{r_s} \rangle$ have a *backward overlap* at $\pi(\boldsymbol{x}^j, \boldsymbol{t}^j)$. Therefore, in total we actually only need to enumerate $\sum_{\boldsymbol{t}^j} |\pi(\boldsymbol{x}^{r_s}, \boldsymbol{t}^{r_s}) \overset{\mathcal{C}}{\bowtie} \pi(\boldsymbol{x}^j, \boldsymbol{t}^j)|$ trails, where the summation is over all $\boldsymbol{t}^j$'s that satisfy one of the following three conditions:

1. $\pi(\boldsymbol{x}^j, \boldsymbol{t}^j) \xrightarrow{\mathcal{C}} \pi(\boldsymbol{x}^{r_e}, \boldsymbol{t}_0^{r_e}), \pi(\boldsymbol{x}^j, \boldsymbol{t}^j) \xrightarrow{\mathcal{C}} \pi(\boldsymbol{x}^{r_e}, \boldsymbol{t}_1^{r_e});$
2. $\pi(\boldsymbol{x}^j, \boldsymbol{t}^j) \xrightarrow{\mathcal{C}} \pi(\boldsymbol{x}^{r_e}, \boldsymbol{t}_0^{r_e}), \pi(\boldsymbol{x}^j, \boldsymbol{t}^j) \xrightarrow{\mathcal{C}} \pi(\boldsymbol{x}^{r_e}, \boldsymbol{t}_1^{r_e});$
3. $\pi(\boldsymbol{x}^j, \boldsymbol{t}^j) \xrightarrow{\mathcal{C}} \pi(\boldsymbol{x}^{r_e}, \boldsymbol{t}_0^{r_e}), \pi(\boldsymbol{x}^j, \boldsymbol{t}^j) \xrightarrow{\mathcal{C}} \pi(\boldsymbol{x}^{r_e}, \boldsymbol{t}_1^{r_e}).$

Condition 3 is exactly the condition that should be satisfied by those $\pi(\boldsymbol{x}^j, \boldsymbol{t}^j)$'s where $\mathsf{SR}\langle \boldsymbol{t}_0^{r_e}, \boldsymbol{t}^{r_s} \rangle$ and $\mathsf{SR}\langle \boldsymbol{t}_1^{r_e}, \boldsymbol{t}^{r_s} \rangle$ have backward overlaps. For m instances denoted by $\mathsf{SR}\langle \boldsymbol{t}_0^{r_e}, \boldsymbol{t}^{r_s} \rangle, \ldots, \mathsf{SR}\langle \boldsymbol{t}_{m-1}^{r_e}, \boldsymbol{t}^{r_s} \rangle$, if there are any two of them that have a backward overlap at $\pi(\boldsymbol{x}^j, \boldsymbol{t}^j)$, we say these m instances have a backward overlap at $\pi(\boldsymbol{x}^j, \boldsymbol{t}^j)$.

Similarly, for two instances denoted by $\mathsf{SR}\langle \boldsymbol{t}^{r_e}, \boldsymbol{t}_0^{r_s} \rangle$ and $\mathsf{SR}\langle \boldsymbol{t}^{r_e}, \boldsymbol{t}_1^{r_s} \rangle$ with the values of flag masks determined as in Lemma 3, we say $\mathsf{SR}\langle \boldsymbol{t}^{r_e}, \boldsymbol{t}_0^{r_s} \rangle$ and $\mathsf{SR}\langle \boldsymbol{t}^{r_e}, \boldsymbol{t}_1^{r_s} \rangle$ have a *forward overlap* at $\pi(\boldsymbol{x}^j, \boldsymbol{t}^j)$ if the $\pi(\boldsymbol{x}^j, \boldsymbol{t}^j)$ satisfies both $\pi(\boldsymbol{x}^{r_s}, \boldsymbol{t}_0^{r_s}) \xrightarrow{\mathcal{C}} \pi(\boldsymbol{x}^j, \boldsymbol{t}^j)$ and $\pi(\boldsymbol{x}^{r_s}, \boldsymbol{t}_1^{r_s}) \xrightarrow{\mathcal{C}} \pi(\boldsymbol{x}^j, \boldsymbol{t}^j)$. The concept of forward overlaps can be extended to multiple instances in the same way as backward overlaps. Naturally, the more backward (resp. forward) overlaps occurs at round j, the more effective we consider the backward (reps. forward) expansion to be.

The forward and backward overlaps can be illustrated by [21, Fig. 1], where we use sold lines to indicate the parts that are precomputed and dashed lines to indicate the parts that are to be computed. The monomial highlighted in red indicates where the forward or backward overlap occurs.

Computing the Superpoly with MITM Framework. As mentioned in Proposition 1, computing the superpoly, i.e., $\mathsf{Coe}\langle z, t_I \rangle$, reduces to solving concrete instances of the form $\mathsf{SR}_{\gamma^{0,\delta}, \gamma^{0,1_c}} \langle \boldsymbol{t}^r, \boldsymbol{t}^0 \rangle$ with $\gamma^{0,\delta}, \gamma^{0,1_c}$ determined by Eq. (3). Assuming $\pi(\boldsymbol{x}^0, \boldsymbol{t}^0) \xrightarrow{\mathcal{C}} \pi(\boldsymbol{x}^r, \boldsymbol{t}^r)$, then we can solve $\mathsf{SR}_{\gamma^{0,\delta}, \gamma^{0,1_c}} \langle \boldsymbol{t}^r, \boldsymbol{t}^0 \rangle$ by applying the forward expansion and backward expansion interchangeably and recursively as follows, where the forward depth r_0 and the backward depth r_1 represent the number of rounds affected each time we use the forward and backward expansion, respectively.

1. Initialize $\boldsymbol{M}^{0,\delta} = \gamma^{0,\delta}, \boldsymbol{M}^{0,1_c} = \gamma^{0,1_c}, \boldsymbol{M}^{0,0_c} = \neg(\gamma^{0,\delta} \vee \gamma^{0,1_c})$ according to Eq. (3). For each $j, 0 < j \leq r$, calculate the values of $\boldsymbol{M}^{j,\delta}, \boldsymbol{M}^{j,1_c}, \boldsymbol{M}^{j,0_c}$ as $\gamma^{j,\delta}, \gamma^{j,1_c}, \gamma^{j,0_c}$ according to the operation rules of flags.
2. Prepare a hash table P whose key is an instance and value is a Boolean polynomial of $\boldsymbol{x}^0$ and initialize P as $P[\mathsf{SR}\langle \boldsymbol{t}^r, \gamma^{0,\delta} \rangle] = 1$. Initialize $r_s = 0, r_e = r$. Prepare a binary variable d to represent the direction of the expansion and initialize $d = 1$. Initialize a Boolean polynomial $p = 0$ to store the results.
3. If $r_e < B$, we flip the value of d. Prepare an empty hash table P_e of the same type as P to store the new instances generated by the expansion.
4. If $d = 0$, we use forward expansion. Namely, for each instance $\mathsf{SR}\langle \boldsymbol{t}^{r_e}, \boldsymbol{t}^{r_s} \rangle$ as a key of P:
   (a) Determine all $\pi(\boldsymbol{x}^{r_s+r_0}, \boldsymbol{t}^{r_s+r_0})$'s that satisfy $\pi(\boldsymbol{x}^{r_s}, \boldsymbol{t}^{r_s}) \xrightarrow{\mathcal{C}} \pi(\boldsymbol{x}^{r_s+r_0}, \boldsymbol{t}^{r_s+r_0})$.
   (b) For each such $\pi(\boldsymbol{x}^{r_s+r_0}, \boldsymbol{t}^{r_s+r_0})$, compute $\mathsf{Sol}\langle \boldsymbol{t}^{r_s+r_0}, \boldsymbol{t}^{r_s} \rangle$ using Proposition 2, and if $\mathsf{Sol}\langle \boldsymbol{t}^{r_s+r_0}, \boldsymbol{t}^{r_s} \rangle$ is not 0, we consider two cases: if the instance $\mathsf{SR}\langle \boldsymbol{t}^{r_e}, \boldsymbol{t}^{r_s+r_0} \rangle$ is already a key of P_e, we update P_e

by $P_e[\mathsf{SR}\langle t^{r_e}, t^{r_s+r_0}\rangle] = P_e[\mathsf{SR}\langle t^{r_e}, t^{r_s+r_0}\rangle] + \mathsf{Expr}\langle \mathsf{Sol}\langle t^{r_s+r_0}, t^{r_s}\rangle, x^0\rangle \cdot P[\mathsf{SR}\langle t^{r_e}, t^{r_s}\rangle]$; otherwise we add the instance $\mathsf{SR}\langle t^{r_e}, t^{r_s+r_0}\rangle$ to P_e by letting $P_e[\mathsf{SR}\langle t^{r_e}, t^{r_s+r_0}\rangle] = \mathsf{Expr}\langle \mathsf{Sol}\langle t^{r_s+r_0}, t^{r_s}\rangle, x^0\rangle \cdot P[\mathsf{SR}\langle t^{r_e}, t^{r_s}\rangle]$.

    (c) Let $P = P_e$ and update r_s by $r_s = r_s + r_0$.

5. If $d = 1$, we use backward expansion. Namely, for each instance $\mathsf{SR}\langle t^{r_e}, t^{r_s}\rangle$ as a key of P:

    (a) Determine all $\pi(x^{r_e-r_1}, t^{r_e-r_1})$'s that satisfy $\pi(x^{r_e-r_1}, t^{r_e-r_1}) \overset{\mathcal{C}}{\leadsto} \pi(x^{r_e}, t^{r_e})$.

    (b) For each such $\pi(x^{r_e-r_1}, t^{r_e-r_1})$, compute $\mathsf{Sol}\langle t^{r_e}, t^{r_e-r_1}\rangle$ using Proposition 2, and if $\mathsf{Sol}\langle t^{r_e}, t^{r_e-r_1}\rangle$ is not 0, we consider two cases: if the instance $\mathsf{SR}\langle t^{r_e-r_1}, t^{r_s}\rangle$ is already a key of P_e, we update P_e by $P_e[\mathsf{SR}\langle t^{r_e-r_1}, t^{r_s}\rangle] = P_e[\mathsf{SR}\langle t^{r_e-r_1}, t^{r_s}\rangle] + \mathsf{Expr}\langle \mathsf{Sol}\langle t^{r_e}, t^{r_e-r_1}\rangle, x^0\rangle \cdot P[\mathsf{SR}\langle t^{r_e}, t^{r_s}\rangle]$; otherwise we add the instance $\mathsf{SR}\langle t^{r_e-r_1}, t^{r_s}\rangle$ to P_e by letting $P_e[\mathsf{SR}\langle t^{r_e-r_1}, t^{r_s}\rangle] = \mathsf{Expr}\langle \mathsf{Sol}\langle t^{r_e}, t^{r_e-r_1}\rangle, x^0\rangle \cdot P[\mathsf{SR}\langle t^{r_e}, t^{r_s}\rangle]$.

    (c) Let $P = P_e$ and update r_e by $r_e = r_e - r_1$.

6. For each instance $\mathsf{SR}\langle t^{r_e}, t^{r_s}\rangle$ as a key of P, if $P[\mathsf{SR}\langle t^{r_e}, t^{r_s}\rangle]$ is 0, we remove $\mathsf{SR}\langle t^{r_e}, t^{r_s}\rangle$ from the keys of P.

7. If the size of P is not larger than N, we jump to Step 3; otherwise we start to solve the instances in P and prepare an empty hash table P_u of the same type as P to store the unsolved instances that will be generated later.

8. For each instance $\mathsf{SR}\langle t^{r_e}, t^{r_s}\rangle$ as a key of P, we solve it using Proposition 2 within a time limit $\tau^{r_e-r_s}$. If the instance is solved within the time limit, we obtain $\mathsf{Sol}\langle t^{r_e}, t^{r_s}\rangle$ and update p by $p = p + \mathsf{Expr}\langle \mathsf{Sol}\langle t^{r_e}, t^{r_s}\rangle, x^0\rangle \cdot P[\mathsf{SR}\langle t^{r_e}, t^{r_s}\rangle]$; if the instance is determined to have the solution 0, we discard it; if the instance is not solved within the time limit, we add the pair to P_u by letting $P_u[\mathsf{SR}\langle t^{r_e}, t^{r_s}\rangle] = P[\mathsf{SR}\langle t^{r_e}, t^{r_s}\rangle]$.

9. If the size of P_u is 0, then p is returned as the final result; otherwise we let $P = P_u$ and jump back to Step 3 to continue expanding and solving instances in P.

As the above process advances, the gap between r_s and r_e decreases progressively, hence we call it a *meet-in-the-middle (MITM)* framework. The parameters $B, N, r_0, r_1, \tau^{r_e-r_s}$ appearing in the process depends on the structure of a cipher, so we will give their values on the spot when applying the framework to a specific cipher. In particular, the time limit $\tau^{r_e-r_s}$ increases as the gap between r_s and r_e shrinks to ensure that more time resources are allocated to solving sufficiently simple instances rather than complex ones. We also set very small values for the forward depth r_0 and the backward depth r_1 (e.g., $r_0 = 5$ and $r_1 = 20$ for TRIVIUM) so that solving instances during the expansion process, namely Step 4b and 5b, can be completed quickly. The way we update P_e in Step 4b and 5b can be thought of as a direct reflection of the role of (forward or backward) overlaps.

For each instance $\mathsf{SR}\langle t^{r_e}, t^{r_s}\rangle$ as a key of P in Step 8, it is very likely $\pi(x^{r_s}, t^{r_s}) \overset{\mathcal{C}}{\nleadsto} \pi(x^{r_e}, t^{r_e})$, resulting in the instance being determined to have the solution 0 and then discarded. Therefore, we can adjust Step 4a to directly identify all $\pi(x^{r_s+r_0}, t^{r_s+r_0})$'s that satisfy both $\pi(x^{r_s}, t^{r_s}) \overset{\mathcal{C}}{\leadsto} \pi(x^{r_s+r_0}, t^{r_s+r_0})$

and $\pi(\boldsymbol{x}^{r_s+r_0}, \boldsymbol{t}^{r_s+r_0}) \overset{\mathcal{C}}{\rightsquigarrow} \pi(\boldsymbol{x}^{r_e}, \boldsymbol{t}^{r_e})$, which can be implemented using the callback interface provided by the Gurobi solver. A similar adjustment can be made to Step 5a. Details on how to use callbacks for expansion are discussed in [21, Sup.Mat. E].

Forward or Backward. We compare the forward expansion and backward expansion strategies heuristically to explain why we set a parameter B in the MITM framework. In Step 3, we have to determine which expansion strategy to adopt for the hash table P. It can be predicted that some instances in P may have forward overlaps at round $r_s + r_0$, while others may have backward overlaps at round $r_e - r_1$. Nevertheless, we observe that for each instance $\mathsf{SR}\langle \boldsymbol{t}^{r_e}, \boldsymbol{t}^{r_s} \rangle$ in P, the Hamming weight of $\boldsymbol{t}^{r_e}$ is much greater than that of $\boldsymbol{t}^{r_s}$. For example, when $r_s = 25, r_e = 289$ for 849-round TRIVIUM with the cube indices chosen as I_3 in Table 2, $wt(\boldsymbol{t}^{r_s})$ is approximately 40, but $wt(\boldsymbol{t}^{r_e})$ is only about 20. This means, if we assume two instances denoted by $\mathsf{SR}\langle \boldsymbol{t}_0^{r_e}, \boldsymbol{t}_0^{r_s} \rangle$ and $\mathsf{SR}\langle \boldsymbol{t}_1^{r_e}, \boldsymbol{t}_1^{r_s} \rangle$ in P are independently stochastic, i.e., the binary vectors $\boldsymbol{t}_0^{r_e}, \boldsymbol{t}_0^{r_s}, \boldsymbol{t}_1^{r_e}, \boldsymbol{t}_1^{r_s}$ are independent and random, then it is more likely that these two instances will have a forward overlap at round $r_s + r_0$ than that they will have a backward overlap at round $r_e - r_1$, and therefore we believe that the forward expansion lessens the amount of trails that must be enumerated to a greater degree compared to the backward expansion.

However, high Hamming weights also present some challenges. One critical limitation of the forward expansion is that the size of the hash table P grows dramatically as the forward depth r_0 increases. While the backward expansion faces a similar issue as the backward depth r_1 rises, P expands at a smaller rate compared to the forward expansion. For this reason, the backward depth r_1 is set greater than the forward depth r_0. If we use the difference between r_s and r_e to evaluate the difficulty of each instance in P, then the backward expansion closes the gap between r_s and r_e much faster than the forward expansion, and the resulting new instances are simpler.

In summary, the faster closure of the gap between r_s and r_e achieved through backward expansion as opposed to forward expansion renders it most suitable when r_e is significantly large (e.g., over 350 for TRIVIUM). In contrast, when r_e falls below a certain threshold B, forward and backward expansion can be applied interchangeably. This allows balancing the benefits and drawbacks of both strategies to optimize performance.

Ultimately, our overall process for computing $\mathsf{Coe}\langle z, t_I \rangle$ can be summarized as follows: we first reduce the superpoly recovery to the instances of the SR problem using Proposition 1 and then solve each instance using the MITM framework (i.e., Step 1 to Step 9). For the implementation of Proposition 2 in the MITM framework, more details can be taken into account for optimization, which are illustrated in [21, Sect. 4.4].

5 Applications

We apply our MITM framework to three stream ciphers that have been targeted in previous research: TRIVIUM, Grain-128AEAD and Kreyvium. As a result, we are able to verify previous results at a much lower time cost, and also recover the exact superpolies for up to 851 rounds of TRIVIUM and up to 899 rounds of Kreyvium. All experiments are conducted using the Gurobi Solver (version 9.1.2) on a workstation equipped with high-speed processors (totally 32 cores and 64 threads). The source code and some of the recovered superpolies are available in our git repository.

More specifically, when referring to the number of rounds for a stream cipher as r, we are considering that the initialization phase of the cipher consists of r rounds, and we assume that we have access to the output bits produced after this initialization phase. We also omit the description of how to construct an MILP model of CMP or MP for a concrete cipher, as they can be found in previous literature [20, 22, 24]. For the cube indices that we will mention later in this section, we also attempt to recover the superpolies by re-running the code provided by [22] on our platform, so that we can compare the time consumption of our MITM framework against the framework presented in [22].

For the cube indices used in this section, we always set the non-cube variables to constant 0, though our MITM framework works no matter what constant values the non-cube variables take.

5.1 Superpoly Recovery for TRIVIUM

TRIVIUM is a hardware-efficient, synchronous stream cipher designed by De Can-nière and Preneel [7]. The specification of TRIVIUM is provided in [21, Sect. 5.1].

Parameters. For the parameters required by the MITM framework, we set B, N, r_0, r_1 to $350, 50\,000, 5, 20$, respectively. The time limit $\tau^{r_e - r_s}$ is selected according to [21, Algorithm 8].

Superpoly Verification for up to 848 Rounds of TRIVIUM. The cube indices of TRIVIUM used for verification are listed in [21, Table 5]. For each cube listed in [21, Table 5], we verified its superpoly using our MITM framework in almost half the time it took in [22]. The verification results are provided in [21, Table 6].

Superpoly Recovery for up to 851 Rounds of TRIVIUM. To the best of our knowledge, currently there is no dedicated method for selecting a good cube that can yield a simple superpoly. However, we notice that using the vector numeric mapping technique published in [45], the authors in [46] discovered two cubes, which we refer to as I_3 and I_4 in Table 2, whose 844-round superpolies are simpler than superpolies of any cubes previously found. This strongly suggests that the superpolies of these two cubes may still maintain manageable complexity even at higher numbers of rounds beyond 844. With this in mind, we applied the MITM framework to these two cubes and successfully recovered the superpolies

Table 2. The cube indices for TRIVIUM up to 851 rounds

I	Indices	Size
I_3	0, 1, 2, 3, 4, 5, 6, 7, 8, 9, 10, 11, 13, 15, 17, 19, 21, 24, 26, 28, 30, 32, 34, 36, 39, 41, 43, 45, 47, 49, 51, 54, 56, 58, 60, 62, 64, 66, 69, 71, 73, 75, 77, 79	44
I_4	0, 1, 2, 3, 4, 5, 6, 7, 8, 9, 10, 11, 13, 15, 17, 19, 22, 24, 26, 28, 30, 32, 34, 37, 39, 41, 43, 45, 47, 49, 52, 54, 56, 58, 60, 62, 64, 67, 69, 71, 73, 75, 77, 79	44

Table 3. Details related to the superpolies recovered for TRIVIUM

I	Rounds	Time Cost	Balancedness[§]	#Monomials[*]	#Key Bits[*]	Degree[*]
I_3	849	24 h	0.50	337 087 128 231	80	32
I_4	849	52 h	0.50	189 293 249 301	80	32
I_3	850	81 h	0.50	3 291 633 158 676	80	34
I_3	851	600 h	0.50	20 129 749 853 208	80	36

[§] The balancedness of each superpoly is estimated by testing 2^{15} random keys.
[*] An upper bound on the number of monomials, the number of involved key bits or the algebraic degree.

for up to 851 rounds of TRIVIUM. The details of the recovered superpolies are given in Table 3. Since the memory required to store the monomials contained in each superpoly exceeds the memory of workstation, we evaluated the number of monomials, the number of involved key bits and the algebraic degree without considering monomial cancellation, and thus the corresponding data in Table 3 is only an upper bound.

We also attempted to reproduce the 851-round superpoly of I_3 using the framework introduced in [22]. Unfortunately, the program had still not terminated even after two months (1440 h). This demonstrates that our MITM framework outperforms previous approaches in terms of computational efficiency and is capable of exceeding what previous work has been able to achieve.

5.2   Superpoly Recovery for Grain-128AEAD

For the cipher Grain-128AEAD that is described in [21, Sup.Mat. G.2], we set the parameters B, N, r_0, r_1 that are required by the MITM framework to $90, 15\,000, 1, 1$, respectively. The time limit $\tau^{r_e - r_s}$ is selected according to [21, Algorithm 9].

Superpoly Verification for up to 192 Rounds of Grain-128AEAD. In [22], the authors recovered a 192-round superpoly with the cube indices chosen as $I = \{0, 1, 2, \ldots, 95\} \backslash \{42, 43\}$. We re-ran the code provided by them on our platform and verified the result after about 45 d. In contrast, our MITM framework only took about 9 d to recover this superpoly, reducing the time to $\frac{1}{5}$ of the original.

5.3 Superpoly Recovery for Kreyvium

In [21, Sup.Mat. G.3], we provide the specification of Kreyvium and discuss the limitations of the effectiveness of our MITM framework on Kreyvium. For the parameters required by the MITM framework, we set B, N, r_0, r_1 to $270, 15\,000, 5, 20$, respectively. The time limit $\tau^{r_e - r_s}$ is selected according to [21, Algorithm 10].

Superpoly Verification for 895-Round Kreyvium. Using the code provided by [22] on our platform, we reproduced the 895-round superpoly of the cube indices $I_0 = \{0, 1, \ldots, 127\} \backslash \{66, 72, 73, 78, 101, 106, 109, 110\}$ in about two weeks. In contrast, our MITM framework took only about 9 d to recover this superpoly.

Superpoly Recovery for up to 899 Rounds of Kreyvium. By adjusting the cube indices I_0 slightly, we finally determine three cube indices that can lead to more than 895 rounds of simple superpolies. These cube indices are referred to as $I_1 = \{0, 1, \ldots, 127\} \backslash \{66, 73, 106, 109, 110\}$, $I_2 = \{0, 1, \ldots, 127\} \backslash \{66, 73, 106, 110\}$ and $I_3 = \{0, 1, \ldots, 127\} \backslash \{66, 73, 85, 87\}$, respectively. The details of the recovered superpolies are given in [21, Table 4].

6 Key Recovery Attack

Based on the memory-efficient Möbius transform proposed by Dinur at EURO-CRYPT 2021 [11], we can mount a key-recovery attack against 851-round TRIVIUM using the superpoly with a time complexity of slightly more than 2^{79} and a memory complexity of about 2^{49} bits. Since in this part we do not bring new techniques, we put the concrete key recovery process in [21, Sect. 6].

Key Recovery for 899-Round Kreyvium. Since the 899-round superpoly of Kreyvium only involves 121 key bits, we can easily mount a key-recovery attack against 899-round Kreyvium with a time complexity of about 2^{127}.

7 Conclusion

In this paper, we analyze algebraically how core monomial trails contribute to the composition of the superpoly, based on the basic definition of core monomial prediction (CMP), thus establishing a theory of superpoly recovery that relies exclusively on CMP. This CMP-based approach can be equivalently linked to MP by means of a variable substitution technique. For a further speedup, we design a meet-in-the-middle (MITM) framework to embed our CMP-based approach. Using this framework, we are able to recover the superpolies for reduced-round versions of the ciphers TRIVIUM and Kreyvium with 851 and 899 rounds, resulting in cube attacks that cover more rounds than previous work.

Acknowledgment. The authors would like to thank the anonymous reviewers for their valuable comments and suggestions to improve the quality of the paper. This research is supported by the National Key Research and Development Program of China (Grant No. 2018YFA0704702), the National Natural Science Foundation of China (Grant No. 62032014, U2336207), Department of Science & Technology of Shandong Province (No. SYS202201), Quan Cheng Laboratory (Grant No. QCLZD202301, QCLZD202306). Kai Hu is supported by the "ANR-NRF project SELECT". The scientific calculations in this paper have been done on the HPC Cloud Platform of Shandong University.

References

1. eSTREAM: the ECRYPT stream cipher project (2018). https://www.ecrypt.eu. org/stream/. Accessed 23 Mar 2021
2. Gurobi Optimization. https://www.gurobi.com
3. ISO/IEC 29192-3:2012: Information technology - Security techniques - Lightweight cryptography - Part 3: stream ciphers. https://www.iso.org/standard/56426.html
4. Aumasson, J.-P., Dinur, I., Meier, W., Shamir, A.: Cube testers and key recovery attacks on reduced-round MD6 and Trivium. In: Dunkelman, O. (ed.) FSE 2009. LNCS, vol. 5665, pp. 1–22. Springer, Heidelberg (2009). https://doi.org/10.1007/978-3-642-03317-9_1
5. Baudrin, J., Canteaut, A., Perrin, L.: Practical cube attack against nonce-misused Ascon. IACR Trans. Symmetric Cryptol. **2022**(4), 120–144 (2022)
6. Boura, C., Coggia, D.: Efficient MILP modelings for sboxes and linear layers of SPN ciphers. IACR Trans. Symmetric Cryptol. **2020**(3), 327–361 (2020)
7. De Cannière, C., Preneel, B.: Trivium. In: Robshaw, M., Billet, O. (eds.) New Stream Cipher Designs. LNCS, vol. 4986, pp. 244–266. Springer, Heidelberg (2008). https://doi.org/10.1007/978-3-540-68351-3_18
8. Canteaut, A., Carpov, S., Fontaine, C., Lepoint, T., Naya-Plasencia, M., Paillier, P., Sirdey, R.: Stream Ciphers: a practical solution for efficient homomorphic-ciphertext compression. J. Cryptol. **31**(3), 885–916 (2018)
9. Che, C., Tian, T.: An experimentally verified attack on 820-round trivium. In: Deng, Y., Yung, M., editors, Information Security and Cryptology - 18th International Conference, Inscrypt 2022, Beijing, China, December 11-13, 2022, Revised Selected Papers, volume 13837 of Lecture Notes in Computer Science, pp. 357–369. Springer, Cham (2022). https://doi.org/10.1007/978-3-031-26553-2_19
10. Delaune, S., Derbez, P., Gontier, A., Prud'homme, C.: A simpler model for recovering superpoly on trivium. In: AlTawy, R., Hülsing, A. (eds.) SAC 2021. LNCS, vol. 13203, pp. 266–285. Springer, Cham (2022). https://doi.org/10.1007/978-3-030-99277-4_13
11. Dinur, I.: Cryptanalytic applications of the polynomial method for solving multivariate equation systems over GF(2). In: Canteaut, A., Standaert, F.-X. (eds.) EUROCRYPT 2021. LNCS, vol. 12696, pp. 374–403. Springer, Cham (2021). https://doi.org/10.1007/978-3-030-77870-5_14
12. Dinur, I., Morawiecki, P., Pieprzyk, J., Srebrny, M., Straus, M.: Cube attacks and cube-attack-like cryptanalysis on the round-reduced Keccak sponge function. In: Oswald, E., Fischlin, M. (eds.) EUROCRYPT 2015. LNCS, vol. 9056, pp. 733–761. Springer, Heidelberg (2015). https://doi.org/10.1007/978-3-662-46800-5_28

13. Dinur, I., Shamir, A.: Cube attacks on tweakable black box polynomials. In: Joux, A. (ed.) EUROCRYPT 2009. LNCS, vol. 5479, pp. 278–299. Springer, Heidelberg (2009). https://doi.org/10.1007/978-3-642-01001-9_16
14. Dinur, I., Shamir, A.: Breaking grain-128 with dynamic cube attacks. In: Joux, A. (ed.) FSE 2011. LNCS, vol. 6733, pp. 167–187. Springer, Heidelberg (2011). https://doi.org/10.1007/978-3-642-21702-9_10
15. Dobraunig, C., Eichlseder, M., Mendel, F., Schläffer, M.: Ascon v1.2: lightweight authenticated encryption and hashing. J. Cryptol. **34**(3), 33 (2021)
16. Fan, H., Hao, Y., Wang, Q., Gong, X., Jiao, L.: Key filtering in cube attacks from the implementation aspect. In: Deng, J., Kolesnikov, V., Schwarzmann, A.A., editors, Cryptology and Network Security - 22nd International Conference, CANS 2023, Augusta, GA, USA, October 31 - November 2, 2023, Proceedings, vol. 14342 of Lecture Notes in Computer Science, pp. 293–317. Springer, Singapore (2023). https://doi.org/10.1007/978-981-99-7563-1_14
17. Fouque, P.-A., Vannet, T.: Improving key recovery to 784 and 799 rounds of trivium using optimized cube attacks. In: Moriai, S. (ed.) FSE 2013. LNCS, vol. 8424, pp. 502–517. Springer, Heidelberg (2014). https://doi.org/10.1007/978-3-662-43933-3_26
18. Funabiki, Y., Todo, Y., Isobe, T., Morii, M.: Improved integral attack on HIGHT. ACISP **2017**, 363–383 (2017)
19. Hao, Y., Jiao, L., Li, C., Meier, W., Todo, Y., Wang, Q.: Links between division property and other cube attack variants. IACR Trans. Symmetric Cryptol. **2020**(1), 363–395 (2020)
20. Hao, Y., Leander, G., Meier, W., Todo, Y., Wang, Q.: Modeling for three-subset division property without unknown subset. In: Canteaut, A., Ishai, Y. (eds.) EUROCRYPT 2020. LNCS, vol. 12105, pp. 466–495. Springer, Cham (2020). https://doi.org/10.1007/978-3-030-45721-1_17
21. He, J., Hu, K., Lei, H., Wang, M.: Massive superpoly recovery with a meet-in-the-middle framework – improved cube attacks on trivium and kreyvium. Cryptology ePrint Archive, Paper 2024/342 (2024). https://eprint.iacr.org/2024/342
22. He, J., Hu, K., Preneel, B., Wang, M.: Stretching cube attacks: improved methods to recover massive superpolies. In: Agrawal, S., Lin, D., editors, Advances in Cryptology - ASIACRYPT 2022 - 28th International Conference on the Theory and Application of Cryptology and Information Security, Taipei, Taiwan, December 5–9, 2022, Proceedings, Part IV, volume 13794 of Lecture Notes in Computer Science, pp. 537–566. Springer, Cham (2022). https://doi.org/10.1007/978-3-031-22972-5_19
23. Hu, K., Sun, S., Todo, Y., Wang, M., Wang, Q.: Massive superpoly recovery with nested monomial predictions. In: Tibouchi, M., Wang, H. (eds.) ASIACRYPT 2021. LNCS, vol. 13090, pp. 392–421. Springer, Cham (2021). https://doi.org/10.1007/978-3-030-92062-3_14
24. Hu, K., Sun, S., Wang, M., Wang, Q.: An algebraic formulation of the division property: revisiting degree evaluations, cube attacks, and key-independent sums. In: Moriai, S., Wang, H. (eds.) ASIACRYPT 2020. LNCS, vol. 12491, pp. 446–476. Springer, Cham (2020). https://doi.org/10.1007/978-3-030-64837-4_15
25. Huang, S., Wang, X., Xu, G., Wang, M., Zhao, J.: Conditional cube attack on reduced-round keccak sponge function. In: Coron, J.-S., Nielsen, J.B., editors, Advances in Cryptology - EUROCRYPT 2017 - 36th Annual International Conference on the Theory and Applications of Cryptographic Techniques, Paris, France, April 30 - May 4, 2017, Proceedings, Part II, volume 10211 of Lecture Notes in Computer Science, pp. 259–288 (2017)

26. Lei, H., He, J., Hu, K., Wang, M.: More balanced polynomials: cube attacks on 810- and 825-round trivium with practical complexities. IACR Cryptol. ePrint Arch., 1237 (2023)

27. Li, Z., Bi, W., Dong, X., Wang, X.: Improved conditional cube attacks on keccak keyed modes with MILP method. In: Takagi, T., Peyrin, T. (eds.) ASIACRYPT 2017. LNCS, vol. 10624, pp. 99–127. Springer, Cham (2017). https://doi.org/10. 1007/978-3-319-70694-8_4

28. Li, Z., Dong, X., Wang, X.: Conditional cube attack on round-reduced ASCON. IACR Trans. Symmetric Cryptol. **2017**(1), 175–202 (2017)

29. Liu, M.: Degree evaluation of NFSR-based cryptosystems. In: Katz, J., Shacham, H. (eds.) CRYPTO 2017. LNCS, vol. 10403, pp. 227–249. Springer, Cham (2017). https://doi.org/10.1007/978-3-319-63697-9_8

30. Liu, M., Yang, J., Wang, W., Lin, D.: Correlation Cube Attacks: from weak-key distinguisher to key recovery. In: Nielsen, J.B., Rijmen, V. (eds.) EUROCRYPT 2018. LNCS, vol. 10821, pp. 715–744. Springer, Cham (2018). https://doi.org/10. 1007/978-3-319-78375-8_23

31. Mroczkowski, P., Szmidt, J.: The cube attack on stream cipher Trivium and quadraticity tests. Fundam. Informaticae **114**(3–4), 309–318 (2012)

32. Rohit, R., Kai, H., Sarkar, S., Sun, S.: Misuse-free key-recovery and distinguishing attacks on 7-round ascon. IACR Trans. Symmetric Cryptol. **2021**(1), 130–155 (2021)

33. Rohit, R., Sarkar, S.: Diving deep into the weak keys of round reduced ascon. IACR Trans. Symmetric Cryptol. **2021**(4), 74–99 (2021)

34. Salam, I., Bartlett, H., Dawson, E., Pieprzyk, J., Simpson, L., Wong, K.K.-H.: Investigating cube attacks on the authenticated encryption stream cipher ACORN. In: Batten, L., Li, G., editors, ATIS 2016, volume 651 of Communications in Computer and Information Science, pp. 15–26 (2016)

35. Sasaki, Yu., Todo, Y.: New algorithm for modeling S-box in MILP based differential and division trail search. In: Farshim, P., Simion, E. (eds.) SecITC 2017. LNCS, vol. 10543, pp. 150–165. Springer, Cham (2017). https://doi.org/10.1007/978-3-319-69284-5_11

36. Song, L., Guo, J., Shi, D., Ling, S.: New MILP Modeling: improved conditional cube attacks on keccak-based constructions. In: Peyrin, T., Galbraith, S. (eds.) ASIACRYPT 2018. LNCS, vol. 11273, pp. 65–95. Springer, Cham (2018). https:// doi.org/10.1007/978-3-030-03329-3_3

37. Sun, L., Wang, W., Wang, M.: Automatic search of bit-based division property for ARX ciphers and word-based division property. In: Takagi, T., Peyrin, T. (eds.) ASIACRYPT 2017. LNCS, vol. 10624, pp. 128–157. Springer, Cham (2017). https://doi.org/10.1007/978-3-319-70694-8_5

38. Sun, L., Wang, W., Wang, M.: MILP-aided bit-based division property for primitives with non-bit-permutation linear layers. IET Inf. Secur. **14**(1), 12–20 (2020)

39. Sun, S., Hu, L., Wang, P., Qiao, K., Ma, X., Song, L.: Automatic security evaluation and (Related-key) differential characteristic search: application to SIMON, PRESENT, LBlock, DES(L) and other bit-oriented block ciphers. In: Sarkar, P., Iwata, T. (eds.) ASIACRYPT 2014. LNCS, vol. 8873, pp. 158–178. Springer, Heidelberg (2014). https://doi.org/10.1007/978-3-662-45611-8_9

40. Sun, Y.: Automatic search of cubes for attacking stream ciphers. IACR Trans. Symmetric Cryptol. **2021**(4), 100–123 (2021)

41. Todo, Y.: Integral cryptanalysis on full MISTY1. In: Gennaro, R., Robshaw, M., editors, CRYPTO 2015, LNCS, vol. 9215, pp. 413–432 (2015)

42. Todo, Y.: Structural evaluation by generalized integral property. In: Oswald, E., Fischlin, M. (eds.) EUROCRYPT 2015. LNCS, vol. 9056, pp. 287–314. Springer, Heidelberg (2015). https://doi.org/10.1007/978-3-662-46800-5_12

43. Todo, Y., Isobe, T., Hao, Y., Meier, W.: Cube attacks on non-blackbox polynomials based on division property. In: Katz, J., Shacham, H. (eds.) CRYPTO 2017. LNCS, vol. 10403, pp. 250–279. Springer, Cham (2017). https://doi.org/10.1007/978-3-319-63697-9_9

44. Todo, Y., Morii, M.: Bit-based division property and application to SIMON family. In: Peyrin, T. (ed.) FSE 2016. LNCS, vol. 9783, pp. 357–377. Springer, Heidelberg (2016). https://doi.org/10.1007/978-3-662-52993-5_18

45. Wang, J., Qin, L., Wu, B.: Correlation cube attack revisited: improved cube search and superpoly recovery techniques. Cryptology ePrint Archive, Paper 2023/1408 (2023). https://eprint.iacr.org/2023/1408

46. Wang, J., Wu, B., Liu, Z.: Improved degree evaluation and superpoly recovery methods with application to trivium. CoRR, abs/2201.06394 (2022)

47. Wang, Q., Grassi, L., Rechberger, C.: Zero-sum partitions of PHOTON permutations. In: Smart, N.P. (ed.) CT-RSA 2018. LNCS, vol. 10808, pp. 279–299. Springer, Cham (2018). https://doi.org/10.1007/978-3-319-76953-0_15

48. Wang, Q., Hao, Y., Todo, Y., Li, C., Isobe, T., Meier, W.: Improved division property based cube attacks exploiting algebraic properties of superpoly. In: Shacham, H., Boldyreva, A. (eds.) CRYPTO 2018. LNCS, vol. 10991, pp. 275–305. Springer, Cham (2018). https://doi.org/10.1007/978-3-319-96884-1_10

49. Wang, S., Hu, B., Guan, J., Zhang, K., Shi, T.: MILP-aided method of searching division property using three subsets and applications. In: Galbraith, S.D., Moriai, S. (eds.) ASIACRYPT 2019. LNCS, vol. 11923, pp. 398–427. Springer, Cham (2019). https://doi.org/10.1007/978-3-030-34618-8_14

50. Xiang, Z., Zhang, W., Bao, Z., Lin, D.: Applying MILP method to searching integral distinguishers based on division property for 6 lightweight block ciphers. In: Cheon, J.H., Takagi, T. (eds.) ASIACRYPT 2016. LNCS, vol. 10031, pp. 648–678. Springer, Heidelberg (2016). https://doi.org/10.1007/978-3-662-53887-6_24

51. Ye, C., Tian, T.: A new framework for finding nonlinear superpolies in cube attacks against trivium-like ciphers. In: Susilo, W., Yang, G. (eds.) ACISP 2018. LNCS, vol. 10946, pp. 172–187. Springer, Cham (2018). https://doi.org/10.1007/978-3-319-93638-3_11

52. Ye, C.-D., Tian, T.: A practical key-recovery attack on 805-round trivium. In: Tibouchi, M., Wang, H. (eds.) ASIACRYPT 2021. LNCS, vol. 13090, pp. 187–213. Springer, Cham (2021). https://doi.org/10.1007/978-3-030-92062-3_7

Diving Deep into the Preimage Security of AES-Like Hashing

Shiyao Chen[4,5] , Jian Guo[3] , Eik List[6], Danping Shi[1,2(✉)] ,
and Tianyu Zhang[3]

[1] Key Laboratory of Cyberspace Security Defense, Institute of Information
Engineering, Chinese Academy of Sciences, Beijing, China
shidanping@iie.ac.cn
[2] School of Cyber Security, University of Chinese Academy of Sciences, Beijing,
China
[3] Division of Mathematical Sciences, School of Physical and Mathematical Sciences,
Nanyang Technological University, Singapore, Singapore
guojian@ntu.edu.sg , tianyu005@e.ntu.edu.sg
[4] Strategic Centre for Research in Privacy-Preserving Technologies and Systems,
Nanyang Technological University, Singapore, Singapore
shiyao.chen@ntu.edu.sg
[5] Digital Trust Centre, Nanyang Technological University, Singapore, Singapore
[6] Weimar, Germany

Abstract. Since the seminal works by Sasaki and Aoki, Meet-in-the-Middle (MITM) attacks are recognized as an effective technique for preimage and collision attacks on hash functions. At Eurocrypt 2021, Bao *et al.* automated MITM attacks on AES-like hashing and improved upon the best manual result. The attack framework has been furnished by subsequent works, yet far from complete. This paper introduces three key contributions dedicated to further generalizing the idea of MITM and refining the automatic model on AES-like hashing. (1) We introduce *S-box linearization* to MITM pseudo-preimage attacks on AES-like hashing. The technique works well with superposition states to preserve information after S-boxes at affordable cost. (2) We propose *distributed initial structures*, an extension on the original concept of initial states, that selects initial degrees of freedom in a more versatile manner to enlarge the search space. (3) We exploit the *structural similarities* between encryption and key schedule in constructions (*e.g.*, Whirlpool and Streebog) to model propagations more accurately and avoid repeated costs. Weaponed with these innovative techniques, we further empower the MITM framework and improve the attack results on AES-like designs for preimage and collision. We obtain the first preimage attacks on 10-round AES-192, 10-round Rijndael-192/256, and 7.75-round Whirlpool, reduced time and/or memory complexities for preimage attacks on 5-, 6-round Whirlpool and 7.5-, 8.5-round Streebog, as well as improved collision attacks on 6- and 6.5-round Whirlpool.

Eik List - visiting independent researcher at Nanyang Technological University, Singapore.

M. Joye and G. Leander (Eds.): EUROCRYPT 2024, LNCS 14651, pp. 398–426, 2024.
https://doi.org/10.1007/978-3-031-58716-0_14

Keywords: Meet-in-the-Middle Attack · S-box Linearization · Distributed Initial Structures · Structural Similiarities · AES · Rijndael · Whirlpool · Streebog

1   Introduction

1.1   Hash Functions

Hash functions map arbitrary long inputs to fixed-length hash values and have been used in a myriad of applications. There are three fundamental security requirements for a cryptographic hash function to fulfill, namely preimage, second-preimage, and collision resistance. This work focuses on the notion of preimage resistance: given a hash function H and a random hash value t, it should be computationally infeasible to find a preimage x such that $H(x) = t$.

To make use of the coexistence of encryption and hashing in embedded systems, a conventional strategy is to construct a hash function from a secure block cipher to minimize hardware or software costs: the encryption function of a block cipher is first transformed into a one-way compression function and then iterated following the Merkle-Damgård design. In 1993, Preneel, Govaerts, and van de Walle [33] identified 12 secure modes for the encryption-compression-function conversion, later known as the PGV modes.

The strategy is highly practical if the underlying block cipher is widely used and has seen a long record of withstanding cryptanalysis, which makes AES the perfect candidate. The MMO mode (one of the PGV modes) instantiated with AES-128 have been standardized by the Zigbee [2] protocol suite and ISO/IEC [24]. Given the high security of AES, several dedicated hash functions are designed with AES-like structures, *e.g.*, the ISO standards Whirlpool [9,23] or the ISO and GOST standard Streebog [1,15,25], which are collectively referred to as AES-like hashing.

1.2   Meet-in-the-Middle Attacks on Block-Cipher-Based Hashing

The Meet-in-the-Middle (MITM) attack is well-known for its effectiveness in cryptanalysis of Double-DES [14] and key recovery. In a series of pioneer works [4,5,36,37], Sasaki and Aoki enlightened the community with MITM attacks applied to the security analyzation of cryptographic hash functions. The core attack framework had been extended ever since by numerous techniques, such as splice-and-cut [4], initial structures [37], indirect and partial matching [4,37], biclique as a formalization of initial structures [26], sieve-in-the-middle [11] and match-boxes [17].

MITM attack on block-cipher-based hash functions is, in essence, a pseudo-preimage attack: the attack splits the computation of the compression function into two chucks, the forward and the backward chunk, so that two portions of input bits, called neutral bits, affect only one of the sub-functions. In such a setting, the chunks are computed independently and end at a common state where their (partial) values are matched. Usually, a third set of bits is shared by both chunks, which is captured in the notion of a 3-subset MITM attack [10].

Sasaki was the first to apply this to a preimage attack on AES hashing modes [35]. However, to avoid the complex relations from the round keys, the key was still fixed to a constant. Sasaki *et al.* then introduced the guess-and-determine strategy [38]. Bao *et al.* [6] revisited the attacks by introducing the degree of freedom from the key space.

At Eurocrypt 2021, Bao *et al.* [7] automated the search for efficient MITM preimage attacks with Mixed-integer Linear Programming (MILP) and applied it to AES hashing modes and Haraka v2. Dong *et al.* [16] later extended this automation model to search for key-recovery and collision attacks and introduced nonlinear constraints for the neutral bits. Later in 2022, Bao *et al.* [8] brought up the concept of superposition bytes, which allowed forward and backward neutral words to propagate simultaneously and independently at a common byte through linear operations in the encryption and key schedule. They also proposed bi-directional attribute propagation and cancellation, *i.e.*, the known values in each chunk are propagated not only in the direction of the chunk but in both directions. Moreover, they integrated the guess-and-determine method into their models. Hua *et al.* [22] then combined guess-and-determine with nonlinearly constrained neutral words in their search for preimage attacks. More recently, Qin *et al.* [34] applied the new framework to Sponges. As a contrast to those very detailed frameworks, Schrottenloher and Stevens proposed a simpler MILP-modeling approach for preimage attacks against keyless permutations [39] and was later extended to ciphers with very light key schedule [40]. While their model was considerably more lightweight and applicable to AES-like permutations, its exclusion of the key schedule made it less effective against the AES than the detailed frameworks.

1.3   Gaps

While previous works on automating MITM on AES-like hashing already provided a groundlaying seminal framework [7,8,16,34], the complexity of the task has left several gaps. Among those, we identified three core challenges:

1. The preimage security evaluation on AES-like hashing has always been at byte-level as the S-box details are abstracted away. Recently, Zhang *et al.* [42] studied the field inversion S-box with algebraic properties and thus can consider the S-box details. However, quoting their words, *this linearizes the non-linear layer of AES, but unfortunately, no attacks better than the current state-of-the-art has been found based on this fact.*
2. The selection of initial states in previous works was limited to two full states, one of them in the encryption function and the other in the key schedule. Initial states could be more scattered, even across several intermediate states. Thus, the artificial limits on initial states had discarded a fraction of the solution pool.

3. It has been a long endeavor to address the dependencies in the model that lead to incorrect measures on the degree of freedom consumption. Particularly, the dependencies due to the structural similarity between the encryption and key schedule in some designs have been overlooked and may lead to duplicate costs.

1.4   Our Contributions

In this work, we have proposed and incorporated three techniques to fill the gaps and improve the state-of-the-art attacks. We would like to point out that the core ideas behind the techniques are fairly generic and expected to have more applications beyond this paper.

Linearizing S-Boxes. We introduce *S-box linearization* (**LIN**) to MITM attacks on AES-like hashing and efficiently incorporate it with the superposition structure. Both propagations at a superposition byte are preserved through the S-box at the cost of guessing over a small pool of *hints*. Making use of the linear relation between propagations, **LIN** checks if a guessed hint is correct efficiently using for- and backward values at S-box input.

In comparison, the study in [42] exploited the algebraic properties of field inversion S-boxes thus resulting in guess-and-determine and announced no improved result on AES. A similar conclusion on their work was also drawn by Liu *et al.* in [29]. The checking phase in plain guess-and-determine requires full information on forward and backward neutral bytes and leads to a cost on degrees of matching, while **LIN** in our proposal uses only local information and spares such cost. To conclude, **LIN** serves as a lightweight alternative to plain guess-and-determine and introduces a new trade-off rule. The technique enables us to mount the first bit-level preimage attacks on AES-like hashing and improve the state-of-the-art.

Distributed Initial Structures. In this work, we further generalize the concept of initial structures, originally proposed by Sasaki and Aoki [37]. We lift the artificial limitation on selecting two full states as initial states and introduce *distributed initial structures* (**DIS**). We now allow the initial states to be distributed in a combination of encryption states and round keys, as long as the total initial degrees of freedom remain the same. An important reflection of this idea is to assign more superposition bytes in the AES key schedule. As only a portion of bytes is propagated through the AES S-box in each key schedule round, more superposition information can be allowed in round keys by the introduction of **DIS**. This has expanded the solution pool by adding more alternatives to the invocation of constraints and allowing more valid propagation patterns.

Structural Similarities. The *structural similarities* (**SIM**) between encryption and key schedule may lead to dependencies across multiple rounds. We observe that values injected into an encryption state by round key addition may propagate through similar sets of operators in encryption and key schedule. Therefore, certain costs of degrees of freedom can be traced back to the same constraints and previous attacks may be suboptimal due to double counting such costs. By modeling the degree consumption more accurately, we enlarged the search space by sparing unnecessary double costs of earlier approaches. Moreover, the approach potentially finds attacks with high concentrations of constraints around the starting points, which could help reduce the memory complexity of the attack.

1.5   Application Results

Our results are as summarized in Table 1. The effectiveness of our proposed techniques is well demonstrated through improved attacks on standards including AES-192 hashing, Whirlpool, and Streebog, as well as the Rijndael hashing family. We argue that the techniques are significant and essential to the breakthroughs.

Both **LIN** and **DIS** are critical for attacking one additional round of AES-192 hashing, i.e. excluding either technique would not yield an attack. Simply using guess-and-determine strategy combined with the AES S-box property also could not improve the attack on Rijndael-192/256. Moreover, the attack advantage on (pseudo-)preimage is non-trivial, *i.e.*, proportional to the size of a subset rather than a fixed constant.

Incorporating **SIM**, we improve the (pseudo-) preimage attacks on 5- and 6-round Whirlpool in terms of time and/or memory complexity. In particular, we achieve a memoryless attack on 5-round Whirlpool. Besides, we present the first preimage attack on 7.75-round Whirlpool, which extends the state-of-the-art by almost a full round while maintaining the same time complexity. What is more, our efficient MILP-based search model improves the 6-round collision attack on Whirlpool and extends it to 6.5 rounds. For Streebog, our approach reduces the time and/or memory complexity on 7.5- and 8.5-round Streebog compared to previous best (pseudo-)preimage attacks.

1.6   Organization

The remainder of this work is structured as follows. In Sect. 2, we provide preliminaries on the MITM attacks and the target designs. Then we elaborate the proposed techniques and their significance in Sect. 3. Thereupon, we present the enhanced MITM framework and MILP modeling in Sect. 4. We detailed pseudo-preimage results of the first attack on 10-round AES-192 hashing and the memoryless attack on 5-round Whirlpool in Sect. 5. Furthermore, other attacks and details of Whirlpool, Rijndael, 8-round AES-192 and Streebog are provided in the full version [12]. Finally, we conclude and discuss in Sect. 6.

2   Preliminaries

2.1   MITM Attacks: Notations and Principle

We provide a high-level overview of MITM pseudo-preimage attacks in Fig. 1 and a list of notations common in all our attack descriptions in Table 2.

Table 1. Results of our improved attacks on AES-like Hashing.

Preimage Attacks

Cipher (target)	#Rounds	T_1 [†]	T_2 [‡]	Memory	Essential technique(s)	References
AES-192 (Hash)	8/12	2^{112}[§]	2^{116}	2^{16}	MITM	[6]
	8/12	$\mathbf{2^{100}}$	$\mathbf{2^{115}}$	2^{96}	**LIN, DIS**, BiDir*	[12, App. B][¶]
	9/12	2^{120}	2^{125}	–	MILP	[7]
	9/12	2^{112}	2^{121}	–	BiDir	[8]
	10/12	2^{124}	2^{127}	2^{124}	**LIN, DIS**, BiDir	Sect. 5.1
Rijndael-192/192 (Hash)	9/12	2^{184}	2^{189}	–	BiDir	[43]
	9/12	$\mathbf{2^{180}}$	$\mathbf{2^{187}}$	2^{180}	**LIN**, BiDir	[12, App. C.1]
Rijndael-192/256 (Hash)	9/12	2^{168}	2^{181}	–	BiDir	[43]
	10/12	$\mathbf{2^{180}}$	2^{187}	2^{180}	**LIN**, BiDir	[12, App. C.2]
Whirlpool (Hash)	5/10	2^{416}	2^{448}	2^{96}	Dedicated	[38]
	5/10	2^{352}	2^{433}	2^{160}	BiDir, MulAK*	[8]
	5/10	$\mathbf{2^{320}}$	$\mathbf{2^{417}}$	$O(1)$	**SIM**, BiDir	Sect. 5.2
	6/10	2^{448}	2^{481}	2^{256}	Dedicated, GnD*	[38]
	6/10	2^{440}	2^{477}	2^{192}	GnD	[8]
	6/10	$\mathbf{2^{416}}$	$\mathbf{2^{465}}$	2^{288}	**SIM**, BiDir, GnD	[12, App. D.1]
	7/10	2^{480}	2^{497}	2^{128}	GnD, MulAK	[8]
	7.75/10	2^{480}	2^{497}	2^{256}	**SIM**, BiDir, GnD	[12, App. D.2]
Streebog-512 (Compression)	7.5/12	2^{496}	–	2^{64}	Dedicated method	[30]
	7.5/12	2^{441}	–	2^{192}	GnD, MulAK	[22]
	7.5/12	$\mathbf{2^{433}}$	–	$\mathbf{2^{177}}$	**SIM**, GnD	[12, App. E.1]
	8.5/12	2^{481}	–	2^{288}	GnD, MulAK	[22]
	8.5/12	2^{481}	–	$\mathbf{2^{129}}$	**SIM**, GnD	[12, App. E.2]
Streebog-512 (Hash)	7.5/12	–	2^{496}	2^{64}	Dedicated method	[30]
	7.5/12	–	$2^{478.25}$	2^{256}	MITM + Multi-collision*	[22]
	7.5/12	–	$\mathbf{2^{474.25}}$	2^{256}	MITM + Multi-collision	[12, App. E.1]
	8.5/12	–	$2^{498.25}$	2^{288}	MITM + Multi-collision	[22]
	8.5/12	–	$\mathbf{2^{498.25}}$	$\mathbf{2^{256}}$	MITM + Multi-collision	[12, App. E.2]

Collision Attacks

Cipher (target)	#Rounds	Time	Memory	Essential technique(s)	References
Whirlpool (Hash)	4.5/10	2^{120}	2^{16}	Rebound	[31]
	4.5/10	2^{64}	2^{16}	Rebound	[28]
	5/10	2^{120}	2^{64}	Super-SBox	[18,27]
	5.5/10	2^{184-s}	2^{s}	Rebound	[28]
	6/10	2^{228}	2^{228}	Quantum	[20]
	6/10	2^{248}	2^{248}	MILP, MITM	[16]
	6/10	$\mathbf{2^{240}}$	$\mathbf{2^{240}}$	New MILP model, MITM	[12, App. A]
	6.5/10	$\mathbf{2^{240}}$	$\mathbf{2^{240}}$	New MILP model, MITM	[12, App. A]

[†] T_1 represents the time complexity of the pseudo-preimage attack on compression function.

[‡] T_2 represents the time complexity of the preimage attack on hash function.

[§] We list only single-target result in [6] for comparison in this table.

* BiDir, MulAK and GnD are techniques introduced to the MITM framework in [8], respectively, short for bi-directional attribute propagation and cancellation, multiple ways of AddRoundKey and guess-and-determine.

[¶] Please refer to the full version of this paper on ePrint [12].

* The attack on the compression function of Streebog is converted into a preimage attack on its hash function using the technique from [3].

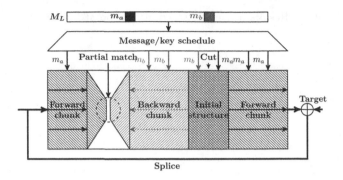

Fig. 1. A high-level overview of MITM attacks [35].

In block-cipher-based hashing, the MITM technique is often used to mount only a pseudo-preimage attack, *i.e.*, a preimage that uses a chaining value different from the fixed initial value of the hash function specification. The pseudo-preimage is later transformed into a preimage on the hash function.

The MITM attack divides the computations into two independent chunks, forward and backward. A byte is called neutral if its value is used only (*i.e.*, is known only) in one of the chunks and has a constant influence on the respective other. Both chunks end at E^+ and E^-, respectively, which are the input and output of a matching operation M. Note that the attack exploits the feed-forward of start and end values in block-cipher-based compression functions. Based on the properties of M, an MITM attack can invoke certain constraints to filter ineligible candidates, which are called partial-match constraints. Those pairs that satisfy these constraints are checked thereupon on larger parts of their states if their combination constitutes a valid pseudo-preimage.

The MITM attack framework [8] with guess-and-determine is described in the following. Without loss of generality, we assume $d_{\mathcal{B}} + g_{\mathcal{B}} \leq d_{\mathcal{R}} + g_{\mathcal{R}}$:

1. Assign arbitrary values to the constants in pre-defined constraints.
2. Compute V^+ and V^- based on the constants.
3. For all tuples $(v^+, g^+, g) \in V^+ \times G^+ \times G$, compute to E^+, obtain m^+ for matching, store (v^+, g^+) in $T^+[m^+, g]$. We have $|T^+| = 2^{d_{\mathcal{B}} + g_{\mathcal{B}} + g_{\mathcal{B}\mathcal{R}}}$
4. For all tuples $(v^-, g^-, g) \in V^- \times G^- \times G$, compute to E^-, obtain m^- for matching.
5. For all (v^+, g^+) in $T^+[m^-, g]$, compute to check if (g^+, g^-, g) is compatible with v^+ and v^-.
6. For compatible (v^+, v^-), check for a full match.
7. If a full match is discovered, compute and return the preimage. Otherwise, revert to Step 1, change the arbitrary values, and repeat the rest.

The computational complexity of the MITM pseudo-preimage attacks is

$$2^{n-(d_{\mathcal{B}}+d_{\mathcal{R}})} \cdot \left(2^{d_{\mathcal{B}}+g_{\mathcal{B}}+g_{\mathcal{B}\mathcal{R}}} + 2^{d_{\mathcal{R}}+g_{\mathcal{R}}+g_{\mathcal{B}\mathcal{R}}} + 2^{d_{\mathcal{B}}+g_{\mathcal{B}}+d_{\mathcal{R}}+g_{\mathcal{R}}+g_{\mathcal{B}\mathcal{R}}-d_{\mathcal{M}}}\right)$$
$$\simeq 2^{n-min(d_{\mathcal{B}}-g_{\mathcal{R}}-g_{\mathcal{B}\mathcal{R}}, d_{\mathcal{R}}-g_{\mathcal{B}}-g_{\mathcal{B}\mathcal{R}}, d_{\mathcal{M}}-g_{\mathcal{B}}-g_{\mathcal{R}}-g_{\mathcal{B}\mathcal{R}})} := 2^l . \tag{1}$$

Table 2. Common notations.

DoF	Degree(s) of freedom
S^{ENC}	Starting state in the encryption
S^{KSA}	Starting state in the key schedule
E^+/E^-	Ending states of forward and backward computations, respectively
M	Matching operation between E^+ and E^-
$d_{\mathcal{B}}/d_{\mathcal{R}}$	DoF of the forward and backward chunk, respectively
$g_{\mathcal{B}}/g_{\mathcal{R}}/g_{\mathcal{BR}}$	DoF of guessed values in the forward, backward, and in both chunks, respectively
$d_{\mathcal{M}}$	Degrees of matching
V^+/V^-	Sets of values for forward and backward neutral bytes satisfying the predefined constraints, with $\|V^+\| = 2^{d_{\mathcal{B}}}$ and $\|V^-\| = 2^{d_{\mathcal{R}}}$, respectively
$G^+/G^-/G$	Sets of guessed values in forward/backward/both chunk(s), with $\|G^+\| = 2^{g_{\mathcal{B}}}$, $\|G^-\| = 2^{g_{\mathcal{R}}}$, and $\|G\| = 2^{g_{\mathcal{BR}}}$
T^+/T^-	Lookup tables constructed at E^+/E^-
$\mathcal{B}^{\text{KSA}}/\mathcal{R}^{\text{KSA}}/\mathcal{G}^{\text{KSA}}$	Sets of indices of forward neutral, backward neutral, and constant bytes in S^{KSA}, respectively
$\mathcal{B}^{\text{ENC}}/\mathcal{R}^{\text{ENC}}/\mathcal{G}^{\text{ENC}}$	Sets of indices of forward neutral, backward neutral, and constant bytes in S^{ENC}, respectively
$\overrightarrow{\iota}/\overleftarrow{\iota}$	Initial DoF of the forward and backward chunk, respectively, with $\overrightarrow{\iota} = \|\mathcal{B}^{\text{ENC}}\| + \|\mathcal{B}^{\text{KSA}}\|$ and $\overleftarrow{\iota} = \|\mathcal{R}^{\text{ENC}}\| + \|\mathcal{R}^{\text{KSA}}\|$
$\overrightarrow{\sigma}/\overleftarrow{\sigma}$	The consumed DoF of the forward and backward chunk, respectively

A pseudo-preimage attack with a computational complexity of 2^l ($l < n - 2$) can be converted to a preimage attack with a computation complexity of $2^{(n+l)/2+1}$ [32]. First, a total of $2^{(n-l)/2}$ pseudo-preimages is obtained. Then, a total of $2^{(n+l)/2+1}$ random values are inserted after the initialization vector IV to obtain $2^{(n+l)/2+1}$ chaining values. Then, one can expect a match between a chaining value and a pseudo-preimage with non-negligible probability, which yields a preimage for the hash function.

2.2 AES-Like Hashing

To start with, we list some common notations in AES-like hashing:

- Nb/Nk: number of columns of a state in the encryption procedure or the secret key. When Nb and Nk are identical, we will denote both by NCOL.
- NROW: number of rows in an encryption or key state.

AES-like hashing refers to hash functions whose compression function follows an AES-like round structure. In this section, we will focus on recalling the necessary details of AES and Whirlpool that are used in this work.

AES. In 2001, the NIST selected a subset of the Rijndael family of block ciphers [13] with a block size of 128 bits and key sizes of 128, 192, or 256 bits (Nb = 4,

Nk $\in \{4, 6, 8\}$, and NROW $= 4$) as the Advanced Encryption Standard. Conventionally, the transposed of a column is referred to as a word, and the word size is thus fixed to $4 \times 8 = 32$ bits. As shown in Fig. 2, an AES round consists of the following operations:

- SubBytes (SB): A non-linear byte-wise substitution.
- ShiftRows (SR): A cyclic left shift on the i-th row by i bytes, for $i \in \{0, 1, 2, 3\}$.
- MixColumns (MC): A column-wise left multiplication of a 4-×-4 maximum-distance-separable matrix.
- AddRoundKey (AK): A bitwise XOR of the round key to the state.

The final round differs in the sense that it omits the MixColumns operation. Before the first round, a whitening key is added to the plaintext.

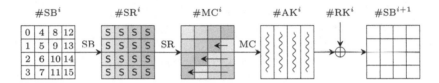

Fig. 2. AES-like round function.

The round keys are expanded from the master key key: Let w be an array of bytes, when $i <$ Nk, the key words are derived directly from the secret key $w[i] = key[i]$. Otherwise, $w[i]$ is calculated as follows:

$$\begin{cases} w[i - \text{Nk}] \oplus \text{Rot}(\text{S}(w[i-1])) \oplus C[i/\text{Nk}] & i \bmod \text{Nk} \equiv 0 \text{ and } \text{Nk} < 8 \\ w[i - \text{Nk}] \oplus \text{S}(w[i-1]) & i \bmod \text{Nk} \equiv 4 \text{ and } \text{Nk} = 8 \\ w[i - \text{Nk}] \oplus w[i-1] & \text{otherwise,} \end{cases} \quad (2)$$

where S denotes the AES S-box, Rot is a left rotation of the input by one byte, and C represents the list of round constants.

The AES-128 in the Matyas-Meyer-Oseas (MMO) mode is used in the standards of the Zigbee protocol suite [2] and ISO/IEC [24]. The MMO mode is defined as the mapping $f : f(H_i, M_i) = E_{H_i}(M_i) \oplus M_i$, where H_i stands for the i-th chaining value, M_i as the i-th message block, and E_k stands for the block cipher encryption under key k.

Whirlpool. In 2000, Rijmen and Barreto [9] designed Whirlpool as a submission to the NESSIE competition that was later tweaked and adopted as an ISO/IEC standard [23]. Whirlpool is a block-cipher-based hash function with a 512-bit hash value, which adopts a 10-round AES-like block cipher with 8×8-byte (NROW = NCOL = 8) keys and plaintexts in Miyaguchi-Preneel mode [33] (MP mode) as its compression function (CF). The MP mode is defined as $f(H_i, M_i) = E_{H_i}(M_i) \oplus M_i \oplus H_i$. It takes the 512-bit chaining value H_i as the key and the 512-bit message block M_i as its plaintext input. Encryption and key schedule essentially use the same round function, except for the fact that the key state has additions with round constants and the encryption state sees additions with the round keys. The round function is depicted in Fig. 3 and consists of:

- **SubBytes** (SB): applies the Substitution-Box to each byte.
- **ShiftColumns** (SC): cyclically shifts the j-column downwards by j bytes.
- **MixRows** (MR): multiplies each row of the state by an MDS matrix.
- **AddRoundKey** (AK): XORs the round key to the state.

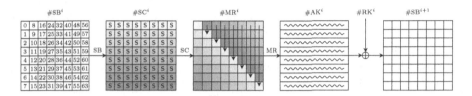

Fig. 3. The round function of Whirlpool.

Note that the final round is a complete round unlike that in the **AES**; a whitening key is added before the first round of encryption as in the **AES**. However, in the MP mode, the whitening key cancels in splice-and-cut MITM attacks due to the feed-forward operation. The key schedule shares the same operations, but replaces **AddRoundKey** by **AddRoundConstants** (AC), which XORs the round constants to the first row of the key state before the result of AC is used as the round key that is added to the state. For more details, we refer the readers to the design paper [9].

Remark 1. Given that the *transposition between row and column* has no impact on attack results, for convenience, we use **ShiftRows** and **MixColumns** instead of **ShiftColumns** and **MixRows** in the rest of paper for **Whirlpool** hereafter. Thus, the states will be *transposed* to correspond with the states of **Whirlpool**.

Remark 2. In the remainder, we will denote a state by the operation that it is used as the direct input for, and will superscript the round index. For example, $\#SB^i$ denotes the state before the SB operation in Round i, as is shown in Figs. 2 and 3.

Remark 3. The Russian national standard **Streebog** follows a similar structure as **Whirlpool**, due to the space limit, we provide the specification of **Streebog** in the full version [12, Appendix E].

3   Advanced Techniques in MITM Attacks

We advance the existing automated MITM frameworks with three generic techniques. Here, we detail the ideas and integration into the augmented framework.

3.1   S-Box Linearization (LIN)

In MITM attacks, we have two sets of states $V^+ = (v_0^+, \ldots, v_{2^{d_b}-1}^+)$ and $V^- = (v_0^-, \ldots, v_{2^{d_r}-1}^-)$ propagating through the cipher. The superposition structure allows any cell of any state $v_{i,j}$ to be represented as the sum of its forward and backward neutral components: $v_{i,j} = v_i^+ \oplus v_j^-$, such that the components v_i^+ and v_j^- can be propagated independently through linear operations. Though, the nonlinear operations, *i.e.*, an S-box S in AES-like ciphers, prevent such trivial linear combinations.

Earlier works in the series of automated MITM attacks on AES-like ciphers had to define propagation rules which either lost knowledge about the cell after the S-box or which consumed one byte degree of freedom for forcing at least one neutral value to be constant before and after the nonlinear operation. We can linearize certain S-boxes partially or fully by restricting the input space or by guessing a hint from a set that is smaller than the input space.

In this work, we consider full linearization with a hint. Thus, we aim at finding a decomposition of S, more precisely, functions $F, G, H : \mathbb{F}_2^b \times \mathbb{F}_2^b \to \mathbb{F}_2^b$ with F and G being linear over $\mathbb{F}_2$ such that

$$S(v^+ \oplus v^-) = F(v^+, H(v^+, v^-)) \oplus G(v^-, H(v^+, v^-)).$$

The range of H is the set of space of hints. Assuming balancedness of H, *i.e.*, $d_{\mathcal{L}} = \dim(\mathrm{range}(H))$, then $2^{d_{\mathcal{L}}}$ elements have to be guessed at most to linearize S, which is beneficial if we find such a function H with $d_{\mathcal{L}} < b$. Then, we add a complexity term of $2^{d_{\mathcal{L}}}$ to the attack for guessing the hint for each combination of (v_i^+, v_j^-) but can propagate a superposition through the S-box.

The S-box of the AES is given by $S(v) = \mathbf{A} \cdot v^{254} \oplus \texttt{0x63}$ for a fixed $\mathbf{A} \in \mathbb{F}_2^{8 \times 8}$. The power map and the XOR is in the field $\mathbb{F}_{2^8}$ with a fixed irreducible polynomial; only the affine layer $\mathbf{A}$ is not defined over this field. At Asiacrypt 2023, Zhang *et al.* [42] observed that one can decompose 254 into $17 \cdot 14 + 16$ and obtain

$$\begin{aligned}(v^+ + v^-)^{254} &= ((v^+ + v^-)^{17})^{14} \cdot (v^+ + v^-)^{16} \\ &= (H(v^+, v^-))^{14} \cdot ((v^+)^{16} + (v^-)^{16}),\end{aligned}$$

where the last equality holds since exponentiation with any power of 2 is linear over $\mathbb{F}_2$. Then according to the following Theorem 1, the hint $H(v^+, v^-)$ can take $|\mathrm{range}(H)| = |\{v^{17} : v \in \mathbb{F}_{2^8}\}| = 16$ values (including the zero element). Thus, one can linearize the AES S-box by guessing at most 16 candidates.

Theorem 1. *Let d be a divisor of $|\mathbb{F}_q^*| = p^n - 1$ where $q = p^n$, and let $X = \{x^d : x \in \mathbb{F}_q^*\}$. The size of X is $|X| = |\mathbb{F}_q^*|/d = (p^n - 1)/d$.*

3.2   Distributed Initial Structures (DIS)

It has been a common approach in MILP-based MITM models to select two independent initial states: S^{ENC} in the encryption function and S^{KSA} in the key schedule, as the generation of round keys is independent of the encryption in most designs. In this work, we generalize the selection of initial states.

In essence, the initial states in MITM attacks are composed of some intermediate bytes in the compression function where we distribute initial DoFs for forward and backward computations. There should be no limitations on where the initial DoF is located, as long as the values of those states can be chosen independently of each other in the actual attack. In other words, the initial DoFs can be distributed to several scattered intermediate states, rather than rigidly selecting two full states in encryption and key schedule, respectively. Previous models implicitly limited the key bytes to depend only on S^{KSA} and not on S^{ENC}, and consequently, shrunk the solution pool.

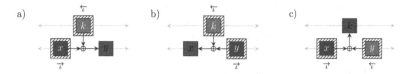

Fig. 4. Conceptual strategies of distributing initial states in two states and a key byte.

Consider an intuitive toy example in Fig. 4. Assume x and y denotes bytes in the encryption and k denote a byte in the key, and we distribute initial DoF in this system for forward and backward computation. The whole system has a total initial DoF of 2. We use $\overrightarrow{\iota}$ and $\overleftarrow{\iota}$ to denote the initial DoF for forward and backward respectively, and the color green ▢ to denote a byte in superposition. Without loss of generality, there are three possible scenarios as depicted in Fig. 4. The previous models covered the first two cases while excluding the third one, wherein the key byte is dependent on the initial DoF from the encryption.

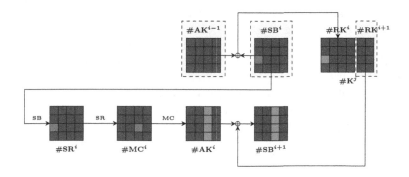

Fig. 5. Example of a distributed initial structure on AES-192.

We extend the above insight to MITM attacks by the introduction of **DIS**. We now distribute the initial DoF to several intermediate states in the compression function, provided that the bytes are independent and there is sufficient information to define all the round keys and all the intermediate encryption states. For example, Fig. 5 describes an example to distribute initial DoF in AES-192. We will distribute initial DoFs in $\#\text{AK}^i$, $\#\text{SB}^{i+1}$ and the rightmost two columns of $\#\text{K}^j$. In this way, we have straightforwardly defined a full intermediate encryption state $\#\text{SB}^{i+1}$, and we can squeeze out a full $\#\text{K}^j$ for key schedule propagations.

The technique is useful in AES, since the key schedule has relatively low confusion and more linear relations can be preserved. In this work, we realize **DIS** in a heuristic manner. We still select S^{ENC} and S^{KSA} respectively to search for attack configurations, but make the exception that superposition bytes are now allowed in S^{KSA} and remain refrained from S^{ENC}. When a configuration is obtained, we check if the initial states can be equivalently chosen to properly define the superposition bytes in S^{KSA} within the maximum available DoF of the target cipher. Our realization of **DIS**, though heuristic, is more tailored to the key schedule and helps extend the analysis of AES-192 by one round.

3.3   Structural Similarities (SIM)

The models by Bao *et al.* and Dong *et al.* could find longer attacks than the manual attacks *e.g.*, by Sasaki [35] since the former effectively used the degree of freedom in key space to obtain reductions in the encryption state. From the XOR of the state with a round key, state bytes in superposition could become single-colored, and forward or backward neutral bytes could become constants. Such concessions are useful and often necessary before and after non-linear operations so that the knowledge of a byte can be propagated further. However, they come at the price of consuming a degree of freedom from the possible solution space.

In previous works, the effects of multiple round-key additions on the state have been usually modeled to be *independent* from each other and the state values. However, constraints from some consecutive rounds may stem from the same source of the neutral words in the key and state, *e.g.*, as depicted in Fig. 6, constraints in states Y^{r_0} and Y^{r_1} are set on the same neutral words in states X^r and $K^{r'}$. Thus, tracing constraints back to such shared sources may enlarge the search space by avoiding duplicate DoF consumption. However, modeling all such dependent constraint relations can become challenging since the relations between all state and key bytes would have to be considered, which can render models infeasible to compute. Nevertheless, we can efficiently model certain special cases, and consider here the *structural similarities* of encryption and key schedule, *e.g.*, Whirlpool and Streebog use almost the same functions for updating key and message, differing only in the usage of round constants. Considering previous best MITM attacks on Whirlpool [8], Bao *et al.* already observed such dependency between encryption and key schedule, however, in their 7-round attacks on Whirlpool, they only used it in a post-processing step to generate the solution space of neutral words. In this work, we include this structural similarity explicitly in our MILP models.

General Concept. For SPNs, we can write the round function as a composition of a nonlinear S-box layer SB, an affine layer $\mathbf{A}$, and a key addition. Assume, the

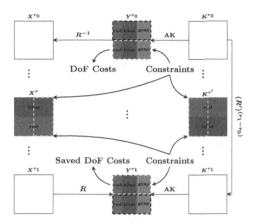

Fig. 6. High-level view of the different constraints connected by key schedule.

key schedule employs the same S-box layer SB, an affine layer $\mathbf{A}'$, and a constant addition. Consider an interval of rounds from i to $i+1$ and assume that we can split the key $\#\mathrm{K}^i$ and the state in the encryption $\#\mathrm{AK}^i$ into an active part, subscripted by a, and a constant part subscripted by c, each: $\#\mathrm{K}^i = \#\mathrm{K}^i_a \| \#\mathrm{K}^i_c$ and $\#\mathrm{AK}^i = \#\mathrm{AK}^i_a \| \#\mathrm{AK}^i_c$. Figure 7 illustrates this setting. If the active parts of the key and encryption state are equal before the S-box layer, then the same values will also be the results in both the encryption and key schedule:

$$\#\mathrm{SB}^{i+1}_a = \#\mathrm{K}^{i+1}_a \Leftrightarrow \#A^{i+1}_a = \#A'^{i+1}_a .$$

If $\#A^{i+1}_a$ and $\#A'^{i+1}_a$ are mapped to the same positions of the state after $\mathbf{A}$ and $\mathbf{A}'$, respectively, then the nonlinear contributions will cancel. Thus, we can define a nonlinear function G and a linear function H such that the active part of the message after the round is given by

$$\#\mathrm{SB}^{i+1}_a = G(\#\mathrm{K}^i_a) \oplus H(\#\mathrm{K}^i_c, \#\mathrm{K}^i_a, \#\mathrm{AK}^i_c) .$$

Note that it does not depend on $\#\mathrm{AK}^i_a$.

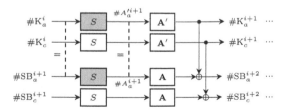

Fig. 7. Exploiting similar operations in the encryption and key schedule.

We can generalize this observation to multiple rounds if the similarities between key schedule and message schedule allow. Given that the diffusion of

AES-like ciphers is usually strong, *i.e.*, an MDS matrix, the number of subsequent rounds where this approach can be employed seems limited to two or three rounds, depending on the round constants and the linear layers. However, it will enlarge the search space and lead to high concentrations of constraints around the starting points, which could help reduce the memory complexity of the attack, as we will demonstrate later in our application results.

4 Enhanced Attack Framework and MILP Model

This section demonstrates our enhanced attack framework, that we call the exceptional MITM framework, and the equipped MILP-based search model.

4.1 Exceptional MITM Framework

We append the following two new notations to Table 2 to reflect the use of **LIN** (Table 3):

Table 3. Additional notations.

$d_{\mathcal{L}}$	DoF consumed by S-Box linearizations
H	Space or set of hints from linearized S-boxes, with $|H| = 2^{d_{\mathcal{L}}}$

Again, without loss of generality, we assume $d_{\mathcal{B}} + g_{\mathcal{B}} \leq d_{\mathcal{R}} + g_{\mathcal{R}}$. The exceptional MITM attack framework is formulated as follows:

1. Assign arbitrary values to the constants in pre-defined constraints.
2. Compute V^+ and V^- based on the constants.
3. For all tuples $(v^+, g^+, g, h^+) \in V^+ \times G^+ \times G \times H$, compute to E^+, obtain m^+ for matching, store (v^+, g^+) in $T^+[m^+, g, h^+]$.
4. For all tuples $(v^-, g^-, g, h^-) \in V^- \times G^- \times G \times H$, compute to E^-, obtain m^- for matching.
5. For all (v^+, g^+) in $T^+[m^-, g, h^-]$ and (v^+, v^-) consistent with h^-, compute to check if (g^+, g^-, g) is compatible with (v^+, v^-).
6. For compatible (v^+, v^-), check for a full match.
7. If a full match is discovered, compute and return the preimage. Otherwise, revert to step 1, change the arbitrary values, and repeat the rest.

The computational complexity of the above attack is evaluated as follows:

$$2^{n-(d_{\mathcal{B}}+d_{\mathcal{R}})} \cdot \left(2^{d_{\mathcal{B}}+g_{\mathcal{B}}+g_{\mathcal{B}\mathcal{R}}+d_{\mathcal{L}}} + 2^{d_{\mathcal{R}}+g_{\mathcal{R}}+g_{\mathcal{B}\mathcal{R}}+d_{\mathcal{L}}} + 2^{d_{\mathcal{B}}+g_{\mathcal{B}}+d_{\mathcal{R}}+g_{\mathcal{R}}+g_{\mathcal{B}\mathcal{R}}-d_{\mathcal{M}}}\right)$$

$$\simeq 2^{n-min(d_{\mathcal{B}}-g_{\mathcal{R}}-g_{\mathcal{B}\mathcal{R}}-d_{\mathcal{L}}, d_{\mathcal{R}}-g_{\mathcal{B}}-g_{\mathcal{B}\mathcal{R}}-d_{\mathcal{L}}, d_{\mathcal{M}}-g_{\mathcal{B}}-g_{\mathcal{R}}-g_{\mathcal{B}\mathcal{R}})}.$$

$$(3)$$

4.2   MILP-Based Search Model

Now we introduce an enhanced MILP model to integrate proposed techniques, including new coloring schemes and corresponding propagation rules in detail.

Color-Encoding Scheme of Neutral Words. We encode different byte types in the superposition structure with three binary variables b, r, and w:.

- A blue cell ■ denotes a forward neutral byte, encoded as $(b, r, w) = (1, 0, 0)$.
- A red cell ■ denotes a backward neutral byte, encoded as $(b, r, w) = (0, 1, 0)$.
- A white cell □ denotes an arbitrary byte, encoded as $(b, r, w) = (0, 0, 1)$.
- A gray cell ■ denotes a constant byte, encoded as $(b, r, w) = (0, 0, 0)$.
- A green cell □ denotes a superposition byte, encoded as $(b, r, w) = (1, 1, 0)$.

In the encoding system, $b = 1$ and $r = 1$ denote that a byte contains forward and backward neutral information, respectively. And $w = 1$ uniquely identifies an arbitrary byte, whose value is unknown, against other byte types. Such construction has high clarity and interpretability, rather than a simple enumeration of the five possible byte types in the superposition structure , and allows a more straightforward realization of propagation rules and efficient counting of DoF. For example, we can easily obtain the initial DoFs $|\mathcal{B}^{\text{ENC}}|$, $|\mathcal{R}^{\text{ENC}}|$, $|\mathcal{B}^{\text{KSA}}|$, and $|\mathcal{R}^{\text{KSA}}|$ by simply summing up b, r encoders in corresponding states.

Our model achieves high efficiencies and makes it possible for better attacks on designs with large state sizes. The new model can formulate attacks on Whirlpool and Streebog in full-sized versions (8×8), while Bao *et al.* 's attack on Whirlpool is limited to 4×4 versions with symmetry patterns [8]. Specifically, our improved MITM attack configurations for Whirlpool can be found within 200 s, and the optimization of MITM collision attack models of 6-round Whirlpool can be finished within just 300 s[1].

In the rest of this chapter, notions b_α, r_α, and w_α are used to represent the encoders of a byte α.

Propagations Through SubBytes. We formulate the SB-rule, a byte-wise propagation rule for SubBytes, with **LIN** integrated.

- When the input byte is not green, the color of the output byte is identical to that of the input byte.
- When the input byte is green, the output byte is either white by default or green with one cost of linearization ($d_{\mathcal{L}}$ incremented by one).

Modeling the SB-rule requires both encoders of the input and output byte as well as one additional encoder to indicate linearization cost. The rule can be converted to MILP constraints with the convex-hull method [41].

Propagations Through MixColumns. The MixColumns operation takes a column as input and outputs a column. Assume that the input is a mix of n_b blue

---

[1] We ran our MILP models with Gurobi 9.5.2 on a desktop computer with 3.6 GHz Intel Core i9 and 16GB 2667 MHz DDR4.

bytes, n_r red bytes, n_c gray bytes, n_g green bytes, and n_w white bytes, the basic rule for the MixColumns operation, MC-rule in short, is formulated as follows:

- When $n_w > 0$, the output contains only white bytes.
- When $n_w = 0$ and $n_b + n_r + n_g = 0$, the output contains only gray bytes.
- When $n_w = n_r = 0$ and $n_b + n_g > 0$, the output contains n'_b blue bytes and n'_c gray bytes, with n'_c consumed DoF from the forward chunk.
- When $n_w = n_b = 0$ and $n_r + n_g > 0$, the output contains n'_r red bytes and n'_c gray bytes, with n'_c consumed DoF from the backward chunk.
- Otherwise, the output is a mix of n'_b blue bytes, n'_r red bytes, n'_c gray bytes, and n'_g green bytes, with $n'_b + n'_c$ consumed DoF from the backward chunk and $n'_r + n'_c$ consumed DoF from the forward chunk.

We use α to denote a byte in the input column and β in the output. To realize the above functionality, we introduce three column-wise encoders Eb, Er, and Ew, which is constructed based on the encoding of input bytes:

$$Eb = \max_{\alpha} b_{\alpha}, \ Er = \max_{\alpha} r_{\alpha}, \ \text{and} \ Ew = \max_{\alpha} w_{\alpha}. \tag{4}$$

Let further $\overrightarrow{\sigma_{\beta}}$ and $\overleftarrow{\sigma_{\beta}}$ be binary variables that respectively track the DoF consumption at byte β (in the output column) for the forward and backward chunk. Then, the MC-rule can be formulated as:

$$\begin{cases} \sum_{\beta} w_{\beta} = \text{NROW} \cdot Ew \\ \sum_{\alpha} b_{\alpha} + \sum_{\beta} b_{\beta} = \text{NROW} \cdot (Eb - Ew) \\ \sum_{\alpha} r_{\alpha} + \sum_{\beta} r_{\beta} = \text{NROW} \cdot (Er - Ew) \\ \text{NROW} \cdot (Eb - Ew) \leq \sum_{\beta} b_{\beta} + \sum_{\beta} \overrightarrow{\sigma_{\beta}} \leq \text{NROW} \cdot \min(Eb, 1 - Ew) \\ \text{NROW} \cdot (Er - Ew) \leq \sum_{\beta} r_{\beta} + \sum_{\beta} \overleftarrow{\sigma_{\beta}} \leq \text{NROW} \cdot \min(Er, 1 - Ew) \end{cases} \tag{5}$$

Integrating Guess-and-Determine Into MixColumns. We introduce a light-weight realization of GnD by integrating its functionality into MC-rule, which is named GnD-MC-rule. We introduce four GnD encoders for an input byte α, g_{α}^w, g_{α}^b, g_{α}^r, and g_{α}^{br}, which satisfy:

$$w_{\alpha} = g_{\alpha}^w + g_{\alpha}^b + g_{\alpha}^r + g_{\alpha}^{br}. \tag{6}$$

The simple constraint ensures that, when an input byte α is non-white, all GnD encoders are 0, meaning no GnD is incurred. Otherwise, when α is white, exactly one GnD encoder equals to 1 with the following meaning:

- $g_{\alpha}^w = 1$: GnD is not activated and byte α remains unknown,
- $g_{\alpha}^b = 1$: α is guessed as blue for forward propagation,
- $g_{\alpha}^r = 1$: α is guessed as red for backward propagation,
- $g_{\alpha}^{br} = 1$: α is guessed as green for both forward and backward propagations.

The GnD-MC-rule is formulated based on MC-rule by a simple tweak on the construction of the column-wise encoders:

$$Eb' = \max_{\alpha}\{b_\alpha, g_\alpha^b, g_\alpha^{br}\}, \ Er' = \max_{\alpha}\{r_\alpha, g_\alpha^r, g_\alpha^{br}\}, \text{ and } Ew' = \max_{\alpha} g_\alpha^w. \qquad (7)$$

We count the guessed DoF by summing up the GnD encoders. Moreover, GnD can be turned off easily for efficiency by adding a simple constraint $w_\alpha = g_\alpha^w$.

XOR with Two Inputs. The XOR-rule models the propagation of variables through a simple XOR operation with two inputs:

- When the input involves a white byte, the output is white.
- When the input contains only gray bytes, the output is gray.
- When the input contains only blue bytes, the output is either blue with no consumption of DoF or gray consuming one DoF from the forward chunk.
- When the input contains only red bytes, the output is either red with no DoF consumption or gray consuming one DoF from the backward chunk.
- When the input is a mixture of red and blue bytes or involves green bytes, the output is green.

Generating the constraints to account for the XOR-rule in MILP is well understood and therefore omitted here.

XOR with Multiple Inputs. In addition to sequentially deriving the round keys following Eq. (2), we propose a new approach to model the AES key schedule. We find the expression of intermediate bytes in terms of bytes in KSA by invoking a sourcing function, which is designed to recursively obtain the parents of an intermediate byte and cancels whenever a byte is XORed an even number of times. Then we propose the n-XOR-rule to determine the coloring of an intermediate byte and the consumed DoF, detailed as follows:

- When the input involves a white byte, the output is white.
- When the input contains only gray bytes, the output is gray.
- When the input contains only blue bytes, the output is either blue with no DoF consumed or gray with 1 DoF consumed from the forward chunk.
- When the input contains only red bytes, the output is either red with no DoF consumed or gray with 1 DoF consumed from the backward chunk.
- When the input contains both red and blue bytes, the output is one of the following:
    - green, with no consumption of DoF,
    - blue, with 1 DoF consumed from the backward chunk,
    - red, with 1 DoF consumed from the forward chunk, or
    - gray, with 1 DoF consumed from each forward and backward chunk.

We denote a byte in the expression of an intermediate byte as γ and introduce three encoders Pb, Pr, and Pw for the intermediate byte that satisfy:

$$Pb = \max_{\gamma} b_\gamma, \ Pr = \max_{\gamma} r_\gamma, \text{ and } Pw = \max_{\gamma} w_\gamma. \qquad (8)$$

The constraints for the n-input XOR rule can be obtained by using the convex-hull method on Pb, Pr, Pw, the encoders of the intermediate byte, and two encoders for DoF costs.

Matching. We deploy two types of matching in our attacks: the XOR-match and the MC-match. The XOR-match is used at the feed-forward that checks E^+, E^-, and $\#RK^{-1}$ byte by byte. If $w_\alpha = 0$ holds for position α in E^+, E^-, and $\#RK^{-1}$, then $m_\alpha = 1$. Otherwise, $m_\alpha = 1$. Then, $d_\mathcal{M}^{\text{XOR}}$ results from:

$$d_\mathcal{M}^{\text{XOR}} = \sum_\alpha m_\alpha. \tag{9}$$

Besides, the MC-match takes the input and output of a MixColumns operation as E^+ and E^- and counts the cumulative non-white bytes at a common column index. Let Δ be a column index and denote the cumulative non-white bytes in E_Δ^+ and E_Δ^- as t_Δ. If there exist $t_\Delta > \text{NROW}$, then we have a $t_\Delta - \text{NROW}$ degrees for matching at column Δ. Otherwise, there are no degrees of matching at column Δ. Then $d_\mathcal{M}^{\text{MC}}$ is given by the sum over all columns:

$$d_\mathcal{M}^{\text{MC}} = \sum_\Delta \max(0, t_\Delta - \text{NROW}). \tag{10}$$

Objective Function. Our search model aims to maximize:

$$\min\{d_\mathcal{B} - g_\mathcal{R} - g_{\mathcal{BR}} - d_\mathcal{L}, d_\mathcal{R} - g_\mathcal{B} - g_{\mathcal{BR}} - d_\mathcal{L}, d_\mathcal{M} - g_\mathcal{B} - g_\mathcal{R} - g_{\mathcal{BR}}\} \tag{11}$$

According to Eq. (3), $\min\{\overrightarrow{d_b}, \overleftarrow{d_r}, \overrightarrow{m}\}$ determines the complexity of an MITM attack. Thus, the search for the optimal MITM attack pattern of given *config* is converted to a maximization problem on objective τ_{Obj}:

5   Applications to AES and Whirlpool

In this section, we briefly describe the *first* 10-round MITM pseudo-preimage attack on the compression function of AES-192 and the *memoryless* 5-round MITM pseudo-preimage attack on the compression function of Whirlpool.

5.1   First MITM Pseudo-preimage Attack on 10-Round AES-192

The previous best MITM pseudo-preimage attack on AES-192 reaches 9 rounds [8]. Adopting **LIN** and **DIS**, we obtain the first MITM pseudo-preimage attack on 10-round AES-192, which is provided in Fig. 8 and summarized below:

- Initial DoF for forward neutral words $\overrightarrow{\iota}$ (■): 39 bytes (16 in $\#AK^5$, 15 bytes in $\#SB^6$, and 8 bytes $\#K^4[16\ldots23]$);
- Initial DoF for backward neutral words $\overleftarrow{\iota}$ (■): 1 byte ($\#SB^6[2]$);
- Consumed DoF in forward computation $\overrightarrow{\sigma}$: 38 bytes;
- Consumed DoF in backward computation $\overleftarrow{\sigma}$: zero bytes;
- Guessed bytes for blue, red, and both colors $g_\mathcal{B}$, $g_\mathcal{R}$, $g_{\mathcal{BR}}$: $g_\mathcal{R} = g_{\mathcal{BR}} = 0$ bytes and $g_\mathcal{B} = 0$ bytes;
- Guessed byte equivalents for linearization: $d_\mathcal{L} = 0.5$ bytes.
- Matching DoF $d_\mathcal{M}$: 1 byte between $\#AT^9$ and $\#SB^0$.
- Remaining DoF: $d_\mathcal{B} - d_\mathcal{L} = 1 - 0.5 = 0.5$ and $d_\mathcal{R} - d_\mathcal{L} = 1 - 0.5 = 0.5$.

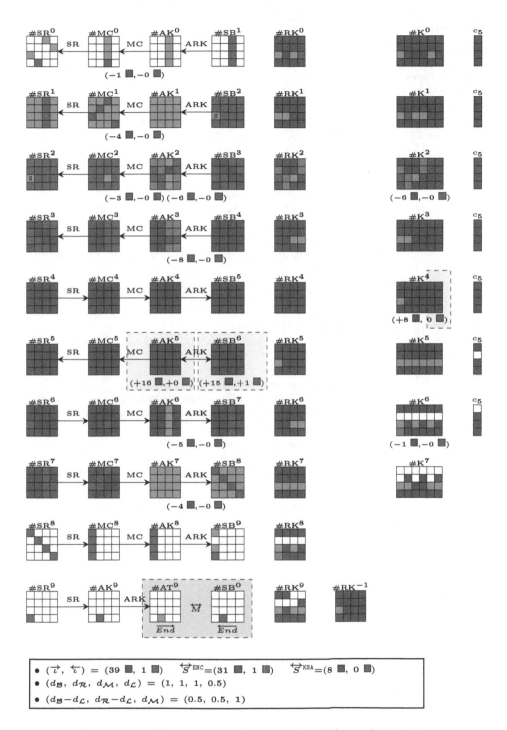

Fig. 8. An MITM pseudo-preimage attack of 10-round AES-192.

Algorithm 1: Computing forward neutral words (blue) for 10-round AES-192.

---

1 Initialize a table $T_{\text{blue}}^{\text{neutral}}$;

2 Fix 6 bytes $\#K^2[1,2,6,7,12,13]$, 6 ■ cells in $\#AK^2$, 3 bytes $\#MC^2[8,9,11]$, 2 bytes $\#MC^1[8,15]$ and $\#AK^3[8..15]$ be all zero.

3 **for** 4 ■ *blue cells* $\#K^4[4,5,6,7] \in (\mathbb{F}_2^8)^4$ **do**

4 $\quad$ Use 4 constants $\#K^2[6,7,12,13]$ to derive $\#K^4[12,13]$, $\#K^3[20,23]$;

5 $\quad$ **for** 3 ■ *blue cells* $\#K^3[18,19,22] \in (\mathbb{F}_2^8)^3$ **do**

6 $\quad\quad$ Use 2 constant $\#K^2[1,2]$ to derive $\#K^4[1,2]$;

7 $\quad\quad$ **for** 6 ■ *blue cells* $\#K^4[8,9,10,11,14,15] \in (\mathbb{F}_2^8)^6$ **do**

8 $\quad\quad\quad$ Derive $\#RK^2[14,15]$ from $\#K^4[6,7,14,15]$;

9 $\quad\quad\quad$ Use 1 constant $\#MC^1[15]$ to derive $\#K^3[21]$ from $\#K^1[20..23] = \#K^4[12..15] \oplus \#K^4[8..11] \oplus \#K^3[20..23]$ and $MC^{-1} \cdot \#K^1[20..23] = (*,*,*,0)$;

10 $\quad\quad\quad$ Derive $\#RK^2[4,5]$ from $\#K^4[4,5]$, $\#K^3[21,22]$;

11 $\quad\quad\quad$ Use 4 constant $\#AK^2[4,5,14,15]$ and $\#RK^2[4,5,14,15]$ to derive $\#SB^3[4,5,14,15]$;

12 $\quad\quad\quad$ **for** 2 ■ *blue cells* $\#K^4[3]$, $\#K^3[16] \in (\mathbb{F}_2^8)^2$ **do**

13 $\quad\quad\quad\quad$ Derive $\#RK^2[3]$ from $\#K^3[16,20]$, $\#K^4[3]$;

14 $\quad\quad\quad\quad$ Use 1 constant $\#AK^2[3]$ to derive $\#SB^3[3]$;

15 $\quad\quad\quad\quad$ Use 1 constant $\#MC^1[8]$ to derive $\#K^3[17]$ from $\#K^1[16..19] = \#K^3[16..19] \oplus \#K^4[4..7] \oplus \#K^4[8..11]$ and $MC^{-1} \cdot \#K^1[16..19] = (0,*,*,*)$;

16 $\quad\quad\quad\quad$ Derive $\#K^4[16..23]$;

17 $\quad\quad\quad\quad$ Use 4 constants $\#AK^2[0]$, $\#MC^2[8,9,11]$ to derive $\#K^4[0]$, $\#SB^3[0,9,10]$ by solving 4 linear Equation (12);
$\quad\quad\quad\quad$ // Now we know all ■ blue cells in $\#SB^3$ and $\#K^4$

18 $\quad\quad\quad\quad$ Derive the blue part of $\#SR^2[2]$;
$\quad\quad\quad\quad$ // Linearization of S-boxes

19 $\quad\quad\quad\quad$ **for** $2^{8 \times 0.5}$ *values of* $c_0 = (\#SR^2[2])^{17}$ **do**

20 $\quad\quad\quad\quad\quad$ Compute 14 constants $(\#MC^0[11]$, $\#MC^1[2,5]$, $\#SB^6[2]$, $\#SB^7[8..11,14]$, $\#SB^8[0,5,10,15]$, $\#K^6[3]) = (c_1,\ldots,c_{14})$;

21 $\quad\quad\quad\quad\quad$ Update the table $T_{\text{blue}}^{\text{neutral}}[c_0,\ldots,c_{14}] \stackrel{\pm}{=}$ (■ in $\#K^4$ and $\#SB^3$);
$\quad\quad\quad\quad\quad$ // For each value of $(c_0,\ldots,c_{14})$, $2^{8 \times (15.5-14.5)} = 2^{8 \times 1}$ candidates expected

22 **return** $T_{\text{blue}}^{\text{neutral}}$;

Compute Initial Values Forward Neutral Bytes (Blue). Note that the value of a byte in this phase represents the value computed from the blue parts. For example, fixing $\#K^2[2]$ to zero means that the blue initial bytes have a zero impact on this byte. To get the initial values of the blue neutral bytes, the following constraints among states $\#SB^3$, $\#K^4$, $\#K^3$ will be enforced.

$$\begin{cases} \#SB^3[0] \oplus \#K^4[0] \oplus S(\#K^3[21]) \oplus S(\#K^3[17] \oplus \#K^3[21]) = \#AK^2[0] \\ MC^{-1} \cdot \begin{pmatrix} \#K^4[0] \oplus \#K^4[8] \\ \#SB^3[9] \oplus \#K^4[1] \oplus \#K^4[9] \\ \#SB^3[10] \oplus \#K^4[2] \oplus \#K^4[10] \\ \#K^4[3] \oplus \#K^4[11] \end{pmatrix} = \begin{pmatrix} \#MC^2[8] \\ \#MC^2[9] \\ * \\ \#MC^2[11] \end{pmatrix} \end{cases}, \quad (12)$$

where $\#AK^2[0]$ and $\#MC^2[8, 9, 11]$ are fixed as zeroes. Algorithm 1 generates the solution space of blue neutral words. The time complexity is upper bounded by $2^{8 \times 15.5} = 2^{124}$ operations.

The MITM Attack Procedure for 10-Round AES-192. For backward neutral words (■ cells), we will iterate over $\#SB^6[2]$. We provide the main attack procedure derived from Fig. 8 in Algorithm 2.

The Attack Complexity. The time complexity of the above MITM pseudo-preimage attack of 10-round AES-192 is about $2^{128-8 \times \min(0.5, 0.5, 1)} = 2^{124}$. The table T^+ dominates the memory complexity with $2^{8 \times 1.5} \approx 2^{12}$. The pre-computation table $T_{\text{blue}}^{\text{neutral}}$ dominates the memory complexity with $2^{8 \times 15.5} = 2^{124}$.

5.2 Improved MITM Preimage Attacks of Whirlpool

We use the **SIM** technique to search for attack configurations of Whirlpool, improved MITM (pseudo-)preimage attacks are obtained for both 5- and 6-round Whirlpool. In particular, we could find an attack on 5-round Whirlpool with $O(1)$ memory and present the first MITM attack on 7.75-round Whirlpool, including the SB, SR, and MC operations in the last round. The previous best (pseudo-)preimage attacks are the 7-round MITM attacks on Whirlpool presented by Bao *et al.* [8] at Crypto 2022.

Improved and Memoryless Preimage Attack of 5-Round Whirlpool. We directly perform search on the full-size 8×8 version for Whirlpool, and our improved search result for 5-round Whirlpool is given in Fig. 9. Compared to the previous best result of 5-round Whirlpool found by Bao *et al.* [8, Figure 13], GnD is still not required but BiDir is utilized (48 ■ cost at Round 0). However, the DoF cost for neutral words is more concentrated at the starting point, *e.g.*, 48 red cells canceled at Round 0 (48 bytes DoF cost will be compensated at Round 1), and another 24 red cells will be canceled at the MC operation for $\#KMC^2$, which makes it more efficient to generate the red neutral words and can improve our attack on 5-round Whirlpool further to *memoryless* when combined with the *same color match*. We elaborate on the attack configuration below.

- Initial DoF for forward neutral words $\overrightarrow{\iota}$ (■): 24 bytes (8 blue cells in $\#SB^1$ and 16 blue cells in $\#KK^0$);
- Initial DoF for backward neutral words $\overleftarrow{\iota}$ (■): 48 bytes (48 red cells in $\#KK^0$ are *set to be equal to the corresponding cells* in $\#SB^1$, then all red bytes can

420   S. Chen et al.

Algorithm 2: MITM attack on 10 rounds of the AES-192 compression function.

---

1 **for** $(c_1, \ldots, c_{14}) \in (\mathbb{F}_2^8)^{14}$ **do**

2 $\quad$ Initialize T^+;

$\quad$ // For blue neutral words

3 $\quad$ **for** *the* $2^{8 \times 0.5}$ *values* c_0 *of the hint pool* **do**

4 $\quad\quad$ Lookup the table $T_{\text{blue}}^{\text{neutral}}[c_0, \cdots, c_{14}]$ to get candidates of ■ blue cells in $\#K^4$ and $\#SB^3$;

5 $\quad\quad$ **for** *the values of* $2^{8 \times 1}$ *in* $\#K^4$ *and* $\#SB^3$ **do**

6 $\quad\quad\quad$ Derive m^+ (the blue part of $\#AT^9[7] = \#RK^9[7] \oplus \#RK^{-1}[7]$) and update the table $T^+[m^+, c_0] \stackrel{\pm}{=}$ [blue neutral bytes];

$\quad\quad\quad$ // $2^{8 \times 0}$ entries for each index in T^+

$\quad$ // For red neutral words

7 $\quad$ **for** *the* $2^{8 \times 0.5}$ *values of* c_0 **do**

8 $\quad\quad$ **for** $\#SB^6[2] \in \mathbb{F}_2^8$ **do**

9 $\quad\quad\quad$ Compute m^- (the red part of $\#AT^9[7] \oplus \#SB^0[7]$), which equals the blue part of $\#AT^9[7]$;

10 $\quad\quad\quad$ Check for entries in $T^+[m^-, c_0]$ to derive 1 blue neutral byte;

11 $\quad\quad\quad$ Check if the red and blue parts of $\#SR^2[2]$ produce c_0;

$\quad\quad\quad$ // $2^{8 \times (14+0.5+1+1-1-0.5)} = 2^{8 \times 15}$ candidates expected

12 $\quad\quad\quad$ Compute the full $\#AT^9$ and $\#SB^0$ in both colors to check the remaining 15 cells;

13 $\quad\quad\quad$ **if** *the full match is found* **then**

$\quad\quad\quad\quad$ // $2^{8 \times (15-15)} = 1$ candidate expected

14 $\quad\quad\quad\quad$ Output the preimage and stop;

---

be canceled to constants marked as zero constant[2] ▨ in $\#AK^0$ and $\#AK^1$, with just 48 bytes DoF cost for XOR operation);

- Consumed DoF for forward $\overrightarrow{\sigma}$: zero;
- Consumed DoF for backward $\overleftarrow{\sigma}$: 24 bytes for $\#KMC^2 \xrightarrow{\text{MC}} \#KK^2$;
- Guessed bytes for blue, red and both colors g_B, g_R, g_{BR}: all zero byte;
- Matching DoF $d_{\mathcal{M}}$: 24 bytes between $\#MC^2$ and $\#AK^2$.

Then, the remaining DoF for the MITM attack is $d_B = 24, d_R = 24, d_{\mathcal{M}} = 24$.

Compute Initial Values for Forward Neutral Words (Blue). As there is no DoF cost for blue neutral words, to obtain the corresponding initial values, one only needs to enumerate values of $24(16 + 8)$ blue cells in $\#KK^0$ and $\#SB^1$.

---

[2] The AddRoundConstant in the key schedule of Whirlpool is the last operation for each round (SB, SR, MC, AC), that is the subkey added into the encryption already involved with the round constant. When using the **SIM** technique, the corresponding cells related to the XOR compensation here will be canceled to all zero constants.

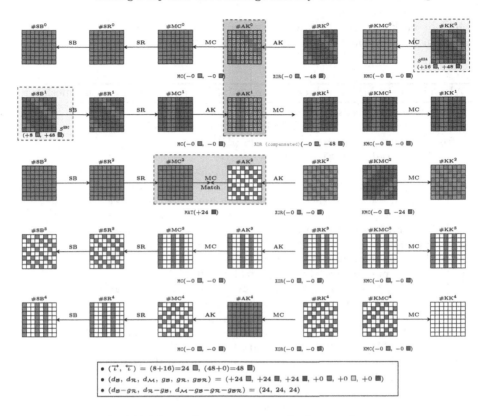

Fig. 9. An MITM pseudo-preimage attack of 5-round `Whirlpool`.

Compute Initial Values for Backward Neutral Bytes (Red). To get the initial values of red neutral words, the constraints among #KMC^2 and #KK^2 are as below

$$\begin{pmatrix} a_0 & - & - & a_9 & - & a_{15} & - & - \\ - & a_3 & - & - & a_{12} & - & a_{18} & - \\ - & - & a_6 & - & - & a_{16} & - & a_{21} \\ a_1 & - & - & a_{10} & - & - & a_{19} & - \\ - & a_4 & - & - & a_{13} & - & - & a_{22} \\ a_2 & - & a_7 & - & - & a_{18} & - & - \\ - & a_5 & - & a_{11} & - & - & a_{21} & - \\ - & - & a_8 & - & a_{14} & - & - & a_{23} \end{pmatrix} = \text{MC} \cdot \begin{pmatrix} \text{\#KMC}^2_0 & \text{\#KMC}^2_8 & \cdots & \text{\#KMC}^2_{48} & \text{\#KMC}^2_{56} \\ \text{\#KMC}^2_1 & - & \cdots & \text{\#KMC}^2_{49} & \text{\#KMC}^2_{57} \\ - & - & \cdots & \text{\#KMC}^2_{50} & \text{\#KMC}^2_{58} \\ - & \text{\#KMC}^2_{11} & \cdots & \text{\#KMC}^2_{51} & - \\ \text{\#KMC}^2_4 & \text{\#KMC}^2_{12} & \cdots & - & - \\ \text{\#KMC}^2_5 & \text{\#KMC}^2_{13} & \cdots & - & \text{\#KMC}^2_{61} \\ \text{\#KMC}^2_6 & \text{\#KMC}^2_{14} & \cdots & \text{\#KMC}^2_{54} & \text{\#KMC}^2_{62} \\ \text{\#KMC}^2_7 & \text{\#KMC}^2_{15} & \cdots & \text{\#KMC}^2_{55} & \text{\#KMC}^2_{63} \end{pmatrix}, \tag{13}$$

where a_i $(0 \le i \le 23)$ are the chosen constants for #KK^2.

The MITM Attack Procedure for 5-Round `Whirlpool`. We provide the *memory-less* attack procedure derived from Fig. 9 in Algorithm 3. The *same-color match* is employed, which is firstly observed by Guo *et al.* [19] in MITM preimage attacks and recently also utilized by Hou *et al.* [21] for MITM attacks on Feistel constructions. It means a match with only blue ■ and gray ▨ (or only red ■ and gray ▨) at the matching point, rather than a mixture of red ■ and blue ■ cells. While gray ▨ cells are fixed as constants, and thus are known in both forward (blue) or backward (red) computations, a same-color match, *e.g.*, only blue or gray, can be performed independently of the red neutral words.

Algorithm 3: MITM attack on 5-round `Whirlpool` compression function

---

1 Fix 8 ■ constant cells in $\#SB^1$ to all zero;

2 Fix 8 constants $(a_{16}, a_{17}, \cdots, a_{23})$ in Equation (13) to all zero;

3 **for** $C = (a_0, a_1, \cdots, a_{15}, a_{16}, \cdots, a_{23}) \in (\mathbb{F}_2^8)^{16}$ **do**

    // For red neutral words

    // As there is no ■ red cell in matching states $\#MC^2$ and
       $\#AK^2$, one does not need a store table T^+ and thus does not
       need to solve the Equation (13) here for back neutral words,
       which can be done after the partial match

    // For blue neutral words

4   **for** *8 ■ blue cells in* $\#SB^1 \in (\mathbb{F}_2^8)^8$ *and 16 ■ blue cells in* $\#KK^0 \in (\mathbb{F}_2^8)^{16}$ **do**

5   Compute forward to the matching state $\#MC^2$;

6   Compute backward to the matching state $\#AK^2$;

       // Only ■ gray and ■ blue cells in matching states here

7   **if** $\#MC^2$ *and* $\#AK^2$ *pass the partial match* **then**

         // $2^{8 \times (16+24-24)} = 2^{8 \times 16}$ candidates expected

8   Solve Equation (13) according to current constant C and obtain
         $2^{8 \times 24}$ $\#KMC^2$ for red neutral words;

9   Compute forward and backward to match the rest 40 cells;

10   **if** *the full match is found* **then**

           // $2^{8 \times (16+24-40)} = 1$ candidate expected

11   Output the preimage and stop;

The Attack Complexity. The time complexity of the above MITM pseudo-preimage attack on 5-round `Whirlpool` is about $2^{512-8 \times \min(24,24,24)} = 2^{320}$.[3] Thanks to the *same color match* between $\#MC^2$ and $\#AK^2$, the partial-matching is independent of backward red neutral words, and the constraints on backward neutral words are *linear*, then the store tables for the partial-matching can be *saved* and thus the memory complexity is $O(1)$.

6   Conclusion

In this work, we advanced the state-of-the-art MITM attacks on `AES`-like hashing. Among the new techniques, **LIN** and **DIS** contributed to the first 10-round preimage attack on `AES-192` and assorted improved results on `Rijndael`-based hashing, while **SIM** better addressed the dependencies and reduced the attack

---

[3] For comparisons, we directly use the calculation method in [8] to provide the time complexity for `Whirlpool`.

complexities on Whirlpool and Streebog. We argued that the ideas behind the new techniques are generic and expected them to have more applications in other attack scenarios.

Open Problems. The fact that the non-linear part of the AES S-box is a single monomial x^{254} allows us to obtain the full output from guessing a space with dimension four. We also investigated the S-boxes of Whirlpool and Streebog and found that their S-boxes possess fewer-dimensional subspaces (yielding parts of the output thus less powerful) for which we could not find better attacks. If more properties of S-boxes are revealed for AES-like hashing, *i.e.*, algebraic properties, better MITM attacks exploiting the **LIN** technique on these target ciphers can be expected. Furthermore, we applied the techniques to all AES/Rijndael variants but could not find other improvements compared to [7,8,16,43]. The relation between the security margin and block-key ratio remains to be further investigated.

Acknowledgements. We would like to thank all anonymous reviewers for their detailed and valuable comments.

This research is supported by the National Key R&D Program of China (Grants No. 2022YFB2701900), the National Natural Science Foundation of China (Grants No. 62172410), the Youth Innovation Promotion Association of Chinese Academy of Sciences, the National Research Foundation, Singapore and Infocomm Media Development Authority under its Trust Tech Funding Initiative and Strategic Capability Research Centres Funding Initiative, the Ministry of Education in Singapore under Grant RG93/23, and the Deutsche Forschungsgemeinschaft (DFG, German Research Foundation) – LI 4223/1-1. Any opinions, findings and conclusions or recommendations expressed in this material are those of the author(s) and do not reflect the views of National Research Foundation, Singapore and Infocomm Media Development Authority.

References

1. Federal Agency on Technical Regulation and Metrology, Information technology - Cryptographic data security - Hash-function, National Standard of the Russian Federation, GOST R 34.11-2012 (2012)
2. ZigBee Alliance. zigbee Specification Revision 22 1.0. Technical report, ZigBee Alliance, April 19 2017 (2017)
3. AlTawy, R., Youssef, A.M.: Preimage attacks on reduced-round Stribog. In: Pointcheval, D., Vergnaud, D. (eds.) AFRICACRYPT 2014. LNCS, vol. 8469, pp. 109–125. Springer, Cham (2014). https://doi.org/10.1007/978-3-319-06734-6_7
4. Aoki, K., Sasaki, Yu.: Preimage attacks on one-block MD4, 63-step MD5 and more. In: Avanzi, R.M., Keliher, L., Sica, F. (eds.) SAC 2008. LNCS, vol. 5381, pp. 103–119. Springer, Heidelberg (2009). https://doi.org/10.1007/978-3-642-04159-4_7
5. Aoki, K., Sasaki, Yu.: Meet-in-the-middle preimage attacks against reduced SHA-0 and SHA-1. In: Halevi, S. (ed.) CRYPTO 2009. LNCS, vol. 5677, pp. 70–89. Springer, Heidelberg (2009). https://doi.org/10.1007/978-3-642-03356-8_5
6. Bao, Z., Ding, L., Guo, J., Wang, H., Zhang, W.: Improved meet-in-the-middle preimage attacks against AES hashing modes. IACR Trans. Symmetric Cryptol. **2019**(4), 318–347 (2019)

7. Bao, Z., et al.: Automatic search of meet-in-the-middle preimage attacks on AES-like hashing. In: Canteaut, A., Standaert, F.-X. (eds.) EUROCRYPT 2021. LNCS, vol. 12696, pp. 771–804. Springer, Cham (2021). https://doi.org/10.1007/978-3-030-77870-5_27

8. Bao, Z., Guo, J., Shi, D., Yi, T.: Superposition meet-in-the-middle attacks: updates on fundamental security of AES-like hashing. In: Dodis, Y., Shrimpton, T. (eds.) CRYPTO 2022. LNCS, vol. 13507. Springer, Cham (2022). https://doi.org/10.1007/978-3-031-15802-5_3

9. Barreto, P.S.L.M., Rijmen, V.: The WHIRLPOOL hashing function. In: First open NESSIE Workshop, Leuven, Belgium, vol. 13, p. 14. Citeseer (2000)

10. Bogdanov, A., Rechberger, C.: A 3-subset meet-in-the-middle attack: cryptanalysis of the lightweight block cipher KTANTAN. In: Biryukov, A., Gong, G., Stinson, D.R. (eds.) SAC 2010. LNCS, vol. 6544, pp. 229–240. Springer, Heidelberg (2011). https://doi.org/10.1007/978-3-642-19574-7_16

11. Canteaut, A., Naya-Plasencia, M., Vayssière, B.: Sieve-in-the-middle: improved MITM attacks. In: Canetti, R., Garay, J.A. (eds.) CRYPTO 2013. LNCS, vol. 8042, pp. 222–240. Springer, Heidelberg (2013). https://doi.org/10.1007/978-3-642-40041-4_13

12. Chen, S., Guo, J., List, E., Shi, D., Zhang, T.: Diving deep into the preimage security of aes-like hashing. Cryptology ePrint Archive, Paper 2024/300 (2024). https://eprint.iacr.org/2024/300

13. Daemen, J., Rijmen, V.: The Design of Rijndael: AES - The Advanced Encryption Standard Information Security and Cryptography. Springer, Heidelberg (2002). https://doi.org/10.1007/978-3-662-04722-4

14. Diffie, W., Hellman, M.E.: Special feature exhaustive cryptanalysis of the NBS data encryption standard. IEEE Comput. 10(6), 74–84 (1977)

15. Dolmatov, V., Degtyarev, A.: GOST R 34.11-2012: Hash Function. RFC 6986, August 2013 (2013)

16. Dong, X., Hua, J., Sun, S., Li, Z., Wang, X., Hu, L.: Meet-in-the-middle attacks revisited: key-recovery, collision, and preimage attacks. In: Malkin, T., Peikert, C. (eds.) CRYPTO 2021. LNCS, vol. 12827, pp. 278–308. Springer, Cham (2021). https://doi.org/10.1007/978-3-030-84252-9_10

17. Fuhr, T., Minaud, B.: Match box meet-in-the-middle attack against KATAN. In: Cid, C., Rechberger, C. (eds.) FSE 2014. LNCS, vol. 8540, pp. 61–81. Springer, Heidelberg (2015). https://doi.org/10.1007/978-3-662-46706-0_4

18. Gilbert, H., Peyrin, T.: Super-Sbox cryptanalysis: improved attacks for AES-like permutations. In: FSE, pp. 365–383 (2010)

19. Guo, J., Ling, S., Rechberger, C., Wang, H.: Advanced meet-in-the-middle preimage attacks: first results on full tiger, and improved results on MD4 and SHA-2. In: Abe, M. (ed.) ASIACRYPT 2010. LNCS, vol. 6477, pp. 56–75. Springer, Heidelberg (2010). https://doi.org/10.1007/978-3-642-17373-8_4

20. Hosoyamada, A., Sasaki, Yu.: Finding hash collisions with quantum computers by using differential trails with smaller probability than birthday bound. In: Canteaut, A., Ishai, Y. (eds.) EUROCRYPT 2020. LNCS, vol. 12106, pp. 249–279. Springer, Cham (2020). https://doi.org/10.1007/978-3-030-45724-2_9

21. Hou, Q., Dong, X., Qin, L., Zhang, G., Wang, X.: Automated meet-in-the-middle attack goes to feistel. In: Guo, J., Steinfeld, R. (eds.) ASIACRYPT 2023, Part III. LNCS, pp. 370–404. Springer, Cham (2023). https://doi.org/10.1007/978-981-99-8727-6_13

22. Hua, J., Dong, X., Sun, S., Zhang, Z., Lei, H., Wang, X.: Improved MITM cryptanalysis on streebog. IACR Trans. Symmetric Cryptol. 2022(2), 63–91 (2022)

23. ISO/IEC. ISO/IEC 10118-3: 2004. IT Security techniques - Hash-functions - Part 3: Dedicated hash-functions (2004)
24. ISO/IEC. ISO/IEC 10118-2: 2010. IT Security techniques - Hash-functions - Part 2: Hash-functions using an n-bit block cipher (2010)
25. ISO/IEC. ISO/IEC 10118-3: 2018. IT Security techniques - Hash-functions - Part 3: Dedicated hash-functions (2018)
26. Khovratovich, D., Rechberger, C., Savelieva, A.: Bicliques for preimages: attacks on skein-512 and the SHA-2 family. In: Fast Software Encryption - 19th International Workshop, FSE 2012, Washington, DC, USA, March 19–21, 2012. Revised Selected Papers, pp. 244–263 (2012)
27. Lamberger, M., Mendel, F., Rechberger, C., Rijmen, V., Schläffer, M.: Rebound distinguishers: results on the full whirlpool compression function. In: Matsui, M. (ed.) ASIACRYPT 2009. LNCS, vol. 5912, pp. 126–143. Springer, Heidelberg (2009). https://doi.org/10.1007/978-3-642-10366-7_8
28. Lamberger, M., Mendel, F., Schläffer, M., Rechberger, C., Rijmen, V.: The rebound attack and subspace distinguishers: application to whirlpool. J. Cryptol. **28**(2), 257–296 (2015)
29. Liu, F., Mahzoun, M., Øygarden, M., Meier, W.: Algebraic attacks on RAIN and AIM using equivalent representations. IACR Trans. Symmetric Cryptol. **2023**(4), 166–186 (2023)
30. Ma, B., Li, B., Hao, R., Li, X.: Improved (Pseudo) preimage attacks on reduced-round GOST and Grøstl-256 and studies on several truncation patterns for AES-like compression functions. In: IWSEC, pp. 79–96 (2015)
31. Mendel, F., Rechberger, C., Schläffer, M., Thomsen, S.S.: The rebound attack: cryptanalysis of reduced whirlpool and grøstl. In: Dunkelman, O. (ed.) FSE 2009. LNCS, vol. 5665, pp. 260–276. Springer, Heidelberg (2009). https://doi.org/10.1007/978-3-642-03317-9_16
32. Menezes, A., van Oorschot, P.C., Vanstone, S.A.: Handbook of Applied Cryptography. CRC Press (1996)
33. Preneel, B., Govaerts, R., Vandewalle, J.: Hash functions based on block ciphers: a synthetic approach. In: Stinson, D.R. (ed.) CRYPTO 1993. LNCS, vol. 773, pp. 368–378. Springer, Heidelberg (1994). https://doi.org/10.1007/3-540-48329-2_31
34. Qin, L., Hua, J., Dong, X., Yan, H., Wang, X.: Meet-in-the-middle preimage attacks on sponge-based hashing. In: Hazay, C., Stam, M. (eds.) EUROCRYPT 2023, IV. LNCS, vol. 14007, pp. 158–188. Springer, Cham (2023). https://doi.org/10.1007/978-3-031-30634-1_6
35. Sasaki, Yu.: Meet-in-the-middle preimage attacks on AES hashing modes and an application to whirlpool. In: Joux, A. (ed.) FSE 2011. LNCS, vol. 6733, pp. 378–396. Springer, Heidelberg (2011). https://doi.org/10.1007/978-3-642-21702-9_22
36. Sasaki, Yu., Aoki, K.: Preimage Attacks on 3, 4, and 5-Pass HAVAL. In: Pieprzyk, J. (ed.) ASIACRYPT 2008. LNCS, vol. 5350, pp. 253–271. Springer, Heidelberg (2008). https://doi.org/10.1007/978-3-540-89255-7_16
37. Sasaki, Yu., Aoki, K.: Finding preimages in full MD5 faster than exhaustive search. In: Joux, A. (ed.) EUROCRYPT 2009. LNCS, vol. 5479, pp. 134–152. Springer, Heidelberg (2009). https://doi.org/10.1007/978-3-642-01001-9_8
38. Sasaki, Yu., Wang, L., Wu, S., Wu, W.: Investigating fundamental security requirements on whirlpool: improved preimage and collision attacks. In: Wang, X., Sako, K. (eds.) ASIACRYPT 2012. LNCS, vol. 7658, pp. 562–579. Springer, Heidelberg (2012). https://doi.org/10.1007/978-3-642-34961-4_34

39. Schrottenloher, A., Stevens, M.: Simplified MITM modeling for permutations: new (quantum) attacks. In: Dodis, Y., Shrimpton, T. (eds.) CRYPTO 2022, Part III. Lecture Notes in Computer Science, vol. 13509, pp. 717–747. Springer, Cham (2022). https://doi.org/10.1007/978-3-031-15982-4_24

40. Schrottenloher, A., Stevens, M.: Simplified modeling of MITM attacks for block ciphers: New (quantum) attacks. IACR Trans. Symmetric Cryptol. **2023**(3), 146–183 (2023)

41. Sun, S., Hu, L., Wang, P., Qiao, K., Ma, X., Song, L.: Automatic security evaluation and (related-key) differential characteristic search: application to SIMON, PRESENT, LBlock, DES(L) and other bit-oriented block ciphers. In: Sarkar, P., Iwata, T. (eds.) ASIACRYPT 2014. LNCS, vol. 8873, pp. 158–178. Springer, Heidelberg (2014). https://doi.org/10.1007/978-3-662-45611-8_9

42. Zhang, K., Qingju Wang, Y.Y., Guo, C., Cui, H.: Algebraic attacks on round-reduced rain and full AIM-III. In: Guo, J., Steinfeld, R. (eds.) ASIACRYPT 2023, Part III. LNCS, vol. 14440, pp. 285–310. Springer, Singapore (2023). https://doi.org/10.1007/978-981-99-8727-6_10

43. Zhang, T.: Comprehensive preimage security evaluations on rijndael-based hashing. In: Zhou, J., et al. (eds.) ACNS 2023. LNCS, vol. 13907, pp. 23–42. Springer, Cham (2023). https://doi.org/10.1007/978-3-031-41181-6_2

Public Key Primitives with Advanced Functionalities (I/II)

Twinkle: Threshold Signatures from DDH with Full Adaptive Security

Renas Bacho[1,3], Julian Loss[1], Stefano Tessaro[2],
Benedikt Wagner[1,3(✉)], and Chenzhi Zhu[2]

[1] CISPA Helmholtz Center for Information Security, Saarbrücken, Germany
{renas.bacho,loss,benedikt.wagner}@cispa.de
[2] Paul G. Allen School of Computer Science & Engineering,
University of Washington, Seattle, USA
{tessaro,zhucz20}@cs.washington.edu
[3] Saarland University, Saarbrücken, Germany

Abstract. Sparkle is the first threshold signature scheme in the pairing-free discrete logarithm setting (Crites, Komlo, Maller, Crypto 2023) to be proven secure under adaptive corruptions. However, without using the algebraic group model, Sparkle's proof imposes an undesirable restriction on the adversary. Namely, for a signing threshold $t < n$, the adversary is restricted to corrupt at most $t/2$ parties. In addition, Sparkle's proof relies on a strong one-more assumption.

In this work, we propose Twinkle, a new threshold signature scheme in the pairing-free setting which overcomes these limitations. Twinkle is the first pairing-free scheme to have a security proof under up to t adaptive corruptions without relying on the algebraic group model. It is also the first such scheme with a security proof under adaptive corruptions from a well-studied non-interactive assumption, namely, the Decisional Diffie-Hellman (DDH) assumption.

We achieve our result in two steps. First, we design a generic scheme based on a linear function that satisfies several abstract properties and prove its adaptive security under a suitable one-more assumption related to this function. In the context of this proof, we also identify a gap in the security proof of Sparkle and develop new techniques to overcome this issue. Second, we give a suitable instantiation of the function for which the corresponding one-more assumption follows from DDH.

Keywords: Threshold Signatures · Adaptive Security · Pairing-Free · Non-Interactive Assumptions

1 Introduction

A threshold signature scheme [36, 37, 70] enables a group of n signers to jointly sign a message as long as more than t of them participate. To this end, each of the n signers holds a share of the secret key associated with the public key of the group. When $t + 1$ of them come together and run a signing protocol for a particular message, they obtain a compact signature (independent in size of t and n) without revealing their secret key shares to each other. On the other hand, no

ⓒ International Association for Cryptologic Research 2024
M. Joye and G. Leander (Eds.): EUROCRYPT 2024, LNCS 14651, pp. 429–459, 2024.
https://doi.org/10.1007/978-3-031-58716-0_15

subset of at most t potentially malicious signers can generate a valid signature. Despite being a well-studied cryptographic primitive, threshold signatures have experienced a renaissance due to their use in cryptocurrencies [64] and other modern applications [30]. This new attention has also led to ongoing standardization efforts [19]. In this work, we study threshold signatures in the pairing-free discrete logarithm setting. As noted in previous works [29,78,79], pairings are not supported in popular libraries and are substantially more expensive to compute, which makes pairing-free solutions appealing.

Static vs. Adaptive Security. When defining security for threshold signatures, the adversary is allowed to concurrently interact with honest signers in the signing protocol. Additionally, it may corrupt up to t out of n parties, thereby learning their secret key material and internal state. Here, we distinguish between *static* corruptions and *adaptive* corruptions. For static corruptions, the adversary declares the set of corrupted parties ahead of time before any messages have been signed. For adaptive corruptions, the adversary can corrupt parties dynamically, depending on previous signatures and corruptions.

Adaptive security is a far stronger notion than static security and matches reality more closely. Unfortunately, proving adaptive security for threshold signatures is highly challenging and previous works in the pairing-free setting rely on strong interactive assumptions to simulate the state of adaptively corrupted parties [28]. This simulation strategy, however, is at odds with rewinding the adversary as part of a security proof. Roughly, if the adversary is allowed to corrupt up to t_c parties, then in the two runs induced by rewinding, it may corrupt up to $2t_c$ parties in total. Thus, for the reduction to obtain meaningful information from the adversary's forgery, it has to be restricted to corrupt at most $t_c \leq t/2$ parties [28]. To bypass this unnatural restriction, prior work heavily relies on the algebraic group model (AGM) [42] in order to avoid rewinding[1]. In summary: to support an arbitrary corruption threshold, one has to use the AGM or sacrifice adaptive security.

1.1 Our Contribution

Motivated by this unsatisfactory state of affairs, we construct Twinkle. Twinkle is the first threshold signature scheme in the pairing-free setting which combines all of the following characteristics:

- *Adaptive Security.* We prove Twinkle secure under adaptive corruptions. Notably, we do not rely on secure erasures of private state.
- *Non-Interactive Assumptions.* Our security proof relies on a non-interactive and well-studied assumption, namely, the DDH assumption. As a slightly more efficient alternative, we give an instantiation based on a one-more variant of CDH, for which we provide evidence of its hardness.

---

[1] Other works resort to heavier machinery such as broadcast channels or non-committing encryption resulting in inefficient protocols.

- *No AGM.* Our security proof does not rely on the algebraic group model, but only on the random oracle model.
- *Arbitrary Threshold.* Twinkle supports an arbitrary corruption threshold $t < n$ for n parties. Essentially, this is established by giving a proof without rewinding.

For a comparison of schemes in the pairing-free discrete logarithm setting, see Table 1. We also emphasize that we achieve our goal without the use of heavy cryptographic techniques, and our scheme is practical. For example, signatures of Twinkle (from DDH) are at most 3 times as large as regular Schnorr signatures [74], and Twinkle has three rounds. In the context of our proof, we also identify a gap in the analysis of Sparkle [28] and develop new proof techniques to fix it in the context of our scheme[2].

Table 1. Comparison of different threshold signature schemes in the discrete logarithm setting without pairings and the two instantiations of our Twinkle scheme. We compare whether the schemes are proven secure under adaptive corruptions and under which assumption and idealized model they are proven. We also compare the corruption thresholds that they support. For all schemes, we assume that there is a trusted dealer distributing key shares securely. For GJKR [48]/StiStr [77], broadcast channels are assumed, which adds rounds when implemented.

Scheme	Rounds	Adaptive	Assumption	Idealization	Corruptions
GJKR [48]/StiStr [77]	≥ 4	✗	DLOG	ROM	$\leq t < n/2$
Lin-UC [63]	3	✗	DLOG	ROM	$\leq t$
Frost [60]	2	✗	DLOG	Custom	$\leq t$
Frost [8, 11, 60]	2	✗	AOMDL	ROM	$\leq t$
Frost2 [8, 11, 27]	2	✗	AOMDL	ROM	$\leq t$
Frost3 [73]/Olaf [25]	2	✗	AOMDL	ROM	$\leq t$
TZ [79]	2	✗	DLOG	ROM	$\leq t$
Sparkle [28]	3	✗	DLOG	ROM	$\leq t$
Sparkle [28]	3	✓	AOMDL	ROM	$\leq t/2$
Sparkle [28]	3	✓	AOMDL	ROM+AGM	$\leq t$
Twinkle (AOMCDH)	3	✓	AOMCDH	ROM	$\leq t$
Twinkle (DDH)	3	✓	DDH	ROM	$0 \leq t$

Conceptually, the design of our threshold signature is inspired by five-move identification schemes, which already have found use in the construction of tightly secure signature schemes [24,49,57]. We achieve our result in two main steps:

1. We first phrase our scheme abstractly using (a variant of) linear function families [23,52,55,69,79]. To prove security under adaptive corruptions, we define a security notion for linear functions resembling a one-more style CDH assumption. This is the step where we identify the gap in the analysis of Sparkle [28].

---

[2] We communicated the gap and our solution to the authors of Sparkle. To be clear, we do not claim that Sparkle is insecure, just that the proof in [28] has a gap.

2. We then instantiate the linear function family such that this one-more notion follows from the (non-interactive) DDH assumption. Note that Tessaro and Zhu [79] showed a related statement, namely, that a suitable one-more variant of DLOG follows from DLOG. In this sense, our work makes a further step in an agenda aimed at replacing interactive assumptions with non-interactive ones. We are confident that this is interesting in its own right.

1.2   Technical Overview

We keep the technical overview self-contained, but some background on Schnorr signatures [58,74], five-move identification [24,49,57], and Sparkle [28] is helpful.

Sparkle and The Problem with Rewinding. As our starting point, let us review the main ideas behind Sparkle [28], and why the use of rewinding limits us to tolerating at most $t/2$ corruptions. For that, we fix a group $\mathbb{G}$ with generator g and prime order p. Each signer $i \in [n]$ holds a secret key share $\mathsf{sk}_i \in \mathbb{Z}_p$ such that $\mathsf{sk}_i = f(i)$ for a polynomial f of degree t. Further, the public key is $\mathsf{pk} = g^{f(0)}$. To sign a message m, a set $S \subseteq [n]$ of signers engage in the following interactive signing protocol, omitting some details:

1. Each party $i \in S$ samples a random $r_i \overset{\$}{\leftarrow} \mathbb{Z}_p$ and computes $R_i = g^{r_i}$. It then sends a hash com_i of R_i, S, and m to the other signers to commit to R_i. We call R_i a *preimage* of com_i. The hash function is modeled as a random oracle.
2. Once a party has received all hashes from the first round, it sends R_i to the other signers to open the commitment.
3. If all commitments are correctly opened, each signer computes the combined nonce $R = \prod_i R_i$. Then, it derives a challenge $c \in \mathbb{Z}_p$ from pk, R, and m using another random oracle. Each signer i computes and sends its response share $s_i := c \cdot \ell_{i,S} \cdot \mathsf{sk}_i + r_i$, where $\ell_{i,S}$ is a Lagrange coefficient. The signature is (c, s), where $s = \sum_i s_i$.

The overall proof strategy adopted in [28] follows a similar paradigm as that of proving Schnorr signatures, with appropriate twists. Namely, one first takes care of simulating signing queries using honest-verifier zero-knowledge (HVZK) and by suitably programming the random oracle. We will come back to this part of the proof later. Then, via rewinding, one can extract the secret key from a forgery. To simulate adaptive corruption queries, the proof of Sparkle relies on a DLOG oracle on each corruption query, i.e., security is proven under the one-more version of DLOG (OMDL). Specifically, getting $t + 1$ DLOG challenges from the OMDL assumption and t-time access to a DLOG oracle, the reduction defines a degree t polynomial "in the exponent", simulates the game as explained, and uses rewinding to solve the final DLOG challenge. Note that if we allow the adversary to corrupt at most t_c parties throughout the experiment, it may corrupt up to $2t_c$ parties over both runs, meaning that the reduction has to query the DLOG oracle up to $2t_c$ times. Therefore, we have to require that $2t_c \leq t$.

How to Avoid Rewinding. Now it should be clear that the restriction on the corruption threshold is induced by the use of rewinding. If we avoid rewinding, we can also remove the restriction. To do so, it is natural to follow existing approaches from the literature on tightly-secure (and thus rewinding-free) signatures. A common approach is to rely on lossy identification [1,56,58] that has already been used in the closely-related multi-signature setting [69]. We find this unsuitable for two reasons. Namely, (a) these schemes rely on the DDH assumption, it is not clear at all what a suitable one-more variant would look like, and (b) the core idea of this technique is to move to a hybrid in which there is no secret key for pk at all. This seems hard to combine with adaptive corruptions. Roughly, this is because if there is no secret key for pk, then at most t of the pk_i can have a secret key, meaning that we would have to guess the set of corruptions. Instead, we take inspiration from five-move identification [24,49,57], for which problems (a) and (b) do not show up. Namely, (a) such schemes rely on the CDH assumption, and (b) there is always a secret key. To explain the idea, we directly focus on our threshold signature scheme. For that, let $h \in \mathbb{G}$ be *derived from the message* via a random oracle. Given h, our signing protocol is as follows:

1. Each signer $i \in S$ samples $r_i \overset{\$}{\leftarrow} \mathbb{Z}_p$ and computes $R_i^{(1)} = g^{r_i}, R_i^{(2)} = h^{r_i}$, and $\mathsf{pk}_i^{(2)} = h^{\mathsf{sk}_i}$. It then sends a hash of $R_i^{(1)}, R_i^{(2)}, \mathsf{pk}_i^{(2)}$ to the other signers.
2. Once a party received all hashes from the first round, it sends $R_i^{(1)}, R_i^{(2)}, \mathsf{pk}_i^{(2)}$.
3. If all commitments are correctly opened, each signer computes the combined nonces $R^{(k)}$ for $k \in \{1,2\}$ and secondary public key $\mathsf{pk}^{(2)}$ in a natural way. Then, it derives a challenge c from $R^{(1)}, R^{(2)}, \mathsf{pk}^{(2)}$, and m and computes $s_i := c \cdot \ell_{i,S} \cdot \mathsf{sk}_i + r_i$. The signature is $(\mathsf{pk}^{(2)}, c, s)$ with $s = \sum_i s_i$.

Intuitively, the signers engage in two executions of Sparkle with generators g and h, respectively, using the same randomness r_i. To understand why we can avoid rewinding with this scheme, let us ignore signing and corruption queries for a moment, and focus on how to turn a forgery $(\mathsf{pk}^{(2)}, c, s)$ into a solution for a hard problem, concretely, CDH. For that, we consider two cases. First, if $\mathsf{pk}^{(2)} = h^{f(0)}$, then $\mathsf{pk}^{(2)}$ is a CDH solution for $\mathsf{pk} = g^{f(0)}$ and h. Indeed, this is what should happen in an honest execution. Second, we can bound the probability that the forgery is valid and $\mathsf{pk}^{(2)} \neq h^{f(0)}$ using a statistical argument. Roughly, (c, s) acts as a statistically sound proof for the statement $\mathsf{pk}^{(2)} = h^{f(0)}$. To simulate adaptive corruptions, for now assume that we can rely on a one-more variant of the CDH assumption, in which we have t-time access to a DLOG oracle. We come back to this later. What remains is to simulate honest parties during the signing. For that, the first trick is to set up h (by programming the random oracle) in a special way. Roughly, we want to be able to translate valid transcripts with respect to g into valid transcripts with respect to h. Once this is established, we can focus on simulating the g-side of the protocol.

A Gap in the Proof of Sparkle. If we only focus on the g-side, our protocol is essentially Sparkle. Therefore, it should be possible to simulate signing exactly as in Sparkle using HVZK. Unfortunately, when looking at this part of Sparkle's proof, we discovered that a certain adversarial behavior is not covered. Namely, the proof does not correctly simulate the case in which the adversary sends inconsistent sets of commitments to different honest parties. It turns out that handling this requires fundamentally new techniques. To understand the gap, it is instructive to consider Sparkle's proof for an example of three signers in a session sid, with two of them being honest, say Signer 1 and 2, and the third one being malicious. Let us assume that Signers 1 and 2 are already in the second round of the protocol. That is, both already sent their commitments com_1 and com_2 and now expect a list of commitments $\mathcal{M} = (com_1, com_2, com_3)$ from the first round as input. In Sparkle's proof, the reduction sends random commitments com_1 and com_2 on behalf of the honest parties. Later, when Signer 1 (resp. 2) gets $\mathcal{M}$, it has to output its second message R_1 (resp. R_2) and program the random oracle at R_1 (resp. R_2) to be com_1 (resp. com_2). The goal of the reduction is to set up R_1 and R_2 using HVZK such that the responses s_1 and s_2 can be computed without using the secret key. To understand how the reduction proceeds, assume that Signer 1 is asked (by the adversary) to reveal his nonce R_1 first. When this happens, the reduction samples a challenge c and a response s_1. It then defines R_1 as $R_1 := g^{s_1} pk_1^{-c\ell_{1,S}}$. Ideally, the reduction would now program the random oracle on the combined nonce $R = R_1 R_2 R_3$ to return c, and output R_1 to the adversary. However, while the reduction can extract R_3 from com_3 by observing the random oracle queries, R_2 is not yet defined at that point. The solution proposed in Sparkle's proof is as follows. Before returning R_1 to the adversary, the reduction also samples s_2 and defines $R_2 := g^{s_2} pk_2^{-c\ell_{2,S}}$. Then, the reduction can compute the combined nonce $R = R_1 R_2 R_3$ and program the random oracle on input R to return c. Later, it can use s_1 and s_2 as responses.

However, as we will argue now, this strategy is flawed[3]. Think about what happens if the first-round messages $\mathcal{M}'$ that Signer 2 sees do not contain com_3, but instead a different[4] commitment com_3' to a nonce $R_3' \neq R_3$. Then, with high probability, the combined nonce R' that Signer 2 will compute is different from R, meaning that its challenge c' will also be different from c, and so s_2 is not a valid response. One naive idea to solve this is to program $R_2 := g^{s_2} pk_2^{-c'\ell_{2,S}}$ for an independent c' when we reveal R_1. In this case, however, the adversary may just choose to submit $\mathcal{M}' = \mathcal{M}$ to Signer 2, making the simulation fail.

Equivalence Classes to the Rescue. The solution we present is very technical, and we sketch a massively simplified solution here. Abstractly speaking, we want to be able to identify whether two queries $q = (sid, i, \mathcal{M})$ and $q' = (sid', i', \mathcal{M}')$ will result in the same combined nonce *before* all commitments com_j in $\mathcal{M}$ and $\mathcal{M}'$ have preimages R_j. To do so, we define an equivalence relation $\sim$ on such queries for which we show two properties.

---

[3] The problem has nothing to do with adaptive security and shows up for a static adversary as well.

[4] Note that in Sparkle, no broadcast channel is assumed, and so this may happen. Also, note that in multi-signatures that follow a similar strategy, e.g. [10], this problem does not show up as there is only one honest signer.

1. First, the equivalence relation is consistent over time, namely, (a) if $q \sim q'$ at some point in time, then $q \sim q'$ at any later point, and (b) if $q \not\sim q'$ at some point in time, then $q \not\sim q'$ at any later point.
2. Second, assume that all commitments in $\mathcal{M}$ and $\mathcal{M}'$ have preimages. Then the resulting combined nonces R and R' are the same if and only if $q \sim q'$.

The technical challenge is that $\sim$ has to stay consistent while also adapting to changes in the random oracle over time. Assuming we have such a relation, we can make the simulation work. Namely, when we have to reveal the nonce R_i of an honest signer i, we first define $c := \mathsf{C}(q)$, where C is a *random oracle on equivalence classes* and is only known to the reduction. That is, C is a random oracle with the additional condition that $\mathsf{C}(q) = \mathsf{C}(q')$ if $q \sim q'$. Then, we define $R_i := g^{s_i} \mathsf{pk}_i^{-c \ell_{i,S}}$. We do not define any other $R_{i'}$ of honest parties at that point, meaning that we also may not know the combined nonce yet. Instead, we carefully delay the random oracle programming of the combined nonce until it is completely known.

Cherry on Top: Non-interactive Assumptions. While the scheme we have so far does its job, we still rely on an interactive assumption, and we are eager to avoid it. For that, it is useful to write our scheme abstractly, replacing every exponentiation with the function $\mathsf{T}(t, x) = t^x$. Note that for almost every $t \in \mathbb{G}$, the function $\mathsf{T}(t, \cdot)$ is a bijection. Our hope is that by instantiating our scheme with a different function with suitable properties, we can show that the corresponding one-more assumption is implied by a non-interactive assumption. Indeed, Tessaro and Zhu [79] recently used a similar strategy to avoid OMDL in certain situations. To do so, they replace the bijective function with a compressing function. In our case, the interactive assumption, written abstractly using T, asks an adversary to win the following game:

- A random g and h are sampled, and random $x_0, \ldots, x_t$ are sampled. Then, g, h, and all $X_i = \mathsf{T}(g, x_i)$ for all $0 \leq i \leq t$ are given to the adversary.
- Roughly, the adversary gets t-time access to an algebraic oracle inverting T. More precisely, the oracle outputs $\sum_{i=0}^{t} \alpha_i x_i$ on input $\alpha_0, \ldots, \alpha_t$.
- The adversary outputs X_i' for all $0 \leq i \leq t$. It wins if all solutions are valid, meaning that there is a z_i such that $\mathsf{T}(g, z_i) = X_i \wedge \mathsf{T}(h, z_i) = X_i'$. Intuitively, the adversary has to "shift" the images X_i from g to h.

Under a suitable instantiation of T and a well-studied non-interactive assumption, we want to show that no adversary can win this game. Unfortunately, if we just use a compressing function as in the case of [79], it is not clear how to make use of the winning condition. Instead, our idea is to use a function that can *dynamically* be switched between a bijective and a compressing mode. A bit more precisely, a proof sketch works as follows:

1. We start with the game we introduced above. With overwhelming probability, the functions $\mathsf{T}_g := \mathsf{T}(g, \cdot)$ and $\mathsf{T}_h := \mathsf{T}(h, \cdot)$ should be bijective.
2. Assume that we can efficiently invert T_h using knowledge of h. Then, we can state our winning condition equivalently by requiring that $\mathsf{T}_h^{-1}(X_i') = x_i$ for all i. Roughly, this means that the adversary has to find the x_i to win.

3. We assume that we can indistinguishably switch g to a mode in which T_g is compressing.
4. Finally, we use a statistical argument to show that the adversary can not win. Intuitively, this is because T_g is compressing and the inversion oracle does not leak too much about the x_i's.

It turns out that, choosing T carefully, we find a function that (1) has all the properties we need for our scheme and (2) allows us to follow our proof sketch under the DDH assumption.

1.3   More on Related Work

We discuss further related work, including threshold signatures from other assumptions, and related cryptographic primitives.

Techniques for Adaptive Security. General techniques for achieving adaptive security have been studied [21,54,65]. Unfortunately, these techniques often rely on heavy cryptographic machinery and assumptions, e.g., secure erasures or broadcast channels.

Other Algebraic Structures. In the pairing setting, a natural construction is the (non-interactive) threshold version of the BLS signature scheme [14,17], which has been modified to achieve adaptive security in [62]. Recently, Bacho and Loss [6] have proven adaptive security of threshold BLS in the AGM. Das et al. have constructed weighted threshold signatures in the pairing-setting [33], and Crites et al. have constructed structure-preserving threshold signatures in the pairing-setting [26]. Threshold signatures have been constructed based on RSA [3,35,41,47,72,75,79]. Notably, adaptive security has been considered in [3]. A few works also have constructed threshold signatures from lattices [2,12,16,32, 51]. Finally, several works have proposed threshold signing protocols for ECDSA signatures [20,22,31,38,43–46,64]. Except for [20], these works focus on static corruptions. For an overview of this line of work, see [5].

Robustness. Recently, there has been renewed interest in robust (Schnorr) threshold signing protocols [13,50,73,76]. Such robust protocols additionally ensure that no malicious party can prevent honest parties from signing. Notably, all of these protocols assume static corruptions.

Multi-signatures. Multi-signatures [10,53] are threshold signatures with $t = n - 1$, i.e., all n parties need to participate in the signing protocol, with the advantage that parties generate their keys independently and come together to sign spontaneously without setting up a shared key. There is a rich literature on multi-signatures, e.g., [4,9,14,15,18,40,66–68,79]. Closest to our work in spirit are the work by Pan and Wagner [69], which avoids rewinding, and the work of Tessaro and Zhu [79], which aims at non-interactive assumptions.

Distributed Key Generation. In principle, one can rely on generic secure multi-party computation to set up key shares for a threshold signature scheme without using a trusted dealer. To get a more efficient solution, dedicated distributed key generation protocols have been studied [21,34,48,54,59,61,71], with some of them being adaptively secure [21,54,59].

2   Preliminaries

By λ we denote the security parameter. We assume all algorithms get λ in unary as input. If X is a finite set, we write $x \xleftarrow{\$} X$ to indicate that x is sampled uniformly at random from X. If $\mathcal{A}$ is a probabilistic algorithm, we write $y := \mathcal{A}(x; \rho)$ to state that y is assigned to the output of $\mathcal{A}$ on input x with random coins ρ. If ρ is sampled uniformly at random, we simply write $y \leftarrow \mathcal{A}(x)$. Further, the notation $y \in \mathcal{A}(x)$ indicates that y is a possible output of $\mathcal{A}$ on input x, i.e., there are random coins ρ such that $\mathcal{A}(x; \rho)$ outputs y.

Threshold Signatures. We define threshold signatures, assuming a trusted key generation, which can be replaced by a distributed key generation in practice. Our syntax matches the three-round structure of our protocol. Namely, a (t, n)-threshold signature scheme is a tuple of PPT algorithms $\mathsf{TS} = (\mathsf{Setup}, \mathsf{Gen}, \mathsf{Sig}, \mathsf{Ver})$, where $\mathsf{Setup}(1^\lambda)$ outputs system parameters par, and $\mathsf{Gen}(\mathsf{par})$ outputs a public key pk and secret key shares $\mathsf{sk}_1, \ldots, \mathsf{sk}_n$. Further, Sig specifies a signing protocol, formally split into four algorithms $(\mathsf{Sig}_0, \mathsf{Sig}_1, \mathsf{Sig}_2, \mathsf{Combine})$. Here, algorithm Sig_j models how the signers locally compute their $(j + 1)$st protocol message pm_{j+1} and advance their state, where $\mathsf{Sig}_0(S, i, \mathsf{sk}_i, \mathsf{m})$ takes as input the signer set S, the index of the signer $i \in [n]$, its secret key share sk_i, and the message m, and Sig_1 (resp. Sig_2) takes as input the current state of the signer and the list $\mathcal{M}_1$ (resp $\mathcal{M}_2$) of all protocol messages from the previous round. Finally, $\mathsf{Combine}(S, \mathsf{m}, \mathcal{M}_1, \mathcal{M}_2, \mathcal{M}_3)$ can be used to publicly turn the transcript into a signature σ, which can then be verified using $\mathsf{Ver}(\mathsf{pk}, \mathsf{m}, \sigma)$. Roughly, we say that the scheme is complete if for any such parameters and keys, a signature generated by a signing protocol among $t + 1$ parties outputs a signature for which Ver outputs 1. For a more formal and precise definition of syntax and completeness, we refer to the full version [7].

   Our security game is in line with the established template and is presented in Fig. 1. First, the adversary gets an honestly generated public key as input. At any point in time, the adversary can start a new signing session with signer set S and message m with session identifier sid by calling an oracle $\mathrm{NEXT}(sid, S, \mathsf{m})$. Additionally, the adversary may adaptively corrupt up to t users via an oracle CORR. Thereby, it learns their secret key and private state in all currently open signing sessions. To interact with honest users in signing sessions, the adversary has access to per-round signing oracles $\mathrm{SIG}_0, \mathrm{SIG}_1, \mathrm{SIG}_2$. Roughly, each signing oracle can be called with respect to a specific honest user i and a session identifier sid, given that the user is already in the respective round for that session (modeled by algorithm $\mathsf{Allowed}$). Further, when calling such an oracle, the adversary inputs the vector of all messages of the previous round. In particular, the adversary could send different messages to two different honest parties within the same session, i.e., we assume no broadcast channels. Additionally, this means that the adversary can arbitrarily decide which message to send to an honest party on behalf of another honest party, i.e., we assume no authenticated channels. Finally, the adversary outputs a forgery (m^*, σ^*). It wins the security game, if it never started a signing session for message m^* and the signature σ^* is valid. Therefore, our notion is (an interactive version of) TS-UF-0 using the terminology of [8,11], which is similar to recent works [25,28].

No Erasures. In our pseudocode, the private state of signer i in session *sid* is stored in state$[sid, i]$, where state is a map. After each signing round, this state is updated. We choose to update the state instead of adding a new state to avoid clutter, which is similar to earlier works [28]. On the downside, this means that potentially, schemes that are secure in our model could rely on erasures, i.e., on safely deleting part of the state of an earlier round before a user gets corrupted. We emphasize that in our scheme, any state in earlier rounds can be computed

---

Game TS-EUF-CMA$_{\text{TS}}^{\mathcal{A}}(\lambda)$

01 par $\leftarrow$ Setup(1^λ)
02 $(\text{pk}, \text{sk}_1, \ldots, \text{sk}_n) \leftarrow$ Gen(par)
03 SIG $:=$ (NEXT, SIG$_0$, SIG$_1$, SIG$_2$)
04 $(m^*, \sigma^*) \leftarrow \mathcal{A}^{\text{SIG}, \text{CORR}}(\text{par}, \text{pk})$
05 if $m^* \in$ Queried : return 0
06 return Ver$(\text{pk}, m^*, \sigma^*)$

Oracle CORR(i)
07 if $|\text{Corrupted}| \geq t$: return $\bot$
08 Corrupted $:=$ Corrupted $\cup \{i\}$
09 return $(\text{sk}_i, \text{state}[\cdot, i])$

Oracle NEXT(sid, S, m)
10 if $|S| \neq t + 1 \vee S \not\subseteq [n]$: return $\bot$
11 if $sid \in$ Sessions : return $\bot$
12 Sessions $:=$ Sessions $\cup \{sid\}$
13 message$[sid] :=$ m, signers$[sid] := S$
14 Queried $:=$ Queried $\cup \{m\}$
15 for $i \in S$: round$[sid, i] := 0$

Oracle SIG$_0(sid, i)$
16 if Allowed$(sid, i, 0, \bot) = 0$:
17   return $\bot$
18 $S :=$ signers$[sid]$
19 $(\text{pm}, St) \leftarrow \text{Sig}_0(S, i, \text{sk}_i, m)$
20 pm$_1[sid, i] :=$ pm, state$[sid, i] := St$
21 round$[sid, i] := 1$
22 return pm

Oracle SIG$_1(sid, i, \mathcal{M}_1)$
23 if Allowed$(sid, i, 1, \mathcal{M}_1) = 0$:
24   return $\bot$
25 $(\text{pm}, St) \leftarrow \text{Sig}_1(\text{state}[sid, i], \mathcal{M}_1)$
26 pm$_2[sid, i] :=$ pm, state$[sid, i] := St$
27 round$[sid, i] := 2$
28 return pm

Oracle SIG$_2(sid, i, \mathcal{M}_2)$
29 if Allowed$(sid, i, 2, \mathcal{M}_2) = 0$:
30   return $\bot$
31 pm $\leftarrow \text{Sig}_2(\text{state}[sid, i], \mathcal{M}_2)$
32 round$[sid, i] := 3$
33 return pm

Alg Allowed$(sid, i, r, \mathcal{M})$
34 if $sid \notin$ Sessions : return 0
35 $S :=$ signers$[sid]$, $H := S \setminus$ Corrupted
36 if $i \notin H$: return 0
37 if round$[sid, i] \neq r$: return 0
38 if $r > 0$:
39   parse $(\text{pm}_i)_{i \in S} := \mathcal{M}$
40   if $\text{pm}_i \neq \text{pm}_r[sid, i]$: return 0
41 return 1

Fig. 1. The game **TS-EUF-CMA** for a (three-round) (t, n)-threshold signature scheme TS $=$ (Setup, Gen, Sig, Ver) and an adversary $\mathcal{A}$.

from the state in the current round and the secret key. This means that our schemes do not rely on erasures.

Definition 1 (TS-EUF-CMA Security). *Let* TS = (Setup, Gen, Sig, Ver) *be a* (t, n)*-threshold signature scheme. Consider the game* **TS-EUF-CMA** *defined in Fig. 1. We say that* TS *is TS-EUF-CMA secure, if for all PPT adversaries* $\mathcal{A}$, *the following advantage is negligible:*

$$\mathsf{Adv}_{\mathcal{A},\mathsf{TS}}^{\mathsf{TS\text{-}EUF\text{-}CMA}}(\lambda) := \Pr\left[\textbf{TS-EUF-CMA}_{\mathsf{TS}}^{\mathcal{A}}(\lambda) \Rightarrow 1\right].$$

3 Our Construction

In this section, we present our new threshold signature scheme. However, before we present it, we first introduce a building block we need, which we call tagged linear function families.

3.1 Tagged Linear Function Families

Similar to what is done in other works [23,52,55,69,79], we use the abstraction of linear function families to describe our scheme in a generic way. However, we slightly change the notion by introducing tags to cover different functions with the same set of parameters.

Definition 2 (Tagged Linear Function Family). *A tagged linear function family is a tuple of PPT algorithms* TLF = (Gen, T) *with the following syntax:*

- Gen$(1^\lambda) \to$ par *takes as input the security parameter* 1^λ *and outputs parameters* par. *We assume that* par *implicitly defines the following sets: A set of scalars* $\mathcal{S}_{\mathsf{par}}$, *which forms a field; a set of tags* $\mathcal{T}_{\mathsf{par}}$; *a domain* $\mathcal{D}_{\mathsf{par}}$ *and a range* $\mathcal{R}_{\mathsf{par}}$, *where each forms a vector space over* $\mathcal{S}_{\mathsf{par}}$. *If* par *is clear from the context, we omit the subscript* par. *We naturally denote the operations of these fields and vector spaces by* + *and* ·, *and assume that these operations can be evaluated efficiently.*
- T$(\mathsf{par}, g, x) \to X$ *is deterministic, takes as input parameters* par, *a tag* $g \in \mathcal{T}$, *a domain element* $x \in \mathcal{D}$, *and outputs a range element* $X \in \mathcal{R}$. *For all parameters* par, *and for all tags* $g \in \mathcal{T}$, *the function* T$(\mathsf{par}, g, \cdot)$ *realizes a homomorphism, i.e.*

$$\forall s \in \mathcal{S}, x, y \in \mathcal{D} : \ \mathsf{T}(\mathsf{par}, g, s \cdot x + y) = s \cdot \mathsf{T}(\mathsf{par}, g, x) + \mathsf{T}(\mathsf{par}, g, y).$$

For T, *we also omit the input* par *if it is clear from the context.*

For our construction, we require that images are uniformly distributed. More precisely, we say that TLF is ε_{r}-regular, if there is a set Reg of pairs (par, g) such that random parameters par and tags g are in Reg with probability at least $1 - \varepsilon_{\mathsf{r}}$, and for each such pair in Reg, T(par, g, x) is uniformly distributed over the range, assuming $x \xleftarrow{\$} \mathcal{D}$. We postpone a more formal definition to the full version [7]. Next, we show that tagged linear function families satisfy a statistical property that turns out to be useful. This property is implicitly present in other works as well, e.g., in [1,56,57,69], and can be interpreted in various ways, e.g., as the soundness of a natural proof system.

Lemma 1. *Let* $\mathsf{TLF} = (\mathsf{Gen}, \mathsf{T})$ *be a tagged linear function family. For every fixed parameters* par *and tags* $g, h \in \mathcal{T}$, *define the set*

$$\mathsf{Im}(\mathsf{par}, g, h) := \left\{ (X_1, X_2) \in \mathcal{R}^2 \mid \exists x \in \mathcal{D} : \ \mathsf{T}(g, x) = X_1 \wedge \mathsf{T}(h, x) = X_2 \right\}.$$

Then, for any (even unbounded) algorithm $\mathcal{A}$, *we have*

$$\Pr \left[\begin{array}{c} (X_1, X_2) \notin \mathsf{Im}(\mathsf{par}, g, h) \\ \wedge\ \mathsf{T}(g, s) = c \cdot X_1 + R_1 \\ \wedge\ \mathsf{T}(h, s) = c \cdot X_2 + R_2 \end{array} \ \middle| \ \begin{array}{c} \mathsf{par} \leftarrow \mathsf{Gen}(1^\lambda), \\ (St, g, h, X_1, X_2, R_1, R_2) \leftarrow \mathcal{A}(\mathsf{par}), \\ c \xleftarrow{\$} \mathcal{S}, \ \ s \leftarrow \mathcal{A}(St, c) \end{array} \right] \leq \frac{1}{|\mathcal{S}|}.$$

The proof of Lemma 1 is postponed to the full version [7]. As another technical tool in our proof, we need our tagged linear function families to be translatable, a notion we define next. Informally, it means that we can rerandomize a given tag g into a tag h, such that we can efficiently compute $\mathsf{T}(h, x)$ from $\mathsf{T}(g, x)$ without knowing x.

Definition 3 (Translatability). *Let* $\mathsf{TLF} = (\mathsf{Gen}, \mathsf{T})$ *be a tagged linear function family. We say that* TLF *is* ε_t-*translatable, if there is a PPT algorithm* Shift *and a deterministic polynomial time algorithm* Translate, *such that the following properties hold:*

- **Well Distributed Tags.** *The statistical distance between the following distributions* $\mathcal{X}_0$ *and* $\mathcal{X}_1$ *is at most* ε_t:

$$\mathcal{X}_0 := \left\{ (\mathsf{par}, g, h) \ \middle| \ \mathsf{par} \leftarrow \mathsf{Gen}(1^\lambda), \ g \xleftarrow{\$} \mathcal{T}, \ h \xleftarrow{\$} \mathcal{T} \right\},$$

$$\mathcal{X}_1 := \left\{ (\mathsf{par}, g, h) \ \middle| \ \mathsf{par} \leftarrow \mathsf{Gen}(1^\lambda), \ g \xleftarrow{\$} \mathcal{T}, \ (h, \mathsf{td}) \leftarrow \mathsf{Shift}(\mathsf{par}, g) \right\}.$$

- **Translation Completeness.** *For every* $\mathsf{par} \in \mathsf{Gen}(1^\lambda)$, *for any* $g \in \mathcal{T}$, *any* $x \in \mathcal{D}$, *and any* $(h, \mathsf{td}) \in \mathsf{Shift}(\mathsf{par}, g)$, *we have*

$$\mathsf{Translate}(\mathsf{td}, \mathsf{T}(g, x)) = \mathsf{T}(h, x) \ and \ \mathsf{InvTranslate}(\mathsf{td}, \mathsf{T}(h, x)) = \mathsf{T}(g, x).$$

Next, we define the main security property that we will require for our construction. Intuitively, it should not be possible for an adversary to translate $\mathsf{T}(g, x)$ into $\mathsf{T}(h, x)$ if g, h and x are chosen randomly. Our actual notion is a one-more variant of this intuition.

Definition 4 (Algebraic Translation Resistance). *Let* $\mathsf{TLF} = (\mathsf{Gen}, \mathsf{T})$ *be a tagged linear function family, and* $t \in \mathbb{N}$ *be a number. Consider the game* **A-TRAN-RES** *defined in Fig. 2. We say that* TLF *is* t-*algebraic translation resistant, if for any PPT algorithm* $\mathcal{A}$, *the following advantage is negligible:*

$$\mathsf{Adv}_{\mathcal{A}, \mathsf{TLF}}^{t\text{-A-TRAN-RES}}(\lambda) := \Pr \left[t\text{-}\mathbf{A\text{-}TRAN\text{-}RES}_{\mathsf{TLF}}^{\mathcal{A}}(\lambda) \Rightarrow 1 \right].$$

Game t-A-TRAN-RES$_{\mathsf{TLF}}^{\mathcal{A}}(\lambda)$	**Oracle $\mathrm{INV}(\alpha_0,\ldots,\alpha_t)$**
01 $\mathsf{par} \leftarrow \mathsf{Gen}(1^\lambda), \quad g,h \overset{\$}{\leftarrow} \mathcal{T}, \quad x_0,\ldots,x_t \overset{\$}{\leftarrow} \mathcal{D}$	07 **if** $q \geq t$: **return** $\bot$
02 **for** $i \in \{0\} \cup [t]$: $X_i := \mathsf{T}(g,x_i)$	08 $q := q+1$
03 $(X_i')_{i=0}^t \leftarrow \mathcal{A}^{\mathrm{INV}}(\mathsf{par}, g, h, (X_i)_{i=0}^t)$	09 $x := \sum_{i=0}^t \alpha_i x_i$
04 **if** $\forall i \in \{0\} \cup [t]\ \exists z \in \mathcal{D}$	10 **return** x
s.t. $\mathsf{T}(g,z) = X_i \wedge \mathsf{T}(h,z) = X_i'$:	
05 **return** 1	
06 **return** 0	

Fig. 2. Game **A-TRAN-RES** for a tagged linear function family $\mathsf{TLF} = (\mathsf{Gen}, \mathsf{T})$ and adversary $\mathcal{A}$.

3.2 Construction

Let $\mathsf{TLF} = (\mathsf{Gen}, \mathsf{T})$ be a tagged linear function family. Further, let $\mathsf{H} \colon \{0,1\}^* \to \mathcal{T}$, $\hat{\mathsf{H}} \colon \{0,1\}^* \to \{0,1\}^{2\lambda}$, $\bar{\mathsf{H}} \colon \{0,1\}^* \to \mathcal{S}$ be random oracles. We construct a (t,n)-treshold signature scheme $\mathsf{Twinkle}[\mathsf{TLF}] = (\mathsf{Setup}, \mathsf{Gen}, \mathsf{Sig}, \mathsf{Ver})$. We assume that there is an implicit injection from $[n]$ into $\mathcal{S}$. Further, let $\ell_{i,S}(x) := \prod_{j \in S \setminus \{i\}} (j-x)/(j-i) \in \mathcal{S}$ denote the ith lagrange coefficient for all $i \in [n]$ and $S \subseteq [n]$, and let $\ell_{i,S} := \ell_{i,S}(0)$. We describe our scheme verbally.

Setup and Key Generation. All parties have access to public parameters $\mathsf{par} \leftarrow \mathsf{TLF.Gen}(1^\lambda)$ which define the function T, and sets $\mathcal{S}, \mathcal{T}, \mathcal{D}$, and $\mathcal{R}$, and to a random tag $g \overset{\$}{\leftarrow} \mathcal{T}$. To generate keys, elements $a_j \overset{\$}{\leftarrow} \mathcal{D}$ for $j \in \{0\} \cup [t]$ are sampled. These elements form the coefficients of a polynomial of degree t. For each $i \in [n]$, we define the key pair $(\mathsf{pk}_i, \mathsf{sk}_i)$ for the ith signer as

$$\mathsf{sk}_i := \sum_{j=0}^t a_j i^j, \quad \mathsf{pk}_i := \mathsf{T}(g, \mathsf{sk}_i).$$

The shared public key is defined as $\mathsf{pk} := \mathsf{pk}_0 := \mathsf{T}(g, a_0)$.

Signing Protocol. Let $S \subseteq [n]$ be a set of signers of size $t+1$. We assume all signers are aware of the set S and a message $\mathsf{m} \in \{0,1\}^*$ to be signed. First, they all compute $h := \mathsf{H}(\mathsf{m})$. Then, they run the following protocol phases to compute the signature:

1. *Commitment Phase.* Each signer $i \in S$ samples $r_i \overset{\$}{\leftarrow} \mathcal{D}$ and computes

$$R_i^{(1)} := \mathsf{T}(g, r_i), \quad R_i^{(2)} := \mathsf{T}(h, r_i), \quad \mathsf{pk}_i^{(2)} := \mathsf{T}(h, \mathsf{sk}_i).$$

Then, each signer $i \in S$ computes a commitment

$$\mathsf{com}_i := \hat{\mathsf{H}}(S, i, R_i^{(1)}, R_i^{(2)}, \mathsf{pk}_i^{(2)})$$

and sends com_i to the other signers.

2. *Opening Phase.* Each signer $i \in S$ sends $R_i^{(1)}, R_i^{(2)}$ and $\mathsf{pk}_i^{(2)}$ to all other signers.

3. *Response Phase.* Each signer $i \in S$ checks that $\mathsf{com}_j = \hat{\mathsf{H}}(S, j, R_j^{(1)}, R_j^{(2)}, \mathsf{pk}_j^{(2)})$ holds for all $j \in S$. If one of these equations does not hold, the signer aborts. Otherwise, the signer defines

$$R^{(1)} := \sum_{j \in S} R_j^{(1)}, \quad R^{(2)} := \sum_{j \in S} R_j^{(2)}, \quad \mathsf{pk}^{(2)} := \sum_{j \in S} \ell_{j,S} \mathsf{pk}_j^{(2)}.$$

The signer computes $c := \bar{\mathsf{H}}(\mathsf{pk}, \mathsf{pk}^{(2)}, R^{(1)}, R^{(2)}, \mathsf{m})$ and $s_i := c \cdot \ell_{i,S} \cdot \mathsf{sk}_i + r_i$. It sends s_i to all other signers.

The signature is $\sigma := (\mathsf{pk}^{(2)}, c, s)$ for $s := \sum_{j \in S} s_j$.

Verification. Let pk be a public key, let $\mathsf{m} \in \{0,1\}^*$ be a message and let $\sigma = (\mathsf{pk}^{(2)}, c, s)$ be a signature. To verify σ with respect to pk and m, one first computes $h := \mathsf{H}(\mathsf{m})$ and $R^{(1)} := \mathsf{T}(g, s) - c \cdot \mathsf{pk}$, $R^{(2)} := \mathsf{T}(h, s) - c \cdot \mathsf{pk}^{(2)}$. Then, one accepts the signature, i.e., outputs 1, if and only if $c = \bar{\mathsf{H}}(\mathsf{pk}, \mathsf{pk}^{(2)}, R^{(1)}, R^{(2)}, \mathsf{m})$.

Theorem 1. *Let* $\mathsf{TLF} = (\mathsf{Gen}, \mathsf{T})$ *be a tagged linear function family and let* $\mathsf{H} \colon \{0,1\}^* \to \mathcal{T}$, $\hat{\mathsf{H}} \colon \{0,1\}^* \to \{0,1\}^{2\lambda}$, $\bar{\mathsf{H}} \colon \{0,1\}^* \to \mathcal{S}$ *be random oracles. Assume that* TLF *is* ε_r-*regular and* ε_t-*translatable. Further, assume that* TLF *is* t-*algebraic translation resistant. Then,* $\mathsf{Twinkle[TLF]}$ *is* TS-EUF-CMA *secure.*

Proof. Fix an adversary $\mathcal{A}$ against the security of $\mathsf{TS} := \mathsf{Twinkle[TLF]}$. We prove the statement by presenting a sequence of games $\mathbf{G_0}$-$\mathbf{G_8}$. All games and associated oracles and algorithms are presented as pseudocode in the full version [7].

Game $\mathbf{G_0}$: This game is the security game $\mathbf{TS}\text{-}\mathbf{EUF}\text{-}\mathbf{CMA}_{\mathsf{TS}}^{\mathcal{A}}$ for threshold signatures. We recall the game to fix some notation. First, the game samples parameters par' for TLF and a tag $g \xleftarrow{\$} \mathcal{T}$. It also samples random coefficients $a_0, \ldots, a_t \xleftarrow{\$} \mathcal{D}$ and computes a public key $\mathsf{pk} := \mathsf{pk}_0 := \mathsf{T}(g, a_0)$ and secret key shares $\mathsf{sk}_i := \sum_{j=0}^{t} a_j i^j$ for each $i \in [n]$. For convenience, denote the corresponding public key shares by $\mathsf{pk}_i := \mathsf{T}(g, \mathsf{sk}_i)$. Then, the game runs $\mathcal{A}$ on input $\mathsf{par} := (\mathsf{par}', g)$ and pk with access to signing oracles, corruption oracles, and random oracles. Concretely, it gets access to random oracles H, $\hat{\mathsf{H}}$, and $\bar{\mathsf{H}}$, which are provided by the game in the standard lazy way using maps $h[\cdot]$, $\hat{h}[\cdot]$, and $\bar{h}[\cdot]$, respectively. The set of corrupted parties is denoted by $\mathsf{Corrupted}$ and the set of queried messages is denoted by $\mathsf{Queried}$. Finally, the adversary outputs a forgery (m^*, σ^*) and the game outputs 1 if $\mathsf{m}^* \notin \mathsf{Queried}$, $|\mathsf{Corrupted}| \leq t$, and σ^* is a valid signature for m^*. We make three purely conceptual changes to the game. First, we will never keep the secret key share sk_i explicitly in the states $\mathsf{state}[sid, i]$ for users i in a session sid, although the scheme description would require this. This is without loss of generality, as the adversary only gets to see the states when it corrupts a user, and in this case it also gets sk_i. Second, we assume the adversary always queried $\mathsf{H}(\mathsf{m}^*)$ before outputting its forgery. Third, we assume that the adversary makes exactly t (distinct) corruption queries. These changes are without loss of generality and do not change the advantage of $\mathcal{A}$. Formally, one could build a wrapper adversary that internally runs $\mathcal{A}$, but makes a query $H(m^*)$ and enough corruption queries before terminating, and on every corruption query includes sk_i in the states before passing the result back to $\mathcal{A}$. Clearly, we have $\mathsf{Adv}_{\mathcal{A},\mathsf{TS}}^{\mathsf{TS\text{-}EUF\text{-}CMA}}(\lambda) = \Pr\left[\mathbf{G}_0 \Rightarrow 1\right]$. The remainder of our proof is split into three parts. In the first part $(\mathbf{G}_1\text{-}\mathbf{G}_3)$, we ensure that the game no longer needs secret key shares sk_i to compute $pk_i^{(2)}$ in the signing oracle. Roughly, this is done by embedding shifted tags $(h, \mathsf{td}) \leftarrow \mathsf{Shift}(\mathsf{par}', g)$ into random oracle H for signing queries, and keeping random tags h for the query related to the forgery. In the second part $(\mathbf{G}_4\text{-}\mathbf{G}_{11})$, we use careful delayed random oracle programming, observability of the random oracle, and an honest-verifier zero-knowledge-style programming to simulate the remaining parts of the signing queries without sk_i. As a result, sk_i is only needed when the adversary corrupts users. In the third part, we analyze $\mathbf{G}_{11}$. This is done by distinguishing two cases. One of the cases is bounded using a statistical argument. The other case is bounded using a reduction breaking the t-algebraic translation resistance of TLF. We now proceed with the details.

Game $\mathbf{G}_1$: In this game, we introduce a map $b[\cdot]$ that maps messages m to bits $b[m] \in \{0, 1\}$. Concretely, whenever a query $H(m)$ is made for which the hash value is not yet defined, the game samples $b[m]$ from a Bernoulli distribution $\mathcal{B}_\gamma$ with parameter $\gamma = 1/(Q_S + 1)$. That is, $b[m]$ is set to 1 with probability $1/(Q_S + 1)$ and to 0 otherwise. The game aborts if $b[m] = 1$ for some message m for which the signing oracle is called, or $b[m^*] = 0$ for the forgery message m^*. Clearly, if no abort occurs, games $\mathbf{G}_0$ and $\mathbf{G}_1$ are the same. Further the view of $\mathcal{A}$ is independent of the map b. We obtain

$$\Pr\left[\mathbf{G}_1 \Rightarrow 1\right] = \gamma\,(1-\gamma)^{Q_S} \cdot \Pr\left[\mathbf{G}_0 \Rightarrow 1\right]$$

Now, we can use the fact $(1 - 1/x)^x \geq 1/4$ for all $x \geq 2$ and get

$$\gamma\,(1-\gamma)^{Q_S} = \frac{1}{Q_S + 1}\left(1 - \frac{1}{Q_S + 1}\right)^{Q_S} = \frac{1}{Q_S}\left(1 - \frac{1}{Q_S + 1}\right)^{Q_S+1} \geq \frac{1}{4Q_S},$$

where the second equality is shown in the full version [7]. In combination, we get $\Pr\left[\mathbf{G}_1 \Rightarrow 1\right] \geq \frac{1}{4Q_S} \cdot \Pr\left[\mathbf{G}_0 \Rightarrow 1\right]$.

Game $\mathbf{G}_2$: In game $\mathbf{G}_2$, we change the way queries to random oracle H are answered. Namely, for a query $H(m)$ for which the hash value $h[m]$ is not yet defined, the game samples $h[m] \xleftarrow{\$} \mathcal{T}$ as a random tag exactly as the previous game did. However, now, if $b[m] = 0$, the game samples $(h, \mathsf{td}) \leftarrow \mathsf{Shift}(\mathsf{par}', g)$ and sets $h[m] := h$. Further, it stores td in a map tr as $tr[m] := \mathsf{td}$. Clearly, $\mathbf{G}_1$ and $\mathbf{G}_2$ are indistinguishable by the ε_t-translatability of TLF. Concretely, one can easily see that $|\Pr\left[\mathbf{G}_1 \Rightarrow 1\right] - \Pr\left[\mathbf{G}_2 \Rightarrow 1\right]| \leq Q_H \varepsilon_t$.

Game $\mathbf{G}_3$: In this game, we change how the values $pk_i^{(2)}$ are computed by the signing oracle. To recall, in the commitment phase of the signing protocol, the signing oracle for user $i \in [n]$ in $\mathbf{G}_2$ would compute the value $\mathsf{pk}_i^{(2)} := \mathsf{T}(h, \mathsf{sk}_i)$, where $h = \mathsf{H}(\mathsf{m})$ and m is the message to be signed. Also, the value $\mathsf{pk}_i^{(2)} := \mathsf{T}(h, \mathsf{sk}_i)$ is recomputed in the opening phase of the signing protocol and included in the output sent to the adversary. From $\mathbf{G}_3$ on, $\mathsf{pk}_i^{(2)}$ is computed differently, namely, as $\mathsf{pk}_i^{(2)} := \mathsf{Translate}(tr[\mathsf{m}], \mathsf{pk}_i)$. Observe that if the game did not abort, we know that $b[\mathsf{m}] = 0$ (see $\mathbf{G}_1$) and therefore h has been generated as $(h, \mathsf{td}) \leftarrow \mathsf{Shift}(\mathsf{par}', g)$ where $tr[\mathsf{m}] = \mathsf{td}$. Thus, it follows from the translatability of TLF, or more concretely from the translation completeness, that the view of $\mathcal{A}$ is not changed. We get $\Pr[\mathbf{G}_2 \Rightarrow 1] = \Pr[\mathbf{G}_3 \Rightarrow 1]$.

Game $\mathbf{G}_4$: In this game, we let the game abort if $(\mathsf{par}', g) \notin \mathsf{Reg}$, where Reg is the set from the regularity definition of TLF. By regularity of TLF, we have $|\Pr[\mathbf{G}_3 \Rightarrow 1] - \Pr[\mathbf{G}_4 \Rightarrow 1]| \le \varepsilon_r$.

Game $\mathbf{G}_5$: In this game, we change the signing oracle again. Specifically, we change the commitment and opening phase. Recall that until now, in the commitment phase for an honest party i in a signer set $S \subseteq [n]$ and message m, an element $r_i \xleftarrow{\$} \mathcal{D}$ is sampled and the party sends a commitment $\mathsf{com}_i := \hat{\mathsf{H}}(S, i, R_i^{(1)}, R_i^{(2)}, \mathsf{pk}_i^{(2)})$ for $R_i^{(1)} := \mathsf{T}(g, r_i), R_i^{(2)} := \mathsf{T}(h, r_i)$, and $\mathsf{pk}_i^{(2)} := \mathsf{Translate}(tr[\mathsf{m}], \mathsf{pk}_i)$. As before, h is defined as $h := \mathsf{H}(\mathsf{m})$. Later, in the opening phase, the party sends $R_i^{(1)}, R_i^{(2)}, \mathsf{pk}_i^{(2)}$. Now, we change this as follows: The signing oracle computes $\mathsf{pk}_i^{(2)}$ as in $\mathbf{G}_4$, but it does not compute $R_i^{(1)}, R_i^{(2)}$ and instead sends a random commitment $\mathsf{com}_i \xleftarrow{\$} \{0,1\}^{2\lambda}$ on behalf of party i. It also inserts an entry (S, i, com_i) into a list Sim that keeps track of these simulated commitments. If there is already an $(S', i') \ne (S, i)$ such that $(S', i', \mathsf{com}_i) \in \mathsf{Sim}$, then the game aborts. Note that there are two situations where the preimage of com_i has to be revealed. Namely, $R_i^{(1)}, R_i^{(2)}, \mathsf{pk}_i^{(2)}$ has to be given to the adversary in the opening phase, and whenever party i is corrupted the game needs to output r_i. To handle this, consider the opening phase or the case where party i is corrupted before it reaches the opening phase. Here, we let the game sample $r_i \xleftarrow{\$} \mathcal{D}$ and define $R_i^{(1)} := \mathsf{T}(g, r_i)$ and $R_i^{(2)} := \mathsf{T}(h, r_i)$. Then, the game checks if $\hat{h}[S, i, R_i^{(1)}, R_i^{(2)}, \mathsf{pk}_i^{(2)}] = \bot$. If it is not, the game aborts. Otherwise, it programs $\hat{h}[S, i, R_i^{(1)}, R_i^{(2)}, \mathsf{pk}_i^{(2)}] := \mathsf{com}_i$ and continues. That is, in the opening phase it would output $R_i^{(1)}, R_i^{(2)}, \mathsf{pk}_i^{(2)}$, and during a corruption, it would output r_i as part of its state. If a corruption occurs after the opening phase, then r_i has already been defined, and corruption is handled as before. Clearly, the view of $\mathcal{A}$ is only affected by this change if $R_i^{(1)}, R_i^{(2)}, \mathsf{pk}_i^{(2)}$ matches a previous query of $\mathcal{A}$ or the same commitment has been sampled by the game twice. The latter event occurs only with probability $Q_S^2/2^{2\lambda}$ by a union bound over all pairs of queries. To bound the former event, we use the regularity of TLF, which implies that $R_i^{(1)}$ is uniform over the range $\mathcal{R}$. Now, for each fixed pair of signing query and random oracle query, the random oracle query matches $R_i^{(1)}, R_i^{(2)}, \mathsf{pk}_i^{(2)}$ with probability at most $1/|\mathcal{R}|$. Thus, the event occurs only with probability $Q_S Q_{\hat{\mathsf{H}}}/2^{2\lambda}$. We get $|\Pr[\mathbf{G}_4 \Rightarrow 1] - \Pr[\mathbf{G}_5 \Rightarrow 1]| \le Q_S Q_{\hat{\mathsf{H}}}/|\mathcal{R}| + Q_S^2/2^{2\lambda}$.

Game G_6: In this game, we rule out collisions for random oracle $\hat{H}$. Namely, the game aborts if there are $x \neq x'$ such that $\hat{h}[x] = \hat{h}[x'] \neq \perp$. Clearly, we have $|\Pr[G_5 \Rightarrow 1] - \Pr[G_6 \Rightarrow 1]| \leq \frac{Q_{\hat{H}}^2}{2^{2\lambda}}$. Subsequent games will internally make use of an algorithm $\hat{H}^{-1}$. On input y the algorithm searches for an x such that $\hat{h}[x] = y$. If no such x is found, or if multiple x are found, then the algorithm returns $\perp$. Otherwise, it returns x. Note that in the latter case the game would abort anyways, and so we can assume that if there is a preimage of y, then this preimage is uniquely determined by y.

Game G_7: In this game, we introduce a list Pending and associated algorithms UpdatePending and AddToPending to manage this list. Intuitively, the list keeps track of honest users i and signing sessions sid for which the game can not yet extract preimages of all commitments sent in the commitment phase. More precisely, the list contains a tuple $(sid, i, \mathcal{M}_1)$ if and only if the following two conditions hold:

- The opening phase oracle $\text{SIG}_1(sid, i, \mathcal{M}_1)$ has been called with valid inputs, i.e., for this query the game did not output $\perp$ due to $\text{Allowed}(sid, i, 1, \mathcal{M}_1) = 0$, and at that point the following was true: For every commitment com_j in $\mathcal{M}_1$ such that $(S, j, \text{com}_j) \notin \text{Sim}$, we have $\hat{H}^{-1}(\text{com}_j) \neq \perp$ and with $(S', k, R^{(1)}, R^{(2)}, \text{pk}^{(2)}) := \hat{H}^{-1}(\text{com}_j)$ we have $S' = S$ and $k = j$, where S is the signer set associated with sid.
- There is a commitment com_j in $\mathcal{M}_1$ such that $\hat{H}^{-1}(\text{com}_j) = \perp$.

To ensure that the list satisfies this invariant, we add a triple $(sid, i, \mathcal{M}_1)$ to Pending when the first condition holds. This is done by algorithm AddToPending. Concretely, whenever $\mathcal{A}$ calls $\text{SIG}_1(sid, i, \mathcal{M}_1)$, the oracle returns $\perp$ in case $\text{Allowed}(sid, i, 1, \mathcal{M}_1) = 0$. If $\text{Allowed}(sid, i, 1, \mathcal{M}_1) = 1$, the game immediately calls $\text{AddToPending}(sid, i, 1, \mathcal{M}_1)$, which checks the first condition of the invariant and inserts the tripe $(sid, i, 1, \mathcal{M}_1)$ into Pending if it holds. Then, the game continues the simulation of SIG_1 as before. Further, we invoke algorithm UpdatePending whenever the map $\hat{h}$ is changed, i.e., during queries to $\hat{H}$, and in corruption and signing oracles (see G_5). On every invocation, the algorithm does the following:

1. Initialize an empty list New.
2. Iterate trough all entries $(sid, i, \mathcal{M}_1)$ in Pending, and do the following:
   (a) Check if the entry has to be removed because it is violating the invariant. That is, check if for all j in the signer set S associated with session sid, we have $\hat{H}^{-1}(\text{com}_j) \neq \perp$, where $\mathcal{M}_1 = (\text{com}_j)_{j \in S}$. If this is not the case, skip this entry and keep it in Pending.
   (b) We know that for all indices $j \in S$, the value $(S'_j, k_j, R^{(1)}_j, R^{(2)}_j, \text{pk}^{(2)}_j)$ $= \hat{H}^{-1}(\text{com}_j)$ exists. Further, it must hold that $S'_j = S$ and $k_j = j$, as otherwise this entry would not have been added to Pending in the first place. Remove the entry from Pending, and determine the combined nonces and secondary public key

$$R^{(1)} = \sum_{j \in S} R_j^{(1)}, \quad R^{(2)} = \sum_{j \in S} R_j^{(2)}, \quad \mathsf{pk}^{(2)} = \sum_{j \in S} \ell_{j,S} \mathsf{pk}_j^{(2)}.$$

(c) Let m be the message associated with the session *sid*.

(d) If $(R^{(1)}, R^{(2)}, \mathsf{pk}^{(2)}, \mathsf{m}) \notin \mathsf{New}$ but $\bar{h}[\mathsf{pk}, \mathsf{pk}^{(2)}, R^{(1)}, R^{(2)}, \mathsf{m}] \neq \bot$, abort the execution of the entire game (see bad event **Defined** below).

(e) Otherwise, sample $\bar{h}[\mathsf{pk}, \mathsf{pk}^{(2)}, R^{(1)}, R^{(2)}, \mathsf{m}] \overset{\$}{\leftarrow} S$ and insert the tuple $(R^{(1)}, R^{(2)}, \mathsf{pk}^{(2)}, \mathsf{m})$ into New.

To summarize, this algorithm removes all entries violating the invariant from the list Pending. For each such entry that is removed, the algorithm computes the combined nonces $R^{(1)}, R^{(2)}$ and secondary public key $\mathsf{pk}^{(2)}$. Roughly, it aborts the execution, if random oracle $\bar{\mathsf{H}}$ for these inputs is already defined. List New ensures that the abort is not triggered if the algorithm itself programmed $\bar{h}$ in a previous iteration within the same invocation. In addition to algorithm UpdatePending, we introduce the following events, on which the game aborts its execution:

- Event BadQuery: This event occurs, if for a random oracle query to $\hat{\mathsf{H}}$ for which the hash value is not yet defined and freshly sampled as com $\overset{\$}{\leftarrow} \{0,1\}^{2\lambda}$, there is an entry $(sid, i, \mathcal{M}_1)$ in Pending such that com is in $\mathcal{M}_1$.
- Event Defined: This event occurs, if the execution is aborted during algorithm UpdatePending.

For shorthand notation, we set Bad := BadQuery $\vee$ Defined. The probability of BadQuery can be bounded as follows: Fix a random oracle query to $\hat{\mathsf{H}}$ for which the hash value is not yet defined. Fix an entry $(sid, i, \mathcal{M}_1)$. Note that over the entire game, there are at most Q_S of these entries. Further, fix an index $j \in [t+1]$. The probability that com collides with the jth entry of $\mathcal{M}_1$ is clearly at most $1/2^{2\lambda}$. With a union bound over all triples of queries, entries, and indices, we get that the probability of BadQuery is at most $Q_{\hat{\mathsf{H}}} Q_S(t+1)/2^{2\lambda}$. Next, we bound the probability of Defined assuming BadQuery does not occur. Under this assumption, one can easily observe that when an entry is removed from list Pending and $R^{(1)} = \sum_{j \in S} R_j^{(1)}$ is the combined first nonce, then there is an $j^* \in S$ such that the game sampled $R_{j^*}^{(1)}$ just before invoking algorithm UpdatePending. Precisely, it must have set $R_{j^*}^{(1)} := \mathsf{T}(g, r)$ for some random $r \overset{\$}{\leftarrow} \mathcal{D}$. By regularity of TLF, this means $R_{j^*}^{(1)}$ is uniform over $\mathcal{R}$, and this means that the combined first nonce $R^{(1)}$ is also uniform. Thus for any fixed entry of in Pending, the probability that $\bar{h}[\mathsf{pk}, \mathsf{pk}^{(2)}, R^{(1)}, R^{(2)}, \mathsf{m}]$ is already defined when the entry is removed, is at most $Q_{\hat{\mathsf{H}}}/|\mathcal{R}|$. With a union bound over all entries we can now bound the probability of Defined by $Q_{\hat{\mathsf{H}}} Q_S/|\mathcal{R}|$. In combination, we get

$$\Pr[\mathsf{Bad}] \leq \Pr[\mathsf{BadQuery}] + \Pr[\mathsf{Defined} \mid \neg\mathsf{BadQuery}] \leq \frac{Q_{\hat{\mathsf{H}}} Q_S(t+1)}{2^{2\lambda}} + \frac{Q_{\hat{\mathsf{H}}} Q_S}{|\mathcal{R}|}.$$

and thus

$$|\Pr\left[\mathbf{G}_6 \Rightarrow 1\right] - \Pr\left[\mathbf{G}_7 \Rightarrow 1\right]| \leq \Pr\left[\mathsf{Bad}\right] \leq \frac{Q_{\hat{\mathsf{H}}} Q_S (t+1)}{2^{2\lambda}} + \frac{Q_{\hat{\mathsf{H}}} Q_S}{|\mathcal{R}|}.$$

Game $\mathbf{G}_8$: In this game, we change algorithm UpdatePending. Specifically, we change what we insert into list New. Recall from the previous game that when we removed an entry $(sid, i, \mathcal{M}_1)$ from Pending, we aborted the game if $(R^{(1)}, R^{(2)}, \mathsf{pk}^{(2)}, \mathsf{m}) \notin$ New but $\bar{h}[\mathsf{pk}, \mathsf{pk}^{(2)}, R^{(1)}, R^{(2)}, \mathsf{m}] \neq \bot$. Otherwise, we inserted tuples $(R^{(1)}, R^{(2)}, \mathsf{pk}^{(2)}, \mathsf{m})$. Now, we instead abort if $(S, R^{(1)}, R^{(2)}, \mathsf{pk}^{(2)}, \mathsf{m}) \notin$ New but $\bar{h}[\mathsf{pk}, \mathsf{pk}^{(2)}, R^{(1)}, R^{(2)}, \mathsf{m}] \neq \bot$, and otherwise insert $(S, R^{(1)}, R^{(2)}, \mathsf{pk}^{(2)}, \mathsf{m})$, where S is the signer set associated with session sid. One can see that the two games can only differ if for two entries $(sid, i, \mathcal{M}_1)$ and $(sid', i', \mathcal{M}_1')$ that are removed from Pending in the same invocation of UpdatePending, the signer sets S and S' differ but the respective tuples $(R^{(1)}, R^{(2)}, \mathsf{pk}^{(2)}, \mathsf{m})$ and $(R'^{(1)}, R'^{(2)}, \mathsf{pk}'^{(2)}, \mathsf{m}')$ are the same and $\bar{h}[\mathsf{pk}, \mathsf{pk}^{(2)}, R^{(1)}, R^{(2)}, \mathsf{m}] \neq \bot$. In this case, game $\mathbf{G}_8$ would abort, but game $\mathbf{G}_7$ would not. We argue that this can not happen: Assume that two entries $(sid, i, \mathcal{M}_1)$ and $(sid', i', \mathcal{M}_1')$ with associated signer sets S and S' are removed from Pending. Then, we know that algorithm UpdatePending has been invoked because the game programmed $\hat{h}$ at some point, say $\hat{h}[S_*, j_*, R_*^{(1)}, R_*^{(2)}, \mathsf{pk}_*^{(2)}] := \mathsf{com}_*$, such that com_* is in both $\mathcal{M}_1$ and $\mathcal{M}_1'$. Thus, the algorithm only removes the entry $(sid, i, \mathcal{M}_1)$ from the list if the first component of $\hat{\mathsf{H}}^{-1}(\mathsf{com}_*)$ is S, i.e., if $S_* = S$. Similarly, it only removes the entry $(sid', i', \mathcal{M}_1')$ if the first the first component of $\hat{\mathsf{H}}^{-1}(\mathsf{com}_*)$ is S', i.e., if $S_* = S'$. Thus, it only removes both if $S = S_* = S'$. With that, we have $\Pr\left[\mathbf{G}_7 \Rightarrow 1\right] = \Pr\left[\mathbf{G}_8 \Rightarrow 1\right]$.

Game $\mathbf{G}_9$: We introduce two more algorithms. Intuitively, these allow us to group tuples of the form $(sid, i, \mathcal{M}_1)$ that have been inserted into list Pending into equivalence classes. To be clear, the relation is defined on all triples in Pending and on all triples that already have been removed from Pending, but not on any other entries. The intuition, roughly, is that such triples lead to the same combined nonces if and only if they are in the same equivalence class. The effect of this is will be that we know the challenge just from the tuple $(sid, i, \mathcal{M}_1)$. We now turn to the details. We introduce an algorithm Equivalent that takes as input two triples $(sid, i, \mathcal{M}_1)$ and $(sid', i', \mathcal{M}_1')$ and decides whether they are equivalent as follows:

1. Let S, S' and m, m' be the signer sets and messages associated with sessions sid and sid', respectively. If $S \neq S'$ or $\mathsf{m} \neq \mathsf{m}'$, the triples are not equivalent.
2. Thus, assume $S = S'$ and write $\mathcal{M}_1 = (\mathsf{com}_j)_{j \in S}$ and $\mathcal{M}_1' = (\mathsf{com}_j')_{j \in S}$. Let $F \subseteq S$ (resp. $F' \subseteq S'$) be the set of indices $j \in S$ (resp $j \in S'$) such that $\hat{\mathsf{H}}^{-1}(\mathsf{com}_j) = \bot$ (resp. $\hat{\mathsf{H}}^{-1}(\mathsf{com}_j') = \bot$). If $(\mathsf{com}_j)_{j \in F} \neq (\mathsf{com}_j')_{j \in F'}$, then the triples are not equivalent.
3. Define $\bar{F} := S \setminus F$ and $\bar{F}' := S \setminus F'$. For each $j \in \bar{F}$, we know that the value $(\tilde{S}_j, k_j, R_j'^{(1)}, R_j'^{(2)}, \mathsf{pk}_j'^{(2)}) = \hat{\mathsf{H}}^{-1}(\mathsf{com}_j')$ exists. Similarly, for each $j \in \bar{F}'$,

we know that the value $(\tilde{S}'_j, k'_j, R'^{(1)}_j, R'^{(2)}_j, \mathsf{pk}'^{(2)}_j) = \hat{\mathsf{H}}^{-1}(\mathsf{com}'_j)$ exists. With these, we can define partially combined nonces and secondary keys

$$\bar{R}^{(1)} := \sum_{j \in \bar{F}} R^{(1)}_j, \quad \bar{R}^{(2)} := \sum_{j \in \bar{F}} R^{(2)}_j \quad \bar{\mathsf{pk}}^{(2)} := \sum_{j \in \bar{F}} \ell_{j,S} \mathsf{pk}^{(2)}_j$$
$$\bar{R}'^{(1)} := \sum_{j \in \bar{F}'} R'^{(1)}_j, \quad \bar{R}'^{(2)} := \sum_{j \in \bar{F}'} R'^{(2)}_j \quad \bar{\mathsf{pk}}'^{(2)} := \sum_{j \in \bar{F}'} \ell_{j,S} \mathsf{pk}'^{(2)}_j.$$

The triples are not equivalent, if $(\bar{R}^{(1)}, \bar{R}^{(2)}, \bar{\mathsf{pk}}^{(2)}) \neq (\bar{R}'^{(1)}, \bar{R}'^{(2)}, \bar{\mathsf{pk}}'^{(2)})$. Otherwise, they are equivalent.

In summary, two triples are equivalent if their signer sets, messages, partially combined nonces and secondary public keys, and remaining commitments match. It is clear that at any fixed point in time during the experiment, this is indeed an equivalence relation. In the following two claims, we argue that this relation is preserved over time. For that, we first make some preliminary observations, using notation as in the definition of equivalence above:

1. The equivalence relation can potentially only change when oracle $\hat{\mathsf{H}}$ is updated during queries to SiG_1 (i.e., the opening phase) or during corruption queries, which may make the sets F and F' change. This is because triples are only inserted into Pending if the only commitments without preimages are simulated, and the preimages of these are only set in such calls (see $\mathbf{G}_7$).
2. The sets F and F' can only get smaller over time, as we assume that no collisions occur.
3. When the oracle is programmed during such calls, say by setting $\hat{h}[S_*, j_*, R^{(1)}_*, R^{(2)}_*, \mathsf{pk}^{(2)}_*] := \mathsf{com}_*$, then it must hold that $(S_*, j_*, \mathsf{com}_*) \in \mathsf{Sim}$. In particular, if in this case some j is removed from F (or F') because com_j (or com'_j) now has a preimage, then it must hold that $\mathsf{com}_* = \mathsf{com}_j$ and $j_* = j$. This is because otherwise, if $j \neq j_*$, then we would have $(\tilde{S}, j, \mathsf{com}_*) \in \mathsf{Sim}$ for some $\tilde{S}$ (because the entry was added to Pending) and $(S_*, j_*, \mathsf{com}_*) \in \mathsf{Sim}$, and such a collision was ruled out in $\mathbf{G}_5$.
4. Again, assume that the oracle is programmed during such calls by setting $\hat{h}[S_*, j_*, R^{(1)}_*, R^{(2)}_*, \mathsf{pk}^{(2)}_*] := \mathsf{com}_*$. Now, assume that both F and F' change. Then, we know (because of the previous observation), that the same $j = j_*$ is removed from both F and F', and $\mathsf{com}_j = \mathsf{com}_* = \mathsf{com}'_j$ is removed from both $(\mathsf{com}_j)_{j \in F}$ and $(\mathsf{com}'_j)_{j \in F'}$. Thus, these lists are the same before the update if and only if they are the same after the update.
5. In the setting of the previous observation, denote the point in time before the update as t_0, and the point in time after the update as t_1. Further, denote the associated partially combined nonces and secondary public keys at time t_b for $b \in \{0, 1\}$ by

$$\bar{R}^{(1)}_b, \ \bar{R}^{(2)}_b, \ \bar{\mathsf{pk}}^{(2)}_b, \text{ and } \bar{R}'^{(1)}_b, \ \bar{R}'^{(2)}_b, \ \bar{\mathsf{pk}}'^{(2)}_b.$$

Now, we observe that

$$\bar{R}^{(1)}_1 = \bar{R}^{(1)}_0 + R^{(1)}_*, \quad \bar{R}^{(2)}_1 = \bar{R}^{(2)}_0 + R^{(2)}_*, \quad \bar{\mathsf{pk}}^{(2)}_1 = \bar{\mathsf{pk}}^{(2)}_0 + \ell_{j_*,S_*} \mathsf{pk}^{(2)}_*.$$

The same holds for $\bar{R}_b^{'(1)}$, $\bar{R}_b^{'(2)}$, and $\bar{\mathsf{pk}}_b^{'(2)}$. Therefore, we see that

$$(\bar{R}_0^{(1)}, \bar{R}_0^{(2)}, \bar{\mathsf{pk}}_0^{(2)}) = (\bar{R}_0^{'(1)}, \bar{R}_0^{'(2)}, \bar{\mathsf{pk}}_0^{'(2)})$$
$$\text{if and only if } (\bar{R}_1^{(1)}, \bar{R}_1^{(2)}, \bar{\mathsf{pk}}_1^{(2)}) = (\bar{R}_1^{'(1)}, \bar{R}_1^{'(2)}, \bar{\mathsf{pk}}_1^{'(2)}).$$

Now, we show that the equivalence relation does not change over time, using our notation from above and the observations we made.

Equivalence Claim 1. If two triples $(sid, i, \mathcal{M}_1)$ and $(sid', i', \mathcal{M}_1')$ are equivalent at some point in time, then they stay equivalent for the rest of the game.

Proof of Equivalence Claim 1. Both signer set and message do not change over time. For the other components that determine whether the triples are equivalent, we consider two cases: Either, on an update of $\hat{\mathsf{H}}$, both do not change. In this case the triples trivially stay equivalent. In the other case, both of them change, as the lists $(\mathsf{com}_j)_{j \in F}$ and $(\mathsf{com}_j')_{j \in F'}$ are the same before the update. Now, it easily follows from our last observation above that the triples stay equivalent.

Equivalence Claim 2. If two triples $(sid, i, \mathcal{M}_1)$ and $(sid', i', \mathcal{M}_1')$ are not equivalent at some point in time, then the probability that they become equivalent later is negligible. Concretely, if Converge is the event that any two non-equivalent triples become equivalent at some point in time, then

$$\Pr[\mathsf{Converge}] \leq \frac{Q_S^2(Q_S + t)}{|\mathcal{R}|}.$$

Proof of Equivalence Claim 2. Clearly, if $\mathsf{m} \neq \mathsf{m}'$ or $S \neq S'$, then the triples will stay non-equivalent. Now, consider an update of $\hat{\mathsf{H}}$ that is caused by a query to $\mathrm{S\scriptstyle IG}_1$ or the corruption oracle and will potentially change the equivalence relation. We consider two cases: In the first case, the lists $(\mathsf{com}_j)_{j \in F}$ and $(\mathsf{com}_j')_{j \in F'}$ are the same before the update. In this case, they either do not change, in which case the triples trivially stay non-equivalent, or they both change, in which case it follows from our last observation above that they stay non-equivalent. In the second case, the lists $(\mathsf{com}_j)_{j \in F}$ and $(\mathsf{com}_j')_{j \in F'}$ are different before the update. If they stay different after the update, the triples stay non-equivalent. If they become the same after the update, this means that an entry was removed from only one of them, say $j = j_*$ from F and thus $\mathsf{com}_j = \mathsf{com}_*$ from $(\mathsf{com}_j)_{j \in F}$. For this case, use notation $\bar{R}_b^{(1)}$ and $\bar{R}_b^{'(1)}$ as in the last observation above and notice that $\bar{R}_1^{'(1)} = \bar{R}_0^{'(1)}$ because $(\mathsf{com}_j')_{j \in F'}$ is not changed during the update. On the other hand, $(\mathsf{com}_j)_{j \in F}$ is changed by the update and we have $\bar{R}_1^{(1)} = \bar{R}_0^{(1)} + R_*^{(1)}$. Thus, if the triples become equivalent, we must have

$$\bar{R}_0^{'(1)} = \bar{R}_1^{'(1)} = \bar{R}_1^{(1)} = \bar{R}_0^{(1)} + R_*^{(1)}.$$

Notice that $R_*^{(1)}$ is sampled in the signing or corruption oracle by sampling some $r_* \xleftarrow{\$} \mathcal{D}$ and setting $R_*^{(1)} = \mathsf{T}(g, r_*)$. Thus, $R_*^{(1)}$ is uniformly distributed over $\mathcal{R}$

by the regularity of TLF and independent of $\bar{R}_0^{'(1)}$ and $\bar{R}_0^{(1)}$, which means that this equation holds with probability at most $1/|\mathcal{R}|$. Taking a union bound over all pairs of triples and all queries to the signing oracle and the corruption oracle, the claim follows.

With our equivalence relation at hand, we introduce an algorithm GetChallenge that behaves as a random oracle on equivalence classes. That is, it assigns each class a random challenge $c \xleftarrow{\$} \mathcal{S}$ in a lazy manner. More precisely, it gets as input a triple $(sid, i, \mathcal{M}_1)$ and checks if a triple in the same equivalence class[5] is already assigned a challenge c. This is done using algorithm Equivalent. If so, it returns this challenge c. If not, it assigns a random challenge $c \xleftarrow{\$} \mathcal{S}$ to the triple $(sid, i, \mathcal{M}_1)$.

These two new algorithms are used in the following way: Recall that in previous games, algorithm UpdatePending would program $\bar{h}[\mathsf{pk}, \mathsf{pk}^{(2)}, R^{(1)}, R^{(2)}, \mathsf{m}] \xleftarrow{\$} \mathcal{S}$ whenever an entry $(sid, i, \mathcal{M}_1)$ is removed from Pending and no abort occurs, where $\mathsf{pk}^{(2)}, R^{(1)}, R^{(2)}, \mathsf{m}$ are the corresponding secondary public keys, combined nonces, and messages. Now, instead of sampling $\bar{h}[\mathsf{pk}, \mathsf{pk}^{(2)}, R^{(1)}, R^{(2)}, \mathsf{m}]$ at random, the algorithm sets $\bar{h}[\mathsf{pk}, \mathsf{pk}^{(2)}, R^{(1)}, R^{(2)}, \mathsf{m}] := \mathsf{GetChallenge}(sid, i, \mathcal{M}_1)$. We need to argue that this way of programming the random oracle does not change the view of the adversary. Concretely, all we need to argue is that two different inputs $x \neq x'$ to random oracle $\bar{\mathsf{H}}$ get independently sampled outputs. Clearly, it is sufficient to consider inputs of the form

$$x = (\mathsf{pk}, \mathsf{pk}^{(2)}, R^{(1)}, R^{(2)}, \mathsf{m}), \quad x' = (\mathsf{pk}, \mathsf{pk}^{'(2)}, R^{'(1)}, R^{'(2)}, \mathsf{m}'),$$

which both are covered by the newly introduced programming in algorithm UpdatePending. Let $(sid, i, \mathcal{M}_1)$ be the entry removed from Pending associated with x and $(sid', i', \mathcal{M}_1')$ be the entry removed from Pending associated with x'. Consider the point in time where the second entry, say $(sid', i', \mathcal{M}_1')$ has been removed. One can see that the outputs $\bar{\mathsf{H}}(x)$ and $\bar{\mathsf{H}}(x')$ are independent, unless at this point in time $(sid, i, \mathcal{M}_1)$ and $(sid', i', \mathcal{M}_1')$ were equivalent. However, by definition of equivalence (algorithm Equivalent), them being equivalent would mean that $\mathsf{m} = \mathsf{m}'$ and $(\mathsf{pk}^{(2)}, R^{(1)}, R^{(2)}) = (\mathsf{pk}^{'(2)}, R^{'(1)}, R^{'(2)})$, as the sets F and F' are both empty because both entries have been removed from Pending. Thus, we would have $x = x'$. This shows that the distribution of random oracle outputs does not change, and so we have $\Pr[\mathbf{G}_8 \Rightarrow 1] = \Pr[\mathbf{G}_9 \Rightarrow 1]$.

Game $\mathbf{G}_{10}$: In this game, we change the signing oracle and corruption oracle. Roughly, we use an honest-verifier zero-knowledge-style simulation to simulate signing without secret keys. Intuitively, we can do that, because now we know the challenge already in the opening phase before fixing nonces. More precisely, recall that until now, signers in the opening phase, i.e., on a query $\mathrm{SIG}_1(sid, i, \mathcal{M}_1)$, sampled a random $r_i \xleftarrow{\$} \mathcal{D}$ and set $R_i^{(1)} := \mathsf{T}(g, r_i)$ and $R_i^{(2)} := \mathsf{T}(h, r_i)$. Later, in the response phase, the signer sent $s_i := c \cdot \ell_{i,S} \cdot \mathsf{sk}_i + r_i$ where

---

[5] It is essential for this algorithm that we have shown that equivalence classes are preserved over time. Otherwise, the behavior of this algorithm would be ambiguous.

$c := \bar{\mathsf{H}}(\mathsf{pk}, \mathsf{pk}^{(2)}, R^{(1)}, R^{(2)}, \mathsf{m})$ and $\mathsf{pk}^{(2)}, R^{(1)}, R^{(2)}$ are the combined secondary public key and nonces. Additionally, when the signer is corrupted, it has to send r_i as part of its state. We change this as follows: In the opening phase, consider two cases: First, if $(sid, i, \mathcal{M}_1)$ has not been added to the list Pending, then the signer sets $c := 0$. Observe that in this case, we can assume that the signer never reaches the response phase for this session due to our changes in $\mathbf{G}_6$ and $\mathbf{G}_7$. Otherwise, it sets $\tilde{c} := \mathsf{GetChallenge}(sid, i, \mathcal{M}_1)$. In both cases, the signer samples $s_i \xleftarrow{\$} \mathcal{D}$ and sets $R_i^{(1)} := \mathsf{T}(g, s_i) - \tilde{c} \cdot \ell_{i,S} \cdot \mathsf{pk}_i$ and $R_i^{(2)} := \mathsf{T}(h, s_i) - \tilde{c} \cdot \ell_{i,S} \cdot \mathsf{pk}_i^{(2)}$. Later, when the signer has to output something in the response phase, it outputs the s_i that it sampled in the opening phase. Further, when the signer is corrupted after the opening phase, it sets $r_i := s_i - \tilde{c} \cdot \ell_{i,S} \cdot \mathsf{sk}_i$. To argue indistinguishability, we need to show that $\tilde{c}$ and $c = \bar{\mathsf{H}}(\mathsf{pk}, \mathsf{pk}^{(2)}, R^{(1)}, R^{(2)}, \mathsf{m})$ are the same. This is established as follows:

1. When the signer is queried in the response phase and does not return $\bot$, we know that the entry $(sid, i, \mathcal{M}_1)$ has been removed from Pending.
2. When it was removed from the list, the combined nonce and secondary public key that have been computed are exactly $R^{(1)}, R^{(2)}$, and $\mathsf{pk}^{(2)}$.
3. Therefore, in the invocation of UpdatePending in which the entry was removed from the list, one of two events happened:
   (a) Either the map $\bar{h}$ has been programmed as $\bar{h}[\mathsf{pk}, \mathsf{pk}^{(2)}, R^{(1)}, R^{(2)}, \mathsf{m}] := \mathsf{GetChallenge}(sid, i, \mathcal{M}_1)$;
   (b) Or, the map $\bar{h}$ has been programmed as $\bar{h}[\mathsf{pk}, \mathsf{pk}^{(2)}, R^{(1)}, R^{(2)}, \mathsf{m}] := \mathsf{GetChallenge}(sid', i', \mathcal{M}_1')$ for some triple $(sid', i', \mathcal{M}_1')$ with the same associated signer set S (see $\mathbf{G}_8$) and message m. In this case, we know that $(sid', i', \mathcal{M}_1')$ is equivalent to $(sid, i, \mathcal{M}_1)$ and therefore $\mathsf{GetChallenge}(sid', i', \mathcal{M}_1')$ returned the same as what the query $\mathsf{GetChallenge}(sid, i, \mathcal{M}_1)$ would have returned at that point.
4. Thus, we only need to argue that the output of $\mathsf{GetChallenge}(sid, i, \mathcal{M}_1)$ did not change over time. This follows from our claims about the stability of equivalence classes over time, assuming event Converge does not occur.

We get

$$|\Pr[\mathbf{G}_9 \Rightarrow 1] - \Pr[\mathbf{G}_{10} \Rightarrow 1]| \leq \Pr[\mathsf{Converge}] \leq \frac{Q_S^2(Q_S + t)}{|\mathcal{R}|}.$$

Game $\mathbf{G}_{11}$: We change the game by no longer assuming that $(\mathsf{par}', g) \in \mathsf{Reg}$. Clearly, we have $|\Pr[\mathbf{G}_{10} \Rightarrow 1] - \Pr[\mathbf{G}_{11} \Rightarrow 1]| \leq \varepsilon_r$.

It remains to bound the probability that game $\mathbf{G}_{11}$ outputs 1. Before turning to that, we emphasize the main property we have established via our changes: We do not longer need secret key shares sk_i to simulate the signer oracle. We only need them on corruption queries. Due to space constraints, we postpone the final part of the proof to the full version [7] and only give a short summary here. To bound the probability that game $\mathbf{G}_{11}$ outputs 1, we consider two cases depending on the final forgery (m^*, σ^*) with $\sigma^* = (\mathsf{pk}^{*(2)}, c^*, s^*)$. First, if there is no $x_0 \in \mathcal{D}$ such that $\mathsf{T}(g, x_0) = \mathsf{pk}$ and $\mathsf{T}(h^*, x_0) = \mathsf{pk}^{*(2)}$, where $h^* = \mathsf{H}(\mathsf{m}^*)$, then we can bound the probability using Lemma 1. Second, if there is such an x_0, then we bound the probability using a reduction against the t-algebraic translation resistance of TLF. The reduction defines all keys from its initial input by interpolation, simulates the signing oracle without any secret keys as in $\mathbf{G}_{11}$, and uses its own oracle to answer corruption queries. From the forgery and the corruption queries, it can then interpolate a solution for t-algebraic translation resistance. See the full version [7] for details. $\square$

4   Instantiations

In this section, we instantiate our threshold signature scheme by providing concrete tagged linear function families.

4.1   Instantiation from (Algebraic) One-More CDH

We can instantiate the tagged linear function family by mapping a tag $h \in \mathbb{G}$ and a domain element $x \in \mathbb{Z}_p$ to $h^x \in \mathbb{G}$. Regularity and translatability are easy to show, and algebraic translation resistance follows from an algebraic one-more variant of CDH. We postpone the details to the full version [7].

4.2   Instantiation from DDH

Here, we present our construction $\mathsf{TLF}_{\mathsf{DDH}} = (\mathsf{Gen}_{\mathsf{DDH}}, \mathsf{T}_{\mathsf{DDH}})$ of a tagged linear function family based on the DDH assumption. Recall that the DDH assumption states that it is hard to distinguish tuples $(\mathbb{G}, p, g, h, g^a, h^a)$ from tuples $(\mathbb{G}, p, g, h, u, v)$, where $\mathbb{G}$ is a cyclic group with generator g and prime order p, h, u, v are random group elements, and $a \in \mathbb{Z}_p$ is a random exponent. From now on, let GGen be an algorithm that takes as input 1^λ and outputs the description of a group $\mathbb{G}$ of prime order p, along with some generator $g \in \mathbb{G}$. Algorithm $\mathsf{Gen}_{\mathsf{DDH}}$ simply runs GGen and outputs the description of $\mathbb{G}$, p, and g as parameters par. We make use of the implicit notation for group elements from [39]. That is, we write $[\boldsymbol{A}] \in \mathbb{G}^{r \times l}$ for the matrix of group elements with exponents given by the matrix $\boldsymbol{A} \in \mathbb{Z}_p^{r \times l}$. Precisely, if $\boldsymbol{A} = (A_{i,j})_{i \in [r], j \in [l]}$, then $[\boldsymbol{A}] := (g^{A_{i,j}})_{i \in [r], j \in [l]}$. With this notation, observe that one can efficiently compute $[\boldsymbol{AB}]$ for any matrices $\boldsymbol{A} \in \mathbb{Z}_p^{r \times l}$, $\boldsymbol{B} \in \mathbb{Z}_p^{l \times s}$ with matching dimensions from either $[\boldsymbol{A}]$ and $\boldsymbol{B}$ or from $\boldsymbol{A}$ and $[\boldsymbol{B}]$. For our tagged linear function family, we define the following sets of scalars, tags, and the domain and range, respectively: $\mathcal{S} := \mathbb{Z}_p$, $\mathcal{T} := \mathbb{G}^{2 \times 2}$, $\mathcal{D} := \mathbb{Z}_p^2$, $\mathcal{R} := \mathbb{G}^2$. Clearly, $\mathcal{D}$ and $\mathcal{R}$ are vector spaces over $\mathcal{S}$. For a tag $[\boldsymbol{G}] \in \mathbb{G}^{2 \times 2}$ and an input $\boldsymbol{x} \in \mathbb{Z}_p^2$, the tagged linear function $\mathsf{T}_{\mathsf{DDH}}$ is defined as $\mathsf{T}_{\mathsf{DDH}}([\boldsymbol{G}], \boldsymbol{x}) := [\boldsymbol{Gx}] \in \mathbb{G}^2$. We emphasize that the tag $[\boldsymbol{G}]$ is given in the group, and the domain element $\boldsymbol{x}$ is given over the field. It is clear that $\mathsf{T}_{\mathsf{DDH}}$ can be computed efficiently and that it is a homomorphism. What remains is to show regularity, translatability and algebraic translation resistance.

Lemma 2. $\mathsf{TLF_{DDH}}$ *is ε_r-regular, where $\varepsilon_r \leq (p+1)/p^2$.*

Lemma 3. $\mathsf{TLF_{DDH}}$ *is ε_t-translatable, where $\varepsilon_t \leq (3+3p)/p^2$.*

Lemma 4. *Let $t \in \mathbb{N}$ be a number polynomial in λ. If the DDH assumption holds relative to GGen, then $\mathsf{TLF_{DDH}}$ is t-algebraic translation resistant.*

We postpone the proofs to the full version [7].

5   Concrete Parameters and Efficiency

Our schemes are slightly less efficient than previous schemes, but they are still in a highly practical regime. Given the strong properties that our schemes achieve from conservative assumptions without the algebraic group model, it is natural to pay such a small price in terms of efficiency. We present a more detailed discussion on efficiency in the full version [7].

Acknowledgments. CISPA authors are funded by the Deutsche Forschungsgemeinschaft (DFG, German Research Foundation) - 507237585, and by the European Union, ERC-2023-STG, Project ID: 101116713. Views and opinions expressed are however those of the author(s) only and do not necessarily reflect those of the European Union. Neither the European Union nor the granting authority can be held responsible for them. Tessaro and Zhu are supported in part by NSF grants CNS- 2026774, CNS-2154174, a JP Morgan Faculty Award, a CISCO Faculty Award, and a gift from Microsoft.

References

1. Abdalla, M., Fouque, P.A., Lyubashevsky, V., Tibouchi, M.: Tightly-secure signatures from lossy identification schemes. In: Pointcheval, D., Johansson, T. (eds.) EUROCRYPT 2012. LNCS, vol. 7237, pp. 572–590. Springer, Heidelberg (2012). https://doi.org/10.1007/978-3-642-29011-4_34
2. Agrawal, S., Stehlé, D., Yadav, A.: Round-optimal lattice-based threshold signatures, revisited. In: Bojanczyk, M., Merelli, E., Woodruff, D.P. (eds.) ICALP 2022. LIPIcs, vol. 229, pp. 8:1–8:20. Schloss Dagstuhl (Jul 2022). https://doi.org/10.4230/LIPIcs.ICALP.2022.8
3. Almansa, J.F., Damgård, I., Nielsen, J.B.: Simplified threshold RSA with adaptive and proactive security. In: Vaudenay, S. (ed.) EUROCRYPT 2006. LNCS, vol. 4004, pp. 593–611. Springer, Heidelberg (2006). https://doi.org/10.1007/11761679_35
4. Alper, H.K., Burdges, J.: Two-round trip schnorr multi-signatures via delinearized witnesses. In: Malkin, T., Peikert, C. (eds.) CRYPTO 2021, Part I. LNCS, vol. 12825, pp. 157–188. Springer, Heidelberg (2021). https://doi.org/10.1007/978-3-030-84242-0_7
5. Aumasson, J.P., Hamelink, A., Shlomovits, O.: A survey of ECDSA threshold signing. Cryptology ePrint Archive, Report 2020/1390 (2020). https://eprint.iacr.org/2020/1390
6. Bacho, R., Loss, J.: On the adaptive security of the threshold BLS signature scheme. In: Yin, H., Stavrou, A., Cremers, C., Shi, E. (eds.) ACM CCS 2022, pp. 193–207. ACM Press (Nov 2022). https://doi.org/10.1145/3548606.3560656

7. Bacho, R., Loss, J., Tessaro, S., Wagner, B., Zhu, C.: Twinkle: Threshold signatures from DDH with full adaptive security. Cryptology ePrint Archive, Paper 2023/1482 (2023). https://eprint.iacr.org/2023/1482

8. Bellare, M., Crites, E.C., Komlo, C., Maller, M., Tessaro, S., Zhu, C.: Better than advertised security for non-interactive threshold signatures. In: Dodis, Y., Shrimpton, T. (eds.) CRYPTO 2022, Part IV. LNCS, vol. 13510, pp. 517–550. Springer, Heidelberg (2022). https://doi.org/10.1007/978-3-031-15985-5_18

9. Bellare, M., Dai, W.: Chain reductions for multi-signatures and the HBMS scheme. In: Tibouchi, M., Wang, H. (eds.) ASIACRYPT 2021, Part IV. LNCS, vol. 13093, pp. 650–678. Springer, Heidelberg (2021). https://doi.org/10.1007/978-3-030-92068-5_22

10. Bellare, M., Neven, G.: Multi-signatures in the plain public-key model and a general forking lemma. In: Juels, A., Wright, R.N., De Capitani di Vimercati, S. (eds.) ACM CCS 2006, pp. 390–399. ACM Press (Oct / Nov 2006). https://doi.org/10.1145/1180405.1180453

11. Bellare, M., Tessaro, S., Zhu, C.: Stronger security for non-interactive threshold signatures: BLS and FROST. Cryptology ePrint Archive, Report 2022/833 (2022). https://eprint.iacr.org/2022/833

12. Bendlin, R., Krehbiel, S., Peikert, C.: How to share a lattice trapdoor: threshold protocols for signatures and (H)IBE. In: Jacobson Jr., M.J., Locasto, M.E., Mohassel, P., Safavi-Naini, R. (eds.) ACNS 13. LNCS, vol. 7954, pp. 218–236. Springer, Heidelberg (2013). https://doi.org/10.1007/978-3-642-38980-1_14

13. Benhamouda, F., Halevi, S., Krawczyk, H., Ma, Y., Rabin, T.: Sprint: High-throughput robust distributed schnorr signatures. Cryptology ePrint Archive, Paper 2023/427 (2023). https://eprint.iacr.org/2023/427

14. Boldyreva, A.: Threshold signatures, multisignatures and blind signatures based on the gap-Diffie-Hellman-group signature scheme. In: Desmedt, Y. (ed.) PKC 2003. LNCS, vol. 2567, pp. 31–46. Springer, Heidelberg (2003). https://doi.org/10.1007/3-540-36288-6_3

15. Boneh, D., Drijvers, M., Neven, G.: Compact multi-signatures for smaller blockchains. In: Peyrin, T., Galbraith, S. (eds.) ASIACRYPT 2018, Part II. LNCS, vol. 11273, pp. 435–464. Springer, Heidelberg (2018). https://doi.org/10.1007/978-3-030-03329-3_15

16. Boneh, D., Gennaro, R., Goldfeder, S., Jain, A., Kim, S., Rasmussen, P.M.R., Sahai, A.: Threshold cryptosystems from threshold fully homomorphic encryption. In: Shacham, H., Boldyreva, A. (eds.) CRYPTO 2018, Part I. LNCS, vol. 10991, pp. 565–596. Springer, Heidelberg (2018). https://doi.org/10.1007/978-3-319-96884-1_19

17. Boneh, D., Lynn, B., Shacham, H.: Short signatures from the Weil pairing. In: Boyd, C. (ed.) ASIACRYPT 2001. LNCS, vol. 2248, pp. 514–532. Springer, Heidelberg (2001). https://doi.org/10.1007/3-540-45682-1_30

18. Boschini, C., Takahashi, A., Tibouchi, M.: MuSig-L: Lattice-based multi-signature with single-round online phase. In: Dodis, Y., Shrimpton, T. (eds.) CRYPTO 2022, Part II. LNCS, vol. 13508, pp. 276–305. Springer, Heidelberg (2022). https://doi.org/10.1007/978-3-031-15979-4_10

19. Brandão, L.T.A.N., Peralta., R.: NIST IR 8214C: First call for multi-party threshold schemes. https://csrc.nist.gov/pubs/ir/8214/c/ipd (2022), (Accessed 12 Sep 2023)

20. Canetti, R., Gennaro, R., Goldfeder, S., Makriyannis, N., Peled, U.: UC non-interactive, proactive, threshold ECDSA with identifiable aborts. In: Ligatti, J., Ou, X., Katz, J., Vigna, G. (eds.) ACM CCS 2020, pp. 1769–1787. ACM Press (Nov 2020). https://doi.org/10.1145/3372297.3423367

21. Canetti, R., Gennaro, R., Jarecki, S., Krawczyk, H., Rabin, T.: Adaptive security for threshold cryptosystems. In: Wiener, M.J. (ed.) CRYPTO 1999. LNCS, vol. 1666, pp. 98–115. Springer, Heidelberg (1999). https://doi.org/10.1007/3-540-48405-1_7

22. Castagnos, G., Catalano, D., Laguillaumie, F., Savasta, F., Tucker, I.: Bandwidth-efficient threshold EC-DSA. In: Kiayias, A., Kohlweiss, M., Wallden, P., Zikas, V. (eds.) PKC 2020, Part II. LNCS, vol. 12111, pp. 266–296. Springer, Heidelberg (2020). https://doi.org/10.1007/978-3-030-45388-6_10

23. Chairattana-Apirom, R., Hanzlik, L., Loss, J., Lysyanskaya, A., Wagner, B.: PI-cut-choo and friends: compact blind signatures via parallel instance cut-and-choose and more. In: Dodis, Y., Shrimpton, T. (eds.) CRYPTO 2022, Part III. LNCS, vol. 13509, pp. 3–31. Springer, Heidelberg (2022). https://doi.org/10.1007/978-3-031-15982-4_1

24. Chevallier-Mames, B.: An efficient CDH-based signature scheme with a tight security reduction. In: Shoup, V. (ed.) CRYPTO 2005. LNCS, vol. 3621, pp. 511–526. Springer, Heidelberg (2002). https://doi.org/10.1007/11535218_31

25. Chu, H., Gerhart, P., Ruffing, T., Schröder, D.: Practical schnorr threshold signatures without the algebraic group model. In: Handschuh, H., Lysyanskaya, A. (eds.) CRYPTO 2023, Part I. LNCS, vol. 14081, pp. 743–773. Springer, Heidelberg (2023). https://doi.org/10.1007/978-3-031-38557-5_24

26. Crites, E., Kohlweiss, M., Preneel, B., Sedaghat, M., Slamanig, D.: Threshold structure-preserving signatures. In: Asiacrypt 2023. Springer-Verlag (2023). https://doi.org/10.1007/978-981-99-8724-5_11

27. Crites, E., Komlo, C., Maller, M.: How to prove schnorr assuming schnorr: Security of multi- and threshold signatures. Cryptology ePrint Archive, Report 2021/1375 (2021). https://eprint.iacr.org/2021/1375

28. Crites, E.C., Komlo, C., Maller, M.: Fully adaptive schnorr threshold signatures. In: Handschuh, H., Lysyanskaya, A. (eds.) CRYPTO 2023, Part I. LNCS, vol. 14081, pp. 678–709. Springer, Heidelberg (2023). https://doi.org/10.1007/978-3-031-38557-5_22

29. Crites, E.C., Komlo, C., Maller, M., Tessaro, S., Zhu, C.: Snowblind: A threshold blind signature in pairing-free groups. In: Handschuh, H., Lysyanskaya, A. (eds.) CRYPTO 2023, Part I. LNCS, vol. 14081, pp. 710–742. Springer, Heidelberg (2023). https://doi.org/10.1007/978-3-031-38557-5_23

30. Dalskov, A.P.K., Orlandi, C., Keller, M., Shrishak, K., Shulman, H.: Securing DNSSEC keys via threshold ECDSA from generic MPC. In: Chen, L., Li, N., Liang, K., Schneider, S.A. (eds.) ESORICS 2020, Part II. LNCS, vol. 12309, pp. 654–673. Springer, Heidelberg (2020). https://doi.org/10.1007/978-3-030-59013-0_32

31. Damgård, I., Jakobsen, T.P., Nielsen, J.B., Pagter, J.I., Østergaard, M.B.: Fast threshold ECDSA with honest majority. In: Galdi, C., Kolesnikov, V. (eds.) SCN 20. LNCS, vol. 12238, pp. 382–400. Springer, Heidelberg (2020). https://doi.org/10.1007/978-3-030-57990-6_19

32. Damgård, I., Orlandi, C., Takahashi, A., Tibouchi, M.: Two-round n-out-of-n and multi-signatures and trapdoor commitment from lattices. In: Garay, J. (ed.) PKC 2021, Part I. LNCS, vol. 12710, pp. 99–130. Springer, Heidelberg (2021). https://doi.org/10.1007/978-3-030-75245-3_5

33. Das, S., Camacho, P., Xiang, Z., Nieto, J., Bunz, B., Ren, L.: Threshold signatures from inner product argument: Succinct, weighted, and multi-threshold. Cryptology ePrint Archive, Paper 2023/598 (2023). https://eprint.iacr.org/2023/598

34. Das, S., Yurek, T., Xiang, Z., Miller, A.K., Kokoris-Kogias, L., Ren, L.: Practical asynchronous distributed key generation. In: 2022 IEEE Symposium on Security and Privacy, pp. 2518–2534. IEEE Computer Society Press (May 2022). https://doi.org/10.1109/SP46214.2022.9833584

35. De Santis, A., Desmedt, Y., Frankel, Y., Yung, M.: How to share a function securely. In: 26th ACM STOC, pp. 522–533. ACM Press (May 1994). https://doi.org/10.1145/195058.195405

36. Desmedt, Y.: Society and group oriented cryptography: a new concept. In: Pomerance, C. (ed.) CRYPTO 1987. LNCS, vol. 293, pp. 120–127. Springer, Heidelberg (1988). https://doi.org/10.1007/3-540-48184-2_8

37. Desmedt, Y., Frankel, Y.: Threshold cryptosystems. In: Brassard, G. (ed.) CRYPTO 1989. LNCS, vol. 435, pp. 307–315. Springer, Heidelberg (1990). https://doi.org/10.1007/0-387-34805-0_28

38. Doerner, J., Kondi, Y., Lee, E., shelat, a.: Threshold ECDSA from ECDSA assumptions: The multiparty case. In: 2019 IEEE Symposium on Security and Privacy, pp. 1051–1066. IEEE Computer Society Press (May 2019). https://doi.org/10.1109/SP.2019.00024

39. Escala, A., Herold, G., Kiltz, E., Ràfols, C., Villar, J.: An algebraic framework for Diffie-Hellman assumptions. In: Canetti, R., Garay, J.A. (eds.) CRYPTO 2013, Part II. LNCS, vol. 8043, pp. 129–147. Springer, Heidelberg (2013). https://doi.org/10.1007/978-3-642-40084-1_8

40. Fleischhacker, N., Simkin, M., Zhang, Z.: Squirrel: efficient synchronized multi-signatures from lattices. In: Yin, H., Stavrou, A., Cremers, C., Shi, E. (eds.) ACM CCS 2022, pp. 1109–1123. ACM Press (Nov 2022). https://doi.org/10.1145/3548606.3560655

41. Frankel, Y., MacKenzie, P.D., Yung, M.: Robust efficient distributed RSA-key generation. In: Coan, B.A., Afek, Y. (eds.) 17th ACM PODC, p. 320. ACM (Jun/Jul 1998). https://doi.org/10.1145/277697.277779

42. Fuchsbauer, G., Kiltz, E., Loss, J.: The algebraic group model and its applications. In: Shacham, H., Boldyreva, A. (eds.) CRYPTO 2018, Part II. LNCS, vol. 10992, pp. 33–62. Springer, Heidelberg (2018). https://doi.org/10.1007/978-3-319-96881-0_2

43. Gągol, A., Kula, J., Straszak, D., Świętek, M.: Threshold ECDSA for decentralized asset custody. Cryptology ePrint Archive, Report 2020/498 (2020). https://eprint.iacr.org/2020/498

44. Gennaro, R., Goldfeder, S.: Fast multiparty threshold ECDSA with fast trustless setup. In: Lie, D., Mannan, M., Backes, M., Wang, X. (eds.) ACM CCS 2018, pp. 1179–1194. ACM Press (Oct 2018). https://doi.org/10.1145/3243734.3243859

45. Gennaro, R., Goldfeder, S.: One round threshold ECDSA with identifiable abort. Cryptology ePrint Archive, Report 2020/540 (2020). https://eprint.iacr.org/2020/540

46. Gennaro, R., Goldfeder, S., Narayanan, A.: Threshold-optimal DSA/ECDSA signatures and an application to bitcoin wallet security. In: Manulis, M., Sadeghi, A.R., Schneider, S. (eds.) ACNS 2016. LNCS, vol. 9696, pp. 156–174. Springer, Heidelberg (2016). https://doi.org/10.1007/978-3-319-39555-5_9

47. Gennaro, R., Halevi, S., Krawczyk, H., Rabin, T.: Threshold RSA for dynamic and ad-hoc groups. In: Smart, N.P. (ed.) EUROCRYPT 2008. LNCS, vol. 4965, pp. 88–107. Springer, Heidelberg (2008). https://doi.org/10.1007/978-3-540-78967-3_6

48. Gennaro, R., Jarecki, S., Krawczyk, H., Rabin, T.: Secure distributed key generation for discrete-log based cryptosystems. J. Cryptol. **20**(1), 51–83 (2007). https://doi.org/10.1007/s00145-006-0347-3

49. Goh, E.J., Jarecki, S., Katz, J., Wang, N.: Efficient signature schemes with tight reductions to the Diffie-Hellman problems. J. Cryptol. **20**(4), 493–514 (2007). https://doi.org/10.1007/s00145-007-0549-3

50. Groth, J., Shoup, V.: Fast batched asynchronous distributed key generation. Cryptology ePrint Archive, Paper 2023/1175 (2023). https://eprint.iacr.org/2023/1175

51. Gur, K.D., Katz, J., Silde, T.: Two-round threshold lattice signatures from threshold homomorphic encryption. Cryptology ePrint Archive, Paper 2023/1318 (2023). https://eprint.iacr.org/2023/1318

52. Hauck, E., Kiltz, E., Loss, J.: A modular treatment of blind signatures from identification schemes. In: Ishai, Y., Rijmen, V. (eds.) EUROCRYPT 2019, Part III. LNCS, vol. 11478, pp. 345–375. Springer, Heidelberg (2019). https://doi.org/10.1007/978-3-030-17659-4_12

53. Itakura, K., Nakamura, K.: A public-key cryptosystem suitable for digital multisignatures. NEC Res. Developm. **71**, 1–8 (1983)

54. Jarecki, S., Lysyanskaya, A.: Adaptively secure threshold cryptography: introducing concurrency, removing erasures. In: Preneel, B. (ed.) EUROCRYPT 2000. LNCS, vol. 1807, pp. 221–242. Springer, Heidelberg (2000). https://doi.org/10.1007/3-540-45539-6_16

55. Katz, J., Loss, J., Rosenberg, M.: Boosting the security of blind signature schemes. In: Tibouchi, M., Wang, H. (eds.) ASIACRYPT 2021, Part IV. LNCS, vol. 13093, pp. 468–492. Springer, Heidelberg (2021). https://doi.org/10.1007/978-3-030-92068-5_16

56. Katz, J., Wang, N.: Efficiency improvements for signature schemes with tight security reductions. In: Jajodia, S., Atluri, V., Jaeger, T. (eds.) ACM CCS 2003, pp. 155–164. ACM Press (Oct 2003). https://doi.org/10.1145/948109.948132

57. Kiltz, E., Loss, J., Pan, J.: Tightly-secure signatures from five-move identification protocols. In: Takagi, T., Peyrin, T. (eds.) ASIACRYPT 2017, Part III. LNCS, vol. 10626, pp. 68–94. Springer, Heidelberg (2017). https://doi.org/10.1007/978-3-319-70700-6_3

58. Kiltz, E., Masny, D., Pan, J.: Optimal security proofs for signatures from identification schemes. In: Robshaw, M., Katz, J. (eds.) CRYPTO 2016, Part II. LNCS, vol. 9815, pp. 33–61. Springer, Heidelberg (2016). https://doi.org/10.1007/978-3-662-53008-5_2

59. Kokoris-Kogias, E., Malkhi, D., Spiegelman, A.: Asynchronous distributed key generation for computationally-secure randomness, consensus, and threshold signatures. In: Ligatti, J., Ou, X., Katz, J., Vigna, G. (eds.) ACM CCS 2020, pp. 1751–1767. ACM Press (Nov 2020). https://doi.org/10.1145/3372297.3423364

60. Komlo, C., Goldberg, I.: FROST: flexible round-optimized Schnorr threshold signatures. In: Dunkelman, O., Jr., M.J.J., O'Flynn, C. (eds.) SAC 2020. LNCS, vol. 12804, pp. 34–65. Springer, Heidelberg (2020). https://doi.org/10.1007/978-3-030-81652-0_2

61. Komlo, C., Goldberg, I., Stebila, D.: A formal treatment of distributed key generation, and new constructions. Cryptology ePrint Archive, Report 2023/292 (2023). https://eprint.iacr.org/2023/292

62. Libert, B., Joye, M., Yung, M.: Born and raised distributively: fully distributed non-interactive adaptively-secure threshold signatures with short shares. In: Halldórsson, M.M., Dolev, S. (eds.) 33rd ACM PODC, pp. 303–312. ACM (Jul 2014). https://doi.org/10.1145/2611462.2611498

63. Lindell, Y.: Simple three-round multiparty schnorr signing with full simulatability. Cryptology ePrint Archive, Report 2022/374 (2022). https://eprint.iacr.org/2022/374

64. Lindell, Y., Nof, A.: Fast secure multiparty ECDSA with practical distributed key generation and applications to cryptocurrency custody. In: Lie, D., Mannan, M., Backes, M., Wang, X. (eds.) ACM CCS 2018, pp. 1837–1854. ACM Press (Oct 2018). https://doi.org/10.1145/3243734.3243788

65. Lysyanskaya, A., Peikert, C.: Adaptive security in the threshold setting: From cryptosystems to signature schemes. In: Boyd, C. (ed.) ASIACRYPT 2001. LNCS, vol. 2248, pp. 331–350. Springer, Heidelberg (2001). https://doi.org/10.1007/3-540-45682-1_20

66. Maxwell, G., Poelstra, A., Seurin, Y., Wuille, P.: Simple schnorr multi-signatures with applications to bitcoin. Des. Codes Cryptogr. **87**(9), 2139–2164 (2019). https://doi.org/10.1007/s10623-019-00608-x

67. Nick, J., Ruffing, T., Seurin, Y.: MuSig2: Simple two-round Schnorr multi-signatures. In: Malkin, T., Peikert, C. (eds.) CRYPTO 2021, Part I. LNCS, vol. 12825, pp. 189–221. Springer, Heidelberg, Virtual Event (2021). https://doi.org/10.1007/978-3-030-84242-0_8

68. Nick, J., Ruffing, T., Seurin, Y., Wuille, P.: MuSig-DN: schnorr multi-signatures with verifiably deterministic nonces. In: Ligatti, J., Ou, X., Katz, J., Vigna, G. (eds.) ACM CCS 2020, pp. 1717–1731. ACM Press (Nov 2020). https://doi.org/10.1145/3372297.3417236

69. Pan, J., Wagner, B.: Chopsticks: fork-free two-round multi-signatures from non-interactive assumptions. In: Hazay, C., Stam, M. (eds.) EUROCRYPT 2023, Part V. LNCS, vol. 14008, pp. 597–627. Springer, Heidelberg (2023). https://doi.org/10.1007/978-3-031-30589-4_21

70. Pedersen, T.P.: A threshold cryptosystem without a trusted party (extended abstract) (rump session). In: Davies, D.W. (ed.) EUROCRYPT 1991. LNCS, vol. 547, pp. 522–526. Springer, Heidelberg (1991). https://doi.org/10.1007/3-540-46416-6_47

71. Pedersen, T.P.: Non-interactive and information-theoretic secure verifiable secret sharing. In: Feigenbaum, J. (ed.) CRYPTO 1991. LNCS, vol. 576, pp. 129–140. Springer, Heidelberg (1992). https://doi.org/10.1007/3-540-46766-1_9

72. Rabin, T.: A simplified approach to threshold and proactive RSA. In: Krawczyk, H. (ed.) CRYPTO 1998. LNCS, vol. 1462, pp. 89–104. Springer, Heidelberg (1998). https://doi.org/10.1007/BFb0055722

73. Ruffing, T., Ronge, V., Jin, E., Schneider-Bensch, J., Schröder, D.: ROAST: robust asynchronous schnorr threshold signatures. In: Yin, H., Stavrou, A., Cremers, C., Shi, E. (eds.) ACM CCS 2022, pp. 2551–2564. ACM Press (Nov 2022). https://doi.org/10.1145/3548606.3560583

74. Schnorr, C.P.: Efficient signature generation by smart cards. J. Cryptol. **4**(3), 161–174 (1991). https://doi.org/10.1007/BF00196725

75. Shoup, V.: Practical threshold signatures. In: Preneel, B. (ed.) EUROCRYPT 2000. LNCS, vol. 1807, pp. 207–220. Springer, Heidelberg (2000). https://doi.org/10.1007/3-540-45539-6_15

76. Shoup, V.: The many faces of schnorr. Cryptology ePrint Archive, Paper 2023/1019 (2023). https://eprint.iacr.org/2023/1019

77. Stinson, D.R., Strobl, R.: Provably secure distributed Schnorr signatures and a (t, n) threshold scheme for implicit certificates. In: Varadharajan, V., Mu, Y. (eds.) ACISP 2001. LNCS, vol. 2119, pp. 417–434. Springer, Heidelberg (2001). https://doi.org/10.1007/3-540-47719-5_33

78. Tessaro, S., Zhu, C.: Short pairing-free blind signatures with exponential security. In: Dunkelman, O., Dziembowski, S. (eds.) EUROCRYPT 2022, Part II. LNCS, vol. 13276, pp. 782–811. Springer, Heidelberg (2022). https://doi.org/10.1007/978-3-031-07085-3_27

79. Tessaro, S., Zhu, C.: Threshold and multi-signature schemes from linear hash functions. In: Hazay, C., Stam, M. (eds.) EUROCRYPT 2023, Part V. LNCS, vol. 14008, pp. 628–658. Springer, Heidelberg (2023). https://doi.org/10.1007/978-3-031-30589-4_22

Toothpicks: More Efficient Fork-Free Two-Round Multi-signatures

Jiaxin Pan[1(✉)] and Benedikt Wagner[2]

[1] University of Kassel, Kassel, Germany
jiaxin.pan@uni-kassel.de

[2] CISPA Helmholtz Center for Information Security, Saarland University, Saarbrücken, Germany
benedikt.wagner@cispa.de

Abstract. Tightly secure cryptographic schemes can be implemented with standardized parameters, while still having a sufficiently high security level backed up by their analysis. In a recent work, Pan and Wagner (Eurocrypt 2023) presented the first tightly secure two-round multi-signature scheme without pairings, called Chopsticks. While this is an interesting first theoretical step, Chopsticks is much less efficient than its non-tight counterparts.

In this work, we close this gap by proposing a new tightly secure two-round multi-signature scheme that is as efficient as non-tight schemes. Our scheme is based on the DDH assumption without pairings. Compared to Chopsticks, we reduce the signature size by more than a factor of 3 and the communication complexity by more than a factor of 2.

Technically, we achieve this as follows: (1) We develop a new pseudorandom path technique, as opposed to the pseudorandom matching technique in Chopsticks. (2) We construct a more efficient commitment scheme with suitable properties, which is an important primitive in both our scheme and Chopsticks. Surprisingly, we observe that the commitment scheme does not have to be binding, enabling our efficient construction.

Keywords: Multi-Signatures · Tightness · Commitment Scheme · Lossy Identification

1 Introduction

A multi-signature scheme [7,33] allows a group of signers to jointly sign a message. Naively, every signer could sign the message locally, and we concatenate the resulting signatures. As the number of signers grows large, this results in impractical signature sizes, and so we aim for a more clever solution with compact signatures, potentially at the cost of introducing interaction. Early constructions of multi-signatures have been presented and analyzed in a variety of models [11,17,21,40,42], mostly differing in how keys are generated, registered, and verified. Nowadays, the accepted de facto standard for multi-signatures is the plain public key model [7], where each signer generates his key pair independently. In this work, we focus on constructions in the said model, proven in the

© International Association for Cryptologic Research 2024
M. Joye and G. Leander (Eds.): EUROCRYPT 2024, LNCS 14651, pp. 460–489, 2024.
https://doi.org/10.1007/978-3-031-58716-0_16

random oracle model [8] from assumptions over cyclic groups without pairings. We look at this problem from the perspective of concrete security, which we explain next.

Concrete Security. Cryptographic security proofs follow a common approach: Assuming the existence of an adversary with advantage ϵ_S against the security of a construction S, we construct a reduction with roughly the same running time that solves some hard underlying problem Π with probability ϵ_Π. Typically, ϵ_Π and ϵ_S are related via a bound of the form $\epsilon_S \leq L \cdot \epsilon_\Pi$, where L is called the *security loss*.

On the one hand, this bound can be treated as a purely qualitative and asymptotic statement, and any polynomial (in the security parameter) L is sufficient to show security. On the other hand, interpreting the bound as a quantitative statement about the concrete security level, it is desirable to minimize L. In the optimal case, L is a small constant, and we call the proof *tight*. There are two ways to interpret the security bound quantitatively: In the first interpretation, we want to achieve 128 bits of security for S. Then, we need to set our parameters such that cryptanalytic results suggest that Π is $128 + \log(L)$ bits hard. Such parameters include, for example, groups over which we implement the scheme. In the second interpretation, we fix parameters for which we believe that Π is 128-bit hard. Then, we are confident in having $128 - \log(L)$ bits of security for our scheme S, according to the concrete security bound. While the first interpretation compensates for the security loss and results in more secure schemes in theory, it is far from what is done in practice, where practitioners use standardized parameters to implement schemes, because these parameters are well-understood and there are highly optimized implementations for them. Using a different cyclic group for every scheme is just not feasible. For that reason, we stick to the second interpretation.

The Price of Tightness. A large body of research is centered around the concept of tightness, and many primitives have been studied in this regard. Prominent examples include public-key encryption [4,5,25,31,32] and key exchange [3,19,27,29,39], as well as signatures [1,4,9,14,20,32,35,36,45] and related primitives [10,16,26,38,46]. Unfortunately, tightness often comes at a price in terms of efficiency. This is particularly true for the first tightly secure constructions of some primitive. For instance, in the first public-key encryption scheme with tight security against chosen-ciphertext attacks, due to Hofheinz and Jager [32], ciphertexts contain a linear (in the security parameter) number of group elements as overhead[1], while the respective non-tight scheme [37] has a constant ciphertext overhead. Clearly, such an overhead is not acceptable in practice, and so researchers strive for the holy grail of concrete security: Tightly secure constructions with minimal efficiency penalty.

Two-Round Multi-signatures. In their seminal work [7], Bellare and Neven not only introduced the plain public key model but also presented constructions of three-round multi-signatures. Their first scheme is based on Schnorr

---

[1] The ciphertext overhead is the size of the ciphertext minus the size of the message.

identification [48]. As typical for Schnorr-based constructions, a rewinding and guessing strategy is used to prove security from the Discrete Logarithm Assumption (DLOG), resulting in a highly non-tight scheme. Their second scheme is tightly secure based on the Decisional Diffie-Hellman (DDH) Assumption. In subsequent works, three-round schemes with so-called key aggregation have been proposed [12,24,41]. With this extension, it is possible to compute a short aggregated key from a set of keys, which can later be used to verify signatures. More recent works concentrate on two-round signing protocols [2,6,13,17,18,43,44,50]. On the downside, many of these schemes require interactive assumptions [2,17,43], and all of them fail to provide meaningful concrete security guarantees due to the use of (double) rewinding[2].

In a recent result, Pan and Wagner [46] constructed the first tightly secure multi-signature scheme, called Chopsticks II. In particular, their scheme neither relies on rewinding, nor on any guessing argument. However, the price of tightness is high: Signatures and communication complexity in Chopsticks II are about 5 times and 3 times as large as in one of the most efficient non-tight two-round schemes, HBMS, respectively.

Our Goal. We aim to reduce the efficiency gap between tight and non-tight two-round multi-signatures. Concretely, we aim for two-round multi-signatures in the pairing-free discrete logarithm setting, based on well-studied assumptions in the random oracle model. Our constructions should have a minimal security loss, and be efficient in terms of signature size and communication complexity.

1.1   Our Contribution

We reach our goal by constructing a new two-round multi-signature scheme that achieves the best of two worlds:

- *Tightness.* Our scheme is tightly secure based on the DDH assumption. When instantiated over a standardized 128-bit secure group, its security guarantee is 126-bit, which is formally supported by our proofs. In contrast, non-tight schemes relying on rewinding do not guarantee any meaningful security level.
- *Efficiency.* Our scheme is as efficient as the state-of-the-art non-tight schemes. Concretely, the communication complexity per signer for our scheme is comparable to HBMS [6] and about 1.5 times smaller than TZ [50] and Musig2 [43]. The signature size is only about 1.5 times larger than for the non-tight schemes. Compared to Chopsticks II [46], this significantly reduces the efficiency cost of tightness. Concretely, our scheme outperforms Chopsticks II by a factor of more than 3 and 2 in terms of signature size and communication complexity, respectively.

In addition, we present a non-tight scheme with an acceptable security loss, namely, linear in the number of signing queries. The advantage of this scheme is that it supports key aggregation. A similar but much less efficient scheme,

---

[2] We do not consider proofs in the (idealized) algebraic group model [23].

Chopsticks I, has been proposed in [46]. We compare our schemes with previous schemes in terms of security (see Table 1) and asymptotic (see Table 2) and concrete (see Table 3) efficiency.

From a technical perspective, our first contribution is a new pseudorandom path technique, as opposed to the pseudorandom matching technique in Chopsticks [46]. This new technique allows us to reduce the size of signatures and communication by a factor of two. Our second technical insight is that, somewhat surprisingly, we do not need a binding commitment as in Chopsticks [46]. Instead, we can significantly relax the binding property of our commitment to hold up to cosets of a certain subspace. This enables more efficient instantiations, further improving the efficiency of our schemes. To show that this relaxation does not introduce problems in terms of security, we identify a strong soundness property many natural lossy identification schemes [1,35,36] have. We are confident that this combination of a weak commitment with lossy identification is of independent interest.

Table 1. Comparison of multi-signature schemes in the discrete logarithm setting without pairings in the plain public key model. We compare the number of rounds, whether the schemes support key aggregation, the assumption the schemes rely on, and the security loss, where Q_H, Q_S denote the number of random oracle and signing queries, respectively, and ϵ denotes the advantage of an adversary against the scheme. For the security loss, we do not consider proofs in the algebraic group model. We do not list [44] as it is prohibitively inefficient due to the use of heavy cryptographic machinery.

Scheme	Rounds	Key Aggregation	Assumption	Loss
BN [7]	3	✗	DLOG	$\Theta(Q_H/\epsilon)$
BN+ [7]	3	✗	DDH	$\Theta(1)$
Musig [12,41]	3	✓	DLOG	$\Theta(Q_H^3/\epsilon^3)$
Musig+ [24]	3	✓	DDH	$\Theta(1)$
Musig2 [43]	2	✓	AOMDL	$\Theta(Q_H^3/\epsilon^3)$
HBMS [6]	2	✓	DLOG	$\Theta(Q_S^4 Q_H^3/\epsilon^3)$
TZ [50]	2	✓	DLOG	$\Theta(Q_H^3/\epsilon^3)$
TSSHO [49]	2	✓	DDH	$\Theta(Q_S)$
Chopsticks I [46]	2	✓	DDH	$\Theta(Q_S)$
Chopsticks II [46]	2	✗	DDH	$\Theta(1)$
Sect. 4.1	2	✓	DDH	$\Theta(Q_S)$
Sect. 4.2	2	✗	DDH	$\Theta(1)$

1.2 Technical Overview

In this paper, we introduce two major technical improvements to the Chopsticks schemes, namely, a novel overall construction strategy and a more efficient commitment scheme that can be used both in Chopsticks and in our schemes.

Table 2. Asymptotic efficiency comparison of multi-signature schemes in the discrete logarithm setting without pairings in the plain public key model. We compare the number of rounds, the size of public keys, the communication complexity per signer, and the signature size. We denote the size of a group element by $\langle \mathbb{G} \rangle$ and the size of a field element by $\langle \mathbb{Z}_p \rangle$. Here, λ is a statistical security parameter, and N is the number of signers. Schemes below the line have two rounds and avoid rewinding, see Table 1. We do not list [44] as it is prohibitively inefficient due to the use of heavy cryptographic machinery.

Scheme	Rounds	Public Key	Communication	Signature
BN [7]	3	$1\langle \mathbb{G} \rangle$	$1\langle \mathbb{G} \rangle + 1\langle \mathbb{Z}_p \rangle + 2\lambda$	$1\langle \mathbb{G} \rangle + 1\langle \mathbb{Z}_p \rangle$
BN+ [7]	3	$2\langle \mathbb{G} \rangle$	$2\langle \mathbb{G} \rangle + 1\langle \mathbb{Z}_p \rangle + 2\lambda$	$2\langle \mathbb{G} \rangle + 1\langle \mathbb{Z}_p \rangle$
Musig [12,41]	3	$1\langle \mathbb{G} \rangle$	$1\langle \mathbb{G} \rangle + 1\langle \mathbb{Z}_p \rangle + 2\lambda$	$1\langle \mathbb{G} \rangle + 1\langle \mathbb{Z}_p \rangle$
Musig+ [24]	3	$2\langle \mathbb{G} \rangle$	$2\langle \mathbb{G} \rangle + 1\langle \mathbb{Z}_p \rangle + 2\lambda$	$2\langle \mathbb{Z}_p \rangle$
Musig2 [43]	2	$1\langle \mathbb{G} \rangle$	$4\langle \mathbb{G} \rangle + 1\langle \mathbb{Z}_p \rangle$	$1\langle \mathbb{G} \rangle + 1\langle \mathbb{Z}_p \rangle$
HBMS [6]	2	$1\langle \mathbb{G} \rangle$	$1\langle \mathbb{G} \rangle + 2\langle \mathbb{Z}_p \rangle$	$1\langle \mathbb{G} \rangle + 2\langle \mathbb{Z}_p \rangle$
TZ [50]	2	$1\langle \mathbb{G} \rangle$	$4\langle \mathbb{G} \rangle + 2\langle \mathbb{Z}_p \rangle$	$1\langle \mathbb{G} \rangle + 2\langle \mathbb{Z}_p \rangle$
TSSHO [49]	2	$2\langle \mathbb{G} \rangle$	$2\langle \mathbb{G} \rangle + 2\langle \mathbb{Z}_p \rangle$	$3\langle \mathbb{Z}_p \rangle$
Chopsticks I [46]	2	$2\langle \mathbb{G} \rangle$	$3\langle \mathbb{G} \rangle + 1\langle \mathbb{Z}_p \rangle + \lambda$	$3\langle \mathbb{G} \rangle + 4\langle \mathbb{Z}_p \rangle$
Chopsticks II [46]	2	$4\langle \mathbb{G} \rangle$	$6\langle \mathbb{G} \rangle + 2\langle \mathbb{Z}_p \rangle + \lambda + 1$	$6\langle \mathbb{G} \rangle + 8\langle \mathbb{Z}_p \rangle + N$
Sect. 4.1	2	$2\langle \mathbb{G} \rangle$	$2\langle \mathbb{G} \rangle + 1\langle \mathbb{Z}_p \rangle + \lambda$	$3\langle \mathbb{Z}_p \rangle + 2\lambda$
Sect. 4.2	2	$4\langle \mathbb{G} \rangle$	$2\langle \mathbb{G} \rangle + 1\langle \mathbb{Z}_p \rangle + \lambda + 1$	$3\langle \mathbb{Z}_p \rangle + 2\lambda + N$

Table 3. Concrete efficiency and security comparison of two-round multi-signature schemes in the discrete logarithm setting without pairings in the plain public key model. We compare the security level guaranteed by the security bound in the random oracle model assuming the underlying assumption is 128-bit hard, the size of public keys, the communication complexity per signer, and the signature size. Sizes are given in bytes and rounded. We do not list [44] as it is prohibitively inefficient due to the use of heavy cryptographic machinery.

Scheme	Security	Public Key	Communication	Signature
Musig2	9	33	164	65
HBMS	−11	33	97	97
TZ	8	33	196	97
TSSHO	106	66	130	96
Chopsticks I	106	66	147	227
Chopsticks II	126	132	278	470
Section 4.1	106	66	114	128
Section 4.2	125	132	114	144

Background. We start with lossy identification schemes [1,35,36]. In such a scheme, there are two ways to set up public keys pk. As usual, one can set up pk with a secret key sk. Alternatively, one can set up pk in lossy mode. In this mode, not even an unbounded prover can make the verifier accept, which is called lossy soundness. This paradigm turns out to be useful when constructing tightly secure Fiat-Shamir style signatures [1,35,36] or three-round multi-signatures [7,24]. To apply it in the two-round setting, Pan and Wagner [46] leveraged a homomorphic dual-mode commitment. Concretely, such a commitment has two ways of setting up commitment keys ck. In the hiding mode, ck is generated in combination with a (weak) equivocation trapdoor. In the other mode, commitments are statistically binding. Given such a commitment and a lossy identification scheme, a signature for a message m contains transcripts of the lossy identification scheme, where some parts are given in a committed form. For these parts, the signature also contains the respective opening information. Importantly, the commitment key is derived from m, e.g., as $ck := H(m)$, where H is a random oracle. Abstractly, Pan and Wagner [46] identified the following properties:

- *Simulation via Secret Keys.* A reduction can simulate the signing oracle using the secret key if pk is in the normal mode. The mode of ck is not relevant.
- *Simulation via Trapdoors.* A reduction can simulate the signing oracle using the trapdoor if ck is in the hiding mode. The mode of pk is not relevant.
- *Forgery.* To show security without rewinding, the adversary must output a forgery with respect to a lossy pk and a binding ck.

The Chopsticks Approach: Pseudorandom Matching. In the proof of their first scheme, Pan and Wagner [46] use these properties by sampling all commitment keys with a trapdoor, allowing them to simulate signing even if the public key is lossy. Only for the forgery message the associated commitment key ck^* is set up to be binding. Then, the proof can be finished without rewinding. On the downside, this approach requires guessing the query defining ck^*, leading to a security loss.

A well-known trick to avoid such a guessing argument is the Katz-Wang approach [28]. Here, each message would specify two commitment keys $ck_0 := H(0, m)$ and $ck_1 := H(1, m)$, and a signer individually would pick a pseudorandom bit b_m for each message and then use ck_{b_m}. It turns out that this trick is not applicable here, as each signer has to use the same commitment key.

To overcome this obstacle, Pan and Wagner proposed the pseudorandom matching technique. Namely, each signer has two public keys pk_0, pk_1, and both message-dependent commitment keys ck_0 and ck_1 are used. That is, the protocol is run twice in parallel and the signature now contains two transcripts instead of one. Importantly, each signer uses the pseudorandom bit b_m to decide which public key to match with which commitment key. We illustrate the pseudorandom matching technique in Fig. 1 (top). In the proof, one can set pk_1 to lossy and always match it with the trapdoor commitment key ck_{1-b_m} for signing queries. In this way, it is possible to simulate the (pk_1, ck_{1-b_m}) side via the trapdoor, and the (pk_0, ck_{b_m}) side via the secret key. At the same time, with probability $1/2$, the

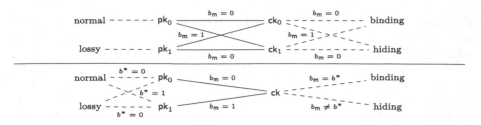

Fig. 1. Visualization of the pseudorandom matching technique from Chopsticks [46] (top), and our new pseudorandom path technique (bottom). Here, b^* is a random bit sampled by the game, b_m is the pseudorandom bit that the signer chooses for message m, normal edges indicate how keys are paired in the scheme, and dotted edges indicate how keys are set up in the proof.

adversary will match the lossy pk_1 with the binding ck_{b_m} for the forgery, finishing the proof. While this is an elegant trick, it introduces a significant overhead for both signature size and communication complexity.

Our Approach: Pseudorandom Paths. We avoid this overhead by using our new pseudorandom path technique, as illustrated in Fig. 1 (bottom). Our first observation is that for the argument used to finish the proof in Chopsticks, only one of the two paths, namely the (pk_1, ck_{b_m}) path, is used. Instead of simply omitting one of the paths, which leads to problems similar to the naive Katz-Wang approach, let us see what happens if we go back to a solution in which there is only one commitment key ck per message m. If we also reduce the number of keys per signer back to one, we end up with the guessing-based solution again. So, we keep the two keys pk_0, pk_1 per signer, and let each signer pseudorandomly decide which key pk_{b_m} to use in the signing interaction. In our proof, we can set up ck with a trapdoor if the lossy key pk_1 is used, and we can set it up in binding mode if the normal key pk_0 is used. Unfortunately, without additional tricks, this strategy is doomed: The adversary could always use pk_0 in its forgery, which is not lossy. In our final solution, we therefore pick a bit b^* at random at the beginning of our simulation. Then, we set pk_{b^*} to normal and pk_{1-b^*} to lossy. We adapt the sampling of ck accordingly. By carrying out all arguments in the correct order, we can argue that in one of four cases, the adversary used the lossy key pk_{1-b^*} with a binding commitment key in its forgery. Let us explain the idea for that with our illustration (Fig. 1, bottom) at hand. Every signature corresponds to a pseudorandom path from the left to the right. The bits are set up in a way that ensures the following:

- *Simulation of Signing.* If pk_{b_m} is used, the path connects the lossy vertex to the trapdoor vertex, or the normal vertex to the binding vertex. In both cases, we can simulate.
- *Forgery.* The probability that the path associated with the forgery starts at the lossy vertex is $1/2$ and conditioned on that, the probability that the path ends at the binding vertex is also $1/2$.

With this technique, communication and signatures now only consist of one transcript of the lossy identification scheme, as opposed to two transcripts in the pseudorandom matching technique.

The Chopsticks Commitment. So far, we have reduced the size of signatures and communication by a factor of two. At this point, the size is mostly dominated by the size of commitments com and openings φ. It is therefore instructive to recall the commitment instantiation from [46] and see if we can optimize it. The instantiation from [46] allows to commit to pairs of group elements $(R_1, R_2) \in \mathbb{G}^2$ via the equation

$$\text{com} = (C_0, C_1, C_2) \in \mathbb{G}^3, \text{ where } \begin{pmatrix} C_0 \\ C_1 \\ C_2 \end{pmatrix} := \begin{pmatrix} A_{1,1}^\alpha \cdot A_{1,2}^\beta \cdot A_{1,3}^\gamma \\ R_1 \cdot A_{2,1}^\alpha \cdot A_{2,2}^\beta \cdot A_{2,3}^\gamma \\ R_2 \cdot A_{3,1}^\alpha \cdot A_{3,2}^\beta \cdot A_{3,3}^\gamma \end{pmatrix}.$$

Here, $\varphi = (\alpha, \beta, \gamma) \in \mathbb{Z}_p^3$ is the commitment randomness and the $A_{i,j} \in \mathbb{G}$ form the commitment key. In terms of exponents, the commitment has the form

$$\mathbf{E} \cdot \begin{pmatrix} \alpha \\ \beta \\ \gamma \end{pmatrix} + \begin{pmatrix} 0 \\ r_1 \\ r_2 \end{pmatrix}$$

for a matrix $\mathbf{E} \in \mathbb{Z}_p^{3 \times 3}$ that determines the commitment key. Now, one can prove that this is statistically hiding if $\mathbf{E}$ has full rank, and it is statistically binding if $\mathbf{E}$ has rank 1. It is one of the main technical contributions of [46] to introduce a weak equivocation trapdoor for this commitment, i.e., a trapdoor that allows to open commitments to messages (R_1, R_2) of a certain structure.

Strawman Commitment. In terms of efficiency, note that the 3×3 commitment key leads to three group elements per commitment and three exponents per opening. To improve it, our naive idea is to replace this 3×3 structure with a 2×2 structure, thereby saving one group element and exponent. Concretely, we could try to drop the first row of the commitment equation, leading to

$$\mathbf{E} \cdot \begin{pmatrix} \beta \\ \gamma \end{pmatrix} + \begin{pmatrix} r_1 \\ r_2 \end{pmatrix}$$

for a matrix $\mathbf{E} \in \mathbb{Z}_p^{2 \times 2}$. Implemented carefully, this is still perfectly hiding with a weak equivocation trapdoor if $\mathbf{E}$ has full rank. Unfortunately, we fail when analyzing the statistically binding mode[3] if $\mathbf{E}$ has rank 1. Concretely, an (unbounded) adversary against binding could output (r_1, r_2) with opening (β, γ) on the one hand, and $(r_1, r_2) + (\beta, \gamma)\mathbf{E}^t$ with opening $(0, 0)$ on the other hand. The first row in the 3×3 scheme prevents this. To save our 2×2 construction without reintroducing such a first row, we thus need additional insights.

---

[3] If we only have a computationally binding mode, the resulting multi-signature scheme needs to rely on rewinding. Therefore, we have to insist on a statistically binding mode.

Coset Binding. As we have seen, our 2×2 scheme is not (statistically) binding, and as such it is not suitable to instantiate the multi-signature construction. However, we make the crucial observation that the scheme is binding *up to a difference in the span of* E. In other words, if we interpret the commitment as a commitment to cosets of the span of E, the scheme is binding. We call this property *coset binding*. It is instructive to pinpoint where the overall multi-signature proof fails if we relax binding to coset binding: In the proof of our multi-signature construction, binding shows up in combination with lossy soundness in the very last proof step. To recall, lossy soundness states that even an unbounded prover can not make a verifier of the lossy identification scheme accept, given that pk is in lossy mode. An accepting transcript of the identification scheme has the form (R, c, s) and satisfies $\mathsf{F}(s) - c \cdot \mathsf{pk} = R$ for a linear function F[4]. Roughly, when constructing an unbounded reduction that breaks lossy soundness, we first guess[5] the random oracle query associated with the forgery. On this query, assume now that the adversary sends a commitment com for R with respect to a binding commitment key. In this case, the reduction would non-efficiently extract the committed pair of group elements $R = (R_1, R_2)$ from com and output it in the lossy soundness game. Further, it would appropriately embed the challenge c from the lossy soundness game. Finally, if the guess was correct, the adversary's forgery contains a valid response s, which the reduction can output. Now, it is clear why coset binding is not enough: The adversary is not bound to $R = (R_1, R_2)$, and it can output a response s that is valid for $R' = (R'_1, R'_2) \neq R$, which is of no use for the reduction.

Coset Lossy Soundness to the Rescue. While coset binding seems to be insufficient at first glance, it still gives us a guarantee we may leverage. Namely, by coset binding, $(R_1 = g^{r_1}, R_2 = g^{r_2})$ and $(R'_1 = g^{r'_1}, R'_2 = g^{r'_2})$ as above have to satisfy that $(r_1, r_2)^t - (r'_1, r'_2)^t$ is in the span of E. We want to understand the impact of this guarantee on the lossy soundness game. For that, imagine a modified lossy soundness game where the final equation $\mathsf{F}(s) - c \cdot \mathsf{pk} = R$ only has to hold up to a difference in the span of E. We call this stronger notion of lossy soundness *coset lossy soundness*. In fact, if we can argue that coset lossy soundness holds, then the reduction sketched above goes through assuming coset binding. For that, our main idea is to set up the binding commitment keys such that the span of E is always contained in the image of F. In this case, we observe that coset lossy soundness is implied by the original lossy soundness notion. This is because, roughly, if $\mathsf{F}(s) - c \cdot \mathsf{pk}$ equals R up to a difference in the span of E, it means that $\mathsf{F}(s) - c \cdot \mathsf{pk} = R + \mathsf{F}(\delta)$ for some δ, and so one can just treat $s - \delta$ as the new s. To summarize our optimized commitment construction, we have seen that lossy soundness of the identification scheme at hand is strong enough

---

[4] We use additive notation when talking about lossy identification from such linear functions in general, and multiplicative notation for the concrete instantiation of the linear function and commitment.

[5] Recall that lossy soundness is a statistical notion, and so guessing is not a problem in terms of tightness at this point.

to compensate for the relaxed binding notion. We are confident that this insight is applicable in other contexts as well.

2   Preliminaries

By $[L] := \{1, \ldots, L\} \subseteq \mathbb{N}$ we denote the set of the first L natural numbers. Let S be a finite set, $\mathcal{D}$ a distribution, and $\mathcal{A}$ be a probabilistic algorithm. The notation $s \xleftarrow{\$} S$ means that s is sampled uniformly at random from S, and $x \leftarrow \mathcal{D}$ means that x is sampled according to $\mathcal{D}$. The notation $s := \mathcal{A}(x; \rho)$ means that $\mathcal{A}$ outputs s on input x with random coins ρ, and when we write $s \leftarrow \mathcal{A}(x)$, we mean that ρ is sampled uniformly at random. We write $s \in \mathcal{A}(x)$ to indicate that there are coins ρ such that $\mathcal{A}$ outputs s on input x with these coins ρ. Throughout the paper, λ will denote the security parameter, and all algorithms get it (in unary) as input. We use standard cryptographic notions like PPT and negligible.

Multi-signatures. We define the syntax and security of multi-signatures in the plain public key model [7]. Following previous works, e.g., [17,18,46], we assume the public keys participating in the signing protocol are given by a set, and we assume that sets can be ordered canonically, e.g. lexicographically. Thus, we can uniquely encode sets $\mathcal{P} = \{\mathsf{pk}_1, \ldots, \mathsf{pk}_N\}$, and we denote such an encoding by $\langle \mathcal{P} \rangle$ throughout the paper. Further, we assume that the honest public key in our security definition is the entry pk_1 in such a set, which is without loss of generality and for simplicity of presentation. In terms of syntax and security, we use the definition from [46]. We postpone a formal definition of key aggregation to our full version [47].

Alg $\mathsf{MS.Exec}(\mathcal{P}, \mathcal{S}, \mathsf{m})$

01 **parse** $\{\mathsf{pk}_1, \ldots, \mathsf{pk}_N\} := \mathcal{P}, \; \{\mathsf{sk}_1, \ldots, \mathsf{sk}_N\} := \mathcal{S}$
02 **for** $i \in [N] : (\mathsf{pm}_{1,i}, St_{1,i}) \leftarrow \mathsf{Sig}_0(\mathcal{P}, \mathsf{sk}, \mathsf{m})$
03 $\mathcal{M}_1 := (\mathsf{pm}_{1,1}, \ldots, \mathsf{pm}_{1,N})$
04 **for** $i \in [N] : (\mathsf{pm}_{2,i}, St_{2,i}) \leftarrow \mathsf{Sig}_1(St_{1,i}, \mathcal{M}_1)$
05 $\mathcal{M}_2 := (\mathsf{pm}_{2,1}, \ldots, \mathsf{pm}_{2,N})$
06 **for** $i \in [N] : \sigma_i \leftarrow \mathsf{Sig}_2(St_{2,i}, \mathcal{M}_2)$
07 **if** $\exists i \neq j \in [N]$ s.t. $\sigma_i \neq \sigma_j :$ **return** $\perp$
08 **return** $\sigma := \sigma_1$

Fig. 2. Algorithm $\mathsf{MS.Exec}$ for a (two-round)multi-signature scheme $\mathsf{MS} = (\mathsf{Setup}, \mathsf{Gen}, \mathsf{Sig}, \mathsf{Ver})$. The algorithm specifies an honest execution of the signing protocol Sig among N signers with public keys $\mathsf{pk}_1, \ldots, \mathsf{pk}_N$ and secret keys $\mathsf{sk}_1, \ldots, \mathsf{sk}_N$ for a message m.

Definition 1 (Multi-Signature Scheme). *A (two-round) multi-signature scheme is a tuple of PPT algorithms* $\mathsf{MS} = (\mathsf{Setup}, \mathsf{Gen}, \mathsf{Sig}, \mathsf{Ver})$ *with the following syntax:*

- Setup(1^λ) → par *takes as input the security parameter* 1^λ *and outputs global system parameters* par. *We assume that* par *implicitly defines sets of public keys, secret keys, messages and signatures, respectively. All algorithms related to* MS *take* par *at least implicitly as input.*
- Gen(par) → (pk, sk) *takes as input system parameters* par, *and outputs a public key* pk *and a secret key* sk.
- Sig = (Sig$_0$, Sig$_1$, Sig$_2$) *is split into three algorithms:*
  - Sig$_0$($\mathcal{P}$, sk, m) → (pm$_1$, St_1) *takes as input a set* $\mathcal{P} = \{pk_1, \ldots, pk_N\}$ *of public keys, a secret key* sk, *and a message* m, *and outputs a protocol message* pm$_1$ *and a state* St_1.
  - Sig$_1$(St_1, $\mathcal{M}_1$) → (pm$_2$, St_2) *takes as input a state* St_1 *and a tuple* $\mathcal{M}_1 = $ (pm$_{1,1}, \ldots,$ pm$_{1,N}$) *of protocol messages, and outputs a protocol message* pm$_2$ *and a state* St_2.
  - Sig$_2$(St_2, $\mathcal{M}_2$) → σ_i *takes as input a state* St_2 *and a tuple* $\mathcal{M}_2 = $ (pm$_{2,1}, \ldots,$ pm$_{2,N}$) *of protocol messages, and outputs a signature* σ.
- Ver($\mathcal{P}$, m, σ) → b *is deterministic, takes as input a set* $\mathcal{P} = \{pk_1, \ldots, pk_N\}$ *of public keys, a message* m, *and a signature* σ, *and outputs a bit* $b \in \{0, 1\}$.

We require that MS *is complete in the following sense. For all* par $\in$ Setup(1^λ), *all* $N = $ poly(λ), *all* (pk$_j$, sk$_j$) $\in$ Gen(par) *for* $j \in [N]$, *and all messages* m, *we have*

$$
\Pr\left[\text{Ver}(\mathcal{P}, \text{m}, \sigma) = 1 \,\middle|\,
\begin{array}{l}
\mathcal{P} = \{pk_1, \ldots, pk_N\}, \mathcal{S} = \{sk_1, \ldots, sk_N\}, \\
\sigma \leftarrow \text{MS.Exec}(\mathcal{P}, \mathcal{S}, \text{m})
\end{array}
\right] = 1,
$$

where algorithm MS.Exec *is defined in Fig. 2.*

Definition 2 (MS-EUF-CMA **Security**). *Let* MS $=$ (Setup, Gen, Sig, Ver) *be a multi-signature scheme and consider the game* **MS-EUF-CMA** *defined in Fig. 3. We say that* MS *is* MS-EUF-CMA *secure, if for all PPT adversaries* $\mathcal{A}$, *the following advantage is negligible:*

$$
\text{Adv}_{\mathcal{A}, \text{MS}}^{\text{MS-EUF-CMA}}(\lambda) := \Pr\left[\textbf{MS-EUF-CMA}_{\text{MS}}^{\mathcal{A}}(\lambda) \Rightarrow 1\right].
$$

Assumptions. In this work, we base our constructions on the well-known DDH assumption over a (family of) cyclic groups $\mathbb{G}$ of prime order p with generator g. To recall, the assumption states that it is infeasible to distinguish $(g, h, g^a, h^a) \in \mathbb{G}^4$ from $(g, h, u, v) \in \mathbb{G}^4$ for $h, u, v \xleftarrow{\$} \mathbb{G}$ and $a \xleftarrow{\$} \mathbb{Z}_p$. For convenience, we define its multi-instance variant Q-DDH. It is well-known that Q-DDH is tightly implied by DDH using random self-reducibility [22]. We postpone the formal definition of both assumptions to our full version [47].

3 Our Building Blocks

In this section, we introduce two building blocks we will use in our constructions. Namely, we make use of linear function families and a special kind of

```
Game MS-EUF-CMA_MS^A(λ)                      Oracle SIG₁(sid, M₁)
01 par ← Setup(1^λ)                          16 if round[sid] ≠ 1 : return ⊥
02 (pk, sk) ← Gen(par)                       17 parse (pm_{1,1}, ..., pm_{1,N}) := M₁
03 SIG := (SIG₀, SIG₁, SIG₂)                 18 if pm₁[sid] ≠ pm_{1,1} : return ⊥
04 (P*, m*, σ*) ← A^SIG(par, pk)             19 round[sid] := round[sid] + 1
05 if pk ∉ P* : return 0                     20 (pm₂, St₂) ← Sig₁(St₁[sid], M₁)
06 if (P*, m*) ∈ Queried : return 0          21 (pm₂[sid], St₂[sid]) := (pm₂, St₂)
07 return Ver(P*, m*, σ*)                    22 return pm₂[sid]

Oracle SIG₀(P, m)                            Oracle SIG₂(sid, M₂)
08 parse {pk₁, ..., pk_N} := P               23 if round[sid] ≠ 2 : return ⊥
09 if pk₁ ≠ pk : return ⊥                    24 parse (pm_{2,1}, ..., pm_{2,N}) := M₂
10 Queried := Queried ∪ {(P, m)}             25 if pm₂[sid] ≠ pm_{2,1} : return ⊥
11 ctr := ctr + 1, sid := ctr                26 round[sid] := round[sid] + 1
12 round[sid] := 1                           27 σ ← Sig₂(St₂[sid], M₂)
13 (pm₁, St₁) ← Sig₀(P, sk, m)               28 return σ
14 (pm₁[sid], St₁[sid]) := (pm₁, St₁)
15 return (pm₁[sid], sid)
```

Fig. 3. The game **MS-EUF-CMA** for a (two-round) multi-signature scheme MS and an adversary $\mathcal{A}$. To simplify the presentation, we assume that the canonical ordering of sets is chosen such that pk is always at the first position if it is included.

commitment scheme. This is similar to what is done in [46]. However, compared to [46], a crucial observation is that we can weaken the requirements for the commitment scheme, thereby enabling a more efficient instantiation. To compensate, we strengthen the requirements for the linear function family in terms of soundness, which is for free in terms of efficiency.

3.1 Linear Functions

Our first building block is a family of linear functions with suitable properties. Linear function families are a widely used abstraction [15,30,34,46,50] that allows us to describe our protocols in a modular and uncluttered fashion. In terms of syntax, we use the definition given in [46].

Definition 3 (Linear Function Family). *A linear function family (LFF) is a tuple of PPT algorithms* LF = (Gen, F) *with the following syntax:*

- Gen(1^λ) → par *takes as input the security parameter 1^λ and outputs parameters* par. *We assume that* par *implicitly defines the following sets:*
  - *A set of scalars $\mathcal{S}_{par}$, which forms a field.*
  - *A domain $\mathcal{D}_{par}$, which forms a vector space over $\mathcal{S}_{par}$.*
  - *A range $\mathcal{R}_{par}$, which forms a vector space over $\mathcal{S}_{par}$.*
  We omit the subscript par *if it is clear from the context, and naturally denote the operations of these fields and vector spaces by + and ·. We assume that these operations can be evaluated efficiently.*

- $\mathsf{F}(\mathsf{par}, x) \to X$ *is deterministic, takes as input parameters* par, *an element* $x \in \mathcal{D}$, *and outputs an element* $X \in \mathcal{R}$. *For all parameters* par, $\mathsf{F}(\mathsf{par}, \cdot)$ *realizes a homomorphism, i.e.*

$$\forall s \in \mathcal{S}, x, y \in \mathcal{D}: \; \mathsf{F}(\mathsf{par}, s \cdot x + y) = s \cdot \mathsf{F}(\mathsf{par}, x) + \mathsf{F}(\mathsf{par}, y).$$

We omit the input par *if it is clear from the context.*

In [46], key indistinguishability and lossy soundness are defined to capture the set of properties that makes linear function families amenable for the use in lossy identification [1]. We recall these definitions from [46]. Further, we introduce strengthened definitions, which allow us to weaken the properties for other building blocks. Concretely, we relax the winning condition for lossy soundness, such that it has to hold up to an arbitrary shift in the image of the linear function, leading to coset lossy soundness. In our full version [47], we also adapt the definition of aggregation lossy soundness from [46] accordingly, leading to coset aggregation lossy soundness. Importantly, we show that the strengthened definitions come for free.

Definition 4 (Key Indistinguishability). *Let* $\mathsf{LF} = (\mathsf{Gen}, \mathsf{F})$ *be a linear function family. We say that* LF *satisfies key indistinguishability, if for any PPT algorithm* $\mathcal{A}$, *the following advantage is negligible:*

$$\mathsf{Adv}_{\mathcal{A}, \mathsf{LF}}^{\mathsf{keydist}}(\lambda) := |\Pr\left[\mathcal{A}(\mathsf{par}, X) = 1 \,\middle|\, \mathsf{par} \leftarrow \mathsf{Gen}(1^\lambda), \; x \xleftarrow{\$} \mathcal{D}, \; X := \mathsf{F}(x)\right]$$
$$- \Pr\left[\mathcal{A}(\mathsf{par}, X) = 1 \,\middle|\, \mathsf{par} \leftarrow \mathsf{Gen}(1^\lambda), \; X \xleftarrow{\$} \mathcal{R}\right]|.$$

Definition 5 (Lossy Soundness). *Let* $\mathsf{LF} = (\mathsf{Gen}, \mathsf{F})$ *be a linear function family. We say that* LF *satisfies* ε_l-*lossy soundness, if for any unbounded algorithm* $\mathcal{A}$, *the following probability is at most* ε_l:

$$\Pr\left[\mathsf{F}(s) - c \cdot X = R \;\middle|\; \begin{array}{l} \mathsf{par} \leftarrow \mathsf{Gen}(1^\lambda), \; X \xleftarrow{\$} \mathcal{R}, \\ (St, R) \leftarrow \mathcal{A}(\mathsf{par}, X), \\ c \xleftarrow{\$} \mathcal{S}, \; s \leftarrow \mathcal{A}(St, c) \end{array}\right].$$

Definition 6 (Coset Lossy Soundness). *Let* $\mathsf{LF} = (\mathsf{Gen}, \mathsf{F})$ *be a linear function family. We say that* LF *satisfies* ε_l-*coset lossy soundness, if for any unbounded algorithm* $\mathcal{A}$, *the following probability is at most* ε_l:

$$\Pr\left[\mathsf{F}(s) - c \cdot X \in R + \mathsf{F}(\mathcal{D}) \;\middle|\; \begin{array}{l} \mathsf{par} \leftarrow \mathsf{Gen}(1^\lambda), \; X \xleftarrow{\$} \mathcal{R}, \\ (St, R) \leftarrow \mathcal{A}(\mathsf{par}, X), \\ c \xleftarrow{\$} \mathcal{S}, \; s \leftarrow \mathcal{A}(St, c) \end{array}\right].$$

Lemma 1. *Let* LF *be a linear function family, such that for any* $\mathsf{par} \in \mathsf{Gen}(1^\lambda)$, *the domain* $\mathcal{D}_{\mathsf{par}}$ *can be enumerated. Then, if* LF *satisfies* ε_l-*lossy soundness, it also satisfies* ε_l-*coset lossy soundness.*

Proof. To prove the claim, it is sufficient to describe an (unbounded) reduction $\mathcal{B}$, that turns any algorithm $\mathcal{A}$ running in the coset lossy soundness game into an algorithm in the lossy soundness game. The reduction $\mathcal{B}$ gets as input parameters par and an element $X \in \mathcal{R}$ from the lossy soundness game. It runs $\mathcal{A}$ on input par and X and gets an output R in return, which it passes to the lossy soundness game. In return, it receives $c \in \mathcal{S}$, and forwards it to $\mathcal{A}$, which outputs $s \in \mathcal{D}$. If $\mathcal{A}$ breaks coset lossy soundness, i.e., $\mathsf{F}(s) - c \cdot X \in R + \mathsf{F}(\mathcal{D})$, then there is a $\delta \in \mathcal{D}$ such that $\mathsf{F}(s) - c \cdot X = R + \mathsf{F}(\delta)$. By enumerating $\mathcal{D}$, the reduction $\mathcal{B}$ finds such a δ and returns $s - \delta$ to the lossy soundness game. As we have $\mathsf{F}(s - \delta) - c \cdot X = R$, $\mathcal{B}$ breaks lossy soundness with the same probability as $\mathcal{A}$ breaks coset lossy soundness, and the claim follows.   □

3.2   Weaker Commitments

In this section, we formally define the syntax and properties of the commitment scheme we require for our construction. Namely, we weaken the commitment definition given in [46]. To recall, the commitment scheme in [46] allows to homomorphically commit to elements in the range of a linear function family. In addition to a statistically binding mode, there is an indistinguishable way of generating commitment keys together with a weak equivocation trapdoor. This trapdoor allows to open commitments to all messages of a certain structure. In comparison to [46], we now also weaken the binding property of the scheme. Concretely, in the binding mode, we only require the commitment to be binding up to any shift in the image of the linear function. Except for this change, we take the definition of [46] verbatim.

Game Q-KEYDIST$_{0,\mathsf{CMT}}^{\mathcal{A}}(\lambda)$	**Game Q-KEYDIST$_{1,\mathsf{CMT}}^{\mathcal{A}}(\lambda)$**
01 par $\leftarrow$ LF.Gen(1^λ), $x \xleftarrow{\$} \mathcal{D}$	06 par $\leftarrow$ LF.Gen(1^λ), $x \xleftarrow{\$} \mathcal{D}$
02 **if** (par, x) $\notin$ Good : **return** 0	07 **if** (par, x) $\notin$ Good : **return** 0
03 **for** $i \in [Q]$: $\mathsf{ck}_i \leftarrow$ BGen(par)	08 **for** $i \in [Q]$: $\mathsf{ck}_i \xleftarrow{\$} \mathcal{K}_{\mathsf{par}}$
04 $\beta \leftarrow \mathcal{A}(\mathsf{par}, x, (\mathsf{ck}_i)_{i \in [Q]})$	09 $\beta \leftarrow \mathcal{A}(\mathsf{par}, x, (\mathsf{ck}_i)_{i \in [Q]})$
05 **return** β	10 **return** β

Fig. 4. The games **KEYDIST$_0$, KEYDIST$_1$** for the definition of a weakly equivocable coset commitment Scheme CMT and an adversary $\mathcal{A}$.

Definition 7 (Weakly Equivocable Coset Commitment Scheme). *Let* LF $= ($LF.Gen$, \mathsf{F})$ *be a linear function family and* $\mathcal{G} = \{\mathcal{G}_{\mathsf{par}}\}, \mathcal{H} = \{\mathcal{H}_{\mathsf{par}}\}$ *be families of subsets of abelian groups with efficiently computable group operations* $\oplus$ *and* $\otimes$*, respectively. Let* $\mathcal{K} = \{\mathcal{K}_{\mathsf{par}}\}$ *be a family of sets. An* $(\varepsilon_{\mathsf{b}}, \varepsilon_{\mathsf{g}}, \varepsilon_{\mathsf{t}})$*-weakly equivocable coset commitment scheme for* LF *with key space* $\mathcal{K}$*, randomness space* $\mathcal{G}$ *and commitment space* $\mathcal{H}$ *is a tuple of PPT algorithms* CMT $= ($BGen, TGen, Com, TCom, TCol$)$ *with the following syntax:*

– BGen(par) $\rightarrow$ ck *takes as input parameters* par, *and outputs a key* ck $\in \mathcal{K}_{\mathsf{par}}$.

- TGen(par, X) → (ck, td) *takes as input parameters* par, *and an element* $X \in \mathcal{R}$, *and outputs a key* ck $\in \mathcal{K}_{par}$ *and a trapdoor* td.
- Com(ck, $R; \varphi$) → com *takes as input a key* ck, *an element* $R \in \mathcal{R}$, *and a randomness* $\varphi \in \mathcal{G}_{par}$, *and outputs a commitment* com $\in \mathcal{H}_{par}$.
- TCom(ck, td) → (com, St) *takes as input a key* ck *and a trapdoor* td, *and outputs a commitment* com $\in \mathcal{H}_{par}$ *and a state* St.
- TCol(St, c) → (φ, R, s) *takes as input a state* St, *and an element* $c \in \mathcal{S}$, *and outputs randomness* $\varphi \in \mathcal{G}_{par}$, *and elements* $R \in \mathcal{R}, s \in \mathcal{D}$.

We omit the subscript par *if it is clear from the context. Further, the algorithms are required to satisfy the following properties:*

- **Homomorphism.** *For all* par $\in$ LF.Gen(1^λ), ck $\in \mathcal{K}_{par}, R_0, R_1 \in \mathcal{R}$ *and* $\varphi_0, \varphi_1 \in \mathcal{G}$, *the following holds:*

$$\text{Com}(\text{ck}, R_0; \varphi_0) \otimes \text{Com}(\text{ck}, R_1; \varphi_1) = \text{Com}(\text{ck}, R_0 + R_1; \varphi_0 \oplus \varphi_1).$$

- **Good Parameters.** *There is a set* Good, *such that membership to* Good *can be decided in polynomial time, and*

$$\Pr\left[(\text{par}, x) \notin \text{Good} \mid \text{par} \leftarrow \text{LF.Gen}(1^\lambda), \; x \xleftarrow{\$} \mathcal{D}\right] \leq \varepsilon_g,$$

- **Uniform Keys.** *For all* (par, x) $\in$ Good, *the following distributions are identical:*

$$\{(\text{par}, x, \text{ck}) \mid \text{ck} \xleftarrow{\$} \mathcal{K}_{par}\} \text{ and } \{(\text{par}, x, \text{ck}) \mid (\text{ck}, \text{td}) \leftarrow \text{TGen}(\text{par}, F(x))\}.$$

- **Weak Trapdoor Property.** *For all* (par, x) $\in$ Good, *and all* $c \in \mathcal{S}$, *the following distributions* $\mathcal{T}_0$ *and* $\mathcal{T}_1$ *have statistical distance at most* ε_t:

$$\mathcal{T}_0 := \left\{ (\text{par}, \text{ck}, \text{td}, x, c, \text{com}, \text{tr}) \; \middle| \; \begin{array}{l} (\text{ck}, \text{td}) \leftarrow \text{TGen}(\text{par}, F(x)) \\ r \xleftarrow{\$} \mathcal{D}, \; R := F(r), \; \varphi \xleftarrow{\$} \mathcal{G}, \\ \text{com} := \text{Com}(\text{ck}, R; \varphi), \\ s := c \cdot x + r, \; \text{tr} := (\varphi, R, s) \end{array} \right\},$$

$$\mathcal{T}_1 := \left\{ (\text{par}, \text{ck}, \text{td}, x, c, \text{com}, \text{tr}) \; \middle| \; \begin{array}{l} (\text{ck}, \text{td}) \leftarrow \text{TGen}(\text{par}, F(x)) \\ (\text{com}, St) \leftarrow \text{TCom}(\text{ck}, \text{td}), \\ \text{tr} \leftarrow \text{TCol}(St, c) \end{array} \right\}.$$

- **Multi-Key Indistinguishability.** *For every* $Q = \text{poly}(\lambda)$ *and any PPT algorithm* $\mathcal{A}$, *the following advantage is negligible:*

$$\text{Adv}_{\mathcal{A}, \text{CMT}}^{Q\text{-keydist}}(\lambda) := \left| \Pr\left[Q\text{-}\mathbf{KEYDIST}_{0, \text{CMT}}^{\mathcal{A}}(\lambda) \Rightarrow 1\right] \right.$$
$$\left. - \Pr\left[Q\text{-}\mathbf{KEYDIST}_{1, \text{CMT}}^{\mathcal{A}}(\lambda) \Rightarrow 1\right] \right|,$$

where games $\mathbf{KEYDIST}_0, \mathbf{KEYDIST}_1$ *are defined in Fig. 4.*
- **Statistical Coset Binding.** *There exists some (potentially unbounded) algorithm* Ext, *such that for every (potentially unbounded) algorithm* $\mathcal{A}$ *the following probability is at most* ε_b:

$$\Pr\left[\begin{array}{l} \text{Com}(\text{ck}, R'; \varphi') = \text{com} \\ \wedge \;\; R' \notin R + F(\mathcal{D}) \end{array} \; \middle| \; \begin{array}{l} \text{par} \leftarrow \text{LF.Gen}(1^\lambda), \\ \text{ck} \leftarrow \text{BGen}(\text{par}), \; (\text{com}, St) \leftarrow \mathcal{A}(\text{ck}), \\ R \leftarrow \text{Ext}(\text{ck}, \text{com}), \; (R', \varphi') \leftarrow \mathcal{A}(St) \end{array} \right].$$

4 Our Constructions

In this section, we present two constructions of efficient two-round multi-signatures that do not rely on rewinding. Both constructions rely on the building blocks introduced before.

4.1 Our Construction with Key Aggregation

In [46], a multi-signature scheme Chopsticks I supporting key aggregation is presented, with a security loss proportional to the number of signing queries and without rewinding. In our full version [47], we show that if we instantiate Chopsticks I with our new building blocks, we get the same properties while improving efficiency.

4.2 Our Tight Construction

Here, we present our construction of a tightly secure two-round multi-signature scheme. For that, let $\mathsf{LF} = (\mathsf{LF.Gen}, \mathsf{F})$ be a linear function family. Let $\mathsf{CMT} = (\mathsf{BGen}, \mathsf{TGen}, \mathsf{Com}, \mathsf{TCom}, \mathsf{TCol})$ be an $(\varepsilon_b, \varepsilon_g, \varepsilon_t)$-weakly equivocable coset commitment scheme for LF with key space $\mathcal{K}$, randomness space $\mathcal{G}$ and commitment space $\mathcal{H}$. Finally, let $\mathsf{H} \colon \{0,1\}^* \to \mathcal{K}$, $\mathsf{H}_b \colon \{0,1\}^* \to \{0,1\}$, and $\mathsf{H}_c \colon \{0,1\}^* \to \mathcal{S}$ be random oracles. We give a verbal description of our scheme $\mathsf{Tooth}[\mathsf{LF}, \mathsf{CMT}] = (\mathsf{Setup}, \mathsf{Gen}, \mathsf{Sig}, \mathsf{Ver})$.

Setup and Key Generation. Our scheme makes use of public parameters $\mathsf{par} \leftarrow \mathsf{LF.Gen}(1^\lambda)$, which define the linear function $\mathsf{F} = \mathsf{F}(\mathsf{par}, \cdot)$. Keys are generated by sampling elements $x_0, x_1 \overset{\$}{\leftarrow} \mathcal{D}$ and a seed $\mathsf{seed} \overset{\$}{\leftarrow} \{0,1\}^\lambda$. Then, the keys are
$$\mathsf{sk} := (x_0, x_1, \mathsf{seed}), \quad \mathsf{pk} := (X_0, X_1) := (\mathsf{F}(x_0), \mathsf{F}(x_1)).$$

Signing Protocol. We consider the setting of a set of N signers with public keys $\mathcal{P} = \{\mathsf{pk}_1, \dots, \mathsf{pk}_N\}$. Let $\mathsf{m} \in \{0,1\}^*$ denote the message that should be signed. In the following, we describe the signing protocol, i.e., algorithms Sig_0, $\mathsf{Sig}_1, \mathsf{Sig}_2$, from the perspective of the first signer. This signer holds a secret key $\mathsf{sk}_1 = (x_{1,0}, x_{1,1}, \mathsf{seed}_1)$ for public key $\mathsf{pk}_1 = (X_{1,0}, X_{1,1})$.

1. *Commitment Phase.* First, a commitment key $\mathsf{ck} := \mathsf{H}(\langle \mathcal{P} \rangle, \mathsf{m})$ is derived from the set of public keys and the message. Further, the signer computes a bit $b_1 := \mathsf{H}_b(\mathsf{seed}_1, \langle \mathcal{P} \rangle, \mathsf{m})$. The signer computes
$$r_1 \overset{\$}{\leftarrow} \mathcal{D}, \quad R_1 := \mathsf{F}(r_1).$$

Then, the signer commits to R_1 using the commitment key ck, i.e., it computes
$$\varphi_1 \overset{\$}{\leftarrow} \mathcal{G}, \quad \mathsf{com}_1 := \mathsf{Com}(\mathsf{ck}, R_1; \varphi_1).$$

Finally, it sends $\mathsf{pm}_{1,1} := (b_1, \mathsf{com}_1)$ as its first message of the protocol to all signers.

2. *Response Phase.* Let $\mathcal{M}_1 = (\mathsf{pm}_{1,1}, \ldots, \mathsf{pm}_{1,N})$ be the list of messages output by the signers in the commitment phase. That is, the message $\mathsf{pm}_{1,i}$ is sent by signer i and has the form $\mathsf{pm}_{1,i} = (b_i, \mathsf{com}_i)$. The signer aggregates these messages by setting

$$B := b_1 \ldots b_N \in \{0,1\}^N, \quad \mathsf{com} := \bigotimes_{i \in [N]} \mathsf{com}_i.$$

Next, a signer specific challenge c_1 is derived and a response s_1 is computed. This is done via

$$c_1 := \mathsf{H}_c(\mathsf{pk}_1, \mathsf{com}, \mathsf{m}, \langle \mathcal{P} \rangle, B), \quad s_1 := c_1 \cdot x_{1,b_1} + r_1.$$

Observe that the signer uses bit b_1 to determine which part of the secret key is used. Finally, the signer sends $\mathsf{pm}_{2,1} := (s_1, \varphi_1)$ as its second message of the protocol to all signers.

3. *Aggregation Phase.* Let $\mathcal{M}_2 = (\mathsf{pm}_{2,1}, \ldots, \mathsf{pm}_{2,N})$ be the list of messages output by the signers in the response phase. That is, the message $\mathsf{pm}_{2,i}$ is sent by signer i and has the form $\mathsf{pm}_{2,i} = (s_i, \varphi_i)$. The signers aggregate the responses and commitment randomness received in the previous messages via

$$s := \sum_{i \in [N]} s_i, \quad \varphi := \bigoplus_{i \in [N]} \varphi_i.$$

Finally, the signature is defined as $\sigma := (\mathsf{com}, \varphi, s, B)$.

Verification. Assume we have a set of public keys $\mathcal{P} = \{\mathsf{pk}_1, \ldots, \mathsf{pk}_N\}$, a message $\mathsf{m} \in \{0,1\}^*$, and a signature $\sigma := (\mathsf{com}, \varphi, s, B)$. To verify σ, write $B = b_1 \ldots b_N \in \{0,1\}^N$ and each public key pk_i as $\mathsf{pk}_i = (X_{i,0}, X_{i,1})$. Then, reconstruct the commitment key $\mathsf{ck} := \mathsf{H}(\langle \mathcal{P} \rangle, \mathsf{m})$ and the signer specific challenges $c_i := \mathsf{H}_c(\mathsf{pk}_i, \mathsf{com}, \mathsf{m}, \langle \mathcal{P} \rangle, B)$ for each $i \in [N]$. The signature is valid, i.e., the verification outputs 1, if and only if

$$\mathsf{com} = \mathsf{Com}\left(\mathsf{ck}, \mathsf{F}(s) - \sum_{i=1}^{N} c_i \cdot X_{i,b_i}; \varphi\right).$$

Lemma 2. *Let* LF *be a linear function family. Let* CMT *be an* $(\varepsilon_\mathsf{b}, \varepsilon_\mathsf{g}, \varepsilon_\mathsf{t})$-*weakly equivocable coset commitment scheme for* LF. *Then* $\mathsf{Tooth}[\mathsf{LF}, \mathsf{CMT}]$ *is complete.*

The proof of Lemma 2 is postponed to our full version [47].

Theorem 1. *Let* LF *be a linear function family that satisfies key indistinguishability and* ε_l-*coset lossy soundness. Let* CMT *be an* $(\varepsilon_\mathsf{b}, \varepsilon_\mathsf{g}, \varepsilon_\mathsf{t})$-*weakly equivocable coset commitment scheme for* LF. *Further, let* $\mathsf{H}: \{0,1\}^* \to \mathcal{K}$, $\mathsf{H}_b: \{0,1\}^* \to \{0,1\}, \mathsf{H}_c: \{0,1\}^* \to \mathcal{S}$ *be random oracles. Then* $\mathsf{Tooth}[\mathsf{LF}, \mathsf{CMT}]$ *is* $\mathsf{MS}\text{-}\mathsf{EUF}\text{-}\mathsf{CMA}$ *secure.*

Concretely, for any PPT algorithm $\mathcal{A}$ that makes at most $Q_H, Q_{H_b}, Q_{H_c}, Q_S$ queries to oracles $H, H_b, H_c, \text{SIG}_0$, respectively, there are PPT algorithms $\mathcal{B}, \mathcal{B}'$ with $\mathbf{T}(\mathcal{B}) \approx \mathbf{T}(\mathcal{A}), \mathbf{T}(\mathcal{B}') \approx \mathbf{T}(\mathcal{A})$ and

$$\mathsf{Adv}^{\text{MS-EUF-CMA}}_{\mathcal{A},\text{Tooth[LF,CMT]}}(\lambda) \leq \frac{Q_{H_b}}{2^\lambda} + 8\varepsilon_g + 4Q_S\varepsilon_t + 4Q_H Q_{H_c}\varepsilon_b + 4Q_{H_c}\varepsilon_I$$
$$+ 4 \cdot \mathsf{Adv}^{Q_H\text{-keydist}}_{\mathcal{B},\text{CMT}}(\lambda) + 4 \cdot \mathsf{Adv}^{\text{keydist}}_{\mathcal{B}',\text{LF}}(\lambda).$$

Proof. Let $\mathcal{A}$ be an adversary against the security of $\text{Tooth}[\text{LF}, \text{CMT}]$. To prove the statement, we give a sequence of games $\mathbf{G}_0, \ldots, \mathbf{G}_8$. We present the games formally in our full version [47], and we verbally describe and analyze them here. **Game $\mathbf{G}_0$:** We start with $\mathbf{G}_0$, which is defined to be the original security game $\mathbf{MS\text{-}EUF\text{-}CMA}^{\mathcal{A}}_{\text{Tooth[LF,CMT]}}$, but we omit the oracle SIG_2 from the game. Observe that this is without loss of generality for the scheme at hand, as this oracle can be run publicly based on the outputs of the other oracles and does not make use of any secret state or key. More concretely, for any adversary $\mathcal{A}$ that calls this oracle, we can build a wrapper adversary that internally simulates the game including oracle SIG_2 for $\mathcal{A}$ and forwards everything else to $\mathbf{G}_0$. This wrapper adversary has the same advantage and running time as $\mathcal{A}$. We now recall the game to fix notation. First, system parameters $\mathsf{par} \leftarrow \mathsf{LF.Gen}(1^\lambda)$ are generated. In addition, the secret and public key of an honest user are generated. Namely, the game samples $\mathsf{seed}_1 \xleftarrow{\$} \{0,1\}^\lambda$ and $x_{1,0}, x_{1,1} \xleftarrow{\$} \mathcal{D}$ and sets $X_{1,0} := \mathsf{F}(x_{1,0})$ and $X_{1,1} := \mathsf{F}(x_{1,1})$. It sets $\mathsf{pk}^* := (X_{1,0}, X_{1,1})$ and runs $\mathcal{A}$ on input $\mathsf{par}, \mathsf{pk}^*$, with access to the following oracles

- Signing oracles SIG_0 and SIG_1: The signing oracles simulate an honest signer in a signing interaction. More precisely, if $\mathcal{A}$ queries $\text{SIG}_0(\mathcal{P}, \mathsf{m})$, a new signing interaction for message m with respect to $\mathcal{P} = \{\mathsf{pk}_1, \ldots, \mathsf{pk}_N\}$ is started, where we assume that $\mathsf{pk}_1 = \mathsf{pk}^*$. For that, first $(\mathcal{P}, \mathsf{m})$ is added to list Queried. Then, the game runs algorithm Sig_0 in the natural way and outputs the result to the adversary. Similarly, when $\mathcal{A}$ calls SIG_1, algorithm Sig_1 is run.
- Random oracles H and H_c: The game simulates random oracles H and H_c for $\mathcal{A}$ by standard lazy sampling. For that, it holds maps h and h_c which map the inputs to their outputs. For example, if $\mathcal{A}$ queries $H(x)$, the game checks if $h[x]$ is defined. If it is not yet defined, it is sampled at random from the output domain of H, i.e., from $\mathcal{K}$. Then, the game returns $h[x]$.
- Random oracle H_b: For H_b, we additionally introduce a level of indirection. This will allow us to distinguish queries to H_b that the game itself issues from the queries that $\mathcal{A}$ issues directly. Concretely, when H_b is queried, the game forwards the query to a random oracle $\bar{H}_b$ with the same interface. Oracle $\bar{H}_b$ is simulated using a map $\bar{h}_b$ via lazy sampling. We emphasize that this oracle $\bar{H}_b$ is not provided to $\mathcal{A}$. Further, the convention for all games will be that the game itself only queries $\bar{H}_b$ and not H_b, for example in oracle SIG_0.

Finally, $\mathcal{A}$ outputs a forgery $(\mathcal{P}^*, \mathsf{m}^*, \sigma^*)$. Write $\mathcal{P}^*$ as $\mathcal{P}^* = \{\mathsf{pk}_1, \ldots, \mathsf{pk}_N\}$ and $\sigma^* = (\mathsf{com}^*, \varphi^*, s^*, B^*)$. Further, write $B^* = b_1^* \ldots b_N^* \in \{0,1\}^N$. Then, the game outputs 0 if $\mathsf{pk}^* \notin \mathcal{P}^*$ or $(\mathcal{P}^*, \mathsf{m}^*) \in \mathsf{Queried}$. Otherwise, we assume that $\mathsf{pk}^* = \mathsf{pk}_1$, and the game outputs 1 if and only if $\mathsf{Ver}(\mathcal{P}^*, \mathsf{m}^*, \sigma^*) = 1$. By definition, we have

$$\mathsf{Adv}_{\mathcal{A},\mathsf{Tooth[LF,CMT]}}^{\mathsf{MS\text{-}EUF\text{-}CMA}}(\lambda) = \Pr[\mathbf{G}_0 \Rightarrow 1].$$

Before we continue, we give an overview of the remaining games and our strategy. In our first step (games $\mathbf{G}_1$ and $\mathbf{G}_2$), we will ensure that for the forgery it holds that $b_1^* = 1 - b^*$ and $\bar{\mathsf{H}}_b(\mathsf{seed}_1, \langle \mathcal{P}^* \rangle, \mathsf{m}^*) = b^*$, for a random bit b^*. Once this is established, we change how we simulate the signing oracles (games $\mathbf{G}_3$ to $\mathbf{G}_6$). Namely, in the case $\bar{\mathsf{H}}_b(\mathsf{seed}_1, \langle \mathcal{P} \rangle, \mathsf{m}) = b^*$, we embed a binding commitment key and simulate signing for $(\mathcal{P}, \mathsf{m})$ honestly, whereas for the other case, we embed a commitment key with a trapdoor and simulate signing by using the trapdoor. The result is that we no longer need $x_{1,1-b^*}$. Now, we switch $X_{1,1-b^*}$ to lossy mode and use the binding property to reduce to lossy soundness (games $\mathbf{G}_7$ and $\mathbf{G}_8$). This works, because the forgery is with respect to a lossy key and a binding commitment key.

Game $\mathbf{G}_1$: This game is the same as $\mathbf{G}_0$, but we introduce a bad event on which the game aborts. Namely, the game sets $\mathsf{bad} := 1$ if $\mathcal{A}$ queries $\mathsf{H}_b(\mathsf{seed}_1, x)$ for any $x \in \{0,1\}^*$. Once $\mathcal{A}$ terminates, the game outputs 0 if $\mathsf{bad} = 1$. Otherwise, it behaves as $\mathbf{G}_0$. It is clear that games $\mathbf{G}_0$ and $\mathbf{G}_1$ only differ if $\mathcal{A}$ makes such a query. Further, the only information about seed_1 that $\mathcal{A}$ gets are the values of $\mathsf{H}_b(\mathsf{seed}_1, \cdot)$. As seed_1 is sampled uniformly at random from $\{0,1\}^\lambda$, we can bound the probability that a fixed query of $\mathcal{A}$ has the form $\mathsf{H}_b(\mathsf{seed}_1, x)$ by $1/2^\lambda$. With a union bound over the queries of $\mathcal{A}$ we obtain

$$|\Pr[\mathbf{G}_0 \Rightarrow 1] - \Pr[\mathbf{G}_1 \Rightarrow 1]| \le \frac{Q_{\mathsf{H}_b}}{2^\lambda}.$$

Game $\mathbf{G}_2$: In this game, we introduce a random bit $b^* \xleftarrow{\$} \{0,1\}$ that is sampled at the beginning of the game. Further, we change the winning condition as follows. When $\mathcal{A}$ outputs the forgery, the game outputs 0, if $b_1^* = b^*$ or $\bar{\mathsf{H}}_b(\mathsf{seed}_1, \langle \mathcal{P}^* \rangle, \mathsf{m}^*) = 1 - b^*$. Otherwise, it continues as $\mathbf{G}_1$ does. In other words, game $\mathbf{G}_2$ outputs 1 if $\mathbf{G}_1$ outputs 1 and the following event occurs:

– Event RightBits: This event occurs, if for $\mathcal{A}$'s final output $(\mathcal{P}^*, \mathsf{m}^*, \sigma^*)$ with $\mathcal{P}^* = \{\mathsf{pk}_1 = \mathsf{pk}^*, \ldots, \mathsf{pk}_N\}, \sigma^* = (\mathsf{com}^*, \varphi^*, s^*, B^*)$, and $B^* = b_1^* \ldots b_N^* \in \{0,1\}^N$, it holds that $b_1^* = 1 - b^*$ and $\bar{\mathsf{H}}_b(\mathsf{seed}_1, \langle \mathcal{P}^* \rangle, \mathsf{m}^*) = b^*$.

If we condition on $\mathbf{G}_1 \Rightarrow 1$, then we claim that b^* and $\bar{\mathsf{H}}_b(\mathsf{seed}_1, \langle \mathcal{P}^* \rangle, \mathsf{m}^*)$ are uniformly random and independent, and independent of $\mathcal{A}$'s view. In particular, they are independent of b_1^*. This is because bit b^* is hidden from $\mathcal{A}$ by construction, and $\bar{\mathsf{H}}_b(\mathsf{seed}_1, \langle \mathcal{P}^* \rangle, \mathsf{m}^*)$ is hidden from $\mathcal{A}$ due to $(\mathcal{P}^*, \mathsf{m}^*) \notin \mathsf{Queried}$ and the change introduced in $\mathbf{G}_1$. Therefore, we have

$$\Pr[\mathsf{RightBits} \mid \mathbf{G}_1 \Rightarrow 1] = \Pr_{b,b^* \xleftarrow{\$} \{0,1\}}[b_1^* = 1 - b^* \wedge b = b^*] = \frac{1}{4}.$$

With this, we obtain

$$\Pr[\mathbf{G}_2 \Rightarrow 1] = \Pr[\mathsf{RightBits} \wedge \mathbf{G}_1 \Rightarrow 1]$$

$$= \Pr[\mathsf{RightBits} \mid \mathbf{G}_1 \Rightarrow 1] \cdot \Pr[\mathbf{G}_1 \Rightarrow 1] = \frac{1}{4} \cdot \Pr[\mathbf{G}_1 \Rightarrow 1].$$

Game $\mathbf{G}_3$: This game is the same as $\mathbf{G}_2$, but we add another abort. Namely, once the game sampled par and $x_{1,0}, x_{1,1}$ at the beginning of the game, it returns 0 and terminates if $(\mathsf{par}, x_{1,1-b^*}) \notin \mathsf{Good}$, where Good is as in the definition of the weakly equivocable coset commitment scheme. Otherwise, it continues as in $\mathbf{G}_2$ does. By the good parameters property of CMT, we have

$$|\Pr[\mathbf{G}_2 \Rightarrow 1] - \Pr[\mathbf{G}_3 \Rightarrow 1]| \le \Pr[(\mathsf{par}, x_{1,1-b^*}) \notin \mathsf{Good}] \le \varepsilon_{\mathsf{g}}.$$

Game $\mathbf{G}_4$: In this game, we change how random oracle H is simulated. Recall that until now, when H is queried on an input $(\langle \mathcal{P} \rangle, \mathsf{m})$ and the output of H is not yet defined, it samples a random commitment key $\mathsf{ck} \xleftarrow{\$} \mathcal{K}$ uniformly at random and defines the output to be this key. From now on, we sample ck differently, distinguishing two cases depending on the bit $b := \bar{\mathsf{H}}_b(\mathsf{seed}_1, \langle \mathcal{P} \rangle, \mathsf{m})$ and the bit b^*. Namely, if $b = 1 - b^*$, then ck is sampled in hiding mode with a trapdoor, i.e., $(\mathsf{ck}, \mathsf{td}) \leftarrow \mathsf{TGen}(\mathsf{par}, X_{1,1-b^*})$. Further, the trapdoor td is stored in a map tr by setting $tr[\langle \mathcal{P} \rangle, \mathsf{m}] := \mathsf{td}$. On the other hand, if $b = b^*$, then ck is sampled in binding mode, i.e., $\mathsf{ck} \leftarrow \mathsf{BGen}(\mathsf{par})$. We now show indistinguishability of $\mathbf{G}_3$ and $\mathbf{G}_4$. First, note that keys sampled in the first case are distributed identically in $\mathbf{G}_3$ and $\mathbf{G}_4$. This follows from the uniform keys property of CMT, which we can apply due to the previous change that ensures that $(\mathsf{par}, x_{1,1-b^*}) \in \mathsf{Good}$. Second, keys sampled in the second case are indistinguishable by the multi-key indistinguishability property of CMT. More precisely, there is a reduction $\mathcal{B}$ that gets as input $\mathsf{par}, x_{1,1-b^*}$, and commitment keys $\mathsf{ck}_1, \dots, \mathsf{ck}_{Q_H}$. It then simulates game $\mathbf{G}_4$ for $\mathcal{A}$, but embedding the commitment keys ck_i whenever random oracle H needs to be simulated and $b = b^*$ as above. In the end, $\mathcal{B}$ outputs whatever the game outputs. Clearly, $\mathcal{B}$'s running time is determined by the running time of $\mathcal{A}$ and it perfectly simulates $\mathbf{G}_4$ if the keys $\mathsf{ck}_1, \dots, \mathsf{ck}_{Q_H}$ are generated via algorithm BGen. Otherwise, if the keys are sampled uniformly at random, it perfectly simulates $\mathbf{G}_3$ for $\mathcal{A}$. For this, it was important that we introduced the indirection via oracle $\bar{\mathsf{H}}_b$ as otherwise the simulation would not be perfect. Concretely, if $\mathcal{B}$ itself had queried H_b instead of $\bar{\mathsf{H}}_b$, then the game would always have output 0, see the change in $\mathbf{G}_2$. We have

$$|\Pr[\mathbf{G}_3 \Rightarrow 1] - \Pr[\mathbf{G}_4 \Rightarrow 1]| \le \mathsf{Adv}_{\mathcal{B}, \mathsf{CMT}}^{Q_H\text{-keydist}}(\lambda).$$

Game $\mathbf{G}_5$: In this game, we change the signing oracle. The result will be that we can simulate the signing oracle without $x_{1,1-b^*}$, but using trapdoors for commitment keys instead. First, we explain how we change oracle SIG_0, which runs Sig_0 in previous games. Recall from the definition of Sig_0, that this means that the oracle on input $\mathcal{P}$ and m samples $r_1 \xleftarrow{\$} \mathcal{D}$, defines $R_1 := \mathsf{F}(r_1)$, computes a bit $b_1 := \mathsf{H}_b(\mathsf{seed}_1, \langle \mathcal{P} \rangle, \mathsf{m})$ and a commitment key $\mathsf{ck} := \mathsf{H}(\langle \mathcal{P} \rangle, \mathsf{m})$, and commits to R_1 by sampling $\varphi_1 \xleftarrow{\$} \mathcal{G}$ and setting $\mathsf{com}_1 := \mathsf{Com}(\mathsf{ck}, R_1; \varphi_1)$. Now, if $b_1 = b^*$, we don't change anything and $\mathbf{G}_5$ behaves as previous games do. However, if $b_1 = 1 - b^*$, the game computes com_1 differently. It computes it as $(\mathsf{com}_1, St_1) \leftarrow \mathsf{TCom}(\mathsf{ck}, tr[\langle \mathcal{P} \rangle, \mathsf{m}])$. Here, recall that if $b_1 = 1 - b^*$, then ck has been generated with a trapdoor that is stored in tr, see $\mathbf{G}_4$. Next, we explain how we change oracle SIG_1, which runs Sig_1 in previous games. To recall, this means that first, a challenge c_1 is computed using the random oracle H_c and all messages of the first round. Then, a response $s_1 := c_1 \cdot x_{1,b_1} + r_1$ is computed, and s_1 and φ_1 is returned to $\mathcal{A}$. Again, we only change the case where $b_1 = 1 - b^*$. Namely, in this case, the game runs $(\varphi_1, R_1, s_1) \leftarrow \mathsf{TCol}(St_1, c_1)$ to compute s_1 and φ_1 instead. Due to the change introduced in $\mathbf{G}_3$, we know that $(\mathsf{par}, x_{1,1-b^*}) \in \mathsf{Good}$, and thus we can apply the weak trapdoor property of CMT for every signing query. We get

$$|\Pr[\mathbf{G}_4 \Rightarrow 1] - \Pr[\mathbf{G}_5 \Rightarrow 1]| \le Q_S \varepsilon_\mathrm{t}.$$

Game $\mathbf{G}_6$: In this game, we undo the change from $\mathbf{G}_3$, namely, we no longer require that $(\mathsf{par}, x_{1,1-b^*}) \in \mathsf{Good}$. With a similar argument as in $\mathbf{G}_3$, we get

$$|\Pr[\mathbf{G}_5 \Rightarrow 1] - \Pr[\mathbf{G}_6 \Rightarrow 1]| \le \varepsilon_\mathrm{g}.$$

Game $\mathbf{G}_7$: In this game, we change how $X_{1,1-b^*}$ is generated. Recall that until now, it is generated by sampling $x_{1,1-b^*} \xleftarrow{\$} \mathcal{D}$ and setting $X_{1,1-b^*} := \mathsf{F}(x_{1,1-b^*})$. From now on, we sample it in lossy mode, i.e., as $X_{1,1-b^*} \xleftarrow{\$} \mathcal{R}$. Observe that $x_{1,1-b^*}$ is used nowhere else during the game, due to our previous changes. Therefore, we can easily bound the distinguishing advantage between $\mathbf{G}_6$ and $\mathbf{G}_7$ by a reduction $\mathcal{B}'$ that runs in the key indistinguishability game of LF and embeds its input in $X_{1,1-b^*}$. We have

$$|\Pr[\mathbf{G}_6 \Rightarrow 1] - \Pr[\mathbf{G}_7 \Rightarrow 1]| \le \mathsf{Adv}^{\mathsf{keydist}}_{\mathcal{B}', \mathsf{LF}}(\lambda).$$

Game $\mathbf{G}_8$: In game $\mathbf{G}_8$, we make use of the statistical coset binding property of CMT. Concretely, we change oracle H_c and the winning condition. Recall that until now, a query $\mathsf{H}_c(\mathsf{pk}, \mathsf{com}, \mathsf{m}, \langle \mathcal{P} \rangle, B)$ is answered in the standard way using lazy sampling. In game $\mathbf{G}_8$, this is still the case, but additionally the extractor Ext for the statistical coset binding property of CMT is run in certain cases. Namely, write $\mathcal{P} = \{\mathsf{pk}_1, \ldots, \mathsf{pk}_N\}$ and $B = b_1 \ldots b_N$. Further, set $b := \bar{\mathsf{H}}_b(\mathsf{seed}_1, \langle \mathcal{P} \rangle, \mathsf{m})$. If pk^* is part of $\mathcal{P}$, i.e., $\mathsf{pk}^* = \mathsf{pk}_1$, and $b = b^*$, then we know that the commitment key $\mathsf{ck} := \mathsf{H}(\langle \mathcal{P} \rangle, \mathsf{m})$ is generated in binding mode by algorithm BGen. This is due to the change in $\mathbf{G}_4$. Now, game $\mathbf{G}_8$ runs $R \leftarrow \mathsf{Ext}(\mathsf{H}(\langle \mathcal{P} \rangle, \mathsf{m}), \mathsf{com})$ and stores R in a map $r[\cdot]$ as $r[\mathsf{com}, \mathsf{m}, \langle \mathcal{P} \rangle, B] := R$. Other than that, the oracle H_c does not change. Next, we describe how the winning condition is changed. For that, assume that $\mathcal{A}$ outputs a forgery $\mathcal{A}$ outputs a forgery $(\mathcal{P}^*, \mathsf{m}^*, \sigma^*)$ with $\mathcal{P}^* = \{\mathsf{pk}_1, \ldots, \mathsf{pk}_N\}$, $\sigma^* = (\mathsf{com}^*, \varphi^*, s^*, B^*)$, and $B^* = b_1^* \ldots b_N^* \in \{0,1\}^N$. Assume that game $\mathbf{G}_7$ does not return 0. Especially, we have $\mathsf{pk}_1 = \mathsf{pk}^*$ and $(\mathcal{P}^*, \mathsf{m}^*) \notin \mathsf{Queried}$, and $\bar{\mathsf{H}}_b(\mathsf{seed}_1, \langle \mathcal{P}^* \rangle, \mathsf{m}^*) = b^*$ (see $\mathbf{G}_2$). Further, the game parses $\mathsf{pk}_i = (X_{i,0}, X_{i,1})$ for every key pk_i in $\mathcal{P}^*$ and defines challenges $c_i^* := \mathsf{H}_c(\mathsf{pk}_i, \mathsf{com}_0^*, \mathsf{m}^*, \langle \mathcal{P}^* \rangle, B^*)$ for all $i \in [N]$ as the verification algorithm does. In particular, now we know, due to $\bar{H}_b(\text{seed}_1, \langle \mathcal{P}^* \rangle, m^*) = b^*$, that $r[\text{com}^*, m^*, \langle \mathcal{P}^* \rangle, B^*]$ is defined. Next, the game defines $R^* := F(s^*) - \sum_{i=1}^{N} c_i^* \cdot X_{i,b_i^*}$ as the verification algorithm does. The game outputs 0 if $R^* \notin r[\text{com}^*, m^*, \langle \mathcal{P}^* \rangle, B^*] + F(\mathcal{D})$. Otherwise, it behaves as $\mathbf{G}_7$ does. Note that if $\mathbf{G}_7$ outputs 1, but $\mathbf{G}_8$ does not, then we know that $\text{com}^* = \text{Com}(\text{ck}, R^*; \varphi^*)$, where $\text{ck} := H(\langle \mathcal{P} \rangle^*, m^*)$. In other words, $\mathbf{G}_7$ and $\mathbf{G}_8$ only differ, if for the forgery, the value $r[\text{com}^*, m^*, \langle \mathcal{P}^* \rangle, B^*]$ that the extractor extracted from commitment com^* is in a different coset than the value to which $\mathcal{A}$ successfully opens com^* in its forgery. We can easily bound the probability of this using the statistical coset binding property of CMT. For that, we sketch an (unbounded) reduction that gets as input the parameters par of the linear function, and a commitment key $\text{ck} \leftarrow \text{BGen}(\text{par})$. Then, it first samples indices $i_H \xleftarrow{\$} [Q_H]$ and $i_{H_c} \xleftarrow{\$} [Q_{H_c}]$ uniformly at random, and then simulates the game $\mathbf{G}_8$ honestly for $\mathcal{A}$, except the i_Hth query to H and the i_{H_c}th query to H_c. In the i_Hth query to H, if it has to sample a binding key, it embeds ck. Otherwise, it aborts. In the i_{H_c}th query to H_c, if it had to run Ext, it instead outputs the commitment com and its state to the statistical coset binding game. Otherwise, it aborts. Finally, when $\mathcal{A}$ outputs its forgery, and the i_Hth query to H and the i_{H_c}th query to H_c are the queries of interest, and $R^* \notin r[\text{com}^*, m^*, \langle \mathcal{P}^* \rangle, B^*] + F(\mathcal{D})$, the reduction outputs R^* and φ^*, thereby winning the statistical coset binding game. It is easy to see that this shows

$$|\Pr[\mathbf{G}_7 \Rightarrow 1] - \Pr[\mathbf{G}_8 \Rightarrow 1]| \le Q_H Q_{H_c} \varepsilon_b.$$

To finish the proof, we bound the probability that $\mathbf{G}_8$ outputs 1 using coset lossy soundness of LF. For that consider the following unbounded reduction:

- The reduction gets as input parameters par and an element $X \in \mathcal{R}$.
- It picks a random index $\hat{i} \xleftarrow{\$} [Q_{H_c}]$. It then simulates game $\mathbf{G}_8$ for $\mathcal{A}$ until $\mathcal{A}$ outputs its forgery, using parameters par and defining $X_{1,1-b^*} := X$ instead of picking it randomly from $\mathcal{R}$. Further, the reduction handles the $\hat{i}$th query to H_c differently.
- Let $H_c(\text{pk}, \text{com}, m, \langle \mathcal{P} \rangle, B)$ be the $\hat{i}$th query to H_c. If the hash value for this query is already defined, the reduction continues as $\mathbf{G}_8$ would do. Otherwise, let $\mathcal{P} = \{\text{pk}_1, \ldots, \text{pk}_N\}$, $B = b_1 \ldots b_N$, and $b := \bar{H}_b(\text{seed}_1, \langle \mathcal{P} \rangle, m)$. The reduction also continues as $\mathbf{G}_8$ would do if pk^* is not in $\mathcal{P}$. Otherwise, assume that $\text{pk}^* = \text{pk}_1$ as usual. If $\text{pk} \neq \text{pk}^*$ or $b \neq b^*$, the reduction also continues as $\mathbf{G}_8$ would do. In other words, the reduction only differs in the case in which $\mathbf{G}_8$ would run the extractor Ext. In this case, the reduction runs Ext as $\mathbf{G}_8$ would do, i.e., it runs $\hat{R} \leftarrow \text{Ext}(H(\langle \mathcal{P} \rangle, m), \text{com})$ and sets $r[\text{com}, m, \langle \mathcal{P} \rangle, B] := \hat{R}$. In addition, the reduction sets $c_i := H_c(\text{pk}_i, \text{com}, m, \langle \mathcal{P} \rangle, B)$ for each $i \in [N] \setminus \{1\}$, and computes

$$R := \hat{R} + \sum_{i=2}^{N} c_i \cdot X_{i,b_i}.$$

Then, the reduction outputs R to the coset lossy soundness game, and in return it receives a challenge $c \in \mathcal{S}$. Finally, the reduction programs $h_c[\text{pk}, \text{com}, m, \langle \mathcal{P} \rangle, B] := c$ and returns this hash value.

– When $\mathcal{A}$ outputs its forgery $(\mathcal{P}^*, \mathsf{m}^*, \sigma^*)$, the reduction does all the verification checks as in $\mathbf{G}_8$. Assuming all of these checks pass, write $\mathcal{P}^* = \{\mathsf{pk}_1 = \mathsf{pk}^*, \ldots, \mathsf{pk}_N\}$, $\sigma^* = (\mathsf{com}^*, \varphi^*, s^*, B^*)$, and $B^* = b_1^* \ldots b_N^* \in \{0,1\}^N$. Additionally, the reduction aborts if the hash value $\mathsf{H}_c(\mathsf{pk}_1, \mathsf{com}^*, \mathsf{m}^*, \langle \mathcal{P}^* \rangle, B^*)$ has not been defined during the $\hat{i}$th query to H_c. Otherwise, the reduction returns $s := s^*$ to the coset lossy soundness game.

One can easily see that the view of $\mathcal{A}$ is independent of the index $\hat{i}$ until a potential abort, and that, assuming the reduction does not abort, the simulation of $\mathbf{G}_8$ is perfect. Now, we want to argue that the reduction breaks coset lossy soundness if $\mathbf{G}_8$ outputs 1, and the index $\hat{i}$ is guessed correctly. Once this is shown, we can conclude with

$$\Pr\left[\mathbf{G}_8 \Rightarrow 1\right] \le Q_{\mathsf{H}_c} \varepsilon_{\mathsf{l}}.$$

To show this claim, we assume that $\mathbf{G}_8$ outputs 1 and the index $\hat{i}$ is guessed correctly. Now, it follows from the condition $\mathsf{H}_b(\mathsf{seed}_1, \langle \mathcal{P}^* \rangle, \mathsf{m}^*) = b^*$ introduced in $\mathbf{G}_2$ that the reduction output R as above to the coset lossy soundness game, received c, and programmed $\mathsf{H}_c(\mathsf{pk}_1, \mathsf{com}^*, \mathsf{m}^*, \langle \mathcal{P}^* \rangle, B^*)$ to be c. It remains to argue that $\mathsf{F}(s) - c \cdot X \in R + \mathsf{F}(\mathcal{D})$. For that, first recall that the change introduced in $\mathbf{G}_8$ ensures that

$$\mathsf{F}(s^*) - \sum_{i=1}^{N} c_i^* \cdot X_{i,b_i^*} \in r[\mathsf{com}^*, \mathsf{m}^*, \langle \mathcal{P}^* \rangle, B^*] + \mathsf{F}(\mathcal{D}).$$

Using the assumption that the index $\hat{i}$ is guessed correctly, this implies

$$\mathsf{F}(s^*) - c \cdot X_{1,b_1^*} - \sum_{i=2}^{N} c_i \cdot X_{i,b_i^*} \in \hat{R} + \mathsf{F}(\mathcal{D}).$$

Now, we rearrange terms and use the condition $b_1^* = 1 - b^*$ introduced in $\mathbf{G}_2$, and get

$$\mathsf{F}(s^*) - c \cdot X_{1,1-b^*} \in \hat{R} + \sum_{i=2}^{N} c_i \cdot X_{i,b_i^*} + \mathsf{F}(\mathcal{D}).$$

If we recall the definition of $s^* = s$, $X_{1,1-b^*} = X$, and the definition of R, then this is exactly the statement we want to show. Concluded. $\square$

5   Our Instantiations

In this section, we instantiate the building blocks introduced in Sect. 3. We present a linear function family and a commitment scheme, both based on DDH.

5.1   Linear Function Family

We use the same linear function family as in [46], which is a linear function family $\mathsf{LF_{DDH}} = (\mathsf{Gen}, \mathsf{F})$ based on the DDH assumption. For that, we assume an algorithm GGen, that outputs the description of a prime order group $\mathbb{G}$ of order p with generator g on input 1^λ. Algorithm Gen runs GGen, samples $h \xleftarrow{\$} \mathbb{G}$, and outputs parameters $\mathsf{par} := (g, h) \in \mathbb{G}^2$. The description of $\mathbb{G}$ is also contained in par and left implicit for the sake of a concise presentation. These parameters define the set of scalars, domain, range, and the function $\mathsf{F}(\mathsf{par}, \cdot)$, which are as follows: $\mathcal{S} := \mathbb{Z}_p$, $\mathcal{D} := \mathbb{Z}_p$, $\mathcal{R} := \mathbb{G} \times \mathbb{G}$, $\mathsf{F}(\mathsf{par}, x) := (g^x, h^x)$. One can easily verify that this is a linear function family. Further, it is shown in [46] that $\mathsf{LF_{DDH}}$ satisfies key indistinguishability, lossy soundness, and aggregation lossy soundness. We conclude that $\mathsf{LF_{DDH}}$ satisfies coset lossy soundness and coset aggregation lossy soundness. The following lemma summarizes this.

Lemma 3. *Assuming that the* DDH *assumption holds relative to* GGen, *the linear function family* $\mathsf{LF_{DDH}}$ *satisfies key indistinguishability. Concretely, for any PPT algorithm $\mathcal{A}$ there is a PPT algorithm $\mathcal{B}$ with $\mathbf{T}(\mathcal{B}) \approx \mathbf{T}(\mathcal{A})$ and*

$$\mathsf{Adv}^{\mathsf{keydist}}_{\mathcal{A}, \mathsf{LF_{DDH}}}(\lambda) \leq \mathsf{Adv}^{\mathsf{DDH}}_{\mathcal{B}, \mathsf{GGen}}(\lambda).$$

Further, the linear function family $\mathsf{LF_{DDH}}$ *satisfies* ε_l*-coset lossy soundness and* ε_al*-coset aggregation lossy soundness for $\varepsilon_\mathsf{l} \leq 3/p$ and $\varepsilon_\mathsf{al} \leq 4/p$.*

5.2   Commitment Scheme

In this section, we present our instantiation of the weakly equivocable coset commitment scheme for the linear function family $\mathsf{LF_{DDH}}$ introduced before. Our commitment scheme shares similarities with the commitment scheme from [46], which uses a 3×3 matrix of group elements as a commitment key. Our crucial observation is that if we replace this 3×3 structure with a more efficient 2×2 structure, we obtain a scheme that is still binding on cosets. We now describe our commitment scheme $\mathsf{CMT_{DDH}} = (\mathsf{BGen}, \mathsf{TGen}, \mathsf{Com}, \mathsf{TCom}, \mathsf{TCol})$ for $\mathsf{LF_{DDH}}$. Assume parameters of $\mathsf{LF_{DDH}}$ are given, specifying a group $\mathbb{G}$. Then, the commitment scheme has key space $\mathcal{K} := \mathbb{G}^{2 \times 2}$, message space $\mathcal{D} = \mathbb{G} \times \mathbb{G}$, randomness space $\mathcal{G} = \mathbb{Z}_p^2$, and commitment space $\mathcal{H} = \mathbb{G}^2$. The spaces $\mathcal{D}, \mathcal{G}$, and $\mathcal{H}$ are associated with the natural componentwise group operations. Next, we describe the algorithms of the commitment scheme verbally.

– $\mathsf{BGen}(\mathsf{par}) \to \mathsf{ck}$: Parse $\mathsf{par} = (g, h)$. Sample $a, b \xleftarrow{\$} \mathbb{Z}_p$ and set

$$\mathsf{ck} := \mathbf{A} := \begin{pmatrix} A_{1,1} & A_{1,2} \\ A_{2,1} & A_{2,2} \end{pmatrix} := \begin{pmatrix} g^a & g^b \\ h^a & h^b \end{pmatrix} \in \mathbb{G}^{2 \times 2}.$$

– $\mathsf{TGen}(\mathsf{par}, X = (X_1, X_2)) \to (\mathsf{ck}, \mathsf{td})$: Sample exponents $d_{i,j} \xleftarrow{\$} \mathbb{Z}_p$ for all $(i, j) \in [2] \times [2]$. Set

$$\mathsf{ck} := \mathbf{A} := \begin{pmatrix} A_{1,1} & A_{1,2} \\ A_{2,1} & A_{2,2} \end{pmatrix} := \begin{pmatrix} X_1^{d_{1,1}} & X_1^{d_{1,2}} \\ X_2^{d_{2,1}} & X_2^{d_{2,2}} \end{pmatrix} \in \mathbb{G}^{2 \times 2}.$$

Further, set td := $(\mathbf{D}, X_1, X_2)$ for

$$\mathbf{D} := \begin{pmatrix} d_{1,1} & d_{1,2} \\ d_{2,1} & d_{2,2} \end{pmatrix} \in \mathbb{Z}_p^{2 \times 2}.$$

- Com$(ck, R = (R_1, R_2); \varphi) \to$ com: Let $\varphi = (\alpha, \beta) \in \mathbb{Z}_p^2$. Compute com := (C_1, C_2) for

$$\begin{pmatrix} C_1 \\ C_2 \end{pmatrix} := \begin{pmatrix} R_1 \cdot A_{1,1}^{\alpha} \cdot A_{1,2}^{\beta} \\ R_2 \cdot A_{2,1}^{\alpha} \cdot A_{2,2}^{\beta} \end{pmatrix}.$$

- TCom$(ck, td) \to (com, St)$: Sample $\rho_1, \rho_2, s \overset{\$}{\leftarrow} \mathbb{Z}_p$. Set $St := (td, \tau, \rho_1, \rho_2, s)$ and compute com := (C_1, C_2) for

$$\begin{pmatrix} C_1 \\ C_2 \end{pmatrix} := \begin{pmatrix} X_1^{\rho_1} \cdot g^s \\ X_2^{\rho_2} \cdot h^s \end{pmatrix}.$$

- TCol$(St, c) \to (\varphi, R, s)$: Set $R := (R_1, R_2) := (g^s \cdot X_1^{-c}, h^s \cdot X_2^{-c})$. Then, if $\mathbf{D}$ is not invertible, return $\bot$. Otherwise, compute $\varphi := (\alpha, \beta)$ for

$$\begin{pmatrix} \alpha \\ \beta \end{pmatrix} = \mathbf{D}^{-1} \cdot \begin{pmatrix} \rho_1 + c \\ \rho_2 + c \end{pmatrix}.$$

Theorem 2. *If the* DDH *assumption holds relative to* GGen, *then* CMT$_{\mathsf{DDH}}$ *is an* $(\varepsilon_b, \varepsilon_g, \varepsilon_t)$*-weakly equivocable coset commitment scheme for* LF$_{\mathsf{DDH}}$*, with*

$$\varepsilon_b = 0, \quad \varepsilon_g \leq 2/p, \quad \varepsilon_t \leq 2/p.$$

Concretely, for any PPT algorithm $\mathcal{A}$*, there is a PPT algorithm* $\mathcal{B}$ *with* $\mathbf{T}(\mathcal{B}) \approx \mathbf{T}(\mathcal{A})$ *and*

$$\mathsf{Adv}_{\mathcal{A}, \mathsf{CMT}_{\mathsf{DDH}}}^{Q\text{-keydist}}(\lambda) \leq \mathsf{Adv}_{\mathcal{A}, \mathsf{GGen}}^{2Q\text{-DDH}}(\lambda)..$$

Due to space limitations, the proof of Theorem 2 is postponed to our full version [47].

6   Efficiency

Here, we analyze the efficiency of our schemes. We first explain minor optimizations that improve signature size and communication complexity. Then, we focus on the asymptotic and concrete efficiency of our schemes.

Further Optimizations. We describe the optimizations for our tight construction in Sect. 4.2, but they also apply to our other scheme. Our first optimization is to reduce the communication complexity by deriving the commitment randomness φ, which consists of two field elements, from a short seed of length λ bit using a random oracle $\bar{\mathsf{H}}: \{0,1\}^* \to \mathbb{Z}_p^2$. Then, instead of sending φ in the second round, each signer sends its seed, and the signers locally derive all φ's and aggregate them. By the unpredictability of the random oracle, the scheme stays secure. Our second optimization allows us to remove the commitment com, which consists of two group elements, from the final signature. The idea is to replace it by a hash of com of length 2λ using another random oracle $\hat{\mathsf{H}}: \{0,1\}^* \to \{0,1\}^{2\lambda}$. Concretely, the signers first complete the signing protocol as before, but to define signer specific challenges, they compute $c_i := \mathsf{H}_c(\mathsf{pk}_i, h, \mathsf{m}, \langle \mathcal{P} \rangle, B)$ for all $i \in [N]$, where $h := \hat{\mathsf{H}}(\mathsf{com})$. In the end, the signature is $\sigma := (h, \varphi, s, B)$. The signature is verified by first recomputing the c_i's as before (using h instead of com) and by checking the commitment after hashing, i.e., using the equation

$$h = \hat{\mathsf{H}}\left(\mathsf{Com}\left(\mathsf{ck}, \mathsf{F}(s) - \sum_{i=1}^{N} c_i \cdot X_{i,b_i}; \varphi\right)\right).$$

In a security proof, we would use the collision-resistance and observability of $\hat{\mathsf{H}}$ to reduce this equation to the original verification equation.

Asymptotics. In Table 2, we compare the asymptotic sizes of public keys and signatures and the communication complexity per signer for our schemes with previous schemes in the pairing-free setting. We see that our schemes are much more efficient than the schemes in [46]. Especially, the asymptotic efficiency of our schemes is comparable with most non-tight or three-round schemes.

Concrete Parameters. We compare the concrete efficiency and security level of two-round multi-signatures in the pairing-free setting in Table 3. Our comparison assumes that all constructions are instantiated with the secp256k1 curve, and we assume security parameter $\lambda = 128$. We compute the concrete security level based on the security bounds (see Table 1) assuming the underlying assumption is 128 bit hard, and assuming $Q_H = 2^{30}$ hash queries and $Q_S = 2^{20}$ signing queries. We see that our tightly secure scheme outperforms Chopsticks II, the only other two-round scheme with comparable security level, by a factor of more than 3 in a signature size, and more than 2 in the communication complexity. Finally, we also remark that our scheme is at least twice as efficient as Chopsticks II in terms of computation.

Acknowledgment. Benedikt Wagner was funded by the Deutsche Forschungsgemeinschaft (DFG, German Research Foundation) – 507237585.

References

1. Abdalla, M., Fouque, P.-A., Lyubashevsky, V., Tibouchi, M.: Tightly-secure signatures from lossy identification schemes. In: Pointcheval, D., Johansson, T. (eds.) EUROCRYPT 2012. LNCS, vol. 7237, pp. 572–590. Springer, Heidelberg (2012). https://doi.org/10.1007/978-3-642-29011-4_34
2. Kılınç Alper, H., Burdges, J.: Two-round trip schnorr multi-signatures via delinearized witnesses. In: Malkin, T., Peikert, C. (eds.) CRYPTO 2021. LNCS, vol. 12825, pp. 157–188. Springer, Cham (2021). https://doi.org/10.1007/978-3-030-84242-0_7

3. Bader, C., Hofheinz, D., Jager, T., Kiltz, E., Li, Y.: Tightly-secure authenticated key exchange. In: Dodis, Y., Nielsen, J.B. (eds.) TCC 2015. LNCS, vol. 9014, pp. 629–658. Springer, Heidelberg (2015). https://doi.org/10.1007/978-3-662-46494-6_26

4. Bader, C., Jager, T., Li, Y., Schäge, S.: On the impossibility of tight cryptographic reductions. In: Fischlin, M., Coron, J.-S. (eds.) EUROCRYPT 2016. LNCS, vol. 9666, pp. 273–304. Springer, Heidelberg (2016). https://doi.org/10.1007/978-3-662-49896-5_10

5. Bellare, M., Boldyreva, A., Micali, S.: Public-key encryption in a multi-user setting: security proofs and improvements. In: Preneel, B. (ed.) EUROCRYPT 2000. LNCS, vol. 1807, pp. 259–274. Springer, Heidelberg (2000). https://doi.org/10.1007/3-540-45539-6_18

6. Bellare, M., Dai, W.: Chain reductions for multi-signatures and the HBMS scheme. In: Tibouchi, M., Wang, H. (eds.) ASIACRYPT 2021. LNCS, vol. 13093, pp. 650–678. Springer, Cham (2021). https://doi.org/10.1007/978-3-030-92068-5_22

7. Bellare, M., Neven, G.: Multi-signatures in the plain public-key model and a general forking lemma. In: Juels, A., Wright, R.N., De Capitani di Vimercati, S. (eds.) ACM CCS 2006, pp. 390–399. ACM Press (Oct / Nov 2006). https://doi.org/10.1145/1180405.1180453

8. Bellare, M., Rogaway, P.: Random oracles are practical: A paradigm for designing efficient protocols. In: Denning, D.E., Pyle, R., Ganesan, R., Sandhu, R.S., Ashby, V. (eds.) ACM CCS 1993, pp. 62–73. ACM Press (Nov 1993). https://doi.org/10.1145/168588.168596

9. Blazy, O., Kakvi, S.A., Kiltz, E., Pan, J.: Tightly-secure signatures from chameleon hash functions. In: Katz, J. (ed.) PKC 2015. LNCS, vol. 9020, pp. 256–279. Springer, Heidelberg (2015). https://doi.org/10.1007/978-3-662-46447-2_12

10. Blazy, O., Kiltz, E., Pan, J.: (Hierarchical) identity-based encryption from affine message authentication. In: Garay, J.A., Gennaro, R. (eds.) CRYPTO 2014. LNCS, vol. 8616, pp. 408–425. Springer, Heidelberg (2014). https://doi.org/10.1007/978-3-662-44371-2_23

11. Boldyreva, A.: Threshold signatures, multisignatures and blind signatures based on the gap-diffie-hellman-group signature scheme. In: Desmedt, Y.G. (ed.) PKC 2003. LNCS, vol. 2567, pp. 31–46. Springer, Heidelberg (2003). https://doi.org/10.1007/3-540-36288-6_3

12. Boneh, D., Drijvers, M., Neven, G.: Compact multi-signatures for smaller blockchains. In: Peyrin, T., Galbraith, S. (eds.) ASIACRYPT 2018. LNCS, vol. 11273, pp. 435–464. Springer, Cham (2018). https://doi.org/10.1007/978-3-030-03329-3_15

13. Boschini, C., Takahashi, A., Tibouchi, M.: MuSig-L: Lattice-based multi-signature with single-round online phase. In: Dodis, Y., Shrimpton, T. (eds.) CRYPTO 2022, Part II. LNCS, vol. 13508, pp. 276–305. Springer, Heidelberg (2022). https://doi.org/10.1007/978-3-031-15979-4_10

14. Boyen, X., Li, Q.: Towards tightly secure lattice short signature and id-based encryption. In: Cheon, J.H., Takagi, T. (eds.) ASIACRYPT 2016. LNCS, vol. 10032, pp. 404–434. Springer, Heidelberg (2016). https://doi.org/10.1007/978-3-662-53890-6_14

15. Chairattana-Apirom, R., Hanzlik, L., Loss, J., Lysyanskaya, A., Wagner, B.: PI-cut-choo and friends: Compact blind signatures via parallel instance cut-and-choose and more. In: Dodis, Y., Shrimpton, T. (eds.) CRYPTO 2022, Part III. LNCS, vol. 13509, pp. 3–31. Springer, Heidelberg (2022). https://doi.org/10.1007/978-3-031-15982-4_1

16. Chen, J., Wee, H.: Fully, (almost) tightly secure IBE and dual system groups. In: Canetti, R., Garay, J.A. (eds.) CRYPTO 2013. LNCS, vol. 8043, pp. 435–460. Springer, Heidelberg (2013). https://doi.org/10.1007/978-3-642-40084-1_25

17. Crites, E., Komlo, C., Maller, M.: How to prove schnorr assuming schnorr: Security of multi- and threshold signatures. Cryptology ePrint Archive, Report 2021/1375 (2021). https://eprint.iacr.org/2021/1375

18. Damgård, I., Orlandi, C., Takahashi, A., Tibouchi, M.: Two-Round n-out-of-n and multi-signatures and trapdoor commitment from lattices. In: Garay, J.A. (ed.) PKC 2021. LNCS, vol. 12710, pp. 99–130. Springer, Cham (2021). https://doi.org/10.1007/978-3-030-75245-3_5

19. Davis, H., Günther, F.: Tighter proofs for the SIGMA and TLS 1.3 key exchange protocols. In: Sako, K., Tippenhauer, N.O. (eds.) ACNS 2021, Part II. LNCS, vol. 12727, pp. 448–479. Springer, Heidelberg (2021). https://doi.org/10.1007/978-3-030-78375-4_18

20. Diemert, D., Gellert, K., Jager, T., Lyu, L.: More efficient digital signatures with tight multi-user security. In: Garay, J.A. (ed.) PKC 2021. LNCS, vol. 12711, pp. 1–31. Springer, Cham (2021). https://doi.org/10.1007/978-3-030-75248-4_1

21. Drijvers, M., et al.: On the security of two-round multi-signatures. In: 2019 IEEE Symposium on Security and Privacy, pp. 1084–1101. IEEE Computer Society Press (May 2019). https://doi.org/10.1109/SP.2019.00050

22. Escala, A., Herold, G., Kiltz, E., Ràfols, C., Villar, J.: An algebraic framework for diffie-hellman assumptions. In: Canetti, R., Garay, J.A. (eds.) CRYPTO 2013. LNCS, vol. 8043, pp. 129–147. Springer, Heidelberg (2013). https://doi.org/10.1007/978-3-642-40084-1_8

23. Fuchsbauer, G., Kiltz, E., Loss, J.: The algebraic group model and its applications. In: Shacham, H., Boldyreva, A. (eds.) CRYPTO 2018. LNCS, vol. 10992, pp. 33–62. Springer, Cham (2018). https://doi.org/10.1007/978-3-319-96881-0_2

24. Fukumitsu, M., Hasegawa, S.: A tightly secure ddh-based multisignature with public-key aggregation. Int. J. Netw. Comput. **11**(2), 319–337 (2021). http://www.ijnc.org/index.php/ijnc/article/view/257

25. Gay, R., Hofheinz, D., Kiltz, E., Wee, H.: Tightly CCA-secure encryption without pairings. In: Fischlin, M., Coron, J.-S. (eds.) EUROCRYPT 2016. LNCS, vol. 9665, pp. 1–27. Springer, Heidelberg (2016). https://doi.org/10.1007/978-3-662-49890-3_1

26. Gay, R., Hofheinz, D., Kohl, L., Pan, J.: More efficient (almost) tightly secure structure-preserving signatures. In: Nielsen, J.B., Rijmen, V. (eds.) EUROCRYPT 2018. LNCS, vol. 10821, pp. 230–258. Springer, Cham (2018). https://doi.org/10.1007/978-3-319-78375-8_8

27. Gjøsteen, K., Jager, T.: Practical and tightly-secure digital signatures and authenticated key exchange. In: Shacham, H., Boldyreva, A. (eds.) CRYPTO 2018. LNCS, vol. 10992, pp. 95–125. Springer, Cham (2018). https://doi.org/10.1007/978-3-319-96881-0_4

28. Goh, E.J., Jarecki, S., Katz, J., Wang, N.: Efficient signature schemes with tight reductions to the Diffie-Hellman problems. J. Cryptol. **20**(4), 493–514 (2007). https://doi.org/10.1007/s00145-007-0549-3

29. Han, S., et al.: Authenticated key exchange and signatures with tight security in the standard model. In: Malkin, T., Peikert, C. (eds.) CRYPTO 2021. LNCS, vol. 12828, pp. 670–700. Springer, Cham (2021). https://doi.org/10.1007/978-3-030-84259-8_23

30. Hauck, E., Kiltz, E., Loss, J.: A modular treatment of blind signatures from identification schemes. In: Ishai, Y., Rijmen, V. (eds.) EUROCRYPT 2019. LNCS, vol. 11478, pp. 345–375. Springer, Cham (2019). https://doi.org/10.1007/978-3-030-17659-4_12

31. Hofheinz, D.: Adaptive partitioning. In: Coron, J.-S., Nielsen, J.B. (eds.) EUROCRYPT 2017. LNCS, vol. 10212, pp. 489–518. Springer, Cham (2017). https://doi.org/10.1007/978-3-319-56617-7_17

32. Hofheinz, D., Jager, T.: Tightly secure signatures and public-key encryption. In: Safavi-Naini, R., Canetti, R. (eds.) CRYPTO 2012. LNCS, vol. 7417, pp. 590–607. Springer, Heidelberg (2012). https://doi.org/10.1007/978-3-642-32009-5_35

33. Itakura, K., Nakamura, K.: A public-key cryptosystem suitable for digital multisignatures. NEC Res. Developm. **71**, 1–8 (1983)

34. Katz, J., Loss, J., Rosenberg, M.: Boosting the security of blind signature schemes. In: Tibouchi, M., Wang, H. (eds.) ASIACRYPT 2021. LNCS, vol. 13093, pp. 468–492. Springer, Cham (2021). https://doi.org/10.1007/978-3-030-92068-5_16

35. Katz, J., Wang, N.: Efficiency improvements for signature schemes with tight security reductions. In: Jajodia, S., Atluri, V., Jaeger, T. (eds.) ACM CCS 2003, pp. 155–164. ACM Press (Oct 2003). https://doi.org/10.1145/948109.948132

36. Kiltz, E., Masny, D., Pan, J.: Optimal security proofs for signatures from identification schemes. In: Robshaw, M., Katz, J. (eds.) CRYPTO 2016. LNCS, vol. 9815, pp. 33–61. Springer, Heidelberg (2016). https://doi.org/10.1007/978-3-662-53008-5_2

37. Kurosawa, K., Desmedt, Y.: A new paradigm of hybrid encryption scheme. In: Franklin, M. (ed.) CRYPTO 2004. LNCS, vol. 3152, pp. 426–442. Springer, Heidelberg (2004). https://doi.org/10.1007/978-3-540-28628-8_26

38. Langrehr, R., Pan, J.: Unbounded HIBE with tight security. In: Moriai, S., Wang, H. (eds.) ASIACRYPT 2020. LNCS, vol. 12492, pp. 129–159. Springer, Cham (2020). https://doi.org/10.1007/978-3-030-64834-3_5

39. Liu, X., Liu, S., Gu, D., Weng, J.: Two-pass authenticated key exchange with explicit authentication and tight security. In: Moriai, S., Wang, H. (eds.) ASIACRYPT 2020. LNCS, vol. 12492, pp. 785–814. Springer, Cham (2020). https://doi.org/10.1007/978-3-030-64834-3_27

40. Lu, S., Ostrovsky, R., Sahai, A., Shacham, H., Waters, B.: Sequential aggregate signatures and multisignatures without random oracles. In: Vaudenay, S. (ed.) EUROCRYPT 2006. LNCS, vol. 4004, pp. 465–485. Springer, Heidelberg (2006). https://doi.org/10.1007/11761679_28

41. Maxwell, G., Poelstra, A., Seurin, Y., Wuille, P.: Simple schnorr multi-signatures with applications to bitcoin. Des. Codes Cryptogr. **87**(9), 2139–2164 (2019). https://doi.org/10.1007/s10623-019-00608-x

42. Micali, S., Ohta, K., Reyzin, L.: Accountable-subgroup multisignatures: Extended abstract. In: Reiter, M.K., Samarati, P. (eds.) ACM CCS 2001, pp. 245–254. ACM Press (Nov 2001). https://doi.org/10.1145/501983.502017

43. Nick, J., Ruffing, T., Seurin, Y.: MuSig2: simple two-round schnorr multisignatures. In: Malkin, T., Peikert, C. (eds.) CRYPTO 2021. LNCS, vol. 12825, pp. 189–221. Springer, Cham (2021). https://doi.org/10.1007/978-3-030-84242-0_8

44. Nick, J., Ruffing, T., Seurin, Y., Wuille, P.: MuSig-DN: Schnorr multi-signatures with verifiably deterministic nonces. In: Ligatti, J., Ou, X., Katz, J., Vigna, G. (eds.) ACM CCS 2020, pp. 1717–1731. ACM Press (Nov 2020). https://doi.org/10.1145/3372297.3417236

45. Pan, J., Wagner, B.: Lattice-based signatures with tight adaptive corruptions and more. In: Hanaoka, G., Shikata, J., Watanabe, Y. (eds.) PKC 2022, Part II. LNCS, vol. 13178, pp. 347–378. Springer, Heidelberg (2022). https://doi.org/10.1007/978-3-030-97131-1_12

46. Pan, J., Wagner, B.: Chopsticks: Fork-free two-round multi-signatures from non-interactive assumptions. In: Hazay, C., Stam, M. (eds.) EUROCRYPT 2023, Part V. LNCS, vol. 14008, pp. 597–627. Springer, Heidelberg (2023). https://doi.org/10.1007/978-3-031-30589-4_21

47. Pan, J., Wagner, B.: Toothpicks: More efficient fork-free two-round multi-signatures. Cryptology ePrint Archive, Paper 2023/1613 (2023). https://eprint.iacr.org/2023/1613

48. Schnorr, C.P.: Efficient signature generation by smart cards. J. Cryptol. 4(3), 161–174 (1991). https://doi.org/10.1007/BF00196725

49. Takemure, K., Sakai, Y., Santoso, B., Hanaoka, G., Ohta, K.: More efficient two-round multi-signature scheme with provably secure parameters. Cryptology ePrint Archive, Report 2023/155 (2023). https://eprint.iacr.org/2023/155

50. Tessaro, S., Zhu, C.: Threshold and multi-signature schemes from linear hash functions. In: Hazay, C., Stam, M. (eds.) EUROCRYPT 2023, Part V. LNCS, vol. 14008, pp. 628–658. Springer, Heidelberg (2023). https://doi.org/10.1007/978-3-031-30589-4_22

Author Index

© International Association for Cryptologic Research 2024
M. Joye and G. Leander (Eds.): EUROCRYPT 2024, LNCS 14651, pp. 491–492, 2024.
https://doi.org/10.1007/978-3-031-58716-0

Printed in the United States
by Baker & Taylor Publisher Services